MW00985362

CHAMBERS

FILM
FACTFINDER

CHAMBERS

CHAMBERS
An imprint of Chambers Harrap Publishers Ltd
7 Hopetoun Crescent
Edinburgh EH7 4AY

www.chambers.co.uk

First published by Chambers Harrap Publishers Ltd 2006

A CIP catalogue record for this book is available from the British Library.

ISBN-13: 978 0 550 10197 6
ISBN-10: 0 550 10197 7

Designed and typeset by Chambers Harrap Publishers Ltd, Edinburgh
Printed and bound in Germany by Bercker

CONTRIBUTORS

EDITOR
Camilla Rockwood

CONTRIBUTORS
Katie Brooks (*Film Reference*)
Allan Hunter (*People in Film*)
Hannah McGill (*100 Notable Films*)
Alan Morrison (*Film Categories and Genres; Film-Producing Countries*)
Michael Munro (*Film Reference*)
Alison Pickering (*People in Film*)
Camilla Rockwood (*Film Reference; People in Film*)
Liam Rodger (*Film Reference*)

PUBLISHING MANAGER
Patrick White

PREPRESS CONTROLLER
Susan Lawrie

PREPRESS MANAGER
Clair Simpson

Acknowledgements

Thanks are due to the following individuals for their suggestions and comments on
the text: Ian Brookes, Hazel Norris, Elaine O'Donoghue, Mary O'Neill, Georges Pilard,
Adam Pinder.

INTRODUCTION

Chambers Film Factfinder is a collection of useful and often fascinating information on many aspects of film, from the early days of silent cinema to the twenty-first century. With wide-ranging coverage and an international scope, it has something to interest everyone from casual film fans to dedicated enthusiasts.

Information is presented in five major sections: People in Film; Film Categories and Genres; Film-Producing Countries; 100 Notable Films; and Film Reference. Carefully researched factual information is combined with a measure of critical analysis, ensuring that each section can entertain as well as inform. Biographies of actors and directors offer suggested career 'highs' and 'lows'; genre and country sections give brief factual histories, alongside lists of key people and films; and the selection of notable films is designed to provoke interest and discussion, rather than representing a 'best-of' list. The reference section includes essential facts, figures and definitions, as well as varied and highly readable lists on such subjects as censored films, memorable dance numbers and notorious commercial flops. Throughout the book, 'fact boxes' provide intriguing snippets of film trivia, bringing added appeal to the text.

Within each section, sub-sections are clearly labelled, while cross-references help to make the reader aware of connections between entries. Further guidance is provided by the detailed contents pages at the front of the book, and by the index of film titles at the back.

Film lovers of all ages, whether seeking reliable facts or simply browsing, will find *Chambers Film Factfinder* an entertaining and thought-provoking read as well as an accessible reference tool.

NOTE

Throughout the book, foreign films are referred to initially by the title deemed to be most familiar to English-speaking audiences. In some cases, this means that a film's original (non-English) title is given first, followed by its English title:

La Règle du jeu (The Rules of the Game)

In other cases, the order may be reversed:

Raise the Red Lantern (Da hong deng long gao gao gua)

In some sections, where space is limited, only one version of a title may be given.

CONTENTS

Contents

100 NOTABLE FILMS   328

FILM REFERENCE   383

Academy Awards®	383	The Hollywood Ten	418
British Academy Film Awards	394	Banned or censored films	420
Golden Raspberry Awards	403	Notorious commercial 'flops'	422
Palme d'Or	405	Spectacular dance numbers	423
Major film festivals	407	'Casts of thousands'	425
Film records	407	Much-filmed literary classics	427
Film-related organizations	409	Actors who have played iconic	
100 American films	411	figures	428
100 British films	413	Film titles in translation	430
The *Sight & Sound* Top Ten poll	416	Glossary of film-related terms	433
Academy Awards® hosts	417		

INDEX OF FILM TITLES   458

PEOPLE IN FILM

SOME NOTABLE ACTORS

A

Abbott, Bud (William Abbott) (1895–1974)

American, born in Asbury Park, New Jersey. A vaudeville performer, he joined forces with **Lou Costello** in 1930 to form a comedy double act. They made their joint film debut in *One Night in the Tropics* (1940) and enjoyed box-office success, if little critical acclaim, for the next 15 years.
Career highs: *Buck Privates* (1941), *Abbott and Costello Meet Frankenstein* (1948)
Career lows: *Africa Screams* (1949), *Dance with Me Henry* (1956)

Adjani, Isabelle Jasmine (1955–)

French, born in Paris. She made her film debut as a teenager in *Le Petit Bougnat* (1969), found some of her best roles in the 1970s, and received Best Actress Academy Award® nominations for *The Story of Adèle H* (1975) and *Camille Claudel* (1988). She was romantically involved with **Warren Beatty**, and later had a child with **Daniel Day-Lewis**.
Career highs: *The Story of Adèle H* (1975), *The Tenant* (1976), *Camille Claudel* (1988)
Career lows: *Ishtar* (1987), *Toxic Affair* (1993), *Diabolique* (1996)

Affleck, Ben(jamin Gezza) (1972–)

American, born in Berkeley, California. Committed to an acting career from an early age, he was a teenage extra in *Field of Dreams* (1989). He appeared extensively on television before his official film debut in *Dazed and Confused* (1993) and shared a Best Original Screenplay Academy Award® for *Good Will Hunting* (1997) with his childhood friend **Matt Damon**.
Career highs: *Good Will Hunting* (1997), *Changing Lanes* (2002)
Career lows: *Gigli* (2003), *Surviving Christmas* (2004)

Alda, Alan (Alphonso Joseph d'Abruzzo) (1936–)

American, born in New York City. The son of actor Robert Alda, he made his film debut in *Gone Are the Days* (1963). He emerged as a leading actor in the late 1960s but found his greatest fame in the long-running television series *M*A*S*H*. He has also directed several pleasing comedies and received a Best Supporting Actor Academy Award® nomination for *The Aviator* (2004).
Career highs: *The Seduction of Joe Tynan* (1979), *The Four Seasons* (1981), *Sweet Liberty* (1985), *Crimes and Misdemeanours* (1989), *The Aviator* (2004)
Career low: *The Extraordinary Seaman* (1968)

Allen, Woody see **Directors**

Allyson, June (Ella Geisman) (1917–   )

American, born in the Bronx, New York City. Trained as a dancer, she appeared on Broadway before making her feature film debut in *Best Foot Forward* (1943). Popular in musicals, she secured her niche as the warm-hearted girl-next-door and supportive wife in MGM films of the 1940s and 1950s. She was married to actor **Dick Powell** until his death in 1963.
Career highs: *Good News* (1947), *Little Women* (1949), *The Glenn Miller Story* (1953), *The Shrike* (1955)
Career lows: *Battle Circus* (1953), *My Man Godfrey* (1957)

Ameche, Don (Dominic Felix Amici) (1908–93)

American, born in Kenosha, Wisconsin. A law student, he pursued an acting career on stage and radio before making his film debut in *The Sins of Man* (1936). A polished light comedian, he was an engaging, breezy all-rounder in Hollywood's Golden Age. He returned after a long absence, winning a Best Supporting Actor Academy Award® for *Cocoon* (1985) and a Venice Film Festival Best Actor award for *Things Change* (1988).
Career highs: *Alexander's Ragtime Band* (1938), *Midnight* (1939), *Heaven Can Wait* (1943), *Cocoon* (1985)
Career lows: *Phantom Caravan* (1954), *Picture Mommy Dead* (1966)

Andrews, (Carver) Dana (1909–92)

American, born in Collins, Mississippi. A student with the Pasadena Playhouse, he was signed to a contract by **Sam Goldwyn** and made his film debut in *The Westerner* (1940). A dependable, underrated leading man in the 1940s, his career faded from the 1950s onwards. He made his final film appearance in *Prince Jack* (1984).
Career highs: *The Ox-Bow Incident* (1943), *A Walk in the Sun* (1945), *The Best Years of Our Lives* (1946), *Boomerang* (1947)
Career lows: *Edge of Doom* (1950), *The Frozen Dead* (1967)

Andrews, Dame Julie (Julia Elizabeth Wells) (1935–   )

English, born in Walton-on-Thames, Surrey. Her four-octave vocal range, clarity of diction and wholesome image helped make her a Broadway star in the 1950s. She won a Best Actress Academy Award® for her film debut as the magical nanny *Mary Poppins* (1964) and married the director **Blake Edwards** in 1969. She was created a Dame in 2000.
Career highs: *Mary Poppins* (1964), *The Sound of Music* (1965), *Victor/Victoria* (1982)
Career low: *Torn Curtain* (1966)

Arkin, Alan (1934–   )

American, born in Brooklyn, New York City. Acting was his only goal from an early age and he had a richly varied theatrical career before his feature film debut in *The Russians Are Coming, The Russians Are Coming* (1966). Very fashionable in the late 1960s and early 1970s, he has also directed films and remains a prolific supporting actor.

Career highs: *The Russians Are Coming, The Russians Are Coming* (1966), *The Heart Is a Lonely Hunter* (1968), *The In-Laws* (1979)
Career low: *Chu Chu and the Philly Flash* (1981)

Arletty (Léonie Bathiat) (1898–1992)

French, born in Courbevoie. The daughter of a miner, she worked in a munitions factory, modelled and appeared extensively on stage before her film debut in *Un chien qui rapporte* (1931). Prolific in the 1930s, she made her best films with director Marcel Carné. An accident in the 1960s left her blind and ended her career.
Career highs: *Hôtel du Nord* (1938), *Le Jour se lève* (1939), *Les Enfants du paradis* (1945)
Career low: *Portrait d'un assassin* (1949)

Arthur, Jean (Gladys Georgianna Greene) (1900–91)

American, born in New York City. The daughter of a photographer, she made her film debut in *Cameo Kirby* (1923). Her apple-cheeked good looks and husky speaking voice made her a particular delight in the 1930s, especially when working for director **Frank Capra**. Notoriously insecure as a performer, she retired from the cinema after *Shane* (1953) but made occasional appearances on stage and television.
Career highs: *Mr Deeds Goes to Town* (1936), *Easy Living* (1937), *Mr Smith Goes to Washington* (1939), *The More the Merrier* (1943)
Career lows: *More Than a Secretary* (1936), *The Impatient Years* (1944)

Astaire, Fred (Frederick Austerlitz) (1899–1987)

American, born in Omaha, Nebraska. He made his film debut in *Dancing Lady* (1933) despite a notoriously unsuccessul screen test. A hardworking perfectionist, his innovative dance routines and debonair personality graced some of the finest Hollywood musicals ever made. He secured an Academy Award® nomination for his supporting role in *The Towering Inferno* (1974).
Career highs: *Top Hat* (1935), *Swing Time* (1936), *The Bandwagon* (1953), *Funny Face* (1957)
Career low: *The Midas Run* (1969)

> ### Testing Times
>
> Screen tests, though they can be an important part of the casting process, are not always reliable indicators of an actor's potential – Fred Astaire's first screen test was famously marked in a studio report: 'Can't act. Can't sing. Can dance a little.' Clark Gable, Shirley Temple, Rock Hudson and Brigitte Bardot all failed early screen tests before moving on to become major stars.

Astor, Mary (Lucille Langhanke) (1906–87)

American, born in Quincy, Illinois. She made her film debut with a small role in *Sentimental Tommy* (1921). A star in the silent era, she survived the transition to sound, becoming a versatile character actress and winning a Best Supporting

Actress Academy Award® for *The Great Lie* (1941). She retired from the screen after *Hush, Hush Sweet Charlotte* (1964).
Career highs: *Dodsworth* (1936), *The Maltese Falcon* (1941), *The Great Lie* (1941), *Act of Violence* (1948)
Career lows: *Return of the Terror* (1934), *Straight from the Heart* (1935)

Attenborough, Sir Richard Samuel (1923–)

English, born in Cambridge. A student at the Royal Academy of Dramatic Art, he made his film debut in *In Which We Serve* (1942). A stalwart character actor for the next 30 years, he later turned to direction, winning an Academy Award® for *Gandhi* (1982), and is now a much-loved elder statesman of the UK film industry.
Career highs (actor): *Brighton Rock* (1947), *Séance on a Wet Afternoon* (1964), *10 Rillington Place* (1971)
Career highs (director): *Gandhi* (1982), *Cry Freedom* (1987), *Shadowlands* (1993)
Career low: *Loot* (1970)

Auteuil, Daniel (1950–)

French, born in Algiers, Algeria. The son of two singers, he was drawn to the stage and made his film debut in *L'Agression* (1975). A powerful presence with a wide-ranging talent, he made an impact internationally in *Jean de Florette* (1986) and has become one of the most distinguished French actors of his generation. He was formerly married to **Emmanuelle Béart**.
Career highs: *Jean de Florette* (1986), *Un Coeur en hiver* (1991), *Le Huitième jour* (1996), *Caché* (2005)
Career lows: *The Lost Son* (1998), *The Escort* (1999)

Aykroyd, Dan (1951–)

Canadian, born in Ottawa, Ontario. A sociology student, he performed with the Second City comedy troupe in Toronto before joining cult television show *Saturday Night Live*. He made his film debut in *Love at First Sight* (1977). A popular comedy star, he later became a character actor, receiving a Best Supporting Actor Academy Award® nomination for *Driving Miss Daisy* (1989).
Career highs: *The Blues Brothers* (1980), *Trading Places* (1983), *Ghostbusters* (1984)
Career lows: *Neighbors* (1981), *Loose Cannons* (1989), *Nothing But Trouble* (1991), *Getting Away with Murder* (1996)

B

Bacall, Lauren (Betty Joan Perske) (1924–)

American, born in New York City. A drama student and model, she was spotted on the cover of *Harper's Bazaar*, taken to Hollywood for a screen test and placed under personal contract to director **Howard Hawks**. She made her film debut opposite **Humphrey Bogart** (whom she later married) in *To Have and Have Not* (1944). She was Academy Award®-nominated as Best Supporting Actress for *The Mirror has Two Faces* (1996).

Career highs: *To Have and Have Not* (1944), *The Big Sleep* (1946), *The Shootist* (1976)
Career lows: *The Gift of Love* (1958), *Shock Treatment* (1964)

Bacon, Kevin (1958–   )

American, born in Philadelphia, Pennsylvania. Intent on an acting career from an early age, he made his film debut in *National Lampoon's Animal House* (1978). A boyish leading man in the 1980s, he matured into a subtle and versatile character actor. He married actress Kyra Sedgwick in 1988.
Career highs: *Diner* (1982), *Footloose* (1984), *JFK* (1991), *The Woodsman* (2004)
Career lows: *Pyrates* (1990), *Beauty Shop* (2005)

Bale, Christian (1974–   )

Welsh, born in Haverfordwest, Pembrokeshire. He was chosen from 4,000 young hopefuls to make his feature film debut in *Empire of the Sun* (1987). He has worked hard to sustain an adult career, dramatically altering his physical appearance and accent according to the demands of his roles. In 2005 he took the title role in *Batman Begins*.
Career highs: *Empire of the Sun* (1987), *American Psycho* (2000), *The Machinist* (2004), *The New World* (2005)
Career lows: *Newsies* (1992), *Swing Kids* (1993), *All the Little Animals* (1998), *Captain Corelli's Mandolin* (2001)

⌐ *Generation Gaps* ⌐

Although in the storyline of *The Graduate* (1967) Anne Bancroft's Mrs Robinson is many years older than the student she seduces (Dustin Hoffman), the actors were in fact only six years apart in age. Similarly, in *The Manchurian Candidate* (1962), Angela Lansbury played the mother of Laurence Harvey, who was just three years her junior, while *Alexander* (2004) saw Angelina Jolie cast as Colin Farrell's mother despite a mere eleven months' age difference.

Bancroft, Anne (Anna Maria Louisa Italiano) (1931–2005)

American, born in the Bronx, New York City. Supporting herself as a salesgirl and English teacher, she began her acting career on radio. She made her film debut in *Don't Bother To Knock* (1952). Her film roles improved after consecutive Tony Awards on Broadway, and she won a Best Actress Academy Award® for *The Miracle Worker* (1962). She was married to **Mel Brooks** from 1964 until her death.
Career highs: *The Miracle Worker* (1962), *The Pumpkin Eater* (1964), *The Graduate* (1967), *The Turning Point* (1977), *Agnes of God* (1985)
Career lows: *The Treasure of the Golden Condor* (1953), *Gorilla at Large* (1954)

Banderas, Antonio (José Antonio Domínguez Bandera) (1960–   )

Spanish, born in Málaga. His original ambition to become a football player ended when he broke his ankle as a teenager. Turning to acting, he made his film debut in *Labyrinth Of Passion* (1982) and worked regularly with director **Pedro Almodóvar** before moving to America in 1992. He married actress **Melanie Griffith** in 1997.

Career highs: *Women on the Verge of a Nervous Breakdown* (1988), *Evita* (1996), *The Mask of Zorro* (1998), *Shrek 2* (2004)
Career lows: *Original Sin* (2001), *The Body* (2001), *Ballistic: Ecks Vs. Sever* (2002)

Bardem, Javier Ángel Encinas (1969–)

Spanish, born on Gran Canaria in the Canary Islands. Born into a family of actors, his original ambition was to become a painter. He was also a rugby player before turning to acting. He made his film debut in *The Ages of Lulu* (1990) and was typecast as a smouldering sex symbol before finding a wider range of roles. He was a Best Actor Academy Award® nominee for *Before Night Falls* (2000).
Career highs: *Jamón, jamón* (1992), *Before Night Falls* (2000), *Mondays in the Sun* (2002), *The Sea Inside* (2004)
Career low: *Between Your Legs* (1998)

Bardot, Brigitte (Camille Javal) (1934–)

French, born in Paris. A ballet student and fashion model, she made her film debut in *Le Trou normand* (1952). *And God Created Woman* (1956) made her an international sex symbol. She retired in 1973 and now devotes herself to animal rights campaigning.
Career highs: *And God Created Woman* (1956), *Contempt* (1963), *Viva Maria* (1965)
Career lows: *Don Juan (ou Si Don Juan était une femme)* (1973), *Colinot* (1973)

Barrymore, Drew Blythe (1975–)

American, born in Los Angeles, California. The daughter of John Barrymore Jr and granddaughter of **John Barrymore**, she was a professional actress almost before she could walk, and endeared herself to cinema-goers in *E.T.* (1982). Overcoming well-publicized adolescent battles with drink and drugs, she emerged as a likeable leading lady at her best in romantic comedies. She is also a successful producer.
Career highs: *E.T. the Extra-Terrestrial* (1982), *Scream* (1996), *The Wedding Planner* (1998), *Charlie's Angels* (2000), *Donnie Darko* (2001)
Career lows: *Riding in Cars with Boys* (2001), *Charlie's Angels: Full Throttle* (2003)

Barrymore, John Sidney Blythe (1882–1942)

American, born in Philadelphia, Pennsylvania. Born into an acting dynasty, he initially resisted his destiny to pursue a career in journalism and commercial art. On stage from 1903, he made his film debut in *An American Citizen* (1913). Sternly handsome, he was known as 'The Great Profile' and became a matinee idol of silent cinema. His later career was blighted by alcoholism.
Career highs: *Beau Brummell* (1924), *Don Juan* (1926), *Grand Hotel* (1932), *Twentieth Century* (1934)
Career low: *The Invisible Woman* (1941), *Playmates* (1941)

Basinger, Kim (1953–)

American, born in Athens, Georgia. A beauty pageant winner and model, she appeared in several television roles before making her film debut in *Hard Country* (1981). Her acting improved with experience, and she won a Best Supporting

Actress Academy Award® for *L.A. Confidential* (1997). She was formerly married to actor Alec Baldwin.
Career highs: *9½ Weeks* (1986), *L.A. Confidential* (1997)
Career lows: *My Stepmother Is an Alien* (1988), *Cool World* (1992)

Bassett, Angela (1958–)

American, born in New York City. After gaining an MFA from Yale University, she pursued an acting career, making her film debut in *F/X* (1996). She received a Best Actress Academy Award® nomination for her portrayal of Tina Turner in *What's Love Got to Do with It* (1993). She is married to actor Courtney B Vance.
Career highs: *Passion Fish* (1992), *What's Love Got to Do with It* (1993), *How Stella Got Her Groove Back* (1998)
Career lows: *Critters 4* (1991), *Supernova* (1999)

Bates, Sir Alan (Arthur Bates) (1934–2003)

English, born in Allestree, Derbyshire. He was a student at the Royal Academy of Dramatic Art, and became an established theatre actor before making his film debut in *The Entertainer* (1960). A vital presence in British cinema during the 1960s, he remained a leading stage and screen actor until his death. He received a Best Actor Academy Award® nomination for *The Fixer* (1968).
Career highs: *Whistle Down the Wind* (1961), *A Kind of Loving* (1962), *Zorba the Greek* (1964), *The Fixer* (1968), *An Unmarried Woman* (1978)
Career lows: *The Wicked Lady* (1983), *Duet For One* (1986), *Docteur M* (1989)

Bates, Kathy (1948–)

American, born in Memphis, Tennessee. The daughter of a mechanical engineer, she studied theatre at the Southern Methodist University in Dallas, Texas. She made her film debut in *Taking Off* (1971) but remained primarily a stage actress until her Academy Award®-winning performance in *Misery* (1990). She has directed episodes of television series *Oz*, *NYPD Blue* and *Six Feet Under*.
Career highs: *Misery* (1990), *Fried Green Tomatoes at the Whistle Stop Cafe* (1991), *Primary Colors* (1998), *About Schmidt* (2002)
Career lows: *The Waterboy* (1998)

Baxter, Anne (1923–85)

American, born in Michigan City, Indiana. The granddaughter of architect Frank Lloyd Wright, she was a child star on Broadway before making her film debut in *Twenty Mule Team* (1940). She developed into an ambitious, hardworking performer who won a Best Supporting Actress Academy Award® for *The Razor's Edge* (1946). Her first husband was actor John Hodiak.
Career highs: *Sunday Dinner for a Soldier* (1944), *The Razor's Edge* (1946), *All About Eve* (1950)
Career lows: *Carnival Story* (1954), *The Come-On* (1956)

Béart, Emmanuelle (1965–)

French, born in St Tropez. The daughter of singer Guy Béart, she made her film debut as a child in *And Hope To Die* (1971). **Robert Altman** encouraged her to

pursue a professional career, and she became a leading star of French cinema in the 1980s. Her rare English-language ventures include *Mission: Impossible* (1996). She was formerly married to **Daniel Auteuil**.

Career highs: *Manon des Sources* (1986), *La Belle noiseuse* (1991), *Un Coeur en hiver* (1992), *Nelly et Monsieur Arnaud* (1995)

Career lows: *Premiers désirs* (1983), *Date with an Angel* (1987)

Beatty, Warren (Warren Beaty) (1937–)

American, born in Richmond, Virginia. The younger brother of **Shirley MacLaine**, he rejected numerous sports scholarships to pursue an acting career in New York. He made his film debut in *Splendor in the Grass* (1961) and subsequently matured into a powerful Hollywood player with an enduring Don Juan reputation. He met **Annette Bening**, whom he later married, during the making of *Bugsy* (1991).

Career highs: *Bonnie and Clyde* (1967), *Reds* (1991), *Bugsy* (1991)

Career lows: *Ishtar* (1987), *Love Affair* (1994), *Town & Country* (2001)

Belmondo, Jean-Paul (1933–)

French, born in Neuilly-sur-Seine. The son of a sculptor, he studied at the Paris Conservatoire and made his name in the theatre before his film debut in *Sois belle et tais-toi* (1957). His craggy good looks and laid-back manner made him the face of the Nouvelle Vague, and he became one of French cinema's most enduring male stars.

Career highs: *Breathless* (1960), *Léon Morin, prêtre* (1961), *Le Voleur* (1967), *Borsalino* (1970), *Les Misérables* (1995)

Career lows: *Le Cerveau* (1969)

Benigni, Roberto (1952–)

Italian, born in Misericordia. Originally intending to become a priest, he later studied accounting before turning to the theatre. He made his film debut in *Berlinguer ti voglio bene* (1977), and his manic energy and surreal approach to comedy have made him one of Italy's biggest box-office stars. He won a Best Actor Academy Award[®] for *Life Is Beautiful* (1997), based on the wartime experiences of his father.

Career highs: *Down by Law* (1986), *Johnny Stecchino* (1991), *Il Mostro* (1994), *Life Is Beautiful* (1997)

Career lows: *Son of the Pink Panther* (1993), *Pinocchio* (2002)

Bening, Annette (1958–)

American, born in Topeka, Kansas. A student at San Francisco's American Conservatory Theater, she concentrated on stage work in New York before making her film debut in *The Great Outdoors* (1988). She met **Warren Beatty**, whom she later married, during the making of *Bugsy* (1991).

Career highs: *The Grifters* (1990), *Bugsy* (1991), *American Beauty* (1999), *Being Julia* (2004)

Career lows: *Love Affair* (1994), *What Planet Are You From?* (2000)

Bergman, Ingrid (1915–82)

Swedish, born in Stockholm. She made her film debut in *Munkbrogreven* (1934) and, after becoming a star in Sweden, her Hollywood debut in *Intermezzo* (1939). She later caused a scandal by leaving her husband for director **Roberto Rossellini**. She received Academy Awards® for *Gaslight* (1944), *Anastasia* (1956) and *Murder on the Orient Express* (1974).

Career highs: *A Woman's Face* (1938), *Casablanca* (1942), *For Whom the Bell Tolls* (1943), *Notorious* (1946), *Autumn Sonata* (1978)
Career lows: *Arch of Triumph* (1948), *Under Capricorn* (1949)

Bernal, Gael García (1978–)

Mexican, born in Guadalajara. A child actor, he appeared in television soap operas, short films and stage productions with his parents before heading to Europe. He studied acting at London's Central School of Speech and Drama and made his first major film appearance in *Amores perros* (2000), quickly emerging as one of the most exciting young actors in world cinema.

Career highs: *Amores perros* (2000), *Y tu mamá también* (2001), *The Motorcycle Diaries* (2003), *Bad Education* (2004)

Berry, Halle (1966–)

American, born in Cleveland, Ohio. A beauty pageant contestant and model, she appeared in the television series *Living Dolls* and *Knots Landing* before making her film debut as a crack addict in *Jungle Fever* (1991). With *Monster's Ball* (2001), she became the first African-American woman to win an Academy Award® for Best Actress.

Career highs: *Jungle Fever* (1991), *Bulworth* (1998), *Monster's Ball* (2001)
Career lows: *Gothika* (2003), *Catwoman* (2004)

Binoche, Juliette (1964–)

French, born in Paris. The daughter of a playwright and stage director, she made her film debut as a teenager in *Liberty Belle* (1983). An increasingly significant figure in the European cinema of the 1990s, she has worked sparingly in English-language films, and won a Best Supporting Actress Academy Award® for *The English Patient* (1996).

Career highs: *Les Amants du Pont Neuf* (1991), *Three Colours: Blue* (1993), *The English Patient* (1996), *Caché* (2005)
Career lows: *Wuthering Heights* (1992), *A Couch in New York* (1996)

Blanchett, Cate (Catherine Elise Blanchett) (1969–)

Australian, born in Melbourne. A student at Australia's National Institute for Dramatic Art, she worked in classical theatre roles and television before making her film debut in *Thank God For Lizzie* (1997). A handful of roles followed before *Elizabeth* (1998) established her on the international scene. She won a Best Supporting Actress Academy Award® playing **Katharine Hepburn** in *The Aviator* (2004).

Career highs: *Elizabeth* (1998), *The Aviator* (2004)
Career low: *The Man Who Cried* (2000)

Blondell, Joan (1909–79)

American, born in New York City. Born into a show-business family, she was a child performer who matured into an eye-catching Broadway actress. Signed to a contract with Warner Brothers, she made her film debut in *Sinners' Holiday* (1930) and spent a decade playing gold-digging chorus girls, wisecracking waitresses and gangsters' molls. She later became a respected character actress.
Career highs: *Gold Diggers of 1933* (1933), *Stand-In* (1937), *A Tree Grows in Brooklyn* (1945), *The Blue Veil* (1951), *Opening Night* (1977)
Career lows: *Off the Record* (1938), *The Kid from Kokomo* (1939), *I Want a Divorce* (1940)

Bloom, Claire (Patricia Claire Blume) (1931–   )

English, born in London. A student at the Guildhall School of Music and Drama, she made her film debut in *Blind Goddess* (1948) and was chosen by **Charlie Chaplin** to appear opposite him in *Limelight* (1952). Despite some impressive highlights, she has had a disappointing film career, enjoying greater success in the theatre. She has been married to **Rod Steiger** and to the writer Philip Roth.
Career highs: *Limelight* (1952), *The Haunting* (1963), *The Spy Who Came in from the Cold* (1965)
Career lows: *Innocents in Paris* (1953), *Déjà Vu* (1985)

Bloom, Orlando Jonathan Blanchard (1977–   )

English, born in Canterbury, Kent. An artistic child, he struggled with dyslexia at school. He trained as an actor in London and made his debut as a rent boy in *Wilde* (1997) before *The Lord of the Rings* trilogy (2001–3), his second film role, brought him international recognition.
Career highs: *The Lord of the Rings: The Fellowship of the Ring* (2001) et seq, *Pirates of the Caribbean: The Curse of the Black Pearl* (2003)
Career lows: *The Calcium Kid* (2004)

Bogarde, Sir Dirk (Derek Jules Ulric Niven van den Bogaerde) (1921–99)

English, born in Hampstead, London. An art student at Chelsea Polytechnic, he worked as an extra on *Come on George* (1940) and made his official film debut in *Dancing with Crime* (1947). He was a popular matinee idol in the 1950s, and gradually extended his range to become a European actor of considerable distinction. He also wrote memoirs and novels.
Career highs: *Doctor in the House* (1953), *Victim* (1961), *The Servant* (1963), *Death in Venice* (1971)
Career lows: *The Singer Not the Song* (1960), *A Bridge Too Far* (1977)

Bogart, Humphrey DeForest (1899–1957)

American, born in New York City. The son of a doctor, he played well-mannered juvenile leads on Broadway before making his feature film debut in *A Devil with Women* (1930). He served a long apprenticeship in supporting roles before establishing himself as a sardonic, lone-wolf tough guy with a streak of nobility. He was married to **Lauren Bacall** from 1945 until his death.

Career highs: *The Maltese Falcon* (1941), *Casablanca* (1942), *The Big Sleep* (1946), *The Treasure of the Sierra Madre* (1948), *The African Queen* (1951)
Career lows: *The Oklahoma Kid* (1939), *The Return of Dr X* (1939)

A Movie Giant

Unusually for a leading man, Humphrey Bogart stood only 5ft 4in/162cm tall. While shooting *Casablanca* (1942), he had to wear three-inch platforms on his shoes in order to bring him level with his co-star, Ingrid Bergman.

Bonham Carter, Helena (1966–)

English, born in London. She was educated at Westminster School before making her film debut in *A Room with a View* (1985). Further 'delicate English rose' roles in period films followed before she sought a more diverse range of parts during the 1990s. Her off-screen partner is director **Tim Burton**.
Career highs: *A Room with a View* (1985), *Howards End* (1992), *Fight Club* (1999)
Career low: *Mary Shelley's Frankenstein* (1994)

Borgnine, Ernest (Ermes Effron Borgnine) (1917–)

American, born in Hamden, Connecticut. A truck driver and gunner's mate during World War II, he subsequently studied acting and made his film debut in *Whistle at Eaton Falls* (1951). A memorably menacing villain in the 1950s, he won a Best Actor Academy Award[®] for *Marty* (1955) and has remained a busy character actor for the past 50 years. His five wives included actresses Katy Jurado and Ethel Merman.
Career highs: *From Here to Eternity* (1953), *Bad Day at Black Rock* (1954), *Marty* (1955), *The Wild Bunch* (1969)
Career lows: *Go Naked in the World* (1961)

Boyer, Charles (1897–1978)

French, born in Figeac. Educated at the Sorbonne, he studied drama at the Paris Conservatoire and made his film debut in *L'Homme du large* (1920). A matinee idol in France, he moved to Hollywood and became known as the international ideal of a sophisticated French lover. He committed suicide days after the death of his wife.
Career highs: *The Garden of Allah* (1936), *Love Affair* (1939), *Gaslight* (1944), *Barefoot in the Park* (1967)
Career low: *Arch of Triumph* (1948)

Branagh, Kenneth Charles (1960–)

Northern Irish, born in Belfast. He joined the Royal Shakespeare Company when he was 23. One of the most praised classical actors of his generation, he made his film debut in *High Season* (1986). He is noted for his film adaptations of Shakespeare, and *Henry V* (1989) earned him Academy Award[®] nominations for Best Actor and Best Director. He was married to **Emma Thompson** from 1989–95.
Career highs: *Henry V* (1989), *Hamlet* (1996), *Harry Potter and the Chamber of Secrets* (2002)
Career lows: *Dead Again* (1991), *Mary Shelley's Frankenstein* (1994), *Celebrity* (1998), *Wild, Wild West* (1999)

PEOPLE IN FILM
Some notable actors

Austrian, born in Alt Aussee. He made his film debut in *The Salzburg Connection* (1972), but remained a dedicated stage actor until his electrifying performance in *Mephisto* (1981) gained him international recognition. A magnetic, unpredictable character actor, he has also directed for both film and theatre.
Career highs: *Mephisto* (1981), *Out of Africa* (1985)
Career lows: *Becoming Colette* (1991)

American, born in Omaha, Nebraska. After studying with acting guru Stella Adler, he made his film debut in *The Men* (1950). The film version of *A Streetcar Named Desire* (1951) established him as an electrifying presence who revolutionized screen acting with a mixture of raw emotion, naturalism and psychological insight. In his later years, he became a reclusive figure who worked infrequently and expressed disdain for his profession.
Career highs: *A Streetcar Named Desire* (1951), *The Wild One* (1953), *On the Waterfront* (1954), *The Godfather* (1972), *Last Tango in Paris* (1972)
Career lows: *Desirée* (1954), *A Countess from Hong Kong* (1967), *Candy* (1968)

American, born in Los Angeles, California. The son of actors Lloyd Bridges and Dorothy Simpson, he made his film debut as a baby in *Born To Be Bad* (1950) and also appeared in his father's television series, *Sea Hunt*. Over the past 30 years, he has developed a body of work that is among the most respected in American cinema.
Career highs: *The Last Picture Show* (1971), *Fat City* (1972), *Starman* (1984), *The Fabulous Baker Boys* (1989), *The Big Lebowski* (1998)
Career lows: *King Kong* (1976), *Somebody Killed Her Husband* (1978), *8 Million Ways to Die* (1986)

American, born in New York City. The son of actor James Broderick, he studied drama and made his film debut in *Max Dugan Returns* (1983). A boyish star of popular teen films in the 1980s, he matured into a successful all-rounder and Broadway star. He married actress Sarah Jessica Parker in 1997.
Career highs: *Ferris Bueller's Day Off* (1986), *Biloxi Blues* (1988), *Election* (1999)
Career lows: *Inspector Gadget* (1999), *The Stepford Wives* (2004)

American, born in Ehrenfeld, Pennsylvania. One of 15 children born to Lithuanian immigrants, he worked as a miner and served in the US Army before pursuing an acting career. He made his film debut in *You're in the Navy Now* (1951) and played numerous supporting roles before emerging as a taciturn, granite-like star of westerns and brutal vigilante thrillers.
Career highs: *The Magnificent Seven* (1960), *The Great Escape* (1963), *Once Upon a Time in the West* (1968), *Death Wish* (1974), *Hard Times* (1975)

Career lows: *Twinky* (1970), *Ten to Midnight* (1983), *Death Wish V: The Face of Death* (1994)

Brooks, Louise (1906–85)

American, born in Cherryvale, Kansas. A dancer and chorus girl, she made her film debut in *Street of Forgotten Men* (1925) and was signed to a contract with Paramount. Journeying to Europe in the late 1920s, she attained cinematic immortality as Lulu in *Pandora's Box* (1928). Her return to Hollywood was badly mishandled, and she retired from the screen in 1938.
Career highs: *A Girl in Every Port* (1928), *Pandora's Box* (1928), *Diary of a Lost Girl* (1929)
Career lows: *Empty Saddles* (1937), *Overland Stage Raiders* (1938)

Brooks, Mel (Melvin Kaminsky) (1926–)

American, born in Brooklyn, New York City. A comedy performer, he was one of the writers for the television series *Your Show of Shows*. He made his feature film debut as the writer-director of *The Producers* (1968). In the 1970s, he found his forte as an irrepressible purveyor of freewheeling movie pastiches blending affection and vulgarity. He was married to **Anne Bancroft** from 1964 until her death.
Career highs: *The Producers* (1968), *Blazing Saddles* (1974), *Young Frankenstein* (1974)
Career lows: *Spaceballs* (1987), *Dracula: Dead and Loving It* (1995)

Brosnan, Pierce (1953–)

Irish, born in Drogheda, County Louth. He made his film debut in *The Long Good Friday* (1980) and found television success as Remington Steele. A commitment to his television work prevented him from replacing **Roger Moore** as James Bond in 1987, but the offer was later repeated, and he played 007 for the first time in *Goldeneye* (1995).
Career highs: *GoldenEye* (1995), *The Thomas Crown Affair* (1999), *The Tailor of Panama* (2001)
Career lows: *Nomads* (1986), *Taffin* (1988)

Brynner, Yul (1915–85)

Russian, born in Vladivostok. A trapeze artist, he came to America in 1941 and found work on stage and television. He made his film debut in *Port of New York* (1949). He won a Best Actor Academy Award® for repeating his stage triumph in the film version of *The King and I* (1956), but later proved difficult to cast.
Career highs: *The King and I* (1956), *The Magnificent Seven* (1960)
Career lows: *The Magic Christian* (1970), *The Light at the Edge of the World* (1971), *Romance of a Horse Thief* (1971)

Bullock, Sandra (1964–)

American, born in Arlington, Virginia. The daughter of German opera singer Helga Bullock, she made her first stage appearance with her mother when she was just eight. She made her film debut in *A Fool and His Money* (1988). Following the success of *Speed* (1994), she became a major star, and has found her greatest popularity in romantic comedies.

Career highs: *Speed* (1994), *While You Were Sleeping* (1995), *Miss Congeniality* (2000), *Crash* (2004)
Career lows: *Speed 2: Cruise Control* (1997), *Miss Congeniality 2: Armed and Fabulous* (2005)

Burstyn, Ellen (Edna Rae Gillooly) (1932–)

American, born in Detroit, Michigan. A dancer and model, she worked on stage and in television before her film debut in *For Those Who Think Young* (1964). Her best film work came in the 1970s, and she won a Best Actress Academy Award® for *Alice Doesn't Live Here Anymore* (1974). She continues to work extensively on stage and television, with occasional film roles.
Career highs: *The King of Marvin Gardens* (1972), *Alice Doesn't Live Here Anymore* (1974), *Resurrection* (1980), *Requiem for a Dream* (2000)
Career lows: *Pit Stop* (1969), *A Dream of Passion* (1978)

Burton, Richard (Richard Walter Jenkins) (1925–84)

Welsh, born in Pontrhydfen. The son of a coalminer, he gained a scholarship to Exeter College, Oxford. A magnetic, brooding stage performer in his youth, he made his film debut in *The Last Days of Dolwyn* (1948). He subsequently pursued a Hollywood career, gaining notoriety for his hell-raising antics and two marriages to **Elizabeth Taylor**.
Career highs: *The Night of the Iguana* (1964), *The Spy Who Came in from the Cold* (1965), *Who's Afraid of Virginia Woolf?* (1966), *The Taming of the Shrew* (1967)
Career lows: *Staircase* (1969), *Hammersmith Is Out* (1972)

Buscemi, Steve (1957–)

American, born in Brooklyn, New York City. A drama student at the Lee Strasberg Institute, he was also a New York firefighter before theatre work led to his film debut in *The Way It Is* (1984). He subsequently became familiar as an invaluable, bug-eyed character actor, often averaging five films in a year. He has also directed.
Career highs: *Reservoir Dogs* (1992), *In the Soup* (1992), *Fargo* (1996), *Ghost World* (2001)

Byrne, Gabriel (1950–)

Irish, born in Dublin. After working as an archaeologist and schoolteacher, he came to acting in his late twenties. Television and stage work led to small film roles and his first important part in *Excalibur* (1981). Frequently cast in brooding, saturnine roles, he has also produced and directed. He was married to the actress Ellen Barkin from 1988–93.
Career highs: *Defence of the Realm* (1985), *Miller's Crossing* (1990), *The Usual Suspects* (1995)
Career lows: *Siesta* (1987), *Hello Again* (1987)

C

Caan, James (1939–)

American, born in Queens, New York City. A university football player, karate expert and rodeo veteran, he studied acting at Stanford Meisner's Neighborhood Playhouse before making his film debut in *Irma La Douce* (1963). A major star in the 1970s, his career faltered in the 1980s.
Career highs: *The Rain People* (1969), *The Godfather* (1972), *The Gambler* (1974), *Thief* (1981), *Misery* (1990)
Career lows: *Harry and Walter Go to New York* (1976), *Another Man, Another Chance* (1977), *Chapter Two* (1979)

Cage, Nicolas (Nicholas Coppola) (1964–)

American, born in Long Beach, California. The nephew of **Francis Ford Coppola**, he began acting as a teenager, making his film debut in *Fast Times at Ridgemont High* (1982). Noted for his quirky, idiosyncratic roles and attention to detail, he has become a mainstay of big-budget blockbusters. He received a Best Actor Academy Award® for *Leaving Las Vegas* (1995).
Career highs: *Moonstruck* (1987), *Wild at Heart* (1990), *Leaving Las Vegas* (1995), *Adaptation* (2002)
Career lows: *Zandalee* (1990), *Gone in Sixty Seconds* (2000)

Cagney, James Francis (1899–1986)

American, born in New York City. A jaunty star of Broadway musicals in the 1920s, he made his film debut in *Sinners' Holiday* (1930). His electrifying performance as a cocky tough guy in *The Public Enemy* (1931) established him as the quintessential screen hoodlum. He received a Best Actor Academy Award® for *Yankee Doodle Dandy* (1942) and retired after *One, Two, Three* (1961), but returned for a final film role in *Ragtime* (1981).
Career highs: *The Public Enemy* (1931), *Angels with Dirty Faces* (1938), *Yankee Doodle Dandy* (1942), *White Heat* (1949), *Love Me Or Leave Me* (1955)
Career low: *The Oklahoma Kid* (1939)

Caine, Sir Michael (Maurice Joseph Micklewhite) (1933–)

English, born in London. The son of a Billingsgate fish porter, he took his name from *The Caine Mutiny* (1954). He made his film debut in *A Hill in Korea* (1956) and played numerous bit-parts before achieving stardom in *Zulu* (1963). His consummate professionalism has improved many mediocre films and enhanced several screen classics. He won Academy Awards® for *Hannah and Her Sisters* (1986) and *The Cider House Rules* (1999), and was knighted in 2000.
Career highs: *Alfie* (1966), *Get Carter* (1971), *Sleuth* (1972), *Educating Rita* (1983), *The Quiet American* (2002)
Career lows: *The Swarm* (1978), *Jaws: The Revenge* (1987)

Carlyle, Robert (1961–)

Scottish, born in Glasgow. As a student in Glasgow he formed the theatre company Rain Dog. He made his film debut in *Silent Scream* (1990), and came to international

notice with his intense portrayal of the psychotic Begbie in *Trainspotting* (1996). A versatile, hardworking actor, he has found some of his most memorable roles on television.
Career highs: *Priest* (1994), *Trainspotting* (1996), *The Full Monty* (1997)
Career low: *Ravenous* (1998)

Carmichael, Ian (1920–)

English, born in Hull, Yorkshire. A cabaret performer, mimic and polished light comedian, he made his film debut in *Bond Street* (1948). He became the embodiment of the dithering English ass in the 1950s comedies of the Boulting Brothers. Later, he was best known for playing Bertie Wooster and Lord Peter Wimsey, both in the theatre and on television.
Career highs: *Private's Progress* (1955), *Lucky Jim* (1957), *I'm All Right Jack* (1959)
Career lows: *Light Up the Sky* (1960), *Double Bunk* (1961)

Caron, Leslie (1931–)

French, born in Boulogne-Billancourt. A ballet student, she was spotted by **Gene Kelly** at the Ballets des Champs-Elysées and invited to Hollywood, where she made her film debut in *An American in Paris* (1951). At her best in MGM musicals of the 1950s, she later tested herself in more dramatic roles and became a character actress in international productions.
Career highs: *An American in Paris* (1951), *Lili* (1953), *Gigi* (1958), *The L-Shaped Room* (1962)
Career lows: *The Subterraneans* (1960), *Valentino* (1977)

Carrey, Jim (1962–)

Canadian, born in Newmarket, Ontario. He worked extensively on the Canadian comedy circuit before moving to the USA and making his film debut in *Finders Keepers* (1984). *Ace Ventura: Pet Detective* (1994) confirmed his appeal as a manic, rubber-faced clown, and he soon became one of Hollywood's highest-paid stars. He has won increasing respect for his dramatic performances.
Career highs: *The Mask* (1994), *The Truman Show* (1998), *Eternal Sunshine of the Spotless Mind* (2004)
Career lows: *Once Bitten* (1985), *Ace Ventura: When Nature Calls* (1995)

Carter, Helena Bonham see **Bonham Carter, Helena**

Cassavetes, John (1929–89)

American, born in New York City. A graduate of the New York Academy Of Dramatic Art, he made his film debut in *Fourteen Hours* (1951). Frequently cast as an angry, alienated youth during the 1950s, he made his directorial debut with the experimental cinéma-verité feature *Shadows* (1959). His skill as an actor was later eclipsed by his ability as a director of emotionally intense, unflinchingly honest contemporary dramas. He was married to **Gena Rowlands**.
Career highs (actor): *Edge of the City* (1957), *The Dirty Dozen* (1967), *Rosemary's Baby* (1968)

Career highs (director): *Faces* (1968), *Husbands* (1970), *A Woman Under the Influence* (1974)

Career lows: *Incubus* (1981), *Big Trouble* (1985)

Chan, Jackie (Chan Kong-Sang) (1954–)

Chinese, born in Hong Kong. Sent to the Peking Opera School as a child, he studied music, dance and martial arts before making his film debut in *Big and Little Wong Tin Bar* (1962). In adulthood, he developed into an incredibly nimble martial arts star, responsible for all of his own death-defying stunts and acrobatic, knockabout routines.

Career highs: *Project A* (1983), *Police Story* (1985), *Armour of God 2: Operation Condor* (1991), *Rush Hour* (1998)

Career lows: *The Cannonball Run* (1980), *The Medallion* (2003)

Chaney, Lon (Alonso Chaney) (1883–1930)

American, born in Colorado Springs, Colorado. The son of deaf-mute parents, he made his film debut in *Poor Jake's Demise* (1913). An all-rounder, he later developed a reputation as silent cinema's 'Man of a Thousand Faces', creating a gallery of screen grotesques involving elaborate disguises and painful contortion of his body. His son, Lon Chaney Jr, followed in his footsteps, achieving fame as the Wolf Man.

Career highs: *The Hunchback of Notre Dame* (1923), *The Phantom of the Opera* (1925), *The Unholy Three* (1925), *London After Midnight* (1927)

Chaplin, Charlie (Sir Charles Spencer Chaplin) (1889–1977)

English, born in London. Born into extreme poverty, he became a music-hall performer. In the USA from 1913, he made his film debut in *Kid Auto Races at Venice* (1914). His plaintive comedy creation of the gentleman tramp with baggy trousers, bowler hat and walking cane endeared him to a vast global audience during the silent era. He was hounded out of the country during the anti-Communist witch-hunts of the 1950s, and spent the rest of his days in Switzerland.

Career highs: *The Kid* (1920), *The Gold Rush* (1924), *City Lights* (1931), *Modern Times* (1936), *Limelight* (1952)

Career low: *A Countess From Hong Kong* (1967)

> ### Man of Many Talents
>
> As well as writing, directing, producing, editing and performing in the acclaimed *City Lights* (1931), Charlie Chaplin composed the film's score himself. He also composed the scores of all his subsequent films.

Charisse, Cyd (Tula Ellice Finklea) (1921–)

American, born in Amarillo, Texas. A ballet student, she joined the Ballets Russes at the age of 14 and toured Europe and America before making her film debut in *Mission to Moscow* (1943). A tall, long-legged beauty, she dazzled in the MGM musicals of the 1950s, and continued to appear on stage and in cabaret well into her seventies.

Career highs: *Singin' in the Rain* (1952), *The Bandwagon* (1953), *Silk Stockings* (1957)
Career lows: *Five Golden Hours* (1960), *Maroc 7* (1967)

Cher (Cherilyn Sarkisian LaPier) (1946–)

American, born in El Centro, California. Along with her husband Sonny Bono, she enjoyed enormous success as a singer in the 1960s. She made her film debut in *Wild on the Beach* (1965). In the 1980s she began to concentrate more on acting, appearing on stage and winning a Best Actress Academy Award® for *Moonstruck* (1987). Her film appearances have grown increasingly rare.
Career highs: *Silkwood* (1983), *Mask* (1985), *Moonstruck* (1987)
Career lows: *Faithful* (1996)

Cheung, Maggie (Cheung Man-Yuk) (1964–)

Chinese, born in Hong Kong. She attended school in England and returned to Hong Kong to work as a model before making her film debut in *Yuen fan* (1984). Following her breakthrough role in **Jackie Chan**'s *Police Story* (1985), she sought out challenging projects that displayed her versatility. A talented comedienne, action star and dramatic actress, she has made some films in English but is best known for her Chinese-language roles.
Career highs: *Days of Being Wild* (1991), *The Actress* (1992), *Irma Vep* (1996), *In the Mood for Love* (2000)
Career low: *Prince Charming* (1984), *Love Hungry Suicide Squad* (1988)

Chevalier, Maurice (1888–1972)

French, born in Menilmontant, Paris. An electrician and apprentice to a metal engraver, he gradually worked his way into show business, making his film debut in *Trop crédules* (1908). He moved to Hollywood in 1929 and enjoyed six years as a roguish star of musicals and romantic comedies, later developing into an avuncular, scene-stealing character actor.
Career highs: *The Love Parade* (1929), *Love Me Tonight* (1932), *One Hour with You* (1932), *Gigi* (1958)
Career low: *A Bedtime Story* (1933), *The Way to Love* (1933)

Chow Yun-Fat (1956–)

Chinese, born in Hong Kong. He began acting at the television station TVB in Hong Kong in 1973, and had his first major role in *The Story of Woo Viet* (1981); he later formed a hugely successful partnership with the director John Woo. A good-looking, athletic and versatile leading man, he made the transition to Hollywood in the late 1990s and went on to star in *Crouching Tiger, Hidden Dragon* (2000).
Career highs: *A Better Tomorrow* (1986), *The Killer* (1989), *Hard Boiled* (1992), *Crouching Tiger, Hidden Dragon* (2000)
Career low: *Massage Girls* (1976)

Christie, Julie Frances (1940–)

English, born in Assam, India. She studied at the Central School of Music and Drama in London before making her film debut in the comedy *Crooks Anonymous* (1962). *Billy Liar* (1963) established her as one of the faces of Swinging Sixties London, and she won a Best Actress Academy Award[®] for *Darling* (1965).
Career highs: *Darling* (1965), *McCabe and Mrs Miller* (1971), *Heat and Dust* (1983), *Afterglow* (1997), *Finding Neverland* (2004)
Career lows: *In Search of Gregory* (1969), *Demon Seed* (1977)

Clift, (Edward) Montgomery (1920–66)

American, born in Omaha, Nebraska. He worked exclusively in the theatre until his film debut in *Red River* (1948) opposite **John Wayne**. A slight, intense figure, he was part of the post-war generation that brought new psychological depth to screen acting. A car accident during the making of *Raintree County* (1957) left him permanently scarred, and he was troubled by poor health during his later career.
Career highs: *The Search* (1948), *A Place in the Sun* (1951), *From Here to Eternity* (1953)
Career low: *The Defector* (1966)

Clooney, George (1961–)

American, born in Maysville, Kentucky. The nephew of singer Rosemary Clooney, he studied journalism before pursuing an acting career. He made his film debut in *Combat High* (1986), and played minor television roles before the hospital drama series *ER* made him a star. He has subsequently proven himself as a dashing leading man and risk-taking producer, and has also directed.
Career highs: *Out of Sight* (1998), *Three Kings* (1999), *O Brother, Where Art Thou?* (2000), *Good Night, and Good Luck* (2005), *Syriana* (2005)
Career lows: *Return of the Killer Tomatoes* (1988), *Batman & Robin* (1997)

Close, Glenn (1947–)

American, born in Greenwich, Connecticut. A drama student and member of the pop group Up With People, she was a vastly experienced stage actress before making her film debut in *The World According to Garp* (1982). Her cinema career flourished in the 1980s, and she continues to balance film and stage work.
Career highs: *The Big Chill* (1983), *Fatal Attraction* (1987), *Dangerous Liaisons* (1988)
Career lows: *Maxie* (1985)

Coburn, James (1928–2002)

American, born in Laurel, Nebraska. He made his film debut in *Ride Lonesome* (1959), and brought a lithe, cheetah-like grace and grinning smile to a succession of westerns, war films and action stories. Despite suffering from chronic arthritis in his later years, he remained prolific, and won a Best Supporting Actor Academy Award[®] for *Affliction* (1997).
Career highs: *The Magnificent Seven* (1960), *Our Man Flint* (1966), *The President's Analyst* (1967), *Affliction* (1997)
Career lows: *Duffy* (1968), *Mr Patman* (1980)

Colbert, Claudette (Lily Claudette Chauchoin) (1903–96)

French, born in Paris. Educated in New York, she became a stenographer before pursuing an acting career. A Broadway star, she made her film debut in *For the Love of Mike* (1927). A leading lady with a merry talent for romantic comedy, she won a Best Actress Academy Award® for *It Happened One Night* (1934). She retired from the screen after *Parrish* (1961), but continued to appear on stage and television.
Career highs: *It Happened One Night* (1934), *Imitation of Life* (1934), *Midnight* (1939), *The Palm Beach Story* (1942)
Career lows: *I Cover the Waterfront* (1933)

Collins, Joan Henrietta (1933–)

English, born in London. A student at the Royal Academy of Dramatic Art, she made her film debut as a teenage beauty contestant in *Lady Godiva Rides Again* (1951). She went to Hollywood as an ambitious starlet in 1955, and has proved a remarkably enduring, good-humoured sex symbol, finding her greatest fame in the television series *Dynasty*.
Career highs: *The Girl in the Red Velvet Swing* (1955), *The Wayward Bus* (1957), *The Stud* (1978)
Career lows: *Can Heironymus Merkin Ever Forget Mercy Humppe and Find True Happiness?* (1969), *Empire of the Ants* (1977), *Homework* (1982)

Colman, Ronald (1891–1958)

English, born in Richmond, Surrey. The son of a silk importer, he worked for the British Steamship Company before serving in the army. An amateur actor, he turned professional and made his film debut in *The Toilers* (1919). In the USA from 1920, he spent 30 years as a dashing matinee idol of rare wit and charm. He won a Best Actor Academy Award® for *A Double Life* (1948)
Career highs: *Bulldog Drummond* (1930), *A Tale of Two Cities* (1935), *Lost Horizon* (1937), *The Prisoner of Zenda* (1937), *Random Harvest* (1942)
Career lows: *Lucky Partners* (1940)

Connery, Sir Sean Thomas (1930–)

Scottish, born in Edinburgh. After a succession of jobs as a milkman, lifeguard, coffin polisher and life model, he pursued an acting career. He became an international star as James Bond in *Dr No* (1962), but struggled to escape from the shadows of the role. Later, he proved himself a powerful dramatic actor and became a much-loved star, winning a Best Supporting Actor Academy Award® for *The Untouchables* (1987).
Career highs: *Goldfinger* (1964), *The Offence* (1972), *The Man Who Would Be King* (1975), *The Untouchables* (1987)
Career lows: *Meteor* (1979), *The Avengers* (1998)

Cooper, Chris (1951–)

American, born in Kansas City, Missouri. Raised on a cattle ranch, he studied agriculture and acting before his first major film role in *Matewan* (1987), which marked the beginning of a series of critically acclaimed performances in independent films. Underappreciated by Hollywood for many years, he

demonstrated his versatility in a variety of character parts before winning a Best Supporting Actor Academy Award® for *Adaptation* (2002).
Career highs: *Lone Star* (1996), *American Beauty* (1999), *Adaptation* (2002), *Silver City* (2004)
Career lows: *Money Train* (1995), *Breast Men* (1997)

Cooper, Gary Frank James (1901–61)

American, born in Helena, Montana. He was a political cartoonist, and began his film career as an extra and stunt rider in silent westerns. His taciturn, self-effacing nature made him a romantic leading man and beloved embodiment of all-American decency. He won Best Actor Academy Awards® for *Sergeant York* (1941) and *High Noon* (1952).
Career highs: *The Virginian* (1929), *Mr Deeds Goes to Town* (1936), *Sergeant York* (1941), *For Whom the Bell Tolls* (1943), *High Noon* (1952)
Career lows: *Good Sam* (1948), *You're in the Navy Now* (1951)

Costello, Lou (Louis Francis Cristillo) (1906–59)

American, born in Paterson, New Jersey. He worked in a wide variety of jobs including newsboy, soda fountain clerk and prizefighter, before moving to Hollywood and becoming a vaudeville performer. He joined forces with **Bud Abbott** in 1930 to form a comedy double act. They made their joint film debut in *One Night in the Tropics* (1940) and enjoyed box-office success, if little critical acclaim, for the next fifteen years.
Career highs: *Buck Privates* (1941), *Abbott and Costello Meet Frankenstein* (1948)
Career lows: *Africa Screams* (1949), *Dance with Me Henry* (1956)

Costner, Kevin (1955–   )

American, born in Lynwood, California. A business major at university, he appeared in low-budget films and bit-parts before his career took off in the 1980s. He won a Best Director Academy Award® for *Dances with Wolves* (1990), but failed to maintain his box-office standing in the new millennium.
Career highs: *Bull Durham* (1988), *Field of Dreams* (1989), *Dances with Wolves* (1990), *Open Range* (2003)
Career lows: *The Postman* (1997), *3000 Miles to Graceland* (2001)

Cotten, Joseph (1905–94)

American, born in Petersburg, Virginia. A football player, salesman and drama critic, he studied acting at the Hickman School of Expression in Washington, DC. He was exclusively a theatre actor until his long association with **Orson Welles** brought him to the cinema, where he proved a dependable leading man over four decades of gradually diminishing standards.
Career highs: *Citizen Kane* (1941), *The Magnificent Ambersons* (1943), *Shadow of a Doubt* (1943), *The Third Man* (1949), *Petulia* (1968)
Career lows: *Beyond the Forest* (1949), *Lady Frankenstein* (1971)

Courtenay, Sir Tom (Thomas Daniel Courtenay) (1937–   )

English, born in Hull. After studying at the Royal Academy of Dramatic Art, he made his film debut as the working-class rebel in *The Loneliness of the Long Distance Runner* (1962). A vital figure in the British cinema of the 1960s, he gradually drifted away from film acting, finding richer rewards in his allegiance to the theatre. He received Academy Award® nominations for *Doctor Zhivago* (1965) and *The Dresser* (1983).
Career highs: *Billy Liar* (1963), *Doctor Zhivago* (1965), *The Dresser* (1983), *Let Him Have It* (1991)
Career lows: *The Day the Fish Came Out* (1967), *Leonard Part 6* (1987)

Crawford, Joan (Lucille Le Sueur) (1906–77)

American, born in San Antonio, Texas. An ambitious Broadway chorus girl and bit-part player, she became the embodiment of the jazz-age flapper and was a star of 1930s melodrama, playing working-class girls with their sights set on wealth and sophistication. Later the epitome of the glamorous Hollywood movie queen, she won a Best Actress Academy Award® for *Mildred Pierce* (1945).
Career highs: *Grand Hotel* (1932), *The Women* (1939), *A Woman's Face* (1941), *Mildred Pierce* (1945), *What Ever Happened to Baby Jane?* (1962)
Career lows: *Ice Follies of 1939* (1939), *Berserk* (1967), *Trog* (1970)

> ### Mutual Dislike
>
> The rivalry between leading ladies Joan Crawford and Bette Davis was legendary, and matters came to a head when they starred together in *What Ever Happened to Baby Jane?* (1962). Crawford later said of her arch-rival, 'Working with Bette Davis was my greatest challenge, and I mean that kindly. She liked to scream and yell. I just sit and knit. During *What Ever Happened to Baby Jane?*, I knitted a scarf from here to Malibu.' (*Variety*, April 1973)

Crosby, Bing (Harry Lillis Crosby) (1904–77)

American, born in Tacoma, Washington. A singer with Paul Whiteman's Rhythm Boys, he made his feature film debut in *King of Jazz* (1930). His relaxed style and intimate crooning revolutionized popular music. He was a hugely popular film star for more than two decades, appearing in light comedies, musicals and the series of *Road to ...* films with **Bob Hope** and Dorothy Lamour. He won a Best Actor Academy Award® for *Going My Way* (1944).
Career highs: *Going My Way* (1944), *The Road to Utopia* (1945), *White Christmas* (1954), *The Country Girl* (1954), *High Society* (1956)
Career lows: *The Emperor Waltz* (1948), *Say One for Me* (1959)

Crowe, Russell Ira (1964–   )

New Zealander, born in Wellington. After appearing as a child star on Australian television, he made his adult film debut in *Prisoners of the Sun* (1990). He quickly established himself as a leading actor in Australian cinema before heading to Hollywood, where he has attracted attention both for his forceful, compelling performances and his ability to attract unsavoury headlines.

Career highs: *Romper Stomper* (1992), *L.A. Confidential* (1997), *The Insider* (1999), *Gladiator* (2000)
Career lows: *Rough Magic* (1995), *Virtuosity* (1995), *Breaking Up* (1997)

Cruise, Tom (Tom Cruise Mapother IV) (1962–)

American, born in Syracuse, New Jersey. He contemplated becoming a priest before dedicating himself to an acting career, and made his film debut in *Endless Love* (1980). He has since developed into one of the most charismatic and driven leading men of his generation. He has previously been married to actress Mimi Rogers and to **Nicole Kidman**, whom he met during the filming of *Days of Thunder* (1990).
Career highs: *Born on the Fourth of July* (1989), *Jerry Maguire* (1996), *Magnolia* (1999), *Collateral* (2004)
Career lows: *Losin' It* (1983), *Legend* (1985)

Cruz, Penélope (Penélope Cruz Sanchez) (1974–)

Spanish, born in Madrid. After studying classical ballet, she worked in television and on music videos before making her film debut in *El Laberinto griego* (1991). An award-winning actress, noted for her collaborations with **Pedro Almodóvar**, she subsequently pursued a Hollywood career but has found her most demanding roles in Europe.
Career highs: *All About My Mother* (1998), *Don't Move* (1993)
Career low: *Woman on Top* (2000)

Crystal, Billy (1947–)

American, born in Long Beach, New York. The son of a concert promoter, he was a successful stand-up comedian before working in television, notably in *Soap* and *Saturday Night Live*. He made his film debut in *Rabbit Test* (1978). An irrepressible, wisecracking imp, he has also written and directed films, and has been a host of the Academy Award[®] ceremonies.
Career highs: *When Harry Met Sally* (1989), *City Slickers* (1991), *Analyze This* (1999)
Career lows: *Memories of Me* (1988), *Fathers' Day* (1997)

Curtis, Jamie Lee (1958–)

American, born in Los Angeles, California. The daughter of **Tony Curtis** and **Janet Leigh**, she worked in television before her film debut in *Halloween* (1978). Initially typecast in horror films, she later revealed a winning flair for comedy. She is married to **Christopher Guest**, who inherited a peerage, thus making her Lady Haden-Guest.
Career highs: *Halloween* (1978), *Trading Places* (1983), *A Fish Called Wanda* (1987)
Career lows: *Perfect* (1985), *Mother's Boys* (1993), *Virus* (1999)

Curtis, Tony (Bernard Schwartz) (1925–)

American, born in the Bronx, New York City. The son of Hungarian immigrants, he served in the US Navy before studying drama. He made his film debut in *Criss Cross* (1948) and quickly rose to stardom in exotic adventure yarns. He later proved

himself an incisive dramatic actor and engaging comedy performer, earning a Best Actor Academy Award® nomination for *The Defiant Ones* (1958).

Career highs: *Sweet Smell of Success* (1957), *The Defiant Ones* (1958), *Some Like It Hot* (1959), *The Boston Strangler* (1968)

Career lows: *The Chastity Belt* (1968), *Where Is Parsifal?* (1984)

Cusack, John Paul (1966–   )

American, born in Evanston, Illinois. The son of director and screenwriter Dick Cusack, he started acting from the age of nine. He made his film debut in *Class* (1983) and appeared in numerous 'teen' films, before seeking a wider range of roles and a career that has balanced mainstream films with quirkier independent ventures. His sister is actress Joan Cusack.

Career highs: *Say Anything* (1989), *The Grifters* (1990), *Grosse Pointe Blank* (1997), *Being John Malkovich* (1999)

Career lows: *Hot Pursuit* (1987), *Identity* (2003)

Cushing, Peter Wilton (1913–94)

English, born in Kenley, Surrey. He studied at the Guildhall School of Music and Drama and appeared in amateur stage productions before heading to Hollywood and making his film debut in *The Man in the Iron Mask* (1939). *The Curse of Frankenstein* (1956) began a long association with Hammer Films, in which he brought a measure of dignity and intelligence to the horror genre.

Career highs: *The Curse of Frankenstein* (1956), *Dracula* (1958), *The Hound of the Baskervilles* (1959), *Star Wars* (1977)

Career low: *Blood Beast Terror* (1967)

D

Dafoe, Willem (1955–   )

American, born in Appleton, Wisconsin. He worked with the experimental Theatre X in Milwaukee, and the avant-garde Wooster Group in New York, before making his film debut in *Heaven's Gate* (1980). Initially typecast by his fierce, menacing features, he gradually found a wider range of roles, earning Best Supporting Actor Academy Award® nominations for *Platoon* (1986) and *Shadow of the Vampire* (2000).

Career highs: *Platoon* (1986), *The Last Temptation of Christ* (1988), *Wild at Heart* (1990), *Shadow of the Vampire* (2000)

Career lows: *Body of Evidence* (1993), *Speed 2: Cruise Control* (1997)

Damon, Matt(hew Paige) (1970–   )

American, born in Cambridge, Massachusetts. A teenage actor, he made his film debut with a single line in *Mystic Pizza* (1988). He came to international prominence during the 1990s, winning an Academy Award® with childhood friend **Ben Affleck** for the screenplay of *Good Will Hunting* (1997). His career has balanced ensemble work with leading roles, and mainstream blockbusters with quirky independent projects.

Career highs: *Good Will Hunting* (1997), *The Talented Mr Ripley* (1999), *The Bourne Identity* (2002)
Career lows: *Rounders* (1998), *The Legend of Bagger Vance* (2000)

Dandridge, Dorothy (1923–65)

American, born in Cleveland, Ohio. The daughter of an actress, she was a dancer, singer and nightclub performer before making her film debut in *A Day at the Races* (1937). The cinema offered her few opportunities to match her talent, although she became the first black woman to receive an Academy Award® nomination for *Carmen Jones* (1954). She died following an overdose, thought to be accidental, at the age of 42.
Career highs: *Carmen Jones* (1954), *The Decks Ran Red* (1958), *Porgy and Bess* (1959)
Career low: *Tarzan's Peril* (1951)

Darrieux, Danielle (1917–)

French, born in Bordeaux. A cello student at the Paris Conservatoire, she made her film debut as a teenager in *Le Bal* (1932). She matured into an elegant beauty whose talent encompassed everything from sophisticated light comedy to stark drama. She briefly attempted a Hollywood career in the late 1930s, but remained in Europe to become one of the continent's most enduring stars.
Career highs: *Mayerling* (1936), *La Ronde* (1950), *Madame De ...* (1953)
Career low: *Bethsabée* (1947)

Davis, Bette (Ruth Elizabeth Davis) (1908–89)

American, born in Lowell, Massachusetts. She arrived in Hollywood in 1930, and made her film debut in *Bad Sister* (1931). Hungry for challenging roles, she became an electrifying star, illuminating a vast gallery of complex female characters. She was an indomitable workhorse, but her later years were marked by too many unworthy ventures. She won Best Actress Academy Awards® for *Dangerous* (1935) and *Jezebel* (1938).
Career highs: *Dark Victory* (1939), *The Little Foxes* (1941), *Now Voyager* (1942), *All About Eve* (1950), *What Ever Happened to Baby Jane?* (1962)
Career lows: *Beyond the Forest* (1949), *Wicked Stepmother* (1989)

> 66
> Evil people ... you never forget them. And that's the aim of any actress – never to be forgotten.
>
> – Bette Davis on her favourite character roles, New York State Theatre programme (1966)
> 99

Davis, Geena (Virginia Elizabeth Davis) (1957–)

American, born in Wareham, Massachusetts. She studied acting at Boston University and subsequently moved to New York, working as a model and waitress before landing a small role in *Tootsie* (1982). She became adept at comedy roles,

winning a Best Supporting Actress Academy Award® for *The Accidental Tourist* (1988).
Career highs: *The Fly* (1986), *The Accidental Tourist* (1988), *Thelma and Louise* (1991), *A League of Their Own* (1992)
Career low: *Cutthroat Island* (1995)

Davis, Judy (1955–)

Australian, born in Perth. A student at the National Institute of Dramatic Art in Sydney, she worked in the theatre before making her film debut in *High Rolling* (1977). She came to international prominence in *My Brilliant Career* (1979), and has played a succession of strong-willed, brittle and emotionally vulnerable characters.
Career highs: *My Brilliant Career* (1979), *A Passage to India* (1984), *Husbands and Wives* (1992)
Career low: *Who Dares Wins* (1982)

Day, Doris (Doris Kappelhoff) (1924–)

American, born in Cincinnati, Ohio. A popular big-band vocalist, she made her film debut in *Romance on the High Seas* (1948). Her sunny personality, charm and apple-pie image made her one of the biggest box-office stars of the 1950s and 1960s. She retired from the screen after *With Six You Get Egg Roll* (1968), and subsequently devoted herself to animal-rights causes.
Career highs: *Calamity Jane* (1953), *Love Me Or Leave Me* (1955), *Pillow Talk* (1959)
Career low: *Caprice* (1967)

Day-Lewis, Daniel (1957–)

English, born in London. The son of poet laureate Cecil Day-Lewis and actress Jill Balcon, he made an early film debut in *Sunday, Bloody Sunday* (1971). He displays a remarkable ability to inhabit the physical and emotional characteristics of a part, as demonstrated in his Academy Award®-winning performance in *My Left Foot* (1989). He has a child with **Isabelle Adjani**, and is married to film-maker Rebecca Miller.
Career highs: *My Beautiful Laundrette* (1985), *My Left Foot* (1989), *In the Name of the Father* (1993), *Gangs of New York* (2002)
Career low: *Stars and Bars* (1988)

Dean, James (1931–55)

American, born in Fairmont, Indiana. He made his film debut in *Fixed Bayonets* (1951). He studied at the Actors Studio and gained substantial experience on television before his first major film role in *East of Eden* (1955). He made only two subsequent films, emerging as an iconic figure, representing the restless rebellion and insecurities of American youth. He died in a car crash at the age of 24.
Career highs: *East of Eden* (1955), *Rebel Without a Cause* (1955), *Giant* (1956)

de Havilland, Olivia Mary (1916–)

American, born in Tokyo, Japan. She was signed by Warner Brothers in 1935, forming a popular partnership with **Errol Flynn**. Often cast as demure, self-effacing characters, she fought for a broader range of roles, winning Best Actress Academy Awards® for *To Each His Own* (1946) and *The Heiress* (1949). Resident in Paris from

the 1950s, she retired from acting in 1988. She is the older sister of **Joan Fontaine**.
Career highs: *The Adventures of Robin Hood* (1938), *Gone with the Wind* (1939), *To Each His Own* (1946), *The Snake Pit* (1948), *The Heiress* (1949)
Career low: *The Adventurers* (1969)

Delon, Alain (1935–)

French, born in Sceaux. After he served as a marine in Indo-China, his handsome matinee-idol looks won him a small role in *Quand la femme s'en mêle* (1958), and within two years he was a major French star. He worked with some of Europe's finest directors in the 1960s, and has made occasional, ill-fated ventures into English-language cinema.
Career highs: *Plein soleil* (1959), *The Leopard* (1963), *Le Samourai* (1967), *Mr Klein* (1976)
Career low: *Airport '79 – Concorde* (1979)

Del Toro, Benicio (1967–)

Puerto Rican, born in Santurce. The son of lawyers, he was partly raised in Pennsylvania and studied business at the University of California in San Diego before heading to New York. A student of acting guru Stella Adler, he worked in television before making his film debut in *Big Top Pee-Wee* (1988). He won a Best Supporting Actor Academy Award® for *Traffic* (2000).
Career highs: *The Usual Suspects* (1995), *Traffic* (2000), *21 Grams* (2003)
Career low: *Excess Baggage* (1997)

Dench, Dame Judi(th Olivia) (1934–)

English, born in York. She studied at the Central School of Speech and Drama, and went on to become one of the most distinguished theatrical performers of her generation. She made her film debut in *The Third Secret* (1964) and began to devote more time to the cinema in the 1990s, winning a Best Supporting Actress Academy Award® for *Shakespeare in Love* (1998).
Career highs: *Four in the Morning* (1965), *Mrs Brown* (1997), *Shakespeare in Love* (1998), *Iris* (2001)
Career low: *The Chronicles of Riddick* (2004)

Deneuve, Catherine (Catherine Dorléac) (1943–)

French, born in Paris. She made her screen debut as a teenager, and her regal blonde beauty has inspired generations of world cinema's finest directors; she endures as an icon of European sophistication. Once married to photographer David Bailey, she has children with director **Roger Vadim** and actor **Marcello Mastroianni**.
Career highs: *The Umbrellas of Cherbourg* (1964), *Repulsion* (1965), *Belle de jour* (1967), *The Last Metro* (1980), *Indochine* (1992)
Career lows: *Mayerling* (1968), *March or Die* (1977)

De Niro, Robert (1943–)

American, born in New York City. After studying acting with Lee Strasberg and Stella Adler, he made his film debut as an extra in *Trois chambres à Manhattan* (1965).

Mean Streets (1973) began a long and fruitful collaboration with **Martin Scorsese** that revealed De Niro's chameleon-like versatility and intense dedication to his craft. He is a prominent figure on New York's film scene through his Tribeca Film Centre and its annual film festival.

Career highs: *Mean Streets* (1973), *Taxi Driver* (1976), *Raging Bull* (1980), *Heat* (1995)

Career lows: *We're No Angels* (1989), *The Adventures of Rocky and Bullwinkle* (2000)

Depardieu, Gérard (1948–)

French, born in Châteauroux. A self-confessed teenage delinquent, he found his salvation in literature and the theatre, making his film debut in *Le Beatnik et le minet* (1965). After his breakthrough role in *Les Valseuses* (1973) he became a dominant figure in French cinema, and has since appeared in more than 150 films. He is a noted *bon viveur* and wine producer.

Career highs: *The Last Metro* (1980), *Danton* (1982), *Le Retour de Martin Guerre* (1982), *Jean de Florette* (1986), *Cyrano de Bergerac* (1990)

Career lows: *I Want To Go Home* (1989), *Bogus* (1996), *102 Dalmatians* (2000)

Depp, Johnny (John Christopher Depp) (1963–)

American, born in Owensboro, Kentucky. He played in a rock group (The Kids) before pursuing an acting career. He made his film debut in *A Nightmare on Elm Street* (1984), and became a teen idol in the television series *21 Jump Street*. He has matured into a versatile actor, noted for his splendidly idiosyncratic career choices and fearless performances, and has also directed.

Career highs: *Edward Scissorhands* (1990), *Ed Wood* (1994), *Donnie Brasco* (1997), *Pirates of the Caribbean: The Curse of the Black Pearl* (2003), *Finding Neverland* (2004)

Career lows: *Private Resort* (1985), *The Astronaut's Wife* (1999), *Secret Window* (2004)

DeVito, Danny (1944–)

American, born in Neptune, New Jersey. He acted in school plays and trained at New York's American Academy of Dramatic Arts before making his film debut in *Lady Liberty* (1971). Television fame in the series *Taxi* led to film work, and he found rich comedy in a number of malevolent or misanthropic roles. He has also directed, and is a noted producer.

Career highs: *Ruthless People* (1986), *Tin Men* (1987), *The War of the Roses* (1989), *Hoffa* (1992)

Career lows: *Going Ape!* (1981), *Wise Guys* (1986), *Death to Smoochy* (2002)

Diaz, Cameron Michelle (1972–)

American, born in San Diego, California. A globetrotting adolescent, she was working as a model when she successfully auditioned for the lead role in *The Mask* (1994). Her comic timing and appealing, vivacious personality have enhanced a number of comedy films and helped her to become one of the highest-paid female stars in Hollywood.

Career highs: *My Best Friend's Wedding* (1997), *There's Something About Mary* (1998), *Charlie's Angels* (2000)
Career lows: *Head above Water* (1996), *The Sweetest Thing* (2002)

DiCaprio, Leonardo (1974–)

American, born in Los Angeles, California. A child actor, he appeared extensively on television before making his film debut in *Critters 3* (1991). A respected young character actor, his career was dramatically affected by the phenomenal international success of *Titanic* (1997). Recently, he has developed a fruitful working relationship with **Martin Scorsese**.
Career highs: *This Boy's Life* (1993), *What's Eating Gilbert Grape?* (1993), *The Aviator* (2004)
Career lows: *Total Eclipse* (1995), *The Man in the Iron Mask* (1998)

Dietrich, Marlene (Maria Magdalena Von Losch) (1901–92)

German, born in Berlin. A student at the Deutsche Theaterschüle, she made her film debut in *Der Kleine Napoleon* (1923). Her performance in *The Blue Angel* (1930) made her an international star and she moved to Hollywood, building an indelible image as an exotic, alluring creature in a succession of lavish star vehicles. Later a cabaret performer of legendary charisma, she made her final film appearance in *Just a Gigolo* (1978) before retiring to quiet seclusion in Paris.
Career highs: *The Blue Angel* (1930), *Morocco* (1930), *Destry Rides Again* (1939), *A Foreign Affair* (1948), *Rancho Notorious* (1952)
Career lows: *Golden Earrings* (1947), *The Monte Carlo Story* (1957)

Marlene in Morocco

In *Morocco* (1930), Marlene Dietrich famously became the first leading lady to kiss another woman on screen. The scene, added to the film at Dietrich's suggestion, was considered extremely provocative at the time but nevertheless escaped cutting by the censor.

Dillon, Matt (1964–)

American, born in New Rochelle, New York. Spotted at school by a casting agent, he made his film debut in *Over the Edge* (1979) and played a number of moody, misunderstood adolescents before finding a wider range of adult roles that showcased his dramatic abilities and comic timing. He has also directed.
Career highs: *Tex* (1982), *The Flamingo Kid* (1984), *Drugstore Cowboy* (1989), *There's Something About Mary* (1998), *Crash* (2004)
Career lows: *The Big Town* (1987), *A Kiss Before Dying* (1991)

Donat, Robert (1905–58)

English, born in Withington, Manchester. Elocution lessons, taken to cure a boyhood stammer, sparked his interest in acting. He made his film debut in *Men of Tomorrow* (1931). His melodious voice, intelligence and grace made him an international star in the 1930s, and he won a Best Actor Academy Award® for *Goodbye, Mr Chips* (1939). His later career was blighted by chronic ill health.

Career highs: *The 39 Steps* (1935), *The Ghost Goes West* (1936), *The Citadel* (1938), *Goodbye, Mr Chips* (1939), *The Winslow Boy* (1948)
Career low: *The Cure for Love* (1949)

Dors, Diana (Diana Mary Fluck) (1931–84)

English, born in Swindon. A student at the Royal Academy of Dramatic Art, she made her film debut in *The Shop at Sly Corner* (1946). As a Rank starlet in the late 1940s, she was enthusiastically and misguidedly promoted as a British sex symbol to rival **Marilyn Monroe**. She cheerfully lived this image to the hilt, and was capable of good performances when challenged.
Career highs: *Yield to the Night* (1956), *Deep End* (1970), *The Amazing Mr Blunden* (1972)
Career lows: *The Amorous Milkman* (1975), *Adventures of a Taxi Driver* (1976), *Adventures of a Private Eye* (1977)

Douglas, Kirk (Issur Danielovich Demsky) (1916–   )

American, born in Amsterdam, New York. The son of Russian immigrants, he worked on stage and radio before making his film debut in *The Strange Love of Martha Ivers* (1946). He was soon established as a leading man, his best roles harnessing the intense drive and dynamism of his own personality. In his eighties he survived a plane crash and a serious stroke, returning to the cinema in *Diamonds* (1999). His son is **Michael Douglas**.
Career highs: *Champion* (1949), *Lust for Life* (1956), *Paths of Glory* (1957), *Spartacus* (1960), *Lonely Are the Brave* (1962)
Career lows: *The Light at the Edge of the World* (1971), *Scalawag* (1973), *The Chosen* (1977)

Douglas, Melvyn (Melvyn Edouard Hesselberg) (1901–81)

American, born in Macon, Georgia. He worked extensively in the theatre before making his film debut in *Tonight or Never* (1931). A dapper, debonair farceur, he abandoned Hollywood in the 1950s, returning a decade later as an authoritative character actor and winning Academy Awards® for *Hud* (1963) and *Being There* (1979). He was married to actress-turned-politician Helen Gahagan; the actress Illeana Douglas is his granddaughter.
Career highs: *Theodora Goes Wild* (1936), *Ninotchka* (1939), *Hud* (1963), *I Never Sang for My Father* (1970), *Being There* (1979)
Career lows: *Nagana* (1933), *There's That Woman Again* (1939)

Douglas, Michael Kirk (1944–   )

American, born in New Brunswick, New Jersey. The son of **Kirk Douglas**, he studied drama at the University of California and made his film debut in *Hail, Hero!* (1969). He became a leading film actor in the 1980s, winning a Best Actor Academy Award® for *Wall Street* (1987). He is married to **Catherine Zeta-Jones**.
Career highs: *Wall Street* (1987), *Fatal Attraction* (1987), *The War of the Roses* (1989), *Wonder Boys* (2000)
Career lows: *Hail, Hero!* (1969), *Shining Through* (1991)

Dreyfuss, Richard Stephan (1947–   )

American, born in Brooklyn, New York City. A child actor, he appeared on stage and television before making his film debut with a tiny role in *The Graduate* (1967). A major star in the 1970s, he won a Best Actor Academy Award® for *The Goodbye Girl* (1977). His struggle to conquer drug addiction affected his star status in the 1980s, but he has maintained a busy career as a character actor on stage and screen.
Career highs: *Jaws* (1975), *Close Encounters of the Third Kind* (1977), *The Goodbye Girl* (1977), *Mr Holland's Opus* (1995)
Career low: *Let It Ride* (1989)

Dunaway, (Dorothy) Faye (1941–   )

American, born in Bascom, Florida. Early Broadway success brought her a personal contract with film-maker **Otto Preminger**. She made her film debut in *The Happening* (1966), and achieved international stardom with *Bonnie and Clyde* (1967). She was a dominant force in 1970s US cinema, winning a Best Actress Academy Award® for *Network* (1976).
Career highs: *Bonnie and Clyde* (1967), *Chinatown* (1974), *Network* (1976), *Barfly* (1987)
Career lows: *Supergirl* (1984), *Dunston Checks In* (1996)

Dunne, Irene Marie (1898–1990)

American, born in Louisville, Kentucky. She made her film debut in *Leathernecking* (1930). Gifted with superb timing, she was equally adept at high farce, romantic comedy, heart-tugging melodrama and musicals. She retired from the cinema in 1952, devoting herself to charitable causes and international politics.
Career highs: *Magnificent Obsession* (1935), *The Awful Truth* (1937), *Love Affair* (1939), *My Favorite Wife* (1940), *I Remember Mama* (1948)
Career low: *It Grows on Trees* (1952)

Durbin, Deanna (Edna Mae Durbin) (1921–   )

Canadian, born in Winnipeg, Manitoba. A high-spirited youngster with a lilting soprano and a charmingly fresh personality, she first appeared in the short film *Every Sunday* (1936). One of the most popular stars of the wartime years, she retired in 1949 and left America to live in France, steadfastly refusing all offers of a comeback.
Career highs: *Three Smart Girls* (1936), *One Hundred Men and a Girl* (1937), *It Started with Eve* (1941), *Lady on a Train* (1945)
Career lows: *Up in Central Park* (1948), *For the Love of Mary* (1949)

Duvall, Robert Selden (1931–   )

American, born in San Diego, California. He served in the US Army before studying drama, and worked extensively in the theatre before making his film debut in *To Kill a Mockingbird* (1962). His career gradually developed until he was recognized as one of the most compelling character actors in American cinema. He won a Best Actor Academy Award® for *Tender Mercies* (1983).

Career highs: *The Godfather* (1972), *The Great Santini* (1979), *Apocalypse Now* (1979), *Tender Mercies* (1983), *The Apostle* (1997)
Career lows: *The Scarlet Letter* (1996), *A Shot at Glory* (2000)

E

Eastwood, Clint (Clinton Eastwood Jr) (1930–   )

American, born in San Francisco, California. Signed to Universal Pictures, he made his film debut in *Revenge of the Creature* (1955). The popularity of the long-running television series *Rawhide* brought him an offer to film a series of spaghetti westerns in Italy, making him an international star. He has also become a distinguished director, winning Academy Awards® for *Unforgiven* (1992) and *Million Dollar Baby* (2004).
Career highs (actor): *A Fistful of Dollars* (1964), *Dirty Harry* (1971), *In the Line of Fire* (1993)
Career highs (director): *Play Misty For Me* (1971), *The Outlaw Josey Wales* (1976), *Unforgiven* (1992), *The Bridges of Madison County* (1995), *Million Dollar Baby* (2004)
Career lows: *The Eiger Sanction* (1975), *The Rookie* (1990), *Blood Work* (2002)

Elliott, Denholm (1922–92)

English, born in Ealing, London. He was a pilot in the Royal Air Force, and spent three years as a POW during World War II. He made his film debut in *Dear Mr Prohack* (1949) and was a stalwart of British cinema in the 1950s. Later, he became a scene-stealing character actor of international distinction. His first wife was actress Virginia McKenna.
Career highs: *Alfie* (1966), *The Apprenticeship of Duddy Kravitz* (1974), *Saint Jack* (1979), *Trading Places* (1983), *A Room with a View* (1985)
Career lows: *Percy* (1970), *Rising Damp* (1980)

Evans, Dame Edith Mary (1888–1976)

English, born in London. She studied acting at night school, made her first stage appearance in 1914 and became one of the great names of the British theatre. She made her film debut in *A Welsh Singer* (1915), but did not embrace the cinema until she was in her sixties, earning Academy Award® nominations for *Tom Jones* (1963), *The Chalk Garden* (1964) and *The Whisperers* (1966).
Career highs: *The Queen of Spades* (1948), *The Importance of Being Earnest* (1952), *The Whisperers* (1966)
Career low: *Craze* (1974)

Everett, Rupert (1959–   )

English, born in Norfolk. Educated at Ampleforth School, he was expelled from London's Central School of Speech and Drama but learnt his craft on the stage, particularly at the Citizens' Theatre in Glasgow. He made his film debut in *A Shocking Accident* (1982). A model, pop singer and novelist, he revitalized his career in the 1990s, and was one of the first openly gay actors to become a major Hollywood star.

Career highs: *Dance with a Stranger* (1985), *My Best Friend's Wedding* (1997), *Shrek 2* (2004)
Career lows: *Hearts of Fire* (1987), *The Next Best Thing* (2000), *Unconditional Love* (2002)

F

Fairbanks, Douglas, Sr (Douglas Elton Ulman) (1883–1939)

American, born in Denver, Colorado. A child performer, he briefly studied at Harvard University, and worked on Wall Street before returning to the stage. He made his film debut in *The Lamb* (1915), and became one of silent cinema's biggest stars as a zestful, devil-may-care swashbuckler in lavish adventure spectacles. His son was **Douglas Fairbanks Jr** , and his second wife was **Mary Pickford**.
Career highs: *The Mark of Zorro* (1920), *The Three Musketeers* (1921), *Robin Hood* (1922), *The Thief of Bagdad* (1924), *The Black Pirate* (1926)
Career low: *Mr Robinson Crusoe* (1932)

Fairbanks, Douglas, Jr (1909–2000)

American, born in New York City. The son of **Douglas Fairbanks Sr**, he followed in his father's footsteps, making his film debut as a teenager in *Stephen Steps Out* (1923). A busy leading man, his greatest successes were as a virile swashbuckler and man of action. He drifted away from the cinema in the 1950s. His first marriage was to **Joan Crawford**.
Career highs: *The Prisoner of Zenda* (1937), *Gunga Din* (1939), *Sinbad the Sailor* (1947)
Career low: *Mimi* (1935)

Falk, Peter (1927–)

American, born in New York City. He worked as an efficiency expert in Connecticut before studying acting with Eva Le Galliene and Sanford Meisner, and made his film debut in *Wind Across the Everglades* (1958). Best known for playing the deceptively dishevelled television sleuth Columbo, he has also displayed his dramatic range in collaborations with director **John Cassavetes**. He was an Academy Award® nominee for *Murder Inc.* (1960) and *Pocketful of Miracles* (1961).
Career highs: *The Great Race* (1965), *A Woman Under the Influence* (1974), *The In-Laws* (1979), *Wings of Desire* (1987)
Career lows: *The Bloody Brood* (1959), *Big Trouble* (1985)

Farrow, Mia (Maria de Lourdes Villiers Farrow) (1945–)

American, born in Los Angeles, California. The daughter of actress Maureen O'Sullivan and director John Farrow, she acted from an early age. A fragile, waif-like figure, she starred in the television soap opera *Peyton Place* and eventually found some tougher roles. She has been married to **Frank Sinatra** and André Previn, and her off-screen relationship with **Woody Allen** ended in acrimony when he left her for her adopted daughter.

Career highs: *Rosemary's Baby* (1968), *Broadway Danny Rose* (1984), *The Purple Rose of Cairo* (1985)
Career lows: *The Great Gatsby* (1974), *Hurricane* (1979)

Faye, Alice (Alice Jeanne Leppert) (1912–98)

American, born in New York City. A teenage member of the Chester Hale Dance Group, she toured the USA and worked as a chorus girl before making her film debut in *George White's Scandals* (1934). She spent the next decade as a warm, sympathetic presence in numerous musicals, but made only a handful of appearances after 1945.
Career highs: *In Old Chicago* (1938), *Alexander's Ragtime Band* (1938), *Tin Pan Alley* (1940)
Career low: *Barricade* (1939)

Fernandel (Fernand Joseph Désiré Contandin) (1903–71)

French, born in Marseille. A docker, bank teller, amateur singer and irrepressible entertainer, he turned professional in 1922, appearing throughout France in cabaret and music halls. He made his film debut in *La meillure bobone* (1930). His plain, horse-like features, big teeth, sly grin and eternal optimism made him a national favourite in rural melodramas and broad farce for the best part of four decades.
Career highs: *Le Rosier de Madame Husson* (1932), *Angèle* (1934), *Le Petit monde de Don Camillo* (1952), *Coiffeur pour dames* (1952)
Career lows: *Le Mystère Saint-Val* (1945), *Coeur de coq* (1947), *Paris Holiday* (1958)

Ferrell, Will (John William Ferrell) (1967–)

American, born in Irvine, California. While working as a sports newscaster after university, he began performing with Los Angeles comedy group The Groundlings, and eventually won a role on the television sketch show *Saturday Night Live*. He appeared in several comedy films, often alongside other *SNL* cast members, before winning the lead role in *Elf* (2003), a surprise hit that made the most of his knack for character-driven physical comedy and proved his box-office appeal.
Career highs: *Old School* (2003), *Elf* (2003), *Anchorman* (2004)
Career lows: *Bewitched* (2005), *Kicking and Screaming* (2005)

Field, Sally (1946–)

American, born in Pasadena, California. She was a perky teenage television star before making her film debut in *The Way West* (1967). She worked hard to become a major film actress, playing indomitable women with spirited intensity and winning Best Actress Academy Awards® for *Norma Rae* (1979) and *Places in the Heart* (1984).
Career highs: *Norma Rae* (1979), *Absence of Malice* (1981), *Places in the Heart* (1984)
Career lows: *Beyond the Poseidon Adventure* (1979)

Fields, W C (William Claude Dukenfield) (1879–1946)

American, born in Philadelphia, Pennsylvania. As a teenager he ran away from home to pursue a show-business career, and became a circus juggler and vaudeville star before making his film debut in *Pool Sharks* (1915). In the sound era, he created and refined the comic character of a bibulous, child-hating misanthrope (not unlike his own personality). Skilled in the art of verbal insult and visual wit, he also favoured outlandish pseudonyms for his screenplays.

Career highs: *It's a Gift* (1934), *David Copperfield* (1935), *The Bank Dick* (1940), *Never Give a Sucker an Even Break* (1941)

Career low: *Poppy* (1936)

> "
> Women are like elephants to me. I like to look at them, but I wouldn't want to own one.
> – W C Fields in *Mississippi* (1935)
> "

Fiennes, Ralph Nathaniel (1962–)

English, born in Suffolk. The eldest son of photographer Mark Fiennes and novelist Jennifer Lash, he attended the Royal Academy of Dramatic Art. Building a career on stage and in television, he made his film debut as Heathcliff in *Wuthering Heights* (1992) and established himself as a brooding, anguished leading man. He received Academy Award® nominations for *Schindler's List* (1993) and *The English Patient* (1996).

Career highs: *Schindler's List* (1993), *Quiz Show* (1994), *The English Patient* (1996), *The Constant Gardener* (2005)

Career low: *The Avengers* (1998)

Finch, (Frederick George) Peter Ingle (1916–77)

Australian, born in London but raised in France, India and Sydney. He made his film debut in *Dad And Dave Come To Town* (1938). After World War II, he became a protégé of **Laurence Olivier** and established himself in the London theatre before slowly building a film career in which he lent conviction to a wide range of characters. He received a posthumous Best Actor Academy Award® for *Network* (1976).

Career highs: *The Trials of Oscar Wilde* (1960), *Far from the Madding Crowd* (1967), *Sunday, Bloody Sunday* (1971), *Network* (1976)

Career lows: *Something to Hide* (1971), *Lost Horizon* (1973)

Finney, Albert (1936–)

English, born in Salford. A student at the Royal Academy of Dramatic Art, he worked in the theatre before making his film debut in *The Entertainer* (1960). *Saturday Night and Sunday Morning* (1960) established him as one of the bright new working-class talents of 1960s British cinema, and his range has stretched from versatile leading man to invaluable character actor. He has received five Academy Award® nominations.

Career highs: *Saturday Night and Sunday Morning* (1960), *Tom Jones* (1963), *Gumshoe* (1971), *Shoot the Moon* (1982), *Under the Volcano* (1984)

Career lows: *Night Must Fall* (1964), *Scrooge* (1970), *Loophole* (1980)

Firth, Colin (1960–)

English, born in Grayshott, Hampshire. His film career began with the 1984 screen adaptation of the play *Another Country*, and he has frequently played diffident, emotionally repressed Englishmen, finding some of his best roles on television.
Career highs: *Another Country* (1984), *Fever Pitch* (1996), *Bridget Jones's Diary* (2001)
Career lows: *Femme Fatale* (1991), *Hope Springs* (2003)

Fishburne, Laurence (1961–)

American, born in Augusta, Georgia. An actor from the age of nine, he made his film debut in *Cornbread, Earl and Me* (1975). *Apocalypse Now* (1979) put him on the map, and he matured into a magnetic leading man of great presence. He earned a Best Actor Academy Award® nomination for *What's Love Got to Do with It* (1993).
Career highs: *Apocalypse Now* (1979), *Boyz n the Hood* (1991), *What's Love Got to Do with It* (1993), *The Matrix* (1999)
Career low: *Event Horizon* (1997)

Flynn, Errol (Leslie Thomson Flynn) (1909–59)

Australian, born in Hobart, Tasmania. The son of a distinguished zoologist, he led a colourful early life before making his feature film debut in *In the Wake of the Bounty* (1933). In Hollywood from 1935, he was a virile, roguish, swashbuckling star until a life of wine, women and hellraising indulgence took its toll.
Career highs: *The Adventures of Robin Hood* (1938), *The Private Lives of Elizabeth and Essex* (1939), *The Sea Hawk* (1940), *Gentleman Jim* (1942)
Career low: *Cuban Rebel Girls* (1959)

Fonda, Henry Jaynes (1905–82)

American, born in Grand Island, Nebraska. Educated at the University of Minnesota, his work with the Omaha Community Playhouse took him to Broadway and Hollywood, where he made his film debut in *The Farmer Takes a Wife* (1935). A tall, soft-spoken figure, he became closely identified with characters that shone with decency, dignity and virtue. He won a Best Actor Academy Award® for *On Golden Pond* (1981), in which his daughter **Jane Fonda** also appeared.
Career highs: *The Grapes of Wrath* (1940), *The Lady Eve* (1941), *My Darling Clementine* (1946), *Twelve Angry Men* (1957), *On Golden Pond* (1981)
Career lows: *The Long Night* (1947), *Tentacles* (1977), *The Swarm* (1978)

Fonda, Jane Seymour (1937–)

American, born in New York City. The daughter of **Henry Fonda**, she made her film debut in *Tall Story* (1960). Her extraordinary career has seen her metamorphose from 1960s sex kitten to 1970s political activist and 1980s fitness queen; she made no films during the 1990s, returning to the screen with *Monster-in-Law* (2005). She has won Best Actress Academy Awards® for *Klute* (1971) and *Coming Home* (1978).
Career highs: *They Shoot Horses, Don't They*? (1969), *Klute* (1971), *Julia* (1977), *Coming Home* (1978), *The China Syndrome* (1979)
Career lows: *The Love Cage* (1964), *The Game Is Over* (1966), *The Bluebird* (1976)

Fonda, Peter Henry (1939–   )

American, born in New York City. The son of actor **Henry Fonda**, he studied at the University of Omaha and worked in the theatre before making his film debut in *Tammy and the Doctor* (1963). A bland leading man, he matured into an anti-establishment rebel and one of the creators of the iconic *Easy Rider* (1969). He received a Best Actor Academy Award® nomination for *Ulee's Gold* (1997).
Career highs: *Lilith* (1964), *Easy Rider* (1969), *Ulee's Gold* (1997)
Career low: *Wanda Nevada* (1979)

Fontaine, Joan (Joan De Beauvoir de Havilland) (1917–   )

American, born in Tokyo, Japan. The younger sister of **Olivia de Havilland**, she was raised in California and made her film debut in *No More Ladies* (1935). A pretty, genteel, ladylike innocent on screen, she won a Best Actress Academy Award® for *Suspicion* (1941). She later played more worldly, sophisticated women, but found few roles that truly tested her talents.
Career highs: *Rebecca* (1940), *Suspicion* (1941), *Letter from an Unknown Woman* (1948)
Career low: *The Emperor Waltz* (1948)

Ford, Glenn (Gwyllyn Samuel Newton Ford) (1916–   )

Canadian, born in Sainte-Christine, Quebec. Raised in California, he worked in casual jobs whilst planning to become an actor. A minor role in a play led to his film debut in *Night in Manhattan* (1937). His popularity grew in the 1940s and he spent 20 years as a dependable leading man, particularly adept at light comedy and westerns. His first wife was dancer Eleanor Powell.
Career highs: *Gilda* (1946), *The Big Heat* (1953), *The Blackboard Jungle* (1955), *3.10 to Yuma* (1957)
Career low: *Happy Birthday to Me* (1981)

Ford, Harrison (1942–   )

American, born in Chicago, Illinois. A student performer, he was signed by Columbia Pictures and made his film debut in *Dead Heat on a Merry-Go-Round* (1966). For some years afterwards he was more employed as a carpenter than an actor, but found stardom as Han Solo in *Star Wars* (1977). A heroic action hero, he received a Best Actor Academy Award® nomination for *Witness* (1985).
Career highs: *Raiders of the Lost Ark* (1981), *Blade Runner* (1982), *Witness* (1985), *Presumed Innocent* (1990), *The Fugitive* (1993)
Career lows: *Regarding Henry* (1991), *Hollywood Homicide* (2003)

What Might Have Been

Harrison Ford will probably always be associated with his role as the archaeologist and adventurer Indiana Jones in several hugely popular films – but if, as nearly happened, the part had gone to Tom Selleck, things might have been very different for both actors' careers. Similarly, Clint Eastwood's iconic performance in *Dirty Harry* (1971) nearly never happened: the role was supposedly written for Frank Sinatra, then offered to John Wayne, Steve McQueen, Jack Nicholson and Paul Newman before Eastwood's turn came. Other performers who may have regretted missing out on certain roles include Molly Ringwald, reported to have turned down the leads in both *Pretty Woman* (1990) and *Ghost* (1990), and Gene Hackman, said to have turned down leads in *One Flew Over the Cuckoo's Nest* (1975) and *Jaws* (1975).

Foster, Jodie (Alicia Christian Foster) (1962–   )

American, born in Los Angeles, California. A performer from the age of three, she worked in television before making her film debut in *Napoleon and Samantha* (1972). She weathered the transition to adult roles, taking time out to study at Yale University and in Paris before returning to the cinema and winning Best Actress Academy Awards® for *The Accused* (1988) and *The Silence of the Lambs* (1991). She has also directed.
Career highs: *Taxi Driver* (1976), *The Accused* (1988), *The Silence of the Lambs* (1991)
Career low: *Mesmerised* (1986)

Fox, Michael J (Michael Andrew Fox) (1961–   )

Canadian, born in Edmonton, Alberta. A professional actor from the age of 15, he adopted the initial J in tribute to the actor Michael J Pollard. A boyish, energetic charmer, he made his film debut in *Midnight Madness* (1980) and enjoyed huge success in the 1980s as Marty McFly in the *Back to the Future* trilogy. He was diagnosed with Parkinson's disease in 1991.
Career highs: *Teen Wolf* (1985), *Back to the Future* (1985), *The Secret of My Success* (1987)
Career low: *Bright Lights, Big City* (1988)

Foxx, Jamie (Eric Morlon Bishop) (1967–   )

American, born in Terrell, Texas. While studying music at university, he began performing stand-up at a local comedy club; he subsequently won a role on the long-running television sketch show *In Living Color*. He balanced television and film work during the 1990s, but did not become a major star until the back-to-back release of *Collateral* and the Ray Charles biopic *Ray* (both 2004), receiving a Best Actor Academy Award® for the latter.
Career highs: *Any Given Sunday* (1999), *Collateral* (2004), *Ray* (2004)
Career lows: *Booty Call* (1997), *Held Up* (1999)

Fraser, Brendan (1968–   )

American, born in Indianapolis, Indiana. He was raised throughout America and Europe before studying theatre in Seattle, Washington. He made his film debut in

Dogfight (1991). A beefy, good-humoured hunk, he at first found his niche in dumb comedy roles before seeking a wider range of parts.
Career highs: *George of the Jungle* (1997), *Gods and Monsters* (1998), *The Mummy* (1999), *The Quiet American* (2002)
Career lows: *Dudley Do-Right* (1999), *Bedazzled* (2000)

Freeman, Morgan (1937–)

American, born in Memphis, Tennessee. He studied in Los Angeles and served in the US Air Force before committing himself to an acting career. Vastly experienced on the stage, his film career developed from the 1980s until he became one of the most admired and authoritative actors working in the medium. He won a Best Supporting Actor Academy Award® for *Million Dollar Baby* (2004).
Career highs: *Glory* (1989), *Unforgiven* (1992), *The Shawshank Redemption* (1994), *Se7en* (1995), *Million Dollar Baby* (2004)
Career low: *The Big Bounce* (2004)

G

Gabin, Jean (Jean Alexis Moncorgé) (1904–76)

French, born in Paris. He was a cabaret performer before making his film debut in *Chacun sa chance* (1930). He quickly became the most popular French star of his generation, lending a stoical, flinty grace to the portrayal of doomed working-class anti-heroes in the 1930s and to more worldly, patriarchal figures in his later years.
Career highs: *Pépé le Moko* (1936), *La Grande illusion* (1937), *Le Quai des brumes* (1938), *La Bête humaine* (1938), *Le Jour se lève* (1939)
Career lows: *Martin Roumagnac* (1946), *Miroir* (1947), *La Marie du port* (1950)

Gable, (William) Clark (1901–60)

American, born in Cadiz, Ohio. A manual labourer, he toured on stage and appeared in silent films before signing a contract with MGM. A rugged, wolfish figure who exuded sex appeal, he won a Best Actor Academy Award® for *It Happened One Night* (1934) and achieved a popularity that saw him voted 'King Of Hollywood' in 1937. His third wife was **Carole Lombard**, who died in a plane crash in 1942.
Career highs: *Red Dust* (1932), *It Happened One Night* (1934), *Mutiny on the Bounty* (1935), *Gone with the Wind* (1939), *The Misfits* (1961)
Career lows: *Parnell* (1937), *Adventure* (1945)

Ganz, Bruno (1941–)

Swiss, born in Zurich. After military service, he moved to Germany and worked in student theatre productions before making his film debut in *Chikita* (1961). He is a powerful stage performer whose film career flourished during the German cinema revival of the 1970s. He has also appeared in English-language productions, including *The Manchurian Candidate* (2004).
Career highs: *The American Friend* (1977), *In the White City* (1983), *Wings of Desire* (1987), *Downfall* (2004)

Garbo, Greta (Greta Lovisa Gustafsson) (1905–90)

Swedish, born in Stockholm. A shop assistant and model, she won a bathing beauty contest and studied at the Royal Dramatic Theatre before making her film debut in *A Fortune Hunter* (1921). In America from 1925, she bewitched audiences with her fine, sphinx-like features, delicate underplaying and air of melancholy mystique. Despite four Academy Award® nominations, she never won, and retired after *Two-Faced Woman* (1941).
Career highs: *Queen Christina* (1933), *Anna Karenina* (1935), *Camille* (1936), *Ninotchka* (1939)
Career low: *Two-Faced Woman* (1941)

> #### Fashion Plate
>
> Greta Garbo is remembered as a style icon of the 1920s and 30s, when her on- and off-screen wardrobes inspired trends for fur collars, berets and rakishly tilted hats. Few of her devoted fans would have known that years earlier, a relatively frumpy 16-year-old Garbo had appeared in the advertising film *How Not to Wear Clothes* (1921), made for the Stockholm department store where she worked as a salesgirl.

Garcia, Andy (Andrés Arturo García Menéndez) (1956–   )

Cuban, born in Havana. His family emigrated to Miami in 1961 and his original intention was to be a basketball player. Illness blighted his student years, and he subsequently moved to Los Angeles, appearing on television and making his film debut in *Blue Skies Again* (1983). He received a Best Supporting Actor Academy Award® nomination for *The Godfather Part III* (1990), and has also directed.
Career highs: *The Untouchables* (1987), *Internal Affairs* (1990), *The Godfather Part III* (1990), *Things to Do in Denver When You're Dead* (1995)
Career low: *Steal Big, Steal Little* (1995)

Gardner, Ava (Lucy Johnson) (1922–90)

American, born in Grabton, North Carolina. Raised in poverty, she worked as a model before signing a contract with MGM. She emerged from the ranks of decorative starlets to play a ravishing *femme fatale* in *The Killers* (1946), and spent a decade as one of the cinema's most glamorous stars. She was married to **Mickey Rooney**, **Frank Sinatra** (who paid her medical bills near the end of her life) and bandleader Artie Shaw.
Career highs: *The Killers* (1946), *Showboat* (1951), *Mogambo* (1953), *The Barefoot Contessa* (1954), *Bhowani Junction* (1956)
Career low: *The Angel Wore Red* (1960)

Garland, Judy (Frances Ethel Gumm) (1922–69)

American, born in Grand Rapids, Minnesota. A performer with show business in her veins, she made her stage debut at the age of three and her film debut in *The Meglin Kiddie Revue* (1929). High-spirited and unaffected, her singing throbbed with emotion; she was magical in musicals and unbearably poignant in drama. Her volatile private life was marked by drink and drug problems, and she married five times.

Career highs: *The Wizard of Oz* (1939), *Meet Me in St Louis* (1944), *The Clock* (1945), *Easter Parade* (1948), *A Star Is Born* (1954)

Garner, James (James Scott Baumgarner) (1928–)

American, born in Norman, Oklahoma. A Korean War veteran, he made his film debut in *Toward the Unknown* (1956). Success in the television series *Maverick* translated into a film career in which he has played likeable, dependable characters. He won a Best Actor Academy Award® nomination for *Murphy's Romance* (1985). **Career highs**: *The Thrill of It All* (1963), *Support Your Local Sheriff* (1969), *Skin Game* (1971), *Victor/Victoria* (1982), *Murphy's Romance* (1985) **Career lows**: *Mister Buddwing* (1966), *How Sweet It Is* (1968)

Garson, Greer (1903–96)

British, born in County Down, Northern Ireland. Originally intent on becoming a teacher, her interest in amateur dramatics led to a professional career. Spotted on stage by Louis B Mayer, she was signed to a contract with MGM and made her mark in ladylike, stiff-upper-lip roles. She won a Best Actress Academy Award® for *Mrs Miniver* (1942). **Career highs**: *Goodbye, Mr Chips* (1939), *Mrs Miniver* (1942), *Random Harvest* (1942), *Madame Curie* (1943) **Career lows**: *Adventure* (1945), *Desire Me* (1947)

Gaynor, Janet (Laura Gainor) (1906–84)

American, born in Philadelphia, Pennsylvania. A peripatetic childhood eventually landed her in Los Angeles, where she became a teenage extra in silent films. She graduated to leading roles and soon became known for playing wholesome, winsome heroines. She won the first ever Best Actress Academy Award® for her performances in the three films from 1927/8 listed below. She retired in 1938, returning to the screen just once for *Bernadine* (1957). **Career highs**: *Sunrise* (1927), *Seventh Heaven* (1927), *Street Angel* (1928), *Sunny Side Up* (1929), *A Star Is Born* (1937) **Career low**: *The Man Who Came Back* (1931), *Three Loves Has Nancy* (1938)

Gere, Richard (1949–)

American, born in Philadelphia, Pennsylvania. He worked in the theatre in London and New York before making his film debut as a pimp in *Report to the Commissioner* (1975). Frequently cast as narcissistic, emotionally aloof characters, he weathered career setbacks to reveal a wider range. He is a passionate spokesman for Tibet and Buddhism. **Career highs**: *American Gigolo* (1980), *An Officer and a Gentleman* (1982), *Internal Affairs* (1989), *Pretty Woman* (1990) **Career lows**: *King David* (1985), *Autumn in New York* (2000)

Giannini, Giancarlo (1942–)

Italian, born in La Spezia. A drama student at the Accademia Nazionale in Rome, he made his film debut in *Fango sulla metropoli* (1965). A long professional association with director **Lina Wertmuller** brought him international recognition, and he

received a Best Actor Academy Award® nomination for *Seven Beauties* (1975). He subsequently appeared in a number of English-language roles.
Career highs: *Swept Away* (1974), *Seven Beauties* (1975), *L'Innocente* (1976), *New York Stories* (1989)
Career low: *Blood Red* (1988)

Gibson, Mel (1956–   )

American–Australian, born in Peekskill, New York. One of eleven children, he moved with his family to Australia in 1968 and later studied at the National Institute of Dramatic Art in Sydney. He made his film debut in *Summer City* (1977) and found cult stardom as *Mad Max* (1979). His boyish good looks, irreverent humour and manic, edgy performances made him a major Hollywood star. He has also directed, winning an Academy Award for *Braveheart* (1995).
Career highs: *Mad Max* (1979), *Lethal Weapon* (1987), *Braveheart* (1995), *What Women Want* (2000), *The Passion of the Christ* (2004)
Career lows: *Air America* (1990), *Bird on a Wire* (1990), *The Million Dollar Hotel* (2000)

Gielgud, Sir (Arthur) John (1904–2000)

English, born in London. One of the most renowned Shakespearean actors of the 20th century, he made his film debut in *Who Is the Man?* (1924), but seemed to regard the medium with some disdain and remained primarily a stage performer until the 1950s. A scene-stealing character actor, he won a Best Supporting Actor Academy Award® as the supercilious butler in *Arthur* (1981).
Career highs: *Becket* (1964), *The Loved One* (1965), *Providence* (1977), *Arthur* (1981)
Career lows: *Caligula* (1977), *Scandalous* (1984)

Gish, Lillian (Lillian Diana de Guiche) (1893–1993)

American, born in Springfield, Ohio. A child performer with her younger sister Dorothy, she made her film debut in *An Unseen Enemy* (1912). The pre-eminent silent actress, she created a gallery of waif-like heroines whose surface frailty concealed inner strength. Abandoned by Hollywood in the sound era, she returned to the stage, making occasional film appearances and touring the world to foster appreciation of silent cinema.
Career highs: *Broken Blossoms* (1919), *The Scarlet Letter* (1926), *The Wind* (1928), *Night of the Hunter* (1955), *The Whales of August* (1987)
Career lows: *Top Man* (1943), *Miss Susie Slagle's* (1945)

Glover, Danny (1946–   )

American, born in San Francisco, California. A member of the Black Actors' Workshop and the American Conservatory Theatre, he made his film debut with a small role in *Escape from Alcatraz* (1979). A commanding character actor, he became a box-office force as the long-suffering elder partner of **Mel Gibson** in *Lethal Weapon* (1987) and its three sequels.

Career highs: *The Color Purple* (1985), *Lethal Weapon* (1987), *To Sleep with Anger* (1990)
Career low: *Gone Fishin'* (1997)

Goldberg, Whoopi (Caryn Elaine Johnson) (1949–   )

American, born in New York City. A high-school dropout who conquered heroin addiction, she moved to California and worked in a mortuary before building a career as a stand-up comic. Spotted by director **Mike Nichols**, she performed a one-woman show on Broadway and won a major role in *The Color Purple* (1985). She won a Best Supporting Actress Academy Award® for *Ghost* (1990).
Career highs: *The Color Purple* (1985), *Ghost* (1990), *Sister Act* (1992)
Career lows: *Burglar* (1987), *The Telephone* (1988), *Homer & Eddie* (1990), *Theodore Rex* (1996)

Gong Li (1966–   )

Chinese, born in Shenyang, Liaoning Province. She studied at the Central Drama Academy in Beijing, and was still a student when she made her film debut in *Red Sorghum* (1987). A fruitful professional and personal association with director **Zhang Yimou** lasted until 1995. She now seems poised for English-language success with the release of *Memoirs of a Geisha* (2005) and *Miami Vice* (2006).
Career highs: *Raise the Red Lantern* (1991), *The Story of Qui Ju* (1992), *Farewell My Concubine* (1993)
Career low: *Chinese Box* (1997)

Gooding, Cuba, Jr (1968–   )

American, born in the Bronx, New York City. Born into a show-business family, he was a dancer and martial-arts expert before working in television drama and making his film debut in *Coming to America* (1988). A dynamic, intense presence, he won a Best Supporting Actor Academy Award® for *Jerry Maguire* (1996), but has since struggled to find worthwhile roles.
Career highs: *Boyz n the Hood* (1991), *Jerry Maguire* (1996), *Men of Honor* (2000)
Career lows: *Chill Factor* (1999), *Boat Trip* (2003), *Radio* (2003)

Grable, Betty (Elizabeth Ruth Grable) (1916–73)

American, born in St Louis, Missouri. A chorus girl at the age of 12, she made her film debut in *Let's Go Places* (1929) and spent a decade toiling in musicals and frothy romances. Her popularity grew during the war years, when her 'Million Dollar Legs' and warm personality made her a forces' sweetheart. She made her last film in 1955.
Career highs: *Down Argentine Way* (1940), *Moon over Miami* (1941), *Springtime in the Rockies* (1942), *How to Marry a Millionaire* (1953)
Career lows: *That Lady in Ermine* (1948), *How to Be Very, Very Popular* (1955)

Granger, Stewart (James Lablanche Stewart) (1913–93)

English, born in London. A student at the Webber-Douglas School of Dramatic Art, he was a stage performer and film extra before becoming a dashing star of wartime costume dramas. In Hollywood from 1950, he played rugged men of action and

athletic swashbucklers. His second wife was **Jean Simmons**.
Career highs: *King Solomon's Mines* (1950), *Scaramouche* (1952), *Moonfleet* (1955)
Career lows: *Woman Hater* (1949), *Gun Glory* (1957)

Grant, Cary (Archibald Alexander Leach) (1904–86)

American, born in Bristol, England. A circus acrobat and clown who moved into legitimate theatre productions, he made his film debut in *Singapore Sue* (1932). A suave, debonair romantic idol, he was a master at comedy roles that required verbal dexterity and physical agility, and received Academy Award® nominations for *Penny Serenade* (1941) and *None But the Lonely Heart* (1944). He retired from the screen in 1966.
Career highs: *Bringing up Baby* (1938), *The Philadelphia Story* (1940), *Notorious* (1946), *North by Northwest* (1959), *Charade* (1963)
Career lows: *Dream Wife* (1953), *The Pride and the Passion* (1957)

Grant, Hugh (1960–)

English, born in London. A student at New College, Oxford, he made his film debut in *Privileged* (1982). His floppy hair and diffident, dithering manner could have doomed him to a career of playing upper-crust fops and hearty juveniles, but his skill as a polished light comedian brought him international stardom.
Career highs: *Four Weddings and a Funeral* (1994), *Notting Hill* (1999), *About a Boy* (2002)
Career lows: *Night Train to Venice* (1993), *Nine Months* (1995)

Grier, Pam (1949–)

American, born in Winston-Salem, North Carolina. The daughter of an Air Force mechanic, she made her film debut in *Beyond the Valley of the Dolls* (1971). The queen of cult blaxploitation B-movies in the 1970s, she built a career playing bad girls and tough women.
Career highs: *Coffy* (1973), *Foxy Brown* (1974), *Jackie Brown* (1997)
Career low: *Drum* (1976)

Griffith, Melanie (1957–)

American, born in New York City. The daughter of actress Tippi Hedren, she made her film debut in *Smith!* (1969). She married actor Don Johnson when she was 14, and in her early career played a succession of empty-headed nymphets. She overcame alcoholism and drug addiction, and later revealed a winning talent for comedy. Divorced from Johnson, she married actor Steven Bauer before remarrying Johnson and then marrying **Antonio Banderas**.
Career highs: *Night Moves* (1975), *Something Wild* (1986), *Working Girl* (1988)
Career lows: *The Bonfire of the Vanities* (1990), *Shining Through* (1992)

Guinness, Sir Alec (1914–2000)

English, born in Marylebone, London. A student at the Fay Compton Studio of Dramatic Art, he made his film debut in *Evensong* (1933) but remained exclusively a stage actor until *Great Expectations* (1946). A self-effacing chameleon, he excelled in Ealing comedies and maintained a distinguished film career alongside his equally

admired stage roles. He received a Best Actor Academy Award® for *The Bridge on the River Kwai* (1957).
Career highs: *Kind Hearts and Coronets* (1949), *The Lavender Hill Mob* (1951), *The Man in the White Suit* (1951), *The Bridge on the River Kwai* (1957), *Tunes of Glory* (1960)
Career lows: *A Majority of One* (1961), *Hitler: The Last Ten Days* (1972), *A Passage to India* (1984)

Gyllenhaal, Jake (Jacob Benjamin Gyllenhaal) (1980–)

American, born in Los Angeles, California. The son of a director and a screenwriter, he began acting in childhood, making his film debut at the age of ten in *City Slickers* (1991). His breakthrough role was as the eponymous *Donnie Darko* (2001), and his three film releases of 2005 saw him maturing into a powerful, versatile leading man. His sister is actress Maggie Gyllenhaal.
Career highs: *Donnie Darko* (2001), *The Good Girl* (2002), *Brokeback Mountain* (2005), *Jarhead* (2005)
Career low: *The Day After Tomorrow* (2004)

H

Hackman, (Eu)Gene Alden (1930–)

American, born in San Bernardino, California. He joined the Marines at 16, and attempted a career in journalism before becoming an actor. He made his film debut in *Mad Dog Coll* (1961) and, as his roles grew in importance, was recognized as one of the most gifted character actors in US cinema. He won Academy Awards® for *The French Connection* (1971) and *Unforgiven* (1992).
Career highs: *I Never Sang for My Father* (1970), *The French Connection* (1971), *The Conversation* (1974), *Mississippi Burning* (1988), *Unforgiven* (1992)
Career lows: *Zandy's Bride* (1974), *Lucky Lady* (1975), *Superman IV: The Quest for Peace* (1987), *Loose Cannons* (1990)

Hanks, Tom (Thomas J Hanks) (1956–)

American, born in Concord, California. He studied in Sacramento, and made his film debut in *He Knows You're Alone* (1981). Success in television comedies led to a film career in which his comic touch and everyman appeal have earned him comparisons with **James Stewart**. He won Best Actor Academy Awards® for *Philadelphia* (1993) and *Forrest Gump* (1994).
Career highs: *Big* (1988), *Philadelphia* (1993), *Forrest Gump* (1994), *Saving Private Ryan* (1998)
Career lows: *He Knows You're Alone* (1981), *The Man with One Red Shoe* (1995), *Bonfire of the Vanities* (1990)

Hardy, Oliver (Norvell Hardy Jr) (1892–1957)

American, born near Atlanta, Georgia. He ran away from home at the age of eight to become a boy singer in a travelling minstrel show, and later entered films with an appearance in the silent short *Outwitting Dad* (1913). He played the straight man to many comedians before teaming up with **Stan Laurel**; their first appearance

together was *A Lucky Dog* (1917), and they later starred together in more than 100 films. Their gentlemanly, bowler-hatted buffoons became one of the most beloved double acts in cinema history.
Career highs: *The Music Box* (1932), *Sons of the Desert* (1933), *Bonnie Scotland* (1935), *Way Out West* (1937)
Career low: *Atoll K* (1950)

Harlow, Jean (Harlean Carpenter) (1911–37)

American, born in Kansas City, Missouri. At 16, she eloped with a millionaire and wound up in Los Angeles, where she made her film debut in *Moran of the Marines* (1928). In the 1930s she became hugely popular as a wisecracking platinum blonde who flaunted her sexuality and poked fun at her own glamorous image. After struggling with kidney disease for most of her life, she died of acute nephritis at the age of 26.
Career highs: *Red Dust* (1932), *Bombshell* (1933), *Dinner at Eight* (1933), *Libeled Lady* (1936)
Career lows: *Reckless* (1935), *Personal Property* (1937)

Harris, Ed(ward Allen) (1949–   )

American, born in Englewood, New Jersey. He made his film debut in *Coma* (1978), and went on to become a character actor of immense range and integrity. He received Academy Award® nominations for *Apollo 13* (1995), *The Truman Show* (1998) and *Pollock* (2000), which he also directed.
Career highs: *The Right Stuff* (1983), *Apollo 13* (1995), *The Truman Show* (1998), *Pollock* (2000), *The Hours* (2002)
Career lows: *Walker* (1987), *Needful Things* (1993), *Milk Money* (1994)

Harris, Richard St John (1930–2002)

Irish, born in Limerick. A student at the London Academy of Music and Dramatic Art, he made his film debut in *Alive and Kicking* (1958). A rugged, forceful supporting performer, he became an international star in the 1960s, and was noted as much for his hellraising antics as for his performances. He enjoyed a career revival in the final decade of his life.
Career highs: *This Sporting Life* (1963), *The Molly Maguires* (1969), *The Field* (1990), *Unforgiven* (1992)
Career lows: *Caprice* (1967), *Tarzan, the Ape Man* (1981)

Harrison, Sir Rex (Reginald Carey Harrison) (1908–90)

English, born in Huyton, Lancashire. A stage actor from the age of 16, he made his film debut in *The Great Game* (1930). A roguish, waspish light comedian, he worked in Hollywood from 1945 but found lasting screen fame repeating his stage triumph as Henry Higgins in *My Fair Lady* (1964), which earned him a Best Actor Academy Award®.
Career highs: *Blithe Spirit* (1945), *The Ghost and Mrs Muir* (1947), *My Fair Lady* (1964)
Career low: *Staircase* (1969)

Don't Bet on That...

Gene Hackman and Dustin Hoffman met as students at California's Pasadena Playhouse Acting School, where legend has it that they were, as a pair, voted 'least likely to succeed' by their classmates (Hackman is also noted for having received one of the lowest grade averages in the school's history). They later moved to New York City, where they briefly shared an apartment before moving on to bigger and better things.

Hart, William S(urrey) (1864–1946)

American, born in Newburgh, New York. An employee of the New York Post Office, he toured the USA with various theatre groups before making his film debut in *The Fugitive* (1913). The cinema's first great cowboy star, he enjoyed his biggest success in 1920s westerns playing chivalrous, stern-faced defenders of truth and justice.
Career highs: *Wild Bill Hickok* (1923), *Singer Jim McKee* (1924), *Tumbleweeds* (1925)

Hawke, Ethan Green (1970–)

American, born in Austin, Texas. A child actor, he made his film debut in *Explorers* (1985) and played his share of sensitive, rebellious adolescents before gravitating towards more challenging adult roles. He won a Best Supporting Actor Academy Award® for *Training Day* (2001) and was also nominated as co-writer of the screenplay for *Before Sunset* (2004). He is divorced from **Uma Thurman**.
Career highs: *Dead Poets Society* (1989), *Before Sunrise* (1995), *Training Day* (2001), *Before Sunset* (2004)
Career lows: *The Newton Boys* (1998), *Taking Lives* (2004)

Hawn, Goldie Jeanne (1945–)

American, born in Washington, DC. She was a dancer and chorus girl before making her film debut in *The One and Only Genuine Original Family Band* (1968). A giggly, endearingly empty-headed blonde in television's *Laugh-In*, she won a Best Supporting Actress Academy Award® for *Cactus Flower* (1969) and has proved to be one of Hollywood's most durable female stars. **Kurt Russell** is her off-screen partner, and actress Kate Hudson is her daughter.
Career highs: *Cactus Flower* (1969), *The Sugarland Express* (1974), *Private Benjamin* (1980)
Career low: *The Duchess and the Dirtwater Fox* (1976)

Hayes, Helen (1900–93)

American, born in Washington, DC. A child actress who became one of the great ladies of the Broadway theatre, she dabbled in film during the silent era and later won a Best Actress Academy Award® for *The Sin of Madelon Claudet* (1931). A Best Supporting Actress Academy Award® for *Airport* (1970) led to a series of film roles as indomitable old ladies, and a stint playing Miss Marple on television.
Career highs: *The Sin of Madelon Claudet* (1931), *A Farewell to Arms* (1932), *What Every Woman Knows* (1934), *Airport* (1970)
Career lows: *The Son-Daughter* (1932), *Vanessa: Her Love Story* (1935)

Hayward, Susan (Edythe Marrener) (1917–75)

American, born in Brooklyn, New York City. She tested for the role of Scarlett O'Hara, and moved to Hollywood to pursue a film career. She eventually found roles that suited her vivid personality and talent for larger-than-life emotional drama, winning a Best Actress Academy Award® for *I Want To Live!* (1958). She died after a long battle with multiple brain tumours.

Career highs: *Smash-Up* (1947), *With a Song in My Heart* (1952), *I'll Cry Tomorrow* (1955), *I Want To Live!* (1958)
Career lows: *The Conqueror* (1956), *Valley of the Dolls* (1967)

Hayworth, Rita (Margarita Carmen Cansino) (1918–87)

American, born in New York City. A distant cousin of **Ginger Rogers**, she pursued a career as a dancer and toured nightclubs in the family act, 'The Dancing Cansinos'. A Hollywood starlet from 1935, she was a ravishing (though not natural) redhead, at her best in escapist musicals. **Orson Welles** was the second of her five husbands.

Career highs: *You Were Never Lovelier* (1942), *Cover Girl* (1944), *Gilda* (1946)
Career low: *Salome* (1953)

Hepburn, Audrey (Audrey Kathleen Ruston) (1929–93)

Belgian, born in Brussels. A ballet student, she made her film debut in *Nederlands in 7 lessen* (1948). Her Broadway performance as Gigi won her the lead in *Roman Holiday* (1953) and a Best Actress Academy Award®. She was Hollywood's fairytale princess for the next decade and retired to Rome in 1968, emerging for a scattering of later roles and for tireless work as a UNICEF ambassador.

Career highs: *Roman Holiday* (1953), *Funny Face* (1957), *Breakfast at Tiffany's* (1961), *My Fair Lady* (1964), *Wait Until Dark* (1967)
Career lows: *Green Mansions* (1959), *Bloodline* (1979)

Hepburn, Katharine Houghton (1907–2003)

American, born in Hartford, Connecticut. Educated at Bryn Mawr College, she worked on the stage before making her film debut in *A Bill of Divorcement* (1932). A vivid personality with an inimitably cadenced speech pattern and an indomitable spirit, she excelled as feisty, unconventional women in everything from screwball comedy to stark drama. She won four Best Actress Academy Awards® and had a long relationship with frequent co-star **Spencer Tracy**.

Career highs: *Little Women* (1933), *The Philadelphia Story* (1940), *Woman of the Year* (1942), *Adam's Rib* (1949), *The African Queen* (1951)
Career lows: *Dragon Seed* (1944), *Song of Love* (1947)

Heston, Charlton (Charles Carter) (1924–   )

American, born in Evanston, Illinois. He made his screen debut in a student version of *Peer Gynt* (1941) and his professional debut in *Dark City* (1950). Tall, ruggedly handsome and granite-jawed, he had the physique and noble bearing for epic roles, and won a Best Actor Academy Award® for *Ben-Hur* (1959). He has also directed, and is an enthusiastic spokesman for the National Rifle Association.

Career highs: *The Ten Commandments* (1956), *Ben-Hur* (1959), *El Cid* (1961), *Will Penny* (1967), *Planet of the Apes* (1968)
Career lows: *The Pigeon that Took Rome* (1962), *Counterpoint* (1968), *The Last Hard Men* (1976), *Mother Lode* (1982)

Hiller, Dame Wendy (1912–2003)

English, born in Bramhall, Cheshire. An actress from childhood, she made her film debut in *Lancashire Luck* (1937) and became a star as Eliza Doolittle in the film version of *Pygmalion* (1938). A woman of the theatre, she worked sparingly in cinema, but won a Best Supporting Actress Academy Award® for *Separate Tables* (1958) and added lustre to several other films.
Career highs: *Pygmalion* (1938), *Major Barbara* (1940), *I Know Where I'm Going* (1945), *Separate Tables* (1958), *Sons and Lovers* (1960)
Career lows: *Sailor of the King* (1953), *The Cat and the Canary* (1979)

Hoffman, Dustin (1937–   )

American, born in Los Angeles, California. The son of a furniture designer, he studied to be a doctor before pursuing an acting career. He spent a decade as a struggling actor in New York before his breakthrough role in *The Graduate* (1967). A magnetic character actor noted for his versatility and uncompromising perfectionism, he has won Best Actor Academy Awards® for *Kramer vs Kramer* (1979) and *Rain Man* (1988).
Career highs: *The Graduate* (1967), *Midnight Cowboy* (1969), *Lenny* (1974), *Kramer vs Kramer* (1979), *Tootsie* (1982)
Career lows: *Alfredo, Alfredo* (1971), *Ishtar* (1987)

Holden, William (William Franklin Beedle Jr) (1918–81)

American, born in O'Fallon, Illinois. As a student at the Pasadena Junior College, he was spotted on stage and signed to a contract by Paramount. A handsome, masculine presence, he made his mark in *Golden Boy* (1939) and was a top attraction in the 1950s. Alcoholism dogged his life, and he bled to death after a drunken fall in his apartment.
Career highs: *Sunset Boulevard* (1950), *Stalag 17* (1953), *The Bridge on the River Kwai* (1957), *The Wild Bunch* (1969), *Network* (1976)
Career lows: *Satan Never Sleeps* (1962), *The Christmas Tree* (1969), *Open Season* (1974)

Holliday, Judy (Judith Tuvim) (1922–65)

American, born in New York City. A telephonist for **Orson Welles'** Mercury Theatre Group, she worked in nightclubs and made her film debut in *Greenwich Village* (1944). Her stage success in *Born Yesterday* was repeated in the 1950 film version, which won her a Best Actress Academy Award® and established her as an endearingly dizzy blonde with a heart of gold.
Career highs: *Adam's Rib* (1949), *Born Yesterday* (1950), *It Should Happen to You* (1954), *Bells are Ringing* (1960)
Career low: *Full of Life* (1956)

Some notable actors

Holm, Sir Ian (Ian Holm Cuthbert) (1931–)

English, born in Goodmayes, Essex. A student at the Royal Academy of Dramatic Art, he worked with the Royal Shakespeare Company and developed a glittering stage career on both sides of the Atlantic before making his film debut in *The Fixer* (1968). A feverishly industrious character actor of range and power, he received an Academy Award® nomination for *Chariots of Fire* (1981).

Career highs: *Chariots of Fire* (1981), *Dance with a Stranger* (1985), *Dreamchild* (1985), *The Sweet Hereafter* (1997), *Joe Gould's Secret* (2000)

Hope, Bob (Leslie Townes Hope) (1903–2003)

American, born in Eltham, London. In the USA from 1907, he was a successful stage comic before making his film debut in *Going Spanish* (1934). His screen persona as a cowardly, wisecracking braggart made him a popular film star for 30 years. A television personality, golfer, philanthropist and tireless entertainer of the armed forces, he became a show-business institution.

Career highs: *The Cat and the Canary* (1939), *The Ghost Breakers* (1940), *The Road to Morocco* (1942), *The Paleface* (1948), *The Seven Little Foys* (1955)

Career lows: *Boy, Did I Get a Wrong Number!* (1966), *Eight on the Lam* (1967), *The Private Navy of Sgt O'Farrell* (1968)

Hopkins, Sir Anthony (1937–)

Welsh, born in Port Talbot. Inspired by **Richard Burton**, he became one of the most electrifying stage actors of his generation and made his film debut in *The Lion in Winter* (1968). He battled alcohol addiction and private demons to become a leading film actor, adept at illuminating the inner lives of the emotionally repressed and eccentric. He won a Best Actor Academy Award® for *The Silence of the Lambs* (1991).

Career highs: *The Elephant Man* (1980), *The Silence of the Lambs* (1991), *The Remains of the Day* (1993), *Shadowlands* (1993)

Career lows: *A Chorus of Disapproval* (1988), *Freejack* (1991), *Bad Company* (2002)

Hopper, Dennis (1936–)

American, born in Dodge City, Kansas. He studied drama with Dorothy McGuire and made his film debut in *Johnny Guitar* (1954). An intense, unremarkable young performer, he became a counterculture icon with *Easy Rider* (1969). He conquered drug and drink addictions, and his career revived in the 1980s; he has played a succession of vicious, eye-catching villains.

Career highs: *Easy Rider* (1969), *Apocalypse Now* (1979), *Blue Velvet* (1986), *Speed* (1994)

Career lows: *The Last Movie* (1971), *The Texas Chainsaw Massacre 2* (1986)

Hoskins, Bob (Robert William Hoskins) (1942–)

English, born in Bury St Edmunds, Suffolk. A Covent Garden porter, window cleaner and truck driver, he became an actor after auditioning for the Unity Theatre and made his film debut in *The National Health* (1973). A forceful, bullet-shaped character actor, he has built an international career and won a Best Actor Academy Award® nomination for *Mona Lisa* (1986). He has also directed.

Career highs: *The Long Good Friday* (1979), *Mona Lisa* (1988), *Who Framed Roger Rabbit* (1988), *Twenty Four Seven* (1997)
Career lows: *The Raggedy Rawney* (1987), *Super Mario Bros.* (1993), *Rainbow* (1995)

Howard, Trevor Wallace (1913–88)

English, born in Cliftonville, Kent. A student at the Royal Academy of Dramatic Art, he worked on stage and served in the army before making his film debut in *The Way Ahead* (1944). A pipe-smoking, cricket-loving, hellraising Englishman, he became a dependable star and incisive character actor who lent his considerable talents to far too many unworthy projects.
Career highs: *Brief Encounter* (1945), *The Third Man* (1949), *Outcast of the Islands* (1951), *The Heart of the Matter* (1953), *Sons and Lovers* (1960)
Career lows: *Twinky* (1969), *The Bawdy Adventures of Tom Jones* (1976), *The Unholy* (1988)

Hudson, Rock (Roy Harold Scherer Jr) (1925–85)

American, born in Winnetka, Illinois. A US Navy veteran, truck driver and postman, he was offered a screen test and made his film debut in *Fighter Squadron* (1948). He was a handsome, amiable figure who rose steadily through the ranks, finding stardom in adventure stories, weepies and romantic comedies, especially in partnership with **Doris Day**. His death, of complications related to AIDS, led to public exposure of his long-concealed homosexuality.
Career highs: *All that Heaven Allows* (1955), *Giant* (1956), *Pillow Talk* (1959), *Seconds* (1966)
Career lows: *Embryo* (1976), *Avalanche* (1978)

Hunt, Helen Elizabeth (1963–)

American, born in Los Angeles, California. A child performer, she appeared on television before making her film debut in *Rollercoaster* (1977). The long-running television series *Mad About You* made her a star in the 1990s, and she won an unexpected Best Actress Academy Award® for *As Good As It Gets* (1997). She was briefly married to actor Hank Azaria.
Career high: *As Good As It Gets* (1997)
Career low: *Trancers II* (1991)

Hunter, Holly (1958–)

American, born in Conyers, Georgia. She studied drama at Carnegie Mellon University in Pittsburgh before making her film debut in *The Burning* (1981). Long associated with the works of playwright Beth Henley on stage, her screen career developed as she revealed the dynamic range and depth of her talent, winning a Best Actress Academy Award® for *The Piano* (1993).
Career highs: *Broadcast News* (1987), *Raising Arizona* (1987), *The Piano* (1993), *Living Out Loud* (1998), *Thirteen* (2003), *The Incredibles* (2004)
Career low: *Animal Behaviour* (1989)

Huppert, Isabelle (1955–   )

French, born in Paris. A drama student at the Paris Conservatoire, she made her film debut as a teenager in *Faustine et le bel été* (1971). She quickly became one of the most industrious figures in French cinema, tackling a dazzling array of roles with a fearless commitment. Latterly, she has been drawn to depictions of extreme sexuality and suffering.
Career highs: *The Lacemaker* (1977), *Violette Nozière* (1978), *Loulou* (1980), *Coup de foudre* (1983), *The Piano Teacher* (2001)
Career lows: *Malina* (1990), *The School of Flesh* (1998)

Hurt, John (1940–   )

English, born in Shirebrook, Derbyshire. A student at the Royal Academy of Dramatic Art, he made his film debut in *The Wild and the Willing* (1962). A hardworking character actor with a distinctive voice, he edged towards leading roles in the 1980s but remains a prolific, scene-stealing supporting player. He received Academy Award[®] nominations for *Midnight Express* (1978) and *The Elephant Man* (1980).
Career highs: *Midnight Express* (1978), *Alien* (1979), *The Elephant Man* (1980), *Scandal* (1989), *Love and Death on Long Island* (1997)
Career lows: *Sinful Davey* (1969), *Partners* (1982)

Going Solo

A cast of thousands is a luxury few film-makers can afford, while the impact of a solo performance can be powerful – so it should come as no surprise that many full-length films have been made with only one actor. *Brontë* (1983) starred Julie Christie as Charlotte Brontë, while Philip Baker Hall portrayed Richard Nixon in Robert Altman's *Secret Honor* (1984). A more unusual example of a single-actor film is *Romeo–Juliet* (1990), an all-cat adaptation of Shakespeare's *Romeo and Juliet* in which John Hurt is the only human performer.

Hurt, William (1950–   )

American, born in Washington, DC. The son of a State Department official, he studied acting at the Juilliard School in New York. He worked on television before making his film debut in *Altered States* (1980). A popular leading man in the 1980s, he won a Best Actor Academy Award[®] for *Kiss of the Spider Woman* (1985).
Career highs: *Body Heat* (1981), *The Big Chill* (1983), *Kiss of the Spider Woman* (1985), *Broadcast News* (1987), *A History of Violence* (2005)
Career lows: *I Love You To Death* (1990), *A Couch in New York* (1996)

Huston, Anjelica (1951–   )

American, born in Santa Monica, California. The daughter of film director **John Huston** and prima ballerina Enrica Soma, she made a disastrous debut in Huston's film *A Walk with Love and Death* (1969). She later emerged from the shadows of her father (and her former lover **Jack Nicholson**) to win a Best Supporting Actress Academy Award[®] for *Prizzi's Honor* (1985).

Career highs: *Prizzi's Honor* (1985), *The Dead* (1987), *Crimes and Misdemeanors* (1989), *The Grifters* (1990), *The Addams Family* (1991)
Career low: *A Walk with Love and Death* (1969)

Hutton, Timothy (1960–   )

American, born in Malibu, California. The son of actor Jim Hutton, he made his film debut with his father in *Never Too Late* (1965). He won a Best Supporting Actor Academy Award® for *Ordinary People* (1980). Although talented and dedicated, he has been unable to maintain the initial impetus of his career. He was briefly married to **Debra Winger**.
Career highs: *Ordinary People* (1980), *Daniel* (1983), *Beautiful Girls* (1996)
Career lows: *Turk 182* (1985), *The Temp* (1993)

I

Irons, Jeremy (1948–   )

English, born in Cowes on the Isle of Wight. A student with the Bristol Old Vic, he worked on the stage and on television before making his film debut in *Nijinsky* (1980). Television acclaim for *Brideshead Revisited* (1981) made his name, and he gave a number of sensitive film portrayals, winning a Best Actor Academy Award® for *Reversal of Fortune* (1990). He is married to actress Sinéad Cusack.
Career highs: *The French Lieutenant's Woman* (1981), *Dead Ringers* (1988), *Reversal of Fortune* (1990)
Career lows: *The House of the Spirits* (1993), *M Butterfly* (1993)

Ives, Burl (Burle Icle Ivanhoe Ives) (1909–95)

American, born in Hunt, Illinois. A football player at school, he later travelled the country and found success as a honey-voiced folk singer, recording more than 40 albums. He made his film debut as a singing cowboy in *Smoky* (1946) and played folksy characters and mean villains in westerns before he won a Best Supporting Actor Academy Award® for *The Big Country* (1958) and secured more prominent roles.
Career highs: *The Big Country* (1958), *Cat on a Hot Tin Roof* (1958), *Our Man in Havana* (1960)
Career lows: *Earthbound* (1981), *Two Moon Junction* (1988)

J

Jackson, Glenda (1936–   )

English, born in Liverpool. She studied at the Royal Academy of Dramatic Art and worked in the theatre before making her film debut in *This Sporting Life* (1963). A commanding, fearless leading lady, she won Best Actress Academy Awards® for *Women in Love* (1969) and *A Touch of Class* (1973). She retired from acting to pursue a political career, and was elected a Labour MP in 1992.
Career highs: *Women in Love* (1969), *Sunday, Bloody Sunday* (1971), *Stevie* (1978)
Career lows: *Lost and Found* (1979), *Beyond Therapy* (1986)

Jackson, Samuel L(eroy) (1948–)

American, born in Washington, DC. Raised in Chattanooga, Tennessee, he sought help from a speech therapist to cure a childhood stammer and was recommended to appear in stage productions. He made his film debut in *Together for Days* (1972), but his cinema career only flourished after he conquered drug addiction. He has become one of the busiest and most commercially successful stars of his generation.
Career highs: *Jungle Fever* (1991), *Pulp Fiction* (1994), *Jackie Brown* (1997), *Changing Lanes* (2002)
Career lows: *Amos & Andrew* (1993), *Deep Blue Sea* (1999)

James, Sid (Sidney Joel Cohen) (1913–76)

South African, born in Johannesburg. He worked as a ladies' hairdresser before wartime service, came to the UK in 1946, and made his film debut in *Black Memory* (1947). He became a valuable supporting player during the 1950s, with his crumpled features, filthy laugh and expert comic timing making him a beloved mainstay of the *Carry On* series.
Career highs: *The Lavender Hill Mob* (1951), *Carry On Cleo* (1963), *The Big Job* (1965), *Carry On Cowboy* (1965), *Carry On Up the Khyber* (1969)
Career low: *Three Hats for Lisa* (1965)

Johnson, Ben (1918–96)

American, born in Foraker, Oklahoma. The son of a rancher, he worked as a ranch hand and rodeo cowboy before drifting into films as a horse-wrangler and stunt double for the likes of **John Wayne** and **Joel McCrea**. An understated actor, he became a favourite of directors **John Ford** and **Sam Peckinpah**, winning a Best Supporting Actor Academy Award® for *The Last Picture Show* (1971).
Career highs: *Wagonmaster* (1950), *One-Eyed Jacks* (1961), *The Last Picture Show* (1971), *The Getaway* (1973)
Career lows: *The Savage Bees* (1976), *The Swarm* (1978)

Johnson, Dame Celia (1908–82)

English, born in Richmond, Surrey. A student at the Royal Academy of Dramatic Art and a stage actress from 1928, she made her film debut in *Dirty Work* (1934). A gentle, ladylike presence, she found her best roles playing understanding wives and loyal sweethearts during the 1940s. She was committed to a life in the theatre, and her subsequent film appearances were rare.
Career highs: *In Which We Serve* (1942), *This Happy Breed* (1944), *Brief Encounter* (1945), *The Prime of Miss Jean Brodie* (1969)
Career low: *The Astonished Heart* (1950)

Johnson, (Charles) Van (1916–)

American, born in Newport, Rhode Island. A Broadway chorus boy and cabaret performer, he made his film debut in *Too Many Girls* (1940). Signed by MGM, he became a teen idol as the boy next door in 1940s musicals and heartwarming melodramas. His popularity faded but his career endured on stage, screen and television.

Career highs: *A Guy Named Joe* (1943), *In the Good Old Summertime* (1949), *Battleground* (1949), *The Bottom of the Bottle* (1956)
Career lows: *The Big Hangover* (1950), *Killer Crocodile* (1988)

Jolie, Angelina (1975–)

American, born in Los Angeles, California. The daughter of actors **Jon Voight** and Marcheline Bertrand, she made her film debut as a child in *Lookin' to Get Out* (1982). Award-winning television roles, pouting beauty and a wild-child reputation brought her cinema stardom, and she won a Best Supporting Actress Academy Award® for *Girl, Interrupted* (1999). She has been married to actors Jonny Lee Miller and **Billy Bob Thornton**, and her partner is **Brad Pitt**.
Career highs: *Girl, Interrupted* (1999), *Lara Croft: Tomb Raider* (2001)
Career lows: *Original Sin* (2001), *Life or Something Like It* (2002), *Beyond Borders* (2003)

Jolson, Al (Asa Yoelson) (c.1886–1950)

Lithuanian, born in Srednike. Arriving in the USA as a child, he ran away from home to join the circus and became a stellar Broadway attraction before making his film debut in the short *April Showers* (1926). An inveterate showman, his exuberant patter and heart-tugging songs in the landmark part-talkie *The Jazz Singer* (1927) ensured his place in cinema history.
Career highs: *The Jazz Singer* (1927), *The Singing Fool* (1928), *Mammy* (1930)
Career lows: *Say It with Songs* (1929), *The Singing Kid* (1936)

> ## A Film of Few Words
>
> *The Jazz Singer* (1927) is famous for being the first feature film to contain dialogue, but its makers originally intended it to feature only recorded music and songs. As it happened, Al Jolson's ad-libbing worked so well that they decided to keep it in; however, the film still only contains two short talking sequences, with a total of 354 words spoken.

Jones, Jennifer (Phyllis Isley) (1919–)

American, born in Tulsa, Oklahoma. A child actress and model, she made her film debut in *New Frontier* (1939). In the 1940s, she brought an ethereal innocence and grace to leading roles, winning a Best Actress Academy Award® for *The Song of Bernadette* (1943). She was married to actor Robert Walker, producer **David O Selznick** and millionaire Norton Simon, and retired after *The Towering Inferno* (1974).
Career highs: *The Song of Bernadette* (1943), *Portrait of Jennie* (1948), *Carrie* (1952)
Career low: *Angel, Angel, Down We Go* (1969)

Jones, Tommy Lee (1946–)

American, born in San Saba, Texas. After studying at Harvard University, where he roomed with Al Gore, he made his film debut in *Love Story* (1970). He appeared in the daytime soap opera *One Life to Live* in the 1970s, but gradually found film roles that served his craggy authority, steely intelligence and deadpan delivery. He won

a Best Supporting Actor Academy Award® for *The Fugitive* (1993), and has also directed.
Career highs: *JFK* (1991), *The Fugitive* (1993), *Men in Black* (1997)
Career lows: *Black Moon Rising* (1986), *Man of the House* (2005)

K

Karloff, Boris (William Henry Pratt) (1887–1969)

English, born in Dulwich. The son of a civil servant, he moved to Canada in 1909 and worked in the theatre, before making his Hollywood debut in 1919. His poignant performance as the monster in *Frankenstein* (1931) established him as an enduring icon of horror films. In life, he was a cricket-loving English gentleman, far removed from the ghouls and madmen he portrayed on screen.
Career highs: *The Criminal Code* (1931), *Frankenstein* (1931), *The Mummy* (1932) *The Bride of Frankenstein* (1935), *Targets* (1968)
Career lows: *The Ape* (1940), *The Strange Door* (1951), *The Black Castle* (1952)

Kaye, Danny (David Daniel Kaminski) (1913–87)

American, born in Brooklyn, New York City. A born entertainer, he worked at odd jobs to support himself before his Broadway breakthrough in *Lady in the Dark* (1941) led to a Hollywood contract and his feature film debut in *Up in Arms* (1944). A popular comedian, he was noted for his tongue-twisting routines, mimicry and expressive features.
Career highs: *The Secret Life of Walter Mitty* (1947), *Hans Christian Andersen* (1952), *White Christmas* (1954), *The Court Jester* (1956)
Career low: *On the Double* (1961)

Keaton, Buster (Joseph Francis Keaton) (1895–1966)

American, born in Piqua, Kansas. Part of his parents' vaudeville act from the age of three, he grew into a remarkably agile, fearless comedy performer, making his film debut in *The Butcher Boy* (1917). He was nicknamed 'The Great Stone Face' because of his solemn, unsmiling features. His career was ruined by alcoholism and studio politics, but he returned to the limelight in the 1950s and lived to see his standing restored as the most inventive and touching of the great silent-era clowns.
Career highs: *Sherlock Junior* (1924), *The Navigator* (1924), *Seven Chances* (1925), *The General* (1927), *Steamboat Bill, Jr* (1928)
Career lows: *Doughboys* (1930), *The Passionate Plumber* (1932), *What! No Beer?* (1933)

Keaton, Diane (Diane Hall) (1946–)

American, born in Los Angeles, California. She studied theatre in New York before making her film debut in *Lovers and Other Strangers* (1970). A long and fruitful association with **Woody Allen** led to some of her best roles, notably the dithering title character in *Annie Hall* (1977), which won her a Best Actress Academy Award®. She is also a respected photographer, and has directed.

Career highs: *Annie Hall* (1977), *Reds* (1981), *Mrs Soffel* (1984), *Something's Got to Give* (2003)
Career lows: *I Will, I Will for Now* (1976), *The Lemon Sisters* (1989)

Keaton, Michael (Michael John Douglas) (1951–   )

American, born in Coraopolis, Pennsylvania. After studying at Kent State University, he moved to Los Angeles. After working as a stand-up comic and television actor, he made his film debut in *Night Shift* (1982). He was the big-screen Batman in two films, and has subsequently sought more diverse roles with varying degrees of success.
Career highs: *Night Shift* (1982), *Beetlejuice* (1988), *Clean and Sober* (1988), *Batman* (1989), *Multiplicity* (1996)
Career lows: *Johnny Dangerously* (1984), *The Squeeze* (1987)

Keel, Howard (Harry Clifford Keel) (1917–2004)

American, born in Gillespie, Illinois. The son of a coalminer, he worked as a mechanic before winning a singing competition and starring in the London production of *Oklahoma!* in 1947. Tall, dark and handsome, with a booming baritone voice, he soon moved into film, making his name in the MGM musicals of the 1950s. He later found renewed popularity in television's *Dallas*.
Career highs: *Annie Get Your Gun* (1950), *Show Boat* (1951), *Kiss Me Kate* (1953), *Calamity Jane* (1953), *Seven Brides for Seven Brothers* (1954)
Career lows: *The Big Fisherman* (1959), *The War Wagon* (1967)

Keitel, Harvey (1939–   )

American, born in Brooklyn, New York City. Formerly a US Marine, he worked as a salesman and court stenographer to support his acting career. A member of the Actors Studio, he made his film debut in *Who's That Knocking at My Door?* (1968), marking the beginning of a long collaboration with **Martin Scorsese**. He is a method actor, known for his intense performances, and has made more than 100 films.
Career highs: *Mean Streets* (1973), *Taxi Driver* (1976), *Fingers* (1977), *Bad Lieutenant* (1992), *The Piano* (1993)
Career lows: *Saturn 3* (1980), *Exposed* (1983), *Wise Guys* (1986), *Head above Water* (1997), *Little Nicky* (2000)

Kelly, Gene (Eugene Curran) (1912–96)

American, born in Pittsburgh, Pennsylvania. An economics graduate, he ran a dance studio and performed a double act with his brother Fred before making a Broadway splash as *Pal Joey* (1939). He made his film debut in *Me and My Gal* (1942), and brought an athletic energy and exuberance to the screen musical in the 1950s. He also directed several films, including *Hello, Dolly!* (1969).
Career highs: *Cover Girl* (1944), *Anchors Aweigh* (1945), *On the Town* (1949), *An American in Paris* (1951), *Singin' in the Rain* (1952)
Career lows: *The Devil Makes Three* (1952), *Viva Knievel* (1977)

Kelly, Grace Patricia (1928–82)

American, born in Philadelphia, Pennsylvania. She made her film debut in *Fourteen Hours* (1951). Graceful, intelligent and poised, she quickly became one of the most admired stars of the era, winning a Best Actress Academy Award[®] for *The Country Girl* (1954). She abandoned her career in 1956 to marry Prince Rainier of Monaco, and devoted herself to her royal duties until her untimely death in a car accident.
Career highs: *Rear Window* (1954), *The Country Girl* (1954), *To Catch a Thief* (1955), *High Society* (1956)
Career low: *Green Fire* (1955)

Kerr, Deborah (Deborah Jane Kerr-Trimmer) (1921–)

Scottish, born in Helensburgh. A trained dancer, she performed with the corps de ballet at Sadler's Wells before concentrating on acting and making her film debut in *Contraband* (1940). A radiant beauty whose ladylike manner restricted her to a career of playing governesses and nuns, she nevertheless revealed a wide dramatic range, earning six Academy Award[®] nominations and receiving a special Academy Award[®] in 1994.
Career highs: *The Life and Death of Colonel Blimp* (1943), *Black Narcissus* (1947), *From Here to Eternity* (1953), *The King and I* (1956), *The Sundowners* (1960)
Career lows: *Dream Wife* (1953), *Prudence and the Pill* (1968)

Kidman, Nicole (1967–)

Australian, born in Honolulu, Hawaii. Committed to acting from an early age, she made her film debut in *Bush Christmas* (1982). An award-winning career led to international roles and *Days of Thunder* (1990), in which she co-starred with **Tom Cruise**, whom she later married. After that marriage ended, she blossomed into a risk-taking dramatic force, winning a Best Actress Academy Award[®] for *The Hours* (2002).
Career highs: *Dead Calm* (1988), *To Die For* (1995), *Moulin Rouge!* (2001), *The Others* (2001), *The Hours* (2002)
Career lows: *Far and Away* (1992), *The Stepford Wives* (2004), *Bewitched* (2005)

Kilmer, Val Edward (1959–)

American, born in Los Angeles, California. He studied at the Hollywood Professional School and the Juilliard School in New York, and made his film debut in the comedy *Top Secret!* (1984). Good-looking and charismatic, he earned a reputation for being difficult, and his career faltered in the late 1990s; he re-emerged as an intriguing character actor. He was married to actress Joanne Whalley.
Career highs: *The Doors* (1991), *Tombstone* (1993), *Kiss, Kiss, Bang, Bang* (2005)
Career lows: *The Real McCoy* (1993), *The Island of Dr Moreau* (1996), *The Saint* (1997)

Kingsley, Sir Ben (Krishna Bhanji) (1943–)

English, born in Scarborough. The son of an Indian physician and an English fashion model, he began his career as a stage actor before making his film debut in *Fear Is the Key* (1972). He continued to work mainly in the theatre until his performance as *Gandhi* (1982), for which he won a Best Actor Academy Award[®].

Career highs: *Gandhi* (1982), *Bugsy* (1991), *Schindler's List* (1993), *Sexy Beast* (2000), *The House of Sand and Fog* (2003).
Career lows: *Harem* (1985), *Parting Shots* (1998), *Spooky House* (1999), *Thunderbirds* (2004)

Kitano, 'Beat' Takeshi (1947–)

Japanese, born in Tokyo. He abandoned his engineering studies to become a stand-up comedian before making his film debut with *Makoto-chan* (1980). In 1989 he began to direct as well as act, and he subsequently became one of Japan's most respected auteurs, often appearing in the films he directed. His prolific output spans many genres, but he is known for combining light-hearted humour with savage violence to startling effect.
Career highs: *Violent Cop* (1989), *Hana-bi* (1997), *Battle Royale* (2000), *Zatoichi* (2003)
Career lows: *Johnny Mnemonic* (1995), *Battle Royale II* (2003)

Kline, Kevin Delaney (1947–)

American, born in St Louis, Missouri. Educated by Benedictine monks, he studied at Indiana University and the Juilliard School. He became a versatile Broadway star before making his film debut in *Sophie's Choice* (1982). He has given sensitive, thoughtful performances in many different genres, winning a Best Supporting Actor Academy Award® for *A Fish Called Wanda* (1988). He is married to the actress Phoebe Cates.
Career highs: *Sophie's Choice* (1982), *A Fish Called Wanda* (1988), *Dave* (1993), *The Ice Storm* (1997)
Career lows: *The January Man* (1989), *Wild Wild West* (1999)

Knightley, Keira Christina (1985–)

English, born in Teddington, Middlesex. The daughter of playwright Sharman McDonald, she made her film debut in *A Village Affair* (1994). She later played the 'decoy' for **Natalie Portman**'s Queen Amidala in *Star Wars: Episode I* (1999), but her breakthrough was a supporting role in the UK sleeper hit *Bend It Like Beckham* (2002). She has since found success in Hollywood, appearing in period adventure films and literary adaptations.
Career highs: *Bend It Like Beckham* (2002), *Pirates of the Caribbean: The Curse of the Black Pearl* (2003), *Pride & Prejudice* (2005)
Career lows: *King Arthur* (2004)

L

Ladd, Alan Walbridge (1913–64)

American, born in Hot Springs, Arkansas. A diving champion at school, he worked at various casual jobs before trying his hand in Hollywood, making his film debut in *Once in a Lifetime* (1932). He spent a decade as an extra and bit-part player before finding his niche as an impassive, cold-hearted tough guy in westerns and film noir thrillers.

Career highs: *This Gun for Hire* (1942), *The Glass Key* (1942), *The Blue Dahlia* (1946), *Shane* (1953)
Career low: *The Black Knight* (1954)

Man on a Box

At 5ft 6in/168cm, Alan Ladd was far from the shortest leading man in Hollywood, but rumours about his supposed lack of height persist – he is sometimes described as having been only 5ft/152cm tall. Whatever the exact figure, cast and crew members have recalled that when Ladd starred opposite the 5ft 8in/173cm Sophia Loren in *Boy on a Dolphin* (1957), he had to stand on a box for two shots in order to kiss her. Adding to the indignity, for a scene where the couple walked along a beach, the crew dug a trench for Loren to walk in so that Ladd would appear taller.

Lamarr, Hedy (Hedwig Eva Maria Kiesler) (1913–2000)

Austrian, born in Vienna. She made her film debut as a teenager in *Geld auf der Strasse* (1930) and gained lasting notoriety for her naked frolics in *Extase* (1933). In Hollywood from 1937, her haughty beauty sustained a 20-year film career. She was married and divorced six times, and her later years were marked by poignant tales of shoplifting charges and unrealized dreams of a comeback.
Career highs: *Extase* (1933), *Algiers* (1938), *Experiment Perilous* (1944)
Career low: *The Female Animal* (1958)

Lancaster, Burt(on Stephen) (1913–94)

American, born in East Harlem, New York City. He left his place at New York University to become a circus acrobat. After wartime service in the US Army, he appeared on Broadway and made his film debut in *The Killers* (1946). A muscular he-man with a dazzling smile, he graduated from swashbucklers to challenging dramatic roles, winning a Best Actor Academy Award® for *Elmer Gantry* (1960).
Career highs: *From Here to Eternity* (1953), *Sweet Smell of Success* (1957), *Elmer Gantry* (1960), *The Birdman of Alcatraz* (1962), *Atlantic City* (1980)
Career low: *La Pelle* (1981)

Lane, Diane (1965–)

American, born in New York City. The daughter of acting coach Burt Lane, she began acting at the age of six and made her film debut in *A Little Romance* (1979). A resilient figure, she has survived career setbacks to emerge as a stronger, more resourceful actress and was Academy Award®-nominated for *Unfaithful* (2002). She is married to actor Josh Brolin.
Career highs: *A Little Romance* (1979), *A Walk on the Moon* (1999), *Unfaithful* (2002)
Career lows: *Priceless Beauty* (1988), *Vital Signs* (1990)

Lange, Jessica (1949–)

American, born in Cloquet, Minnesota. She studied drama in Paris, and was a waitress and model before making her film debut in the poorly-received *King Kong* (1976). She worked hard to gain critical respect, and has won Academy

Awards® for *Tootsie* (1982) and *Blue Sky* (1994). She has a child with dancer Mikhail Baryshnikov, and her off-screen partner is playwright Sam Shepard.
Career highs: *Frances* (1982), *Tootsie* (1982), *Country* (1984), *Sweet Dreams* (1985), *Blue Sky* (1994)
Career lows: *King Kong* (1976), *How to Beat The High Co$t of Living* (1980), *Hush* (1998)

Lansbury, Angela (1925–   )

American, born in London. The granddaughter of Labour politician George Lansbury, she was evacuated to the USA in 1940 and worked as a nightclub act before making her film debut in *Gaslight* (1944). A scene-stealing character actress, she eventually became one of the great Broadway stars, and found lasting television success as Jessica Fletcher in the long-running series *Murder, She Wrote*.
Career highs: *The Harvey Girls* (1946), *State of the Union* (1948), *The Dark at the Top of the Stairs* (1960), *The Manchurian Candidate* (1962)
Career lows: *Tenth Avenue Angel* (1948), *Mutiny* (1952)

Lau, Andy (Lau Tak-Wah) (1961–   )

Chinese, born in Hong Kong. He began acting at the television station TVB in Hong Kong before moving into film roles, and has since appeared in over 100 films. He is also a highly successful pop musician in China.
Career highs: *God of Gamblers* (1989), *Days of Being Wild* (1991), *Infernal Affairs* (2002)
Career low: *The Crazy Companies* (1988)

Laughton, Charles (1899–1962)

English, born in Scarborough. The son of an hotelier, he studied at the Royal Academy of Dramatic Art before embarking on a glittering stage career. He made his film debut in *Bluebottles* (1928). During the 1930s he created a vivid gallery of characters, although lesser roles could bring out the ham in him. He directed the extraordinary *The Night of the Hunter* (1955) and was married to actress Elsa Lanchester, who claimed after his death that he had been tortured by his repressed homosexuality.
Career highs: *The Private Life of Henry VIII* (1933), *Ruggles of Red Gap* (1935), *Mutiny on the Bounty* (1935), *The Hunchback of Notre Dame* (1939), *Witness for the Prosecution* (1957)
Career lows: *The Strange Door* (1951), *Abbott and Costello Meet Captain Kidd* (1952)

Laurel, Stan (Arthur Stanley Jefferson) (1890–1965)

American, born in Lancashire, England. A music-hall performer from his teenage years, he toured America with the Fred Karno troupe, understudying **Charlie Chaplin**, and made his film debut in *Nuts in May* (1917). Popular in the silent era, he first worked with **Oliver Hardy** on *A Lucky Dog* (1917), and the two later starred together in more than 100 films. Their gentlemanly, bowler-hatted buffoons became one of the most beloved double acts in cinema history.

Career highs: *The Music Box* (1932), *Sons of the Desert* (1933), *Bonnie Scotland* (1935), *Way Out West* (1937)
Career low: *Atoll K* (1950)

Law, (David) Jude (1972–   )

English, born in Lewisham, London. The son of schoolteachers, he joined the National Youth Music Theatre when he was twelve, and appeared on stage and in the daytime television soap opera *Families* before making his film debut in *Shopping* (1994). A handsome, charismatic figure, he quickly gained international prominence and has tackled a wide range of character parts and star roles.
Career highs: *Wilde* (1997), *The Talented Mr Ripley* (1999), *Cold Mountain* (2003)
Career lows: *Music from Another Room* (1988), *Love, Honor and Obey* (2000)

Lee, Bruce (Lee Yuen-Kam) (1940–73)

American, born in San Francisco, California. Raised in Hong Kong, he made his film debut at the age of six in *The Birth of Mankind* (1946). After studying philosophy at the University of Washington, he appeared in the television series *The Green Hornet*, and went on to build a film career. Back in Hong Kong, he became the first superstar of kung fu films before his mysterious death from cerebral edema. His son was the actor Brandon Lee.
Career highs: *Fists of Fury* (1972), *Enter the Dragon* (1973)
Career low: *The Big Boss* (1971)

> ### Brandon Lee and The Crow
>
> Brandon Lee, the 28-year-old actor son of kung fu superstar Bruce Lee, was accidentally killed by a faulty prop revolver while filming a scene for *The Crow* (1994). Following his death the film was partially rewritten and completed, using stand-ins and digital technology to recreate Lee's image onscreen. The fact that Lee's early death was a sad parallel to his famous father's gave rise to a number of conspiracy theories and rumours, including one which suggested (incorrectly) that footage of his fatal accident had actually been used in the final cut of the film.

Lee, Christopher Frank Carandini (1922–   )

English, born in London. An office clerk, he served in the Royal Air Force before making his film debut in *Corridor of Mirrors* (1948). He spent a decade as an all-purpose character actor before his portrayals of Frankenstein's monster and Count Dracula led to a long career of playing fantasy roles, which he invested with dignity and pathos. He found a greater variety of challenging roles from the 1970s onwards.
Career highs: *Dracula* (1958), *The Wicker Man* (1973), *The Man with the Golden Gun* (1974), *Jinnah* (1998), *The Lord of the Rings: The Fellowship of the Ring* (2001)
Career lows: *The Castle of Fu Manchu* (1970), *Meat Cleaver Massacre* (1977), *Police Academy: Mission To Moscow* (1994)

Leigh, Janet (Jeanette Helen Morrison) (1927–2004)

American, born in Merced, California. Spotted by actress **Norma Shearer**, she made her film debut in *The Romance of Rosy Ridge* (1947) and was signed to MGM where she played loyal sweethearts and costume drama maidens. She fought for more diverse roles, and won an Academy Award® nomination as the ill-fated Marion in *Psycho* (1960). Her third marriage was to **Tony Curtis**, and their daughter is **Jamie Lee Curtis**.

Career highs: *Touch of Evil* (1958), *Psycho* (1960), *The Manchurian Candidate* (1962)
Career lows: *Jet Pilot* (1950), *Night of the Lepus* (1972)

Leigh, Vivien (Vivian Mary Hartley) (1913–67)

English, born in Darjeeling, India. A student at the Royal Academy of Dramatic Art, she made her professional debut in the film *Things are Looking Up* (1934). She became a leading lady of British cinema before securing the role of Scarlett O'Hara in *Gone with the Wind* (1939), which won her a Best Actress Academy Award®. She won a second Academy Award® for *A Streetcar Named Desire* (1951), and was married to **Laurence Olivier**.

Career highs: *St Martin's Lane* (1938), *Gone with the Wind* (1939), *Waterloo Bridge* (1940), *A Streetcar Named Desire* (1951)
Career lows: *Caesar and Cleopatra* (1945), *Anna Karenina* (1948)

Lemmon, Jack (John Uhler Lemmon III) (1925–2001)

American, born in Boston, Massachusetts. A graduate of Harvard University, he served in the US Navy and was a prolific television and stage actor before making his film debut in *It Should Happen to You* (1954). His sublime comic touch and dramatic range made him unrivalled as an interpreter of the urban underdog, plagued by insecurities and neuroses. He won Academy Awards® for *Mister Roberts* (1955) and *Save the Tiger* (1973).

Career highs: *Mister Roberts* (1955), *Some Like It Hot* (1959), *The Apartment* (1960), *Days of Wine and Roses* (1962), *Missing* (1981)
Career lows: *Buddy Buddy* (1981), *Getting Away with Murder* (1995)

Leung, Tony (Leung Chiu-Wai) (1962–)

Chinese, born in Hong Kong. He began acting at the television station TVB in Hong Kong, and gradually moved into film roles, building a career as a sensitive, intense leading man in a range of independent and commercial films. His partnership with director Wong Kar-Wei, begun during the 1990s, has brought him international recognition.

Career highs: *City of Sadness* (1989), *Chungking Express* (1994), *Happy Together* (1997), *In the Mood for Love* (2000)

Lewis, Jerry (Joseph Levitch) (1926–)

American, born in Newark, New Jersey. Born into a show-business family, he was a nightclub comic before joining **Dean Martin** in a double act. They made their joint film debut in *My Friend Irma* (1949). After their partnership ended in 1956, Lewis enjoyed a decade as an inventive, multi-talented screen comic before his popularity faded. He became a noted philanthropist, and later returned to the screen in occasional character parts.

Career highs: *The Bellboy* (1960), *Cinderfella* (1960), *The Nutty Professor* (1963), *The King of Comedy* (1982)
Career lows: *Way...Way Out* (1966), *Hook, Line & Sinker* (1969), *Which Way to the Front?* (1970)

Li, Jet (Li Lian Jie) (1963–)

Chinese, born in Beijing. The youngest of five children, he trained in wushu from the age of eight and became China's national champion before making the move into film with *Shaolin Temple* (1979). His dazzling athleticism and appealing screen presence soon made him a major action star in Asia, and he crossed over into English-language films with *Lethal Weapon 4* (1998).
Career highs: *Once Upon a Time in China* (1991), *Hero* (2002), *Unleashed* (2005)
Career low (director): *Born to Defend* (1986)
Career lows (actor): *Romeo Must Die* (2000), *Cradle 2 the Grave* (2003)

Lloyd, Harold Clayton (1893–1971)

American, born in Burchard, Nebraska. He studied acting in San Diego, California and worked in the theatre before entering the film industry as an extra. He eventually developed the screen persona of a shy, bespectacled boy-next-door, anxious to make good and perennially involved in hair-raising adventures. The daredevil comic of silent cinema, he retired after *Mad Wednesday* (1947).
Career highs: *Safety Last* (1923), *The Freshman* (1925), *For Heaven's Sake* (1926), *Kid Brother* (1927), *Speedy* (1928)
Career low: *Mad Wednesday* (1947)

Lockwood, Margaret (1916–90)

English, born in Karachi, India. A student at the Italia Conti School, she gained six years' worth of stage experience before making her film debut in *Lorna Doone* (1934). Immensely popular as the wicked lady of British cinema in the 1940s, she retired from the cinema in 1955, returning for a final appearance in *The Slipper and the Rose* (1976).
Career highs: *Bank Holiday* (1938), *The Lady Vanishes* (1938), *The Man in Grey* (1943), *The Wicked Lady* (1945), *Jassy* (1947)
Career lows: *Look Before You Love* (1948), *Madness of the Heart* (1948)

Lollobrigida, (Lui)gina (1927–)

Italian, born in Subiaco. The daughter of a carpenter, she studied to become a commercial artist, but became a model and made her film debut in *L'Elisir d'amore* (1946). She was a popular European sex symbol during the 1950s, and worked in the USA from 1956. Later, she became a respected photographer.
Career highs: *Fanfan la Tulipe* (1951), *Bread, Love and Jealousy* (1954), *Beautiful But Dangerous* (1955), *Trapeze* (1956)
Career lows: *Go Naked in the World* (1961), *Cervantes* (1967)

Lombard, Carole (Jane Alice Peters) (1908–42)

American, born in Fort Wayne, Indiana. Spotted by director Allan Dwan, she was cast in *A Perfect Crime* (1921), and worked in comedy shorts and features before

signing with Paramount in 1930. A glamorous, witty performer with a flair for screwball comedy, she married **Clark Gable** and was one of Hollywood's most popular stars at the time of her death in a plane crash.
Career highs: *Twentieth Century* (1934), *My Man Godfrey* (1936), *Nothing Sacred* (1937), *To Be or Not To Be* (1942)
Career lows: *The Gay Bride* (1934), *Rumba* (1935), *Fools for Scandal* (1938)

Lopez, Jennifer (1969–   )

American, born in the Bronx, New York City. She took singing and dancing lessons from the age of five, and made her film debut in *My Little Girl* (1986) before moving to Los Angeles in 1990 to pursue her show-business dreams. She became a bestselling recording artist and the highest paid Latina actress in the world, noted as much for her diva reputation, shapely derrière and range of perfumes as for her performances.
Career highs: *Selena* (1997), *Out of Sight* (1998), *Maid in Manhattan* (2002)
Career lows: *Enough* (2002), *Gigli* (2003)

Loren, Sophia (Sofia Scicolone) (1934–   )

Italian, born in Rome. Raised in dire poverty, she was a teenage beauty queen and began working as a film extra in 1950. Under contract to her future husband, producer Carlo Ponti, she blossomed into a breathtaking beauty with a talent for earthy drama and vivacious comedy. She won a Best Actress Academy Award® for *Two Women* (1960), and her ageless glamour remains undiminished.
Career highs: *Heller in Pink Tights* (1960), *Two Women* (1960), *Yesterday, Today and Tomorrow* (1963), *Marriage – Italian Style* (1964), *A Special Day* (1977)
Career lows: *A Breath of Scandal* (1960), *A Countess from Hong Kong* (1966), *Brief Encounter* (1974)

Lorre, Peter (Laszlo Löwenstein) (1904–64)

Hungarian, born in Rosenberg. He ran away from home to become a travelling actor, and made a striking early impression on film as the child-murderer in *M* (1931). He fled to Britain from Hitler's Germany in 1933 and was in Hollywood from 1935, where he excelled as velvety-voiced villains, deranged killers and snivelling underlings. He also directed *Der Verlorene* (1951).
Career highs: *M* (1931), *The Man who Knew Too Much* (1934), *Mad Love* (1935), *Crime and Punishment* (1935), *The Maltese Falcon* (1941)
Career lows: *Island of Doomed Men* (1940), *You'll Find Out* (1940), *The Story of Mankind* (1957)

Loy, Myrna (Myrna Adele Williams) (1905–93)

American, born in Radersburg, Montana. Of Welsh ancestry, she moved to Los Angeles in 1919 and worked as a chorus girl before being spotted by **Rudolph Valentino** and signed to a film contract. She made her film debut in *Pretty Ladies* (1925) and survived the transition to sound, emerging as an elegant comedienne who was voted the Queen of Hollywood in 1937.

Career highs: *The Animal Kingdom* (1932), *The Thin Man* (1934), *Libeled Lady* (1936), *I Love You Again* (1940), *The Best Years of Our Lives* (1946)
Career lows: *The Barbarian* (1933), *Parnell* (1937)

Lugosi, Bela (Bela Ferenc Denzso Blasko) (1882–1956)

Hungarian, born in Lugos. The son of a banker, he studied at the Budapest Academy of Theatrical Arts and was a stage star before making his film debut in *A Leopard* (1917). In the USA from the 1920s onwards, he was a sensation on Broadway as Dracula and repeated the role on film. He became typecast in horror films, and his later years were blighted by drug addiction and ill health. He died during the production of *Plan 9 from Outer Space* (1956), frequently voted the worst film ever made.
Career highs: *Dracula* (1931), *White Zombie* (1932), *The Black Cat* (1934), *The Son of Frankenstein* (1939)
Career lows: *Spooks Run Wild* (1941), *Bela Lugosi Meets a Brooklyn Vampire* (1952), *The Black Sleep* (1956), *Plan 9 from Outer Space* (1956)

Lupino, Ida (1918–95)

English, born in Brixton, London. The daughter of comedian Stanley Lupino, she trained at the Royal Academy of Dramatic Art and made her film debut in *Her First Affaire* (1932). In 1933 she went to Hollywood, where she survived years of thankless roles before winning acclaim as an intense dramatic actress. She was also a trailblazer, producing, writing and directing films in an era when such endeavours were largely a male preserve.
Career highs (actress): *They Drive by Night* (1940), *High Sierra* (1941), *The Hard Way* (1943), *Road House* (1948), *On Dangerous Ground* (1951)
Career highs (director): *The Bigamist* (1953), *The Hitch-Hiker* (1953)
Career lows: *Escape Me Never* (1947), *Food of the Gods* (1976)

M

McConaughey, Matthew David (1969–)

American, born in Uvalde, Texas. He dropped out of university and was attending film school when a chance meeting with director Richard Linklater secured him his first role in *Dazed and Confused* (1993). Tall, handsome and blue-eyed, he was quickly hailed as a new **Paul Newman**, but struggled to maintain the initial momentum of his career. He has enjoyed his greatest success in romantic comedies, and has also directed.
Career highs: *Dazed and Confused* (1993), *Lone Star* (1996), *A Time to Kill* (1996)
Career lows: *The Return of the Texas Chainsaw Massacre* (1995), *Larger than Life* (1996), *The Newton Boys* (1998)

McCrea, Joel Albert (1905–90)

American, born in Pasadena, California. A student at Pomona State College, he made his film debut as an extra in *A Self-Made Failure* (1924). Handsome and dependable, he was an undervalued performer whose range extended from urgent drama to madcap comedy and the many westerns that filled his later years. He was

a rancher in real life, and was married to actress Frances Dee.
Career highs: *Union Pacific* (1939), *Foreign Correspondent* (1940), *Sullivan's Travels* (1941), *The Palm Beach Story* (1942), *Ride the High Country* (1962)
Career lows: *The Great Moment* (1944), *Cry Blood, Apache* (1970)

MacDonald, Jeanette (1901–65)

American, born in Philadelphia, Pennsylvania. A trained singer and dancer, she made her New York debut as a chorus girl in *The Demi-Tasse Revue* (1920). Broadway success led to her film debut in *The Love Parade* (1929). A vibrant soprano who became known as 'the Iron Butterfly', she was also a spirited comedienne and enjoyed huge popularity in screen operettas, partnered by Nelson Eddy.
Career highs: *Love Me Tonight* (1932), *The Merry Widow* (1934), *Rose Marie* (1936), *San Francisco* (1936), *Maytime* (1937)
Career lows: *I Married an Angel* (1942), *Cairo* (1942)

McDormand, Frances (1957–)

American, born in Chicago, Illinois. The daughter of a Disciples of Christ minister, she graduated from the Yale School of Drama and made her film debut in *Blood Simple* (1984), later marrying the film's director **Joel Coen**. A smart, committed performer, she has been an asset to many films and won a Best Actress Academy Award® for her performance as pregnant cop Marge Gunderson in *Fargo* (1996).
Career highs: *Mississippi Burning* (1988), *Fargo* (1996), *Wonder Boys* (2000), *Almost Famous* (2000), *Laurel Canyon* (2002)

McDowall, Roddy (Roderick Andrew Anthony Jude McDowall) (1928–99)

English, born in London. A child actor, he made his film debut in *Murder in the Family* (1938). Evacuated to the USA during World War II, he resumed his career as the devoted companion of Lassie and Flicka in family features. He weathered the transition to adult roles, enjoying renewed fame as Cornelius in the *Planet of the Apes* series. He was also a photographer, and a dedicated collector of Hollywood lore and memorabilia.
Career highs: *How Green was My Valley* (1941), *Lassie Come Home* (1943), *My Friend Flicka* (1943), *Planet of the Apes* (1968), *Fright Night* (1988)
Career lows: *Tuna Clipper* (1949), *Killer Shark* (1950)

McGregor, Ewan (1971–)

Scottish, born in Crieff. The son of two schoolteachers, he left school at 16 to pursue an acting career. He studied at London's Guildhall School of Music and Drama, making his film debut in *Being Human* (1994). An ambitious, hardworking actor, he has combined independent ventures with Hollywood blockbusters.
Career highs: *Trainspotting* (1996), *Moulin Rouge!* (2001), *Young Adam* (1993)
Career lows: *Serpent's Kiss* (1997), *Eye of the Beholder* (1999)

McKellen, Sir Ian Murray (1939–)

English, born in Burnley, Lancashire. A student of English literature at Cambridge University, he intended to be a journalist before the acting bug bit. He made his film debut in *A Touch of Love* (1969), but remained primarily a stage actor until the 1990s, when he concentrated his energies on a screen career. He has been a significant activist for gay rights.

Career highs: *Richard III* (1995), *Gods and Monsters* (1998), *The Lord of the Rings: The Fellowship of the Ring* (2001), et seq

Career low: *Jack & Sarah* (1995)

MacLaine, Shirley (Shirley MacLean Beaty) (1934–)

American, born in Richmond, Virginia. The elder sister of **Warren Beatty**, she was a chorus girl, model and understudy before her Broadway triumph in *The Pajama Game* (1954). She made her film debut in *The Trouble with Harry* (1955), and brought charm and heartbreaking vulnerability to a wide range of characters. She won a Best Actress Academy Award® for *Terms of Endearment* (1983). She has written several volumes of autobiography, and is known for her belief in reincarnation.

Career highs: *Some Came Running* (1958), *The Apartment* (1960), *Sweet Charity* (1968), *The Turning Point* (1977), *Terms of Endearment* (1983)

Career lows: *Two Loves* (1960), *John Goldfarb, Please Come Home* (1965)

MacMurray, Fred(erick Martin) (1908–91)

American, born in Kankakee, Illinois. The son of a concert violinist, his original intention was to become a saxophonist. He made his film debut as an extra in *Girls Gone Wild* (1928) but continued to work as a musician before Broadway success took him to Hollywood in 1934. A genial, easy-going performer, usually cast as solid citizens and nice guys, he impressed most in less sympathetic roles.

Career highs: *Remember the Night* (1940), *Double Indemnity* (1944), *The Caine Mutiny* (1954), *Pushover* (1954), *The Apartment* (1960)

Career lows: *The Miracle of the Bells* (1948), *The Swarm* (1978)

McQueen, (Terence) Steve(n) (1930–80)

American, born in Beech Grove, Indiana. A juvenile delinquent and US Marine, he moved to New York City and worked in various jobs whilst studying acting at the Neighborhood Playhouse. He made his film debut as an extra in *Somebody Up There Likes Me* (1956), and quickly graduated to leading roles. During the 1960s, his image as a taciturn, ice-cool loner made him an international star.

Career highs: *The Great Escape* (1963), *The Sand Pebbles* (1966), *Bullitt* (1968), *The Thomas Crown Affair* (1968), *Papillon* (1973)

Career lows: *The Blob* (1958), *The Hunter* (1980)

Madonna (Madonna Louise Veronica Ciccone) (1958–)

American, born in Bay City, Michigan. She trained as a dancer at the University of Michigan before heading to New York City, and made her film debut in the low-budget *A Certain Sacrifice* (1985). She has intermittently pursued an acting career in the shadow of her enormous success as an iconic pop diva. Her notable performances have been few, her disasters rather more frequent. Previously married to **Sean Penn**, she is now married to director Guy Ritchie.

Career highs: *Desperately Seeking Susan* (1985), *Snake Eyes* (1993), *Evita* (1996)

Career lows: *Shanghai Surprise* (1986), *Body of Evidence* (1993), *The Next Best Thing* (2000), *Swept Away* (2002)

Magnani, Anna (1908–73)

Italian, born in Rome. A student at the Corso Eleanora Duse at Santa Cecilia, she was a nightclub singer and stage actress before making her film debut in *Scampolo* (1927). Her film career flourished during the late 1940s, and she subsequently brought a fiery, extravagant intensity to international roles, winning a Best Actress Academy Award® for *The Rose Tattoo* (1955).
Career highs: *Rome – Open City* (1945), *Amore* (1948), *The Golden Coach* (1952), *The Rose Tattoo* (1955), *Mamma Roma* (1962)
Career lows: *Nella città l'inferno* (1958), *Risate di gioia* (1961)

Maguire, Tobey (Tobias Vincent Maguire) (1975–   )

American, born in Santa Monica, California. Originally intent on becoming a chef, he turned to acting as an adolescent, appearing in commercials and television series. He matured into a sensitive, soulful character actor before his appearance as comic-book hero *Spider-Man* (2002) catapulted him to stardom. He is a renowned poker player.
Career highs: *The Ice Storm* (1997), *Wonder Boys* (2000), *Spider-Man* (2002)

Malkovich, John Gavin (1953–   )

American, born in Benton, Illinois. A founding member of the Steppenwolf theatre company, he gained extensive stage and television experience before making his film debut in *Places in the Heart* (1984). He is a valuable and versatile character actor, and has brought insight and intelligence to a wide range of roles in international productions. He has also designed a range of clothes.
Career highs: *Places in the Heart* (1984), *Dangerous Liaisons* (1988), *In the Line of Fire* (1993), *Being John Malkovich* (1999)
Career lows: *Eleni* (1985), *Rounders* (1998)

March, Fredric (Fredric Ernest McIntyre Bickel) (1897–1975)

American, born in Racine, Wisconsin. A stage actor and model, he worked as an extra in silent films, but it was Broadway success that led to his flourishing career in Hollywood from 1930. He was a handsome, self-effacing leading man whose range extended from costume drama to screwball comedy. He won Best Actor Academy Awards® for *Dr Jekyll and Mr Hyde* (1931) and *The Best Years of Our Lives* (1946).
Career highs: *The Royal Family of Broadway* (1930), *Dr Jekyll and Mr Hyde* (1931), *A Star is Born* (1937), *The Best Years of Our Lives* (1946), *Death of a Salesman* (1951)
Career low: *Inherit the Wind* (1960)

Martin, Dean (Dino Paul Crocetti) (1917–95)

American, born in Steubenville, Ohio. A boxer and croupier, he turned to professional singing and teamed up with **Jerry Lewis** in 1945 to form a beloved comic double act. They made their joint film debut in *My Friend Irma* (1949). After the partnership ended in 1956, he flourished as a solo performer, chart-topping

crooner, straight actor (notably as the laid-back secret agent Matt Helm) and relaxed, easy-going Rat Pack crony.
Career highs: *Rio Bravo* (1959), *The Bells Are Ringing* (1960), *Kiss Me Stupid* (1964)
Career lows: *How to Save a Marriage and Ruin Your Life* (1968), *Mr Ricco* (1975)

Martin, Steve (1945–)

American, born in Waco, Texas. After studying philosophy and drama, he worked as a stand-up comic and comedy writer before making his film debut in the short *The Absent-Minded Waiter* (1977). His physical dexterity and manic inventiveness made him an inspired comedy performer, and he has proved effective in dramatic roles. He is also a novelist, playwright and noted art collector.
Career highs: *The Jerk* (1979), *The Man with Two Brains* (1983), *All of Me* (1984), *Roxanne* (1987)
Career lows: *Leap of Faith* (1992), *Mixed Nuts* (1994), *Novocaine* (2001), *Looney Toons: Back in Action* (2003)

Marvin, Lee (1924–87)

American, born in New York City. After service in the US Marines, he worked on stage and television before making his film debut in *You're in the Navy Now* (1951). A memorably menacing villain, he matured into a tough, flinty leading man, noted for his hellraising exploits. He won a Best Actor Academy Award® for *Cat Ballou* (1965).
Career highs: *The Big Heat* (1953), *Bad Day at Black Rock* (1954), *Cat Ballou* (1965), *The Dirty Dozen* (1967), *Point Blank* (1967)
Career lows: *The Klansman* (1974), *Avalanche Express* (1979)

Marx, Groucho (Julius Henry Marx) (1895–1977)

American, born in New York City. The son of German immigrants, he joined with his brothers Chico, Harpo and Zeppo to form an anarchic comedy act named the Four Nightingales, later renamed the Marx Brothers. Hugely popular, they made their official film debut in *The Cocoanuts* (1929) and their final team appearance in *Love Happy* (1949).
Career highs: *Monkey Business* (1931), *Horse Feathers* (1932), *Duck Soup* (1933), *A Night at the Opera* (1935), *A Day at the Races* (1937)
Career low: *The Big Store* (1941), *Love Happy* (1949)

Making an Impression

The forecourt of Grauman's Chinese Theatre on Hollywood Boulevard is famously paved with the cement handprints, footprints and signatures of screen actors from as long ago as the 1920s. Some stars have left a more distinctive type of mark: the imprints of Betty Grable's legs, Bob Hope's nose, Groucho Marx's cigar and Roy Rogers's gun can all be seen in the cement.

Mason, James Neville (1909–84)

English, born in Huddersfield. After studying architecture he turned to acting, working on stage before making his film debut in *Late Extra* (1935). He attained

stardom as a suave, saturnine villain in British costume dramas, before moving to Hollywood and becoming one of the most prolific and reliable of screen performers.
Career highs: *Odd Man Out* (1946), *A Star Is Born* (1954), *Bigger than Life* (1956), *Child's Play* (1972), *The Verdict* (1982)
Career lows: *Forever Darling* (1956), *Bad Man's River* (1971), *Mandingo* (1975)

Mastroianni, Marcello (1923–96)

Italian, born in Fontana Liri. The son of a carpenter, he trained as a draughtsman. He was interned in a Nazi labour camp during World War II, then became a cashier in Rome. He pursued amateur dramatics as a hobby, before turning professional and making his film debut in *I Miserabli* (1947). During a long, productive career, he played a wide variety of roles with immense charm, delicacy and sincerity. **Catherine Deneuve** is the mother of his daughter Chiara, also an actress.
Career highs: *La Dolce vita* (1960), *Divorce – Italian Style* (1961), *8½* (1963), *A Special Day* (1977), *Dark Eyes* (1987)
Career lows: *Diamonds for Breakfast* (1968), *A Place for Lovers* (1968), *Sunflower* (1969)

Matthau, Walter (1920–2000)

American, born in New York City. He was a radio operator during World War II, then studied acting with Erwin Piscator, working on stage before making his film debut in *The Kentuckian* (1955). A lugubrious bloodhound of an actor, he graduated from villains and supporting parts to the comedy roles that made him famous, winning a Best Supporting Academy Award® for *The Fortune Cookie* (1966).
Career highs: *The Fortune Cookie* (1966), *The Odd Couple* (1968), *Kotch* (1971), *The Taking of Pelham One Two Three* (1974), *The Sunshine Boys* (1975)
Career lows: *Buddy Buddy* (1981), *Pirates* (1986)

Would You Mind Spelling That?

Walter Matthau's original surname is often incorrectly given as Matuschanskayasky – many of his obituaries even included this rather unlikely-sounding 'fact'. The origin of the mistake is that Matthau, unhappy with the way his role in *Earthquake* (1974) had been edited, requested that he be credited under this elaborate pseudonym in much the same spirit that disgruntled directors sometimes opt to hide behind the name 'Alan Smithee'. For years afterwards, Matthau's fondness for pulling the wool over interviewers' eyes led him to encourage the misunderstanding about his birth name, which still persists today.

Mature, Victor (Victor Joseph Maturi) (1915–99)

American, born in Louisville, Kentucky. A stage actor with the Pasadena Playhouse, he made his film debut in *The Housekeeper's Daughter* (1939). A brawny, wavy-haired slab of beefcake, dubbed 'the Hunk', he swaggered and grinned his way through 30 years of musicals, westerns and costume dramas, giving occasional hints that he was more talented than his critics might care to admit.
Career highs: *One Million BC* (1940), *My Darling Clementine* (1946), *Samson and Delilah* (1949), *The Robe* (1953)

Career lows: *Affair with a Stranger* (1953), *The Sharkfighters* (1956), *Hannibal* (1960)

Midler, Bette (1945–)

American, born in Paterson, New Jersey. Raised in Honolulu, she made her film debut with a bit part in *Hawaii* (1966). A brassy, flamboyant entertainer in the gay bathhouses of New York City, she became a huge mainstream success as a sassy singer and caustic comedy performer on Broadway, television and the stage. She earned Best Actress Academy Award® nominations for *The Rose* (1979) and *For The Boys* (1991).
Career highs: *The Rose* (1979), *Ruthless People* (1986), *Beaches* (1988), *The First Wives Club* (1996)
Career lows: *Jinxed!* (1982), *Stella* (1990), *Isn't She Great* (2000)

Mifune, Toshirô (1920–97)

Japanese, born in Tsingtao, China. After army service in World War II, he made his film debut in *These Foolish Things* (1946). *Drunken Angel* (1948) began his long association with director **Akira Kurosawa**, and he remains best known to western audiences for his virile portraits of samurai warriors in Kurosawa films.
Career highs: *Rashômon* (1950), *Seven Samurai* (1955), *Throne of Blood* (1957), *Yojimbo* (1961), *Hell in the Pacific* (1968)
Career lows: *1941* (1979), *Inchon* (1980)

Milland, Ray (Reginald Truscott-Jones) (1905–86)

Welsh, born in Neath, Glamorganshire. He served as a Royal Guardsman before touring as a dancer and making his film debut in *The Plaything* (1929). In Hollywood from 1931, he played mainly breezy juveniles and solid citizens, although he was always a more interesting actor when his character's intentions were less than honourable. He won a Best Actor Academy Award® for *The Lost Weekend* (1945), and later directed.
Career highs: *The Uninvited* (1944), *The Lost Weekend* (1945), *Alias Nick Beal* (1949), *Dial M for Murder* (1954), *X: The Man with the X-Ray Eyes* (1963)
Career lows: *Jamaica Run* (1953), *The Thing with Two Heads* (1972)

Miller, Ann (Johnnie Lucille Collier) (1923–2004)

American, born in Houston, Texas. A child performer, she made her film debut as an extra in *Anne of Green Gables* (1934). She is best remembered as a dynamic, long-legged tap queen of MGM musicals, whose dancing was once recorded at 500 taps per minute. She later enjoyed Broadway success, and returned to film after a long absence for *Mulholland Drive* (2001).
Career highs: *Easter Parade* (1948), *On the Town* (1949), *Kiss Me Kate* (1953)
Career low: *The Great American Pastime* (1956)

Mills, Sir John Lewis Ernest Watts (1908–2005)

English, born in North Elmham, Norfolk. The son of a teacher, he performed in amateur dramatics before turning professional, working as a chorus boy and a West End actor. He made his film debut in *The Midshipmaid* (1932). A boyish juvenile, he

later played stiff-upper-lip British heroes and won a Best Supporting Actor Academy Award[®] for *Ryan's Daughter* (1970). His 70-year film career concluded with *Bright Young Things* (2003).
Career highs: *In Which We Serve* (1942), *Great Expectations* (1946), *Scott of the Antarctic* (1948), *Ice Cold in Alex* (1958), *Tunes of Glory* (1960)
Career lows: *War and Peace* (1956), *A Black Veil for Lisa* (1969), *Dulcima* (1971)

— *Take 15* —

> A scene in *Ice Cold in Alex* (1958) required leading man John Mills to down a glass of lager in a single draught. Perhaps unfortunately for him, no non-alcoholic substitute drink looked convincing on film, and real lager had to be used. Mills later recalled that by the time the final version was shot he was genuinely drunk, and spent the rest of that day stumbling into scenery.

Minnelli, Liza May (1946–)

American, born in Los Angeles, California. The daughter of **Judy Garland** and **Vincente Minnelli**, she made her film debut for her father in *In the Good Old Summertime* (1949). A Broadway star in the 1960s, she won a Best Actress Academy Award[®] for her electrifying performance as Sally Bowles in *Cabaret* (1972), but has had too few chances to shine since then.
Career highs: *The Sterile Cuckoo* (1969), *Cabaret* (1972), *New York, New York* (1977)
Career lows: *A Matter of Time* (1976), *Rent-a-Cop* (1988)

Mirren, Dame Helen (Ilyena Lydia Mironoff) (1945–)

English, born in Chiswick, London. A member of the National Youth Theatre and the Royal Shakespeare Company, she made her film debut in *A Midsummer Night's Dream* (1968). A fearless performer, she maintains a balance between stage and screen roles, and became widely known during the 1990s for her leading role in the *Prime Suspect* series of television dramas.
Career highs: *The Long Good Friday* (1980), *Cal* (1984), *The Madness of King George* (1994), *Calendar Girls* (2003)
Career lows: *Caligula* (1977), *Hussy* (1979)

Mitchum, Robert Charles (1917–97)

American, born in Bridgeport, Connecticut. After a colourful adolescence as a labourer, vagrant and professional boxer, he made his film debut as an extra in *Hoppy Serves a Writ* (1943). A burly figure, he exuded sleepy-eyed charisma, and his facade of indifference concealed the heart of a true professional and a great actor. His career was undamaged by the scandal surrounding his arrest and imprisonment for possession of marijuana in 1948.
Career highs: *Out of the Past* (1947), *Night of the Hunter* (1955), *The Sundowners* (1960), *El Dorado* (1967), *Farewell, My Lovely* (1975)
Career lows: *Desire Me* (1947), *The Big Sleep* (1978)

Mix, Tom (Thomas Hezikiah) (1880–1940)

American, born in Mix Run, Pennsylvania. A sergeant in the US Army Artillery, he was a bartender and deputy sheriff before touring in Wild West shows. He made his acting debut in *Life in the Great Southwest* (1913). Dressed in an oversized cowboy hat and pure white clothes, he was a precursor of **John Wayne** in his embodiment of the honest, naive western hero. He married five times, and died in a car accident.
Career highs: *Riders of the Purple Sage* (1925), *The Rainbow Trail* (1925), *The Great K & A Train Robbery* (1926)

Monroe, Marilyn (Norma Jean Mortenson) (1926–62)

American, born in Los Angeles, California. After an unhappy childhood spent in foster homes, she became a photographer's model and made her film debut in *Scudda Hoo! Scudda Hay!* (1948). Just another blonde sex symbol at first, her ripe beauty, childlike vulnerability and flair for light comedy, combined with a willingness to send herself up occasionally, made her one of the greatest of Hollywood icons. Her early death cemented the legend.
Career highs: *Gentlemen Prefer Blondes* (1953), *How to Marry a Millionaire* (1953), *The Seven Year Itch* (1955), *Bus Stop* (1956), *Some Like it Hot* (1959)
Career low: *Don't Bother to Knock* (1952)

Montand, Yves (Ivo Livi) (1921–91)

Italian, born in Monsummano, Tuscany. Raised in Marseilles, France, he worked in a factory before developing a cabaret act as a singing cowboy. He then became a protégé of Edith Piaf, and made his film debut in *Étoile sans lumière* (1945). A live performer of legendary magnetism, he brought dour presence and skilled underplaying to his film roles. He was married to **Simone Signoret** and, famously, involved with **Marilyn Monroe**.
Career highs: *Le Salaire de la peur* (1953), *La guerre est finie* (1966), *Z* (1968), *State of Siege* (1973), *Jean de Florette* (1986)
Career lows: *Sanctuary* (1961), *On a Clear Day You Can See Forever* (1970)

Moore, Demi (Demi Gene Guynes) (1962–)

American, born in Roswell, New Mexico. After a troubled childhood, she left school at 16 to pursue a modelling and acting career. She appeared on the daytime soap opera *General Hospital*, and made her film debut in *Choices* (1981). Ambition, a knack for self-publicity, and marriage to **Bruce Willis** helped to make her the highest-paid actress of the 1990s, but she has made few films since then.
Career highs: *St Elmo's Fire* (1985), *Ghost* (1990), *Mortal Thoughts* (1991)
Career lows: *Parasite* (1982), *Wisdom* (1986), *The Seventh Sign* (1988), *The Scarlet Letter* (1995), *Striptease* (1996)

Moore, Julianne (Julie Ann Smith) (1960–)

American, born in Fayetteville, North Carolina. She attended Boston University and worked off-Broadway, learning her trade in daytime soap operas and television miniseries. Eye-catching supporting performances eventually earned her lead roles that showcased her versatility and depth.

Career highs: *Safe* (1994), *Boogie Nights* (1997), *Far from Heaven* (2002), *The Hours* (2002)
Career lows: *Psycho* (1998), *Laws of Attraction* (2004)

Moore, Roger George (1927–)

English, born in London. A student at the Royal Academy of Dramatic Art, he made his film debut in *Caesar and Cleopatra* (1945). A move to Hollywood in the 1950s did not result in lasting cinema success, but his dashing good looks proved ideal for television series like *The Saint* and *The Persuaders*. He played secret agent James Bond from *Live and Let Die* (1973) to *A View to a Kill* (1985).
Career highs: *The Last Time I Saw Paris* (1954), *The Man who Haunted Himself* (1970), *Live and Let Die* (1973)
Career lows: *That Lucky Touch* (1975), *Sunday Lovers* (1980), *Bullseye!* (1990), *Fire, Ice and Dynamite* (1990), *Boat Trip* (2003)

Moorehead, Agnes Robertson (1900–74)

American, born in Clinton, Massachusetts. The daughter of a Presbyterian minister, she studied at the University of Wisconsin and taught English before embarking on an acting career. She was a member of **Orson Welles'** Mercury Theater Group, and made her film debut in *Citizen Kane* (1941). A versatile, scene-stealing character actress, she later found widespread popularity in the television series *Bewitched*.
Career highs: *The Magnificent Ambersons* (1942), *Mrs Parkington* (1944), *Johnny Belinda* (1948), *Caged* (1950)
Career lows: *The Adventures of Captain Fabian* (1951), *The Conqueror* (1956)

More, Kenneth (1914–82)

English, born in Gerrards Cross, Buckinghamshire. After working as an apprentice engineer and fur trapper in Canada, he became a stage-hand at the Windmill Theatre and found work as an extra in *Look Up and Laugh* (1935). His career moved into top gear during the 1950s, when he embodied a hearty sense of British pluck in war films and comedies.
Career highs: *Genevieve* (1953), *Doctor in the House* (1954), *Reach for the Sky* (1956), *The Greengage Summer* (1961), *The Comedy Man* (1963)
Career low: *Fräulein Doktor* (1968)

Moreau, Jeanne (1928–)

French, born in Paris. After studying drama, she made her film debut in *Dernier amour* (1948). She became one of France's most respected film performers, closely associated with the Nouvelle Vague and bringing vivid life to a succession of complex, sensual, world-weary women. She has also directed, and was once married to director William Friedkin.
Career highs: *Les Amants* (1958), *La notte* (1961), *Eve* (1962), *Jules et Jim* (1962), *Diary of a Chambermaid* (1964)
Career low: *Your Ticket Is No Longer Valid* (1981)

Mortensen, Viggo (1958–)

American, born in New York City. The eldest son of a Danish father and American mother, he spent his childhood in South America. After studying in New York, he appeared as an extra in *Witness* (1985). His career moved into a higher gear with the success of the *Lord of the Rings* trilogy of films. He is also a painter, poet, jazz musician and photographer.

Career highs: *The Indian Runner* (1991), *The Lord of the Rings: The Fellowship of the Ring* (2001) et seq, *A History of Violence* (2005)

Career lows: *Leatherface: Texas Chainsaw Massacre III* (1990), *Psycho* (1998)

Muni, Paul (Muni Weisenfreund) (1895–1967)

American, born in Lemberg, Austria. The son of actors, he emigrated with them to America as a child and worked in the theatre before making his film debut in *The Valiant* (1929). In the 1930s, he was prized for his use of disguise and dignified impersonation of noble historical figures, winning a Best Actor Academy Award® for *The Story of Louis Pasteur* (1936).

Career highs: *Scarface* (1932), *I Am a Fugitive from a Chain Gang* (1932), *The Story of Louis Pasteur* (1936), *The Life of Emile Zola* (1937)

Career lows: *The Woman I Love* (1937), *A Song to Remember* (1945)

Murphy, Eddie (Edward Regan) (1961–)

American, born in Brooklyn, New York City. The son of a New York policeman, he was the class clown who became a professional entertainer. A member of the *Saturday Night Live* team in the early 1980s, he made his film debut in *48 Hrs* (1982) and became a top box-office attraction as an irreverent, edgy clown. He later restricted himself to more family-friendly fare.

Career highs: *48 Hrs* (1982), *Trading Places* (1983), *Beverly Hills Cop* (1984), *Shrek* (2001)

Career lows: *Harlem Nights* (1989), *The Adventures of Pluto Nash* (2002), *I Spy* (2002)

Multiple Personalities

Over the years, many actors – particularly comedians – have attempted the feat of playing several roles within one film. As well as showing off a performer's virtuosity, this trick can usually be relied upon to drum up some publicity, even if the film in question has little else going for it. Some of the most memorable examples have been *Kind Hearts and Coronets* (1949), in which Alec Guinness played eight different roles; *Dr Strangelove or: How I Learned to Stop Worrying and Love the Bomb* (1964), in which Peter Sellers played three roles; and *The Nutty Professor* (1996) and *Nutty Professor II: The Klumps* (2000), in which Eddie Murphy played most of the large Klump family (seven and eight roles respectively). Perhaps even more impressively, in the days before sophisticated make-up, prosthetics and digital retouching, a British actor named Rolf Leslie is on record as having played 27 separate roles in *Sixty Years a Queen* (1913), an early Ealing Studios film about the life of Queen Victoria.

Murray, Bill (William James Murray) (1950–   )

American, born in Wilmette, Illinois. The son of a lumber salesman, he worked as a stand-up comic with Chicago's Second City company and with *Saturday Night Live* before lending his voice to the cartoon *Jungle Burger* (1975). A lugubrious, deadpan comedian, he has recently tackled complex dramatic roles, earning a Best Actor Academy Award® nomination for *Lost in Translation* (2003).
Career highs: *Ghostbusters* (1984), *Groundhog Day* (1993), *Rushmore* (1998), *Lost in Translation* (2003), *Broken Flowers* (2005)
Career lows: *The Razor's Edge* (1984), *The Man Who Knew Too Little* (1997)

Myers, Mike (1963–   )

Canadian, born in Scarborough, Ontario. A child performer, he worked in television before making his film debut in *Elvis Stories* (1989). A member of the Canadian offshoot of the Second City comedy ensemble, and a stalwart of *Saturday Night Live*, he has enjoyed his greatest solo success as the creator of spoof Swinging Sixties spy Austin Powers.
Career highs: *Wayne's World* (1992), *Austin Powers: International Man of Mystery* (1997), *Shrek* (2001)
Career low: *The Cat in the Hat* (2003)

N

Neagle, Dame Anna (Marjorie Robertson) (1904–86)

English, born in London. A trained dancer, she made her film debut in *Those Who Love* (1929). She was married to director Herbert Wilcox, who guided her through 30 years of ladylike appearances in historical dramas, musicals and fairytale romances. She was especially popular in the post-war years. She retired from the screen in 1959, but continued to appear on stage.
Career highs: *Nell Gwyn* (1934), *Victoria the Great* (1937), *Spring in Park Lane* (1948)
Career lows: *My Teenage Daughter* (1956), *The Lady Is a Square* (1959)

Neal, Patricia (1926–   )

American, born in Packard, Kentucky. After studying drama at Northwestern University, she worked on Broadway before making her film debut in *John Loves Mary* (1949). She rarely found the roles that matched her abilities, but won a Best Actress Academy Award® for *Hud* (1963). Famously in love with **Gary Cooper**, she married the author Roald Dahl, and survived family tragedies and a series of strokes during the 1960s.
Career highs: *The Hasty Heart* (1949), *The Breaking Point* (1950), *A Face in the Crowd* (1957), *Hud* (1963), *The Subject Was Roses* (1968)
Career lows: *Washington Story* (1952), *Stranger from Venus* (1954)

Neeson, Liam (William John Neeson) (1952–   )

Northern Irish, born in Ballymena. A truck driver and amateur boxer in his youth, he joined the Belfast Lyric Players Theatre and made some minor film appearances before **John Boorman** chose him for *Excalibur* (1981). In the USA from 1986, he

became a major star of stage and screen, winning a Best Actor Academy Award®
nomination for *Schindler's List* (1993). He is married to actress Natasha Richardson.
Career highs: *Schindler's List* (1993), *Michael Collins* (1996), *Kinsey* (2004)
Career lows: *Satisfaction* (1988), *The Haunting* (1999)

Neill, Sam (Nigel Neill) (1947–   )

Northern Irish, born in Omagh. Raised in New Zealand, he studied English
literature and worked in the theatre before making his film debut in *Ashes* (1975).
His performance in *My Brilliant Career* (1979) brought him a champion in **James
Mason** and an international career as a wry, authoritative leading man.
Career highs: *My Brilliant Career* (1979), *Dead Calm* (1988), *The Piano* (1993),
Jurassic Park (1993), *The Dish* (2000)
Career lows: *The Final Conflict* (1981), *Event Horizon* (1997)

Newman, Paul Leonard (1925–   )

American, born in Cleveland, Ohio. A student at the Yale School of Drama and
the Actors Studio in New York City, he made a disastrous film debut in *The Silver
Chalice* (1954). Handsome and blue-eyed, with a steely intelligence and a rebellious
attitude, he became one of Hollywood's biggest stars, winning a Best Actor
Academy Award® for *The Color of Money* (1986). His is married to actress Joanne
Woodward.
Career highs: *The Hustler* (1961), *Hud* (1963), *Cool Hand Luke* (1967), *Absence of
Malice* (1981), *The Verdict* (1982)
Career lows: *The Silver Chalice* (1954), *Quintet* (1979), *When Time Ran Out...* (1980),
Blaze (1990)

Nicholson, Jack (1937–   )

American, born in Neptune, New Jersey. An actor in high school, he made his film
debut in *The Cry Baby Killer* (1958). He spent a decade in low-budget productions
before appearing in *Easy Rider* (1969). A charismatic personality, he became the
dominant actor of his generation, and has won Academy Awards® for *One Flew
Over the Cuckoo's Nest* (1975), *Terms of Endearment* (1983) and *As Good as it Gets*
(1997).
Career highs: *Five Easy Pieces* (1970), *The Last Detail* (1973), *Chinatown* (1974),
One Flew Over the Cuckoo's Nest (1975), *About Schmidt* (2002)
Career lows: *The Cry Baby Killer* (1958), *Man Trouble* (1992)

Nielsen, Leslie William (1926–   )

Canadian, born in Regina, Saskatchewan. He studied at the Academy of Radio Arts
in Toronto. After working as a radio announcer and disc jockey, and performing at
New York's Neighborhood Playhouse, he made his film debut in *The Vagabond King*
(1956). A solid character actor, he showed his funny side in *Airplane!* (1980), and
spent the next 20 years lending deadpan dignity to silly spoofs.
Career highs: *Forbidden Planet* (1956), *Airplane!* (1980), *The Naked Gun: From the
Files of Police Squad* (1988)
Career lows: *Repossessed* (1990), *Spy Hard* (1996), *Wrongfully Accused* (1998)

Niven, David (James David Graham Nevins) (1910–83)

English, born in London. He attended Sandhurst Military Academy and served with the Highland Light Infantry, before sailing for Canada and winding up in Hollywood as an extra. He quickly rose through the ranks to become an urbane leading man and polished light comedian, winning a Best Actor Academy Award® for *Separate Tables* (1958). He also published two bestselling volumes of autobiography.
Career highs: *The Dawn Patrol* (1938), *A Matter of Life and Death* (1946), *Around the World in 80 Days* (1956), *Separate Tables* (1958)
Career lows: *Bonnie Prince Charlie* (1948), *The Statue* (1969)

Noiret, Philippe (1930–   )

French, born in Lille. He performed in school plays before studying with Roger Blin, and made his film debut in *Gigi* (1948). A popular stage actor and cabaret performer, he worked more consistently in the cinema from 1960 onwards, moving from scene-stealing supporting player to highly respected star performer in the course of over 150 film roles. His range has been emphasized by a long collaboration with director **Bertrand Tavernier**.
Career highs: *Zazie dans le Métro* (1960), *Coup de torchon* (1981), *Cinema Paradiso* (1989), *Life and Nothing But* (1989), *Il Postino* (1994)
Career lows: *Mister Freedom* (1968), *Sweet Torture* (1971)

Nolte, Nick (1940–   )

American, born in Omaha, Nebraska. He was an athlete in college, then spent ten years in regional theatre before starting to work in television. He made his film debut in *The Feather Farm* (1965) and actively sought a film career from the 1970s. A powerful presence, he has battled alcohol and drug addictions, winning Best Actor Academy Award® nominations for *The Prince of Tides* (1991) and *Affliction* (1997).
Career highs: *Who'll Stop the Rain* (1978), *Under Fire* (1983), *Q&A* (1990), *The Prince of Tides* (1991), *Affliction* (1997)
Career lows: *The Deep* (1977), *Hulk* (2003)

Norton, Edward James (1969–   )

American, born in Columbia, Maryland. After graduating from Yale University, he worked in the New York theatre, where he was spotted by playwright Edward Albee and asked to appear with the Signature Theatre Company. He was Academy Award®-nominated for his screen debut in *Primal Fear* (1996) and is a committed, socially aware actor whose career choices have wavered between the creatively challenging and the bewildering. He has also directed.
Career highs: *Primal Fear* (1996), *American History X* (1998), *Fight Club* (1999)
Career low: *The Score* (2001)

Novak, Kim (Marilyn Pauline Novak) (1933–   )

American, born in Chicago, Illinois. She moved to Los Angeles and was working as a model when she made her film debut as a decorative extra in *The Veils of Bagdad* (1953). Signed to Columbia, she emerged as a platinum-haired, ice-cool sex symbol during the late 1950s, but challenging roles exposed her modest dramatic range.

Some notable actors

Career highs: *Vertigo* (1958), *Bell, Book and Candle* (1958), *Kiss Me Stupid* (1964)
Career lows: *Of Human Bondage* (1964), *The Amorous Adventures of Moll Flanders* (1965), *The Legend of Lylah Clare* (1968)

O

Oates, Warren (1928–82)

American, born in Depoy, Kentucky. After serving as a US Marine, he made his film debut in *Up Periscope* (1959), and his leering grin and throaty voice made him an excellent villain. His long association with director **Sam Peckinpah** brought him a wider range of roles. His life is the subject of the documentary *Warren Oates: Across the Border* (1993).
Career highs: *The Wild Bunch* (1969), *Two-Lane Blacktop* (1971), *Dillinger* (1973), *Cockfighter* (1974), *Bring Me the Head of Alfredo Garcia* (1974)
Career lows: *Race with the Devil* (1975), *Drum* (1976), *Dixie Dynamite* (1976)

Oberon, Merle (Estelle Merle O'Brien Thompson) (1911–79)

Anglo-Indian, born in Bombay, India. In Britain from the late 1920s, she worked as a dance hostess and film extra before being signed to a contract by film mogul **Alexander Korda**, who became her first husband. She became a Hollywood star in the 1930s, but drifted away from the cinema in the 1950s. A dark-haired beauty, she took pains throughout her life to conceal her Eurasian parentage, falsely claiming to have been born and raised in Tasmania.
Career highs: *The Private Life of Henry VIII* (1933), *The Dark Angel* (1936), *Wuthering Heights* (1939), *Lydia* (1941)
Career lows: *A Song to Remember* (1945), *Of Love and Desire* (1963), *Interval* (1973)

O'Connor, Donald David Dixon Ronald (1925–2003)

American, born in Chicago. Born into a show-business family, he was performing from an early age, and made his film debut in *Melody for Two* (1937). A brash, live-wire performer in modest Universal musicals of the 1940s, he is best remembered for his show-stopping 'Make 'em laugh' routine in the MGM classic *Singin' in the Rain* (1952).
Career highs: *Francis* (1949), *Singin' in the Rain* (1952), *Call Me Madam* (1953)
Career lows: *Anything Goes* (1956), *The Wonders of Aladdin* (1961)

O'Hara, Maureen (Maureen FitzSimons) (1920–   )

Irish, born in Dublin. A radio and stage performer, she made her film debut in *Kicking the Moon Around* (1938). In the USA from 1939, her flame-haired beauty and spitfire personality made her a star of colourful swashbucklers, and she frequently played opposite **John Wayne**. She returned to the screen after a 20-year absence in *Only the Lonely* (1991).
Career highs: *How Green Was My Valley* (1941), *The Black Swan* (1942), *This Land Is Mine* (1943), *The Quiet Man* (1952)
Career lows: *Bagdad* (1949), *Lady Godiva* (1955), *How Do I Love Thee?* (1970)

Oldman, (Leonard) Gary (1958–   )

English, born in New Cross, London. A member of the Greenwich Young People's Theatre, he made his film debut in *Remembrance* (1982). He has an uncanny ability to lose himself within a character, but after a sensational start, he has not always found the roles that would best serve his talents. He was once married to **Uma Thurman**, and has also directed (the harrowing *Nil by Mouth* (1997)).
Career highs: *Sid and Nancy* (1986), *Prick Up Your Ears* (1987), *JFK* (1991)
Career lows: *Track 29* (1988), *The Scarlet Letter* (1995)

Olivier, Laurence Kerr (Baron Olivier of Brighton) (1907–89)

English, born in Dorking. His school appearance as Katherina in *The Taming of the Shrew* began a career as one of the greatest Shakespearean actors of the 20th century. He made his film debut in the short *Hocus Pocus* (1930) and became a matinee idol during the 1930s (despite refusing the studio's request that he change his name to 'Larry Oliver'). He later produced, directed and played in acclaimed films of *Henry V* (1944), *Hamlet* (1948) and *Richard III* (1955). After 1974, he appeared chiefly in films and in television productions. He was married three times, to the actresses Jill Esmond, **Vivien Leigh** and Joan Plowright.
Career highs: *Wuthering Heights* (1939), *Rebecca* (1940), *Henry V* (1944), *Carrie* (1952), *The Entertainer* (1960), *Sleuth* (1972)
Career lows: *The Prince and the Showgirl* (1957), *The Betsy* (1978), *Inchon* (1980)

O'Neal, Ryan (1941–   )

American, born in Los Angeles, California. He was a bit-part actor in countless television series before his big break in the soap opera *Peyton Place* and his film debut in *The Big Bounce* (1969). A handsome, sandy-haired man, he was a major star in the 1970s but has struggled to sustain his career since then. His daughter Tatum O'Neal appeared with him in *Paper Moon* at the age of nine, and went on to win an Academy Award[®] for her performance.
Career highs: *Love Story* (1970), *What's Up, Doc?* (1972), *Paper Moon* (1973), *Barry Lyndon* (1975)
Career lows: *Partners* (1982), *Fever Pitch* (1985), *Faithful* (1996)

> **"**
> Acting is a masochistic form of exhibitionism. It is not quite the occupation of an adult.
> – Laurence Olivier, *Time* magazine (3 July 1978)
> **"**

O'Toole, Peter Seamus (1932–   )

Irish, born in Connemara. He was a journalist with the *Yorkshire Evening Post* and served with the British submarine corps before attending the Royal Academy of Dramatic Art. He made a few films before his star-making performance as a mercurial *Lawrence of Arabia* (1962), and gave a decade of dazzling screen performances before his career became more uneven. He has received seven Academy Award[®] nominations, but has never won.

Career highs: *Lawrence of Arabia* (1962), *The Lion in Winter* (1968), *The Ruling Class* (1972), *The Stuntman* (1980), *My Favourite Year* (1982)
Career low: *Caligula* (1977)

Owen, Clive (1964–)

English, born in Coventry. Inspired to become an actor by his appearance in a school production of *Oliver!*, he studied at the Royal Academy of Dramatic Art and made his film debut in *Vroom* (1988). Television success led to more film roles, and he eventually came to international prominence as the result of a long, steady climb to the top.
Career highs: *Close My Eyes* (1991), *Croupier* (1998), *Closer* (2004)
Career low: *Beyond Borders* (2003)

P

Pacino, Al(fred James) (1940–)

American, born in East Harlem, New York City. The son of a stonemason, he was raised by his mother and his Sicilian grandparents. A movie buff as a child, he later studied acting, and made his film debut as a junkie in *Me, Natalie* (1969). He went on to become one of the most magnetic actors of his generation, winning a Best Actor Academy Award® for *Scent of a Woman* (1993).
Career highs: *The Godfather* (1972), *Serpico* (1973), *Dog Day Afternoon* (1975), *Scarface* (1983), *Scent of a Woman* (1993), *Heat* (1995)
Career lows: *Bobby Deerfield* (1977), *Revolution* (1985), *Gigli* (2003)

Page, Geraldine (1924–87)

American, born in Kirksville, Missouri. She studied at the Goodman Theater School, and made her film debut in *Out of the Night* (1948). Noted on Broadway for her association with the works of Tennessee Williams, she eventually moved on to more challenging film roles and received eight Academy Award® nominations, winning a Best Actress award for *The Trip to Bountiful* (1985).
Career highs: *Hondo* (1953), *Summer and Smoke* (1961), *Sweet Bird of Youth* (1962), *Interiors* (1978), *The Trip to Bountiful* (1985)

Palance, Jack (Vladimir Palanuik) (1919–)

American, born in Latimer Mines, Pennsylvania. The son of a coalminer, he was a professional heavyweight boxer before distinguished wartime service that earned him a Purple Heart. Plastic surgery to correct burn injuries left him with a taut, menacing appearance that made him a chilling screen villain. He made his film debut in *Panic in the Streets* (1950) and won a Best Supporting Actor Academy Award® for *City Slickers* (1991).
Career highs: *Sudden Fear* (1952), *Shane* (1953), *Attack!* (1956), *Bagdad Cafe* (1987), *City Slickers* (1991)
Career lows: *Sword of the Conqueror* (1961), *Che!* (1969), *The Sensuous Nurse* (1975), *Cocaine Cowboys* (1979), *Outlaw of Gor* (1989)

Paltrow, Gwyneth (1973–   )

American, born in Los Angeles, California. The daughter of actress Blythe Danner and director Bruce Paltrow, she made her film debut as a teenager in *Shout* (1991). Her career developed with a variety of supporting roles that displayed her grace, elegance and skill with accents. She won a Best Actress Academy Award® for *Shakespeare in Love* (1998). She has had relationships with leading men **Brad Pitt** and **Ben Affleck**, and is married to the musician Chris Martin.
Career highs: *Flesh and Bone* (1993), *Emma* (1996), *Shakespeare in Love* (1998)
Career lows: *Hush* (1998), *View from the Top* (2003)

Parker, Eleanor Jean (1922–   )

American, born in Cedarville, Ohio. Spotted by a Warner Brothers talent agent when she was just 18, she made her film debut in *They Died with Their Boots On* (1941). A strong leading lady in the 1950s, she remains an undervalued talent, best known for her role as the Baroness in *The Sound of Music* (1965).
Career highs: *Voice of the Turtle* (1947), *Caged* (1950), *The Detective Story* (1951), *Interrupted Melody* (1955), *Lizzie* (1957)
Career lows: *Of Human Bondage* (1946), *Sunburn* (1979)

Parton, Dolly Rebecca (1946–   )

American, born in Sevierville, Tennessee. One of 12 children born to a tobacco-farming family, she was raised in the Smokey Mountains, and was performing by the age of 12. A legendary country-and-western singer/songwriter, she made her film debut in *9 to 5* (1980) and her blonde, bubbly, self-deprecating personality has been effectively used in a handful of film and television roles.
Career highs: *9 to 5* (1980), *The Best Little Whorehouse in Texas* (1982), *Steel Magnolias* (1989)
Career low: *Rhinestone* (1984)

Peck, (Eldred) Gregory (1916–2003)

American, born in La Jolla, California. Educated at San Diego State College, he was a stage actor before making his film debut in *Days of Glory* (1944). A handsome, sincere young man, his best-remembered performances exuded the same decency and virtue that marked his off-camera nature. He won a Best Actor Academy Award® for *To Kill a Mockingbird* (1962).
Career highs: *The Keys of the Kingdom* (1944), *Gentleman's Agreement* (1947), *The Gunfighter* (1950), *Roman Holiday* (1953), *To Kill a Mockingbird* (1962)
Career lows: *Beloved Infidel* (1959), *The Boys from Brazil* (1978)

Penn, Sean Justin (1960–   )

American, born in Burbank, California. The son of director Leo Penn and actress Eileen Ryan, he studied with drama coach Peggy Feury and made his film debut in *Taps* (1981). His bad-boy image initially distracted from his talent as an intense, driven method actor and thoughtful director. He won a Best Actor Academy Award® for *Mystic River* (2003). Previously married to **Madonna**, he is now married to actress Robin Wright. The actor Chris Penn was his brother.

Career highs: *Fast Times at Ridgemont High* (1982), *Colors* (1988), *Dead Man Walking* (1995), *Sweet and Lowdown* (1999), *Mystic River* (2003)
Career low: *Shanghai Surprise* (1986)

Perkins, Anthony (1932–92)

American, born in New York City. The son of actor Osgood Perkins, he began performing as a teenager and made his film debut in *The Actress* (1953). Boyish, gauche and gangly, he mainly played sensitive young men before his performance as Norman Bates in *Psycho* (1960) doomed him to a lifetime of neurotic, unbalanced characters. He also directed, and was married to the actress Berry Berenson.
Career highs: *Friendly Persuasion* (1956), *Fear Strikes Out* (1957), *Psycho* (1960), *The Trial* (1963), *Pretty Poison* (1968)
Career low: *Edge of Sanity* (1989)

Pfeiffer, Michelle (1957–)

American, born in Santa Ana, California. A supermarket checkout girl and beauty-pageant winner, she was a model and worked on television before making her film debut in *Falling in Love Again* (1980). A typical Californian beauty, she emerged from the ranks of pretty newcomers to prove herself a versatile actress. She is married to television executive David E Kelley.
Career highs: *Scarface* (1983), *Dangerous Liaisons* (1988), *Married to the Mob* (1988), *The Fabulous Baker Boys* (1989), *Love Field* (1991)
Career lows: *Grease 2* (1982), *The Story of Us* (1999)

Phillippe, (Matthew) Ryan (1974–)

American, born in New Castle, Delaware. An actor from childhood, he first gained attention as daytime television's first gay teenager in the soap *One Life to Live*, and made his film debut in *Crimson Tide* (1995). His seductive performance in *Cruel Intentions* (1999) made him a teen heart-throb, but he has since sought a wider range of parts. He is married to **Reese Witherspoon**.
Career highs: *Cruel Intentions* (1999), *Igby Goes Down* (2002)
Career low: *Company Man* (2000)

Phoenix, Joaquin Rafael (1974–)

American, born in San Juan, Puerto Rico. He is the son of Children of God missionaries, and the younger brother of **River Phoenix**. A child actor on television, he made his film debut in *Space Camp* (1986). Frequently cast in anguished, misfit adolescent roles, he grew into a talented character actor whose star has been in the ascendant since *Gladiator* (2000).
Career highs: *To Die For* (1995), *Gladiator* (2000), *Buffalo Soldiers* (2001), *Walk the Line* (2005)
Career low: *U Turn* (1997)

Phoenix, River (1970–93)

American, born in Madras, Oregon. He was the son of Children of God missionaries, and the older brother of **Joaquin Phoenix**. He made his film debut in *Explorers* (1985), and soon gained a cult following as a sensitive young actor of immense

promise. He died of an accidental drug overdose outside the Viper Room nightclub in Los Angeles.
Career highs: *Stand By Me* (1986), *Running on Empty* (1988), *My Own Private Idaho* (1991), *Dogfight* (1991)
Career lows: *Little Nikita* (1988), *Silent Tongue* (1993)

Piccoli, (Jean Daniel) Michel (1925–)

French, born in Paris. The son of musicians, he made his film debut in *Sortilèges* (1945). In the course of his more than 200 film appearances he has worked with many of the great names in world cinema, and is especially noted for his work with **Luis Buñuel**. His second wife was singer/actress Juliette Gréco.
Career highs: *Belle de jour* (1967), *The Discreet Charm of the Bourgeoisie* (1972), *Leap into the Void* (1980), *La Belle noiseuse* (1991), *I'm Going Home* (2001)

Pickford, Mary (Gladys Marie Smith) (1893–1979)

Canadian, born in Toronto, Ontario. A stage performer from the age of five, she had her first substantial screen role in *The Violin Maker of Cremona* (1909). Her golden curls, beauty, wit and innocent charm helped make her cinema's first major star, famous on an unprecedented scale. She was also a shrewd businesswoman who established the United Artists Corporation along with **Charlie Chaplin**, **D W Griffith** and her second husband **Douglas Fairbanks Sr**. Her acting career ended soon after the arrival of sound, and she later struggled with alcoholism.
Career highs: *Rebecca of Sunnybrook Farm* (1917), *Pollyana* (1920), *Little Lord Fauntleroy* (1921), *Sparrows* (1926), *Coquette* (1929)
Career lows: *The Taming of the Shrew* (1929), *Secrets* (1933)

Pitt, (William) Brad(ley) (1963–)

American, born in Shawnee, Oklahoma. His early roles included a part in the television series *Dallas*. His portrayal of a seductive hitch-hiker in *Thelma And Louise* (1991) led to stardom. He has maintained his status as a soulful leading man whilst attempting increasingly demanding roles. He was formerly married to actress Jennifer Aniston, and his partner is **Angelina Jolie**; he has also pursued a passionate interest in architecture.
Career highs: *A River Runs Through It* (1992), *Se7en* (1995), *Fight Club* (1999)
Career lows: *Cutting Class* (1989), *Meet Joe Black* (1998)

Pleasence, Donald (1919–95)

English, born in Worksop, Nottinghamshire. The son of a stationmaster, he joined the RAF during World War II, and was held in a Nazi prison camp. He resumed his stage career in the 1940s, making his film debut in *Orders Are Orders* (1954). Over the next 40 years, he made over 200 film and television appearances, portraying a gallery of oddballs, scientists and black-hearted villains with apparent relish.
Career highs: *The Caretaker* (1963), *The Great Escape* (1963), *Cul-de-Sac* (1966), *You Only Live Twice* (1967), *Halloween* (1978) et seq
Career lows: *Frankenstein's Great Aunt Tillie* (1983), *Where is Parsifal?* (1983), *Buried Alive* (1989), *River of Death* (1989)

Plummer, (Arthur) Christopher Orme (1927–)

Canadian, born in Toronto, Ontario. A distinguished stage actor, he made his film debut in *Wind Across the Everglades* (1958). A leading man after the phenomenal success of *The Sound of Music* (1965), he has become a prolific character actor, noted for his incisive, scene-stealing supporting roles. His daughter is actress Amanda Plummer.

Career highs: *The Sound of Music* (1965), *The Man Who Would Be King* (1975), *The Silent Partner* (1978), *The Insider* (1999)
Career lows: *Nobody Runs Forever* (1968), *Lock Up Your Daughters* (1969)

Poitier, Sidney (1924–)

American, born in Miami, Florida. Raised in the Bahamas, he served in the US Army before embarking on an acting career with the American Negro Theater. He made his film debut in the documentary *From Whom Cometh My Help* (1949). In Hollywood from 1950, his warm presence and clean-cut image blazed a trail for all black actors. He won a Best Actor Academy Award® for *Lilies of the Field* (1963), and has also directed.

Career highs: *No Way Out* (1950), *The Blackboard Jungle* (1955), *The Defiant Ones* (1958), *Lilies of the Field* (1963), *In the Heat of the Night* (1967)
Career lows: *The Long Ships* (1963), *A Warm December* (1973)

Portman, Natalie (Natalie Hershlag) (1981–)

American, born in Jerusalem, Israel. She moved to the USA at the age of three and was a child model before making her film debut in *Léon* (1994). Her delicate beauty and sensitive performances have found her work with some of Hollywood's best-known directors, but her role in the much-hyped *Star Wars* franchise, despite mixed reviews for the films, made her an international household name.

Career highs: *Léon* (1994), *Star Wars: Episode I – The Phantom Menace* (1999), *Closer* (2004)
Career low: *Mars Attacks!* (1996)

Powell, Dick (Richard Ewing Powell) (1904–63)

American, born in Mountain View, Arkansas. A student at Little Rock College with a passion for music, he worked in several bands before being spotted by a talent scout and making his film debut in *Street Scene* (1931). He was a baby-faced crooner in 1930s musicals, but reinvented himself in tough-guy roles during the 1940s, and later directed. He was married to actresses **Joan Blondell** and **June Allyson**.

Career highs: *42nd Street* (1933), *Dames* (1934), *Christmas in July* (1940), *Farewell, My Lovely* (1945), *The Bad and the Beautiful* (1952)
Career lows: *Riding High* (1943), *The Conqueror* (1956)

Powell, William Horatio (1892–1984)

American, born in Pittsburgh, Pennsylvania. The son of an accountant, he worked as a clerk before moving to New York City and studying at the American Academy of Dramatic Arts. Stage work led to his film debut in *Sherlock Holmes* (1922). Initially cast in villainous roles, he later established himself as an urbane, polished light

comedian. He retired after *Mister Roberts* (1955).
Career highs: *Jewel Robbery* (1932), *One Way Passage* (1932), *The Thin Man* (1934), *My Man Godfrey* (1936), *Life with Father* (1947)
Career lows: *The Heavenly Body* (1944), *The Hoodlum Saint* (1946)

Power, Tyrone Edmund, Jr (1913–58)

American, born in Cincinnati, Ohio. The son of theatre actor Tyrone Power, he followed in his father's footsteps, making his film debut in *Tom Brown of Culver* (1932). A very dashing young man, he became a boyish star of costume dramas and lightweight musicals but struggled to handle more challenging parts. He died of a heart attack whilst filming *Solomon and Sheba (1959)*.
Career highs: *The Mark of Zorro* (1940), *Blood and Sand* (1941), *Nightmare Alley* (1947), *Witness for the Prosecution* (1957)
Career lows: *The Razor's Edge* (1946), *The Sun Also Rises* (1957)

Presley, Elvis Aron (1935–77)

American, born in Tupelo, Mississippi. A truck driver who became the 'King of Rock'n'Roll', he made his film debut in *Love Me Tender* (1956). Early films reveal his raw magnetism, hip-swivelling sex appeal and genuine acting abilities but he eventually settled for bland, assembly-line star vehicles that effectively killed off his screen career. He turned down the opportunity to make a screen comeback in the 1976 version of *A Star Is Born*.
Career highs: *Jailhouse Rock* (1957), *King Creole* (1958), *Flaming Star* (1960), *Elvis: That's the Way It Is* (1970)
Career lows: *Stay Away Joe* (1968), *Charro!* (1969)

Preston, Robert Meservey (1917–87)

American, born in Newton Highlands, Massachusetts. A performer in amateur dramatics, he was spotted by a Paramount talent scout, and made his film debut in *King of Alcatraz* (1938). Often cast as hearty villains and second-division heroes, he triumphed on Broadway in *The Music Man*, a role he repeated on film.
Career highs: *Union Pacific* (1939), *The Macomber Affair* (1947), *The Music Man* (1962), *Child's Play* (1972), *Victor/Victoria* (1982)
Career lows: *Moon Over Burma* (1940), *My Outlaw Brother* (1951)

Price, Vincent Leonard (1911–93)

American, born in St Louis, Missouri. A graduate of Yale University and a student of fine arts at the Courtauld in London, he made his film debut in *Service de Luxe* (1938). A hardworking supporting actor, his performance in *House of Wax* (1953) established him as a master of the horror genre. He was a noted art expert and gourmand, and was married to the actress Coral Browne.
Career highs: *Laura* (1944), *The Baron of Arizona* (1949), *The Pit and the Pendulum* (1961), *Witchfinder General* (1968), *Theatre of Blood* (1973)
Career lows: *The Story of Mankind* (1947), *Dr Goldfoot and the Girl Bombs* (1966), *Percy's Progress* (1974), *Bloodbath at the House of Death* (1984)

Pryor, Richard (1940–2005)

American, born in Peoria, Illinois. A childhood spent hanging around pool halls and nightclubs gave him a taste for performing, and after serving in the US Army he began to work as a stand-up comic. He made his film debut in *The Busy Body* (1967). A raw, hard-hitting performer, he eventually gained mainstream success. He was diagnosed with multiple sclerosis in 1986, but continued to perform live for many years.

Career highs: *Silver Streak* (1976), *Blue Collar* (1978), *Richard Pryor – Live in Concert* (1979), *Stir Crazy* (1980)
Career lows: *The Toy* (1982), *Jo Jo Dancer, Your Life is Calling* (1986), *Another You* (1991)

Puri, Om (1947–)

Indian, born in Ambala. He studied at New Delhi's National School of Drama and worked extensively in theatre before moving to Bombay and making his film debut in *Ghashiram Kotwal* (1976). Numerous Bollywood roles followed before he made his western film debut in *Gandhi* (1982). His range and versatility have made him one of India's most respected actors, and his profile in the west has grown steadily over the past two decades.

Career highs: *Sadgati* (1981), *My Son the Fanatic* (1997), *East is East* (1998)
Career low: *City of Joy* (1992)

Q

Quaid, Dennis William (1954–)

American, born in Houston, Texas. The younger brother of actor Randy Quaid, he made his film debut in *Crazy Mama* (1975). A charismatic actor with a lopsided grin, he endured and flourished as a leading man, overcoming career setbacks, cocaine addiction and the failure of his marriage to **Meg Ryan**. He also performs with his band The Sharks, and has directed.

Career highs: *The Right Stuff* (1983), *The Big Easy* (1987), *The Savior* (1988), *Far from Heaven* (2002)
Career lows: *Jaws 3-D* (1983), *Come See the Paradise (1990)*

Quayle, Sir Anthony (1913–89)

English, born in Ainsdale, Lancashire. A student at the Royal Academy of Dramatic Art, he appeared as an extra in several 1930s films. After serving in World War II he was primarily a stage actor, but he became more active in the cinema during the 1950s and 1960s, winning an Academy Award® nomination for *Anne of the Thousand Days* (1969).

Career highs: *Ice Cold in Alex* (1958), *Lawrence of Arabia* (1962), *Anne of the Thousand Days* (1969), *The Legend of the Holy Drinker* (1988)
Career low: *The Chosen* (1977)

Quinn, Anthony Rudolf Oaxaca (1915–2001)

Mexican, born in Chihuahua. He toiled as a boxer, butcher, janitor and labourer whilst supporting his ambition to become an actor. He made his film debut in

Parole (1936) and played numerous virile villains and impassive 'Red Indians' before establishing himself as an international star. He made more than 150 films, winning Best Supporting Actor Academy Awards® for both *Viva Zapata* (1952) and *Lust for Life* (1956).

Career highs: *Viva Zapata* (1952), *La Strada* (1954), *Lust for Life* (1956), *Zorba the Greek* (1964)

Career lows: *The Magus* (1968), *The Shoes of the Fisherman* (1968), *Flap* (1970), *Ghosts Can't Do It* (1990)

R

Raft, George (George Ranft) (1895–1980)

American, born in New York City. Raised in Hell's Kitchen, he was a prizefighter and dancehall gigolo before making his film debut in *Queen of the Night Clubs* (1929). Frequently cast as lounge lizards and grim-faced gangsters, he rejected many of the roles that made **Humphrey Bogart** famous. He was later known more for his dubious gangland associates than his acting achievements.

Career highs: *Scarface* (1932), *Bolero* (1934), *Each Dawn I Die* (1939), *They Drive by Night* (1940)

Career lows: *Red Light* (1949), *A Dangerous Profession* (1949)

Raimu (Jules August César Muraire) (1883–1946)

French, born in Toulon. The son of a shopkeeper, he became a stage actor and music-hall performer before making his film debut in *L'Homme nu* (1912). An immensely popular stage star during the 1920s, he returned to the cinema in *Le Blanc et le noir* (1931) and became one of the most beloved French stars of his generation.

Career highs: *Marius* (1931), *Fanny* (1932), *César* (1936), *La Femme du boulanger* (1938), *Les Inconnus dans la maison* (1942)

Career low: *Le Héros de la Marne* (1938)

Rainer, Luise (1910–)

German, born in Düsseldorf. A teenage performer, she worked with director Max Reinhardt on stage, and made her film debut in *Sehnsucht 202* (1932). In Hollywood from 1935, her delicate, dewy-eyed charm won her consecutive Best Actress Academy Awards® for *The Great Ziegfeld* (1936) and *The Good Earth* (1937), but her career as a star was short-lived. She made occasional appearances on stage and television, returning to the cinema after a 50-year absence for *The Gambler* (1997).

Career highs: *The Great Ziegfeld* (1936), *The Good Earth* (1937)

Career low: *Hostages* (1943)

Rains, Claude (1889–1967)

English, born in London. A child actor, he worked extensively on the stage before making his film debut in *Build Thy House* (1920). In Hollywood from 1933, he was an urbane, exceptional supporting actor, bringing wit and intelligence to a gallery of velvet-voiced villains, long-suffering husbands and characters with shifting allegiances. He received four Academy Award® nominations, but never won.

Career highs: *The Adventures of Robin Hood* (1938), *Mr Smith Goes to Washington* (1939), *Casablanca* (1942), *Mr Skeffington* (1944), *Notorious* (1946)
Career lows: *Hearts Divided* (1936), *Strange Holiday* (1942)

Rampling, Charlotte (1945–)

English, born in Sturmer, Essex. The daughter of a NATO commander and a painter, she worked as a model before making her film debut in *The Knack* (1965). One of the best-known faces of the Swinging Sixties, she found her most challenging roles in European films. In recent years she has enjoyed a career revival with roles that highlight her soulful maturity and emotional depth.
Career highs: *The Night Porter* (1974), *Stardust Memories* (1980), *The Verdict* (1982), *Under the Sand* (2000), *The Swimming Pool* (2003)
Career lows: *The Long Duel* (1967), *Foxtrot* (1976), *Orca: Killer Whale* (1977), *Mascara* (1987)

Rathbone, Basil (1892–1967)

English, born in Johannesburg, South Africa. Educated in England, he worked as a stage actor from 1911 and made his film debut in *Innocent* (1921). In America from 1922, he became known as a suavely sinister villain in costume dramas and swashbucklers. He is remembered as the definitive screen Sherlock Holmes, having played the role in 14 films from *The Hound of the Baskervilles* (1939) to *Dressed to Kill* (1946).
Career highs: *David Copperfield* (1935), *The Adventures of Robin Hood* (1938), *The Hound of the Baskervilles* (1939), *The Mark of Zorro* (1940), *The Last Hurrah* (1958)
Career lows: *Love from a Stranger* (1937), *The Black Sleep* (1956), *The Ghost in the Invisible Bikini* (1966), *Hillbillys in a Haunted House* (1967)

Reagan, Ronald Wilson (1911–2004)

American, born in Tampico, Illinois. An athletic youngster, he became a lifeguard and radio sports commentator before signing to Warner Brothers and making his film debut in *Love Is on the Air* (1937). A genial presence, though with limited dramatic ability, he retired from the screen after *The Killers* (1964). He was later elected Governor of California and, eventually, 40th President of the United States. He was married to actresses **Jane Wyman** and Nancy Davis.
Career highs: *Knute Rockne: All American* (1940), *King's Row* (1942), *The Hasty Heart* (1949)
Career low: *Hellcats of the Navy* (1957)

Redford, (Charles) Robert (1937–)

American, born in Santa Monica, California. He earned a baseball scholarship to the University of Colorado and later studied art in Europe before committing himself to an acting career. He made his film debut in *War Hunt* (1962), and had become a reluctant sex symbol by the end of the decade. He has also directed, winning an Academy Award® for *Ordinary People* (1980), and founded the influential Sundance Institute in 1981.
Career highs: *Butch Cassidy and the Sundance Kid* (1969), *The Way We Were* (1973), *All the President's Men* (1976), *Ordinary People* (1980), *Quiz Show* (1994)

Career lows: *The Great Gatsby* (1974), *Havana* (1990), *Up Close and Personal* (1996), *The Last Castle* (2001)

> ## All in the Family
>
> Acting 'dynasties' spanning two or more generations are not uncommon in the world of film: notable examples include the Redgraves (Michael, Vanessa, Lynn, Corin and others), the Fondas (Henry, Jane, Peter and Bridget), and the Wayans (Keenen Ivory, Damon, Kim, Marlon, Shawn, Damien and others). However, the only family to produce three generations of Oscar® winners so far has been the Hustons: Walter (Best Supporting Actor, *The Treasure of the Sierra Madre*, 1948), John (Best Director for the same film) and Anjelica (Best Supporting Actress, *Prizzi's Honor*, 1985).

Redgrave, Lynn Rachel (1943–)

English, born in London. The youngest daughter of **Michael Redgrave** and actress Rachel Kempson, she studied at London's Central School of Music and Drama and worked in the theatre before making her film debut in *Tom Jones* (1963). Her poignant performance in *Georgy Girl* (1966) confirmed her talent, and she remains a hardworking stage and film actress.
Career highs: *Girl with Green Eyes* (1964), *Georgy Girl* (1966), *The National Health* (1973), *Shine* (1996), *Gods and Monsters* (1998)
Career lows: *Last of the Mobile Hot-Shots* (1970), *The Happy Hooker* (1975)

Redgrave, Sir Michael Scudamore (1908–85)

English, born in Bristol. The son of actor Roy Redgrave, he was educated at Cambridge University and worked as a teacher before embarking on a distinguished stage career. He made his film debut in *The Lady Vanishes* (1938), and became a popular leading man and character actor. His children Corin, **Lynn** and **Vanessa Redgrave** have all followed in the family tradition.
Career highs: *The Lady Vanishes* (1938), *Kipps* (1941), *Dead of Night* (1945), *The Browning Version* (1951), *Time Without Pity* (1957)
Career lows: *The Green Scarf* (1954), *Connecting Rooms* (1969), *Goodbye Gemini* (1970)

Redgrave, Vanessa (1937–)

English, born in London. The eldest daughter of **Michael Redgrave** and actress Rachel Kempson, she trained at London's Central School of Speech and Drama and made her film debut opposite her father in *Behind the Mask* (1958). Her luminous grace, conviction and integrity have served a vast range of characterizations, winning her a Best Supporting Actress Academy Award® for *Julia* (1977).
Career highs: *Morgan* (1966), *Isadora* (1968), *Julia* (1977), *The Bostonians* (1984), *Howards End* (1992)
Career low: *Bear Island* (1979)

Reed, (Robert) Oliver (1937–99)

English, born in London. The nephew of film director **Carol Reed**, he began working as an extra in films during the late 1950s. His brawny physique and brooding manner made him a major star a decade later, but the quality of his roles diminished as his reputation as a hellraiser grew. After his death, digital technology was used to complete his unfinished scenes in *Gladiator* (2000).

Career highs: *Women in Love* (1969), *The Three Musketeers* (1973), *Castaway* (1987), *Gladiator* (2000)

Career lows: *Dr Heckyl and Mr Hype* (1980), *Venom* (1982), *Fanny Hill* (1983), *Spasms* (1984)

Reeve, Christopher (1952–2004)

American, born in New York City. A performer from the age of nine, he studied at New York City's Juilliard School, and made his film debut in *Gray Lady Down* (1977). His deft playing of the mild-mannered Clark Kent and his superhero alter ego made him an ideal *Superman* (1978). He was paralysed by a riding accident in 1995, but continued to act, direct and campaign for research into spinal injuries.

Career highs: *Superman* (1978), *Somewhere in Time* (1980), *Street Smart* (1987)

Career lows: *Monsignor* (1982), *Superman IV – The Quest for Peace* (1987)

Reeves, Keanu (1964–)

American, born in Beirut, Lebanon. After travelling widely as a child, he left school at the age of 15 to study acting. Appearances on stage and television led to his film debut in *Youngblood* (1986). The success of the two *Bill & Ted* movies typecast him as an airheaded adolescent, but he matured into a likeable and ambitious all-rounder. He also plays in the band Dogstar.

Career highs: *Bill & Ted's Excellent Adventure* (1989), *My Own Private Idaho* (1991), *Speed* (1994), *The Matrix* (1999)

Career lows: *Bram Stoker's Dracula* (1992), *Chain Reaction* (1996)

Reilly, John C(hristopher) (1965–)

American, born in Chicago, Illinois. After training at the Goodman School of Drama, he worked with the Steppenwolf Theatre Company before making his film debut in *Casualties of War* (1989). Initially underappreciated, perhaps because of his relatively homely appearance, he has steadily built a reputation as an intelligent and charismatic performer with a vast range. He received a Best Supporting Actor Academy Award® nomination for *Chicago* (2002).

Career highs: *Casualties of War* (1989), *Hard Eight* (1996), *Boogie Nights* (1997), *Magnolia* (1999), *Chicago* (2002)

Career lows: *The River Wild* (1994), *Never Been Kissed* (1999)

Remick, Lee (1935–91)

American, born in Quincy, Massachusetts. The daughter of an actress, she was committed to the profession from an early age, working on stage and television. She was spotted by **Elia Kazan**, who cast her in her film debut, *A Face in the Crowd* (1957). A sensitive, hardworking actress, she found few roles that matched her abilities.

Career highs: *Anatomy of a Murder* (1959), *Wild River* (1960), *Days of Wine and Roses* (1962), *Baby, the Rain Must Fall* (1965), *The Europeans* (1979)

Career lows: *Sanctuary* (1961), *The Medusa Touch* (1978)

Reno, Jean (Don Juan Moreno y Jederique Jimenez) (1948–)

Spanish, born in Casablanca, Morocco. He moved to France as a teenager, and worked on stage and television before making his film debut in *L'Hypothèse du tableau volé* (1978). A hulking bear of a man, he was initially cast mainly in villainous roles, but his work with director **Luc Besson** brought him to international attention and gradually broadened the scope of his career.
Career highs: *Nikita* (1989), *Les Visiteurs* (1992), *Léon* (1994), *Roseanna's Grave* (1996)
Career lows: *Jet Lag* (2002), *Rollerball* (2002)

Reynolds, Burt(on Leon, Jr) (1936–)

American, born in Waycross, Georgia. A college football star, he won a scholarship to the Hyde Park Playhouse in New York, and worked on stage and television before making his film debut in *Angel Baby* (1961). His swaggering, light-hearted, macho image made him a top box-office star in the 1970s. He found renewed popularity with television roles during the 1990s, and in 1997 received an Academy Award® nomination for *Boogie Nights*.
Career highs: *Deliverance* (1972), *The Longest Yard* (1974), *Smokey and the Bandit* (1977), *Breaking In* (1989), *Boogie Nights* (1987)
Career lows: *Stroker Ace* (1983), *Heat* (1987), *Malone* (1987), *Cop and a Half* (1993)

Reynolds, Debbie (Mary Frances Reynolds) (1932–)

American, born in El Paso, Texas. Raised in Los Angeles, she was a teenage beauty queen who made her film debut in *June Bride* (1948). A cute, irrepressible star of musicals and romantic comedies, she flourished in the 1950s and 1960s. She continues to work on stage and television, with occasional film roles.
Career highs: *Singin' in the Rain* (1952), *Tammy and the Bachelor* (1957), *The Unsinkable Molly Brown* (1964), *What's the Matter with Helen?* (1971), *Mother* (1996)
Career lows: *The Singing Nun* (1966), *How Sweet It Is* (1968)

Richardson, Miranda (1958–)

English, born in Southport, Lancashire. She studied at the Old Vic Theatre School in Bristol. Stage and television work followed before her breakthrough performance as Ruth Ellis in *Dance with a Stranger* (1985). She remains a versatile, unpredictable scene-stealer, drawn to unconventional material.
Career highs: *Dance with a Stranger* (1985), *Damage* (1992), *Tom and Viv* (1994), *Spider* (2002)

Richardson, Sir Ralph David (1902–83)

English, born in Cheltenham, Gloucestershire. He worked in an insurance company before deciding to become an actor, and established his reputation with the Birmingham Repertory Company from 1926. West End success led to his film debut in *The Ghoul* (1933). One of the great knights of the British theatre, he was an eccentric, unpredictable but often mesmerizing film performer.

Career highs: *South Riding* (1938), *The Fallen Idol* (1948), *The Heiress* (1949), *Long Day's Journey into Night* (1962), *Greystoke* (1984)
Career low: *Invitation to the Wedding* (1983)

Ritter, Thelma (1905–69)

American, born in New York City. A child performer, she supported herself with odd jobs while studying at the American Academy of Dramatic Arts, and made her Broadway debut in 1926. She married, and was semi-retired, before making her film debut in *Miracle on 34th Street* (1947). A gravelly-voiced character actress, she received six Academy Award® nominations but never won.
Career highs: *All About Eve* (1950), *Pickup on South Street* (1953), *Pillow Talk* (1959), *The Misfits* (1961), *Birdman of Alcatraz* (1962)

Robards, Jason, Jr (1922–2000)

American, born in Chicago, Illinois. The son of actor Jason Robards Sr, he received the Navy Cross for his wartime service, and went on to study drama. Long associated with the plays of Eugene O'Neill on stage, he made his film debut in *The Journey* (1959). He won Best Supporting Actor Academy Awards® for both *All the President's Men* (1976) and *Julia* (1977). His third wife was actress **Lauren Bacall**.
Career highs: *Long Day's Journey into Night* (1962), *All the President's Men* (1976), *Julia* (1977), *Melvin and Howard* (1980), *Magnolia* (1999)
Career lows: *Hurricane* (1979), *Raise the Titanic* (1980), *Caboblanco* (1980)

Robbins, Tim(othy Francis) (1958–)

American, born in West Covina, California. The son of folk singer Gil Robbins, he was a child actor who later studied at the University of California and formed the Actors' Gang theatre group. He made his film debut in *Toy Soldiers* (1984), and continued to work extensively in mainstream film and television roles whilst maintaining his involvement with radical theatre work. He won a Best Supporting Actor Academy Award® for *Mystic River* (2003), and has also directed. His off-screen partner is **Susan Sarandon**, and both are noted for their interest in political issues.
Career highs: *Bull Durham* (1988), *The Player* (1992), *The Shawshank Redemption* (1994), *Dead Man Walking* (1995), *Mystic River* (2003)
Career lows: *Howard the Duck* (1986), *Erik the Viking* (1989)

Roberts, Julia (1967–)

American, born in Smyrna, Georgia. The younger sister of actor Eric Roberts, she made her film debut in *Baja Oklahoma* (1988). Her performance in the Cinderella romance *Pretty Woman* (1990) elevated her to the front rank of stardom. Although best known for romantic comedies, she has increasingly tackled dramatic roles, winning a Best Actress Academy Award® for *Erin Brockovich* (2000).
Career highs: *Steel Magnolias* (1989), *Pretty Woman* (1990), *My Best Friend's Wedding* (1997), *Erin Brockovich* (2000)
Career lows: *Satisfaction* (1988), *Mary Reilly* (1996)

Robertson, Cliff (1925–)

American, born in La Jolla, California. A merchant marine during World War II, he subsequently worked on stage and television before securing a significant film role in *Picnic* (1955). A handsome, reliable performer, he won a Best Actor Academy Award® for *Charly* (1968) and subsequently pursued his ambition to write and direct, most notably on *J W Coop* (1972).
Career highs: *Underworld USA* (1961), *The Best Man* (1964), *Charly* (1968), *J W Coop* (1972)
Career lows: *Dominique* (1978), *Class* (1983)

Robinson, Edward G (Emanuel Goldenberg) (1893–1973)

American, born in Bucharest, Romania. After emigrating to the USA at the turn of the 20th century, he studied at the American Academy of Dramatic Arts in New York City. He made his film debut in *The Bright Shawl* (1923), but it was his pugnacious performance as an Al Capone-style gangster in *Little Caesar* (1930) that brought him stardom. He was a noted art collector.
Career highs: *Little Caesar* (1930), *Dr Ehrlich's Magic Bullet* (1940), *Double Indemnity* (1944), *Scarlet Street* (1945), *Key Largo* (1948)
Career lows: *Tampico* (1944), *My Daughter Joy* (1950)

Robson, Dame Flora McKenzie (1902–84)

English, born in South Shields, Durham. A student at the Royal Academy of Dramatic Art, she worked in the theatre before making her film debut in *Gentleman of Paris* (1931). Working in British and American films, she played historical roles and character parts, and was frequently cast as wounded spinsters and formidable old ladies.
Career highs: *Fire over England* (1937), *Wuthering Heights* (1939), *Poison Pen* (1939), *The Sea Hawk* (1940), *Guns at Batasi* (1964), *Seven Women* (1966)
Career low: *Saratoga Trunk* (1945)

Rogers, Ginger (Virginia Katherine McMath) (1911–95)

American, born in Independence, Missouri. A child performer, she appeared in vaudeville before making her film debut in the short *Campus Sweethearts* (1928). She is fondly remembered for her sublime screen partnership with **Fred Astaire** in ten musicals, but she also won a Best Actress Academy Award® for a dramatic role in *Kitty Foyle* (1940). She retired from the screen after *Harlow* (1965), but remained an indefatigable stage performer.
Career highs: *Top Hat* (1935), *Swing Time* (1936), *Stage Door* (1937), *Vivacious Lady* (1938), *Kitty Foyle* (1940)
Career lows: *Lady in the Dark* (1944), *Heartbeat* (1946), *Quick, Let's Get Married* (1964)

Rooney, Mickey (Joseph Yule Jr) (1920–)

American, born in Brooklyn, New York City. Born into a show-business family, he was a performer from the age of two and made his film debut in *Not to Be Trusted* (1926). His performance as the wholesome, all-American boy-next-door Andy Hardy in several films earned him great public affection. He matured into a hardworking

trouper, appearing in more than 250 films. One of his eight marriages was to **Ava Gardner**.

Career highs: *A Midsummer Night's Dream* (1935), *Boys Town* (1938), *The Human Comedy* (1943), *Baby Face Nelson* (1957), *The Black Stallion* (1979)

Career lows: *He's a Cockeyed Wonder* (1950), *The Atomic Kid* (1954), *The Private Lives of Adam and Eve* (1960)

Small Wonder

Mickey Rooney's first film role – as a cigar-chomping adult midget in *Not to Be Trusted* (1926) – was almost too convincing for his own good: it gave rise to a rather mean-spirited rumour that Rooney, then a rising child star, was in fact a midget posing as a child.

Rossellini, Isabella (1952–)

Italian, born in Rome. The daughter of **Ingrid Bergman** and **Roberto Rossellini**, she worked as a television journalist and model before making her film debut with her mother in *A Matter of Time* (1976). She continued to dabble in acting before fully committing to the profession from the late 1980s. She was briefly married to **Martin Scorsese**.

Career highs: *Blue Velvet* (1986), *Cousins* (1989), *Fearless* (1993), *The Saddest Music in the World* (2003)

Career low: *Siesta* (1987)

Roth, Tim (Timothy Simon Smith) (1961–)

English, born in London. He studied sculpture at Camberwell Art College before dropping out to follow an acting career. Eye-catching television performances led to his film debut in *The Hit* (1984). In the USA from the early 1990s, he has played a wide range of supporting roles, winning an Academy Award® nomination for *Rob Roy* (1995). He also directed *The War Zone* (1999).

Career highs: *The Hit* (1984), *Vincent & Theo* (1990), *Reservoir Dogs* (1992), *Rob Roy* (1995), *The War Zone* (1999)

Career lows: *Four Rooms* (1995), *Invincible* (2001)

Roundtree, Richard (1937–)

American, born in New Rochelle, New York. He won a football scholarship to study at Southern Illinois University and subsequently worked with the Negro Ensemble Theatre in New York City before making his film debut in *What Do You Say to a Naked Lady?* (1970). His performance as cool, super-stud detective John Shaft made him the first star of blaxploitation cinema.

Career highs: *Shaft* (1971), *Q – The Winged Serpent* (1982), *Original Gangstas* (1996)

Career lows: *A Game for Vultures* (1979), *Killpoint* (1984), *Party Line* (1988), *Maniac Cop* (1988), *Crack House* (1989)

Rourke, Mickey (Philip Andre Rourke Jr) (c.1956–)

American, born in Schenectady, New York. Raised in Miami, Florida, he was an amateur boxer before turning to acting and making his film debut in *1941* (1979). His rebellious persona made him a star in the 1980s, but after leaving the profession to become a professional boxer, he struggled to regain his former stature.

Career highs: *Diner* (1982), *Rumblefish* (1983), *9½ Weeks* (1986), *Barfly* (1987), *Sin City* (2005)

Career lows: *Francesco* (1989), *Wild Orchid* (1990), *Another 9½ Weeks* (1997), *Double Team* (1997), *They Crawl* (2001)

Rowlands, Gena (Virginia Cathryn Rowlands) (1930–)

American, born in Madison, Wisconsin. The daughter of a politician, she studied at New York's American Academy of Dramatic Arts, and worked on Broadway and in television before making her film debut in *The High Cost of Loving* (1958). She was married to **John Cassavetes** from 1954 until his death, and gave powerful, emotionally raw performances in some of his best films.

Career highs: *Faces* (1968), *Minnie and Moskowitz* (1971), *A Woman Under the Influence* (1974), *Gloria* (1980), *Another Woman* (1988)

Career lows: *Machine Gun McCain* (1968), *The Skeleton Key* (2005)

Rush, Geoffrey (1951–)

Australian, born in Toowoomba, Queensland. Raised in Brisbane, he studied at the University of Queensland before pursuing an acting career. He made his film debut in *Hoodwink* (1981) but was primarily a respected stage actor before his Academy Award®-winning performance as the troubled pianist David Helfgott in *Shine* (1996).

Career highs: *Shine* (1996), *Shakespeare in Love* (1998), *Quills* (2000)

Russell, (Ernestine) Jane (Geraldine) (1921–)

American, born in Bemidji, Minnesota. A chiropodist's assistant and occasional model, she was spotted by **Howard Hughes**, who launched her cinema career in a blaze of publicity with *The Outlaw* (1943). Although her ability as an actress was limited, her voluptuous figure and sense of humour earned her a 20-year career as a screen siren.

Career highs: *The Outlaw* (1943), *The Paleface* (1948), *Gentlemen Prefer Blondes* (1953)

Career lows: *Young Widow* (1946), *The Fuzzy Pink Nightgown* (1957)

Russell, Kurt Vogel (1951–)

American, born in Springfield, Massachusetts. A television actor from the age of six, he made his film debut in the Elvis Presley vehicle *It Happened at the World's Fair* (1962), and spent the next decade performing in wholesome Disney comedies. He then played professional baseball before reappearing as an adult actor, frequently cast as a brawny man of action. His off-screen partner is **Goldie Hawn**.

Career highs: *Escape from New York* (1981), *The Mean Season* (1985), *Backdraft* (1991), *Dark Blue* (2003)
Career lows: *Captain Ron* (1992), *Soldier* (1998), *3000 Miles to Graceland* (2001)

Russell, Rosalind (1908–76)

American, born in Waterbury, Connecticut. A student at the American Academy of Dramatic Arts in New York City, she worked on Broadway before making her film debut in *Evelyn Prentice* (1934). She was a superb comedy actress who excelled at playing smart, wisecracking career women; however, her later attempts to tackle more heavyweight dramatic roles met with limited success.
Career highs: *Craig's Wife* (1936), *The Women* (1939), *His Girl Friday* (1940), *Auntie Mame* (1958), *Gypsy* (1962)
Career lows: *Mourning Becomes Electra* (1947), *A Majority of One* (1962)

Russo, Rene Marie (1954–)

American, born in Burbank, California. She worked in countless low-paid jobs before she was spotted at a Rolling Stones concert and offered a modelling contract. After a successful career as a fashion model she studied drama, finding work in television before making her film debut in *Major League* (1989).
Career highs: *Lethal Weapon 3* (1992), *Get Shorty* (1995), *The Thomas Crown Affair* (1999)
Career low: *The Adventures of Rocky and Bullwinkle* (2000)

Rutherford, Dame Margaret (1892–1972)

English, born in London. She worked in the theatre for a decade before making her film debut in *Dusty Ermine* (1936), and subsequently became one of the country's most beloved character stars, with a sublime comic touch. Noted for her on-screen portrayal of Agatha Christie's sleuth Miss Marple, she also won a Best Supporting Actress Academy Award[®] for *The V.I.P.s* (1963).
Career highs: *Blithe Spirit* (1945), *The Happiest Days of Your Life* (1950), *The Importance of Being Earnest* (1952), *The V.I.P.s* (1963), *Chimes at Midnight* (1966)
Career low: *Meet Me at Dawn* (1946)

Ryan, Meg (Margaret Mary Emily Ann Hyra) (1961–)

American, born in Bethel, Connecticut. The daughter of teachers, she performed in amateur dramatics before making her film debut in *Rich and Famous* (1981). She then studied journalism at New York University before devoting herself to an acting career. Hugely popular in romantic comedy roles, she has also displayed a flinty dramatic talent. She is divorced from actor **Dennis Quaid**.
Career highs: *When Harry Met Sally* (1989), *Sleepless in Seattle* (1993), *When a Man Loves a Woman* (1994), *In the Cut* (2003)
Career lows: *Hanging Up* (2000), *Against the Ropes* (2004)

Ryan, Robert (1909–73)

American, born in Chicago, Illinois. A boxing champion at Dartmouth College, he majored in dramatic literature and intended to become a journalist until he developed an interest in amateur dramatics. He made his film debut in *Golden Gloves* (1940), and spent the next 30 years bringing insight and depth to a wide range of characters, from mean-spirited villains to anguished heroes and leathery men of the west.

Career highs: *Crossfire* (1947), *The Set-Up* (1949), *Bad Day at Black Rock* (1954), *Billy Budd* (1962), *The Wild Bunch* (1969), *The Iceman Cometh* (1973)

Career lows: *Escape to Burma* (1955), *The Canadians* (1961)

Ryder, Winona (Winona Laura Horowitz) (1971–)

American, born in Winona, Minnesota. Named after her hometown, she was raised partly in a Californian commune and began acting in her early teens, working in the theatre before making her film debut in *Lucas* (1986). As a sensitive, talented young actress she received two Academy Award® nominations, but her adult career appeared to be faltering before her 2001 arrest and conviction for shoplifting.

Career highs: *Heathers* (1989), *Edward Scissorhands* (1990), *The Age of Innocence* (1993), *Little Women* (1994)

Career lows: *Autumn in New York* (2000), *Lost Souls* (2000), *Mr Deeds* (2002)

S

Saint, Eva Marie (1924–)

American, born in Newark, New Jersey. A student at the University of Ohio, she worked in radio and television before making her Academy Award®-winning debut in *On the Waterfront* (1954). A warm, intelligent presence, she has worked sparingly during the course of her long career.

Career highs: *On the Waterfront* (1954), *North by Northwest* (1959), *All Fall Down* (1962), *Loving* (1970)

Career low: *Cancel My Reservation* (1972)

Sanders, George (1906–72)

Russian, born in St Petersburg. Raised in Britain and educated at Brighton College, he worked in the textile business before committing himself to the stage. He made his film debut in *Find the Lady* (1936), and excelled in subsequent roles as suave villains and world-weary cads. He won a Best Supporting Actor Academy Award® for *All About Eve* (1950). His four wives included both Zsa Zsa Gabor and her sister, Magda.

Career highs: *The Moon and Sixpence* (1942), *All About Eve* (1950), *Voyage to Italy* (1953), *Call Me Madam* (1953)

Career lows: *The Candy Man* (1969), *The Body Stealers* (1969), *Psychomania* (1972)

Sandler, Adam Richard (1966–   )

American, born in Brooklyn, New York City. While attending New York University, he pursued a career in stand-up comedy at nightclubs. He made his film debut in *Going Overboard* (1989), but it was his stint on *Saturday Night Live* that became the springboard to a lasting film career in goofball comedy vehicles.
Career highs: *The Wedding Singer* (1998), *Fifty First Dates* (2004)
Career lows: *Little Nicky* (2000), *Eight Crazy Nights* (2002), *Mr Deeds* (2002)

Sarandon, Susan (Susan Abigail Tomalin) (1946–   )

American, born in New York City. She studied at the Catholic University in Washington, DC, where she met her future husband Chris Sarandon. She made her film debut in *Joe* (1970) and subsequently matured into one of the finest screen actresses of her generation, winning a Best Actress Academy Award® for *Dead Man Walking* (1995). Her off-screen partner is **Tim Robbins**, and both are noted for their interest in political issues and new theatre.
Career highs: *Atlantic City* (1980), *Thelma and Louise* (1981), *Bull Durham* (1988), *Lorenzo's Oil* (1992), *Dead Man Walking* (1995)
Career lows: *The Other Side of Midnight* (1977), *Something Short of Paradise* (1979)

Scacchi, Greta (Greta Gracco) (1960–   )

English, born in Milan, Italy. Raised in Milan, London and Australia, she studied at the Bristol Old Vic and worked as a model before learning German to make her film debut in *Das Zweite Gesicht* (1982). Her graceful good looks and talent won her a number of high-profile roles in the 1980s, but she later found a wider range of opportunities in the theatre.
Career highs: *Heat and Dust* (1983), *White Mischief* (1988), *Presumed Innocent* (1990), *The Player* (1992)
Career low: *Turtle Beach* (1992)

Scheider, Roy Richard (1932–   )

American, born in Orange, New Jersey. An athletic youngster, he was a baseball player and boxer before studying drama and serving in the US Air Force. He made his film debut in *Curse of the Living Corpse* (1963), and was a dynamic, rugged presence in a number of key 1970s films before his career began to fade.
Career highs: *The French Connection* (1971), *Klute* (1971), *Jaws* (1975), *All That Jazz* (1979)
Career lows: *Sorcerer* (1977), *Still of the Night* (1982), *The Men's Club* (1986)

Schell, Maximilian (1930–   )

Austrian, born in Vienna. Raised in a theatrical family, he made his stage debut at the age of three, and was a vastly experienced actor before his film debut in *Kinder, Mütter und ein General* (1955). He appeared in international productions from 1958, and won a Best Actor Academy Award® for *Judgment at Nuremberg* (1961). He has also written, produced and directed, most notably the documentary *Marlene* (1984) on Marlene Dietrich.

Career highs: *Judgment at Nuremberg* (1961), *Topkapi* (1964), *The Man in the Glass Booth* (1975), *Julia* (1977)
Career lows: *Krakatoa, East of Java* (1968), *Pope Joan* (1972)

Schwarzenegger, Arnold Alois (1947–)

Austrian, born in Thal, near Graz. A dedicated body-builder, he was named Mr Germany in 1966 and subsequently became the youngest ever Mr Universe. He made his film debut in *Hercules Goes to New York* (1969), and gradually became one of the leading action stars of his generation. He later switched his focus to the pursuit of political office, and was elected Governor of California in 2003.
Career highs: *The Terminator* (1984), *Total Recall* (1990), *True Lies* (1994)
Career lows: *Last Action Hero* (1993), *Collateral Damage* (2001)

Scofield, (David) Paul (1922–)

English, born in Hurstpierpoint, Sussex. The son of a headmaster, he appeared in school plays and studied with the London Mask Theatre before making his stage debut in 1940. He has remained primarily a stage actor throughout his long career, but made his film debut in *That Lady* (1955) and won a Best Actor Academy Award® repeating his stage performance as Sir Thomas More in *A Man for All Seasons* (1966).
Career highs: *A Man for All Seasons* (1966), *King Lear* (1971), *Quiz Show* (1994)

Scott, George C(ampbell) (1927–99)

American, born in Wise, Virginia. The son of a mine surveyor, he served in the Marine Corps and studied journalism before dedicating himself to acting. He made his film debut in *The Hanging Tree* (1958), and emerged as a dynamic, authoritative leading man who famously rejected his Best Actor Academy Award® for *Patton* (1970). His son is actor Campbell Scott.
Career highs: *Anatomy of a Murder* (1959), *The Hustler* (1961), *Petulia* (1968), *Patton* (1970), *The Hospital* (1971)
Career low: *The Savage Is Loose* (1974)

Scott, (George) Randolph (1898–1987)

American, born in Orange County, Virginia. Educated at the University of North Carolina, he entered the film industry as an extra in *Sharpshooters* (1928). He endured as a handsome, easy-going and rather stolid leading man, but really made his mark as the leathery, hard-bitten star of some excellent Budd Boetticher westerns in the 1950s. He retired in 1962 as one of Hollywood's wealthiest stars.
Career highs: *My Favorite Wife* (1940), *Seven Men from Now* (1956), *Buchanan Rides Alone* (1958), *Ride Lonesome* (1959), *Ride the High Country* (1962)
Career lows: *Captain Kidd* (1945), *Christmas Eve* (1947)

Scott-Thomas, Kristin (1960–)

English, born in Redruth, Cornwall. The daughter of a pilot who died when she was four, she suffered another tragedy when her stepfather died in similar circumstances. After working in France as a teenager, she has continued to make

her home there. Her English cinema career blossomed in the mid-1990s with films such as *Four Weddings and a Funeral* (1994) and *The English Patient* (1996).
Career highs: *A Handful of Dust* (1987), *Four Weddings and a Funeral* (1994), *The English Patient* (1996)
Career lows: *Under the Cherry Moon* (1986), *Random Hearts* (1999)

Seberg, Jean (1938–79)

American, born in Marshalltown, Iowa. Ambitious to become an actress, she was chosen from a nationwide search to make her film debut in *Saint Joan* (1957). Although criticized for her inexperience, she persevered to build an erratic international career, but problems with drink and drugs and an anguished private life led her to commit suicide.
Career highs: *Bonjour Tristesse* (1958), *Breathless* (1960), *Lilith* (1964)
Career low: *Kill!* (1972)

Segal, George (1934–)

American, born in Great Neck, Long Island. A graduate of Columbia University, he worked on the stage and in some distinguished television productions before making his film debut in *The Young Doctors* (1961). A versatile leading star of the 1970s, he won acclaim for his skill at playing wry comic roles, but was unable to sustain his popularity.
Career highs: *Who's Afraid of Virginia Woolf?* (1966), *Loving* (1970), *The Owl and the Pussycat* (1970), *California Split* (1974)
Career lows: *The Black Bird* (1975), *The Duchess and the Dirtwater Fox* (1976)

Sellers, Peter (1925–80)

English, born in London. He was a child actor, and served his apprenticeship as an Entertainments National Service Association entertainer during World War II. A huge success on radio's *The Goon Show*, he made his film debut in *Penny Points to Paradise* (1951). His talent for mimicry and comic timing made him an international star, and he is fondly remembered as the hapless Inspector Clouseau in the Pink Panther films.
Career highs: *I'm All Right Jack* (1959), *Only Two Can Play* (1961), *The Pink Panther* (1963), *Dr Strangelove* (1964), *Being There* (1979)
Career lows: *Where Does It Hurt?* (1972), *Soft Beds, Hard Battles* (1973), *The Blockhouse* (1973), *Ghost in the Noonday Sun* (1973)

Pink Panther Pastiche

Following Peter Sellers's death in 1980, old clips and out-takes from his popular Pink Panther films were used by director Blake Edwards as a basis for *The Trail of the Pink Panther* (1982), which has the dubious distinction of being the first and only film ever to have been conceived after the death of its star. Unsurprisingly, this ill-advised venture was not a success, and even led to Sellers's widow successfully suing the film-makers for violation of the actor's contractual rights.

Serrault, Michel (1928–)

French, born in Brunoy, Essonne. He originally trained to be a singer, before making his film debut in *Comment réussir en amour* (1952). A versatile stage and film actor, he has appeared in 150 films, revealing a sprightly talent for farce as well as playing a wide range of character parts.
Career highs: *La Cage aux folles* (1978), *Garde à vue* (1981), *Docteur Petiot* (1990), *Nelly & Monsieur Arnaud* (1995)
Career low: *Assassin(s)* (1997)

Sharif, Omar (Michael Shalhoub) (1932–)

Egyptian, born in Alexandria. The son of a wealthy merchant, he worked in his father's business before making his film debut in *The Blazing Sun* (1954). A major star of Egyptian cinema, he found international fame after his Academy Award®-nominated performance in *Lawrence of Arabia* (1962). He has played dashing leading men in many exotic tales, and is also a world-class bridge player.
Career highs: *Lawrence of Arabia* (1962), *Dr Zhivago* (1965), *Funny Girl* (1968), *Monsieur Ibrahim et les fleurs du Coran* (2003)
Career lows: *The Appointment* (1969), *Che!* (1969)

Shaw, Robert (1927–78)

English, born in Westhoughton, Lancashire. The son of a doctor, he studied at the Royal Academy of Dramatic Art before making his stage debut in 1949. He made his film debut in *The Lavender Hill Mob* (1951), and was a popular television star in the 1950s before gradually attaining more prominent film roles in the 1960s. A Hollywood favourite during the 1970s, he was also a novelist and playwright.
Career highs: *From Russia with Love* (1963), *A Man for All Seasons* (1966), *The Sting* (1973), *Jaws* (1975)
Career lows: *Custer of the West* (1967), *Force 10 from Navarone* (1978), *Avalanche Express* (1979)

Shearer, Norma (Edith Norma Fisher) (1904–83)

Canadian, born in Montreal, Quebec. Trained as a pianist, she started working in films as a teenage extra, but quickly rose to become a star noted for her poise, chic beauty and authority. She married studio executive Irving Thalberg, who helped advance her career, and she won a Best Actress Academy Award® for *The Divorcee* (1930). Less focused on her career after Thalberg's death, she retired in 1942.
Career highs: *He Who Gets Slapped* (1924), *The Divorcee* (1930), *Marie Antoinette* (1938), *The Women* (1939)
Career low: *Her Cardboard Lover* (1942)

Sheen, Martin (Ramon Estevez) (1940–)

American, born in Dayton, Ohio. He appeared in a television soap opera and on Broadway before making his film debut in *The Incident* (1967). An intelligent, sincere actor, he is frequently cast as politicians and presidents, and his roles have reflected his off-screen activism on a number of liberal causes. The actors Emilio Estevez and Charlie Sheen are his sons.

Career highs: *The Subject Was Roses* (1968), *Badlands* (1973), *Apocalypse Now* (1979), *Da* (1988)
Career low: *The Cassandra Crossing* (1977)

Sheridan, Ann (Clara Lou Sheridan) (1915–67)

American, born in Denton, Texas. After winning a beauty contest prize of a Hollywood screen test, she made her film debut in *Search for Beauty* (1934) and built a career on the sassy sex appeal that made her a match for the tough guys at Warner Brothers in the 1940s. Nicknamed the 'Oomph Girl', she made her last film in 1957.
Career highs: *Torrid Zone* (1940), *They Drive by Night* (1940), *The Man Who Came To Dinner* (1941), *King's Row* (1942), *I Was a Male War Bride* (1949)
Career low: *Woman and the Hunter* (1957)

Sidney, Sylvia (Sophia Kosow) (1910–99)

American, born in New York City. After studying acting as a teenager, she made her film debut in *Broadway Lights* (1927). A sensitive, soulful star, she appeared in socially conscious dramas during the 1930s. After a period of concentrating on stage work, she resumed her film career as a character actress, making her final appearance in *Mars Attacks!* (1996). Her second husband was actor Luther Adler.
Career highs: *An American Tragedy* (1931), *Street Scene* (1931), *Fury* (1936), *You Only Live Twice* (1937), *Summer Wishes, Winter Dreams* (1973)
Career lows: *Good Dame* (1934), *Behold My Wife!* (1934), *Love From a Stranger* (1947)

Signoret, Simone (Simon-Henriette Charlotte Kaminker) (1921–85)

German, born in Wiesbaden. Raised in Paris, she became a film extra in 1942 and soon moved on to leading roles. A languorous, heavy-lidded blonde, she was frequently cast as prostitutes and courtesans, but matured into one of France's most admired character actresses and won a Best Actress Academy Award® for *Room at the Top* (1959). She was married to **Yves Montand**.
Career highs: *La Ronde* (1950), *Casque d'Or* (1952), *Les Diaboliques* (1954), *Room at the Top* (1959), *Madame Rosa* (1977)
Career low: *Four Days Leave* (1950)

Sim, Alastair (1900–76)

Scottish, born in Edinburgh. The son of a tailor, he lectured in elocution at the University of Edinburgh before pursuing an acting career. He made his film debut in *Riverside Murder* (1935) and gradually established himself as a leading performer on stage and screen, equally adept at mirthful or menacing characterizations.
Career highs: *Green for Danger* (1946), *The Happiest Days of Your Life* (1950), *Scrooge* (1951), *The Belles of St Trinian's* (1954), *An Inspector Calls* (1954)

Simmons, Jean Merilyn (1929–   )

English, born in London. She was a model and bit-part player before making her film debut in *Give Us the Moon* (1944). A breathtakingly beautiful young woman of rare ability, she worked in Hollywood from 1952, and enjoyed a decade of front-rank stardom. She was married to actor **Stewart Granger** and to director Richard Brooks.

Career highs: *Great Expectations* (1946), *The Actress* (1953), *Guys and Dolls* (1955), *Elmer Gantry* (1960), *The Happy Ending* (1969)

Career lows: *Mister Buddwing* (1966), *Say Hello to Yesterday* (1970), *Mr Sycamore* (1975)

Simon, (François) Michel (1895–1975)

Swiss, born in Geneva. He was a boxer, a photographer and an acrobat before settling on a career as an actor. He made his film debut in *La Galerie des monstres* (1924). A beloved character actor, he brought vivid life to his portrayals of tramps, peasants, uncouth dreamers and brutish suitors.

Career highs: *Boudu sauvé des eaux* (1932), *L'Atalante* (1934), *Le Quai des brumes* (1938), *Panique* (1946), *La Beauté du diable* (1949)

Sinatra, Frank (Francis Albert Sinatra) (1915–98)

American, born in Hoboken, New Jersey. As an amateur singer, beloved of 1940s bobbysoxers, he made his film debut in *Las Vegas Night* (1941). A breezy presence in screen musicals and an incomparable interpreter of the Great American Songbook, he won a Best Supporting Actor Academy Award® for *From Here to Eternity* (1953) and gave some impressive dramatic performances before drifting away from the cinema after 1970. His four wives included **Ava Gardner** and **Mia Farrow**.

Career highs: *On the Town* (1949), *From Here to Eternity* (1953), *The Man with the Golden Arm* (1955), *Some Came Running* (1958), *The Manchurian Candidate* (1962)

Career lows: *The Miracle of the Bells* (1948), *The Kissing Bandit* (1948)

Skarsgård, Stellan (1951–)

Swedish, born in Gothenburg. He was a teenage star in the television series *Bombi Bitt och jag* (1968) and became a leading light of Stockholm's Royal Dramatic Theatre before building a reputation as a character actor on film. The success of *Breaking the Waves* (1996) brought him an international career.

Career highs: *The Simple-Minded Murderer* (1982), *The Ox* (1991), *Breaking the Waves* (1996), *Insomnia* (1997), *Taking Sides* (2001)

Career low: *Passion of Mind* (2000)

Slater, Christian (Christian Michael Leonard Hawkins) (1969–)

American, born in New York City. He was a child actor in television soap operas and stage musicals before his first major film appearance in *The Legend of Billie Jean* (1985). His dynamic performances and rebellious bad-boy image made him very popular during the early 1990s.

Career highs: *Heathers* (1989), *Pump Up the Volume* (1991), *Untamed Heart* (1993)

Career lows: *Kuffs* (1992), *Churchill – The Hollywood Years* (2004)

Smith, Dame Maggie (Margaret Natalie Smith) (1934–   )

English, born in Ilford, Essex. She was a student at the Oxford Playhouse School, then made her stage debut in 1952 and her film debut in *Nowhere To Go* (1958). Her inimitable vocal range and timing have enabled her to portray vulnerability to both dramatic and comic effect. An Academy Award® favourite, she has won for both *The Prime of Miss Jean Brodie* (1969) and *California Suite* (1978). She was married to actor Robert Stephens and is the mother of actor Toby Stephens.
Career highs: *The Prime of Miss Jean Brodie* (1969), *California Suite* (1978), *A Private Function* (1984), *A Room with a View* (1985), *Gosford Park* (2001)
Career low: *Travels with My Aunt* (1972)

Smith, Will (Willard Christopher Smith Jr) (1968–   )

American, born in Philadelphia, Pennsylvania. He was a successful teenage rap artist and his fame grew with the television series *The Fresh Prince of Bel-Air* during the early 1990s. He made his film debut in *Where the Day Takes You* (1992), and quickly emerged as one of the most charismatic actors of his generation, winning a Best Actor Academy Award® nomination for *Ali* (2001). His second wife is actress Jada Pinkett.
Career highs: *Independence Day* (1996), *Men in Black* (1997), *Ali* (2001), *Hitch* (2005)
Career lows: *Wild Wild West* (1999), *Men in Black II* (2002)

Snipes, Wesley (1962–   )

American, born in the Bronx, New York City. After attending the High School for the Performing Arts, he was part of a puppet theatre troupe called Struttin' Street Stuff. He appeared on Broadway and on television before making his film debut in *Wildcats* (1986). Tall, athletic and good-looking, he has constantly tested himself as an actor but is now most frequently cast as an action star.
Career highs: *Jungle Fever* (1991), *Demolition Man* (1993), *One Night Stand* (1997), *Blade* (1998)
Career lows: *The Fan* (1996), *The Art of War* (2000), *Liberty Stand Still* (2002)

Sondergaard, Gale (Edith Holm Sondergaard) (1899–1985)

American, born in Litchfield, Minnesota. She worked in the New York theatre before reluctantly moving to Hollywood, where she won the first Best Supporting Actress Academy Award® for *Anthony Adverse* (1936). She was soon typecast as exotic villains and wicked ladies. A victim of the anti-Communist blacklist, she was absent from the screen for 20 years, returning only for a handful of supporting roles.
Career highs: *Anthony Adverse* (1936), *The Cat and the Canary* (1939), *The Letter* (1940), *Sherlock Holmes and the Spider Woman* (1944), *Anna and the King of Siam* (1946)
Career lows: *The Spider Woman Strikes Back* (1946), *Slaves* (1969)

Sothern, Ann (Harriette Arlene Lake) (1909–2001)

American, born in Valley City, North Dakota. After studying at the University of Washington, she trained as a singer and made her film debut in *Broadway Nights* (1927). A warm, likeable performer, ideally cast as a sassy, wisecracking blonde in

the long-running *Maisie* series of films, she later impressed as a blowsy character actress and received an Academy Award® nomination for *The Whales of August* (1987).
Career highs: *Folies Bergère* (1935), *Maisie* (1939), *Panama Hattie* (1942), *A Letter To Three Wives* (1949), *The Whales of August* (1987)
Career low: *The Manitou* (1978)

Spacek, Sissy (Mary Elizabeth Spacek) (1949–)

American, born in Quitman, Texas. The cousin of **Rip Torn**, she made her film debut as an extra in *Trash* (1970). A youthful, freckle-faced woman, she was often cast as tormented innocents, notably in *Carrie* (1976), but went on to tackle a wide range of characters, winning a Best Actress Academy Award® as Loretta Lynn in *Coal Miner's Daughter* (1980).
Career highs: *Badlands* (1973), *Carrie* (1976), *Coal Miner's Daughter* (1980), *Missing* (1981), *In the Bedroom* (2001)
Career lows: *Violets Are Blue* (1985), *The Ring 2* (2005)

Spacey, Kevin (Kevin Spacey Fowler) (1959–)

American, born in South Orange, New Jersey. Raised in California, he was a rebellious, delinquent adolescent who found a purpose in life through acting. He attended New York's Juilliard School and began a distinguished stage career before making his film debut in *Heartburn* (1986). His steely intelligence and sardonic humour have enlivened a range of unsettling characters, and he has won Academy Awards® for *The Usual Suspects* (1995) and *American Beauty* (1999).
Career highs: *The Usual Suspects* (1995), *Se7en* (1995), *L.A. Confidential* (1997), *American Beauty* (1999)
Career low: *Pay It Forward* (2000)

Spall, Timothy (1957–)

English, born in Battersea, London. A member of the National Youth Theatre, he studied at the Royal Academy of Dramatic Art and worked with the Royal Shakespeare Company. He made his film debut in *Quadrophenia* (1979) and became a much-loved character actor, lending pathos and dignity to a wide range of roles and noted for his work with director **Mike Leigh**.
Career highs: *Secrets & Lies* (1996), *Topsy Turvy* (1999), *All Or Nothing* (2001), *Nicholas Nickleby* (2002)

Stack, Robert (Charles Langford Modini Stack) (1919–2003)

American, born in Los Angeles, California. He made his film debut kissing Deanna Durbin in *First Kiss* (1939). He served in the US Navy during World War II, and was an undervalued leading man in the 1950s before television claimed him for the long-running series *The Untouchables*.
Career highs: *To Be Or Not to Be* (1942), *The Bullfighter and the Lady* (1951), *The High and the Mighty* (1954), *Written on the Wind* (1956), *Tarnished Angels* (1957)
Career lows: *Bwana Devil* (1952), *The Gift of Love* (1958)

Stallone, Sylvester (1946–)

American, born in New York City. The son of a Sicilian immigrant, he worked at odd jobs before drifting into acting. After a series of minor parts in films including *Bananas* (1971), he gained stardom as an underdog boxer in *Rocky* (1976), which he also wrote. Four *Rocky* sequels and his role as a Vietnam veteran in the *Rambo* series maintained his star status for the next 20 years. He also directs.

Career highs: *Rocky* (1976), *First Blood* (1982), *Cliffhanger* (1993)

Career lows: *Cobra* (1986), *Over the Top* (1987), *Lock Up* (1989), *Stop! or My Mom Will Shoot* (1992), *Driven* (2001)

> **"**
>
> It's true – I was thinking of Rimbaud ... I was reading Rimbaud when my wife came from the supermarket [with] some apples. Rambo apples! Of such accidents...
>
> – David Morrell, creator of Rambo, *Knave* magazine (1986)
>
> **"**

Stamp, Terence (1939–)

English, born in Stepney, London. A student at the Webber-Douglas Academy, he made his film debut in *Billy Budd* (1962), for which he received an Academy Award® nomination. He became an iconic, enigmatic star during the 1960s, but took time away from his career for a spiritual journey to India in the 1970s before returning to the screen in supporting roles.

Career highs: *Billy Budd* (1962), *The Collector* (1965), *The Mind of Mr Soames* (1970), *The Hit* (1984), *Priscilla, Queen of the Desert* (1994)

Career lows: *Blue* (1968), *Monster Island* (1980), *Link* (1985)

Stanton, Harry Dean (1926–)

American, born in West Irvine, Kentucky. After wartime service in the US Navy, he worked in the theatre before making his film debut in *Tomahawk Trail* (1957). He became a welcome presence in westerns and war films, and attained cult status with his poignant performance in *Paris, Texas* (1984). He is also a singer and guitarist with the Harry Dean Stanton Band.

Career highs: *Alien* (1979), *Wise Blood* (1979), *One from the Heart* (1982), *Paris, Texas* (1984), *Repo Man* (1984)

Career low: *The Mini-Skirt Mob* (1968), *Dream a Little Dream* (1989)

Stanwyck, Barbara (Ruby Stevens) (1907–90)

American, born in Brooklyn, New York City. A performer from the age of 13, she was a dancer and stage actress before making her film debut in *Broadway Nights* (1927). She became one of the most hardworking, versatile and professional performers of her time, frequently cast as gutsy pioneer women, sultry *femmes fatales* and professional women torn between career and romance. Her second husband was **Robert Taylor**.

Career highs: *Stella Dallas* (1937), *The Lady Eve* (1941), *Ball of Fire* (1941), *Double Indemnity* (1944), *Clash by Night* (1952)
Career lows: *Cry Wolf* (1947), *Escape to Burma* (1955)

Steiger, Rod(ney Stephen) (1925–2002)

American, born in Westhampton, Long Island. Born into a show-business family, he served in the US Navy before studying at the Actors Studio in New York. He worked extensively in television before making his film debut in *Teresa* (1951). An intense, dynamic method actor, he was a powerful screen presence with a tendency to overwhelm a role in his later years. He won a Best Actor Academy Award® for *In the Heat of the Night* (1967).
Career highs: *On the Waterfront* (1954), *The Pawnbroker* (1965), *Doctor Zhivago* (1965), *In the Heat of the Night* (1967), *No Way to Treat a Lady* (1968)
Career lows: *The Unholy Wife* (1957), *Three into Two Won't Go* (1969), *Wolf Lake* (1978), *American Gothic* (1988)

Stewart, James Maitland (1908–97)

American, born in Indiana, Pennsylvania. He studied architecture at Princeton University, worked in summer stock and made his New York stage debut in 1932. His first film was *Murder Man* (1935). Tall and gangly, with a distinctive hesitant drawl, he progressed from roles as shy suitors and country boys to play flinty men of the west and perverse romantics; as his career developed, he became one of the most beloved screen actors of all time. He won a Best Actor Academy Award® for *The Philadelphia Story* (1940).
Career highs: *Mr Smith Goes to Washington* (1939), *The Philadelphia Story* (1940), *It's a Wonderful Life* (1946), *Vertigo* (1958), *Anatomy of a Murder* (1959)
Career lows: *Seventh Heaven* (1937), *Pot o' Gold* (1941)

Stiller, Ben(jamin) (1965–   )

American, born in New York City. The son of comedians Jerry Stiller and Anne Meara, he dropped out of UCLA to pursue a theatre career and made his film debut in *Empire of the Sun* (1987). He joined the *Saturday Night Live* team and had his own television series before establishing himself as a director and screen comic, playing uptight characters defined by their neuroses.
Career highs: *There's Something About Mary* (1998), *Meet the Parents* (2000)
Career low: *Envy* (2004)

Stone, Sharon Vonne (1958–   )

American, born in Meadville, Pennsylvania. A teenage beauty-pageant winner, she was a successful model before making her film debut in *Stardust Memories* (1980). For the next decade she remained an unremarkable B-movie starlet, but after she famously crossed her legs in *Basic Instinct* (1992) her career took on new momentum. She survived a brain aneurysm in 2001, but recovered and resumed her career.
Career highs: *Total Recall* (1990), *Basic Instinct* (1992), *Casino* (1995), *Broken Flowers* (2005)
Career lows: *Scissors* (1991), *Diabolique* (1996), *Catwoman* (2004)

Streep, Meryl (Mary Louise Streep) (1949–)

American, born in Summit, New Jersey. After graduating from Vassar College and Yale School of Drama, she made her film debut in *Julia* (1977). She quickly became one of the most admired American performers of her generation, earning 13 Academy Award® nominations to date and winning the award for both *Kramer vs Kramer* (1979) and *Sophie's Choice* (1982).
Career highs: *Kramer vs Kramer* (1979), *The French Lieutenant's Woman* (1981), *Sophie's Choice* (1982), *A Cry in the Dark* (1989), *The Bridges of Madison County* (1995)
Career lows: *Still of the Night* (1982), *Defending Your Life* (1991), *The House of the Spirits* (1993)

Streisand, Barbra (Barbara Joan Rosen) (1942–)

American, born in Brooklyn, New York City. As a teenager she performed in Greenwich Village amateur talent contests. She became the toast of Broadway in the 1960s, and won a Best Actress Academy Award® for her film debut *Funny Girl* (1968), in which she repeated her stage role as Fanny Brice. A gifted singer and comedienne, and an accomplished director, she won a further Academy Award® as co-writer of the song 'Evergreen'.
Career highs: *Funny Girl* (1968), *What's Up, Doc?* (1972), *The Way We Were* (1973), *Yentl* (1983), *Prince of Tides* (1991)
Career lows: *Nuts* (1987), *The Mirror Has Two Faces* (1996)

Sullavan, Margaret Brooke (1911–60)

American, born in Norfolk, Virginia. A student at Baltimore University, she appeared on Broadway before making her film debut in *Only Yesterday* (1933). A radiant, husky-voiced actress with a delicate, vulnerable quality, she was especially poignant in the four films she made with **James Stewart**. Her four husbands included **Henry Fonda** and director **William Wyler**. She committed suicide.
Career highs: *The Good Fairy* (1935), *Three Comrades* (1938), *The Shop Around the Corner* (1940), *The Mortal Storm* (1940), *Back Street* (1941)

Sutherland, Donald McNicol (1934–)

Canadian, born in Saint John, New Brunswick. A student at the University of Toronto, he worked in local radio before moving to London and studying at the Royal Academy of Dramatic Art. He made his film debut in *The World Ten Times Over* (1963) and put his gaunt features and wry, anti-authoritarian image to the service of some highly varied and often eccentric dramatic roles. His son is actor Kiefer Sutherland.
Career highs: *M*A*S*H* (1970), *Klute* (1971), *Don't Look Now* (1973), *Fellini's Casanova* (1976), *Ordinary People* (1980)
Career lows: *Lady Ice* (1973), *S*P*Y*S** (1974), *The Day of the Locust* (1975)

Swank, Hilary Ann (1974–)

American, born in Lincoln, Nebraska. She made her film debut in *Buffy the Vampire Slayer* (1992). Tall and athletic, she proved difficult to cast, but won Best Actress

Academy Awards® for demanding roles in *Boys Don't Cry* (1999) and *Million Dollar Baby* (2004).
Career highs: *Boys Don't Cry* (1999), *Million Dollar Baby* (2004)
Career low: *The Affair of the Necklace* (2001)

Swanson, Gloria (Gloria May Josephine Svensson) (1897–1983)

American, born in Chicago, Illinois. She worked as a clerk, and was studying to become a singer when she appeared as an extra in silent films and began her acting career. A former Mack Sennett Bathing Beauty, she exuded a glamour and sophistication that made her one of the greatest stars of silent cinema, and made an electrifying if short-lived comeback in *Sunset Boulevard* (1950). She was married six times.
Career highs: *Male and Female* (1919), *Madame Sans-Gêne* (1925), *Sadie Thompson* (1928), *Queen Kelly* (1928), *Sunset Boulevard* (1950)
Career lows: *Tonight or Never* (1931), *Nero's Weekend* (1956)

Swayze, Patrick Wayne (1952–   )

American, born in Houston, Texas. A dancer from the age of four, he became a star athlete, professional ice-skater and ballet dancer before making his film debut in *Skatetown USA* (1979). He enjoyed his greatest success as the star of *Dirty Dancing* (1987), but his time at the top was brief.
Career highs: *Dirty Dancing* (1987), *Ghost* (1990), *Point Break* (1991), *Donnie Darko* (2001)
Career lows: *Steel Dawn* (1987), *Father Hood* (1993)

Swinton, (Katherine Ma)Tilda (1960–   )

English, born in London. She studied at Cambridge University and worked with the Royal Shakespeare Company. She made her film debut in *Caravaggio* (1986), the beginning of a long association with director Derek Jarman. Tall and pale-skinned, she can appear strikingly androgynous, and is fearless in her choice of projects.
Career highs: *Edward II* (1991), *Orlando* (1992), *Love Is the Devil* (1998), *The Deep End* (2001), *The Chronicles of Narnia: The Lion, the Witch and the Wardrobe* (2005)
Career low: *Female Perversions* (1997)

T

Tandy, Jessica (1909–94)

American, born in London. She made her film debut in *The Indiscretions of Eve* (1932), but was primarily a stage actress until late in her career, when she won a Best Actress Academy Award® for *Driving Miss Daisy* (1989). She was married to her second husband, actor Hume Cronyn, from 1942 until her death.
Career highs: *The Birds* (1963), *Driving Miss Daisy* (1989), *Fried Green Tomatoes at the Whistle Stop Cafe* (1991)
Career low: *Batteries Not Included* (1987)

Tati, Jacques (Jacques Tatischeff) (1908–82)

French, born in Le Pecq. A talented rugby player in his youth, he became a mimic and cabaret performer, and made his film debut in the short *Oscar, champion de tennis* (1932). An incomparable physical comedian, he gained lasting fame as the lugubrious, pipe-smoking Monsieur Hulot in several films.
Career highs: *Jour de fête* (1949), *Monsieur Hulot's Holiday* (1952), *Mon oncle* (1958), *Playtime* (1967)
Career low: *Traffic* (1971)

Tautou, Audrey (1978–)

French, born in Beaumont. She studied acting at school, and worked in television before her first major film role in *Vénus beauté (institut)* (1999) won her a César award for Most Promising Actress. International recognition followed with *Amélie* (2001), and she subsequently found high-profile roles in both French and English-language productions.
Career highs: *Vénus beauté (institut)* (1999), *Amélie* (2001), *Dirty Pretty Things* (2002)
Career lows: *Épouse-moi* (2000), *Les Marins perdus* (2003)

Taylor, Dame Elizabeth Rosemond (1932–)

English, born in London. A child actress, she made her film debut in *There's One Born Every Minute* (1942). One of the screen's great beauties, with sparkling violet eyes, she has at times received more attention for her private life and many marriages (two to **Richard Burton**) than for her dramatic abilities. She won Best Actress Academy Awards® for *Butterfield 8* (1960) and *Who's Afraid of Virginia Woolf?* (1966).
Career highs: *National Velvet* (1944), *A Place in the Sun* (1951), *Giant* (1956), *Cat on a Hot Tin Roof* (1958), *Who's Afraid of Virginia Woolf?* (1966)
Career lows: *Boom* (1968), *Hammersmith Is Out* (1972)

Taylor, Robert (Spangler Arlington Brugh) (1911–69)

American, born in Filley, Nebraska. The son of a doctor, he studied music before appearances in amateur dramatics led to an acting career. He made his film debut in *Handy Andy* (1934), and his dashing good looks made him a popular matinee idol during the 1930s. After naval service in World War II, he resumed his career playing tougher roles in westerns and war films. His first wife was **Barbara Stanwyck**.
Career highs: *Magnificent Obsession* (1935), *Camille* (1936), *Waterloo Bridge* (1940), *Devil's Doorway* (1950), *Ivanhoe* (1952)
Career lows: *Lucky Night* (1939), *Undercurrent* (1946)

Taylor, Rod (Rodney Sturt Taylor) (1929–)

Australian, born in Sydney. He studied art and engineering before amateur acting led him to a professional career. He made his film debut in *The Stewart Expedition* (1951). In Hollywood from 1955, he became a brawny, likeable leading man in a variety of 1960s films before moving into supporting roles.

Career highs: *The Time Machine* (1960), *The Birds* (1963), *Hotel* (1967), *Dark of the Sun* (1968)
Career low: *Nobody Runs Forever* (1968)

Temple, Shirley Jane (1928–)

American, born in Santa Monica, California. A precociously talented child, she was appearing in short films by the time she was four years old. A golden-haired moppet who spread sweetness and cheer during the Great Depression, she received 135,000 gifts from a grateful world on her eighth birthday. She retired after *A Kiss for Corliss* (1949), and later built a career as a diplomat.
Career highs: *Little Miss Marker* (1934), *The Little Colonel* (1935), *Wee Willie Winkie* (1937), *Heidi* (1937)
Career lows: *Young People* (1940), *Honeymoon* (1947)

Peculiar Policies

Unusual insurance policies have long had their place in Hollywood – Betty Grable's celebrated legs were famously insured for more than a million dollars, and similar examples abound. Even basic life cover for a star can sometimes be complicated: in the 1930s, Lloyd's of London agreed to insure the life of child actress Shirley Temple on the rather odd condition that no payment would be made if the seven-year-old met death or injury while drunk.

Terry-Thomas (Thomas Terry Hoar-Stevens) (1911–90)

English, born in Finchley, London. After service in World War II he became a stand-up comic. His film career flourished in Hollywood from the 1950s onwards, as he came to embody the caricature of a silly-ass, upper-crust Englishman. He suffered from Parkinson's disease in later life, and his final decade was beset with poor health and financial hardship.
Career highs: *Private's Progress* (1956), *Too Many Crooks* (1958), *tom thumb* (1958), *How to Murder Your Wife* (1965), *Arabella* (1967)
Career lows: *His and Hers* (1960), *Spanish Fly* (1976)

Thewlis, David (David Wheeler) (1963–)

English, born in Blackpool. After studying at the Guildhall School of Music and Drama, he worked in television before making his film debut in *Road* (1987). His powerful performance in *Naked* (1993) led to an international career, and he has also written and directed. He was previously married to film-maker Sara Sugarman, and his off-screen partner is actress Anna Friel.
Career highs: *Life Is Sweet* (1991), *Naked* (1993), *Besieged* (1998)
Career lows: *Total Eclipse* (1995), *The Island of Dr Moreau* (1996)

Thompson, Emma (1959–)

English, born in Paddington, London. The daughter of actress Phyllida Law and *The Magic Roundabout*'s Eric Thompson, she studied at Cambridge University and performed with the Cambridge Footlights. She made her film debut in *The Tall Guy* (1989). A woman of great intelligence and effortless wit, she won a Best Actress

Academy Award® for *Howards End* (1992) and a screenplay Academy Award® for her adaptation of *Sense and Sensibility* (1995). She was previously married to **Kenneth Branagh**, and is now married to actor Greg Wise.
Career highs: *Howards End* (1992), *The Remains of the Day* (1993), *In the Name of the Father* (1993), *Sense and Sensibility* (1995), *Nanny McPhee* (2005)
Career lows: *Junior* (1994), *Imagining Argentina* (2003)

Thornton, Billy Bob (1955–)

American, born in Hot Springs, Arkansas. He moved to Los Angeles in 1981 and made his film debut in *Hunter's Blood* (1987). Also a writer and director, he won an Academy Award® for the screenplay of *Sling Blade* (1996), and has become an increasingly popular star in misanthropic, darkly comic roles. He was formerly married to **Angelina Jolie**.
Career highs: *Sling Blade* (1996), *Monster's Ball* (2001), *The Man Who Wasn't There* (2001), *Bad Santa* (2003)
Career low: *South of Heaven, West of Hell* (2000)

Thurman, Uma Karunna (1970–)

American, born in Boston, Massachusetts. The daughter of a college professor and a psychotherapist, she attended the Professional Children's School and made her film debut in *Kiss Daddy Good Night* (1987). A willowy beauty, she has played romantic comedy, costume drama and violent action adventure with equal spirit. She has been married to **Gary Oldman** and **Ethan Hawke**.
Career highs: *Dangerous Liaisons* (1988), *Henry & June* (1990), *Pulp Fiction* (1994), *Kill Bill Volumes 1 & 2* (2003–4)
Career lows: *Even Cowgirls Get the Blues* (1994), *The Avengers* (1998)

Tierney, Gene Eliza (1920–91)

American, born in Brooklyn, New York City. Raised in a wealthy family, she was educated in Switzerland and appeared on Broadway before making her film debut in *The Return of Frank James* (1940). A bewitching beauty, she tackled some demanding roles in the 1940s, and made her final film appearance in *The Pleasure Seekers* (1964). Her later life was marred by ill health, family tragedy and a nervous breakdown.
Career highs: *Laura* (1944), *Leave Her to Heaven* (1945), *The Ghost and Mrs Muir* (1947), *Whirlpool* (1949)
Career low: *Personal Affair* (1953)

Todd, Richard (Richard Andrew Palethorpe-Todd) (1919–)

Irish, born in Dublin. He studied at the Italia Conti school and worked in repertory theatre before distinguished service in the army during World War II. He made his film debut in *For Them That Trespass* (1949) and received a Best Actor Academy Award® nomination for *The Hasty Heart* (1949). A rather stiff, earnest actor on film, he became a hardworking theatre stalwart.
Career highs: *The Hasty Heart* (1949), *A Man Called Peter* (1955), *The Dambusters* (1955)
Career lows: *The Naked Earth* (1958), *Never Let Go* (1960)

Torn, Rip (Elmore Rual Torn) (1931–   )

American, born in Temple, Texas. After moving to New York, he studied at the Actors Studio and made his film debut in *Baby Doll* (1956). He has played his share of avuncular Southerners and sly villains. His exit from *Easy Rider* (1969) allowed **Jack Nicholson** to give his star-making performance. He was married to actresses Ann Wedgeworth and **Geraldine Page**.
Career highs: *Tropic of Cancer* (1970), *Payday* (1973), *Heartland* (1979), *Cross Creek* (1983), *Dodgeball* (2004)
Career lows: *A Stranger Is Watching* (1982), *Beer* (1985)

Tracy, Spencer Bonadventure (1901–67)

American, born in Milwaukee, Wisconsin. Educated at Rippon College, he also studied at New York's American Academy of Dramatic Arts, and was an established theatre actor before making his feature film debut in *Up the River* (1930). A master of unpretentious, understated acting, he excelled in everything from social drama to battle-of-the-sexes comedies and won consecutive Best Actor Academy Awards® for *Captains Courageous* (1937) and *Boys Town* (1938). **Katharine Hepburn** was his off-screen partner for 25 years.
Career highs: *Captains Courageous* (1937), *Boys Town* (1938), *Adam's Rib* (1949), *Father of the Bride* (1950), *Bad Day at Black Rock* (1955)
Career lows: *Dr Jeykll and Mr Hyde* (1941), *The Sea of Grass* (1947)

Travolta, John (1954–   )

American, born in Engelwood, New Jersey. Encouraged to follow his show-business ambitions, he studied dance and performed in musicals as a teenager. He made his film debut in *The Devil's Rain* (1975), and his Academy Award®-nominated performance as the narcissistic Tony Manero in *Saturday Night Fever* (1977) made him an international star. His fading career was revived by his appearance in *Pulp Fiction* (1994). He is married to actress Kelly Preston.
Career highs: *Saturday Night Fever* (1977), *Grease* (1978), *Pulp Fiction* (1994), *Get Shorty* (1995), *Primary Colors* (1998)
Career lows: *Moment by Moment* (1978), *Battlefield Earth* (2000), *Be Cool* (2005)

Trevor, Claire (Claire Wemlinger) (1909–2000)

American, born in New York City. She studied at the American Academy of Dramatic Arts and worked in the theatre before making her film debut in *Life in the Raw* (1933). A scene-stealing supporting actress and B-movie star, she made an indelible impression as the shopsoiled Dallas in *Stagecoach* (1939). She won a Best Supporting Actress Academy Award® for *Key Largo* (1948). She was a noted patron of the arts in her later years.
Career highs: *Dead End* (1937), *Stagecoach* (1939), *Murder, My Sweet* (1944), *Key Largo* (1948), *The High and the Mighty* (1954)

Trintignant, Jean-Louis (1930–   )

French, born in Port-St Esprit. The son of a wealthy industrialist, he abandoned his legal studies to become an actor, and made his film debut in the short *Peauchinef* (1955). His pale-skinned impassivity initially saw him cast as sensitive, vulnerable young men, but he impressed in a wide range of roles for some of Europe's best directors.

Career highs: *Un homme et une femme* (1966), *Z* (1968), *The Conformist* (1969), *My Night With Maud* (1969), *Three Colours: Red* (1994)

Career low: *Così dolce... così perversa* (1969)

Turner, Kathleen (1954–)

American, born in Springfield, Missouri. The daughter of a diplomat, she studied at the Central School of Speech and Drama in London. She appeared in the television soap opera *The Doctors* before making her film debut as the sultry *femme fatale* in *Body Heat* (1981). An ambitious, husky-voiced leading lady, she received a Best Actress Academy Award® nomination for *Peggy Sue Got Married* (1986), but is now more gainfully employed on stage.

Career highs: *Body Heat* (1981), *Romancing the Stone* (1984), *Prizzi's Honor* (1985), *Peggy Sue Got Married* (1986), *The War of the Roses* (1989)

Career lows: *V I Warshawski* (1991), *Baby Geniuses* (1999)

Turner, Lana (Julia Jean Mildred Frances Turner) (1920–95)

American, born in Wallace, Idaho. Legend has it that as a teenager she was spotted sipping soda at a drugstore on Sunset Boulevard and asked if she would like to be in the movies. She duly made her film debut as an extra in *A Star Is Born* (1937), signed with MGM and blossomed into a glamorous movie queen. She earned a Best Actress Academy Award® nomination for *Peyton Place* (1957). In 1958, her daughter stabbed to death her gangland lover Johnny Stompanato.

Career highs: *The Postman Always Rings Twice* (1946), *The Bad and the Beautiful* (1952), *Peyton Place* (1957), *Imitation of Life* (1959)

Career lows: *The Big Cube* (1969), *Persecution* (1974)

Turturro, John (1957–)

American, born in Brooklyn, New York City. He studied at Yale School of Drama and made his film debut as an extra in *Raging Bull* (1980). He has appeared in more than 60 films, his anguished features, frizzy mop of hair and sharp intelligence capturing a gallery of characters that ranges from the sympathetic to the grotesque. He also writes and directs.

Career highs: *Five Corners* (1987), *Barton Fink* (1991), *Mac* (1992), *Quiz Show* (1994), *The Truce* (1997)

Career low: *Brain Donors* (1992)

U

Ullmann, Liv Johanne (1939–)

Norwegian, born in Tokyo, Japan. Raised in Canada, she was a drama student at the Webber-Douglas School in London before beginning her acting career with a repertory company in Norway. She made her film debut in *Fools in the Mountains* (1957). Her reputation rests on a long association with **Ingmar Bergman**, in which she laid bare the inner turmoil of women experiencing various emotional and sexual crises. Later, she also became a director of great skill and sensitivity.

Career highs: *Persona* (1966), *The Shame* (1968), *The Emigrants* (1972), *Scenes From a Marriage* (1973), *Face to Face* (1975)
Career lows: *Pope Joan* (1972), *Lost Horizon* (1973)

Ustinov, Sir Peter Alexander (1921–2004)

English, born in London. Of Russian descent, he trained with actor Michael St Denis and made his stage debut in 1938. His film debut followed in the short *Hullo Fame* (1940). A much-loved man of many talents, he was a playwright, author, director, inimitable raconteur and charity worker. He won Best Supporting Actor Academy Awards® for *Spartacus* (1960) and *Topkapi* (1964).
Career highs: *Spartacus* (1960), *Billy Budd* (1962), *Topkapi* (1964), *Hot Millions* (1968), *Death on the Nile* (1978)
Career low: *Hammersmith Is Out* (1972), *Memed My Hawk* (1984)

V

Valentino, Rudolph (Rodolpho Alphonso Guglielmi di Valentina d'Antonguolla) (1895–1926)

Italian, born in Castellaneta. The son of an army vet, he studied agriculture before leaving Italy for New York City, where he worked as a dancer and gigolo. He began his film career as an extra, and progressed to playing villains before his smouldering performance in *The Four Horsemen of the Apocalypse* (1921) helped to establish him as the silent screen's greatest lover. His early death from peritonitis provoked public mourning around the world.
Career highs: *The Four Horsemen of the Apocalypse* (1921), *The Sheik* (1921), *Blood and Sand* (1922), *Cobra* (1925), *The Eagle* (1925)

> **❝**
> When will we be rid of all these effeminate youths,
> pomaded, powdered, bejeweled and bedizened, in
> the image of Rudy – that painted pansy?
>
> – From an editorial on Rudolph Valentino entitled
> 'Pink Powder Puff', *Chicago Tribune* (1926)
> **❞**

Van Cleef, Lee (1925–89)

American, born in Somerville, New Jersey. He served in the US Navy and worked as an office administrator before amateur dramatics led him to a professional acting career. He made his film debut in *The Showdown* (1950). His hawk-nosed, beady-eyed appearance made him a memorable western villain, and in the 1960s he graduated to starring roles in spaghetti westerns.
Career highs: *High Noon* (1952), *For a Few Dollars More* (1965), *The Good, the Bad and the Ugly* (1966), *Sabata* (1969)
Career low: *Kid Vengeance* (1977)

Van Damme, Jean-Claude (Jean-Claude Camille François Van Varenberg) (1960–)

Belgian, born in Brussels. He studied ballet and martial arts from an early age, and became a karate champion. After moving to Los Angeles, he worked at odd jobs before breaking into the movies with *Monaco Forever* (1984). Dubbed 'the Muscles from Brussels', he became a popular action star, although that popularity has waned in recent years. He has also written and directed.
Career highs: *Universal Soldier* (1992), *Timecop* (1994), *Sudden Death* (1995)
Career low: *Universal Soldier – The Return* (1999)

Van Dyke, Dick (Richard Wayne Van Dyke) (1925–)

American, born in West Plains, Missouri. He served in the US Air Force during World War II before pursuing an acting career. He worked in radio and as a game show host before Broadway success led to his film debut in *Bye Bye Birdie* (1963). An all-round entertainer, his greatest success came in long-running television series.
Career highs: *Mary Poppins* (1964), *Chitty Chitty Bang Bang* (1967), *Cold Turkey* (1971)
Career lows: *Some Kind of a Nut* (1969), *The Runner Stumbles* (1979)

Vaughn, Vince(nt Anthony) (1970–)

American, born in Minneapolis, Minnesota. Drawn to performing, he moved to Los Angeles as a teenager and eventually made his film debut with a bit part in *For the Boys* (1991). His role in *Swingers* (1996) brought him to the attention of Hollywood and a career more successful for his broad comedy roles as part of the Frat Pack than for his dramatic performances.
Career highs: *Swingers* (1996), *Dodgeball* (2004), *The Wedding Crashers* (2005)
Career lows: *Psycho* (1998), *Be Cool* (2005)

Veidt, Conrad (Hans Konrad Weidt) (1893–1943)

German, born in Berlin. He studied at the Hohenzollern Gymnasium, worked in the theatre with Max Reinhardt and served in the army before making his film debut in *Der Spion* (1916). A tall, gaunt figure, his soulful performance in *The Cabinet of Dr Caligari* (1920) made him a leading figure in German Expressionism. He made his Hollywood debut in *The Beloved Rogue* (1927) but was later typecast in villainous roles.
Career highs: *The Cabinet of Dr Caligari* (1920), *The Hands of Orlac* (1924), *Der Student von Prag* (1926), *The Thief of Bagdad* (1940), *Casablanca* (1942)
Career low: *Nazi Agent* (1942)

Vitti, Monica (Maria Luisa Ceciarelli) (1931–)

Italian, born in Rome. Raised in Milan, she studied at the Accademia d'Arte Drammatica in Rome and worked in the theatre before making her film debut in *Ridere Ridere Ridere* (1955). She remains best known for her landmark collaborations with director **Michelangelo Antonioni**, exploring a sense of unease and alienation from the world. She has also played comedy roles and later directed.

Career highs: *L'Avventura* (1960), *La Notte* (1961), *Eclipse* (1962), *The Red Desert* (1964)
Career low: *The Chastity Belt* (1967)

Voight, Jon(athan) (1938–)

American, born in Yonkers, New York. The son of a professional golfer, he worked on stage before making his film debut in *Fearless Frank* (1967). He became a star with his performance as the small-town hustler in *Midnight Cowboy* (1969) and won a Best Actor Academy Award® for *Coming Home* (1978). Always a maverick, he remains a prolific character actor. His daughter is actress **Angelina Jolie**.
Career highs: *Midnight Cowboy* (1969), *The Revolutionary* (1970), *Deliverance* (1972), *Coming Home* (1978), *Runaway Train* (1985)
Career lows: *Lookin' to Get Out* (1982), *Anaconda* (1997)

Volonté, Gian Maria (1933–94)

Italian, born in Milan. He studied at the Accademia Nazionale di Arte Drammatica, and made his film debut in *La Ragazza con la valigia* (1960). He became known to international audiences as villainous characters in the spaghetti westerns of the 1960s. Later, he tackled a more demanding range of serious dramatic roles that reflected his own left-wing views and interest in issues of social justice.
Career highs: *Investigation of a Citizen Above Suspicion* (1970), *Sacco and Vanzetti* (1971), *Lucky Luciano* (1973), *Christ Stopped at Eboli* (1979), *Open Doors* (1990)

Von Sydow, Max Carl Adolf (1929–)

Swedish, born in Lund. He studied at the Royal Academy in Stockholm, and made his film debut in *Only a Mother* (1949). Tall, lean and gaunt, he became a favourite of **Ingmar Bergman**, eloquently expressing the troubled inner lives of his guilt-ridden characters. He embarked on an international career after his portrayal of Christ in *The Greatest Story Ever Told* (1965). He has also directed.
Career highs: *The Seventh Seal* (1957), *The Shame* (1968), *The Emigrants* (1971), *The Exorcist* (1973), *Pelle the Conqueror* (1988)
Career low: *Hurricane* (1979)

W

Wagner, Robert John (1930–)

American, born in Detroit, Michigan. Raised in Los Angeles, he was discovered by a talent scout and made his film debut in *The Happy Years* (1950). His matinee-idol good looks made him a popular young star in the 1950s, but his greatest success was in television. Widowed by the drowning of wife **Natalie Wood** in 1981, he later married actress Jill St John.
Career highs: *With a Song in My Heart* (1952), *A Kiss Before Dying* (1956), *The Mountain* (1956), *Winning* (1969)
Career lows: *All the Fine Young Cannibals* (1960)

Wahlberg, Mark Robert Michael (1971–)

American, born in Dorchester, Massachusetts. The youngest of nine children, he drifted into a life of petty crime and delinquency, serving a brief jail sentence, before finding success as a bad-boy rapper (known as Marky Mark) and becoming an underwear model for Calvin Klein. He made his film debut in *Renaissance Man* (1994), and silenced his critics with an accomplished performance as a porn star in *Boogie Nights* (1997).
Career highs: *Boogie Nights* (1997), *Three Kings* (1999), *I Heart Huckabees* (2004)
Career lows: *Planet of the Apes* (2001), *The Truth About Charlie* (2002)

Walbrook, Anton (Adolf Anton Wilhelm Wohlbrück) (1896–1967)

Austrian, born in Vienna. Born into a family of circus clowns, he worked extensively in the theatre, and is believed to have made his film debut in *Marionetten* (1918). A matinee idol in 1930s Europe, he moved to Britain in 1937, lending soulful style and elegant charm to a range of roles.
Career highs: *Maskerade* (1934), *Gaslight* (1940), *The Red Shoes* (1948), *La Ronde* (1950), *Lola Montès* (1955)
Career low: *The Man from Morocco* (1944)

Walken, Christopher (Ronald Walken) (1943–)

American, born in Queens, New York City. A child performer in television soap operas, he performed on Broadway before making his film debut in *Me and My Brother* (1968). An intense, charismatic all-rounder, he is best known for the chilling menace of his villainous roles and is also an accomplished dancer. He won a Best Supporting Actor Academy Award® for *The Deer Hunter* (1978).
Career highs: *The Deer Hunter* (1978), *Pennies from Heaven* (1981), *At Close Range* (1986), *Pulp Fiction* (1994), *Catch Me If You Can* (2002)
Career low: *The Country Bears* (2002)

Wallach, Eli (1915–)

American, born in Brooklyn, New York City. He made his Broadway debut in 1945, and his film debut in *Baby Doll* (1956). He brought a menacing, rasping intensity to villainous roles in some of the best westerns of the 1960s. He is married to actress Anne Jackson.
Career highs: *Baby Doll* (1956), *The Magnificent Seven* (1960), *The Misfits* (1961), *The Good, the Bad and the Ugly* (1966)
Career low: *How to Save a Marriage and Ruin Your Life* (1968)

Walters, Julie (Julia Mary Walters) (1950–)

English, born in Birmingham. She originally trained to become a nurse before turning to drama. She worked extensively on stage and television, often collaborating with comedian Victoria Wood, before making her film debut in *Educating Rita* (1983). Shunning all Hollywood offers, she has become a beloved character actress in Britain, working across a wide spectrum from broad comedy to heartbreaking pathos on stage, screen and television.

Career highs: *Educating Rita* (1983), *Personal Services* (1987), *Billy Elliot* (2000), *Calendar Girls* (2003)
Career lows: *She'll Be Wearing Pink Pyjamas* (1984), *Car Trouble* (1985), *Killing Dad* (1989)

Washington, Denzel, Jr (1954–   )

American, born in Mount Vernon, New York. The son of a Pentecostal preacher and a beautician, he originally studied medicine and considered becoming a journalist before following an acting career. He appeared off-Broadway and in several television movies before making his film debut in *Carbon Copy* (1981). A handsome, charismatic leading man, he has won Academy Awards® for *Glory* (1989) and *Training Day* (2001).
Career highs: *Cry Freedom* (1987), *Glory* (1989), *Malcolm X* (1992), *The Hurricane* (1999), *Training Day* (2001)
Career lows: *Ricochet* (1991), *Virtuosity* (1995)

Watson, Emily Anita (1967–   )

English, born in Islington, London. The daughter of an architect and an English professor, she studied English literature and worked with the Royal Shakespeare Company before making her film debut in *Breaking the Waves* (1996) as a last-minute replacement for Helena Bonham Carter. As a leading lady, she has been drawn to eccentric, offbeat material.
Career highs: *Breaking the Waves* (1996), *Hilary and Jackie* (1998), *Angela's Ashes* (1999), *Gosford Park* (2001)
Career lows: *Trixie* (2000), *Equilibrium* (2002)

Watts, Naomi (1968–   )

English, born in Shoreham, Sussex. The daughter of Pink Floyd sound engineer Peter Watts, she was raised in Australia. Roles in commercials led to her film debut in *For Love Alone* (1986). She struggled to build a substantial film career, but finally won recognition for her dramatic abilities in *Mulholland Drive* (2001) and received a Best Actress Academy Award® nomination for *21 Grams* (2003).
Career highs: *Mulholland Drive* (2001), *The Ring* (2002), *21 Grams* (2003), *King Kong* (2005)
Career low: *Children of the Corn IV: The Gathering* (1996)

Wayne, John (Marion Morrison) (1907–79)

American, born in Winterset, Iowa. He was raised in California and attended university on a football scholarship. He worked as a prop man and extra in the film industry before his first starring role in *The Big Trail* (1930). Much admired for the decency and integrity he brought to his portrayals of the cowboy, he won a Best Actor Academy Award® for *True Grit* (1969).
Career highs: *Stagecoach* (1939), *Red River* (1948), *The Quiet Man* (1952), *The Searchers* (1956), *True Grit* (1969), *The Shootist* (1976)
Career lows: *The Conqueror* (1956), *The Green Berets* (1968)

> "
> I'd been friendly with John Ford for ten years. He came to me with the script of *Stagecoach* and said, 'Who the hell can play the Ringo Kid?' I said there's only one guy: Lloyd Nolan. Ford said, 'Oh Jesus, can't you play it?'
>
> – John Wayne, *Time* magazine (8 August 1969)
> "

Weaver, Sigourney (Susan Alexandra Weaver) (1949–)

American, born in New York City. She took the name Sigourney from a character in *The Great Gatsby*. After studying at Stanford University and Yale School of Drama, she worked in the theatre and in a television soap opera before making her film debut in *Annie Hall* (1977). Tall, elegant and intelligent, she won her greatest popularity as Ripley in the *Alien* series, but has played a wide range of comic and dramatic parts.
Career highs: *Aliens* (1986), *Gorillas in the Mist* (1988), *Working Girl* (1988), *The Ice Storm* (1997), *A Map of the World* (1999)
Career low: *Company Man* (2000)

Webb, Clifton (Webb Parmalee Hollenbeck) (1889–1966)

American, born in Indianapolis, Indiana. He was a child performer, and became a successful leading man in Broadway musical comedies before making his film debut in *Polly with a Past* (1920). He was primarily a theatre performer until his waspish performance as gossip columnist Waldo Lydecker in *Laura* (1944) led to a Hollywood career of playing misanthropic roles in sentimental comedies.
Career highs: *Laura* (1944), *Sitting Pretty* (1948), *Cheaper by the Dozen* (1950), *Dreamboat* (1952), *Three Coins in a Fountain* (1954)
Career low: *Mr Belvedere Goes to College* (1949)

Weissmuller, Johnny (Peter John Weissmuller) (1904–84)

American, born in Freidorf, Romania. After emigrating to the USA, he claimed to have been born in Windber, Pennsylvania so that he could represent America in the Olympics, where he won five gold medals for swimming during the 1920s. He made his film debut in *Glorifying the American Girl* (1929). His brawny physique, athleticism and trademark yodel made him the definitive screen Tarzan in a dozen films from 1932 to 1948.
Career highs: *Tarzan the Ape Man* (1932), *Tarzan and His Mate* (1934), *Tarzan Escapes* (1936)
Career low: *Cannibal Attack* (1954), *Jungle Moon Men* (1955), *Devil Goddess* (1955)

Weisz, Rachel (1971–)

English, born in London. She was a teenage model before studying English at Cambridge University. She formed the student theatre company Talking Tongues, and subsequently worked on stage and television before making her film debut in

Death Machine (1995). The blockbuster success of *The Mummy* (1999) earned her an international career.
Career highs: *The Mummy* (1999), *The Shape of Things* (2003), *The Constant Gardener* (2005)
Career low: *Chain Reaction* (1996)

Welch, Raquel (Raquel Tejada) (1940–)

American, born in Chicago, Illinois. The daughter of a Bolivian-born engineer, she was a teenage beauty queen and pin-up before embarking on a film career with a bit-part in *A House is Not a Home* (1964). A leading sex symbol of the 1960s, her film career faded after a decade, but she has maintained her celebrity on stage, television and in cabaret.
Career highs: *One Million Years BC* (1966), *Fantastic Voyage* (1966), *The Three Musketeers* (1973)
Career low: *Myra Breckinridge* (1970)

Weld, Tuesday (Susan Ker Weld) (1943–)

American, born in New York City. A child model, she became the family breadwinner and made her official film debut in *Rock Rock Rock* (1956). Initially an unremarkable sex-kitten starlet, she soon revealed real potential and matured into a formidable dramatic actress. Wary of stardom, she rejected such high-profile films as *Lolita* (1962) and *Bonnie And Clyde* (1967). Her second husband was actor and comedian Dudley Moore.
Career highs: *The Cincinnati Kid* (1965), *Lord Love a Duck* (1996), *Pretty Poison* (1968), *I Walk the Line* (1970), *Looking for Mr Goodbar* (1977)
Career low: *Sex Kittens Go to College* (1960)

Welles, Orson (1915–85)

American, born in Kenosha, Wisconsin. A child prodigy, he performed with the Gate Theatre in Dublin, stunned Broadway with his innovative theatre productions and shocked America with his radio adaptation of *The War of the Worlds* (1938). His official cinema debut *Citizen Kane* (1941) is frequently chosen as the greatest film ever made. He spent his career battling for authorial independence and proper financing, but left a rich legacy of daring filmmaking and larger-than-life performances.
Career highs (actor): *Citizen Kane* (1941), *The Third Man* (1949), *Othello* (1952), *Touch of Evil* (1958), *Compulsion* (1959)
Career highs (director): *Citizen Kane* (1941), *The Magnificent Ambersons* (1942), *The Lady from Shanghai* (1948), *Othello* (1952), *Touch of Evil* (1958)
Career lows: *Trouble in the Glen* (1954), *Where Is Parsifal?* (1983)

West, Mae (1892–1980)

American, born in Brooklyn, New York City. The daughter of a heavyweight boxer, she was steeped in show business, and worked in vaudeville as 'The Baby Vamp'. Notorious for her risqué stage shows during the 1920s, she made her film debut in *Night After Night* (1932). She was famed for her cheerful vulgarity and inventive way with innuendo, and was the scourge of 1930s moralists. She made only two appearances on film after 1943.

Career highs: *She Done Him Wrong* (1933), *I'm No Angel* (1933), *Klondike Annie* (1936), *My Little Chickadee* (1940)

Career low: *Sextette* (1978)

Not Just a Pretty Face

As well as performing, Mae West was a director, playwright and novelist. Her first play, *Sex* (1926), was considered so shocking that it led to her imprisonment on obscenity charges; she followed it with *The Drag* (1927), a play about homosexuals which was banned from Broadway but found a receptive audience in nearby Paterson, New Jersey. *Diamond Lil* (1928) finally brought her Broadway success, and West went on to write a number of other plays and novels whose unflinching treatment of challenging social and sexual themes have kept them in print to this day.

White, Pearl Fay (1889–1938)

American, born in Green Ridge, Missouri. A farmer's daughter, she acted from the age of six, performing with touring theatre companies and with a circus. She made her film debut in *The Life of Buffalo Bill* (1910). *The Perils of Pauline* (1914) established her as the queen of daredevil adventure in cliffhanging serials for which she often performed her own stunts. She retired to Paris in 1924.

Career highs: *The Perils of Pauline* (1914), *The Exploits of Elaine* (1915), *The Fatal Ring* (1917), *The Lightning Raider* (1918)

Widmark, Richard (1914–)

American, born in Sunrise, Minnesota. The son of a travelling salesman, he studied at Lake Forest College before heading to New York and building a career in radio dramas. He made an electrifying film debut as the giggling psychopath Tommy Udo in *Kiss of Death* (1947), and was typecast as a villain until he sought a wider range. An undervalued all-rounder, he excelled in noir thrillers and westerns.

Career highs: *Kiss of Death* (1947), *Panic in the Streets* (1950), *No Way Out* (1950), *Madigan* (1968), *When the Legends Die* (1972)

Career lows: *Saint Joan* (1957), *The Tunnel of Love* (1958)

Wilde, Cornel(ius) (1915–89)

American, born in New York City. The son of a Hungarian immigrant, he intended to become a surgeon. Amateur drama led to a professional career and a contract with Warner Brothers where he made his film debut in *The Lady with Red Hair* (1940). The handsome star of swashbuckling tales and exotic adventure yarns, he later became an accomplished director.

Career highs: *A Song to Remember* (1945), *The Big Combo* (1955), *The Naked Prey* (1966), *Beach Red* (1967).

Career lows: *Saadia* (1953), *Hot Blood* (1956).

Wilder, Gene (Jerome Silberman) (1933–)

American, born in Milwaukee, Wisconsin. He studied at the University of Iowa and served in the US Army before deciding on an acting career. A number of distinguished Broadway roles followed before he made his film debut in *Bonnie and Clyde* (1967). A manic comedy performer, he has frequently collaborated with **Mel Brooks** and **Richard Pryor**, and has also written and directed.
Career highs: *The Producers* (1968), *Willy Wonka and the Chocolate Factory* (1971), *Blazing Saddles* (1974), *Young Frankenstein* (1974), *Silver Streak* (1976)
Career lows: *Rhinoceros* (1974), *Another You* (1991)

Williams, Esther Jane (1922–)

American, born in Los Angeles, California. She worked in a department store before her record-breaking prowess in the swimming pool brought her national attention. She was signed by an MGM talent scout, and made her film debut in *Andy Hardy's Double Life* (1942). She became a star of spectacular aqua-musical entertainments based around her swimming skills.
Career highs: *Bathing Beauty* (1944), *Take Me Out to the Ball Game* (1948), *Million Dollar Mermaid* (1952), *Dangerous When Wet* (1953).
Career low: *The Hoodlum Saint* (1946)

Williams, Robin (1951–)

American, born in Chicago, Illinois. A political science major at Claremont Men's College, he also studied acting at the Juilliard School. His success as a manic, freewheeling stand-up comic led to television roles, notably the series *Mork and Mindy* (1978–81). He made his film debut in *Popeye* (1980) and built a career in iconoclastic comedy roles before tackling more dramatic material. He won a Best Supporting Actor Academy Award® for *Good Will Hunting* (1997).
Career highs: *Good Morning, Vietnam* (1987), *Dead Poets Society* (1989), *The Fisher King* (1991), *Mrs Doubtfire* (1993), *Good Will Hunting* (1997)
Career lows: *Hook* (1991), *Jack* (1996), *Fathers' Day* (1997)

Willis, (Walter) Bruce (1955–)

American, born in Idar-Oberstein, Germany. Raised in New Jersey, he worked as a security guard and played in a blues band before studying drama at Montclair State College. He worked on Broadway and made his film debut in *The First Deadly Sin* (1980). Television success in *Moonlighting* (1985–9) led to a film career as an implacable action hero and wry comedian. He was previously married to **Demi Moore**.
Career highs: *Die Hard* (1988), *Pulp Fiction* (1994), *Nobody's Fool* (1994), *The Sixth Sense* (1999)
Career lows: *Bonfire of the Vanities* (1990), *Hudson Hawk* (1991), *Breakfast of Champions* (1999), *The Whole Ten Yards* (2004)

Wilson, Owen Cunningham (1968–)

American, born in Dallas, Texas. A troublemaker in his youth, he was expelled from St Mark's Academy and never completed his degree at the University of Texas in Austin. He did meet director **Wes Anderson** there, and collaborated with him on

the screenplay of *Bottle Rocket* (1996), which also became his screen debut. A wry, laid-back charmer with a prominent broken nose, he has attained modest success in comedy roles.
Career highs: *Shanghai Noon* (2000), *The Royal Tenenbaums* (2001), *The Wedding Crashers* (2005)
Career lows: *The Haunting* (1999), *Behind Enemy Lines* (2001), *I Spy* (2002)

Winger, (Mary) Debra (1955–)

American, born in Cleveland, Ohio. She worked as a waitress and at a kibbutz in Israel before commercials and small television roles led to her film debut in *Slumber Party '57* (1977). A smouldering, uncompromising star in the 1980s, she took a lengthy sabbatical in the 1990s, returning in *Big Bad Love* (2002).
Career highs: *Urban Cowboy* (1980), *An Officer and a Gentleman* (1982), *Terms of Endearment* (1983), *Black Widow* (1987), *Shadowlands* (1993)
Career low: *Everybody Wins* (1990)

Winslet, Kate Elizabeth (1975–)

English, born in Reading, Berkshire. Part of an acting family, she made her professional debut aged eleven, dancing in a cereal commercial. She worked on stage and television before making her film debut in *Heavenly Creatures* (1994). Her role in *Titanic* (1997) made her an international star, but she has continued to seek out challenging roles rather than confine herself to blockbusters. Her second husband is director **Sam Mendes**.
Career highs: *Heavenly Creatures* (1994), *Sense and Sensibility* (1995), *Titanic* (1997), *Iris* (2001), *Eternal Sunshine of the Spotless Mind* (2004)

Winstone, Ray (1957–)

English, born in Hackney, London. An amateur boxer in his youth, he studied acting at the Corona School and worked in television before making his film debut in *Scum* (1979). Initially often cast in violent, aggressive roles, his film career gained momentum in the late 1990s, leading to diverse roles in a number of international productions.
Career highs: *Scum* (1979), *Nil by Mouth* (1997), *The War Zone* (1999), *Sexy Beast* (2000)
Career lows: *Darkness Falls* (1998), *Love, Honour and Obey* (2000)

Winters, Shelley (Shirley Schrift) (1920–2006)

American, born in East St Louis, Illinois. Theatre work led to her film debut in *What A Woman!* (1943), and to a prolific, enduring career as a character actress. She won Best Supporting Actress Academy Awards® for *The Diary of Anne Frank* (1959) and *A Patch of Blue* (1965).
Career highs: *A Place in the Sun* (1951), *The Diary of Anne Frank* (1959), *Lolita* (1962), *A Patch of Blue* (1965), *The Poseidon Adventure* (1972)
Career lows: *Fanny Hill* (1983), *Ellie* (1984), *Déjà Vu* (1985)

Wisdom, Sir Norman (1915–)

English, born in London. Raised in an orphanage, he joined the army, where he discovered his talent to entertain. After working as a stand-up comic, he made his film debut in *A Date with a Dream* (1948). The success of *Trouble in Store* (1953) began a 15-year run as a top British box-office attraction in a series of sentimental, slapstick vehicles in which he played the amiable underdog.
Career highs: *Trouble in Store* (1953), *One Good Turn* (1954), *Man of the Moment* (1955), *The Night They Raided Minsky's* (1968)
Career low: *What's Good for the Goose* (1969)

Withers, Googie (Georgette Lizette Withers) (1917–)

English, born in Karachi, Pakistan. A child performer, she was a professional dancer from the age of twelve, working in London musicals and revues before making her film debut in *The Girl in the Crowd* (1934). Popular in the 1940s as wicked ladies in British melodramas, she later starred in the television series *Within These Walls* (1974–5). She has been married to actor John McCallum since 1948, and still appears on the stage.
Career highs: *Pink String and Sealing Wax* (1945), *It Always Rains on Sunday* (1947), *Night and the City* (1950), *Country Life* (1994), *Shine* (1996)
Career lows: *Once Upon a Dream* (1948), *Traveller's Joy* (1949)

Witherspoon, (Laura Jean) Reese (1976–)

American, born in Baton Rouge, Louisiana. She was raised in Germany and Nashville, Tennessee, and was a child model before making her film debut in *The Man in the Moon* (1991). A rising star in the 1990s, she was catapulted into the A-list by her perky comic performance in *Legally Blonde* (2001). She is married to **Ryan Phillippe**.
Career highs: *Freeway* (1996), *Election* (1999), *Legally Blonde* (2001), *Walk the Line* (2005)
Career low: *Legally Blonde 2: Red, White and Blonde* (2003)

Wong, Anna May (Wong Liu Tsong) (1905–61)

American, born in Los Angeles, California. A pupil at Hollywood High School, she was a photographer's model as a teenager and is believed to have made her film debut in *The Red Lantern* (1919). The success of *The Toll of the Sea* (1922) helped establish her as cinema's first major Chinese-American star, but her ambitions were constantly thwarted by the stereotypical roles offered by Hollywood. She later found starring roles on television, and was making a comeback in supporting roles at the time of her death.
Career highs: *The Toll of the Sea* (1922), *The Thief of Bagdad* (1924), *Piccadilly* (1929), *Shanghai Express* (1932), *Daughter of Shanghai* (1937)
Career low: *Lady From Chungking* (1942).

Wood, Elijah Jordan (1981–)

American, born in Cedar Rapids, Iowa. As a child performer he appeared in commercials and on television before making his film debut in *Back to the Future Part II* (1989). He weathered the transition to adult roles, and has found his greatest

success to date playing Frodo Baggins in the *Lord of the Rings* trilogy of films. He has subsequently sought tougher, more dramatically demanding roles.
Career highs: *Avalon* (1990), *The Good Son* (1993), *The Ice Storm* (1997), *The Lord of the Rings: The Fellowship of the Ring* (2001) et seq
Career lows: *North* (1994), *Green Street* (2005)

Wood, Natalie (Natasha Gurdin) (1938–81)

American, born in San Francisco, California. As a child performer she made her film debut in *Happy Land* (1943). She made a successful transition to adult roles, becoming a vivacious, committed leading lady of the 1960s, but lacked the depth of talent to match her ambitions. She was twice married to actor **Robert Wagner**, and drowned off Catalina Island in mysterious circumstances.
Career highs: *Miracle on 34th Street* (1947), *Rebel Without a Cause* (1955), *Splendor in the Grass* (1961), *Love with the Proper Stranger* (1963)
Career lows: *Penelope* (1966), *Peeper* (1975), *Meteor* (1979), *The Last Married Couple in America* (1980)

Woods, James Howard (1947–)

American, born in Vernal, Utah. A keen amateur actor, he found work on Broadway before making his film debut in *The Visitors* (1972). He is an electric, versatile character actor, the searing intensity of whose work can easily steal the limelight in a film; he has produced a gallery of memorable performances.
Career highs: *The Onion Field* (1979), *Once Upon a Time in America* (1984), *Salvador* (1986), *Ghosts of Mississippi* (1996).
Career low: *The Boost* (1988)

Woodward, Joanne Gignilliat Trimmier (1930–)

American, born in Thomasville, Georgia. A graduate of Louisiana State University, she later moved to New York and studied at the Actors Studio. She made her film debut in *Count Three and Pray* (1955) and won a Best Actress Academy Award® for *The Three Faces Of Eve* (1957). Her film career has been uneven, and some of her best work has been on television. She has been married to actor **Paul Newman** since 1958.
Career highs: *The Three Faces of Eve* (1957), *The Stripper* (1963), *A Fine Madness* (1966), *Rachel Rachel* (1968), *Summer Wishes, Winter Dreams* (1973)
Career low: *Signpost to Murder* (1964)

Wray, (Vina) Fay (1907–2004)

Canadian, born in Cardston, Alberta. Raised in Los Angeles, she became an actress as a teenager, appearing in short comedies like *Gasoline Love* (1923). Her popularity grew during the late 1920s, and she eventually achieved lasting fame as the screaming beauty who attracted the beast that was *King Kong* (1933). She retired from the cinema in 1958, but continued to act occasionally on stage and television.
Career highs: *The Wedding March* (1928), *The Most Dangerous Game* (1932), *King Kong* (1933), *The Mystery of the Wax Museum* (1933)
Career low: *Dragstrip Riot* (1958)

Wright, (Muriel) Teresa (1918–2005)

American, born in New York City. Always intent on becoming an actress, she worked at the Wharf Theatre before making her Broadway debut in 1938. She made her film debut in *The Little Foxes* (1941) and quickly established herself as an acute interpreter of sensitive young women, winning a Best Supporting Actress Academy Award® for *Mrs Miniver* (1942). The cinema never made the most of her talent, although she remained a respected character actress.
Career highs: *The Pride of the Yankees* (1941), *Mrs Miniver* (1942), *Shadow of a Doubt* (1943), *The Best Years of Our Lives* (1946), *The Men* (1950)
Career lows: *The Imperfect Lady* (1947), *The Restless Years* (1958)

Wyman, Jane (Sarah Jane Fulks) (1914–)

American, born in St Joseph, Missouri. Trained as a dancer and supported by an ambitious mother, she became a singer and a bit-part player in the movies from 1932. A hardworking starlet, she eventually secured more demanding roles, winning a Best Actress Academy Award® for *Johnny Belinda* (1948). Famed for the 'Wyman weepies' of the 1950s, she later starred in the television series *Falcon Crest* (1981–90). Actor and future US President **Ronald Reagan** was the second of her four husbands.
Career highs: *The Yearling* (1946), *Johnny Belinda* (1948), *The Blue Veil* (1951), *Magnificent Obsession* (1954), *All That Heaven Allows* (1955)
Career lows: *The Lady Takes a Sailor* (1949), *How to Commit Marriage* (1969)

> *Take a Deep Breath ...*
>
> Jane Wyman and her co-star Regis Toomey shared the longest ever screen kiss in a commercial feature film – their record-breaking clinch in *You're in the Army Now* (1941) lasts for three minutes and five seconds.

Y

Yeoh, Michelle (Yeoh Chu-Kheng) (1962–)

Malaysian, born in Ipoh. As a teenager she moved to London to study at the Royal Academy of Dance; she later won the Miss Malaysia beauty pageant before an appearance in a television commercial with **Jackie Chan** kick-started her film career. A graceful fighter with a charismatic screen presence, she quickly developed into one of Asia's most popular martial arts stars, but is best known to western audiences for *Tomorrow Never Dies* (1997) and *Crouching Tiger, Hidden Dragon* (2000).
Career highs: *Police Story 3: Super Cop* (1992), *The Soong Sisters* (1997), *Crouching Tiger, Hidden Dragon* (2000)

York, Michael (Michael York-Johnson) (1942–)

English, born in Fulmer, Buckinghamshire. A member of the National Youth Theatre, he also performed with the Oxford University Dramatic Society and worked at the National Theatre before making his film debut in *The Taming of the Shrew* (1967).

A dashing, fair-haired leading man, his best roles came early in his career, but he remains a youthful and prolific performer.
Career highs: *Accident* (1967), *Cabaret* (1972), *The Three Musketeers* (1973), *Logan's Run* (1976)
Career lows: *Lost Horizon* (1973), *Seven Nights in Japan* (1976)

York, Susannah (Susannah Yolande Fletcher) (1941–)

English, born in London. A student at the Royal Academy of Dramatic Art, she worked in the theatre before making her film debut as a teenager in *Tunes of Glory* (1960). Blonde, blue-eyed and intelligent, she became an international star in the 1960s, securing an Academy Award[®] nomination for *They Shoot Horses, Don't They?* (1969). Her film career faded in the 1980s, and she is now primarily a theatre performer.
Career highs: *Tunes of Glory* (1960), *The Greengage Summer* (1961), *The Killing of Sister George* (1968), *They Shoot Horses, Don't They?* (1969)
Career lows: *The Awakening* (1980), *Prettykill* (1987)

Young, Loretta (Gretchen Michaela Young) (1913–2000)

American, born in Salt Lake City, Utah. A child performer, she is believed to have made her film debut in *The Only Way* (1917). She continued to appear as an extra during the silent era but soon rose to become a leading lady in the 1930s, exuding a wholesome beauty and elegance. She won a Best Actress Academy Award[®] for *The Farmer's Daughter* (1947). She made her last film in 1953, but continued to appear on television.
Career highs: *Taxi* (1932), *Zoo in Budapest* (1933), *Man's Castle* (1933), *The Stranger* (1946), *The Farmer's Daughter* (1947)
Career lows: *Ramona* (1936), *China* (1943)

Young, Robert George (1907–98)

American, born in Chicago, Illinois. He was a reporter and salesman before making the leap from amateur theatricals to professional performing. He made his film debut in *The Black Camel* (1931) and proved an affable, dependable leading man. He battled with alcoholism, and retired from the screen after *Secret of the Incas* (1954), but enjoyed enormous success in the long-running television series *Father Knows Best* and *Marcus Welby, M.D.*
Career highs: *H.M. Pulham Esq.* (1941), *Claudia* (1943), *The Enchanted Cottage* (1945), *They Won't Believe Me* (1947), *Crossfire* (1947)
Career lows: *Cairo* (1942), *The Half-Breed* (1952)

Z

Zellweger, Renée Kathleen (1969–)

American, born in Katy, Texas. She worked in television before making her film debut with a brief appearance in *Dazed and Confused* (1993). Her performance in *Jerry Maguire* (1996) endeared her to audiences and led to starring roles. She won a Best Supporting Actress Academy Award[®] for *Cold Mountain* (2003).

Career highs: *Jerry Maguire* (1996), *Nurse Betty* (2000), *Bridget Jones' Diary* (2001), *Chicago* (2002), *Cold Mountain* (2003)
Career lows: *Texas Chainsaw Massacre: The Next Generation* (1994)

Renée Undercover

In order to prepare for her role in *Bridget Jones' Diary* (2001), Renée Zellweger spent several weeks working as an office intern at a well-known London publishing company. Her unsuspecting colleagues (who knew her as 'Bridget Cavendish') noticed that their new work experience girl bore a strong resemblance to a certain Hollywood actress, but still accepted her as genuine and tried to help her with tips on breaking into the book business. One of them later told a newspaper, 'I did wonder why she'd stuck a small picture of Jim Carrey on the side of her computer, but didn't really dwell on it.' (*The Daily Telegraph*, 26 March 2001)

Zeta-Jones, Catherine (1969–)

Welsh, born in Swansea. She performed in amateur productions and appeared in several musicals before making her film debut in *Les 1001 nuits* (1990). Continually improving, she carved out a career in Hollywood and won a Best Supporting Actress Academy Award® for *Chicago* (2002). She is married to **Michael Douglas**.
Career highs: *The Mask of Zorro* (1998), *Traffic* (2000), *Chicago* (2002)
Career lows: *Splitting Heirs* (1993), *The Haunting* (1999)

Zetterling, Mai Elizabeth (1925–94)

Swedish, born in Västerås. Always intent on becoming an actress, she made her professional stage debut as a teenager and her film debut in *Lasse-Maja* (1941). She appeared in international productions from the late 1940s, and later directed documentaries and features that expressed her feminist views and social concerns. She returned to acting towards the end of her life.
Career highs: *Frenzy* (1944), *Frieda* (1947), *Loving Couples* (1964), *Night Games* (1966), *Scrubbers* (1982)
Career lows: *The Lost People* (1949), *The Romantic Age* (1949)

Zhang Ziyi (1979–)

Chinese, born in Beijing. A trained dancer, she studied at Beijing's Central Drama Academy and, after meeting **Zhang Yimou** during an audition for a shampoo commercial, won the leading role in his *The Road Home* (2000). In *Crouching Tiger, Hidden Dragon* (2000) she drew upon her dance skills to compensate for a lack of martial arts training, and she has since appeared in several high-profile Chinese and international films.
Career highs: *The Road Home* (2000), *Crouching Tiger, Hidden Dragon* (2000), *House of Flying Daggers* (2004), *2046* (2004), *Memoirs of a Geisha* (2005)

SOME NOTABLE DIRECTORS

A

Aldrich, Robert (1918–83)

American, born in Cranston, Rhode Island. He started in the film industry as a production clerk at RKO and rose through the ranks to become an assistant director. He made his directorial debut with *The Big Leaguer* (1953), and created a powerful body of work offering muscular explorations of violence, the struggle for survival and the way individual character is revealed under extreme stress.
Career highs: *Kiss Me Deadly* (1955), *Attack!* (1956), *What Ever Happened to Baby Jane?* (1962), *The Flight of the Phoenix* (1965), *The Dirty Dozen* (1967)
Career low: *The Legend of Lylah Clare* (1968)

Allen, Woody (Allen Stewart Konigsberg) (1935–)

American, born in Brooklyn, New York City. A comedy writer turned nightclub performer, he made his film debut in *What's New Pussycat?* (1965). Releasing a new film each year, he has become the quintessential New York film-maker, offering comic insights into love and death, show-business nostalgia and the intricate workings of the human heart. His career was temporarily eclipsed by scandal when he left his off-screen partner **Mia Farrow** for her adopted daughter Soon-Yi Previn, whom he later married.
Career highs: *Annie Hall* (1977), *Manhattan* (1979), *Broadway Danny Rose* (1984), *Hannah and Her Sisters* (1986), *Crimes and Misdemeanors* (1989)
Career lows: *Casino Royale* (1967), *Hollywood Endings* (2002)

Almodóvar, Pedro (Pedro Almodóvar Caballero) (1951–)

Spanish, born in Calzada de Calatrava. A maverick talent, he worked in the theatre before beginning to make short films on Super 8, and graduated to features in 1978. He took full advantage of the post-Franco cultural freedom to develop a distinctive directorial style, and has matured from the 'bad boy' of Spanish cinema into a sophisticated European auteur. He is noted for creating sublime melodramas and writing superb roles for women.
Career highs: *Matador* (1986), *Women on the Verge of a Nervous Breakdown* (1988), *Live Flesh* (1997), *All About My Mother* (1988), *Talk to Her* (2002)
Career low: *High Heels* (1991)

Altman, Robert (1925–)

American, born in Kansas City, Missouri. He directed industrial documentaries before making his feature film debut with *The Delinquents* (1957). Television work during the 1960s led him to a second chance at a feature film career, and he developed a distinctive style involving large ensemble casts, overlapping dialogue and kaleidoscopic narratives. His work frequently explores the unheroic reality of cherished American myths, and questions the validity of the 'American Dream'.
Career highs: *M*A*S*H* (1970), *McCabe and Mrs Miller* (1971), *Nashville* (1975), *The Player* (1992), *Short Cuts* (1993), *Gosford Park* (2001)
Career lows: *Quintet* (1979), *Beyond Therapy* (1987)

Altman's Early Years

Long before beginning his career as a film director, Robert Altman briefly pursued a decidedly less glamorous line of work: dog tattooing. Just after World War II, Altman and an acquaintance established a business tattooing identification numbers onto unfortunate pet dogs, a scheme they hoped would quickly make them rich. Despite being invited to Washington, DC to tattoo President Harry S Truman's dog, they failed to make a success of the business, and eventually went their separate ways. Asked in a 2001 interview whether he regretted giving up dog tattooing for film-making, Altman enigmatically replied, 'Well … they're both about the same.'

Angelopoulos, Theo (1935–)

Greek, born in Athens. He was a law student in Athens and at the Sorbonne, and became a film critic, actor and producer before making his directorial debut with *The Broadcast* (1968). He established his international reputation with the epic *The Travelling Players* (1975), and is known for his meditative, melancholy explorations of landscape, history and the relationship between past events and current politics.
Career highs: *Days of '36* (1972), *The Travelling Players* (1975), *Landscape in the Mist* (1988), *Ulysses' Gaze* (1995), *Eternity and a Day* (1998)

Antonioni, Michelangelo (1912–)

Italian, born in Ferrara. He studied political economy at Bologna University and worked as a film critic before becoming an assistant director in 1942. He made his feature film debut with *Story of a Love Affair* (1950). *L'Avventura* (1960) became his career-defining film, offering a hypnotic exploration of alienation and the impossibility of meaningful communication in the modern world.
Career highs: *L'Avventura* (1960), *The Eclipse* (1962), *The Red Desert* (1964), *Blow-Up* (1966), *The Passenger* (1975)
Career lows: *The Oberwald Mystery* (1979), *Beyond the Clouds* (1995)

Arzner, Dorothy (1900–79)

American, born in San Francisco, California. She studied medicine at the University of Southern California, and was a volunteer ambulance driver during World War I. She began her film career as a script typist, later worked as an editor, and made her directorial debut with *Fashions for Women* (1927). The only major female director working in the Hollywood studio system of her time, she retired in 1943; she later taught film (**Francis Ford Coppola** was one of her students) and made training films and commercials.
Career highs: *Merrily We Go to Hell* (1932), *Christopher Strong* (1933), *Craig's Wife* (1936), *Dance, Girl, Dance* (1940)
Career low: *Nana* (1934)

Ashby, William Hal (1929–88)

American, born in Ogden, Utah. The son of a dairy farmer, he dropped out of university and moved to California, finding employment in the film industry as a clerk. He worked his way up the ladder to become a much-respected editor before

making his directorial debut with *The Landlord* (1970). He was an exceptional director of actors, but his career faded as he battled with alcohol and drug problems.
Career highs: *Harold and Maude* (1970), *The Last Detail* (1973), *Shampoo* (1975), *Bound for Glory* (1976), *Coming Home* (1978)
Career lows: *Second Hand Hearts* (1980), *Eight Million Ways to Die* (1986)

Attenborough, Sir Richard see **Actors**

B

Bergman, (Ernst) Ingmar (1918–)

Swedish, born in Uppsala. The son of a Lutheran clergyman, he studied art history and literature at the University of Stockholm and worked in the theatre before gaining employment in the script department of Svensk Filmindustri. He made his directorial debut with *Crisis* (1945) and became one of the world's most admired directors, noted for his austere explorations of spirituality and suffering. He announced his retirement from film with *Fanny and Alexander* (1982), but continued to work in the theatre and direct for television.
Career highs: *Smiles of a Summer Night* (1955), *Wild Strawberries* (1957), *The Seventh Seal* (1957), *Persona* (1966), *Cries and Whispers* (1972)
Career low: *Now About These Women* (1964)

Berkeley, Busby (William Berkeley Enos) (1895–1976)

American, born in Los Angeles, California. Educated at a military academy, he served in the US Army before working in the theatre. He was hired by producer **Samuel Goldwyn** to devise the musical numbers for the film *Whoopee!* (1930), and stayed in Hollywood to build a career as an innovative choreographer and director. He was noted for his dazzling camerawork and kaleidoscopic routines involving multitudes of chorus girls. Alcoholism and ill health blighted his later career.
Career highs: *Roman Scandals* (as dance director, 1932), *42nd Street* (as choreographer, 1933), *Gold Diggers of 1933* (as dance director, 1933), *Dames* (as dance director, 1934), *Babes in Arms* (1939)
Career low: *Comet over Broadway* (1938)

Bertolucci, Bernardo (1941–)

Italian, born in Parma. An amateur film-maker and poet, he became an assistant to **Pier Paolo Pasolini** before making his directorial debut with *The Grim Reaper* (1962). He is a visual stylist whose films often tackle the tensions between conventionality and rebellion, or explore the relationship between politics, sex and violence. He won a Best Director Academy Award[®] for *The Last Emperor* (1987).
Career highs: *The Spider's Stratagem* (1969), *The Conformist* (1970), *Last Tango in Paris* (1972), *The Last Emperor* (1987)
Career low: *Little Buddha* (1993)

Boetticher, Budd (Oscar Boetticher, Jr) (1916–2001)

American, born in Chicago, Illinois. The son of a hardware retailer, he attended Ohio State University, where he excelled at sport. After moving to Mexico and becoming a professional matador, he worked as a technical adviser on *Blood and Sand* (1941), in which bullfighting featured prominently. He stayed in Hollywood, eventually making his directorial debut with *The Missing Juror* (1944), and went on to direct a number of lean, flinty westerns starring **Randolph Scott** before his disaster-strewn private life led to the ruin of his career.

Career highs: *The Bullfighter and the Lady* (1951), *Seven Men from Now* (1956), *The Tall T* (1957), *Buchanan Rides Alone* (1958)
Career low: *A Time for Dying* (1969)

Bogdanovich, Peter (1939–   )

American, born in Kingston, New York. After studying acting in the 1950s, he worked in the theatre and in journalism before making his directorial debut with *Targets* (1967). *The Last Picture Show* (1971) established him as a leading American director. Following a critical fall from grace in the late 1970s, he was caught up in a high-profile tragedy when his girlfriend, model Dorothy Stratten, was murdered by her jealous husband; the events were dramatized in Bob Fosse's 1983 film *Star 80* (with Roger Rees as Bogdanovich). He continues to direct, and also acts, notably in the television series *The Sopranos*.

Career highs: *Targets* (1967), *The Last Picture Show* (1971), *Paper Moon* (1973), *Saint Jack* (1979), *Mask* (1985)
Career lows: *At Long Last Love* (1985), *Illegally Yours* (1988)

Boorman, John (1933–   )

English, born in Shepperton, Middlesex. He worked as a journalist before moving into television, where he worked as an assistant film editor and eventually began directing documentaries. He made his feature film debut with *Catch Us If You Can* (1965), and went on to build an international career. Heavily influenced by the Arthurian legends, his films show a subtle use of colour and often include mythological resonances or involve some form of quest.

Career highs: *Point Blank* (1967), *Hell in the Pacific* (1968), *Deliverance* (1972), *Excalibur* (1981), *Hope and Glory* (1987)
Career low: *Exorcist II: The Heretic* (1977)

Boyle, Danny (1956–   )

English, born in Bury, Lancashire. He worked extensively in the theatre before moving into television, and made his feature film debut with the thriller *Shallow Grave* (1994). He gained an international reputation with the success of *Trainspotting* (1996).

Career highs: *Shallow Grave* (1994), *Trainspotting* (1996), *28 Days Later* (2002)
Career low: *A Life Less Ordinary* (1997)

Bresson, Robert (1901–99)

French, born in Bromont-Lamothe. Initially a painter, he worked as a scriptwriter before making his directorial debut with *Les Affaires publiques* (1934). A prisoner of war in Germany, he returned to directing with *Les Anges du péché* (1943). His modest but influential body of work is noted for its use of non-professional actors, avoidance of conventional dramatic manipulation and austere focus on suffering, saintliness and redemption.
Career highs: *Diary of a Country Priest* (1950), *A Man Escaped* (1956), *Pickpocket* (1959), *Au Hasard, Balthazar* (1966), *L'Argent* (1983)
Career low: *The Devil, Probably* (1977)

Brooks, Mel (Melvin Kaminsky) (1926–)

American, born in Brooklyn, New York City. A comedy performer, he was one of the writers for the television series *Your Show of Shows*. He made his feature film debut as the writer-director of *The Producers* (1968). In the 1970s, he found his forte as an irrepressible purveyor of freewheeling movie pastiches blending affection and vulgarity. He was married to **Anne Bancroft** from 1964 until her death.
Career highs: *The Producers* (1968), *Blazing Saddles* (1974), *Young Frankenstein* (1974)
Career lows: *Spaceballs* (1987), *Dracula: Dead and Loving It* (1995)

Buñuel, Luis (1900–83)

Spanish, born in Calanda. Educated at Madrid University, he then went to Paris, where he worked as an assistant to director Jean Epstein. His fascination with the Surrealist movement led him to collaborate with Salvador Dalí. His best films use black comedy, sly satire and alarming surrealistic imagery to express his hatred of the Catholic church and his disregard for conventional morality.
Career highs: *Los Olvidados* (1950), *Viridiana* (1961), *Belle de jour* (1967), *Tristana* (1970), *The Discreet Charm of the Bourgeoisie* (1972), *That Obscure Object of Desire* (1977)
Career low: *Susana* (1951)

Burton, Tim (1960–)

American, born in Burbank, California. A teenage cartoonist, he won a Disney fellowship and worked as an animator before directing the shorts *Vincent* (1982) and *Frankenweenie* (1984). He made his feature film debut with *Pee-wee's Big Adventure* (1985). His films are rich in gothic fantasy and ghoulish humour, often displaying a love of the macabre, a strong visual sensibility, and empathy with outsiders and underdogs.
Career highs: *Beetlejuice* (1988), *Batman* (1989), *Edward Scissorhands* (1990), *Ed Wood* (1994)
Career low: *Planet of the Apes* (2001)

C

Cameron, James Francis (1954–)

Canadian, born in Kapuskasing, Ontario. He studied physics at California State University before working for producer **Roger Corman**. He made his directorial debut with *Piranha Part Two: The Spawning* (1981). *The Terminator* (1984) was his first major success, and led to a career defined by science fiction, fantasy, adventure and big-budget spectacle. His 1997 film *Titanic* won a record-equalling eleven Academy Awards®, including Best Director.
Career highs: *The Terminator* (1984), *Aliens* (1986), *Terminator 2: Judgment Day* (1991), *Titanic* (1997)
Career low: *Piranha Part Two: The Spawning* (1981)

Campion, Jane (1954–)

New Zealander, born in Wellington. After graduating from the Australian Film, Television and Radio School in Sydney, she made award-winning short films including *Peel* (1982) and *Passionless Moments* (1983). She made her feature film debut with *Sweetie* (1989). Her work frequently displays an interest in the thin line between rationality and insanity, and examines both the power and the perils of love. She won a Best Original Screenplay Academy Award® for *The Piano* (1993).
Career highs: *Sweetie* (1989), *An Angel at My Table* (1990), *The Piano* (1993), *Portrait of a Lady* (1996)
Career low: *Holy Smoke* (1999)

Capra, Frank (1897–1991)

American, born in Palermo, Italy. Raised in California from the age of six, he studied chemical engineering, taught ballistics and eventually entered the film industry as a prop man and joke-writer. He made his directorial debut with *Fultah Fisher's Boarding House* (1922), and became known for films that celebrated the common man and his search for justice and decency. He won Best Director Academy Awards® for *It Happened One Night* (1934), *Mr Deeds Goes to Town* (1936) and *You Can't Take It with You* (1938).
Career highs: *It Happened One Night* (1934), *Mr Deeds Goes to Town* (1936), *Lost Horizon* (1937), *Mr Smith Goes to Washington* (1939), *It's a Wonderful Life* (1946)
Career low: *A Hole in the Head* (1959)

Carné, Marcel (1909–96)

French, born in Paris. He worked in a bank, a grocery and an insurance company before securing the position of assistant to director Jacques Feyder. He also worked with **René Clair** before directing his own first feature, *Jenny* (1936). In collaboration with writer Jacques Prévert, he made a series of romantic melodramas capturing the fatalistic mood of the years leading up to World War II. His post-war career was markedly less successful.
Career highs: *Drôle de drame* (1937), *Le Quai des brumes* (1938), *Hôtel du Nord* (1938), *Le Jour se lève* (1939), *Les Enfants du paradis* (1945)
Career low: *Les Tricheurs* (1958)

Cassavetes, John (1929–89)

American, born in New York City. A graduate of the New York Academy Of Dramatic Art, he made his film debut in *Fourteen Hours* (1951). Frequently cast as an angry, alienated youth during the 1950s, he made his directorial debut with the experimental cinema-verité feature *Shadows* (1959). His skill as an actor was later eclipsed by his ability as a director of emotionally intense, unflinchingly honest contemporary dramas. He was married to **Gena Rowlands**.

Career highs (actor): *Edge of the City* (1957), *The Dirty Dozen* (1967), *Rosemary's Baby* (1968)

Career highs (director): *Faces* (1968), *Husbands* (1970), *A Woman Under the Influence* (1974)

Career lows: *Incubus* (1981), *Big Trouble* (1985)

Chabrol, Claude (1930–)

French, born in Paris. He studied pharmacy and law before becoming a film critic, and went on to make his directorial debut with *Beau Serge* (1958). Credited as an architect of the Nouvelle Vague movement, he has frequently been compared to **Alfred Hitchcock** in his fondness for depicting murder, suspense and the seething emotions concealed beneath the most respectable of middle-class veneers.

Career highs: *Les Biches* (1968), *La Femme infidèle* (1969), *Le Boucher* (1969), *Violette Nozière* (1977), *Une Affaire de femmes* (1988).

Career lows: *The Twist* (1976), *Dr M* (1989)

Chaplin, Charlie (Sir Charles Spencer Chaplin) see **Actors**

Chen Kaige (Chen Aige) (1952–)

Chinese, born in Beijing. The son of director Chen Huaiai, he worked on a rubber plantation and served in the army before attending the Beijing Film Academy. He made his feature debut with *Yellow Earth* (1984), an innovative film which attracted international attention and won the Best Film award at the Berlin Film Festival. A key member of China's Fifth Generation group of film-makers, he has made occasional forays into English-language cinema, but his reputation rests with his Chinese films.

Career highs: *Yellow Earth* (1984), *The Big Parade* (1986), *Farewell My Concubine* (1993)

Career low: *Killing Me Softly* (2001)

Clair, René (René Lucien Chomette) (1898–1981)

French, born in Paris. A member of the Ambulance Corps during World War I, he was a journalist, poet and actor before making his directorial debut with the comic fantasy *Paris qui dort* (1923). His early sound films have a rare wit, elegance and lightness of touch. He came to Britain in 1935, then spent the war years in Hollywood before returning to France. He retired after *Les Fêtes galantes* (1965), but continued to work in the theatre.

Career highs: *Sous les toits de Paris* (1930), *Le Million* (1931), *À nous la liberté* (1931), *Les Belles de nuit* (1952), *Les Grandes manoeuvres* (1955)

Career low: *Break the News* (1937)

Clouzot, Henri-Georges (1907–77)

French, born in Niort. Educated at a naval school in Brest, he studied law and political science and worked as a journalist before entering the film industry. He was a scriptwriter before making his directorial debut with the thriller *L'Assassin habite au 21* (1942). A master of suspense, his films reveal a pessimistic view of human morality. His later career was affected by ill health.
Career highs: *Le Corbeau* (1943), *Quai des Orfèvres* (1947), *The Wages of Fear* (1953), *Les Diaboliques* (1955)
Career low: *La Prisonnière* (1968)

Coen, Ethan (1957–)

American, born in Minneapolis, Minnesota. The son of academics, he studied at Princeton University and went on to establish his reputation working in collaboration with his brother **Joel Coen**. The brothers made their debut with *Blood Simple* (1984), which Ethan produced and co-wrote. Admired for the innovative style and wit of their films, they have brought their distinctive black humour to hard-boiled crime yarns and screwball comedies, and won a Best Original Screenplay Academy Award® for *Fargo* (1996).
Career highs: *Blood Simple* (1984), *Miller's Crossing* (1990), *Fargo* (1996), *O Brother, Where Art Thou?* (2000)
Career low: *The Ladykillers* (2004)

Coen, Joel (1954–)

American, born in St Louis Park, Minnesota. The son of academics, he studied at Simon's Rock College and at the University of New York, and went on to establish his reputation working in collaboration with his brother **Ethan Coen**. The brothers made their debut with *Blood Simple* (1984). Admired for the innovative style and wit of their films, they have brought their distinctive black humour to hard-boiled crime yarns and screwball comedies, and won a Best Original Screenplay Academy Award® for *Fargo* (1996). Joel is married to **Frances McDormand**.
Career highs: *Blood Simple* (1984), *Miller's Crossing* (1990), *Fargo* (1996), *O Brother, Where Art Thou?* (2000)
Career low: *The Ladykillers* (2004)

Coppola, Francis Ford (1939–)

American, born in Detroit, Michigan. He studied film at the University of California in Los Angeles and worked as a scriptwriter before moving into directing in the early 1960s. One of the great American film-makers of the 1970s, he shared Best Adapted Screenplay Academy Awards® for *Patton* (1970) and *The Godfather* (1972), and won Academy Awards® for Screenplay, Direction and Best Picture for *The Godfather Part II* (1974). His daughter is the director Sofia Coppola.
Career highs: *The Godfather* (1972), *The Conversation* (1974), *The Godfather Part II* (1974), *Apocalypse Now* (1979)
Career lows: *Tonight for Sure* (1961), *Jack* (1996)

You Have to Start Somewhere

Though he is regarded as one of the greatest American film-makers of recent decades, Francis Ford Coppola's first solo effort as a director gave little indication of the talent he would later develop. *Tonight for Sure* (1962), which Coppola also co-wrote, was a soft-core comedy western of the type known as 'nudie-cuties'. Cobbled together using leftover footage from other projects alongside some new scenes, this unpromising debut is – with good reason – rarely seen today.

Costa-Gavras, Constantin (Konstantinos Gavras) (1933–   )

Greek, born in Klivia. The son of a Greek bureaucrat, he was a promising ballet dancer before his father's outspoken political beliefs forced the family to relocate to France. He studied literature and film-making, working as an assistant before making his directorial debut with *The Sleeping Car Murders* (1965). He is a master of the political thriller, illuminating injustice and human rights abuses through compelling individual stories. He shared a Best Adapted Screenplay Academy Award® for *Missing* (1981).
Career highs: *Z* (1969), *The Confession* (1970), *State of Siege* (1973), *Missing* (1982)
Career lows: *Hanna K* (1983), *Mad City* (1997)

Cronenberg, David Paul (1943–   )

Canadian, born in Toronto, Ontario. The son of a musician mother and a father who wrote for pulp fiction magazines, he began directing short, experimental films as a student at the University of Toronto. He made his feature debut with *Shivers* (1974), and has created a body of work that explores man's vulnerability to the forces that lie within the body, whether in the form of disease, mental illness, violence or sexual obsession. He has also acted.
Career highs: *The Brood* (1979), *Videodrome* (1982), *The Fly* (1986), *Dead Ringers* (1988), *A History of Violence* (2005)
Career low: *M. Butterfly* (1993)

Cukor, George D(ewey) (1899–1983)

American, born in New York City. Originally a man of the theatre, he moved to Hollywood as a dialogue director and made his solo directorial debut with *Tarnished Lady* (1931). Drawn to screen adaptations of classic novels and plays, he was noted for his sensitive handling of major stars and for his ten-film partnership with **Katharine Hepburn**. He won a Best Director Academy Award® for *My Fair Lady* (1964).
Career highs: *Camille* (1936), *The Women* (1939), *The Philadelphia Story* (1940), *A Star Is Born* (1954), *My Fair Lady* (1964)
Career low: *Rich and Famous* (1981)

Curtiz, Michael (Mihaly Kertész) (1888–1962)

Hungarian, born in Budapest. Originally a stage actor, he directed the first Hungarian feature film, *The Last Bohemian* (1912). He worked throughout Europe before making his Hollywood debut with *The Third Degree* (1926). Under contract to Warner Brothers for 20 years, he brought a sense of crisp narrative drive, pace

and professionalism to every conceivable genre. He won a Best Director Academy Award® for *Casablanca* (1942).
Career highs: *The Adventures of Robin Hood* (1938), *The Sea Hawk* (1940), *Casablanca* (1942), *Yankee Doodle Dandy* (1942), *Mildred Pierce* (1945)
Career lows: *The Scarlet Hour* (1956), *The Vagabond King* (1956)

D

Davies, Terence (1945–   )

English, born in Liverpool. He initially worked as an actor and novelist before joining the National Film School, where he made an extraordinary trio of short films that lyrically reflected the agony and the ecstasy of his life as a gay man and a Catholic. His best films have included fragments of autobiography, and he has also proved a sensitive director of literary adaptations.
Career highs: *The Terence Davies Trilogy* (1983), *Distant Voices, Still Lives* (1988), *The Long Day Closes* (1992), *The House of Mirth* (2000)

De Mille, Cecil B(lount) (1881–1959)

American, born in Ashfield, Massachusetts. The son of an Episcopalian minister, he attended the Pennsylvania Military Academy and worked as an actor, stage manager and playwright before making his directorial debut with the first of his two versions of *The Squaw Man* (1914). He was an extravagant showman with a penchant for lavish, action-packed spectaculars, their plots often culled from the Bible.
Career highs: *Male and Female* (1919), *King of Kings* (1927), *Reap the Wild Wind* (1942), *The Greatest Show on Earth* (1952), *The Ten Commandments* (1956)
Career lows: *The Squaw Man* (1931), *The Story of Dr Wassell* (1944)

Demme, Jonathan (1944–   )

American, born in Baldwin, New York. He initially studied to become a veterinarian and briefly served in the US Air Force before working in the publicity department of Embassy Pictures. He then went to work for **Roger Corman**, making his directorial debut with *Caged Heat* (1974). He graduated from exploitation fare to more prestigious ventures, winning a Best Director Academy Award® for *The Silence of the Lambs* (1991).
Career highs: *Citizens Band* (1977), *Melvin and Howard* (1980), *Stop Making Sense* (1984), *Something Wild* (1986), *The Silence of the Lambs* (1991)
Career lows: *Beloved* (1998), *The Truth about Charlie* (2002)

Demy, Jacques (1931–90)

French, born in Pontchâteau. He studied art and film, and made several short films before directing the feature *Lola* (1960). He gained international attention with *The Umbrellas of Cherbourg* (1964) and was subsequently noted for his charming, whimsical musicals and light, frivolous comedies. He was married to fellow film-maker Agnes Varda from 1962 until his death.

Career highs: *Lola* (1960), *Bay of the Angels* (1962), *The Umbrellas of Cherbourg* (1964), *The Magic Donkey* (1970)
Career low: *Model Shop* (1969)

De Sica, Vittorio (1902–74)

Italian, born in Sora. He studied accountancy at Rome University before becoming an actor and making his film debut in *Il Processo Clémenceau* (1918). A matinée idol in the 1930s, he made his directorial debut with *Rose Scarletti* (1940) and became an influential figure in the neo-realist movement. His later films are less distinguished, and he also returned to acting as an avuncular, scene-stealing presence in character parts.
Career highs: *Shoeshine* (1946), *Bicycle Thieves* (1948), *Miracle in Milan* (1950), *Umberto D* (1952), *Two Women* (1961)
Career lows: *A Place for Lovers* (1969), *The Voyage* (1974)

Disney, Walt see **Producers**

Donen, Stanley (1924–   )

American, born in Columbia, South Carolina. Trained as a dancer, he made his mark as a performer on the Broadway stage before being hired by MGM as a dance director. He co-directed *On the Town* (1949) with Gene Kelly before directing a succession of memorable musicals and polished light entertainments. He has not directed for the cinema since *Blame It on Rio* (1984).
Career highs: *On the Town* (1949), *Singin' in the Rain* (1952), *Seven Brides for Seven Brothers* (1954), *Funny Face* (1956), *Charade* (1963)
Career lows: *Staircase* (1969), *Saturn 3* (1980)

Douglas, Bill (1934–91)

Scottish, born in Newcraighall near Edinburgh. The illegitimate son of a miner, he endured a childhood of grinding misery and penury that would form the basis of his famed autobiographical trilogy. He completed his National Service and worked as an actor before directing short films that led to *My Childhood* (1972). He was an uncompromising perfectionist whose best films are austere, rigorously unsentimental and bleakly poetic.
Career highs: *My Childhood* (1972), *My Ain Folk* (1973), *My Way Home* (1977), *Comrades* (1986)

Dreyer, Carl Theodor (1889–1968)

Danish, born in Copenhagen. Raised in a strict Lutheran family, he was a reporter before entering the film industry as a scriptwriter. He made his directorial debut with *The President* (1919). Fascinated by spiritual themes and the influence of guilt and evil on the human soul, he was also an exacting perfectionist and a technical pioneer in his editing, composition and use of close-ups.
Career highs: *The Parson's Widow* (1920), *The Passion of Joan of Arc* (1928), *Vampyr* (1932), *Day of Wrath* (1943), *Ordet* (1955)

Dwan, Allan (Joseph Aloysius Dwan) (1885–1981)

Canadian, born in Toronto, Ontario. He studied at Notre Dame University, intending to become an electrical engineer. His expertise with lighting brought him into the film industry, where he made his directorial debut with *Branding a Bad Man* (1911). A true pioneer, he made more than 300 films in his 50-year career, working in every genre from adventure classics to B-movie westerns.

Career highs: *Robin Hood* (1922), *Suez* (1938), *The Three Musketeers* (1939), *Sands of Iwo Jima* (1949), *Silver Lode* (1954)

Career lows: *Enchanted Island* (1958), *The Most Dangerous Man Alive* (1961)

E

Eastwood, Clint see **Actors**

Edwards, Blake (William Blake McEdwards) (1922–   )

American, born in Tulsa, Oklahoma. He was an actor and prolific screenwriter before turning director with *Bring Your Smile Along* (1955). His career reached its peak in the 1960s, when he proved to be a master of polished light comedy and social drama. His later career was dominated by the Pink Panther series and a succession of strained adult farces. He is married to **Julie Andrews**.

Career highs: *Breakfast at Tiffany's* (1961), *Days of Wine and Roses* (1962), *The Pink Panther* (1963), *A Shot in the Dark* (1964), *Victor/Victoria* (1982)

Career lows: *Switch* (1991), *Son of the Pink Panther* (1993)

Eisenstein, Sergei Mikhailovitch (1898–1948)

Russian, born in Riga, Latvia. The son of an architectural engineer, he served with the Red Army and worked in the theatre before making his directorial debut with *Strike* (1924). He was drawn to the celebration of heroic collective struggles, and his films were a fusion of art and propaganda, making pioneering use of editing and montage. Ill health and political difficulties curtailed his later career.

Career highs: *Strike* (1924), *Battleship Potemkin* (1925), *October* (1928), *Alexander Nevsky* (1938), *Ivan the Terrible* (1942–6)

F

Fassbinder, Rainer Werner (1946–82)

German, born in Bad Wörishofen, Bavaria. He studied drama and worked with fringe theatre companies before directing the film *The City Tramp* (1965). Staggeringly prolific, he often made four films in one year. He became a key figure of the New German Cinema, attacking the country's economic miracle through stories of personal failure, frustration and oppression. During his later career, he concentrated on stylized melodramas. He died following an overdose of sleeping pills and cocaine.

Career highs: *The Bitter Tears of Petra Von Kant* (1972), *Fear Eats the Soul* (1974), *Fox and His Friends* (1975), *The Marriage of Maria Braun* (1978), *Lola* (1981)

Career low: *Despair* (1978)

Fellini, Federico (1920–93)

Italian, born in Rimini. He worked as a comic strip artist before becoming a screenwriter, and made his solo directorial debut with *The White Sheik* (1951). His international reputation grew throughout the 1950s, culminating in the success of *La Dolce vita* (1960). His later films became increasingly autobiographical and reflected his love of extravagant fantasy, dreams and the grotesque. He was married to the actress Guilietta Masina.

Career highs: *I Vitelloni* (1953), *La Strada* (1954), *La Dolce vita* (1960), *8½* (1963), *Amarcord* (1973)

Career lows: *Orchestra Rehearsal* (1978), *The Voice of the Moon* (1990)

Flaherty, Robert Joseph (1884–1951)

American, born in Iron Mountain, Michigan. The son of a miner, he worked as an explorer and surveyor for the Canadian Grand Trunk Railroad and developed an interest in Inuit culture that he eventually committed to film in *Nanook of the North* (1922). He is hailed as the first documentary film-maker, his naive, poetic films capturing the struggles of cultures on the brink of fundamental change.

Career highs: *Nanook of the North* (1922), *Moana* (1926), *Man of Aran* (1934), *Louisiana Story* (1948)

Fleming, Victor (1889–1949)

American, born in La Canada, California. He worked as a mechanic and professional racing driver before entering the film industry as an assistant cameraman in 1910. His technical expertise developed as he worked with **Allan Dwan** and **D W Griffith**, and he made his directorial debut with *When the Clouds Roll By* (1919). Noted for his sensitive direction of major stars and his fondness for literary adaptations, he won a Best Director Academy Award® for *Gone with the Wind* (1939).

Career highs: *The Virginian* (1929), *Red Dust* (1932), *Captains Courageous* (1937), *The Wizard of Oz* (1939), *Gone with the Wind* (1939)

Career lows: *Adventure* (1945), *Joan of Arc* (1948)

Ford, John (Sean Aloysius O'Fearna) (1894–1973)

American, born in Cape Elizabeth, Maine. The son of Irish immigrants, he arrived in Hollywood in 1914 to join his brother Francis, and worked as an actor and stuntman before directing *The Tornado* (1917). Throughout his long and prolific career, he was an affectionate, patriotic chronicler of US history and the mythology of how the West was won. He won Best Director Academy Awards® for *The Informer* (1935), *The Grapes of Wrath* (1940), *How Green Was My Valley* (1941) and *The Quiet Man* (1952).

Career highs: *Stagecoach* (1939), *The Grapes of Wrath* (1940), *My Darling Clementine* (1946), *The Searchers* (1956), *The Man Who Shot Liberty Valance* (1962)

Career lows: *The Plough and the Stars* (1936), *When Willie Comes Marching Home* (1950)

Forman, Miloš (1932–)

American, born in Cáslav, Czechoslovakia (now in the Czech Republic). He studied drama and film, worked as a screenwriter and directed documentaries before making his fictional film debut with *Peter and Pavla* (1963). A key figure in the flowering of Czech cinema during the 1960s, he moved to New York City in 1968 and subsequently pursued a US career, winning Best Director Academy Awards® for both *One Flew Over the Cuckoo's Nest* (1975) and *Amadeus* (1984).
Career highs: *A Blonde in Love* (1965), *The Fireman's Ball* (1967), *Taking Off* (1971), *One Flew Over the Cuckoo's Nest* (1975), *Amadeus* (1984)
Career low: *Hair* (1979)

Forsyth, Bill (William David Forsyth) (1946–)

Scottish, born in Glasgow. The son of a plumber, he worked for a film production company before directing documentaries and short films. His low-budget social comedy *That Sinking Feeling* (1979) was a landmark in Scottish film-making, and his international reputation was established with the success of *Gregory's Girl* (1980). His films offer a melancholy view of the world, punctuated by wry observation and sharp insights into human nature.
Career highs: *That Sinking Feeling* (1979), *Gregory's Girl* (1980), *Local Hero* (1983), *Housekeeping* (1987)
Career lows: *Being Human* (1993), *Gregory's Two Girls* (1999)

Frankenheimer, John (1930–2002)

American, born in Malba, New York. He served in the US Air Force before joining the CBS television network, where he is thought to have directed in excess of 100 television plays. He made his cinema debut with *The Young Stranger* (1957). In the 1960s, he made a dazzling succession of thoughtful, action-packed thrillers, but his career faltered in the 1970s.
Career highs: *All Fall Down* (1961), *Birdman of Alcatraz* (1962), *The Manchurian Candidate* (1962), *Seven Days in May* (1963), *The Train* (1964)
Career lows: *The Extraordinary Seaman* (1968), *The Island of Dr Moreau* (1996)

Fuller, Samuel Michael (1911–97)

American, born in Worcester, Massachusetts. He worked as a crime reporter and fiction writer before moving to Hollywood, where he became a scriptwriter. After serving with distinction in World War II, he made his directorial debut with *I Shot Jesse James* (1948). His best films, though not known for their political subtlety, have all the impact and fury of a tabloid headline; his rasping growl and cigar-chomping figure were also seen in a number of acting roles.
Career highs: *Park Row* (1952), *Pickup on South Street* (1953), *40 Guns* (1957), *Shock Corridor* (1963), *The Big Red One* (1980)
Career lows: *Thieves after Dark* (1983), *Street of No Return* (1989)

G

Gance, Abel (1889–1981)

French, born in Paris. He worked as a law-office clerk, then became a stage actor and scriptwriter before making his directorial debut with *La Digue* (1911). He was a technical innovator whose obsession with the life of Napoleon Bonaparte led him to make the silent epic *Napoléon* (1927). His sound career was less dazzling, although he continued to direct until the 1960s.
Career highs: *J'Accuse* (1919), *La Roue* (1923), *Napoléon* (1927)
Career low: *The Battle of Austerlitz* (1960)

Gilliam, Terry Vance (1940–)

American, born in Medicine Lake, Minnesota. He studied at Occidental College in Los Angeles, where he founded the magazine *Fang*. In Britain from the 1960s, he worked as an animator and writer before forming part of the Monty Python team. He co-directed *Monty Python and the Holy Grail* (1975), and his subsequent films celebrate the power of the imagination to transcend the awful realities of daily life.
Career highs: *Brazil* (1985), *The Fisher King* (1991), *Twelve Monkeys* (1995)
Career lows: *Fear and Loathing in Las Vegas* (1998), *Tideland* (2005)

A Cervantes Catastrophe

While it is not uncommon for a film production to be abandoned in its early stages, disasters on the scale of Terry Gilliam's attempted adaptation of Miguel de Cervantes's novel *Don Quixote* are relatively rare. Gilliam spent more than ten years developing the ill-fated project (*The Man Who Killed Don Quixote*), only to see it overwhelmed soon after filming had started by a devastating combination of personal and logistical problems, including the lead actor falling ill and a location sited next to a NATO bombing range. Film-makers Keith Fulton and Louis Pepe were on hand, shooting a 'making of' feature, as events unfolded; but Gilliam probably took little comfort from the fact that their resulting documentary *Lost in La Mancha* (2002) went on to become a critical success.

Godard, Jean-Luc (1930–)

French, born in Paris. He studied at the Sorbonne, and immersed himself in film culture at the Cinémathèque Française. He was a critic before turning to direction with the short film *Opération béton* (1954). A leading figure of the Nouvelle Vague movement, he became increasingly radical and experimental as he stepped back from conventional narrative to concentrate on the power of the image, his political concerns and the state of the world.
Career highs: *Breathless* (1960), *Vivre sa vie* (1962), *Le Mépris* (1963), *Alphaville* (1965), *Weekend* (1967)
Career lows: *Number Two* (1975), *King Lear* (1987), *Hélas pour moi* (1993)

Grierson, John (1898–1972)

Scottish, born in Deanston, Stirlingshire. He studied philosophy at Glasgow University before a Rockefeller Fellowship took him to America, where he developed an interest in mass communication. He subsequently established the Empire Marketing Board Film Unit, and became the founding father of the UK

documentary movement. He later headed the GPO Film Unit, established the National Film Board of Canada and presented the television documentary series *This Wonderful World* (1957–65).
Career highs: *Drifters* (1929), *Song of Ceylon* (1934) (producer/co-writer), *Night Mail* (1936) (producer)

Griffith, D(avid Lewelyn) W(ark) (1875–1948)

American, born in Floydsfork, Kentucky. The son of a Confederate officer, he worked as an actor and journalist before being hired to write film scripts by the Edison Company. He subsequently directed more than 500 short dramas, continually refining and developing his cinematic technique. Increasingly drawn to epic themes and lavish productions, he was the most admired US director of the silent era, but his career faded with the coming of sound and his health was destroyed by alcoholism.
Career highs: *The Birth of a Nation* (1915), *Intolerance* (1916), *Broken Blossoms* (1919), *Way Down East* (1920), *Orphans of the Storm* (1922)
Career lows: *The Battle of the Sexes* (1928), *The Struggle* (1931)

Güney, Yilmaz (Yilmaz Pütün) (1937–84)

Turkish, born in Adana. He studied law at Ankara and economics in Istanbul. He was a screenwriter and novelist before making his directorial debut with *The Horse, the Woman and the Gun* (1966). His films reflect his concerns about the injustice and oppression in his country. Arrested several times for alleged subversive activities, he was eventually imprisoned on a false murder charge. He continued to run his film company from jail and managed to escape to Switzerland in 1981, but died three years later at the age of 47.
Career highs: *The Herd* (1978), *The Enemy* (1979), *Yol* (1982), *The Wall* (1983)

H

Hawks, Howard Winchester (1896–1977)

American, born in Goshen, Indiana. He studied mechanical engineering at Cornell University and worked in the film industry as a prop man before serving in World War I. He returned to the cinema as a scriptwriter, and made his directorial debut with *The Road to Glory* (1926). He went on to work with some of Hollywood's biggest stars, and proved an expert at screwball comedy as well as at tough action pictures that explored male friendship and masculine values.
Career highs: *Scarface* (1932), *Bringing up Baby* (1938), *The Big Sleep* (1946), *Red River* (1948), *Rio Bravo* (1959)
Career low: *A Song is Born* (1948)

Haynes, Todd (1961–)

American, born in Los Angeles, California. He majored in art and semiotics at Brown University, and made his directorial debut with the short film *Assassins* (1985). He began to attract attention with *Superstar: The Karen Carpenter Story* (1987), a biography of the singer made using Barbie® dolls. Part of the New Queer Cinema, he has moved closer to the mainstream whilst still creating films about outsiders and transgression.

Career highs: *Poison* (1991), *Safe* (1995), *Far from Heaven* (2002)
Career low: *Velvet Goldmine* (1998)

Herzog, Werner (Werner Stipetic) (1942–)

German, born in Munich. He studied literature and theatre, worked in American television and directed a number of short films before making his feature debut with *Signs of Life* (1967). An important figure in the New German Cinema of the 1970s, he has used his fascination with obsessive individuals and their heroic struggles to inform his work. Recently he has concentrated on documentaries, with impressive results.
Career highs: *Aguirre: The Wrath of God* (1972), *The Enigma of Kaspar Hauser* (1974), *Heart of Glass* (1976), *Woyzeck* (1978), *Fitzcarraldo* (1982)
Career low: *Invincible* (2001)

Hitchcock, Sir Alfred Joseph (1899–1980)

English, born in London. A student of drawing and design at London University, he entered the film industry as a designer of title cards for silent films. His first notable success came with the thriller *The Lodger* (1926). He directed Britain's first talking picture, *Blackmail* (1929), and went on to build a reputation as the Master of Suspense. His impressive body of work is noted for its dark wit, ice-cool blonde heroines and increasing psychological complexity. He never won an Academy Award® despite receiving six Best Director nominations.
Career highs: *Blackmail* (1929), *The Thirty-Nine Steps* (1935), *Shadow of a Doubt* (1943), *Vertigo* (1958), *Psycho* (1960)
Career lows: *The Paradine Case* (1947), *Under Capricorn* (1949)

— Clever Cameos —

One of Alfred Hitchcock's trademarks as a director was the cameo appearance he made in each of his films from *The Lodger* (1927) onwards. He appeared as a passer-by, missing a bus, wearing a cowboy hat, winding a clock or struggling to carry a cumbersome double bass. Even *Lifeboat* (1944), which is set entirely within the confines of the eponymous tiny craft, features Hitchcock – who had recently lost a considerable amount of weight – in the 'before' and 'after' photos of an advertisement for 'Reduco Obesity Slayer', visible on a newspaper being read by one of the boat's passengers.

Hou Hsiao-Hsien (1947–)

Taiwanese, born in Guangdong Province, China. He studied film at the National Taiwan College of Arts, and worked as a scriptwriter and assistant director before making his directorial debut with *Cute Girl* (1980). His gentle, meticulously composed, static films are marked by a nostalgia for the Taiwan of his youth and a desire to confront how the country has been marked by economic and social changes.
Career highs: *The Time to Live and the Time to Die* (1985), *City of Sadness* (1989), *The Puppetmaster* (1993), *Flowers of Shanghai* (1998)
Career lows: *The Green, Green Grass of Home* (1982), *Goodbye South, Goodbye* (1996)

Howard, Ron (1953–   )

American, born in Duncan, Oklahoma. The son of actors, he made his film debut as a small child in *Frontier Woman* (1956) and matured into the popular star of television series *Happy Days* (1974–80). He made his directorial debut with the low-budget *Grand Theft Auto* (1977), and has since become a proficient purveyor of increasingly accomplished mainstream entertainments. He won a Best Director Academy Award® for *A Beautiful Mind* (2001). Actress Bryce Dallas Howard is his daughter.
Career highs: *Splash* (1984), *Apollo 13* (1985), *A Beautiful Mind* (2001), *Cinderella Man* (2005)
Career low: *Grand Theft Auto* (1977)

Huston, John Marcellus (1906–87)

American, born in Nevada, Missouri. The son of actor Walter Huston, he was a boxer, painter, reporter and honorary member of the Mexican cavalry before making his way to Hollywood. A respected screenwriter, he made his directorial debut with *The Maltese Falcon* (1941). A master storyteller enthralled by grand adventures and larger than life characters, he won a Best Director Academy Award® for *The Treasure of the Sierra Madre* (1948). Actors **Anjelica Huston** and Danny Huston are his children.
Career highs: *The Maltese Falcon* (1941), *The Treasure of the Sierra Madre* (1947), *The African Queen* (1951), *Fat City* (1972), *The Dead* (1987)
Career lows: *A Walk with Love and Death* (1969), *Phobia* (1980)

I

Ichikawa, Kon (1915–   )

Japanese, born in Uji-Yamada. He studied animation, and worked in the animation department at J O Studios, eventually making his directorial debut with the puppet film *A Girl of Dojo Temple* (1946). Once dubbed the 'Japanese Frank Capra', he made a number of comedies satirizing Japanese social mores, but later concentrated on bleak antiwar dramas and tales of dark obsession.
Career highs: *The Burmese Harp* (1956), *Conflagration* (1958), *Fires on the Plain* (1959), *The Key* (1959), *An Actor's Revenge* (1963)

Ivory, James (1928–   )

American, born in Berkeley, California. He studied architecture and fine art at the University of Oregon and subsequently studied film-making at the University of Southern California. He directed a number of short films before forming a partnership with producer Ismail Merchant. Their initial films explored Indian culture and the clash between east and west but their greatest renown came with a series of refined literary adaptations.
Career highs: *Shakespeare Wallah* (1965), *A Room with a View* (1985), *Maurice* (1987), *Howards End* (1992), *The Remains of the Day* (1993)
Career lows: *Savages* (1972), *Slaves of New York* (1989)

J

Jackson, Peter (1961–   )

New Zealander, born in Pukerua Bay. An enthusiastic amateur film-maker as a child, he gradually refined his efforts and eventually made his feature debut with the low-budget splatter film *Bad Taste* (1987). Initially regarded mainly as a director of gory horror films, he won a different level of recognition and acclaim for his work on the Lord of the Rings trilogy of films, winning a Best Director Academy Award® for *The Lord of the Rings: The Return of the King* (2003).
Career highs: *Braindead* (1992), *Heavenly Creatures* (1994), *The Lord of the Rings: The Fellowship of the Ring* (2001), *The Lord of the Rings: The Two Towers* (2002), *The Lord of the Rings: The Return of the King* (2003)

> ## ▬ *Sausages Again* ▬
>
> In his early days as a committed amateur director, Peter Jackson spent considerable time and effort devising his own special effects on an extremely tight budget. For the gory zombie horror *Bad Taste* (1987) he even created latex prosthetic zombie heads, which he baked at home in such large quantities that his family, denied access to their own oven, reportedly spent several weeks eating fried sausages for dinner.

Jarman, (Michael) Derek Elworthy (1942–94)

English, born in Northwood, Essex. He studied at the Slade School of Fine Art, and worked as a painter and set designer while making home movies and short films. He made his feature debut with *Sebastiane* (1976). He used film as an intimate form of self-expression, and his lyrical, experimental and innovative work reflected his experiences as a homosexual man and his distress at Britain's social and moral decline.
Career highs: *Sebastiane* (1976), *Jubilee* (1978), *Caravaggio* (1986), *Edward II* (1991), *Blue* (1993)
Career low: *The Last of England* (1987)

Jarmusch, Jim (1953–   )

American, born in Akron, Ohio. He studied film at New York University, where he was a teaching assistant to **Nicholas Ray**. He made his directorial debut with *Permanent Vacation* (1980) and won the Camera d'Or award at the Cannes Film Festival for *Stranger than Paradise* (1984). He is an uncompromising independent whose films are distinguished by deadpan wit, laconic performances and luminous cinematography.
Career highs: *Stranger than Paradise* (1984), *Down by Law* (1986), *Dead Man* (1995), *Broken Flowers* (2005)

Jennings, Humphrey (1907–50)

English, born in Walberswick, Suffolk. He was a gifted scholar who worked as a writer, painter and photographer before joining the British government's GPO Film Unit in 1934. There, he was a scenic designer and editor before making his directorial debut with *Post Haste* (1934). His talent flourished during wartime, when he made poetic, heartfelt documentaries capturing the spirit of ordinary people. He fell to his death from a cliff whilst scouting locations in Greece.

Career highs: *London Can Take It* (1940), *Listen to Britain* (1942), *Fires Were Started* (1943), *A Diary for Timothy* (1945)

Jewison, Norman (1926–)

Canadian, born in Toronto, Ontario. He served in the Canadian Navy during World War II, studied at the University of Toronto and worked extensively in television before making his directorial debut with *Forty Pounds of Trouble* (1962). Initially a director of breezy comedies, he has tackled a wide variety of genres and shown a particular fondness for stories highlighting social issues and racial tensions.

Career highs: *The Cincinnati Kid* (1965), *In the Heat of the Night* (1967), *The Thomas Crown Affair* (1968), *Moonstruck* (1987)

Career lows: *Gaily, Gaily* (1969), *Bogus* (1996)

Jordan, Neil (1950–)

Irish, born in County Sligo. He read history and literature at University College, Dublin and subsequently helped to form the Irish Writers' Cooperative. An acclaimed novelist, he was a script consultant on *Excalibur* (1981) before making his directorial debut with the thriller *Angel* (1982). His best films have a dream-like intensity, reflecting a love of fantasy and a deep romanticism. He won a Best Original Screenplay Academy Award® for *The Crying Game* (1992).

Career highs: *Angel* (1982), *The Company of Wolves* (1984), *Mona Lisa* (1996), *The Crying Game* (1992), *The Butcher Boy* (1997)

Career lows: *High Spirits* (1987), *We're No Angels* (1989), *In Dreams* (1999)

K

Kaurismäki, Aki (1957–)

Finnish, born in Orimattila. He worked as an artist, dishwasher, builder, postman and machinist before collaborating with his elder brother, film-maker Mika Kaurismäki; as a team, they became key figures in the development of Finnish cinema. He was a writer and assistant before directing his first feature, *Crime and Punishment* (1983), and gradually built an international reputation. His films are characterized by their deadpan humour, melancholy feel and sympathetic portrayals of outsiders.

Career highs: *Hamlet Goes Business* (1987), *The Match Factory Girl* (1989), *Drifting Clouds* (1996), *The Man Without a Past* (2002)

Career low: *Leningrad Cowboys Meet Moses* (1993)

Kazan, Elia (Elia Kazanjoglou) (1909–2003)

American, born in Istanbul, Turkey. In the USA from 1913, he was an actor and a stage director before making his film debut with *A Tree Grows in Brooklyn* (1945). He proved a sympathetic director of method acting's greatest stars in the 1950s, and won Best Director Academy Awards® for *Gentleman's Agreement* (1947) and *On The Waterfront* (1954). He abandoned the cinema after *The Last Tycoon* (1976) and wrote novels.

Career highs: *Boomerang* (1947), *Panic in the Streets* (1950), *A Streetcar Named Desire* (1951), *On the Waterfront* (1954), *Wild River* (1960)
Career lows: *The Sea of Grass* (1947), *The Arrangement* (1969)

Kiarostami, Abbas (1940–)

Iranian, born in Tehran. He studied fine art and worked as a graphic designer before making his directorial debut with *The Bread and Alley* (1970). A key figure in Iranian film-making, he eschews conventional narrative and professional actors to offer deceptively simple poetic reflections on everyday life and death in his country.
Career highs: *Close Up* (1990), *Through the Olive Trees* (1994), *Taste of Cherry* (1997), *The Wind Will Carry Us* (1999), *Ten* (2002)
Career low: *Five* (2004)

Kieslowski, Krzysztof (1941–96)

Polish, born in Warsaw. After briefly attempting to train as a fireman, he studied at the Lodz Film Academy and worked extensively in television before making his cinema debut with *The Scar* (1976). His growing international reputation was confirmed by the *Dekalog* (1988–9), commissioned for Polish television but later distributed internationally. His later work offers a soulful investigation of the random nature of human existence and the infinite quest for love and happiness.
Career highs: *Camera Buff* (1979), *A Short Film About Killing* (1988), *The Double Life of Veronique* (1991), *Three Colours: Blue* (1993), *Three Colours: Red* (1994)

Kubrick, Stanley (1928–99)

American, born in the Bronx, New York City. He was a teenage photographer for *Look* magazine before directing documentary shorts and making his feature debut with *Fear and Desire* (1953). He gained critical respect for a number of taut thrillers before attempting an increasingly ambitious range of work. Resident in the UK from the 1960s, he was a painstaking craftsman, drawn to films that explored the erosion of human values.
Career highs: *The Killing* (1956), *Paths of Glory* (1957), *Dr Strangelove* (1964), *2001: A Space Odyssey* (1968), *A Clockwork Orange* (1971)
Career low: *Eyes Wide Shut* (1999)

Kurosawa, Akira (1910–98)

Japanese, born in Tokyo. He studied art and worked as a painter and illustrator before entering the film industry, making his directorial debut with *Judo Saga* (1943). He began to attract international attention with *Drunken Angel* (1948). A visual stylist and master storyteller, his reputation rests on his dazzling samurai films and blood-drenched adaptations of Shakespearean plots. He was the first Japanese film-maker to become widely known in the West.
Career highs: *Rashômon* (1950), *Living* (1952), *Seven Samurai* (1954), *Yojimbo* (1961), *Kagemusha* (1980)
Career lows: *Rhapsody in August* (1991), *Madadayo* (1993)

Kusturica, Emir (1954–)

Bosnian, born in Sarajevo. An amateur film-maker, he studied at the Academy of Performing Arts (FAMU) in Prague before making his feature debut with *Do You Remember Dolly Bell?* (1981). His recent films have addressed the history and divisions in his country and the folly of war, using manic, scattershot narratives that convey a buoyant, passionate humanism. He has also acted, and is a member of the rock band No Smoking.
Career highs: *Do You Remember Dolly Bell?* (1981), *When Father Was Away on Business* (1985), *Underground* (1995)

L

Lang, Fritz (1890–1976)

Austrian, born in Vienna. The son of an architect, he studied engineering and travelled extensively before serving in World War I. He then worked as a screenwriter, and made his directorial debut with *The Halfbreed* (1919). Fascinated by violence, cruelty and the criminal mind, he produced memorable silent epics; after fleeing Nazi Germany, he settled in California to direct westerns, thrillers and social dramas with equal distinction.
Career highs: *Metropolis* (1926), *M* (1931), *Fury* (1936), *You Only Live Once* (1937), *The Woman in the Window* (1944)
Career lows: *Secret Beyond the Door* (1948), *Human Desire* (1954)

Lean, Sir David (1908–91)

English, born in Croydon. The son of a chartered accountant, he entered the film industry as a tea-boy at Gaumont Studios and rose through the ranks, working as a camera operator, assistant director and highly respected editor. He co-directed *In Which We Serve* (1942) with Noel Coward, and subsequently became renowned for his meticulous craftsmanship, skilful storytelling and epic vision. He won Best Director Academy Awards® for *The Bridge on the River Kwai* (1957) and *Lawrence of Arabia* (1962).
Career highs: *Brief Encounter* (1945), *Great Expectations* (1946), *Oliver Twist* (1948), *The Bridge on the River Kwai* (1957), *Lawrence of Arabia* (1962)
Career lows: *The Passionate Friends* (1948), *Madeleine* (1949)

Lee, Ang (1954–)

Taiwanese, born in Taipei. He studied at the National Taiwan College of Arts before moving to the USA and studying film production at New York University, where he worked with fellow student **Spike Lee**. He made his directorial debut with *Pushing Hands* (1981), and became noted for his sensitive explorations of generational and cultural conflict.
Career highs: *The Wedding Banquet* (1993), *Sense and Sensibility* (1995), *The Ice Storm* (1997), *Crouching Tiger, Hidden Dragon* (2000), *Brokeback Mountain* (2005)
Career low: *The Hulk* (2003)

Lee, Spike (Shelton Jackson Lee) (1956–)

American, born in Atlanta, Georgia. The eldest son of jazz musician Bill Lee, he studied at Morehouse College and New York University's Institute of Film and Television. He made his directorial debut with the short *Last Hustle in Brooklyn* (1977) and his feature debut with *She's Gotta Have It* (1986). Exploring all aspects of black culture and history, he has combined provocative social comment with stylish film-making.

Career highs: *She's Gotta Have It* (1986), *Do the Right Thing* (1989), *Jungle Fever* (1991), *Malcolm X* (1992)

Career lows: *Girl 6* (1996), *Bamboozled* (2000)

Leigh, Mike (1943–)

English, born in Salford, Greater Manchester. The son of a doctor, he studied theatre and film, and built a formidable reputation in the theatre for a style of working based on extensive, guided group improvisations. He made his cinema debut with *Bleak Moments* (1971) and went on to create a body of work noted for its truthful and compassionate dramatization of everyday lives and universal concerns.

Career highs: *Life Is Sweet* (1991), *Naked* (1993), *Secrets & Lies* (1996), *Topsy Turvy* (1999), *Vera Drake* (2004)

Leisen, James Mitchell (1898–1972)

American, born in Menominee, Michigan. The son of a brewery owner, he studied architecture and worked in the art department of the *Chicago Tribune* before entering the film industry in 1919. He was a designer of sets and costumes for directors including **Cecil B De Mille** and **Ernst Lubitsch** before making his directorial debut with *Cradle Song* (1933) and proved adept at breezy comedy, lyrical romance and heartfelt melodrama.

Career highs: *Easy Living* (1937), *Midnight* (1939), *Remember the Night* (1940), *Hold Back the Dawn* (1941), *To Each His Own* (1946)

Career lows: *Bride of Vengeance* (1949), *Tonight We Sing* (1953)

Lelouch, Claude (1937–)

French, born in Paris. A prize-winning amateur film-maker in his teenage years, he made his feature debut with *The Right of Man* (1960). He achieved enormous international success with *A Man and a Woman* (1966), sharing a Best Original Screenplay Academy Award®. He has been a prolific director of lyrical, light-hearted entertainments, slickly celebrating romance and the power of love.

Career highs: *A Man and a Woman* (1966), *Life, Love, Death* (1969), *Happy New Year* (1973), *And Now My Love* (1974), *Les Misérables* (1995)

Career lows: *Bolero* (1981), *Edith and Marcel* (1983)

Leone, Sergio (1921–89)

Italian, born in Rome. The son of director Vincenzo Leone, he studied law before working as an assistant film director, screenwriter and bit-part actor. He made his official directorial debut with *The Colossus of Rhodes* (1961). He made his name with spaghetti westerns, bringing a stylized approach to the savage history of America and making a star of **Clint Eastwood**.

Career highs: *A Fistful of Dollars* (1964), *The Good, the Bad and the Ugly* (1966), *Once Upon a Time in the West* (1968), *Once Upon a Time in America* (1984).

Lester, Richard (1932–)

American, born in Philadelphia, Pennsylvania. A talented, precocious child, he was a composer and vocalist in his teenage years and a television director by the age of 20. He settled in the UK in the 1950s, collaborating on a number of projects with **Peter Sellers** before making his feature film debut with *It's Trad, Dad!* (1962). He brought energy and exuberance to a wide range of films, retiring after the documentary *Get Back* (1991).
Career highs: *A Hard Day's Night* (1964), *Help!* (1965), *Petulia* (1968), *The Three Musketeers* (1973), *Robin and Marian* (1976)
Career low: *Finders Keepers* (1984)

Levinson, Barry (1942–)

American, born in Baltimore, Maryland. He studied broadcast journalism and worked in local television before heading to California, where he became a comedy performer and writer. He made his directorial debut with the autobiographical *Diner* (1982) and has interspersed wise and witty reflections on his beloved home city of Baltimore with more anonymous studio productions, winning a Best Director Academy Award® for *Rain Man* (1988).
Career highs: *Diner* (1982), *Tin Men* (1987), *Good Morning, Vietnam* (1987), *Rain Man* (1988), *Avalon* (1990)
Career lows: *Toys* (1992), *Jimmy Hollywood* (1994), *Sphere* (1998)

Loach, Ken(neth) (1936–)

English, born in Nuneaton. The son of an electrician, he studied law at Oxford University and worked as an actor before training as a television director and joining the BBC, where he directed episodes of *Z Cars* and made his mark with the hard-hitting television play *Cathy Come Home* (1966). He made his cinema debut with *Poor Cow* (1967), and has since created a distinguished body of work examining social issues and political ideas through the everyday lives and experiences of ordinary people.
Career highs: *Kes* (1969), *Looks and Smiles* (1981), *Riff-Raff* (1991), *Raining Stones* (1993), *My Name Is Joe* (1998)

Losey, Joseph Walton (1909–84)

American, born in La Crosse, Wisconsin. He studied English literature at Harvard University, wrote arts reviews and directed for the New York stage before studying film with **Sergei Eisenstein** in Moscow. He made his directorial debut with the marionette short *Pete Roleum and His Cousins* (1939) and his feature debut with *The Boy with Green Hair* (1948). Blacklisted during the McCarthy era, he moved to Europe, embarking on fruitful collaborations with Harold Pinter and **Dirk Bogarde**.
Career highs: *The Boy with Green Hair* (1948), *The Servant* (1963), *Accident* (1967), *The Go-Between* (1971), *Mr Klein* (1976)
Career low: *Boom* (1968)

Lubitsch, Ernst (1892–1947)

German, born in Berlin. He was a teenage actor on stage and screen before making his directorial debut with *Fräulein Seifenschaum* (1914) and making a name for himself as a director of comedies and costume dramas. Brought to Hollywood by **Mary Pickford**, he became a master of sophisticated comedy, known for the 'Lubitsch touch' – a mixture of wit, urbanity and sex with great critical and popular appeal. His use of sparkling dialogue in the sound era only enhanced his reputation. **Career highs**: *Lady Windermere's Fan* (1925), *The Student Prince in Old Heidelberg* (1927), *Trouble in Paradise* (1932), *The Shop around the Corner* (1940), *Heaven Can Wait* (1943)

Lucas, George Walton (1944–   )

American, born in Modesto, California. Raised on a walnut ranch, he studied film at the University of Southern California and made a number of shorts before securing an internship at Warner Brothers. He made his feature debut with the science-fiction story *THX 1138* (1971). The phenomenal success of *Star Wars* (1977) transformed him into an influential producer, technical innovator and owner of his own film empire. It also kept him away from directing for the next two decades. **Career highs**: *THX 1138* (1971), *American Graffiti* (1973), *Star Wars* (1977) **Career lows**: *Howard the Duck* (1986) (producer), *Star Wars: Episode 1 – The Phantom Menace* (1999)

Luhrmann, Baz(mark) Anthony (1962–   )

Australian, born in New South Wales. Raised in rural Australia, he studied at the National Institute of Dramatic Art, and went on to serve as artistic director of the Sydney Theatre Company and as a director for Australian Opera. He took the Cannes Film Festival by storm with *Strictly Ballroom* (1992). His three films have been sweeping, swooning explorations of love, death and the transformative power of art. **Career highs**: *Strictly Ballroom* (1992), *Romeo + Juliet* (1996), *Moulin Rouge!* (2001)

Lumet, Sidney (1924–   )

American, born in Philadelphia, Pennsylvania. The son of an actor, he made his stage debut opposite his father in 1928, subsequently appearing on Broadway and in the cinema. He served with the Army Signal Corps, then directed extensively for television before making his cinema debut with *Twelve Angry Men* (1957). Fascinated by crime and punishment, he has guided a number of actors to their finest screen performances. **Career highs**: *Twelve Angry Men* (1957), *The Pawnbroker* (1965), *Dog Day Afternoon* (1975), *Network* (1976), *The Verdict* (1982) **Career lows**: *Last of the Mobile Hot Shots* (1970), *Gloria* (1999)

Lumière, Auguste (1862–1954) and Louis (1864–1948)

French, both born in Besançon, France. The brothers were both employed at their father's photographic supplies factory in Lyons, and after his retirement they concentrated on the production and projection of moving film. They gave the first public cinema performance of their efforts in December 1895 with a programme of ten films capturing fragments of everyday life. Both devoted their later years to research.

Lynch, David Keith (1946–)

American, born in Missoula, Montana. The son of a research scientist, he studied painting before experimenting with film, making his directorial debut with the short film *The Alphabet* (1967). He made his feature film debut with *Eraserhead* (1976) and subsequently became known for his dark, sometimes nightmarishly intense thrillers and his fascination with the perverse, sometimes surreal underside of small-town American life.

Career highs: *Eraserhead* (1976), *The Elephant Man* (1980), *Blue Velvet* (1996), *The Straight Story* (1999), *Mulholland Drive* (2001)

Career lows: *Dune* (1984), *Twin Peaks: Fire Walk with Me* (1992)

Lynch's Lunches

The US restaurant chain Bob's Big Boy has its oldest remaining branch in Los Angeles, California, where its 1940s-style architecture makes it a point of interest for local historians and, occasionally, an ideal site for location filming (it appears in *Heat* (1995) as well as *Austin Powers 2: The Spy Who Shagged Me* (1999)). The restaurant is also famous locally as the place where David Lynch ate lunch every day for over seven years during the 1970s. The director would typically arrive at 2.30pm because, as he has since told interviewers, the chocolate milkshakes were always better after the lunch rush was over.

M

Malick, Terrence (1943–)

American, born in Waco, Texas. He studied at Harvard and Oxford University, taught philosophy at MIT and attended the American Film Institute before making his directorial debut with *Badlands* (1973). A 20-year break between his second and third features made him a notoriously reclusive figure; his few films have been lyrical, visually painstaking creations.

Career highs: *Badlands* (1973), *Days of Heaven* (1978), *The New World* (2005)

Malle, Louis (1932–95)

French, born in Thumeries, near Lille. He studied at the Institut des Hautes Études Cinématographiques and worked as an assistant to Jacques Cousteau and **Robert Bresson** before making his directorial debut with *Lift to the Scaffold* (1957). His work displays a sensitive understanding of adolescence, and a willingness to explore the dark corners of his country's past. He won a Best Original Screenplay Academy Award® for *Dearest Love* (1971), and was married to the actress Candice Bergen.

Career highs: *The Lovers* (1958), *Dearest Love* (1971), *Lacombe Lucien* (1974), *Atlantic City* (1980), *Au revoir les enfants* (1987)

Career low: *Crackers* (1984)

Mankiewicz, Joseph Leo (1909–83)

American, born in Wilkes-Barre, Pennsylvania. He was a reporter for the *Chicago Tribune* in Berlin, and worked as a screenwriter and producer before making his belated directorial debut with *Dragonwyck* (1946). Noted for his diamond-sharp dialogue and sophistication, he is the only film-maker to have won Academy Awards® for both writing and directing two years in a row. He retired after *Sleuth* (1972).

Career highs: *The Ghost and Mrs Muir* (1947), *A Letter to Three Wives* (1949), *All About Eve* (1950), *Guys and Dolls* (1955), *Sleuth* (1972)

Career low: *Somewhere in the Night* (1946)

Mann, Anthony (Emil Anton Bundesmann) (1906–67)

American, born in San Diego, California. He moved to New York City at the age of ten, and began his career as a child performer before working as a stage manager and Broadway director. His career in film began when **David O Selznick** hired him as a talent scout and screen-test director. He made his directorial debut with *Dr Broadway* (1942), and became noted for his stylish handling of punchy, low-budget thrillers, as well as a series of lean, flinty westerns, eight of which starred **James Stewart**.

Career highs: *T-Men* (1947), *The Naked Spur* (1953), *The Glenn Miller Story* (1953), *The Man from Laramie* (1955), *El Cid* (1961)

Career lows: *Sing Your Way Home* (1945), *The Bamboo Blonde* (1946)

Mann, Michael Kenneth (1943–   )

American, born in Chicago, Illinois. He studied at the University of Wisconsin before training at the London Film School and directing a number of documentaries and commercials. He wrote scripts for television series including *Starsky and Hutch* and *Vega$* before making his debut as a feature film director with *Thief* (1981). He has brought a strong visual flair to a number of stylish, moody thrillers, as well as to the acclaimed literary adaptation *Last of the Mohicans* (1992) and the biopic *Ali* (2001).

Career highs: *Thief* (1981), *Manhunter* (1986), *Heat* (1995), *The Insider* (1999)

Career low: *The Keep* (1983)

Méliès, (Marie-)Georges(-Jean) (1861–1938)

French, born in Paris. The son of a shoe manufacturer, he was a talented painter and sculptor with a passion for the arts. In 1888 he bought a theatre in Paris, where he began presenting his own magic lantern shows. Inspired by the work of the **Lumière** brothers, he enthusiastically embraced the new medium of film and made over 500 shorts using equipment he built himself. A lover of fantasy and showmanship and a pioneer in the field of special effects, he was underappreciated in his time, and ceased making films in 1912. He was belatedly honoured by the French government in 1931.

Career highs: *Cinderella* (1900), *Voyage to the Moon* (1902), *The Man with the Rubber Head* (1902), *The Impossible Voyage* (1904), *The Conquest of the Pole* (1912)

Melville, Jean-Pierre (Jean-Pierre Grumbach) (1917–73)

French, born in Paris. An amateur film-maker as a child, he served in the French Army and made short films before his feature debut *Le Silence de la mer* (1947). An admirer of American pulp fiction and gangster films, he became known for his own tense, terse thrillers exploring friendship, betrayal, loyalty and the code of honour among thieves. He also acted.

Career highs: *Bob le flambeur* (1955), *Le Doulos* (1962), *Le Samouraï* (1967), *L'Armée des ombres* (1969), *Le Cercle rouge* (1970)
Career low: *Quand tu liras cette lettre* (1952)

Mendes, Sam(uel Alexander) (1965–   )

English, born in Reading, Berkshire. He studied at Cambridge University and became a theatre director, joining the Royal Shakespeare Company and later becoming artistic director of London's Donmar Warehouse. He made his film debut with *American Beauty* (1999) for which he received a Best Director Academy Award®. He is married to **Kate Winslet**.

Career highs: *American Beauty* (1999), *Road to Perdition* (2002), *Jarhead* (2005)

Minghella, Anthony (1954–   )

English, born in Ryde, Isle of Wight. He studied and then taught literature at the University of Hull before writing plays and television scripts. He made his film debut with *Truly, Madly, Deeply* (1991) and went on to prove himself a master of epic literary adaptations, winning a Best Director Academy Award® for *The English Patient* (1996).

Career highs: *Truly, Madly, Deeply* (1991), *The English Patient* (1996), *The Talented Mr Ripley* (1999)
Career low: *Mr Wonderful* (1993)

Minnelli, Vincente (Lester Anthony Minnelli) (1903–86)

American, born in Chicago, Illinois. Raised in a travelling theatrical family, he began performing as a child. He later worked as a stage designer before moving to New York City and establishing himself as a costume designer and Broadway director. In Hollywood from 1940, he made his directorial debut with *Cabin in the Sky* (1943). He directed lavish MGM musicals and full-blown melodramas with equal aplomb, winning a Best Director Academy Award® for *Gigi* (1958). He was married to **Judy Garland**, and their daughter is **Liza Minnelli**.

Career highs: *Meet Me in St Louis* (1944), *An American in Paris* (1951), *The Bandwagon* (1953), *Lust for Life* (1956), *Gigi* (1958)
Career lows: *Undercurrent* (1946), *A Matter of Time* (1976)

Mizoguchi, Kenji (1898–1956)

Japanese, born in Tokyo. The son of a carpenter, he grew up in abject poverty and was apprenticed to a pharmacist before studying at the Aohashi Western Painting Research Institute and finding work as an assistant film director. His directorial debut was *The Resurrection of Love* (1922). Regarded as one of the greatest artists of world cinema, he brought a painterly sensibility and lyrical grace to radical, hard-hitting social dramas.

Career highs: *Sisters of the Gion* (1936), *The Story of the Late Chrysanthemums* (1939), *The Life of Oharu* (1952), *Ugetsu Monogatari* (1953), *Sansho the Bailiff* (1954)
Career low: *Tales of the Taira Clan* (1955)

Murnau, F W (Friedrich Wilhelm Plumpe) (1888–1931)

German, born in Bielefeld. He studied philology, art history and literature before becoming an actor. After serving as a combat pilot during World War I, he made his directorial debut with *The Boy in Blue* (1919). He was a master of the macabre and the lyrical, and is regarded as one of the silent era's most innovative and influential directors. He moved to the USA in 1926, and his career was ripe with promise when he died in a car crash.
Career highs: *Nosferatu* (1922), *The Last Laugh* (1924), *Tartuffe* (1925), *Faust* (1926), *Sunrise* (1927)

N

Nichols, Mike (Michael Igor Peschkowsky) (1931–)

American, born in Berlin, Germany. His family escaped Nazi Germany by moving to the USA, where Nichols later studied at the University of Chicago. He directed the early comedies of Neil Simon on Broadway before launching his film career with an explosive film adaptation of Edward Albee's stage play *Who's Afraid of Virginia Woolf?* (1966). Unconventional but topical choices of material followed, cementing his reputation. He frequently works with comedic partner and screenwriter/director Elaine May, and is one of a handful of people to have won a Tony, Grammy, Emmy and Academy Award®.
Career highs: *Who's Afraid of Virginia Woolf?* (1966), *The Graduate* (1967), *Catch-22* (1970), *Silkwood* (1983), *Working Girl* (1988)
Career low: *The Day of the Dolphin* (1973)

O

Olmi, Ermanno (1931–)

Italian, born in Bergamo. He began his career as a documentary short maker at the Edison-Volta electric company. Working in the neorealist vein, he later took as his subject matter the unhurried, bucolic surroundings of his native Bergamo region. His low-budget productions used ordinary Italian peasants as actors and retained a documentary style. *The Tree of Wooden Clogs* (1978) won the Palme d'Or at Cannes.
Career highs: *Il Posto* (1961), *The Fiancés* (1963), *The Tree of Wooden Clogs* (1978)
Career low: *And There Came a Man* (1965)

Ophüls, Max (Max Oppenheimer) (1902–57)

French, born in Saarbrücken, Germany. Ophüls chose French nationality in the plebiscite of 1934, and spent the 1930s making films in his adoptive country. He later sought exile in the USA, where his stylish and sumptuous camerawork reached its pinnacle in a series of films revolving around tragic love affairs. His son is the documentarist Marcel Ophüls.

Career highs: *Letter from an Unknown Woman* (1948), *La Ronde* (1950), *Lola Montès* (1955)

Oshima, Nagisa (1932–)

Japanese, born in Kyoto. He joined the Shochiku Ofuna Studio in 1954 before later forming his own production company, Sozosha, in 1965. A controversial New Wave film-maker, he is notorious for the challenging political and erotic themes of his work. The highly controversial *Ai no corrida* (1976) portrayed an obsessive relationship that resulted in strangulation and castration. Today he works as a television chat-show host.
Career highs: *A Town of Love and Hope* (1959), *Ai no corrida* (1976), *Ai no borei* (1978), *Merry Christmas, Mr Lawrence* (1983)
Career low: *Max mon amour* (1986)

Ozon, François (1967–)

French, born in Paris. He studied directing at the Fondation Européenne pour la Maîtrise de l'Image et du Son (FEMIS) film school in Paris, and made numerous acclaimed short films before his full-length debut, *Sitcom* (1998). His film *8 femmes* (2002), which featured several of the great female stars of French cinema, attracted widespread attention. He has developed a fruitful artistic relationship with **Charlotte Rampling** in his recent works.
Career highs: *8 femmes* (2002), *Swimming Pool* (2003), *5x2* (2004)
Career low: *Sitcom* (1998)

Ozu, Yasujiro (1903–63)

Japanese, born in Tokyo. A film devotee from childhood, he began his film career as an assistant cameraman at the Shochiku Ofuna Studio. His early work was heavily influenced by Hollywood, but his post-World War II output dealt almost invariably with the lives of Japanese middle-class families, and relationships between parents and their children. He was known for filming from a static low camera angle. *Tokyo Story* (1953), considered his masterpiece, is frequently cited as one of the greatest films ever made.
Career highs: *A Story of Floating Weeds* (1934), *The Flavour of Green Tea over Rice* (1952), *Tokyo Story* (1953), *An Autumn Afternoon* (1962)
Career low: *The Sword of Penitence* (1927)

P

Pasolini, Pier Paolo (1922–75)

Italian, born in Bologna. He studied art at the University of Bologna. Following army service in World War II he joined the Communist Party, but was expelled in 1949 following a sexual scandal involving young boys. He was a published poet and novelist before making his film debut with *Accattone!* (1961). His early work typically focused on low-life characters and people on the margins of society, but he later ventured into exploring religious and mythical themes. He was brutally murdered, reportedly during an encounter with a male prostitute.

Career highs: *Accattone!* (1961), *The Gospel According to St Matthew* (1964), *Oedipus Rex* (1967), *Medea* (1970)

Peckinpah, (David) Sam(uel) (1925–84)

American, born in Fresno, California. Raised on a ranch, he was a troublesome teenager and was sent to military school before serving in the US Marines during World War II. He later studied theatre, and joined the film industry as an assistant to director Don Siegel. His film debut was *The Deadly Companions* (1961), and he subsequently became famous for his groundbreaking slow-motion portrayal of violence on-screen, including a notorious rape scene in *Straw Dogs* (1971) that led to the film being banned in the UK for almost 20 years.
Career highs: *The Wild Bunch* (1969), *Straw Dogs* (1971), *Pat Garrett and Billy the Kid* (1973)
Career lows: *Major Dundee* (1965), *Convoy* (1978)

Polanski, Roman (1933–)

French–Polish, born in Paris, France. After moving to Poland, his parents were sent to Nazi concentration camps, where his mother died; in 1945 he was reunited with his father. He studied at Lodz film school and worked in the UK before relocating to Hollywood. His life has been marked by tragedy and scandal (notably the murder of his wife, actress Sharon Tate) and his pessimistic but darkly humorous films often explore the nature of evil and personal corruption. He now lives and works in France, where he settled in the 1970s after fleeing the USA following a charge of statutory rape.
Career highs: *Repulsion* (1965), *Rosemary's Baby* (1968), *Chinatown* (1974), *Death and the Maiden* (1994), *The Pianist* (2002)
Career lows: *Pirates* (1985), *The Ninth Gate* (1999)

Pontecorvo, Gillo (Gilberto Pontecorvo) (1919–)

Italian, born in Pisa. He studied chemistry and worked as a journalist before making his directorial debut with *Missione Timiriazev* (1953). His masterpiece, the documentary-styled *The Battle of Algiers* (1965), was a Golden Lion winner at the Venice Film Festival, though initially banned in France. He was the director of the Venice Film Festival from 1992–6.
Career highs: *Kapò* (1959), *The Battle of Algiers* (1965), *Burn!* (1968)

Powell, Michael Latham (1905–90)

English, born in Bekesbourne, near Canterbury. Powell worked for MGM in Nice and at Elstree Studios, assisting on some of **Alfred Hitchcock**'s early films. He formed an enviable artistic partnership with the Hungarian émigré Emeric Pressburger in which they created films distinguished by bold imagery, fantastical strands and the use of Technicolor. *Peeping Tom* (1960), a voyeuristic murder story now regarded as a classic, was derided by the critics of the time and effectively ended Powell's creative career. He was married to film editor **Thelma Schoonmaker**.
Career highs: *The Thief of Bagdad* (1940), *The Life and Death of Colonel Blimp* (1943), *A Matter of Life and Death* (1946), *Black Narcissus* (1947), *The Red Shoes* (1948), *Peeping Tom* (1960)

Preminger, Otto Ludwig (1905–86)

American, born in Vienna, Austria. He studied law before joining a theatre company, and emigrated to the USA in 1935, becoming naturalized in 1943. He moved to Hollywood, where he worked as an actor before making his name as a director with *Laura* (1944). His films boldly tackled controversial themes such as drug addiction, rape, Jewish repatriation, homosexuality and racism. He had a child with Gypsy Rose Lee.

Career highs: *Laura* (1944), *The Man with the Golden Arm* (1955), *Anatomy of a Murder* (1959), *Exodus* (1960), *Advise & Consent* (1962)
Career lows: *Saint Joan* (1957), *Skidoo* (1968)

Burned on the Set

During the filming of *Saint Joan* (1957), Otto Preminger – who had a reputation as something of a tyrant – is said to have been particularly hard on the film's young star, Jean Seberg. While the actress was chained to a post atop a pile of wood in preparation for her execution scene, the flames that were intended to suggest her burning at the stake shot up higher than planned and began to actually scorch her. Ignoring protests from cast and crew, Preminger reportedly refused to let Seberg be rescued until he had the shot he wanted.

R

Ray, Nicholas (Raymond Nicholas Kienzle Jr) (1911–79)

American, born in Galesville, Wisconsin. He studied architecture with Frank Lloyd Wright before turning to theatre and film. A maverick auteur, he expressed in his films a pessimistic and critical view of American society, frequently featuring disaffected 'loners' as protagonists. He retired from directing in the early 1960s, but continued to teach and collaborate with other film-makers. He was the subject of **Wim Wenders'** *Lightning over Water* (1980), a documentary filmed shortly before his death from cancer.

Career highs: *In a Lonely Place* (1950), *Johnny Guitar* (1954), *Rebel Without a Cause* (1955)
Career low: *Flying Leathernecks* (1951)

Ray, Satyajit (1921–92)

Indian, born in Calcutta. Ray graduated from Santiniketan University and initially worked as a commercial artist in an advertising agency. Encouraged by **Jean Renoir** to make films, he won international recognition with his debut *Pather Panchali* (1955), the first part of the Apu trilogy, an understated, affectionate portrait of social change in rural India. Considered India's greatest film-maker, Ray received a Lifetime Achievement Academy Award® in 1992, accepting it from his hospital bed shortly before his death.

Career highs: *Pather Panchali* (1955), *Aparajitu* (1957), *The World of Apu* (1959)

Reed, Sir Carol (1906–76)

English, born in London. The illegitimate son of actor-manager Sir Herbert
Beerbohm Tree, Reed began his career as an assistant to writer Edgar Wallace at
British Lion Studios. After wartime propaganda films featuring portrayals of working-
class life, he directed a number of Graham Greene adaptations, most famously *The
Third Man* (1949), set in the sinister underworld of post-war partitioned Vienna.
Reed was awarded a knighthood in 1952 – the first film director to be so honoured –
and won an Academy Award® for *Oliver!* (1968), starring his nephew **Oliver Reed**.
Career highs: *The Stars Look Down* (1939), *The Way Ahead* (1944), *Odd Man Out*
(1947), *The Fallen Idol* (1948), *The Third Man* (1949), *Oliver!* (1968)
Career low: *Flap* (1970)

Renoir, Jean (1894–1979)

American, born in Paris, France. The son of impressionist painter Pierre-Auguste
Renoir, he studied philosophy and mathematics before serving in World War I. He
later married actress Catherine Hessling, and established a film company primarily
for her benefit. His *La grande illusion* (1937) was the first foreign-language film to be
nominated for a Best Picture Academy Award®; the controversial satire *La Règle du
jeu* (1939) was initially banned in France. In 1941, he moved to the USA and became
a naturalized US citizen.
Career highs: *Une partie de campagne* (1936), *La grande illusion* (1937), *La Règle
du jeu* (1939), *The Southerner* (1945)
Career low: *Nana* (1926)

Resnais, Alain (1922–)

French, born in Vannes. He studied at the Institut des Hautes Études
Cinématographiques, where he made a series of prize-winning short documentaries
including *Night and Fog* (1955), a haunting evocation of the horror of Nazi
concentration camps. He made his feature-length debut with *Hiroshima mon amour*
(1959). He was a key figure in the Nouvelle Vague movement, but has made few
films in recent years.
Career highs: *Night and Fog* (1955), *Hiroshima mon amour* (1959), *Last Year in
Marienbad* (1961), *Stavisky* (1974)

Riefenstahl, Leni (Helene Bertha Amalie Riefenstahl) (1902–2003)

German, born in Berlin. She studied fine art and ballet, and was a professional
dancer before making her film debut in *Der Heilige Berg* (1926). She later moved
into directing and, after being appointed as film adviser to the Nazi Party, made
a series of propagandist documentaries including *Triumph of the Will* (1935) and
Olympia (1938). She was interned by the Allies after World War II, and upon release
became a photojournalist.
Career highs: *The Blue Light* (1931), *Triumph of the Will* (1935), *Olympia* (1938),
Tiefland (1943)

Rocha, Glauber (1938–81)

Brazilian, born in Vitória da Conquista. He studied law before becoming a theatre
director and film critic, then helped to create the Brazilian *cinema novo*, a

movement concerned with the underdeveloped status of the country and the search for Brazilian identity. He made his debut as a director with the short *Pátio* (1959), and was known for his radical, provocative approach to directing and his preference for using non-actors in his films.
Career highs: *Black God, White Devil* (1964), *Terra em Transe* (1967), *Antonio das Mortes* (1969)

Roeg, Nicolas (1928–)

English, born in London. His early career as a cinematographer included work on *Lawrence of Arabia* (1962) and *Far from the Madding Crowd* (1967). His debut as a director was *Performance* (1970), featuring Mick Jagger, and he later worked with David Bowie in *The Man Who Fell to Earth* (1976). An individualistic director, he is known for demanding and complex films, often with disturbing themes. He is married to the actress Theresa Russell.
Career highs: *Performance* (1970), *Walkabout* (1971), *Don't Look Now* (1973)
Career low: *Castaway* (1986)

Rohmer, Eric (Jean-Marie Maurice Schérer) (1920–)

French, born in Nancy. He worked as a journalist, teacher, novelist and critic before becoming a director. His films, usually grouped into series or cycles, are subtle, intimate explorations of contemporary relationships. A key member of the Nouvelle Vague movement, he is known for the slow pace and dense, highbrow dialogue of his films, qualities which tend to divide critical opinion.
Career highs: *Ma nuit chez Maud* (1969), *Le genou de Claire* (1970), *Die Marquise von O…* (1976)

Rosi, Francesco (1922–)

Italian, born in Naples. After studying law, serving in the military and working as a radio journalist, he entered films in the 1940s as an assistant to **Luchino Visconti.** His first solo effort as a director was *La Sfida* (1958). He is an uncompromisingly political director, known for forceful exposés of the influence of gangsters and corruption in Italian politics.
Career highs: *Salvatore Giuliano* (1962), *Il caso Mattei* (1972), *Cadaveri eccellenti* (1976)
Career low: *C'era una volta* (1967)

Rossellini, Roberto (1906–77)

Italian, born in Rome. An amateur film-maker from his youth, he was recruited to work on propaganda films for the Fascist government. His two masterpieces, *Roma, città aperta* (1945) and *Paisà* (1946), were filmed in Rome during the grim final months of World War II. Largely filmed with non-professional actors and in a grainy black-and-white documentary style, the films ushered in the neorealist movement in Italy. His love affair with the married actress **Ingrid Bergman** (whom he later married, 1949–57) caused a scandal; actress **Isabella Rossellini** is their daughter.
Career highs: *Roma, città aperta* (1945), *Paisà* (1946), *Il Generale della Rovere* (1959)
Career low: *Europa '51* (1952)

S

Salles, Walter, Jr (1956–)

Brazilian, born in Rio de Janeiro. Raised partly in France and the USA, he was a documentary film-maker before moving into feature films, and continues to cast non-professional actors in his films, which often deal with themes of exile and the search for identity. His road movie *The Motorcycle Diaries* (2004) is a film about the young Che Guevara.

Career highs: *Central Station* (1998), *Behind the Sun* (2001), *The Motorcycle Diaries* (2004).

Sanjinés, Jorge (1937–)

Bolivian, born in La Paz. He studied philosophy before enrolling at the Chilean Film Institute, then formed a film collective in Bolivia, where he directed documentary shorts. His first feature was *Ukamau* (1966), performed by impoverished native peasants in the local Aymara language. His best-known film, *Blood of the Condor* (1969), was initially banned by the Bolivian government because of its militantly political content.

Career highs: *Ukamau* (1966), *Blood of the Condor* (1969)

Saura, Carlos (1932–)

Spanish, born in Huesca. He worked as a stills photographer before studying film in Madrid, made his feature debut with *Los Golfos* (1960), and went on to attract international attention with *La Caza* (1966). He defied government censors to expose the social, sexual and religious repression of Franco's Spain; latterly he has turned his attention to flamenco-based films. His long-term partner was the actress Geraldine Chaplin, daughter of **Charlie Chaplin**.

Career highs: *La Caza* (1966), *Cría cuervos* (1976), *Bodas de sangre* (1981), *Carmen* (1983)

Career low: *¡Dispara!* (1993)

Sayles, John Thomas (1950–)

American, born in Schenectady, New York. He studied psychology and worked in a variety of odd jobs while writing fiction, eventually branching out to write screenplays for producer **Roger Corman** and others. His directorial debut was *Return of the Secaucus 7* (1980). An independent film-maker, he frequently uses ensemble casts in his films, many of which have social and political themes. He is also an actor, and has published several novels.

Career highs: *Matewan* (1987), *City of Hope* (1991), *Lone Star* (1996)

Scorsese, Martin (1942–)

American, born in Queens, New York City. A sickly child, he at one stage planned to become a priest before opting instead to study film at New York University, where he later taught. His films, often set in and around his home city, frequently contain autobiographical elements, and he has forged a number of long-lasting creative partnerships, notably with **Robert De Niro** and editor **Thelma Schoonmaker**. Regarded by many as the most influential director of his generation, Scorsese has

been nominated for seven Academy Awards® but has yet to win.
Career highs: *Mean Streets* (1973), *Taxi Driver* (1976), *Raging Bull* (1980), *Goodfellas* (1990), *Gangs of New York* (2002)
Career low: *New York, New York* (1977)

Scott, Sir Ridley (1937–   )

English, born in South Shields, County Durham. He studied at London's Royal College of Art, then worked for the BBC as a set designer and director before branching out into commercials and then into feature films. The often spectacular visual composition of his work has earned him the nickname 'The Rembrandt of Light'. He owns Shepperton film studios with his younger brother, the director Tony Scott, and despite a career lull during the mid-1990s, is one of the most successful British directors in Hollywood.
Career highs: *Alien* (1979), *Blade Runner* (1982), *Thelma & Louise* (1991), *Gladiator* (2000)
Career lows: *1492: Conquest of Paradise* (1992), *White Squall* (1996), *G I Jane* (1997)

Sembène, Ousmane (1923–   )

Senegalese, born in Ziguinchor. After working as a fisherman and construction worker and serving in the French army during World War II, he won a scholarship to study film-making in Moscow and made his debut as a director with the short *Borom Sarret* (1963). *Mandabi* (1968), his second feature film, was the first African film to be made in an African language (Wolof). Since then, he has often directed films in Wolof or Diola as well as in French, and frequently uses the clash between African and European cultures as a theme of his work.
Career highs: *La Noire de…* (1966), *Mandabi* (1968), *Ceddo* (1977), *Camp de Thiaroye* (1987)

Sirk, Douglas (Claus Detlef Sierck) (1900–87)

Danish–American, born in Hamburg, Germany. From 1923 to 1936 he was a theatre director in Germany, moving to the USA before the outbreak of World War II. During the 1950s, he became famous for creating lavish melodramas for Universal Studios, often starring **Rock Hudson**. Often derided by critics at the peak of his career, his work was subsequently acclaimed for its blend of highly theatrical Technicolor histrionics and sharp social criticism.
Career highs: *Magnificent Obsession* (1954), *All That Heaven Allows* (1955), *The Tarnished Angels* (1957), *Imitation of Life* (1959), *Written on the Wind* (1956)
Career lows: *Slightly French* (1949), *Taza, Son of Cochise* (1954)

Sjöström, Victor (1879–1960)

Swedish, born in Silbodal. Orphaned as a teenager, he began a career as an actor before joining the Svenska Bio film company. His skill at adapting the work of classic Swedish writers for the screen gave Swedish cinema a new-found popular appeal. In Hollywood from 1923, he worked (as 'Victor Seastrom') with such luminaries of the silent age as **Lillian Gish** and **Greta Garbo** before returning to acting, notably appearing in **Ingmar Bergman**'s *Wild Strawberries* (1957) at the age of 78.

Career highs: *Ingeborg Holm* (1913), *Thy Soul Shall Bear Witness* (1920), *The Scarlet Letter* (1926), *The Wind* (1928)
Career low: *Under the Red Robe* (1937)

Soderbergh, Steven (1963–)

American, born in Atlanta, Georgia. An amateur film-maker as a teenager, he was initially unsuccessful in Hollywood but, on his second serious attempt at a film career, quickly found mainstream success. His debut feature, the low-budget *sex, lies, and videotape* (1989), won the Palme d'Or at Cannes, making him the youngest-ever directorial winner there. He is frequently the cinematographer on his own films, credited under the pseudonym Peter Andrews.
Career highs: *sex, lies, and videotape* (1989), *Out of Sight* (1998), *Traffic* (2000), *Erin Brockovich* (2000)
Career lows: *Kafka* (1991), *Gray's Anatomy* (1996), *Full Frontal* (2002)

Spielberg, Steven (1946–)

American, born in Cincinnati, Ohio. He began directing short films as a child, and studied film at California State University before beginning his career in television. He moved on to mainstream family films, then graduated to the challenging and harrowing epics that won him Best Director Academy Award® nods: *Schindler's List* (1993) and *Saving Private Ryan* (1998). A box-office legend, he has made many of the most commercially and artistically successful films of all time, as well as a number of crowd-pleasing, sentimental efforts. In 1994 he founded his own production company, Amblin Entertainment; he was also a founder of Dreamworks SKG.
Career highs: *Jaws* (1975), *Raiders of the Lost Ark* (1981), *E.T. the Extra-Terrestrial* (1982), *Schindler's List* (1993), *Saving Private Ryan* (1998)
Career lows: *Always* (1989), *Hook* (1991), *The Terminal* (2004)

Stevens, George (1904–75)

American, born in Oakland, California. The son of two actors, he began performing at the age of five. As a cinematographer in the 1920s he worked on **Laurel** and **Hardy** short films, graduating to comedy features a decade later. He headed the Army Signal Corps Special Motion Picture Unit during World War II, and his footage of the Nazi concentration camp at Dachau was used to indict war criminals at the Nuremberg war trial. His classic films of the 1950s were notably more sombre in tone as a result of his wartime experiences.
Career highs: *Swing Time* (1936), *Woman of the Year* (1942), *A Place in the Sun* (1951), *Shane* (1953), *Giant* (1956)
Career low: *The Only Game in Town* (1970)

Stone, Oliver (1946–)

American, born in New York City. Following several years as a teacher and soldier in Vietnam, he studied film at New York University (where he was taught by **Martin Scorsese**) and made his feature debut with *Seizure* (1974). His often controversial work frequently examines events from recent US history, particularly the Vietnam War; the violence of war, and of society in general, is a recurring theme in his work.

He has won three Academy Awards[®]: for the screenplay of *Midnight Express* (1978), and as Best Director for *Platoon* (1986) and *Born on the Fourth of July* (1989).
Career highs: *Platoon* (1986), *Salvador* (1986), *Born on the Fourth of July* (1989), *JFK* (1991)
Career lows: *Seizure* (1974), *U-Turn* (1997)

Stroheim, Erich von (Erich Oswald Stroheim) (1885–1957)

Austrian–American, born in Vienna. After working as a supervisor in his father's straw hat factory he emigrated to the USA, where he began his Hollywood career playing on-screen villains. He turned to writing and directing after World War I. His films reflect his sharp eye for detail, as well as his tendency to massively overrun in terms of length and budget. This flamboyance led to his becoming a victim of the studio system's controlling tendencies, and he was never given the opportunity to make a sound film; after 1933 he returned to acting, appearing notably in both *La grande illusion* (1937) and *Sunset Boulevard* (1950).
Career highs: *Blind Husbands* (1919), *Greed* (1924), *The Wedding March* (1928)
Career low: *Queen Kelly* (1928)

Epic Proportions

Erich von Stroheim's passion for authentic detail and his insistence on time-consuming, painstaking explorations of his characters' psychology were his defining characteristics as a director. Both are apparent in his masterpiece *Greed* (1924), an impressively faithful adaptation of Frank Norris's 1899 novel *McTeague*. Stroheim's original 42-reel cut of the film was more than seven hours long, and had to be cut – without his approval – to less than a quarter of its original length before it was considered suitable for commercial release. Stroheim is said to have remarked of the director who cut the film on his behalf, 'The only thing he had on his mind was his hat!'

Sturges, Preston (Edmund Preston Biden) (1898–1959)

American, born in Chicago, Illinois. Educated in the USA and Europe, he worked in the cosmetics industry and in 1920 invented a 'kiss-proof' lipstick ('Red-Red Rouge'), before beginning a career as a dramatist. He went on to write some of the wittiest and most sophisticated scripts ever filmed in Hollywood – inventive, freewheeling comedies that combined wit, slapstick and social concerns. By 1940 he had taken over the direction of his own projects, and in 1944 he was Academy Award[®]-nominated for two scripts, *The Miracle of Morgan's Creek* and *Hail the Conquering Hero*.
Career highs: *The Great McGinty* (1940), *The Lady Eve* (1941), *Sullivan's Travels* (1941), *The Miracle of Morgan's Creek* (1944), *Hail the Conquering Hero* (1944)
Career low: *The French, They Are a Funny Race* (1955)

Szabó, István (1938–   )

Hungarian, born in Budapest. A graduate of Budapest's Academy of Film Art, he worked in short features and television films until the release of his highly praised feature *Mephisto* (1981). His most famous films star the Austrian actor Klaus Maria

Brandauer, and are both character studies and studies of political corruption. In the 1990s he started to produce work in the English language.
Career highs: *Mephisto* (1981), *Colonel Redl* (1984), *Sunshine* (1999)
Career low: *Hanussen* (1988)

T

Tarantino, Quentin (1963–   )

American, born in Knoxville, Tennessee. After working as a video clerk while studying acting, he used the sale of an early screenplay to raise money for his first directorial venture, *Reservoir Dogs* (1992), a violent heist movie that became a huge success. Noted for his witty dialogue, non-linear narratives and distinctive use of music, he has since blended humour with stylish violence to great effect, and achieved cult status as a director. He also works as an actor and producer.
Career highs: *Reservoir Dogs* (1992), *Pulp Fiction* (1994), *Jackie Brown* (1997), *Kill Bill: Vol. 1* (2003), *Kill Bill: Vol. 2* (2004)
Career low: *Four Rooms* (segment 'The Man from Hollywood') (1995)

Tarkovsky, Andrei Arsenevich (1932–86)

Russian, born in Zavrzhe, USSR (now Belarus). The son of poet Arseni Tarkovsky, he was educated at Moscow's Institute of Oriental Languages and at the state film school VGIK. His films, deeply personal and spiritual, often feature dreamy lyrical scenes and long takes. The release of *Andrei Rublev* was held up for several years by the Soviet authorities, and Tarkovsky left the country in the 1980s for Italy, Sweden and finally France, where he died of lung cancer.
Career highs: *Ivan's Childhood* (1962), *Andrei Rublev* (1969), *The Sacrifice* (1986)

Truffaut, François (1932–84)

French, born in Paris. His early life as an unhappy child, reform school pupil and army deserter later formed elements of his more autobiographical works. A passionate film lover with a particular affection for obscure American B-pictures, he entered the film industry as a critic, worked for *Cahiers du cinéma* magazine under his mentor André Bazin, and ultimately became an integral part of the Nouvelle Vague movement. French actress Fanny Ardant was his off-screen partner.
Career highs: *The 400 Blows* (1959), *Jules et Jim* (1961), *La nuit américaine* (1973)

Dialogue Difficulties

Despite his lifelong love of US film, François Truffaut never learned to speak English. This proved something of a handicap when he began work on his only English-language production, *Fahrenheit 451* (1966), an adaptation of the novel by Ray Bradbury. The film's screenplay (on which Truffaut collaborated with French writer Jean-Louis Richard) unsurprisingly contained some rather stilted English dialogue, and the director's relative inability to communicate with his cast in English did not improve matters. Truffaut is said to have been far more pleased with the version of the film that was dubbed into French under his supervision.

V

Van Sant, Gus, Jr (1952–   )

American, born in Louisville, Kentucky. He was educated at the Rhode Island School of Design, where he studied painting before turning to cinema. He began his career directing television commercials, then made his feature debut with *Mala Noche* (1985). Many of his films feature dysfunctional characters on the margins of society. He is also a published author, photographer and musician.

Career highs: *Drugstore Cowboy* (1989), *My Own Private Idaho* (1991), *To Die For* (1995), *Good Will Hunting* (1997), *Elephant* (2003)

Career lows: *Even Cowgirls Get the Blues* (1994), *Psycho* (1998)

Vidor, King Wallis (1894–1982)

American, born in Galveston, Texas. Having survived the Galveston hurricane of 1900, then the worst natural disaster in US history, he used it as the subject of his first film *Hurricane in Galveston* (1913). A director for over 60 years, his output included both silent films and talkies. The Academy Award®-nominated *Hallelujah!* (1929) was the first Hollywood film to have an all-black cast. Vidor was also the uncredited director of the black-and-white Kansas sequence in *The Wizard of Oz* (1939).

Career highs: *The Big Parade* (1925), *The Crowd* (1928), *The Champ* (1931), *Duel in the Sun* (1946), *The Fountainhead* (1949), *War and Peace* (1956)

Career lows: *Ruby Gentry* (1952), *Solomon and Sheba* (1959)

A Setback for Solomon

Filming of King Vidor's biblical epic *Solomon and Sheba* (1959) was thrown off course when the star, Tyrone Power, collapsed and died of a heart attack. Although more than half of Power's scenes had already been completed, Vidor had for some reason started with the actor's long shots and left most of his close-ups to last, so it was impossible to complete the film without replacing him and starting again. Yul Brynner took over the role, although some footage of Power – seen from a distance – remained in the final cut.

Vigo, Jean (1905–34)

French, born in Paris. The son of an anarchist who died mysteriously in prison, Vigo spent his childhood at boarding schools, often suffering from poor health. He made his directorial debut with *À propos de Nice* (1930), and used his unhappy schooldays as the stimulus for the banned *Zéro de Conduite* (1933). His masterpiece, *L'Atalante* (1934), was mangled by the censor and not fully restored until 1990. He died at the age of 29, with just four films to his credit.

Career highs: *Zéro de conduite* (1933), *L'Atalante* (1934)

Visconti, Luchino (Count Don Luchino Visconti Di Morone) (1906–76)

Italian, born in Milan. After military service and a period spent breeding racehorses, he became an assistant to **Jean Renoir**. He became a pioneer of Italian neorealism with *Ossessione* (1942), the first film to be attributed to the movement, and developed into a director with an operatic touch, creating stunning literary adaptations that often focused on class and moral decay. He also directed plays, ballets and operas.

Career highs: *Ossessione* (1943), *Senso* (1954), *The Leopard* (1963), *Death in Venice* (1971)

Career low: *Le Streghe* (1967)

Von Sternberg, Josef (Jonas Sternberg) (1894–1969)

Austrian, born in Vienna. Von Sternberg was brought up in the USA, and worked on silent films in 1920s Hollywood as a scriptwriter, cameraman and director. In Germany to direct *The Blue Angel* (1930), he discovered **Marlene Dietrich**, whom he cast in that film as well as another six of his Hollywood features. His films were noted for their strong visual imagery and atmospheric use of lighting.

Career highs: *The Blue Angel* (1930), *Morocco* (1930), *Shanghai Express* (1932), *The Devil is a Woman* (1935)

Career low: *Jet Pilot* (1957)

von Trier, Lars (Lars Trier) (1956–)

Danish, born in Copenhagen. The son of radical, nudist, Communist parents, he became interested in film during his unhappy childhood and went on to train at the Danish Film School, where he added 'von' to his name. In 1995 he co-authored the Dogme 95 manifesto, advocating austerity and the rejection of artifice in film-making. He has become Denmark's pre-eminent film-maker, known for his experimental techniques and his often unsettling subject matter.

Career highs: *Europa* (1991), *Breaking the Waves* (1996), *Dancer in the Dark* (2000)

W

Wajda, Andrzej (1926–)

Polish, born in Suwalki. As a youngster, he fought with the Resistance movement against the Nazi occupation of Poland. He studied at Lodz film school after World War II, making his directorial debut with the short *The Bad Boy* (1950). His work has documented the effects of the war, as well as political developments including the rise of the Solidarity movement. Exiled to France in the 1980s, he subsequently returned to his homeland and served as a Polish senator (1989–91).

Career highs: *Kanal* (1956), *Ashes and Diamonds* (1958), *Man of Marble* (1977), *Man of Iron* (1981), *Danton* (1983)

Walsh, Raoul (Albert Edward Walsh) (1887–1980)

American, born in New York City. As a child, he ran away from home, working as a cowboy before becoming a stage actor and eventually finding work in the film industry. He played John Wilkes Booth in **D W Griffith**'s *Birth of a Nation* (1916), and began his directorial career as Griffith's assistant; his output consisted mainly of westerns, gangster films and action dramas. He lost an eye in a car accident while filming *In Old Arizona* in 1929, and wore an eye patch thereafter. His first wife was silent film actress Miriam Cooper, who appeared in many of his films.

Career highs: *The Big Trail* (1930), *The Roaring Twenties* (1939), *They Died with Their Boots On* (1941), *White Heat* (1949)

Warhol, Andy (Andrew Warhola) (1928–87)

American, born in Pittsburgh, Pennsylvania. He studied art and designed advertisements for women's shoes before reinventing himself as leader of the Pop Art movement. His directorial debut was a five-hour silent observation of a sleeping man, *Sleep* (1963), and his early filmic career was characterized by experimental but plotless (critics would assert pointless) compositions such as the eight-hour stationary shot of the Empire State Building, *Empire* (1964). His later work incorporated improvised dialogue, colour and graphic sexual content.
Career highs: *My Hustler* (1965), *The Chelsea Girls* (1966), *Lonesome Cowboys* (1969)

Watkins, Peter (1935–   )

English, born in Surbiton. Watkins was educated at Cambridge University and the Royal Academy of Dramatic Art, and became a BBC documentary film-maker. *The War Game* (1966), a documentary-style depiction of a Soviet nuclear attack on Britain, won a Best Documentary Academy Award® despite being banned by the BBC. Watkins subsequently worked abroad, continuing to direct movies with a political message and non-professional actors.
Career highs: *Culloden* (1964), *The War Game* (1965)
Career low: *Privilege* (1967)

Weir, Peter Lindsay (1944–   )

Australian, born in Sydney. He studied at the University of Sydney before joining Australia's Commonwealth Film Unit, and made his feature debut with *The Cars That Ate Paris* (1975). Having found early success in his home country, he moved to Hollywood, where his characteristic themes of physical and cultural isolation, and the mysteries of the natural world, were used to good effect in numerous mainstream productions.
Career highs: *Picnic at Hanging Rock* (1975), *Gallipoli* (1981), *The Year of Living Dangerously* (1982), *Witness* (1985), *Master and Commander: The Far Side of the World* (2003)
Career lows: *The Mosquito Coast* (1986), *Fearless* (1993)

Welles, (George) Orson (1915–85)

American, born in Kenosha, Wisconsin. A child prodigy, he performed with the Gate Theatre in Dublin, stunned Broadway with his innovative theatre productions and shocked America with his radio adaptation of *The War of the Worlds* (1938). His official cinema debut *Citizen Kane* (1941) is regarded by many as the greatest film ever made. He spent his career battling for authorial independence and proper financing, and left a rich legacy of daring film-making and larger-than-life performances.
Career highs (actor): *Citizen Kane* (1941), *The Third Man* (1949), *Othello* (1952), *Touch of Evil* (1958), *Compulsion* (1959)

Career highs (director): *Citizen Kane* (1941), *The Magnificent Ambersons* (1942), *The Lady from Shanghai* (1948), *Othello* (1952), *Touch of Evil* (1958)
Career lows: *Trouble in the Glen* (1954), *Where Is Parsifal?* (1983)

Wellman, William A(ugustus) (1896–1975)

American, born in Brookline, Massachusetts. After dropping out of high school, he served in the French Foreign Legion and was a US pilot in World War I, and a stunt pilot thereafter. He entered the film industry after a chance meeting with **Douglas Fairbanks**, and after a spell as an actor made his directorial debut with *Second Hand Love* (1923). His aviation film *Wings* (1927) was the first film to win a Best Picture Academy Award®.
Career highs: *The Public Enemy* (1931), *A Star Is Born* (1937) *The Ox-Bow Incident* (1943)

Wenders, (Ernst) Wi(lhel)m (1945–)

German, born in Düsseldorf. A fan of American films from his early childhood, he lived in Paris for a time before studying film at Munich's Academy of Film and Television. He began his career as a critic before developing into one of the leading exponents of the New German Cinema. Themes of isolation and alienation characterize his films, which often feature journeys in search of enlightenment.
Career highs: *The Scarlet Letter* (1973), *Paris, Texas* (1984), *Wings of Desire* (1987), *Buena Vista Social Club* (1999)
Career low: *Hammett* (1982)

Wertmüller, Lina (Arcangela Felice Assunta Wertmüller von Elgg) (1928–)

Italian, born in Rome. Wertmüller began her career as an actress and, through her friendship with **Marcello Mastroianni**, was introduced to **Federico Fellini**, who employed her as an assistant director on *8½*. Her best-known film, *Seven Beauties* (1976), set in a Nazi concentration camp, gained her an Academy Award® nomination as Best Director, the first for a woman. A prolific director, she is known for mixing sexual and political themes in her work, and notorious for her wordy film titles.
Career highs: *Love and Anarchy* (1973), *Swept Away... by an Unusual Destiny in the Blue Sea of August* (1974), *Seven Beauties* (1976)
Career low: *The End of the World in Our Usual Bed in a Night Full of Rain* (1977)

Whale, James (1889–1957)

English, born in Dudley. He was a newspaper cartoonist before turning to acting as a hobby while he was a prisoner during World War I. After the war he worked on the stage before moving to Hollywood in 1930; he then became a successful director in many genres, but is best remembered for his witty and stylish horror films. He died by drowning in his swimming pool. His life and career were portrayed in the 1998 film *Gods and Monsters*.
Career highs: *Frankenstein* (1931), *The Old Dark House* (1932), *The Invisible Man* (1933), *Bride of Frankenstein* (1935), *Show Boat* (1936)

Wilder, Billy (Samuel Wilder) (1906–2002)

American, born in Sucha, Austria. After studying law, he worked as a journalist, crime reporter, screenwriter and 'taxi dancer' in Vienna, Paris and Berlin, then moved to the USA in 1933; his mother died in a Nazi concentration camp. In Hollywood, he worked as a screenwriter before making his solo directorial debut with *The Major and the Minor* (1942). During more than 50 years of film-making, he produced a mixture of daring, provocative comedies and satires that crackled with witty dialogue and brought him both critical and popular acclaim.

Career highs: *Double Indemnity* (1944), *The Lost Weekend* (1945), *Sunset Boulevard* (1950), *Stalag 17* (1953), *Some Like It Hot* (1959), *The Apartment* (1960)
Career lows: *Irma La Douce* (1963), *Kiss Me, Stupid* (1964)

Winterbottom, Michael (1961–)

English, born in Blackburn. After studying at Oxford, he worked as a television editor before moving into directing documentaries. His first feature film was *Butterfly Kiss* (1995). He is known for creating stark and edgy dramas, often filmed using hand-held cameras and improvisational techniques.

Career highs: *Go Now* (1995), *In This World* (2002), *24 Hour Party People* (2003)
Career low: *The Claim* (2000)

Wise, Robert (1914–2005)

American, born in Winchester, Indiana. After entering the film industry as an assistant cutter, he received an Academy Award® nomination as editor of *Citizen Kane* (1941) and subsequently began directing. He excelled in a range of genres, from science fiction to dramas and musicals, and won Best Picture and Best Director Academy Awards® for both *West Side Story* (1961) and *The Sound of Music* (1965).

Career highs: *The Day the Earth Stood Still* (1951), *West Side Story* (1961), *The Sound of Music* (1965)
Career low: *Star!* (1968)

Wiseman, Frederick (1930–)

American, born in Boston, Massachusetts. After studying law at Yale University, he became a documentary film-maker; his first major work, *Titicut Follies* (1967), was a controversial exposé of life inside a state hospital for the criminally insane. He subsequently turned his camera onto other US institutions – schools, hospitals, courts and the police force – using a distinctive non-chronological style without narration. He has also made fictional films.

Career highs: *Titicut Follies* (1967), *High School* (1968), *Law and Order* (1969), *Hospital* (1970)
Career low: *Ballet* (1995)

Wyler, William (1902–81)

American, born in Mülhausen, Germany (now Mulhouse, France). He was invited to the USA by his cousin **Carl Laemmle**, the head of Universal Pictures, and after working his way up from the publicity department, made his directorial debut with *Crook Buster* (1925). Noted for his slow pace of working and meticulous attention to detail, he was nominated a record twelve times for the Best Director Academy Award®, winning on three occasions.

Career highs: *The Little Foxes* (1941), *Mrs Miniver* (1942), *The Best Years of Our Lives* (1946), *Ben-Hur* (1959)

Z

Zhang Yimou (1951–)

Chinese, born in Xian, Shanxi Province. He studied at the Beijing Film Academy and began his career as a cinematographer, making his directorial debut with *Red Sorghum* (1987). His early films were often suppressed by the Chinese authorities for political reasons, despite finding critical favour abroad. He is now one of the best-known and most influential members of China's Fifth Generation movement, a group of directors whose careers began after the Cultural Revolution; he has recently become known for lavish, digitally-enhanced historical action epics that showcase his love of dramatic, colourful visuals.

Career highs: *Red Sorghum* (1987), *Ju Dou* (1990), *Raise the Red Lantern* (1991), *Hero* (2002)

Career low: *Codename Cougar* (1987)

Zinnemann, Fred (1907–97)

Austrian, born in Vienna. After studying law he turned to a film career, beginning as an assistant cameraman. In 1929 he moved to Hollywood, where he worked his way up from extra to director; his first notable solo effort was *The Search* (1948). His films are often concerned with conflicts of conscience and the moral dilemmas of reluctant heroes; his vast range as a director included westerns, thrillers, musicals and historical dramas. He was nominated seven times for the Best Director Academy Award®, winning twice.

Career highs: *High Noon* (1952), *From Here to Eternity* (1953), *A Man for All Seasons* (1966), *Julia* (1977)

SOME NOTABLE PRODUCERS

Corman, Roger William (1926–)

American, born in Detroit, Michigan. He worked as a messenger boy at Twentieth-Century Fox before moving to England to study at Oxford University. He later returned to Hollywood, and was closely associated with the independent American International Pictures, known for exploitation films. He produced and directed entertaining low-budget films across many genres during the 1960s; his horror films in particular are regarded as cult classics. From the 1970s onwards he was less active as a director, but remained a noted independent producer and distributor, lending his support to the careers of up-and-coming directors including **Francis Ford Coppola** and **Martin Scorsese**.

Corman's Cameos

Several directors who were given early career breaks by producer Roger Corman eventually became well-known in their own right. Some of his protégés later paid homage to Corman by inviting him to make cameo appearances in their films – hence his small roles in *The Godfather, Part II* (1974), *The Silence of the Lambs* (1991) and *The Manchurian Candidate* (2004), among others.

De Laurentiis, Dino (Agostino De Laurentiis) (1919–)

Italian, born in Torre Annunziata. The son of a pasta manufacturer, he trained as an actor before turning to production. His first international hit was *Riso amaro* (1949) starring the actress Silvana Mangano, whom he later married. During the 1950s and 60s he established himself as an international producer, working with fellow producer Carlo Ponti before building his own studio complex, Dinocittà, near Rome. He became known for expensive, visually spectacular films, produced on a grand scale. Changes to government funding of the Italian film industry drove him to Hollywood in the 1970s, but his success there was limited.

Disney, Walt(er Elias) (1901–66)

American, born in Chicago, Illinois. He worked as a commercial artist before setting up a small Hollywood studio, where he collaborated with animator Ub Iwerks on animated cartoons. He was largely responsible for the creation of Mickey Mouse (initially providing Mickey's voice himself), Donald Duck and Goofy, and was the driving force behind *Snow White and the Seven Dwarfs* (1937). The Walt Disney name became a global business empire, producing full-length cartoons and family films. In 1955 he opened a theme park, Disneyland, in California; others have since opened in Florida (1971), Tokyo (1983), Paris (1992) and Hong Kong (2005).

Goldwyn, Samuel (Samuel Goldfish) (1882–1974)

American, born in Warsaw, Poland. Orphaned at a young age, he worked as a successful glove salesman before co-founding a film company with his brother-in-law, vaudeville producer Jesse L Lasky, and **Cecil B De Mille**. Their first film, *The Squaw Man* (1914), was a hit, providing them with funds for more ambitious projects. In 1917 he co-founded Goldwyn Pictures, which subsequently merged with rivals to form the Metro-Goldwyn-Mayer (MGM) Company. He later established the independent Samuel Goldwyn Productions. His instinctive business sense and attention to detail brought him lasting fame and fortune, and he was also a noted philanthropist.

Goldwynisms

Polish-born Samuel Goldwyn was famous for the malapropisms, or 'Goldwynisms', that resulted from his combination of imperfect English and genuine wit. Sayings attributed to him include 'A verbal contract isn't worth the paper it's written on', 'Gentlemen, include me out' and 'They stayed away in droves'.

Korda, Sir Alexander (Sándor Laszlo Kellner) (1893–1956)

British, born in Pusztatúrpáztó, Hungary. After working as a journalist in Budapest he became a film publicist and subtitle-writer there, later moving into directing and production. He worked in Vienna, Berlin and Hollywood before moving to the UK, where he founded London Film Productions in 1932 with his brothers Vincent (an art director) and Zoltàn (a director). A charismatic, flamboyant figure, he is thought to have served as partial inspiration for the character of Boris Lermontov in Powell and Pressburger's classic *The Red Shoes* (1948), which he produced. In 1942 he became the first film producer to receive a knighthood.

Laemmle, Carl, Sr (1867–1939)

American, born in Laupheim, Germany. He moved to the USA in 1917 to seek his fortune, and invested his savings in a nickelodeon. Success led him to expand into film distribution and production. As founder of the Independent Motion Picture Company of America (1909) he was instrumental in the creation of the star system during the silent era, establishing the popular actress Florence Lawrence as the face of his company. A pioneering producer and bold businessman, he later became head of Universal Studios, but sold the company in 1935. His son Carl Laemmle Jr was also a film producer.

Mayer, Louis B(urt) (Eliezer Mayer) (1885–1957)

American, born in Minsk, Russia. His family emigrated to Canada when he was three, and he was working as a scrap metal dealer by the age of eight. In 1907 he opened one of the earliest custom-designed cinemas. He subsequently acquired a chain of movie theatres in New England, set up a film production company in Los Angeles, and in 1924 became vice-president of the newly merged Metro-Goldwyn-Mayer (MGM) Company. He wielded enormous power within the film industry for over 20 years, overseeing such successes as *Grand Hotel* (1932) and *Ninotchka* (1939), and helped to establish the Academy of Motion Picture Arts and Sciences in 1927.

Selznick, David O(liver) (1902–65)

American, born in Pittsburgh, Ohio. He worked for his father in film distribution and promotion before becoming a producer with the short film *Will He Conquer Dempsey?* (1923). Employment as a story editor and associate producer at MGM and Paramount led to his appointment as vice-president in charge of production at RKO. He was known for masterminding every aspect of a production, and for the long, detailed memos he sent to colleagues. In 1937 he formed his own production company, which produced the hugely successful screen adaptation of *Gone with the Wind* (1939). His second wife was **Jennifer Jones**.

Thalberg, Irving G(rant) (1899–1936)

American, born in New York City. He began his career as secretary to **Carl Laemmle** at Universal Studios. Promoted to general manager, he played a key role in the formation of MGM, where he then became head of production. Nicknamed 'The Boy Wonder', he was renowned for his obsessive devotion to his work; among the films he helped put into production were *Grand Hotel* (1932) and

Camille (1936). Plagued by illness since childhood, he died of pneumonia at 37; an Academy Award® is still given in his name, honouring consistent excellence in film production. He was married to **Norma Shearer**.

The Last Tycoon

The character of Monroe Stahr in *The Last Tycoon*, the final unfinished novel by US author F Scott Fitzgerald, is said to have been inspired by the life of Irving G Thalberg. In the early 1930s Fitzgerald had worked as a screenwriter at MGM, where he met and admired the driven, energetic producer.

Warner, Jack Leonard (Jack Leonard Eichelbaum) (1892–1978)

American, born in London, Ontario, Canada. The youngest son of a large, impoverished Polish immigrant family, he embarked upon a show-business career as a boy soprano before joining with his brothers to form a film distribution company. They eventually moved into production, and built a studio in Los Angeles in 1919. The sensational popularity of the first 'talkie', *The Jazz Singer* (1927), saw Warner Brothers blossom into a major studio, specializing in gangster films, musicals and historical biographies. Warner spent decades as a hard-headed, sometimes ruthless head of production before selling his interest in the studio in the late 1960s.

Zanuck, Darryl F(rancis) (1902–79)

American, born in Wahoo, Nebraska. After service in the National Guard, he held a variety of odd jobs before becoming a screenwriter at Warner Brothers in 1924. He was eventually promoted to head of production, but left the company following a rift with Harry Warner. He co-founded Twentieth-Century Pictures (1933) and, after its merger with Fox Films (1935), became vice-president of Twentieth-Century Fox Films Corporation, where his productions included *The Grapes of Wrath* (1940). Following World War II he took control of the studio, and remained there – apart from a six-year gap during which he worked in Europe – until 1971.

Credit Conflict

Modern films often list large teams of producers, rather than single names, in their credits. However, if such a film wins the Academy Award® for Best Picture, it can be difficult to decide which producers should actually accept – and keep – the coveted Oscar® statuettes. When *Shakespeare in Love* (1998) won in 1999, disagreements over this issue were widely reported by the media. The Academy of Motion Picture Arts and Sciences subsequently decided that only the three producers who had made the most significant contributions to a film could receive Oscars® for Best Picture. This, however, led to acrimonious debate within nominated production teams over who was most deserving, and the 2005 awards were notable for the awkwardness surrounding producer credits for Best Picture nominees *The Aviator*, *Million Dollar Baby* and *Ray* (all 2004). In a further attempt to resolve the issue, the Academy announced in 2006 that it would hand over full responsibility for decisions on producer eligibility to the Producers Guild of America (PGA). Strict guidelines were drawn up, with the aim of evaluating each producer's contribution as fairly as possible, but it remains to be seen whether this will be a lasting solution.

SOME NOTABLE CINEMATOGRAPHERS

Bitzer, Billy (Johann Gottlob Wilhelm Bitzer) (1872–1944)

American, born in Roxbury, Massachusetts. He worked as a silversmith before becoming a cameraman in the early days of motion-picture photography, when he joined the newly-formed film company that would later become famous as Biograph. He worked closely with **D W Griffith** for 16 years, photographing almost all of Griffith's shorts and feature films. Together they were responsible for a number of significant developments in film technique, including the close-up, the slow fade and the iris shot. Bitzer retired from film-making in the 1920s, and subsequently became a film researcher at the Museum of Modern Art in New York City.

Cardiff, Jack (1914–)

English, born in Yarmouth. A child actor from the age of four, he moved behind the camera at the age of 13 as an assistant and devoted himself to learning the mechanics of cinematography. He was camera operator on the UK's first Technicolor production, *Wings of the Morning* (1937), and went on to become a renowned director of photography and colour expert, celebrated for his work on such films as *Black Narcissus* (1947) and *The Red Shoes* (1948). Later in his career he moved into directing, but he remains best known for his accomplishments as a cinematographer.

> ### Smell-O-Vision
>
> Jack Cardiff has the dubious distinction of having directed the first – and only – Smell-O-Vision film, *Scent of Mystery* (1960). Smell-O-Vision was a system of presentation involving a 'smell track' which prompted the release of particular odours, including peaches and wine, through tubes directly to the audience at predetermined points in the film.

Doyle, Christopher (1952–)

Australian, born in Sydney. After several years travelling and working in a variety of jobs including cow-herding and oil drilling, he moved to Taiwan, where he co-founded the country's first modern theatre, Lanling Theatre Workshop. He took up cinematography in his early 30s, and his innovative work with **Wong Kar-Wai** (notably on *Chungking Express*, 1994) brought him international attention. He has since become one of modern cinema's most celebrated and sought-after cinematographers, noted for his perfectionism and distinctive visual style. He continues to work mainly, though not exclusively, on Asian films, and has also directed (*Away with Words*, 1999).

Figueroa, Gabriel (Gabriel Figueroa Mateos) (1907–97)

Mexican, born in Mexico City. He was orphaned as a young boy, and worked to support himself while pursuing his love of painting and photography. He studied at Mexico's Conservatorio Nacional and ran a photography studio before taking up cinematography in 1932. From 1935–6 he was in Hollywood, where he assisted

Gregg Toland; he then returned to Mexico and went on to build an international reputation as a prolific and visionary cameraman. He worked with **Luis Buñuel**, **John Ford** and **John Huston**, but his most celebrated long-term collaboration was with the eminent Mexican director Emilio Fernández.

Howe, James Wong (Wong Tung-Jim) (1899–1976)

American, born in Canton (now Guangzhou), China. He moved to the USA at the age of five, and was a professional boxer before his fascination with photography led to a job as a cutting-room assistant in 1917. By 1922 he had been promoted to director of photography. Renowned for his skill with lighting, he endeared himself to leading ladies with his knack for obscuring flaws and creating flattering images. He was also a technical innovator – one of the first cinematographers to employ hand-held camera techniques and make use of deep focus – and occasionally directed.

Kovács, László (1933–   )

Hungarian, born in Budapest. He trained at Budapest's Academy of Drama and Film Art before relocating to Hollywood in the mid-1950s, initially working under the name Leslie Kovacs. His skilful work on low-budget films with **Roger Corman** attracted the attention of critics and brought him into contact with young directors including **Peter Fonda** and **Peter Bogdanovich**, with whom he collaborated on such films as *Easy Rider* (1969), *What's Up Doc?* (1971) and *Paper Moon* (1973).

Schüfftan, Eugen (1893–1977)

American, born in Breslau, Germany (now Wrocław, Poland). Trained at Breslau's Academy of Arts, he was a painter before moving into the film industry in 1920. A pioneering visual effects specialist, in the 1920s he developed what became known around the world as the 'Schüfftan process', filming miniature models with the aid of mirrors to give the effect of full-sized sets (first used in *Metropolis*, 1927). He was a noted cinematographer in France (where he worked on such films as *Le quai des brumes*, 1938), Germany and the UK as well as in the USA, where he settled in 1941.

Toland, Gregg (1904–48)

American, born in Charleston, Illinois. He entered the film industry as an office boy at 15, and quickly moved into camera work. Promoted to director of photography early in the sound era, he gained a reputation as a brilliant technical innovator with a unique artistic vision. He collaborated with directors including **John Ford**, **Orson Welles** and **William Wyler**, and was responsible for the development of the deep-focus technique – employed to striking effect in *Citizen Kane* (1941) – as well as countless other innovations in his field; his pioneering work was cut short by his early death of a heart attack.

SOME NOTABLE EDITORS

Booth, Margaret (1898–2002)

American, born in Los Angeles, California. She began cutting film for **D W Griffith**, and in 1921 moved to **Louis B Mayer**'s studio, which later became MGM. She was the first woman to achieve success in her field, and worked as MGM's supervising film editor from 1939 to 1968, eventually leaving the studio to return to more hands-on editing assignments with various independent film-makers. Her film credits include *Mutiny on the Bounty* (1935) and *The Way We Were* (1973). She received an Academy Award® for overall career achievement in 1977, and continued to work until the age of 88.

Murch, Walter (1943–)

American, born in New York City. He studied film at the University of Southern California, and began his career as sound editor on **Francis Ford Coppola**'s *The Rain People* (1969). A noted film editor as well as sound editor and mixer, he was the first to use the term 'sound designer'. He received an Academy Award® for his work on *Apocalypse Now* (1979), and was also nominated for *The Conversation* (1974) and *Julia* (1977). He has directed one film (the unsuccessful *Return to Oz*, 1985), and contributed to the screenplays of *THX 1138* (1971) and *The Black Stallion* (1979).

Schoonmaker, Thelma (1945–)

American, born in Algeria. The daughter of an oil company worker, she spent much of her childhood in Africa. She met **Martin Scorsese** at New York University, and has been closely associated with his films since his debut, *Who's That Knocking at My Door?* (1968). She has been influential in helping create Scorsese's distinctive visual style, and is one of the leading editors in contemporary US cinema. She received an Academy Award® for her work on *Raging Bull* (1980), and was also nominated for *Goodfellas* (1990) and *Woodstock* (1970). She was married to **Michael Powell** until his death in 1990.

SOME NOTABLE FILM COMPOSERS

Bernstein, Elmer (1922–2004)

American, born in New York City. He trained at New York's Juilliard School of Music and worked as a composer for radio, television and low-budget films before making his name with the groundbreaking jazz score for *The Man with the Golden Arm* (1955). He composed a number of classic film scores during the 1950s and 60s (notably *The Magnificent Seven*, 1960, and *The Great Escape*, 1963), and continued to work steadily in later decades, receiving the fourteenth and final Academy Award® nomination of his career for *Far from Heaven* (2002).

Goldsmith, Jerry (Jerrald King Goldsmith) (1929–2004)

American, born in Pasadena, California. He studied at the University of Southern California, where **Miklós Rózsa** was one of his teachers, and began his career composing for the CBS radio network. He worked extensively in radio and television before making his feature film breakthrough with the score for *Freud* (1962), which earned him an Academy Award® nomination. For the next four decades he continued – unusually for a major film composer – to balance television work (notably the theme for *The Waltons*) with film scores (including *Chinatown*, 1974, and *L.A. Confidential*, 1997).

Herrmann, Bernard (1911–75)

American, born in New York City. He studied at the Juilliard School of Music and was a composer and conductor for CBS radio, where he worked with **Orson Welles** on the 1938 broadcast of *The War of the Worlds*. He accompanied Welles to Hollywood to score *Citizen Kane* (1941), his first work on a feature film. Although he disliked being pigeonholed as a film composer, he went on to provide some of the most famous scores of 1950s and 60s cinema, particularly on **Alfred Hitchcock** films including *Vertigo* (1958) and *Psycho* (1960). He relocated to the UK in the late 1960s.

Herrmann and Hitchcock

Notoriously irascible, Bernard Herrmann routinely ignored the specific instructions of film directors regarding music, and he made no exception for his long-term collaborator Alfred Hitchcock. For the shower scene in *Psycho* (1960) Hitchcock was adamant that he wanted no music whatsoever, but Herrmann persisted and ultimately won the argument, providing the shrill, shrieking music that helped to make the scene so shocking and memorable. Despite this happy outcome, an almost identical disagreement took place over the scoring of a murder sequence in *Torn Curtain* (1966), leading to the permanent severing of relations between the two men.

Korngold, Erich Wolfgang (1897–1957)

American, born in Brno, Moravia (now in Czech Republic). The son of a music critic, he was known throughout Germany from the age of 12 for his chamber, orchestral and stage music compositions (the eminent composer Gustav Mahler reportedly described him as 'a genius'). He was made a professor at the Vienna State Academy of Music in 1930, but moved to Hollywood a few years later to escape Hitler's annexation of Austria. He became an influential film composer, receiving Academy Awards® for *Anthony Adverse* (1936) and *Robin Hood* (1938), but continued to compose operas and concert pieces.

Morricone, Ennio (1928–)

Italian, born in Rome. He studied music at the Conservatorio di Santa Cecilia in Rome and began his career composing for theatre, radio and television. He turned to film composition in the early 1960s, making his breakthrough with the stylized score for the spaghetti western *A Fistful of Dollars* (1964), which marked the beginning of his long professional association with **Sergio Leone**. Though best known for his highly influential work with Leone, he has had a prolific career in international cinema, with nearly 400 film scores in many genres to his credit.

Rózsa, Miklós (1907–95)

American, born in Budapest, Hungary. The son of a successful industrialist, he studied the violin from the age of five and developed an interest in modern music while still at school. His early career as a composer took him to London, where he was invited to provide the score for *Knight without Armour* (1937) (produced by his countryman **Alexander Korda**). He relocated to Hollywood in 1940 and established a stellar reputation with innovative scores for such films as *Double Indemnity* (1944) and *Spellbound* (1945). He was also a Professor of Film Music at the University of Southern California (1945–65).

Rota, Nino (Nini Rota Rinaldi) (1911–79)

Italian, born in Milan. Raised in a musical family, he studied music and composition in Italy and the USA, as well as completing a degree in literature. He balanced a long teaching career at Italy's Bari Conservatory with numerous compositions for ballet, opera and film. His work as a film composer is best remembered for the 25-year creative partnership with **Federico Fellini** that saw him compose the scores for *La strada* (1954) and *Amarcord* (1974) among others; he also worked with **Luchino Visconti**, Franco Zeffirelli and **Francis Ford Coppola**.

Williams, John Towner (1932–)

American, born in Floral Park, Long Island, New York. The son of a professional musician, he trained at New York's Juilliard School of Music and started his career as a jazz pianist. In the late 1950s he began composing for television, turning to film in the 1960s. He made a name for himself as a composer of scores for disaster films such as *The Towering Inferno* (1974), and established a fruitful professional association with **Steven Spielberg** from 1974, providing the score for *Jaws* (1975); his prolific output also includes the scores for *Star Wars* (1977) and *E.T. the Extra-Terrestrial* (1982).

FILM CATEGORIES AND GENRES

ACTION AND ADVENTURE

History

Cinema, more than any other art form, has an immediacy that can set the pulse racing by catapulting viewers into death-defying situations in far-off times and places. Pirates, outlaws, spies and renegade cops are among the larger-than-life characters onto whom audiences can project their own heroic fantasies. Within this escapist form of entertainment, stunts add a visceral thrill to the emotional impact of a story – as early as the 1890s, showmen were eliciting gasps by fixing cameras to the front of trains for a 'phantom ride'. The swashbucklers of the silent era brought exciting physical movement to costume dramas, leading to increasingly high standards of spectacle and set design. Bursts of action became important components of many genres, from World War II-inspired films to the historical epics of the 1950s. The relaxation of censorship laws in the late 1960s allowed action scenes to become more graphically violent, although scale was still of primary importance, as evidenced by the disaster-themed adventures of the 1970s. By the 1980s, action in US cinema had become synonymous with the popcorn buzz of high-concept blockbusters and the oiled muscles of superstars such as Sylvester Stallone and Arnold Schwarzenegger.

The genre today

Although Hollywood's big-budget adventures dominate the global box office, they have recently started to respond to foreign influences – notably the slow-motion gunfights of Hong Kong cinema and the invisible-wire acrobatic techniques of Asian kung fu epics. Increasingly sophisticated computer effects have helped to push action spectacle to unprecedented levels, although one result of this trend is that many action blockbusters now resemble a series of stunt set pieces, only loosely linked by a plot.

Key figures

Jerry Bruckheimer (1945–   )
Producer who, along with his late partner Don Simpson, is mostly responsible for the high-concept blockbuster style of the 1980s, which combines simple storylines with explosive action, loud music and fast editing.

Douglas Fairbanks, Sr (1883–1939)
Actor-producer who set the mould for swashbuckler heroes with gymnastic displays of choreographed stunt work in *Robin Hood* (1922) and *The Black Pirate* (1926).

Steve McQueen (1930–80)
Actor with a casually cool, tough and independent screen presence who achieved superstar status, often performing his own stunts – particularly those involving cars or motorbikes, as in *The Great Escape* (1963).

Arnold Schwarzenegger (1947–   )
Austrian bodybuilder-turned-actor who exploited his muscle-bound, physically

unstoppable screen persona – notably as *The Terminator* (1984) – during his political campaign to become governor of California.

Sir Ridley Scott (1937–)
Director and producer of superior, action-fuelled genre films (*Alien*, 1979; *Blade Runner*, 1982; *Gladiator*, 2000) who brings real drama to his lavishly mounted set pieces.

Raoul Walsh (1887–1980)
Director with a well-earned reputation as a hellraiser, who began his career by shooting battle scenes for D W Griffith, and was at his best when dealing with complex characters openly hungering for adventure.

Sigourney Weaver (1949–)
Actress who became one of Hollywood's few well-known action heroines by starring in the *Alien* series (1979–97) as Ripley, a character defined as much by her maternal instincts as by her skill with a flame-thrower.

> ## Bruce's Pop Past
>
> Action star Bruce Willis recorded two albums in the 1980s – *The Return of Bruno* and *If It Don't Kill You, It Just Makes You Stronger*. The former, which accompanied a spoof 'rockumentary' of the same title, included the singles 'Respect Yourself' and 'Under the Boardwalk', which managed to reach Number 7 and Number 2 respectively in the UK charts.

Key films

The Mark of Zorro
Fred Niblo, USA, 1920
The film that put acrobatic movement at the very heart of the period adventure casts Douglas Fairbanks, Sr as Mexico's swordfighting champion of the oppressed.

Tarzan the Ape Man
W S Van Dyke, USA, 1932
Johnny Weissmuller's yodelling jungle call echoes around the first Tarzan talkie; although the exotic vine-swinging and animal-wrestling action continued in many sequels, the lusty romance with Tarzan's 'mate' Jane was later toned down.

The Adventures of Robin Hood
Michael Curtiz and William Keighley, USA, 1938
Errol Flynn brings a twinkle to the eye of medieval England's underdog folk hero as he and villainous Basil Rathbone indulge in the greatest swordfight ever to grace the costumed swashbuckler genre.

Seven Samurai (Shichinin no samurai)
Akira Kurosawa, Japan, 1954
Kurosawa's samurai adventure was a key influence on action cinema, using telephoto lenses and multiple camera set-ups for filming its dynamic battle scenes.

The French Connection
William Friedkin, USA, 1971
Bullitt (1968) made the car chase a staple ingredient of action cinema, but this

morally shady cop thriller added extra excitement by shooting its landmark subway chase guerrilla-style, only inches away from the toes of real-life New Yorkers.

Enter the Dragon
Robert Clouse, USA/Hong Kong, 1973
Bruce Lee lit the fuse of the kung fu explosion with *The Big Boss* (1971), but it was this Hollywood-funded story of a fighter sent into a Bond-style villain's lair that truly revolutionized action cinema's hand-to-hand fight scenes.

Raiders of the Lost Ark
Steven Spielberg, USA, 1981
Spielberg nailed the formula for the modern family adventure by looking back to early matinée serials. Here, archaeologist Indiana Jones uses bravery, wit and intelligence to beat the Nazis to a priceless religious artefact.

Lethal Weapon
Richard Donner, USA, 1987
This early example of the burgeoning subgenre of mismatched buddy movies pairs a loose-cannon cop (Mel Gibson) with a cool-headed partner (Danny Glover), establishing a winning box-office formula of smart-ass comedy quips alternating with bursts of adrenaline-pumping action.

Terminator 2: Judgment Day
James Cameron, USA, 1991
The action movie entered the digital age with *T2*, as realistic computer effects allowed the evil T-1000 cyborg to morph like liquid metal before the audience's very eyes.

Festivals

Festival du Film Aventures
Held annually since 1990 in Valenciennes, France.
Website: www.festival-valenciennes.com
Top prizes: Grand Prix; Prix Rémy Julienne (named after a French action star, 1930–)

Further viewing

The Thief of Bagdad (1924), *Captain Blood* (1935), *The Four Feathers* (1939), *Ben-Hur* (1959), *The Wild Bunch* (1969), *Rambo: First Blood, Part II* (1985), *Aliens* (1986), *Top Gun* (1986), *Die Hard* (1988), *The Killer* (1989), *The Matrix* (1999)

The James Bond franchise

The first actor to play James Bond wasn't Sean Connery. It was Barry Nelson, who starred in an hour-long television production of *Casino Royale* in 1954. The previous year, Ian Fleming had created the super-suave British secret agent in his book of the same name; he went on to write another eleven Bond novels and two short-story collections, with the franchise continuing in print after his death in 1964. Connery slipped into the tuxedo in 1962 for the first in the long-running cinema franchise following the exploits of 007, the man with a licence to kill for queen and country. Tapping into the fears and preoccupations of the Cold War period, the Bond films provided an action-packed fantasy mix of girls, gadgets, villains, henchmen and hi-tech lairs in exotic locations. Australian actor George Lazenby lasted only one film in the role (*On Her Majesty's Secret Service*, 1969), with Connery being coaxed back for *Diamonds Are Forever* (1971) and for rival production *Never Say Never Again* (1983). Roger Moore brought a lighter, more comedic touch to Bond's lethal style from *Live and Let Die* (1973) onwards, before Timothy Dalton tried out a colder, tougher style in *The Living Daylights* (1987) and *Licence to Kill* (1989). The struggling series was reborn for the blockbuster age with *GoldenEye* (1995), in which Pierce Brosnan borrowed from the Connery approach, giving playboy sexiness a deadly edge. The other unofficial entry into the Bond canon was spy spoof *Casino Royale* (1967); that particular story will finally be given a proper adventure makeover as the 21st official James Bond film, due to be released in 2006 with Daniel Craig in the lead role.

Official James Bond films

Dr No (1962), *From Russia with Love* (1963), *Goldfinger* (1963), *Thunderball* (1965), *You Only Live Twice* (1967), *On Her Majesty's Secret Service* (1969), *Diamonds Are Forever* (1971), *Live and Let Die* (1973), *The Man with the Golden Gun* (1974), *The Spy Who Loved Me* (1977), *Moonraker* (1979), *For Your Eyes Only* (1981), *Octopussy* (1983), *A View to a Kill* (1985), *The Living Daylights* (1987), *Licence to Kill* (1989), *GoldenEye* (1995), *Tomorrow Never Dies* (1997), *The World Is Not Enough* (1999), *Die Another Day* (2002), *Casino Royale* (2006)

Unofficial James Bond films

Casino Royale (1967), *Never Say Never Again* (1983)

Actors who have played James Bond

Sean Connery (1962–7, 1971, 1983), George Lazenby (1969), Roger Moore (1973–85), Timothy Dalton (1987–9), Pierce Brosnan (1995–2002), Daniel Craig (2006–)

Some Bond villains and henchmen

Dr No (Joseph Wiseman), Auric Goldfinger (Gert Fröbe), Oddjob (Harold Sakata in *Goldfinger*, 1963), Ernst Stavro Blofeld (Donald Pleasence in *You Only Live Twice*, 1967; Telly Savalas in *On Her Majesty's Secret Service*, 1969; Charles Gray in *Diamonds Are Forever*, 1971), Francisco Scaramanga (Christopher Lee in *The Man with the Golden Gun*, 1974), Nick Nack (Hervé Villechaize in *The Man with the Golden Gun*, 1974), Jaws (Richard Kiel in *The Spy Who Loved Me*, 1977, and *Moonraker*, 1979), May Day (Grace Jones in *A View to a Kill*, 1985), Renard (Robert Carlyle in *The World Is Not Enough*, 1999)

Some 'Bond girls'

Honey Rider (Ursula Andress in *Dr No*, 1962), Pussy Galore (Honor Blackman in *Goldfinger*, 1963), Tiffany Case (Jill St John in *Diamonds Are Forever*, 1971), Mary Goodnight (Britt Ekland in *The Man with the Golden Gun*, 1974), Wai Lin (Michelle Yeoh in *Tomorrow Never Dies*, 1997), Jinx (Halle Berry in *Die Another Day*, 2002)

Other Bond characters

M (Bernard Lee, 1962–79; Robert Brown, 1983–9; Judi Dench, 1995–), Miss Moneypenny (Lois Maxwell, 1962–85; Caroline Bliss, 1987–9; Samantha Bond, 1995–), Q (Desmond Llewelyn, 1963–99; John Cleese, 2002–)

ANIMATION

History

The origins of cinema lie not only in photography, but also in the Victorian era's 'magic lantern' slide shows and zoetrope devices that used a flickering sequence of pictures to give the illusion of movement. This was a type of early animation: a process of bringing the inanimate to life via drawings, puppets, silhouettes or objects photographed frame by frame. Short cartoons were popular additions to cinema programmes in the silent era and the 1930s, with Felix the Cat, Popeye and Betty Boop rivalling human stars in terms of popularity. In the 1940s, Warner Brothers showcased the slapstick violence of Tex Avery and Chuck Jones in the Looney Tunes and Merrie Melodies series (starring, amongst others, Bugs Bunny and Daffy Duck), while MGM worked up strings of manic gags for Tom and Jerry. From the late 1930s onwards, it was Walt Disney who dominated the feature end of the medium.

If Hollywood saw animation as an industry, Europe treated it as more of an art form. Various schools – particularly those in Czechoslovakia and Yugoslavia – excelled in political satire. It was not until the 1970s that the USA brought an underground flavour to the cartoon world in such X-rated, comic-inspired romps as *Fritz the Cat* (1972). Stop-motion techniques, whereby models are manipulated frame by frame, had added wonder to fantasy films such as *The Lost World* (1926) and *King Kong* (1933), but these were eventually surpassed by amazingly realistic computer graphics such as those used to create the dinosaurs in *Jurassic Park* (1993).

The genre today

In box-office terms, traditional 'drawn' animation has been dwarfed by its computer-generated counterpart since the mid-1990s, despite film spin-offs from children's television channel Nickelodeon (including *The Rugrats Movie*, 1998) and cartoon sequels produced by Disney solely for the DVD market.

Key figures

Walt Disney (1901–66)
Studio head whose taste for sentimental, song-filled fairy tales and cartoon adaptations of children's books turned animation into a Hollywood industry and powerful box-office force. His commercial empire has expanded to include live-action films, merchandising, television programmes and theme parks.

Ray Harryhausen (1920–)
US animator specializing in 'Dynamation' stop-motion techniques, which brought life to mythical beasts, dinosaurs and fighting skeletons in fantasy films such as *Jason and the Argonauts* (1963) and *One Million Years B.C.* (1966).

Jim Henson (1936–90)
Director, producer, puppeteer and creator of The Muppets, whose foamy, hand-operated characters – including Kermit the Frog and Miss Piggy – spilled over from their long-running television show into six big-screen outings.

John Lasseter (1957–)
Director, producer and co-founder of Pixar, the company that revolutionized animation with computer-generated features including *Toy Story* (1995), *Finding Nemo* (2003) and *The Incredibles* (2004).

Norman McLaren (1914–87)
Scottish animator whose work for the GPO Film Unit and the National Film Board of Canada saw him scratching and painting directly onto celluloid to create jazzy, abstract and experimental short films.

Hayao Miyazaki (1941–)
Director whose work with Studio Ghibli combines folk tales with a distinctively Eastern spirituality, avoiding the sci-fi themes that dominate most Japanese anime.

Nick Park (1958–)
Director (and creator of the much-loved characters Wallace and Gromit) whose mastery of Bristol-based Aardman Animations' plasticine-modelling technique won him three Best Animated Short Academy Awards® before he tackled the feature-length *Chicken Run* (2000).

Wladyslaw Starewicz (1882–1965)
Polish animator whose pioneering use of stop-frame puppet animation – particularly with insects and animals – gives a distinctive look to his fables and fairy tales.

The Last Laugh

Mel Blanc, the voice behind countless cartoon icons including Bugs Bunny, Porky Pig, Daffy Duck, Elmer Fudd, Foghorn Leghorn, Sylvester and Tweety Pie is buried in the Hollywood Forever cemetery in Los Angeles. The inscription on his headstone reads 'That's All Folks'.

Key films

Steamboat Willie
Walt Disney and Ub Iwerks, USA, 1928
The talkie debut of Mortimer (later Mickey) Mouse put sound effects and music to ingenious comic use, and helped to establish the rodent as the world's greatest cartoon icon.

Snow White and the Seven Dwarfs
USA, 1937
Based on the fairy tale by the Brothers Grimm, the world's first feature-length colour cartoon with sound was groundbreaking in its creation of depth and space, achieved through multiple layers of background detail and foreground characters.

Animal Farm
John Halas and Joy Batchelor, UK, 1954
George Orwell's farmyard satire on 20th-century totalitarianism provided the source for the UK's first feature-length cartoon, which avoids the cutesy characterization of Disney's talking animals.

Akira
Katsuhiro Otomo, Japan, 1988
The first of the 'anime' (Japanese animation) blockbusters – released in the USA in 1989 and in the UK in 1990 – paints a high-tech vision of a post-apocalyptic Tokyo.

Beauty and the Beast
Gary Trousdale and Kirk Wise, USA, 1991
Disney's revival of fortunes was secured by the success of this fairy tale, whose ballroom sequence marked the studio's first use of computer animation.

Toy Story
John Lasseter, USA, 1995
The first animated feature to be entirely computer-generated brings the secret world of toys to life, as cowboy doll Woody and spaceman doll Buzz team up on a rescue mission.

Shrek
Andrew Adamson and Vicky Jenson, USA, 2001
This cheeky subversion of the fairy-tale universe was proof that another studio (DreamWorks) could usurp Disney's throne and establish computer animation as the genre's dominant technique.

Spirited Away (Sen to Chihiro no kamikakushi)
Hayao Miyazaki, Japan, 2001
By winning the Best Animated Feature Academy Award® and succeeding at the international box office, Miyazaki's story of a young girl lost in a beguiling Oriental spirit world showed that traditional 'drawn' animation had not yet been rendered obsolete by computers.

Festivals

Festival International du Film d'Animation
Held annually since 1960 in Annecy, France.
Website: www.annecy.org
Top prize: Annecy Cristal

Further viewing

Fantasia (1940), *Bambi* (1942), *Neighbours* (1952), *Watership Down* (1978), *Who Framed Roger Rabbit* (1988), *The Nightmare Before Christmas* (1993), *The Lion King* (1994), *Princess Mononoke* (1997), *South Park: Bigger, Longer & Uncut* (1999), *Chicken Run* (2000), *Belleville Rendez-vous* (2003)

CHILDREN'S FILMS

History

Cinema was several decades old before the industry began making an effort to cater specifically for children. A steady stream of comic moments or adventure thrills would hold the attention of young viewers, even more so if the heroes on screen were their own age and size. Saturday matinées, free from parental supervision, became a national pastime in Britain as children lapped up cartoons, cliffhanger serials and short features such as those produced by the Children's Film Foundation in the UK from 1951 onwards. Child actors including Jackie Coogan, Shirley Temple and Mickey Rooney (in the wholesome Andy Hardy series) became household names, as did animal stars from Rin Tin Tin to Lassie, Flipper and Black Beauty. Animation was the preferred format for family entertainment, with Disney topping the box-office rankings decade after decade. Since the 1970s, however, Hollywood – ever mindful of the widest possible audience – has reinvented the family adventure in the blockbuster form of *Star Wars* (1977), *Raiders of the Lost Ark* (1981) and other summer hits.

The genre today

Most major children's films are now released to coincide with school holidays, and are heavily marketed through merchandising and fast-food restaurant tie-ins. The creation in the UK of a 12A certificate has allowed children under the previously restricted age of 15 freer access to the fantasy violence of many comic-book adaptations.

Key figures

Macaulay Culkin (1980–)
Actor who became famous as a kid defending his house from burglars in *Home Alone* (1990), before becoming the highest-paid child actor in history ($8 million for 1994's *Richie Rich*).

Rin Tin Tin (1918–32)
Cinema's most popular canine star, whose screen adventures are thought to have saved Warner Brothers in the late 1920s and early 1930s, was discovered as a German Shepherd puppy in a bombed-out kennel in wartime France.

Shirley Temple (1928–)
The archetypal child actor whose golden ringlets and precocious singing and dancing talents made her a cutesy, cherubic star in talkies including *The Littlest Rebel* (1935).

Key films

Chitty Chitty Bang Bang
Ken Hughes, UK, 1968
A mixture of whimsical imagination, hummable songs and colourful production design by Ken Adams has ensured that this tale of an inventor and a magical car continues to delight young audiences.

The Railway Children
Lionel Jeffries, UK, 1970
This perennial favourite of Bank Holiday television schedules is an enduring example of the literary nostalgia that runs through much of children's cinema in the UK.

E.T. the Extra-Terrestrial
Steven Spielberg, USA, 1982
This lovely but emotionally manipulative sci-fi fantasy about a young boy who befriends a stranded alien broke box-office records with its depiction of a world in which children are resourceful and adults are not to be trusted.

Precocious Prize-winners

Several child stars have won Oscars® at a tender age. Shirley Temple was given a special 'Juvenile Award' at six, while Tatum O'Neal (ten) and Anna Paquin (eleven) were named Best Supporting Actress for, respectively, *Paper Moon* (1973) and *The Piano* (1993). The youngest ever nominee for a Best Actress Academy Award® was 13-year-old Keisha Castle-Hughes, for *Whale Rider* (2002).

Festivals

Cinemagic
Held annually since 1989 in Belfast, Northern Ireland.
The UK's largest festival aimed at viewers aged 4–18.
Website: www.cinemagic.org.uk
Top prize: Best Feature (chosen by young people's jury)

Further viewing

The Wizard of Oz (1939), *Lassie Come Home* (1943), *Willy Wonka & the Chocolate Factory* (1971), *The Black Stallion* (1979), *The NeverEnding Story* (1984), *The Princess Bride* (1987), *The Lion King* (1994), *Toy Story* (1995)

The Harry Potter franchise

The idea for a story about a boy wizard first popped into author J K Rowling's head while she was on a train from Manchester to London in 1990. Seven years later, *Harry Potter and the Philosopher's Stone* was published by Bloomsbury. In 1998 the first sequel, *Harry Potter and the Chamber of Secrets*, went straight to the top of the bestseller lists, and a phenomenon was born. Warner Brothers bought the rights for the first two books for a seven-figure sum, although two further instalments – *Harry Potter and the Prisoner of Azkaban* and *Harry Potter and the Goblet of Fire* – were published before the first film hit the big screen in 2001. It now sits at number three in the all time worldwide box-office charts, with a take of over $968 million. Warner Brothers announced a bold plan to shoot the seven-part franchise with the same young cast and, after Chris Columbus directed the first two films, each new movie – reflecting the increasing maturity of the characters in darker themes – was to be tackled by a different director.

Harry Potter and the Order of the Phoenix is due for release in the summer of 2007, with a relative unknown (David Yates) as director. With the sixth book, *Harry Potter and the Half-Blood Prince* (2005), selling over two million copies on the first day of its publication, all that now awaits fans in print is the final book.

Harry Potter films

Harry Potter and the Philosopher's Stone (Chris Columbus, 2001), *Harry Potter and the Chamber of Secrets* (Chris Columbus, 2002), *Harry Potter and the Prisoner of Azkaban* (Alfonso Cuarón, 2004), *Harry Potter and the Goblet of Fire* (Mike Newell, 2005)

Key characters

Harry Potter (Daniel Radcliffe), Ron Weasley (Rupert Grint), Hermione Granger (Emma Watson), Draco Malfoy (Tom Felton), Albus Dumbledore (Richard Harris in the first two films; Michael Gambon in subsequent instalments), Professor Minerva McGonagall (Maggie Smith), Professor Severus Snape (Alan Rickman), Rubeus Hagrid (Robbie Coltrane), Professor Quirrell (Ian Hart), Professor Gilderoy Lockhart (Kenneth Branagh), Sirius Black (Gary Oldman), Professor Lupin (David Thewlis), Lord Voldemort/Tom Marvolo Riddle (Ralph Fiennes)

COMEDY

History

Ever since a naughty boy stood on a gardener's hose in the Lumière brothers' short *L'Arroseur arrosé* (1895), cinema laughter has helped people to forget their daily woes. Vaudeville supplied the first silent-screen comedians, as broad physical comedy – the pratfall, the custard pie fight, the banana skin – made the audience chuckle regardless of its native tongue. In Europe, French clowns André Deed and Max Linder were the first comedy stars, but it was in Hollywood that the madcap antics of Mack Sennett's Keystone Kops, Harry Langdon, Harold Lloyd, Buster Keaton and Charlie Chaplin turned comedy into a global phenomenon.

The arrival of sound made comedy a matter of verbal as well as visual wit. Films in the 1930s crackled with Mae West's innuendoes, W C Fields's cynical quips and the rapid-fire dialogue of the battle-of-the-sexes screwball comedy. Until the end of the 1950s, comic teams – Abbott and Costello, the Three Stooges, Dean Martin and Jerry Lewis – dominated the field. The arrival of television sitcoms forced cinema to up the stakes with expensive all-star spectaculars. It wasn't until the late 1960s that a relaxation in censorship freshened up the genre, allowing it to deal with adult subjects and use swearing to comic effect. A new breed of comedians including Chevy Chase, Mike Myers and Adam Sandler earned their stripes on television and the stand-up stage before making the move into film. Meanwhile, Hollywood recognized a shift in audience demographics and so churned out high-school, gross-out and romantic comedies (and countless sequels) for younger multiplex crowds.

The genre today

As far as Hollywood is concerned, it's a diet of gross-out for the boys and romantic comedies for the girls, with only independent film-makers and writers – notably Wes Anderson, Alexander Payne and Charlie Kaufman – equalling the intelligence and sophistication of the best of their predecessors.

Key figures

Woody Allen (1935–)
Actor, writer and director who was a television gag writer and stand-up comedian in the 1960s before bringing his self-deprecating, angst-filled brand of humour to the screen in a series of films, produced at the rate of almost one per year.

Mel Brooks (1926–)
Actor, writer and director who hit a peak with his feature debut *The Producers* (1968), followed by a series of genre parodies (1974's *Blazing Saddles* and *Young Frankenstein*) which later descended into lame single-film spoofs (*Spaceballs*, 1987).

Jim Carrey (1962–   )
Actor who relies on excessive energy and facial contortions in his comedy work, and who became the first Hollywood star to demand – and receive – $20 million for a single film (*The Cable Guy*, 1996).

Charlie Chaplin (1889–1977)
Actor, director and creator of the hugely popular 'Little Tramp' character, Chaplin put power into the hands of performers rather than producers when he set up his own studio in 1918. He established comedy as an art form by bringing sentiment and feeling into pratfall routines.

Peter Farrelly (1956–   ) and Bobby Farrelly (1958–   )
Director-writer-producer duo who made their names as purveyors of politically-incorrect gross-out humour in the 1990s, although there is always a sweet romance or friendship apparent beneath the filth and bad-taste gags.

Cary Grant (1904–86)
Actor and former acrobat who had the physical poise and verbal dexterity to handle anything that the screwball-comedy genre could throw at him.

Buster Keaton (1895–1966)
Actor who brought death-defying stunts and big-scale thrills into silent comedies including *The General* (1927), but whose expressionless face was not well-suited to the demands of talkies.

Stan Laurel (1890–1965) and Oliver Hardy (1892–1957)
Comedy duo paired by Hal Roach, whose visual mismatch – skinny cry-baby Stan and chubby, exasperated Ollie – brought extra humour to a series of shorts and features in which their characters' friendship and shabby dignity were sorely tested.

Marx Brothers (Chico (Leonard, 1891–1961), Harpo (Adolph Arthur, 1893–1964), Groucho (Julius Henry, 1895–1977) and Zeppo (Herbert, 1901–79))
Actor-writer team of brothers – ad-libbing Groucho, hustling Chico, mute Harpo and bland Zeppo – who tested their anarchic brand of quick-fire gags and vaudeville musical interludes on live audiences before going in front of the camera.

Monty Python (John Cleese (1939–   ), Terry Gilliam (1940–   ), Graham Chapman (1941–89), Terry Jones (1942–   ), Eric Idle (1943–   ) and Michael Palin (1943–   ))
Actor-writer-director team whose very British, university-educated, slightly surreal style of humour betrays its television sketch-show origins even in such 'narrative' features as *Monty Python and the Holy Grail* (1975) and *Monty Python's Life of Brian* (1979).

Eddie Murphy (1961–   )
Actor who turned the 1980s Hollywood comedy on its head when he left behind television's *Saturday Night Live* to combine sex appeal, cocky attitude, motor-mouth quips and gun-toting action in *48 Hrs* (1982) and *Beverley Hills Cop* (1984).

Peter Sellers (1925–80)
Actor who developed his multiple characters and silly voices on radio's *The Goon Show* before achieving international stardom and playboy status as the vowel-mangling, incompetent Inspector Clouseau in the Pink Panther series of films.

Preston Sturges (1898–1959)

Writer and director (the first Hollywood figure to be credited as 'writer-director') who developed the pace and tone of the screwball comedy in a series of fearless satires on such US institutions as patriotism, marriage and motherhood.

Blowing the Budget

In order to get his first break as a director, Preston Sturges agreed to make *The Great McGinty* (1940) for a fee of just one dollar. Before he actually started shooting the film (for which he went on to win a Best Original Screenplay Academy Award®) Paramount Studio's legal department graciously upped his fee – to $10.

Key films

The Gold Rush
Charlie Chaplin, USA, 1925

The Little Tramp falls in love while seeking his fortune in Alaska, where he is forced to eat his own worn-out boots – a classic image that illustrates the complexity of Chaplin's art by being simultaneously funny, sad, desperate and brave.

Bringing Up Baby
Howard Hawks, USA, 1938

The organized chaos and lightning-paced verbal wit of the screwball comedy was never better than this, in which socialite Katharine Hepburn scuppers the wedding plans of dinosaur expert Cary Grant.

Some Like It Hot
Billy Wilder, USA, 1959

The American Film Institute's number-one comedy proves that cross-dressing is good for a giggle in any era, as Jack Lemmon and Tony Curtis attempt to escape from the mob by joining an all-girl jazz band that includes ditzy blonde Marilyn Monroe.

Dr Strangelove: Or, How I Learned to Stop Worrying and Love the Bomb
Stanley Kubrick, UK, 1964

Fear of nuclear war fed the black-comedy aspects of Terry Southern's satirical screenplay, as Peter Sellers took on three roles – the US President, an RAF captain and a wheelchair-bound, ex-Nazi scientist.

*M*A*S*H*
Robert Altman, USA, 1970

Altman's Korean War comedy chimed with anti-Vietnam feelings and woke up Hollywood studios to a younger market with its depiction of two army doctors alternating between life-saving operations and a series of pranks that show no respect for rank.

Annie Hall
Woody Allen, USA, 1977

Marking the transition between Allen's early films and his later maturity as a film-maker, this romance between anxious Alvy Singer (Allen) and kooky Annie Hall

(Diane Keaton) won four major Academy Awards®, bringing credibility to the comedy genre.

National Lampoon's Animal House
John Landis, USA, 1978
With its party mood and cheerful treatment of sex, drugs and rock'n'roll, this rowdy campus comedy made the most of its adult rating, turned John Belushi into a star and established television's *Saturday Night Live* as a breeding ground for new comic talent.

Airplane!
Jim Abrahams, David Zucker and Jerry Zucker, USA, 1980
Fired up by a string of silly visual gags and puns, this disaster-movie spoof ushered in a run of lowest-common-denominator parodies, including *The Naked Gun* (1988).

When Harry Met Sally...
Rob Reiner, USA, 1989
Built on the understanding that romantic sparring is at the heart of the best comedies, screenwriter Nora Ephron's witty examination of modern relationships gave birth to the contemporary 'rom-com' genre.

American Pie
Paul Weitz, USA, 1999
Although it features more likeable characters than many films of its type, this marks the point in the evolution of the Hollywood teen comedy at which the appeal of scatological, sex-crazed 'highlights' became more of a selling point than the overall story.

Bridget Jones's Diary
Sharon Maguire, UK, 2001
British production company Working Title brought together two of mainstream culture's most lucrative entertainment genres – the chick-lit novel and the romantic comedy film – in this story of an unattached, chardonnay-guzzling thirtysomething trying to win her ideal man.

Festivals

Comedia
Held annually since 1997 in Montreal, Canada. Part of the Just For Laughs Comedy Festival for stand-up comedians, street theatre and television shows.
Website: www.hahaha.com
Top prize: Comedia Award

Further viewing

Safety Last (1923), *Duck Soup* (1933), *It Happened One Night* (1934), *His Girl Friday* (1939), *The Philadelphia Story* (1940), *Adam's Rib* (1949), *Kind Hearts and Coronets* (1949), *Monsieur Hulot's Holiday* (1953), *The Apartment* (1960), *Divorce Italian Style* (1961), *The Graduate* (1967), *Local Hero* (1983), *Crocodile Dundee* (1986), *Pretty Woman* (1990), *Clerks* (1994), *Four Weddings and a Funeral* (1994), *The Big Lebowski* (1998), *Lost in Translation* (2003), *Sideways* (2004)

The Carry On franchise

The most commercially successful comedy series in British film history began with what was designed to be a one-off farce about army life, *Carry On Sergeant* (1958). Embraced by the public, the film quickly spawned a sequel, and then another, until there were a total of 31 entries in the series, all directed by Gerald Thomas and produced by Peter Rogers. Early films concentrated on institutions (hospitals, schools, police) before turning to parodies of current cinema trends (ancient epics, Bond films, Hammer Horror). The team of regulars attacked their stereotyped roles with gusto, relishing every excruciating pun and double entendre. Carry On films were, in a sense, the motion-picture equivalent of the British seaside postcard: smutty and sex-obsessed, yet strangely innocent and old-fashioned. The series floundered in the 1970s, when rival comedies began to treat sex in a less coy manner. Comeback attempt *Carry On Columbus* (1992), with many of the original cast now dead and replaced by contemporary comedians, was a resounding flop.

Carry On films

Carry On Sergeant (1958), *... Nurse* (1959), *... Teacher* (1959), *... Constable* (1959), *... Regardless* (1961), *... Cruising* (1962), *... Cabby* (1963), *... Jack* (1963), *... Spying* (1964), *... Cleo* (1964), *... Cowboy* (1965), *... Screaming!* (1966), *... Don't Lose Your Head* (1966), *... Follow That Camel* (1967), *... Doctor* (1967), *... Up the Khyber* (1968), *... Camping* (1969), *... Again Doctor* (1969), *... Up the Jungle* (1970), *... Loving* (1970), *... Henry* (1971), *... at Your Convenience* (1971), *... Matron* (1972), *... Abroad* (1972), *... Girls* (1973), *... Dick* (1974), *... Behind* (1975), *... England* (1976), *That's Carry On* (1978), *... Emmannuelle* (1978), *... Columbus* (1992)

Carry On regulars

Numbers in brackets represent the number of Carry On films in which each performer appeared.
Bernard Bresslaw (14), Peter Butterworth (16), Kenneth Connor (17), Jim Dale (11), Jack Douglas (8), Charles Hawtrey (23), Hattie Jacques (14), Sid James (19), Leslie Phillips (4), Patsy Rowlands (9), Terry Scott (7), Joan Sims (24), Kenneth Williams (25), Barbara Windsor (9)

COMIC-BOOK ADAPTATIONS

History

If cinema is a source of escapist adventure, then why not present audiences with heroes who can fly, change shape or use superpowers to combat evil villains with a twisted desire to take over the world? Hollywood has found a ready-made treasure trove of such characters and stories in the pages of comic books published by Marvel, DC Comics and Dark Horse. The roots of the screen superhero can be traced back to the serial thrillers of the 1930s, which featured the to-be-continued adventures of Buck Rogers and Flash Gordon. In the 1940s – with the USA at war – Captain America, Superman and Batman waved the Stars and Stripes. The development of computerized special effects unlocked the potential of comic-book characters in the late 1970s and, by the 1990s, blockbusters featuring costumed heroes with alliterative identities had become a significant box-office phenomenon.

A more thoughtful, independent film-making culture subsequently sprang up around the underground 'graphic novel' and comic scene, with such films as *Ghost World* (2000) and *American Splendor* (2003).

The genre today

Sequels and franchises featuring big-name superheroes have become summer event movies, while other comic-book stars – such as *Daredevil* (2003) – provide hit-or-miss fodder for the rest of the year. Japan dedicates a section of its film industry to transforming 'manga' comics into high-tech 'anime' films.

Key figures

Danny Elfman (1953–)
Composer of choice for comic-book movies (and for director Tim Burton), whose driving orchestral scores have a gothic flavour which has worked well as theme music for *Batman* (1989), *Darkman* (1990), *Dick Tracy* (1990), *Spider-Man* (2002) and *Hulk* (2003).

Christopher Reeve (1952–2004)
Actor who brought a dramatic seriousness to the role of Superman in four screen outings between 1978 and 1987, and who was much praised for his courage after he was confined to a wheelchair following a riding accident in 1995.

Bryan Singer (1965–)
Director and producer whose love of comic books brought both fanboy credibility and depth of character to the X-Men films, before he resurrected the Man of Steel in *Superman Returns* (2006).

Key films

Superman
Richard Donner, USA, 1978
The first modern comic-book blockbuster transformed the superhero from camp crusader into action star, using special effects to convince the world that a man could fly.

Spider-Man
Sam Raimi, USA, 2002
The comic-book movie was confirmed as a 21st-century box-office champion when this story of web-swinging wonder Peter Parker secured a record-breaking opening weekend take of $114 million in the USA.

Sin City
Robert Rodriguez and Frank Miller, USA, 2005
With a nod to hard-boiled pulp fiction and noir cinema, Rodriguez's digital treatment of Miller's graphic novel series uses stark black and white to illustrate the ruthless codes of morality and honour in a hyperviolent world.

Notable Names

In the world of comic books, it's often possible to spot heroes and villains by their alliterative names. Examples include Reed Richards and Sue Storm (*Fantastic Four*), Clark Kent, Lois Lane and Lex Luther (*Superman*), Peter Parker (*Spider-Man*), Matt Murdock (*Daredevil*) and Bruce Banner (*Hulk*).

Festivals

Comic-Con International Independent Film Festival
Held annually since 2001 in San Diego, California, USA. Part of a large comic book convention, with an emphasis on cinema featuring superheroes, science fiction and fantasy.
Website: www.comic-con.org
Top prize: Judges' Choice

Further viewing

Dick Tracy (1990), *The Crow* (1994), *Blade* (1998), *X-Men* (2000), *From Hell* (2001), *Road to Perdition* (2002), *Hellboy* (2004), *A History of Violence* (2005)

The Batman franchise

Batman, created by Bob Kane, first hit the news-stands in *Detective Comics* #27 in May 1939. The title of the publication reflected the fact that this was not a hero with superpowers, but a human crime-fighter driven to avenge the murder of his parents by a mugger. Hiding his identity beneath Batman's mask and cape, playboy Bruce Wayne uses his millions to develop gadgets and vehicles that give him the edge over a series of grotesque villains.

The darker side of Gotham City's night-time vigilante was ignored in the 1966 *Batman* television series, with its cartoonish biff-bang-pow antics, and its spin-off movie. Director Tim Burton restored some of the story's gothic sensibility in the much-hyped blockbuster *Batman* (1989), which drew heavily upon Frank Miller's 1986 reassessment of the character in comic-book form, *Batman: The Dark Knight Returns*. A profitable film franchise for Warner Brothers had now been launched: after a Burton sequel, the series again veered off into camp theatrics for two instalments made under the directorial eye of Joel Schumacher. Christopher Nolan, working from a script by David S Goyer, wiped the slate clean in 2005 with *Batman Begins*, the first in the Warner Brothers series to closely examine the roots of the character and dwell on his schizophrenic tendencies.

Batman films

Batman (Leslie H Martinson, 1966), *Batman* (Tim Burton, 1989), *Batman Returns* (Tim Burton, 1992), *Batman Forever* (Joel Schumacher, 1995), *Batman & Robin* (Joel Schumacher, 1997), *Batman Begins* (Christopher Nolan, 2005)

Batman spin-offs

The Batman (Columbia Pictures' 15-episode serial, 1943), *Batman: Mask of the Phantasm* (animated feature devised from Warner Brothers' animated television series, 1993)

Adam West (1966), Michael Keaton (1989–92), Val Kilmer (1995), George Clooney (1997), Christian Bale (2005)

Key Batman villains

The Joker (Cesar Romero in *Batman*, 1966; Jack Nicholson in *Batman*, 1989), The Penguin (Burgess Meredith in *Batman*, 1966; Danny DeVito in *Batman Returns*, 1992), The Riddler (Frank Gorshin in *Batman*, 1966; Jim Carrey in *Batman Forever*, 1995), Catwoman (Lee Meriwether in *Batman*, 1966; Michelle Pfeiffer in *Batman Returns*, 1992), Two-Face (Tommy Lee Jones in *Batman Forever*, 1995), Mr Freeze (Arnold Schwarzenegger in *Batman & Robin*, 1997), Poison Ivy (Uma Thurman in *Batman & Robin*, 1997), Henri Ducard (Liam Neeson in *Batman Begins*, 2005), Scarecrow (Cillian Murphy in *Batman Begins*, 2005)

Other major characters

Robin (Burt Ward, 1966; Chris O'Donnell, 1995–7), Alfred Pennyworth (Alan Napier, 1966; Michael Gough, 1989–97; Michael Caine, 2005), Commissioner Gordon (Neil Hamilton, 1966; Pat Hingle, 1989–97; Gary Oldman, 2005)

CRIME AND GANGSTER FILMS

History

Audiences love rubbing shoulders with criminals in the knowledge that they can dip into the world of crime, experience the rush that comes from breaking the law, and slip back safely into their everyday lives when the lights go up. The very first feature film, *The Great Train Robbery* (1903), thrilled viewers with its bandits, murders, chase and shoot-out, but it wasn't until sound came along that the crime genre really got going. Led by Warner Brothers, the rise of gangster movies in the 1930s filled cinema screens with hyperactive, self-destructive characters who rose and fell to a cacophony of bullets, police sirens, snarled threats and speakeasy jazz. Official outcries over the glorification of gangsters switched the focus to equally ruthless lawmen, and crime in 1940s cinema often focused on detectives mired in shady mysteries. Throughout the following decade the tone became darker, as the genre probed the psychology of violence. By the 1960s, the outlaw status of the criminal appealed to the counterculture generation, with films such as *Bonnie and Clyde* (1967) becoming more graphically violent. Crime as an organized business, particularly Mafia-related, was a key theme during the 1970s. Meanwhile, cop movies took an ambivalent approach, with *The French Connection* (1971), *Dirty Harry* (1971) and vigilante fantasy *Death Wish* (1974) placing one foot on either side of the moral divide. By the 1980s, Hollywood had absorbed the crime genre into the high-concept action thriller.

The genre today

In recent years Hollywood has added a hip-hop gloss to depictions of urban street crime, but the UK film industry continues to display a fascination with wide-boy gangsters who aim too high. The genre has looked to the Far East for inspiration, drawing upon a wealth of high-octane cop and killer movies from Hong Kong, Japan and South Korea.

Key figures

Humphrey Bogart (1899–1957)
Actor who began his career playing callous gangsters before specializing in the portrayal of flawed, cynical private detectives in such films as *The Maltese Falcon* (1941).

James Cagney (1899–1986)
Actor famed for playing tough hoods with a streetwise snarl in early gangster films such as *The Public Enemy* (1931). He drew on his vaudeville background as a song-and-dance man to bring energy, charisma and poise to his performances.

Clint Eastwood (1930–)
Actor and director who first played a cop in *Coogan's Bluff* (1968), but became Hollywood's number one star in the 1970s thanks to his role as misogynistic 'vigilante with a badge' Harry Callaghan in *Dirty Harry* (1971) and its sequels.

Takeshi Kitano (1947–)
Japanese actor and director whose typically expressionless characters alternate between bursts of violence, acts of tenderness and disrespect for their bosses, regardless of whether they are police officers (*Violent Cop*, 1989) or yakuza gangsters (*Sonatine*, 1993).

Jean-Pierre Melville (1917–73)
Director and writer whose films depict a less tense, more poetic mood within underworld settings, examining the loyalties, betrayals and existential loneliness of the criminal class in the likes of *Bob le flambeur* (1955) and *Le Samouraï* (1967).

Al Pacino (1940–)
Actor who has played both dogged cops – *Serpico* (1973), *Heat* (1995) – and a range of iconic criminals, from the corrupted innocence of Michael Corleone (*The Godfather*, 1972) to the rampaging ego of Tony Montana (*Scarface*, 1983).

Edward G Robinson (1893–1973)
Actor, blessed with raw talent rather than matinée-idol looks, who played a string of aggressive gangsters before maturing into more sympathetic and complex character parts.

Quentin Tarantino (1963–)
Director, screenwriter and actor with a knack for working distinctive pop-culture dialogue into crime subgenres such as the heist-gone-wrong (*Reservoir Dogs*, 1992) and the lovers-on-the-run (*True Romance*, 1993), and who brought the independent sector into the Hollywood mainstream with the success of *Pulp Fiction* (1994).

Key films

Little Caesar
Mervyn Le Roy, USA, 1930
The first gangster talkie set the pattern for the decade's typical 'rise and fall' story structure, with Edward G Robinson's repellent, power-hungry Rico ruthlessly shooting his way to the top before crashing to the gutter.

Scarface, the Shame of a Nation
Howard Hawks, USA, 1932
One of several early gangster films drawn from contemporary headlines, with Paul Muni playing a barely disguised version of Al Capone; in Brian De Palma's 1983 remake, the character became a megalomaniac Cuban drug lord (Al Pacino).

The Big Sleep
Howard Hawks, USA, 1946
The Hollywood crime movie edged closer to film noir and hard-boiled pulp fiction as Raymond Chandler's smart-mouthed, cynical private detective Philip Marlowe (Humphrey Bogart) was entangled in the web of a near-impenetrable case.

Rififi (Du Rififi chez les hommes)
Jules Dassin, France, 1955
Although there had been earlier heist movies (such as 1950's *The Asphalt Jungle*), the silent 30-minute set piece at the centre of this film inspired a crime subgenre that dwelt on the detailed planning and execution of complicated robberies.

Chinatown
Roman Polanski, USA, 1974
In 1930s Los Angeles, private detective J J Gittes (Jack Nicholson) trawls through an amoral world that's rotten from top to bottom, encountering shady business deals, political corruption and incest.

The Godfather Part II
Francis Ford Coppola, USA, 1974
The superior sequel to Coppola's groundbreaking original presents crime as a business empire rather than a neighbourhood protection racket, directly comparing (through flashback) the rise to power of father and son at a similar age.

Goodfellas
Martin Scorsese, USA, 1990
Scorsese's bravura camera flourishes underline the seductive appeal of the modern gangster world in this violent morality tale centring on professional hoodlum Henry Hill.

Reservoir Dogs
Quentin Tarantino, USA, 1992
A botched heist forms the backdrop to a series of smart conversations and violent stand-offs between cool-suited gangsters, in the film that encouraged hundreds of independent film-makers to try their hands at low-budget gunplay.

Heat
Michael Mann, USA, 1995
Brilliantly choreographed action scenes interrupt soulful meditations on the loneliness of cop and crook, seen here as two sides of the same coin in the film that brought Al Pacino and Robert De Niro together on screen for the first time.

Lock, Stock and Two Smoking Barrels
Guy Ritchie, UK, 1998
With more style than substance, and a well-chosen soundtrack to match, Ritchie's story of four London lads getting out of their depth inspired a flood of inferior 'mockney' Brit-crime imitators.

The Coens' Creation

Roderick Jaynes, the editor of Joel and Ethan Coen's darkly comic crime film *Fargo* (1996), was nominated for an Academy Award® despite being merely a pseudonym for the film-maker brothers. To keep up the ploy, the Coens invented a biography for Mr Jaynes, claiming that he had begun his career as tea boy at Shepperton Studios in the 1930s and was the world's foremost collector of nude paintings of Margaret Thatcher.

Festivals

Crime Scene
Held annually since 2001 in London, England. Crime genre film and literature festival run by the British Film Institute.
Website: www.bfi.org.uk

Further viewing

M (1931), *The Thin Man* (1934), *Angels with Dirty Faces* (1938), *High Sierra* (1941), *White Heat* (1949), *Point Blank* (1967), *Bullitt* (1968), *Get Carter* (1971), *Klute* (1971), *Shaft* (1971), *Mean Streets* (1973), *The Long Good Friday* (1980), *A Better Tomorrow* (1986), *The Untouchables* (1987), *Se7en* (1995), *The Usual Suspects* (1995), *L.A. Confidential* (1997), *Ocean's Eleven* (2001)

The Sherlock Holmes franchise

Edinburgh-born Sir Arthur Conan Doyle published his first Sherlock Holmes novel, *A Study in Scarlet*, in 1887. The first screen version of a Holmes story, a 30-second short film called *Sherlock Holmes Baffled*, appeared c.1900; in the decades since, the consulting detective has become the most frequently filmed fictional character in cinema history. British stage star Eille Norwood became the first actor to be identified with the role through a series of silent shorts made in the 1920s. Arthur Wontner proved popular with the critics for his take on the role in the 1930s, but was eclipsed when Basil Rathbone slipped on the famous deerstalker hat in 20th Century Fox's *The Hound of the Baskervilles* (1939). With Nigel Bruce cast as an amiably bumbling Dr Watson, Rathbone made one further Holmes film for Fox – *The Adventures of Sherlock Holmes* (1939) – before the franchise shifted to Universal Studios in the 1940s. Universal unapologetically updated the Victorian detective's cases to contemporary times, with villain Professor Moriarty remodelled as a Nazi spymaster. In the UK, Hammer Films tried its hand with Peter Cushing in the lead for a 1959 version of *The Hound of the Baskervilles*; other interesting big-screen casting choices have included Michael Caine as a drunken Holmes in *Without a Clue* (1988) and Peter Cook in yet another version of *The Hound of the Baskervilles* (1978). It is perhaps on television that Conan Doyle's creation has been most faithfully treated, especially in Granada's series (1984–94) starring Jeremy Brett. Other small-screen Holmeses have included Roger Moore (1976), Tom Baker (1982), Charlton Heston (1991), Christopher Lee (1991–2) and Rupert Everett (2004).

Key Sherlock Holmes films

Sherlock Junior (Buster Keaton, USA, 1924), *The Hound of the Baskervilles* (Sidney Lanfield, USA, 1939), *The Scarlet Claw* (Roy William Neill, USA, 1944), *The Hound of the Baskervilles* (Terence Fisher, UK, 1959), *The Private Life of Sherlock Holmes* (Billy Wilder, UK, 1970), *The Adventures of Sherlock Holmes' Smarter Brother* (Gene Wilder, USA, 1975), *Murder by Decree* (Bob Clark, UK/Canada, 1978), *Young Sherlock Holmes* (Barry Levinson, USA, 1985)

Some actors who have played Sherlock Holmes

Numbers in brackets represent the number of Holmes film and television adaptations in which each actor appeared.
Jeremy Brett (41), Peter Cushing (17), Vasili Livanov (11), Eille Norwood (47), Basil Rathbone (14), Arthur Wontner (5)

DISASTER FILMS

History

Early film-makers soon discovered that scenes of catastrophe were a big-money draw for audiences eager to witness destruction on a grand scale. On the silent screen, ancient regimes and biblical cities were routinely felled by the righteous wrath of a higher moral power, as in the Babylon section of D W Griffith's *Intolerance* (1916). In the 1930s, US audiences preferred their disaster closer to home, thrilling to the sight of New York City under water (*Deluge*, 1933) or Atlanta in flames (*Gone with the Wind*, 1939). After World War II, Japan's devastation inspired the trampled-city rampages of the Godzilla series, while US audiences were encouraged by various films to fear annihilation from outer space.

The 1970s marked the glory years of the Hollywood disaster movie, which stuck to a formula in which stereotyped characters, often played by an all-star cast, overcame potentially lethal obstacles caused by a big-budget set piece. By the following decade, such clichés were being spoofed in the likes of *Airplane!* (1980). Increased use of computer-generated effects allowed the disaster movie to merge with the summer blockbuster in the 1990s, showing tourist landmarks across the world succumbing to the forces of nature or the invasion plans of alien races.

The genre today

The media-witnessed events of 11 September, 2001, and the destruction wreaked by severe weather events such as Hurricane Katrina, have affected the tone of disaster movies more than any other genre. Blockbusters such as Steven Spielberg's *War of the Worlds* (2005) now inevitably bring to mind images of global terrorism and real-life disaster.

Key figures

Irwin Allen (1916–91)
Producer and director, nicknamed 'The Master of Disaster', whose big-budget, escapist movies of the 1970s display star power to match their destructive spectacle.

Roland Emmerich (1955–   )
German-born director who uses computer-generated effects to create awesome scenes of urban destruction in Hollywood summer blockbusters such as *Independence Day* (1996), *Godzilla* (1998) and *The Day After Tomorrow* (2004).

George Kennedy (1925–   )
Veteran actor who enjoyed a run of success in 1970s disaster movies, playing mechanic and general airline expert Joe Patroni in all four *Airport* films, and a Los Angeles cop in *Earthquake* (1974).

Key films

The Last Days of Pompeii (Gli ultimi giorni di Pompei)
Luigi Maggi, Italy, 1908
The first (but certainly not the last) film version of this story recreates the eruption of Mount Vesuvius in a grand style, kicking off a series of early Italian-made costume epics considered at the time to be the best in the world.

San Francisco
W S Van Dyke, USA, 1936
The San Francisco earthquake of 1906 provides an exciting climax to the otherwise clichéd romance between a singer (Jeanette MacDonald) and a roguish nightclub owner (Clark Gable).

Airport
George Seaton, USA, 1970
The first of the definitive disaster movies of the 1970s, in which a bomb is discovered on an airliner, was nominated for ten Academy Awards®, won Best Supporting Actress for Helen Hayes and went on to inspire three sequels.

The Poseidon Adventure
Ronald Neame, USA, 1972
When a luxury liner is flipped over by a tidal wave, the survivors – including Gene Hackman, Shelley Winters and Ernest Borgnine – must engineer their own escape by working their way upwards to the hull.

The Towering Inferno
John Guillermin and Irwin Allen, USA, 1974
Paul Newman and Steve McQueen provide the disaster genre with a heavyweight star pairing, playing an architect and fire chief combating a blaze in a newly built skyscraper.

The Day after Tomorrow
Roland Emmerich, USA, 2004
This post-9/11 release takes a more human, less gung-ho approach than earlier disaster movies, depicting New York City struck by a tidal wave which is followed by a new Ice Age.

Documentaries

Further viewing

The War of the Worlds (1953), *A Night to Remember* (1958), *Earthquake* (1974), *Alive* (1993), *Twister* (1996), *Independence Day* (1997), *Armageddon* (1998)

DOCUMENTARIES

History

Very early films such as the Lumière brothers' footage of workers leaving a factory are known as 'actualities' rather than documentaries. The latter term only came into common usage after a *New York Sun* reporter used it in a review of Robert Flaherty's South Seas-set film *Moana* (1926). Documentaries use factual information to convey reality as it is, not as invented for fiction. Of course, the true meaning of these 'real' images can be manipulated through editing, carefully worded interview questions, selection of camera set-ups and the inclusion of archive footage.

The documentary form came of age in the 1920s with a series of European portraits of urban life, known as 'city symphonies'. During World War II, documentaries fell prey to propaganda, rousing the patriotic spirit and demonizing the enemy. Russian and Dutch schools developed the form's avant-garde potential, while the British documentary movement of the 1930s established a more worthy educational tone. As equipment became more portable in the late 1950s, two overwhelmingly influential styles emerged. In the USA and Canada, 'Direct Cinema' eschewed planning and film-maker interference in favour of a spontaneous, fly-on-the-wall approach. In France, the cinéma-vérité style was similar in its immediacy, but included film-maker interviews during which the very presence of a camera crew encouraged subjects to part more readily with answers.

The genre today

Cheap and widely available digital camcorders have opened up the documentary format to new voices from wider backgrounds, with a growing network of independent cinemas using digital projection to allow them to be seen. Strong box-office returns for the likes of *Super Size Me* (2004) and *March of the Penguins* (2005) have also given documentaries a mainstream commercial boost.

Key figures

Nick Broomfield (1948–   )
British director who uses his own self-deprecating, bumbling on-screen presence to convey the difficulty of making a film and to tease answers out of his interview subjects, who have included Hollywood madam Heidi Fleiss and serial killer Aileen Wuournos.

Robert Flaherty (1884–1951)
US director who used a technique of reconstructing certain scenes within his films, adding drama to such nostalgic depictions of mankind struggling against nature as *Man of Aran* (1934).

Documentaries

John Grierson (1898–1972)
Producer who, in the interwar period, headed government bodies including the GPO Film Unit and the National Film Board of Canada, and who believed that documentaries should play an educational role in society.

Albert Maysles (1926–) and David Maysles (1932–87)
Film-maker brothers who used the objective Direct Cinema approach to capture unadorned reality in *Salesman* (1969) and *Grey Gardens* (1975).

Michael Moore (1954–)
Director and political satirist who, in his books, television series and films (including *Roger and Me*, 1989, *Bowling for Columbine*, 2002 and *Fahrenheit 9/11*, 2004) airs controversial political opinions and highlights conflicts between ordinary people and big institutions.

Frederick Wiseman (1930–)
Director who has made effective use of the fly-on-the-wall style for four decades, documenting the workings of US institutions including hospitals, department stores and schools.

_ A Mixed Bag _

Werner Herzog, the German director of *Aguirre: The Wrath of God* (1972) and *Fitzcarraldo* (1982), has also made a number of documentaries about larger-than-life individuals and eccentrics. His subjects include cattle auctioneers, a champion ski-jumper who works as a carpenter, a TV evangelist, an activist working to protect grizzly bears and the sole survivor of a Peruvian plane crash.

Key films

Nanook of the North
Robert Flaherty, USA, 1922
The first documentary to adapt the structure of narrative fiction to real-life footage, using reconstructed scenes to reveal the hardships facing an Inuit family in Alaska.

Man with a Movie Camera (Chelovek s kino-apparatom)
Dziga Vertov, USSR, 1929
Vertov uses various camera tricks to manipulate footage of everyday life in a Soviet city, flaunting the fact that the film-maker has the power to control the audience's perception of reality.

Triumph of the Will (Triumph des Willens)
Leni Riefenstahl, Germany, 1935
Commissioned by Hitler himself, this notorious document of the Nazi Party's 1934 rally in Nuremberg is immaculately designed, choreographed and edited to glorify its political subject.

Fires Were Started
Humphrey Jennings, UK, 1943
Jennings captures the quiet dignity of Londoners caught up in the Blitz, depicting firemen fighting a blaze that was reconstructed for the cameras.

Gimme Shelter
Albert and David Maysles, USA, 1970
Direct Cinema cameras captured history as it happened when Hell's Angels security guards killed an audience member at a Rolling Stones concert; the repeated use of footage of the death raised questions about the ethics of documentary techniques.

The Sorrow and the Pity (Le Chagrin et la pitié)
Marcel Ophüls, France/Germany/Switzerland, 1969
Ophüls tackled the sensitive subjects of Nazi collaboration and the myth of the French Resistance in cinéma-vérité interviews conducted with the citizens of Clermont-Ferrand, who contradict one another as well as the evidence of archive footage.

Hearts of Darkness: A Filmmaker's Apocalypse
Fax Bahr and George Hickenlooper, USA, 1991
This documentary on the making of *Apocalypse Now* (1979) uses intimate on-set footage to show the extreme pressure placed on director Francis Ford Coppola as his production spun out of control.

When We Were Kings
Leon Gast, USA, 1996
This record of the 1974 championship fight known as the Rumble in the Jungle is also a window onto the birth of Black Pride, and a portrait of Muhammad Ali at his height.

Fahrenheit 9/11
Michael Moore, USA, 2004
This aggressive, challenging indictment of the Bush administration, focusing on the aftermath of the 11 September 2001 terrorist attacks and the build-up to war in Iraq, became the highest-grossing documentary of all time in the USA.

Festivals

International Documentary Festival Amsterdam
Held annually since 1998 in Amsterdam, The Netherlands.
Website: www.idfa.nl
Top prizes: Joris Ivens Prize (for films over 60 minutes), Silver Wolf (for films under 60 minutes)

Further viewing

Grass (1925), *Berlin, Symphony of a City* (1928), *Night Mail* (1936), *Olympiad* (1938), *Le Monde du Silence* (1956), *Night and Fog* (1956), *Chronicle of a Summer* (1961), *Don't Look Back* (1967), *Hearts and Minds* (1974), *The Battle of Chile* (1975–9), *Harlan County USA* (1976), *The Last Waltz* (1978), *Koyaanisqatsi* (1983), *The Times of Harvey Milk* (1984), *Shoah* (1985), *Hoop Dreams* (1994)

EPICS

History

In movie terms, the word 'epic' has now come to mean any film with an unusually long running time. In its purest form, however, it refers to the story of a heroic individual whose adventures, trials and tribulations carry an instructive moral message. The Italians were the first to bring epic scope to the cinema screen in a series of silent films from 1905 onwards which depicted awe-inspiring religious spectacles or the destruction of ancient cities. Hollywood quickly picked up on the trend, bringing more mobile camerawork to the static tableaux and giving production designers the budget to recreate the past on a huge scale.

The Hollywood epics of the 1930s attracted audiences with the promise of scantily-clad slaves and fierce battles, but sent them home with a Christian message fresh in their minds. Meanwhile, around the world, nationalistic epics such as Russia's *Alexander Nevsky* (1938) were produced to stir patriotic hearts. In the 1950s, Hollywood tried to combat the growing appeal of television by experimenting with various widescreen and colour processes, and rousing the spirits with musical scores by the likes of Miklós Rósza. Back in Italy, the *peplum* (quickly-made mythic adventures featuring musclemen with swords and voluptuous women in skimpy togas) proved popular. By the 1960s, however, a younger audience was demanding more contemporary themes, and the rise of science-fiction adventures laden with special effects sounded the genre's death knell.

The genre today

Hopes for the revival of the historical epic rested on the muscular shoulders of Ridley Scott's *Gladiator* (2000), but the blockbuster-budgeted *Troy* (2004), *Alexander* (2004) and *Kingdom of Heaven* (2005) have failed to meet expectations.

Key figures

Dino De Laurentiis (1919–   )
Legendary Italian producer of *King Kong* (1976) and *Red Dragon* (2002) who, along with producing partner Carlo Ponti, encouraged Hollywood studios to come to Rome to shoot epics such as *Ulysses* (1954).

Cecil B De Mille (1881–1959)
Director and producer, regarded as US cinema's greatest showman, whose big-budget epics promoted Christian values beneath the thrills and spectacle.

Charlton Heston (1924–   )
Actor whose tall, muscular frame conveyed courage and chivalry, whether he was playing Old Testament prophet Moses in *The Ten Commandments* (1956) or a medieval warrior in *El Cid* (1961).

Victor Mature (1915–99)
Actor with a burly build well-suited to Hollywood's historical epics, including *Samson and Delilah* (1949) and *The Robe* (1953); he moved to Italy in the 1960s to take on a series of toga-and-sandals roles.

Key films

Quo Vadis?
Enrico Guazzoni, Italy, 1912
One of the first films to run to more than an hour in length, this biblical epic, mostly shot in static tableaux, filled the Royal Albert Hall on its London engagement.

The Ten Commandments
Cecil B De Mille, USA, 1956
De Mille's last film – a remake of his own 1925 version – used cutting-edge special effects to depict the parting of the Red Sea and the liberation of the Jews from Egyptian slavery.

Hercules (Le Fatiche di Ercole)
Pietro Francisci, Italy, 1958
The success of this film in the USA paved the way for a number of other Italian myth-based, sword-and-sandal epics, and made former Mr Universe Steve Reeves a star.

Ben-Hur
William Wyler, USA, 1959
The winner of eleven Academy Awards® and, at $15 million, the most expensive film of its day, this story of a heroic individual's fight against Roman tyranny features a climactic chariot race that remains a key moment in the history of action cinema.

Lawrence of Arabia
David Lean, UK, 1962
British Imperial adventures had long been a staple of epic cinema, and here, against a backdrop of shimmering desert scenes, Peter O'Toole brought a near-mystic aura to his portrayal of an army officer who leads the Arabs to victory against the Turks.

Cleopatra
Joseph L Mankiewicz, USA, 1963
The gossip-column scandals, production disasters and swollen budget of this film killed both studio and public appetites for overindulgent blockbusters, as Elizabeth Taylor and Richard Burton's off-screen love affair distracted everyone involved from the job at hand.

Jason and the Argonauts
Don Chaffey, US/UK, 1963
Greek mythology was excellent source material for stop-motion animator Ray Harryhausen, who created swordfighting skeletons and a giant man of bronze for this fantasy epic.

Gandhi
Richard Attenborough, UK, 1982
This Academy Award®-winning biopic about the man who peaceably ended British rule in India drew its epic story from recent rather than ancient history, using a cast of thousands to depict the life of a humble individual.

Gladiator
Ridley Scott, USA, 2000
The sword-and-sandals epic was reborn for the digital age, as Scott rebuilt the Colosseum from computer pixels and Russell Crowe proved himself a worthy successor to the epic stars of old.

The Lord of the Rings trilogy
Peter Jackson, New Zealand/USA, 2001–3
To reflect the scale of J R R Tolkien's epic literary saga, Jackson released his film adaptation in three annual instalments.

Standing Up for Spartacus

Towards the end of *Spartacus* (1960) the conquered slave army rises one by one, prompted by Antoninus (Tony Curtis), with each man shouting 'I'm Spartacus!' in order to save their leader (Kirk Douglas) from the wrath of Rome. In 2003, this scene was voted number one in *Empire* magazine's '50 Movie Moments to Make a Grown Man Cry' poll.

Further viewing

Cabiria (1914), *Intolerance* (1916), *Ben-Hur* (1925), *Napoléon* (1927), *Gone with the Wind* (1939), *Fabiola* (1949), *Quo Vadis?* (1951), *The Greatest Show on Earth* (1952), *The Vikings* (1958), *Spartacus* (1960), *War and Peace* (1968), *Braveheart* (1995)

FILM NOIR

History

Classic film noir emerged just after World War II as the meeting point between a sombre European visual style and a typically American pulp-fiction setting. Although the phrase is French, meaning 'black film', the cinematic influences that shaped the genre were more obviously German. Film-makers including Billy Wilder, who had fled from the Nazis to the USA, were directly inspired by the shadowy frames of German Expressionist films and the snappy dialogue of US crime novels by the likes of Raymond Chandler, Dashiell Hammett and Cornell Woolrich.

Set in cynical and unforgiving underworlds, these fatalistic films distinguished themselves from previous gangster and detective tales through sharp contrasts of light and shade, mirroring the stories' harsh morality. Film noir also reflected psychological trends; Freudian fears took shape in predatory *femmes fatales*, and a cast of characters made up of amnesiacs, schizophrenics and dead men provided their own obituary voiceovers. By the 1950s, the pessimism of World War II had developed into the paranoia of the Cold War, ensuring fresh inspiration for film noir's tense and claustrophobic moods.

The genre today

Neo-noir, as it is often called, has freely fused the dark visual style and moody themes of classic film noir with other genres, using colour photography and a gorier approach to bloodletting. The results now span the black-comedy style of the Coen brothers (*Blood Simple*, 1984; *Fargo*, 1996), the dialogue-driven violence of Quentin Tarantino and the disturbingly surreal visions of David Lynch (*Blue Velvet*, 1986; *Lost Highway*, 1997).

Key figures

John Alton (1901–96)
Cinematographer, born in Austria-Hungary, whose use of deep focus and high-contrast photography created the rich black shadows that define the expressionistic film noir look.

Humphrey Bogart (1899–1957)
Actor who became the most important male star of the film noir genre when he developed his tough-guy gangster act of the 1930s into a more cynical, bemused approach.

Henry Hathaway (1898–1985)
Director whose use of real locations in *The House on 92nd Street* (1945), *Kiss of Death* (1947) and *Call Northside 777* (1948) gave film noir an authentic, semi-documentary quality.

Fritz Lang (1890–1976)
Austrian director whose film-noir obsessions with fate and forbidden desire (*Scarlet Street*, 1945; *The Big Heat*, 1953) can be traced back to his German urban thriller *M* (1931).

Robert Siodmak (1900–73)
German director who fled Nazi persecution and whose stylish noirs (including the 1946 version of *The Killers*) dwell on cruelty, betrayal and death.

Barbara Stanwyck (1907–90)
Actress who, despite her blonde hair, became film noir's iconic *femme fatale* for her cold but erotic performance in *Double Indemnity* (1944).

Chandler the Critic

Hard-boiled crime novelist Raymond Chandler was hired by Paramount to adapt fellow pulp stylist James M Cain's novel *Double Indemnity* (1944) for the screen. Chandler wasn't impressed by the source material, describing Cain in a letter to his publisher as 'the kind of writer I detest … a dirty little boy with a piece of chalk and a board fence and nobody looking'.

Key films

Port of Shadows (Le Quai des brumes)
Marcel Carné, France, 1938
Jean Gabin stars in this French precursor to film noir, which overflows with doomed romance, foggy locations and a remarkably pessimistic poetic realism.

The Maltese Falcon
John Huston, USA, 1941
This third screen version of Dashiell Hammett's novel crystallizes several noir elements: the hard-boiled dialogue, the cynical detective, the *femme fatale* and the oddball assortment of crooks.

Double Indemnity
Billy Wilder, USA, 1944
Greed, lust and betrayal – the staple diet of film noir – come to the fore as cocky salesman Fred MacMurray is seduced by Barbara Stanwyck into killing her husband for his life insurance.

Sunset Boulevard
Billy Wilder, USA, 1950
Floating face down in a swimming pool, William Holden narrates the lead-up to his own murder in this blackest and most cynical of Hollywood's self-examinations.

Kiss Me Deadly
Robert Aldrich, USA, 1955
The brutal pulp style of novelist Mickey Spillane – combined with Cold War paranoia and twisted camera angles – gives the classic noir genre a disturbing edge.

Le Samouraï
Jean-Pierre Melville, France, 1967
Steely blues replace black shadows, but otherwise the key noir ingredients are present in this French existentialist thriller which emphasizes the lonely life of its assassin anti-hero, played by Alain Delon.

Blue Velvet
David Lynch, USA, 1986
Lynch reveals a psychotic noir underbelly beneath the white picket fences of suburban America when naïve Kyle MacLachlan is drawn into a sadomasochistic relationship between singer Isabella Rossellini and crime boss Dennis Hopper.

Se7en
David Fincher, USA, 1995
Fincher's gory, nightmarish twist on a serial killer's cat-and-mouse game is laden with post-modern pessimism, while Darius Khondji's underlit interiors are the epitome of colour-noir photography.

Festivals

Noir In Festival
Held annually since 1991 at Courmayeur in the Italian Alps.
Website: www.noirfest.com
Top prizes: Mystery Awards (for film); Raymond Chandler Award and Giorgio Scerbanenco Award (for books)

Further viewing

Laura (1944), *Farewell, My Lovely* (1945), *Gilda* (1946), *The Killers* (1946), *Build My Gallows High* (1947), *DOA* (1949), *The Big Heat* (1953), *Touch of Evil* (1958), *The Long Goodbye* (1973), *Body Heat* (1981), *Blood Simple* (1985)

HORROR

History

Film versions of *Dr Jekyll and Mr Hyde* (1908) and *Frankenstein* (1910) appeared early in the silent era in the USA, but it was the twisted poetic designs and psychological terrors of German Expressionism – particularly *The Cabinet of Dr Caligari* (1920) – that set the horror genre in motion. Hollywood took control in the 1930s, when Universal Studios instigated a cycle of horror films with the 1931 double whammy of *Dracula* and *Frankenstein*. The eerie, fairytale mood of these films was hugely influential, but by the 1940s the series had run out of steam and the studio was desperately throwing its horror icons together in formulaic sequels.

It took a small company based in Bray, England to pump blood back into the genre in the late 1950s. Hammer Studios shook up the Universal back catalogue, splashing gore across the screen and increasing the sex factor in their gothic tales. By the following decade, the genre was already focusing on a new type of monster – the human homicidal maniac. The nuclear family was blown apart in the 1970s as children became monsters – *The Exorcist* (1973), *The Omen* (1976), *The Brood* (1979) – and cannibalistic families stalked the quiet corners of America. After an exploitation boom during the early video era, the horror film – always the black sheep of the cinema family – was finally accepted by the Hollywood majors. Top stars such as Tom Cruise (*Interview with the Vampire*, 1994), Jack Nicholson (*Wolf*, 1994) and Robert De Niro (*Mary Shelley's Frankenstein*, 1994) embraced the shadows.

The genre today

While Hollywood works its way through a trend for remaking the classic horror movies of the 1970s, the genre has been revived by a flood of ghostly tales from the Far East (although these too are undergoing the Hollywood remake treatment).

Key figures

Dario Argento (1940–)
Italian director who became the master of the gory set piece, bringing an artistic eye and bold camera moves to murder scenes in *Suspiria* (1976) and *Inferno* (1980).

Wes Craven (1939–)
Director who has twice revitalized the horror genre, first with the wisecracks of child-killer Freddy Krueger in *A Nightmare on Elm Street* (1984), then with the post-modern pop culture references of *Scream* (1996) and its sequels.

Christopher Lee (1922–)
English actor with a prolific and wide-ranging output including regular stints in the Hammer Horror series, in which he played both Frankenstein's monster and Dracula.

Boris Karloff (1887–1969)
English actor whose heavy eyebrows and quietly menacing demeanour led to his typecasting in the horror genre, particularly after his surprisingly sympathetic performance as the tragic monster in Universal's *Frankenstein* (1931).

Stephen King (1947–   )
Author whose novels and short stories have provided the basis for more than 70 feature films, miniseries and television adaptations, including genre classics *Carrie* (1976) and *The Shining* (1980), plus prison movie *The Shawshank Redemption* (1994).

Val Lewton (1904–51)
Russian-born producer and former story editor whose films for RKO between 1942 and 1946 – including *Cat People* (1942) and *I Walked with a Zombie* (1943) – sustained a dark, poetic mood by suggesting horrors that were left unseen.

Bela Lugosi (1882–1956)
Hungarian actor who used his native accent to good effect in *Dracula* (1931) before taking on a stream of horror roles that declined in quality in the late 1940s and early 1950s, partly because of his alcoholism and morphine addiction.

Vincent Price (1911–93)
Actor who worked onstage with Orson Welles in the 1930s before his pencil-thin moustache and suave malevolence typecast him as a hammy horror villain, although his talent shines in Roger Corman's Poe cycle and *Witchfinder General* (1968).

A Never-Ending Story

The 'after-the-colon' subtitles of sequels to the horror classic *A Nightmare on Elm Street* (1984) are: *Freddy's Revenge* (1985), *Dream Warriors* (1987), *The Dream Master* (1988) and *The Dream Child* (1989). Further instalments were entitled *Freddy's Dead: The Final Nightmare* (1991), *Wes Craven's New Nightmare* (1994) and *Freddy Vs Jason* (2003).

Key films

Frankenstein
James Whale, USA, 1931
The influence of German Expressionism can be seen in the striking images of Universal's adaptation of Mary Shelley's novel, with Colin Clive playing God as the mad scientist and Boris Karloff winning sympathy as the childlike monster.

Psycho
Alfred Hitchcock, USA, 1960
Years ahead of its time in probing the schizophrenic recesses of a serial killer's mind, Hitchcock's voyeuristic, blackly comic horror is world-class film-making, from the sustained tension within the Bates Motel to the cut-and-slash of the famous shower scene.

Night of the Living Dead
George A Romero, USA, 1968
The dead rise from their graves to consume the living in Romero's pessimistic, terrifyingly contemporary horror film, which drew upon current politics and spawned three direct sequels, as well as a horde of gory zombie imitations.

The Exorcist
William Friedkin, USA, 1973
Hollywood finally embraced the 'disreputable' horror genre with this blockbuster tale of demonic possession, making the eternal battle between good and evil graphically explicit with groundbreaking special effects make-up by Dick Smith.

The Texas Chain Saw Massacre
Tobe Hooper, USA, 1974
Young city slickers become fresh meat for hick cannibals, including chainsaw-wielding freak Leatherface, in a relentless (but not bloody) film that was branded by censors 'the pornography of terror' and banned in the UK for 23 years.

Halloween
John Carpenter, USA, 1978
Horror became a rollercoaster ride, filled with sudden scares and brief rest periods, as escaped psycho and modern-day bogeyman Michael Myers slashed his way through his hometown with a particularly phallic knife.

The Evil Dead
Sam Raimi, USA, 1981
Demonized by campaigner Mary Whitehouse as the number one video nasty, Raimi's cartoonish, gory and ferociously funny debut is now revered as the horror classic that introduced the fast, low-to-the-ground tracking shot.

The Silence of the Lambs
Jonathan Demme, USA, 1991
As the iconic Hannibal Lecter, Anthony Hopkins plays the horror-movie serial killer as a charming, intellectual monster, helping this adaptation of Thomas Harris's bestselling novel to become one of only three films ever to scoop all five major Academy Awards[®].

The Blair Witch Project
Daniel Myrick and Eduardo Sanchez, USA, 1999
Digital video and internet hype turned this low-budget independent film, which used hand-held camerawork to create intense, claustrophobic intimacy with three characters lost in the woods, into a worldwide phenomenon.

Festivals

Gérardmer Festival du Film Fantastique
Held annually since 1994 in Gérardmer, France. Festival specializing in horror, science fiction and fantasy.
Website: www.gerardmer-fantasticart.com
Top prize: Grand Prix

Further viewing

Häxan (1922), *The Phantom of the Opera* (1925), *Freaks* (1932), *King Kong* (1933), *Bride of Frankenstein* (1935), *Eyes Without a Face* (1959), *Black Sunday* (1960), *The Birds* (1963), *The Haunting* (1963), *Onibaba* (1965), *Rosemary's Baby* (1968), *Don't Look Now* (1973), *The Wicker Man* (1973), *Friday the 13th* (1980), *Henry: Portrait of a Serial Killer* (1986), *Hellraiser* (1987), *The Others* (2001)

The Dracula franchise

The first major 'Dracula' film did not actually feature a vampire called Dracula. The main character was Graf Orlok, played by German actor Max Schreck, whose bald, skeletal head and fearsome talons made him look like a skinned bat. Even the film's title – *Nosferatu* (1922) – had to be changed because of copyright wrangles with the estate of Bram Stoker, the Irish author whose vampire novel *Dracula* had been published in 1897. Nevertheless, this classic of German Expressionism was more faithful to the book than Universal Studios' more famous *Dracula* (1931). Hungarian actor Bela Lugosi had played the role on stage and was drafted in when the original choice, silent star Lon Chaney, died. A Spanish version starring Carlos Villarias was shot simultaneously on the same sets. Universal dusted off Dracula's fangs and cape for a further four sequels, not to mention an Abbott and Costello comedy.

The first great British Dracula was Christopher Lee, who brought a dark, handsome sensuality to the Count in the 1958 Hammer Films version. Hammer officially bought up the rights to the Universal monster movies of the 1930s, setting up their own Dracula franchise with eight sequels which thrust the Count's name somewhere into the title. Other vampire movies have stalked the cinemas over the decades, using the Dracula name even when the vampire in question bears no resemblance to Stoker's creation. This unauthorized Count has bitten an African prince in a blaxploitation flick (*Blacula*, 1972) and taken on a Wild West outlaw (*Billy the Kid Versus Dracula*, 1965). Elsewhere, his heritage has been linked to 15th-century warlord Vlad the Impaler (*Bram Stoker's Dracula*, 1992) and, remarkably, Judas Iscariot (*Dracula 2000*, 2000).

Key Dracula films

Nosferatu (F W Murnau, Germany, 1922), *Dracula* (Tod Browning, USA, 1931), *Dracula's Daughter* (Lambert Hillyer, USA, 1936), *Drakula Istanbulda* (Mehmet Muhtar, Turkey, 1953), *Dracula* (Terence Fisher, UK, 1958), *Andy Warhol's Dracula* (Paul Morrissey, USA, 1973), *The Monster Squad* (Fred Dekker, 1987), *Bram Stoker's Dracula* (Francis Ford Coppola, 1992)

Key Dracula performances

Bela Lugosi (*Dracula*, 1931), John Carradine (*House of Frankenstein*, 1944), Christopher Lee (*Dracula*, 1958), Udo Kier (*Blood for Dracula*, 1974), Frank Langella (*Dracula*, 1979), George Hamilton (*Love at First Bite*, 1979), Klaus Kinski (*Nosferatu*, 1979), David Carradine (*Sundown*, 1988), Gary Oldman (*Bram Stoker's Dracula*, 1992), Leslie Nielsen (*Dracula: Dead and Loving It*, 1995), Richard Roxburgh (*Van Helsing*, 2004)

INDEPENDENT FILM

History

An obvious question when discussing independent cinema is: independent of what? It can be said that the term refers to films and film-makers not funded or employed by the major Hollywood studios. However, from a global perspective this distinction is not always helpful, as true independence might require a film-maker to be free of state funding, should that involve some degree of censorship and artistic control. Every film-producing country, therefore, has an independent sector in which films outside the formulaic mainstream treat sidelined subjects in a more daring style, usually with a low budget to protect the film-maker's personal vision.

In the USA, the first independent of note was United Artists, formed by Charlie Chaplin, Mary Pickford, Douglas Fairbanks Sr and D W Griffith in order to control the marketing and distribution of their own work. In the 1930s, smaller companies on so-called 'Poverty Row', such as Monogram and Republic, made quick and cheap B-movies for cinemas not on the mainstream circuit. The rise of youth culture led to a boom in independent features to fill drive-in double bills and the heyday of American International Pictures (AIP), which provided a launch pad for many of the young Hollywood players of the early 1970s. In the late 1980s, a new generation of film-makers – many showcased at Robert Redford's Sundance Film Festival – created a body of work that emphasized script and performance over special effects.

The genre today

'Independent' is now as much a style as anything else, after 20th Century Fox formed its own indie-style arm (Fox Searchlight) and heavyweight independent company Miramax formed an alliance with Disney. Cable television, DVD and video have opened new markets for independent product, just as the cheap availability of digital equipment has increased access for new film-makers.

Key figures

John Cassavetes (1929–89)
Actor and director who used his fees from acting roles (*Rosemary's Baby*, 1968) to personally finance his directorial work, which drew strong performances from actors including his wife, Gena Rowlands, emphasizing mood and character over narrative.

Roger Corman (1926–)
Director and producer whose work for AIP and his own company, New World Pictures, brought some social significance to the exploitation market, and who mentored the debuts of Jack Nicholson, Monte Hellman and Francis Ford Coppola.

Samuel Goldwyn (1882–1974)
Producer, born in the Warsaw ghetto, who had a talent for making both popular and prestige pictures from the silent era onwards, and whose best work was done in collaboration with director William Wyler (*The Best Years of Our Lives*, 1946).

Jim Jarmusch (1953–)
Silver-haired US writer-director whose films have a hip, deadpan humour and frequently feature loners dislocated from the world around them, whether it be the Wild West (*Dead Man*, 1995) or the urban jungle (*Ghost Dog*, 1999).

Spike Lee (1957–)
Director, producer, writer and actor who gave young black America an angry cinematic voice in *She's Gotta Have It* (1986), and who has since alternated studio-financed work with privately-funded, smaller independent projects.

Russ Meyer (1922–2004)
Director and producer nicknamed 'King of the Nudies', who also wrote, shot and edited his softcore sexploitation films, all of which contain a unique blend of satire, cartoon violence, overheated melodrama and actresses with unfeasibly large breasts.

John Sayles (1950–   )
Director whose Hollywood-writer-for-hire sideline funds his own politically committed films (made with long-time producing partner Maggie Renzi), which explore such issues as unionization, political corruption and big-business exploitation.

John Waters (1947–   )
Director, nicknamed the 'Pope of Trash', whose bad-taste, cult-hit movies – particularly *Pink Flamingos* (1972), starring Divine – tackle taboos in a kitsch and crudely witty manner.

Sweet Sweetback's Baadasssss Song
Melvin Van Peebles, USA, 1971
The blaxploitation fad began in a genuinely radical, from-the-streets mood, with director-star Van Peebles playing a black stud who gets the better of 'the Man' to the sound of an Earth, Wind & Fire funk score.

Eraserhead
David Lynch, USA, 1977
With its surreal, nightmarish imagery and unsettling post-industrial soundtrack, this cult hit on the midnight movie circuit proved that the independent arena could accommodate a director-artist like David Lynch.

sex, lies and videotape
Steven Soderbergh, USA, 1989
Modern US independent cinema came of age when Soderbergh's intimate examination of deceit and duplicity in modern relationships electrified the Sundance Film Festival and won the Palme d'Or at Cannes a few months later.

Clerks
Kevin Smith, USA, 1994
Made for only $27,000, Smith's profanity-fuelled tale of life in a convenience store proved that good dialogue can make a film's grainy visual quality irrelevant, thus inspiring a wave of can-do, low-budget 'Generation X' film-makers.

The Blair Witch Project
Daniel Myrick and Eduardo Sanchez, USA, 1999
The limitations of digital video were exploited to good effect by this indie horror film, which used a groundbreaking internet campaign to persuade audiences that the shaky footage they were watching really had been shot by a film crew lost in the woods.

Musicals

Festivals

Sundance Film Festival
Held annually since 1985 in Park City, Utah, USA.
Website: www.sundance.org
Top prize: Grand Jury Prize

Further viewing

Flaming Creatures (1963), *Scorpio Rising* (1963), *Easy Rider* (1969), *Trash* (1970), *Two-Lane Blacktop* (1971), *Tracks* (1976), *Halloween* (1978), *Down by Law* (1986), *Slacker* (1991), *Safe* (1995), *Happiness* (1998), *Sideways* (2004)

MUSICALS

History

Most countries routinely churn out folksy musicals, operettas and pop-star vehicles geared towards local tastes, but few of these – apart from the elaborate products of India's Bollywood industry – have traditionally found audiences beyond their own borders. The arrival of sound introduced song to the cinema, but despite its title, *The Jazz Singer* (1927) actually amazed audiences with its snippets of spoken dialogue rather than its musical numbers. It wasn't until 1929, with the Marx Brothers' vaudeville show *The Cocoanuts* and MGM's all-singing, all-dancing backstage drama *The Broadway Melody*, that Hollywood turned the stage musical into a cinematic art form.

Throughout the 1930s, Hollywood kidnapped performers, writers and packages of songs from the Broadway stage. During the Depression, US audiences favoured the escapism of behind-the-scenes, putting-on-a-show spectaculars and the fluid dance moves of Fred Astaire and Ginger Rogers. The musical truly came of age, however, at MGM in the late 1940s and early 1950s, when song-and-dance interludes were made to move the plot along rather than distracting from it, and films sparkled with a high standard of scriptwriting and production design. The rock'n'roll era saw many pop idols briefly transformed into film stars, while the traditional musical played safe by splashing successful Broadway shows across screens in colourful, extravagant style. The genre toughened up its subject matter in the 1970s, but by the end of the decade the disco phenomenon had crept into the picture. The musical finally lost steam in the 1980s, as older audiences headed to the theatre and younger viewers tuned in to MTV.

The genre today

Regular bursts of pop songs on a movie soundtrack now frequently take the place of musical numbers, as Hollywood shies away from embracing the traditional genre despite the success of *Chicago* (2002). Musical biopics remain in vogue, however, telling the life stories of Ray Charles (*Ray*, 2004) and Johnny Cash (*Walk the Line*, 2005).

Musicals

Fred Astaire (1899–1987)
Actor and dancer with a graceful ballroom and tap style (which he preferred to have framed in a full-body shot), who made a series of musicals with dance partner Ginger Rogers in the 1930s before revealing a talent for comedy in later solo work.

Busby Berkeley (1895–1976)
Choreographer and director whose lavish spectacles used intricate camera moves and unusual angles to fill the screen with dancers arranged in geometric patterns.

Bing Crosby (1903–77)
Actor and singer whose relaxed crooning style features in seven 'Road to ...' films with co-star Bob Hope, as well as on bestselling single 'White Christmas' from *Holiday Inn* (1942).

Doris Day (1924–)
Actress whose virginal, girl-next-door persona proved popular opposite Rock Hudson in 1950s sex comedies, and who was as comfortable taking the lead in *Calamity Jane* (1953) as singing the odd song in *The Man Who Knew Too Much* (1956).

Bob Fosse (1927–87)
Director, choreographer and dancer who fused modern Broadway with European arthouse influences to create a cynical, self-critical view of the musical in *Sweet Charity* (1969), *Cabaret* (1972) and the semi-autobiographical *All That Jazz* (1979).

Arthur Freed (1894–1973)
Producer and lyricist who joined MGM in 1929 with composer Nacio Herb Brown, and led the studio's musical unit through the golden era of the 1940s and 1950s with a series of genre classics that seamlessly integrated song, speech and dance.

Judy Garland (1922–69)
Actress and singer who first appeared alongside Mickey Rooney in the Andy Hardy series before *The Wizard of Oz* (1939) turned her into a genre icon.

Gene Kelly (1912–96)
Actor-dancer, director and choreographer whose collaborations with director Stanley Donen from *On the Town* (1949) onwards revitalized the Hollywood musical, showcasing his acrobatic agility as well as his artistic pretensions.

Elvis Presley (1935–77)
Singer and actor, nicknamed 'The King', whose teen rock'n'roll movies (including *Jailhouse Rock*, 1957) showcased his greatest hits but were generally of poor quality, with only Don Siegel's *Flaming Star* (1960) revealing much dramatic ability.

Frank Sinatra (1915–98)
Actor and singer who made the leap from bobbysoxer idol to musical star before toughening up his image with a Best Supporting Actor Academy Award® win for *From Here to Eternity* (1953).

Barbra Streisand (1942–   )
Actress and singer whose inimitable ability to build up the dramatic power of a song made her a star in late 1960s musicals such as *Funny Girl* (1968) and *Hello, Dolly!* (1969), and who later showed talent as a comedienne and director.

Key films

The Love Parade
Ernst Lubitsch, USA, 1929
Lubitsch's first sound film broke new ground by integrating songs into its plot.

42nd Street
Lloyd Bacon, USA, 1933
The first of many backstage 'putting-on-a-show' musicals casts Ruby Keeler as a chorus girl who becomes an overnight star when the leading lady twists her ankle.

Top Hat
Mark Sandrich, USA, 1935
The Fred Astaire and Ginger Rogers partnership was at its height when the pair danced their duets in art deco settings to an Irving Berlin score.

The Wizard of Oz
Victor Fleming, USA, 1939
Part fantasy, part road movie, this perennial family favourite gave Judy Garland her signature song ('Over the Rainbow') and heralded the arrival of the Arthur Freed era at MGM.

Singin' in the Rain
Stanley Donen and Gene Kelly, USA, 1952
Betty Comden and Adolph Green's witty script elevates a package of Arthur Freed and Nacio Herb Brown songs into a glorious nostalgia piece about the arrival of sound in Hollywood, while Gene Kelly's splashing solo for the title song remains one of the most joyously uplifting moments in cinema history.

West Side Story
Robert Wise and Jerome Robbins, USA, 1961
Serious issues of racism and juvenile delinquency are tackled in this Manhattan-set Romeo and Juliet story, which is powered by Leonard Bernstein's jazzy score and Jerome Robbins' dynamic choreography.

The Sound of Music
Robert Wise, USA, 1965
Chirpy tunes, the wholesome presence of Julie Andrews and a sentimental storyline made this a massive box-office hit which, unfortunately, ushered in a spate of bloated and obscenely expensive musical copycats.

Cabaret
Bob Fosse, USA, 1972
The decadent nightlife of Berlin between the wars provides an atmospheric backdrop for Academy Award®-winners Liza Minnelli and Joel Grey, singing on the cabaret stage as the Nazis rise to power.

Saturday Night Fever
John Badham, USA, 1977
This X-certificate musical strutted onto the disco floor to the chart-topping sound of the Bee Gees; John Travolta's dance moves, oozing with masculine sexuality, struck a chord with working-class audiences longing for a weekend blow-out.

Moulin Rouge!
Baz Luhrmann, Australia/USA, 2001
Using the visual language of pop videos and a melting-pot of musical influences stretching from opera to Nirvana to Bollywood, Luhrmann concocts a heady love story, capturing at least one seminal musical moment as cameras swirl around Ewan McGregor launching into 'Your Song' on a Parisian rooftop.

Dubbing for Drew

In Woody Allen's first and only film musical, *Everyone Says I Love You* (1996), Drew Barrymore was the only actor whose singing voice was dubbed (by Olivia Hayman). The variable vocal talents of Barrymore's co-stars – including Alan Alda, Billy Crudup, Edward Norton, Natalie Portman, Julia Roberts and Tim Roth – can be heard on the soundtrack album.

Further viewing

Hallelujah (1929), *Meet Me in St Louis* (1944), *On the Town* (1949), *An American in Paris* (1951), *Seven Brides for Seven Brothers* (1954), *A Star is Born* (1954), *The Umbrellas of Cherbourg* (1964), *The Rocky Horror Picture Show* (1975), *Tommy* (1975), *Grease* (1978), *Fame* (1980), *Dancer in the Dark* (2000), *8 Mile* (2002)

ROAD MOVIES

History

The wide expanse of the cinema screen is an ideal backdrop on which to project images of the open highway. The road movie can be seen as the cinematic equivalent of the age-old literary device of a physical journey or odyssey which mirrors a hero's spiritual journey. Wagon-trail westerns, space-exploration adventures and ancient epics have all taken this approach, but it took the car-culture obsession of the USA to turn it into a definable cinema genre.

In the road movies of the 1930s, detours and chance meetings typically brought characters into contact with 'ordinary' people who, sometimes unwittingly, taught them life lessons. Later, the open road – free from the laws of the city – provided an escape route for outlaws and liberated an alienated generation seeking an alternative to the rat race. However, these uncharted lands also held dangers for city slickers, as seen in 1970s horror films. This was the key decade for the road movie, when personal stories were set in untamed corners of America and revved-up engines, car chases and destructive stunts provided thrills.

The genre today

The on-location, improvised structure of road movies suits independent film-makers, who have broadened the genre's traditional themes to include gay characters (*The Living End*, 1992) and foreign settings (*The Motorcycle Diaries*, 2004).

Key figures

Burt Reynolds (1936–)
Actor who became one of the top box-office stars of the 1970s, and whose presence behind a steering wheel guaranteed action on the road in *Smokey and the Bandit* (1977) and *The Cannonball Run* (1981).

Wim Wenders (1945–)
German director whose protagonists often feel like exiles in their own homeland (as in 1976's *Kings of the Road* and 1984's *Paris, Texas*), and who often shoots from inside moving cars, emphasizing their detachment from the landscapes through which they pass.

Key films

It Happened One Night
Frank Capra, USA, 1934
The standard for 1930s road movies, in which characters are freed from their class backgrounds and brought into contact with 'real people' during unplanned detours, was set by this Academy Award®-sweeping comedy about a hitch-hiking heiress and a journalist.

Bonnie & Clyde
Arthur Penn, USA, 1967
Warren Beatty and Faye Dunaway star as the eponymous 1930s robbers whose violent and passionate story established the pattern for subsequent lovers-on-the-run road movies including *Badlands* (1971) and *Natural Born Killers* (1994).

Easy Rider
Dennis Hopper, USA, 1969
The image of Harley-Davidson choppers on the open road should represent freedom, but what Dennis Hopper and Peter Fonda experience in this film is a growing sense of alienation compounded by bad acid trips and redneck hostility.

Thelma & Louise
Ridley Scott, USA, 1991
Callie Khouri's Oscar®-winning screenplay challenged the road movie's traditional gender stereotypes and rejected its conventions, with a story of two women fleeing together from a dead-end marriage and the consequences of shooting a rapist.

The Straight Story
David Lynch, USA, 1999
Based on a true story, this tale of a stubborn old man crossing the plains of the Midwest on a motorized lawnmower to visit his sick brother displays folksy humour and warmth; a sharp contrast to Lynch's violent, surreal take on the road movie, *Wild at Heart* (1990).

The Motorcyle Diaries (Diarios de motocicleta)
Walter Salles, Argentina/Chile/Peru/US/UK/Germany/France, 2004
The traditional boundaries of the road movie melt away as the young Che Guevara travels with a friend across the borders of South America on a journey of personal and political discovery.

> ### A Love of the Road
> German director Wim Wenders, who has several road movies to his credit, sums up his affinity with the genre thus: 'I sometimes think that the emotion in my films comes only from the motion.' (Quoted in *Wim Wenders* by Jan Dawson, 1976)

Further viewing

The Grapes of Wrath (1940), *Vanishing Point* (1971), *Two-Lane Blacktop* (1971), *Convoy* (1978), *The Adventures of Priscilla, Queen of the Desert* (1994)

ROMANCE

History

As film stars are among the world's most beautiful people, it is surely appropriate that they should be shown to fall in love with one another for our viewing pleasure. This is the essential appeal of the big-screen romance, a genre in which emotional resonance is more of a priority than superficial action. The first film that could in any way be described as romantic was Thomas Edison's *The Kiss* (1896), a 20-second shot of two stage actors sharing a passionate embrace. During the more eroticized silent era, vampish Theda Bara and smouldering Rudolph Valentino set hearts aflutter. In the 1930s, humour became part of the genre, with screwball comedies throwing all manner of obstacles into the path of quick-witted lovers. Love itself became dangerous in the films noirs of the 1940s; later in the century, even after the advent of a more relaxed censorship system, it became clear that explicit sex and on-screen nudity would never take the place of true romance.

The genre today

In modern romance films, the emphasis has shifted from straight love stories and tear-jerkers to romantic comedies designed to appeal to the widest possible audience. Outside Europe, however, women's roles are still often weak and badly written.

Key figures

George Cukor (1899–1983)
Director with a talent for bringing out career-best performances from actresses and for ensuring that his heroines were at least the equals of the men they loved, carrying their romantic relationships to a satisfying conclusion.

John Gilbert (1899–1936)
A suave lover of the silent screen who became famous for a series of roles opposite Greta Garbo – including *Flesh and the Devil* (1927) – but whose high-pitched voice was said to be the cause of his quick decline in the sound era.

Douglas Sirk (1900–1987)
Director, born in Germany, who became master of the Hollywood melodrama in the 1950s, often depicting repressed female characters trapped by social convention in a loveless existence (*All That Heaven Allows*, 1955).

Key films

The Sheik
George Melford, USA, 1921
Legions of female fans swooned at the sight of Rudolph Valentino, wrapped in white robes against a desert backdrop, kidnapping an English aristocrat to be his bride.

Brief Encounter
David Lean, UK, 1945
British reserve and rigid social codes intensify the unconsummated passions of a middle-aged couple, in a film that forgoes surface glamour to concentrate instead on powerful emotion.

Breakfast at Tiffany's
Blake Edwards, USA, 1961
Audrey Hepburn is at her most delightful as Holly Golightly, projecting aloof sophistication while falling in love with a struggling writer (George Peppard).

Dr Zhivago
David Lean, USA/UK, 1965
Set against the backdrop of World War I and the Russian Revolution, Lean's adaptation of Boris Pasternak's novel presents the love between doctor-poet Yuri and the beautiful Lara as an inescapable, enduring force (thus excusing his adultery).

Love Story
Arthur Hiller, USA, 1970
A simple 'weepie' formula – boy meets girl, boy loses girl to terminal cancer – combined with a syrupy theme song and birthday-card sentiments ('Love means never having to say you're sorry') guaranteed tear-stained hankies and a box-office smash.

Amélie (Le fabuleux destin d'Amélie Poulain)
Jean-Pierre Jeunet, France, 2001
A touch of fantasy made cinematic magic of this comedy-romance about a sweet Parisian girl who sorts out other people's love lives while remaining single herself.

Festivals

International Love Film Festival
Held annually since 1985 in Mons, Belgium. Festival specializing in films with a romantic theme.
Website: www.festival-film-amour.be
Top prizes: Grand Prix and Coup de Coeur

Further viewing

City Lights (1931), *Gone with the Wind* (1939), *Casablanca* (1942), *Letter from an Unknown Woman* (1948), *Written on the Wind* (1956), *Cyrano De Bergerac* (1990), *Ghost* (1990), *The English Patient* (1996), *Romeo + Juliet* (1996), *Titanic* (1997), *In the Mood for Love* (2000), *My Big Fat Greek Wedding* (2002)

SCIENCE FICTION

History

Cinema was still in its infancy when, in French film pioneer George Méliès' *A Trip to the Moon* (1902), man stepped onto an alien landscape for the first time. Here was an early indication that science fiction might be the ideal genre to exploit the visual possibilities of cinema's escapist fantasies. The best science fiction, however, also has a philosophical quality, using futuristic scenarios to ask big questions about how we live today. Fear of technological progress and the unknown (in the shape of mad scientists, alien invaders and rogue computers) also plays a part.

Although space rockets and a countdown sequence had been seen as early as 1929 in Fritz Lang's *Woman in the Moon*, the first golden age of 'sci-fi' did not arrive until the 1950s. *Destination Moon* (1950) portrayed the space programme as a noble and patriotic endeavour, but as the decade progressed, apprehension of nuclear attacks and Communist infiltration inspired innumerable silly drive-in features filled with cheap monsters and flying saucers. In 1968, *2001: A Space Odyssey* bestowed some much-needed intellectual weight upon the genre, which then began to explore frontiers beyond humanity's solar system. The modern Hollywood blockbuster took flight with *Star Wars* (1977) as improved special effects raised the standard of big-screen spectacle. In the 1980s, science fiction crossed over with the action genre in films such as *The Terminator* (1984), *Aliens* (1986) and *Robocop* (1987). In the 1990s, the genre commandeered the disaster movie, raining meteor showers and alien death rays onto the cities of the world.

The genre today

Science fiction remains a summer blockbuster playground for film-makers with access to multimillion-dollar budgets. However, independent films such as *Cube* (1997), *Pi* (1998) and *Primer* (2004) prove that there is still a place for thoughtful genre pieces.

Key figures

Jack Arnold (1916–92)
Director who brought a simple, effective narrative tension and atmospheric use of landscape to 1950s B-movies including *It Came from Outer Space* (1953), *The Creature from the Black Lagoon* (1954) and *The Incredible Shrinking Man* (1957).

Michael Crichton (1942–   )
Writer and director (trained as a doctor at Harvard) whose books and films often feature science and technology run amok, such as the gunslinger robot in *Westworld* (1973) and the dinosaurs in *Jurassic Park* (1993).

George Lucas (1944–   )
Director and writer behind the Star Wars series, who visualized a cold, dehumanized, oppressive future in his feature debut, *THX 1138* (1971).

Steven Spielberg (1946–   )
Director and producer whose fascination with science fiction has manifested itself in the generally optimistic *Close Encounters of the Third Kind* (1977) and *E.T.* (1982) as well as the darker *Artificial Intelligence: AI* (2001), *Minority Report* (2002) and *War of the Worlds* (2005).

Key films

Metropolis
Fritz Lang, Germany, 1927
The futuristic cityscapes and robot design of this silent German masterpiece defined the look of the science fiction genre for decades.

Things to Come
William Cameron Menzies, UK, 1936
The first major British science fiction film placed H G Wells's prophetic original story inside Vincent Korda's huge, gleaming sets to debate big ideas about how science can save man from destruction.

The Day the Earth Stood Still
Robert Wise, USA, 1951
Good alien Klaatu (Michael Rennie) descends, god-like, from the stars, bringing with him his robot-weapon Gort as well as a dire warning for humankind to mend its warmongering ways.

2001: A Space Odyssey
Stanley Kubrick, UK/USA, 1968
Kubrick and co-writer Arthur C Clarke draw a direct line from prehistoric apes' discovery of tools to futuristic man's space exploration, presenting a cold, ambiguous but visually stunning portrait of hostile technology and alien intelligence.

The Planet of the Apes
Franklin J Schaffner, USA, 1969
Nuclear fears meet a civil-rights theme in this tale of an astronaut (Charlton Heston) trapped on a planet where the social roles of apes and humans have been reversed.

Silent Running
Douglas Trumbull, USA, 1972
Science fiction tackled environmental issues with this story of an interstellar greenhouse keeper (Bruce Dern) taking drastic action to save the last of Earth's plant life.

Solaris
Andrei Tarkovsky, Russia, 1972
In a big-screen echo of Cold War rivalry, the Soviet film industry responded to *2001: A Space Odyssey* (1968) with this cerebral, metaphysical story of an alien planet which turns the unconscious desires of a space-station crew into physical form.

Close Encounters of the Third Kind
Steven Spielberg, USA, 1977
Science fiction is at its most idealistic and hopeful here, as peaceful aliens communicate with Earth and make first contact in a memorable climactic sequence.

Alien
Ridley Scott, UK/USA, 1979
Sigourney Weaver's strong heroine and H R Giger's ferocious alien designs made this film much more than a gory 'haunted house' film transplanted into space; several sequels followed.

Star Trek: The Motion Picture
Robert Wise, USA, 1979
One of television's landmark science fiction series kicked off a long-running cinema franchise with its original cast intact, revelling in its bigger budget and lingering over tiny design details to please fans.

Blade Runner
Ridley Scott, USA, 1982
The future is presented here not as a gleaming utopia but as a dirty, rain-drenched, overinhabited city in which a detective (Harrison Ford) must track down renegade 'replicants' – androids whose near-perfect blend of man and machine touches elemental fears.

Jurassic Park
Steven Spielberg, USA, 1993
Computerized special effects entered a new era as live human actors appeared to walk with dinosaurs in a film that played on anxieties over cutting-edge science spinning out of control.

The Matrix
Andy and Larry Wachowski, USA, 1999
Science fiction shifted into cyberspace with this first of a three-film cycle, in which philosophical questions about free will, illusion and reality were combined with action-driven special effects.

Three New Titles

Hammer Studios' popular trilogy of science fiction films featuring the character of Professor Bernard Quatermass were all retitled for the US market. *The Quatermass Experiment* (1955) became *The Creeping Unknown*, *Quatermass II* (1957) became *Enemy from Space* and *Quatermass and the Pit* (1967) became *Five Million Years to Earth*.

Festivals

Festival International du Film Fantastique
Held annually since 1983 in Brussels, Belgium.
Website: www.bifff.org
Top prize: The Raven

Further viewing

The Thing from Another World (1951), *When Worlds Collide* (1951), *The War of the Worlds* (1953), *Them!* (1954), *This Island Earth* (1955), *Forbidden Planet* (1956), *Logan's Run* (1976), *Outland* (1981), *Tetsuo* (1988), *Total Recall* (1990), *12 Monkeys* (1995), *Gattaca* (1997), *Eternal Sunshine of the Spotless Mind* (2004)

The Star Wars franchise

Not all stories begin at the beginning. In 1977, space adventure *Star Wars* launched into 'Episode IV' of what writer-director George Lucas claimed would be a nine-part series. In some ways, there was nothing particularly original about his epic tale of good versus evil; Lucas openly borrowed from early Flash Gordon science fiction serials, swashbucklers, westerns, comic books and even Akira Kurosawa's *The Hidden Fortress* (1958). The result was a sweeping story about young Luke Skywalker's transformation into a Jedi Knight, fighting against the oppressive Empire and black-masked villain Darth Vader. *Star Wars* struck a chord with a generation of young filmgoers who lapped up its myths and thrilling fight scenes, transforming it into an immensely profitable franchise and merchandising phenomenon for 20th Century Fox.

Lucas's special-effects company, Industrial Light and Magic, continued to develop groundbreaking visual effects and sound design in the film's sequels. The director also tinkered with upgraded effects sequences in 'special editions' of the films for later rereleases. After a gap of 16 years, Lucas returned to the director's chair for a second Star Wars trilogy (set earlier than the events of the first films), which divided opinion amongst fans as well as critics; however, with its completion in 2005, the entire six-part series took on a new narrative dimension. Viewed as a whole, the series was no longer simply the story of Luke, but a chronicle of the growth, corruption and eventual redemption of his father, Anakin Skywalker. Lucas has also fleshed out the Star Wars universe with related stories in comic-book and video-game formats, but has stated that he has no intention to direct a third group of films.

Star Wars films

Star Wars: Episode IV – A New Hope (George Lucas, 1977), *Star Wars: Episode V – The Empire Strikes Back* (Irvin Kershner, 1980), *Star Wars: Episode VI – Return of the Jedi* (Richard Marquand, 1983), *Star Wars: Episode I – The Phantom Menace* (George Lucas, 1999), *Star Wars: Episode II – Attack of the Clones* (George Lucas, 2002), *Star Wars: Episode III – Revenge of the Sith* (George Lucas, 2005)

Key characters

Luke Skywalker (Mark Hamill), Princess Leia (Carrie Fisher), Han Solo (Harrison Ford), C-3PO (Anthony Daniels), R2-D2 (Kenny Baker), Chewbacca (Peter Mayhew), Darth Vader (James Earl Jones, voice; David Prowse, body), Obi-Wan Kenobi (Alec Guinness, *Episodes IV–VI*; Ewan McGregor, *Episodes I–III*), Yoda (Frank Oz), Anakin Skywalker (Sebastian Shaw, *Episode VI*; Jake Lloyd, *Episode I*; Hayden Christensen, *Episodes II–III*), Senator Palpatine/The Emperor/Darth Sidious (Ian McDiarmid), Qui-Gon Jinn (Liam Neeson), Padmé Amidala (Natalie Portman), Jar Jar Binks (Ahmed Best), Count Dooku (Christopher Lee)

SILENT FILM

History

After the novelty factor of the Lumière brothers' single-shot 'moving pictures' began to wear thin, cinema quickly developed a sophisticated language of its own as film-makers experimented with camera tricks, editing theories and narrative methods. Screenings during the silent era were almost never truly silent: films were often accompanied by live music on piano, organ or even an entire orchestra, while in Japan *benshi* narrators narrated the story from a position beside the screen. Wartime bombings and lack of archive preservation have meant that the majority of Japan's silent cinema, as in China and India, is lost to history.

Before World War I, it was Europe that dominated the world market, offering French comedies, spicy Danish melodramas and Italian costume epics. After the war, other countries began to make significant contributions: German Expressionism's twisted visual style brought psychological depth to silent cinema, while the 'montage' techniques beloved of Russian directors bestowed additional power and meaning on sequences of images. However, as Hollywood's studio system steadily expanded, US product began to flood the market. These were the glory days of comedians, matinée idols and adventurers. The silents reached such a peak of visual sophistication that, when Al Jolson started singing 'Mammy' in *The Jazz Singer* (1927), many saw it as a sign that cinema's greatest era had come to an end.

The genre today

Now that the artistic and historical importance of silent cinema is more widely understood, studio and government-funded archives are doing more to preserve original negatives (made on highly flammable nitrate). The DVD market, which demands superior sound and picture quality, has provided a major financial incentive to restorers.

Key figures

Lon Chaney (1883–1930)
Actor, immortalized as 'The Man of a Thousand Faces', who devised his own make-up to create a gallery of sympathetic misfits in such silent classics as *The Hunchback of Notre Dame* (1923) and *The Phantom of the Opera* (1925).

Charlie Chaplin (1889–1977)
Actor and director whose 'Little Tramp' persona became the most recognized cinema character in the world, and whose talent behind the camera matured from devising slapstick gags for Mack Sennett's Keystone shorts to creating a bold mix of sentimentality and humour in his feature-length films.

Greta Garbo (1905–90)
Swedish actress who became silent Hollywood's most enigmatic and radiant star, particularly when cast in romantic dramas opposite John Gilbert.

Lillian Gish (1893–1993)
Actress, best known for her work with D W Griffith (including *Broken Blossoms*, 1919), whose screen characters were typically pure of spirit, defiant and inwardly strong – virtues that helped them overcome much suffering and oppression.

D W Griffith (1875–1948)
Director whose innovative use of close-ups, intertitles, flashbacks and parallel editing was strikingly effective, and helped to develop cinema as a medium for storytelling.

Buster Keaton (1895–1966)
Actor whose signature role was an underdog caught up in a world determined to crush his body and spirit, and whose distinctively emotionless expression was at odds with the physical energy he brought to dangerous stunt work.

Mary Pickford (1893–1979)
The silent era's most popular actress (nicknamed 'America's Sweetheart' despite being born in Canada), who played spirited women and adolescent girls while proving to be a shrewd businesswoman off-screen as a quarter-partner of United Artists.

Rudolph Valentino (1895–1926)
Actor whose physical grace, handsome looks and burning 'animal magnetism' made him the greatest lover of the silent screen era, and whose funeral was attended by thousands of female fans.

Arab Death?

The term 'vamp', meaning a sultry temptress, was coined when silent star Theda Bara played a character called The Vampire in *A Fool There Was* (1915). Her phoney biography stated that her name was an anagram of 'Arab Death' and that she was the daughter of a French artist and an Egyptian princess, born in the Sahara desert. The far more prosaic truth is that she was born Theodosia Burr Goodman, daughter of a tailor, in Cincinnati, Ohio.

Key films

Cabiria
Giovanni Pastrone, Italy, 1914
Packing a volcano, pirates, slavery, human sacrifice, Hannibal and the Romans into its original four-hour running time, this is the Italian costume epic at its height.

Intolerance
D W Griffith, USA, 1916
The art of visual storytelling was taken to a new level by Griffith's innovative use of close-ups and intercutting in four stories linked by themes of intolerance and persecution.

The Cabinet of Dr Caligari (Das Kabinett des Doktor Caligari)
Robert Wiene, Germany, 1919
This masterpiece of German Expressionism uses dramatically twisted two-dimensional sets which lend it a disturbing, dream-like quality.

The Kid
Charlie Chaplin, USA, 1921
Chaplin's first feature was inspired by his own impoverished childhood; the long

format allowed him to develop rounded characters rather than resort to quickfire gags, marking his rise from popular comedian to the era's foremost actor-director.

Greed
Erich von Stroheim, USA, 1924
Von Stroheim sought to capture the naturalism of his source material, Frank Norris's 1899 novel *McTeague: A Story of San Francisco*, by shooting on location, bringing an authentic tone to this harsh morality tale.

Battleship Potemkin (Bronenosets Potyomkin)
Sergei Eisenstein, USSR, 1925
This stirring story of mutiny and massacre is notable for its skilful use of montage to create meaning; its influence is still felt in cinema today.

Napoléon
Abel Gance, France, 1927
Screenings of a restored print of *Napoléon* in 1980 proved that the power of the great silent masterpieces was undiminished – Gance's dynamic camera movements and rapid editing techniques celebrate cinema as pure spectacle.

Sunrise: A Song of Two Humans
F W Murnau, USA, 1927
It took a group of European film-makers working on a Hollywood budget to create what is arguably the greatest ever Expressionist film, combining vivid symbolic imagery with a melodramatic plot about marriage, murder and redemption.

The Passion of Joan of Arc (La Passion de Jeanne d'Arc)
Carl Theodor Dreyer, France, 1928
Dreyer's compressed version of the trial and execution of the French saint is silent cinema at its most pared down and spiritually intense, with the Danish director using detailed close-ups of facial expressions to stunning effect.

The Wind
Victor Sjöström, USA, 1928
The great Swedish director's best Hollywood work continues his study of humanity beset by the elements and environment, as ranchers including Lillian Gish battle for their livelihoods against the storms and sands of Texas.

Festivals

Pordenone Silent Film Festival (Le Giornate del Cinema Muto)
Held annually since 1982 in Sacile and Pordenone, Italy.
Website: www.cinetecadelfriuli.org
Top prize: Jean Mitry Award (for services to restoration of film)

Further viewing

A Trip to the Moon (1902), *The Birth of a Nation* (1915), *Foolish Wives* (1922), *Nosferatu* (1922), *The Thief of Bagdad* (1924), *Ben-Hur* (1925), *The Freshman* (1925), *The Gold Rush* (1925), *Strike* (1925), *Flesh and the Devil* (1926), *The Lodger* (1926), *Mother* (1926), *An Italian Straw Hat* (1927), *Metropolis* (1927), *The Crowd* (1928), *Pandora's Box* (1929)

SPORTS FILMS

History

Sports films are a relatively recent cinema phenomenon, although immediately after World War II a handful of 'sports noir' boxing films – including *Body and Soul* (1947), *Champion* (1949) and *The Harder They Fall* (1956) – presented the ring as a magnet for greed and corruption. In the 1970s Hollywood began to use sport as a backdrop for formulaic fairytale films in which every underdog had its day: athletic losers were typically shown pulling themselves together to score a crucial last-minute goal, home run, basket, point or punch. The resulting body of films was one of cinema's most clichéd genres, but proved irresistibly crowd-pleasing nonetheless. American football, soccer and baseball form the core of the sports film catalogue, but a veritable Olympic Games of disciplines have been represented: from cricket (*Lagaan*, 2001) to weightlifting (*Pumping Iron*, 1977), tennis (*Wimbledon*, 2004), cycling (*Breaking Away*, 1979), bobsleighing (*Cool Runnings*, 1993) and indoor bowls (*Blackball*, 2003), no sport is sacred.

The genre today

The sports film is still a contender. Prestige dramas such as *Seabiscuit* (2003) and *Cinderella Man* (2005) compete for Academy Awards®, while the fairytale formula has now become fodder for multiplex remakes such as *The Bad News Bears* (2005) and *The Longest Yard* (2005).

Key figures

Ron Shelton (1945–)
Director, screenwriter and former minor-league baseball player who has used sports subjects including golf (*Tin Cup*, 1996), boxing (*Play It to the Bone*, 1999) and basketball (*White Men Can't Jump*, 1992) to examine masculine bonding and mid-life crises.

Key films

Olympiad
Leni Riefenstahl, Germany, 1936
This official documentary of the 1936 Berlin Olympics brilliantly captures the grace and strength of the athletes' bodies while also featuring shots of Hitler, and has been condemned as Nazi propaganda.

The Longest Yard
Robert Aldrich, USA, 1974
A grudge American football match between prison inmates and sadistic guards becomes the means by which a disgraced quarterback (Burt Reynolds) begins to regain his dignity and self-respect.

Raging Bull
Martin Scorsese, USA, 1980
Domestic violence and sporting violence, beautifully edited in brutal black and white close-ups, alternate in this biopic of boxer Jake LaMotta, the role that won Robert De Niro a Best Actor Academy Award®.

Bull Durham
Ron Shelton, USA, 1988
The film that restarted the trend for Hollywood sports movies offers an insider's view of baseball, but won a wide audience by presenting its story of a veteran rookie and ageing groupie as a romantic comedy.

Further viewing

The Hustler (1961), *Big Wednesday* (1978), *Chariots of Fire* (1981), *Eight Men Out* (1988), *Field of Dreams* (1989), *Hoop Dreams* (1994), *When We Were Kings* (1996), *Friday Night Lights* (2004), *Million Dollar Baby* (2004)

The Rocky franchise

On 24 March 1975, little-known New Jersey boxer Chuck Wepner lost to Muhammad Ali in the 15th round of a world title bout. Struggling actor Sylvester Stallone, watching on television, was inspired to write a screenplay. The following year, *Rocky* won Academy Awards[®] for Best Picture and Best Director (John G Avildsen), and turned Stallone into an overnight star. The original story made a working-class hero of mumbling loan-shark heavy Rocky Balboa, plucked from obscurity to fight world champ Apollo Creed. Subsequent sequels, however, with MGM building a franchise and Stallone writing and directing, became ever more sentimental, as Rocky suffered personal tragedies by the dozen. *Rocky IV* (1985) featured a particularly embarrassing sequence in which Stallone – now also in the public conscience as gung-ho hero Rambo – delivered an excruciatingly patriotic speech on a Cold War theme. A sixth instalment entitled *Rocky Balboa*, with Stallone back as director, began shooting early in 2006.

Rocky films

Rocky (John G Avildsen, 1976), *Rocky II* (Sylvester Stallone, 1979), *Rocky III* (Sylvester Stallone, 1982), *Rocky IV* (Sylvester Stallone, 1985), *Rocky V* (John G Avildsen, 1990), *Rocky Balboa* (Sylvester Stallone, 2006)

Rocky's opponents

Apollo Creed (Carl Weathers in *Rocky* and *Rocky II*); Clubber Lang (Mr T in *Rocky III*); Ivan Drago (Dolph Lundgren in *Rocky IV*); Tommy Gunn (Tommy Morrison in *Rocky V*)

Other major characters

Rocky Balboa (Sylvester Stallone), Adrian (Talia Shire), Paulie (Burt Young), Mickey Goldmill (Burgess Meredith), Rocky Jr (Sage Stallone)

THRILLERS

History

Almost all films tell a story, but those known as thrillers are specifically designed to generate excitement and suspense, engaging audiences mentally rather than simply dazzling them with stunts and spectacle. Thrillers hold back information, delay the release of tension and pull viewers in to share the sense of threat felt by the hero. The roots of the modern thriller can be found in the cliffhanger climaxes of silent serials such as French director Louis Feuillade's *Fantômas* (1913–14) and *Judex* (1916–17) or the near-death escapes of US heroine Pearl White in *The Perils of Pauline* (1914). Different genres have been adapted to the thriller format in different eras – noir mysteries in the 1940s, spy dramas in the 1950s and political conspiracy films in the 1970s. From the 1980s onwards, the thriller has been a reliable way for Hollywood studios to attract multiplex audiences, although the misogynistic undertones of films such as *Fatal Attraction* (1987), *Single White Female* (1992) and *Basic Instinct* (1992) have attracted criticism.

The genre today

Keeping the audience on the edge of their seats remains the primary task for directors in many mainstream genres; however, the mainstream Hollywood thriller now seems to be judged as much on the cleverness of its twists as on its credibility.

Key figures

Claude Chabrol (1930–)
French director, screenwriter and former critic for *Cahiers du Cinéma* with over 50 films to his credit; his studies of bourgeois characters dealing with guilt, crime and punishment have seen him compared to Alfred Hitchcock.

Constantin Costa-Gavras (1933–)
Greek director whose films – including *Z* (1969), *State of Siege* (1973) and *Missing* (1982) – feature political themes that are at least as important as the thriller devices he uses to entertain the audience.

Joe Ezsterhas (1944–)
Screenwriter whose work – including *Jagged Edge* (1985) and *Basic Instinct* (1992) – defined the glossy Hollywood thriller of the late 20th century by prioritizing plot twists over character development.

Alfred Hitchcock (1899–1980)
Director celebrated for his uncanny ability to manipulate an audience's emotions in darkly humorous, brilliantly constructed, psychologically troubling tales of heroes – and, characteristically, icy blonde heroines – caught up in situations beyond their control.

M Night Shyamalan (1970–)
Director, producer, screenwriter and actor whose use of unforeseen plot twists in *The Sixth Sense* (1999) and *Unbreakable* (2000) have heavily influenced the modern thriller script.

Key films

The Spiral Staircase
Robert Siodmak, USA, 1945
With roots in both film noir and Gothic horror, this tale of a mute maid stalked by an insane killer uses mood rather than mystery to build a level of palpable tension.

The Wages of Fear (Le Salaire de peur)
Henri-Georges Clouzot, France, 1953
The first foreign-language film to be widely distributed in the UK and USA had audiences holding their breath in anticipation of the worst as a group of sweat-

drenched truckers transport a cargo of nitroglycerine along the bumpy roads of South America.

Les Diaboliques
Henri-Georges Clouzot, France, 1955
The plans of a sickly schoolteacher to murder her husband go awry when his corpse disappears, leading to a wonderful, much-imitated grand guignol climax.

Vertigo
Alfred Hitchcock, USA, 1958
Romantic obsession befuddles hero James Stewart as he attempts to make over a girl (Kim Novak) into the double of his dead lover.

North by Northwest
Alfred Hitchcock, USA, 1959
A classic case of mistaken identity sends an advertising man (Cary Grant) scurrying through a series of plot twists peppered with chase scenes and high-adrenaline set pieces, notably an attack by cropduster plane and a precarious climactic chase on Mount Rushmore.

The Manchurian Candidate
John Frankenheimer, USA, 1962
Post-McCarthy witch hunts and pre-Kennedy assassination, this political thriller about a Communist brainwashing plot to take over the White House is given an extra edge by its bold black humour and cynical take on heroism.

The Conversation
Francis Ford Coppola, USA, 1974
The US public's post-Watergate concerns about surveillance and invasion of privacy are reflected in this portrait of a bugging specialist who suffers a moral crisis when he pieces together a tape that reveals details of a planned murder.

Jagged Edge
Richard Marquand, USA, 1985
Courtroom drama meets glossy sex thriller in a film that playfully manipulates audiences' perception of a man accused of savagely murdering his wife.

Thirteen Days
Roger Donaldson, USA, 2000
Historical fact proves as nerve-wracking as any fictional thriller in this depiction of the US administration's attempts to defuse the apocalyptic tension caused by the Cuban Missile Crisis.

Festivals

Festival du Film Policier
Held annually since 1982 in Cognac, France. International festival specializing in thrillers, whodunnits, cop movies, courtroom dramas and films noirs.
Website: www.festival.cognac.fr
Top prize: Grand Prix

Further viewing

Notorious (1946), *Rear Window* (1954), *The Night of the Hunter* (1955), *Cape Fear* (1962), *Fail-Safe* (1964), *Duel* (1971), *The Day of the Jackal* (1973), *The Parallax View* (1974), *Illustrious Corpses* (1976), *The Vanishing* (1988), *Memento* (2000), *Caché* (2005)

WAR FILMS

History

History is frequently discussed in terms of defeats and victories on the battlefield, and it is little wonder that the drama and spectacle of war have proved a popular subject for film-makers. Understandably, the global conflicts of World Wars I and II have dominated the genre, although less well-known episodes from history, such as medieval clan disputes in Japan and 19th-century Imperial adventures in the UK, have also been dramatized.

A flurry of jingoistic movies appeared in Hollywood during the early days of World War I, but it was not until the mid-1920s that film-makers began to reflect on the human cost of the conflict. A similar cycle was apparent during and after World War II. At first, patriotic dramas and documentaries demonized the enemy, saluted the courage of the fighting men and praised the spirit of the home front. By the mid-1950s, however, a sour, sceptical vision, recognizing the futility of war, was apparent in films such as *The Bridge on the River Kwai* (1957). As the 1960s wore on, war films became merely an excuse for exciting, all-star adventures that kept well clear of politics; however, the Vietnam experience – reflected in films of the late 1970s and the mid-1980s – introduced a major change of tone, as nightly news coverage had made western viewers unsure of the morality of the conflict carried out in their names. In the 1990s, however, the focus shifted back to World War II with the poetic realism of *The Thin Red Line* (1998) and the graphic but sentimental *Saving Private Ryan* (1998).

The genre today

Saturation coverage of the conflict in Iraq – and shifting public opinion about its legality – have temporarily pushed war films off the production agenda while film-makers assess the market appeal of a subject matter that dominates real life.

Key figures

Sam Fuller (1911–97)
Director, writer and producer who drew on his first-hand experience of army service in tough, unsentimental B-movies about World War II and Korea, including *Fixed Bayonets* (1951) and *The Big Red One* (1980).

Jack Hawkins (1910–73)
British actor with a rugged appeal and hardy screen presence, whose portrayals of stiff-upper-lipped officers contained a more ruthless streak than previous incarnations.

Lewis Milestone (1895–1980)
Director who served with the US Army during World War I and whose war movies – including *A Walk in the Sun* (1945) and *Pork Chop Hill* (1959) – show the effects of the brutality of war on the ordinary soldier.

Oliver Stone (1946–)
Director, writer and producer whose tour of duty in the Vietnam War brought unprecedented authenticity to a trilogy of films examining aspects of the conflict – *Platoon* (1986), *Born on the Fourth of July* (1989) and *Heaven & Earth* (1993).

John Wayne (1907–79)
Actor who presented a strong, masculine and very patriotic brand of heroism whether wearing army fatigues or cowboy chaps, and whose second film as director, *The Green Berets* (1968), was a pro-war rallying call for the Vietnam era.

Twelve Angry Men?

The military prisoners who made up *The Dirty Dozen* (1967), led by Lee Marvin, were played by Charles Bronson, Jim Brown, Ben Carruthers, John Cassavetes, Stuart Cooper, Trini López, Colin Maitland, Al Mancini, Telly Savalas, Donald Sutherland, Tom Busby and Clint Walker.

Key films

All Quiet on the Western Front
Lewis Milestone, USA, 1930
Based on Erich Maria Remarque's novel, the first major war film of the sound era follows a group of German boys who become disillusioned with the patriotic cause and dislocated from home life when they witness death and terror in the trenches.

Hell's Angels
Howard Hughes, USA, 1930
Utilizing the resources of his private air fleet, Hughes's cinematic folly – three years in the making – contains some of the most thrilling air battles ever committed to celluloid.

La Grande Illusion
Jean Renoir, France, 1937
One of the greatest pacifist films ever made – the prototype for subsequent prisoner-of-war movies – celebrates the common bond between men of different classes and races, blaming war, rather than individual soldiers, for blood spilled in the name of nationalism.

The Dam Busters
Michael Anderson, UK, 1954
British cinema celebrates the success of a key campaign in World War II, praising not only the heroism of the pilots who flew the mission to destroy German dams, but also the ingenuity of the scientist who devised the bouncing bomb.

The Longest Day
Ken Annakin, Andrew Marton and Bernhard Wicki, USA, 1962
The D-day landings are depicted with the most impressive spectacle that the 1960s

war film could muster – a three-hour running time, black and white photography and an all-star cast including John Wayne, Henry Fonda, Robert Mitchum and Richard Burton.

The Great Escape
John Sturges, USA, 1963
Using a prisoner-of-war camp as a colourful setting for an adventure plot, this perennial television favourite contrasts British soldiers' collective efforts to escape with the insouciant individualism of their fellow prisoner, US officer Steve McQueen.

The Deer Hunter
Michael Cimino, USA, 1978
The devastating effects of the Vietnam War on blue-collar America are illustrated by the before-during-after structure of this controversial Academy Award®-winner, in which three army veterans are tormented by the after-effects of psychological torture.

Apocalypse Now
Francis Ford Coppola, USA, 1979
Coppola takes a metaphorical approach to the Vietnam experience in particular and the insanity of war in general, adapting Joseph Conrad's 1899 novella *Heart of Darkness* into the tale of a US soldier's mission to locate and kill a renegade officer.

Das Boot
Wolfgang Petersen, Germany, 1981
International audiences responded well to this sympathetic take on the dangerous, claustrophobic missions carried out by Germany's U-boat crews, showing that all men are terrified victims in wartime.

Come and See (Idi i smotri)
Elem Klimov, Russia, 1985
A nightmarishly poetic usage of harrowing images of German atrocities committed in Belarus in 1943, witnessed by a young survivor who becomes a resistance fighter after seeing his neighbours being burned alive by an SS division.

Platoon
Oliver Stone, USA, 1986
Lauded by veterans for the authentic feel it brought to scenes of firefights and jungle locations, Stone's searing portrait of the Vietnam War centres on rival US officers' battle for the soul of a rookie soldier.

Schindler's List
Steven Spielberg, USA, 1993
Spielberg's Holocaust drama is based on the true story of a German industrialist who saved his Jewish workers from the concentration camps, and won acclaim for its depiction of genocide and the moral void within Nazi officer Amon Goeth (Ralph Fiennes).

Land and Freedom
Ken Loach, UK/Spain/Germany/Italy, 1995
Loach presents the Spanish Civil War as a tragedy of political in-fighting and

betrayal, alternating gun battles with informed debate and presenting an entirely unsentimental portrait of international brotherhood.

Further viewing

The Big Parade (1925), *Wings* (1927), *In Which We Serve* (1942), *The Life And Death of Colonel Blimp* (1943), *Guadalcanal Diary* (1944), *Story Of G.I. Joe* (1945), *A Generation* (1955), *Paths of Glory* (1957), *Battle of Algiers* (1966), *The Dirty Dozen* (1967), *M*A*S*H* (1970), *Patton* (1970), *Kagemusha* (1980), *Full Metal Jacket* (1987), *Three Kings* (1999), *Black Hawk Down* (2001), *Pearl Harbor* (2001)

WESTERNS

History

Many other film genres belong to the whole of world cinema, but the western belongs to America. It was on the big screen that the USA rewrote its history of frontier pioneers, wagon trains, savage 'redskins', gunslingers, ranchers and cattlemen. Western themes appeared in moving picture shows as early as 1898, when the real cowboy era was still a living memory. By 1908, cinema had its first western hero in Bronco Billy, played by G M Anderson, and its first notable director in Thomas H Ince, on whose film *Custer's Last Raid* (1912) a number of Sioux were employed as extras. The first silent western features were hymns to the pioneer spirit, but soon it was the promise of white-hatted US heroes shooting from the hip on horseback that gripped audiences in exciting matinée serials and B-movies.

Although *Cimarron* (1931) won a Best Picture Academy Award®, it wasn't until 1939 that the major Hollywood studios properly entered the fray. For the next two decades, the western was the leading Hollywood genre. After World War II, the psychological and social dimensions of the western expanded, with film-makers using colour and stretching the size of the screen. Native Americans began to receive more respectful treatment in the likes of *Broken Arrow* (1950), but by the 1960s, young audiences were rejecting this most traditional of genres. Italy's more cynical, stylized 'spaghetti westerns' better suited new tastes, and Hollywood westerns had to become more graphically violent and critical of US history in order to capture the modern mood. By the end of the 1970s, however, the great names in the genre – John Ford, John Wayne, Howard Hawks – were gone, and the western struggled to find its footing in the era of the blockbuster.

The genre today

Despite the efforts of Clint Eastwood and Kevin Costner, and attempts to revive the western as a teen movie (*Young Guns*, 1988), romantic adventure (*The Last of the Mohicans*, 1992) or existentialist independent (*Dead Man*, 1995), this old-fashioned genre is more out of favour with the paying public than ever.

Key figures

Kevin Costner (1955–)
Actor and director who keeps flying the flag for westerns in modern Hollywood, playing the title role in *Wyatt Earp* (1994) and making his Academy Award®-winning directorial debut with *Dances with Wolves* (1990).

Clint Eastwood (1930–   )
Actor and director who left 1960s television show *Rawhide* to star in a trio of spaghetti westerns as a cheroot-chewing, nameless bounty hunter; on returning to Hollywood, he adapted the Italian formula for *High Plains Drifter* (1973), the first of many westerns – including Academy Award®-winner *Unforgiven* (1992) – that he has also directed.

Henry Fonda (1905–82)
Actor most often cast as a tough but honest symbol of integrity, but who played some darker, more complex characters in westerns such as *Fort Apache* (1948).

John Ford (1894–1973)
The greatest western director of all time typically used the genre to celebrate the community spirit of pioneers, settlers and cavalry soldiers, and turned the wind-sculpted rocks of Monument Valley into the genre's definitive backdrop.

Sergio Leone (1921–89)
Italian writer-director who transported the lone cowboy into a grotesque black-comedy world in a series of spaghetti westerns which brilliantly used widescreen frames and depth of focus to create dramatic compositions.

Anthony Mann (1906–67)
Director whose film noir background informed his series of westerns in the 1950s – including several starring James Stewart – which featured darker psychological themes, violent action and tragic, conflicted heroes.

Tom Mix (1880–1940)
Actor and former rodeo rider who was the first cowboy star to treat the genre as stunt-driven, fantasy entertainment, more worthy of a Wild West Show than a history book.

Sam Peckinpah (1925–84)
Director whose hard-living lifestyle caused inevitable clashes with the studios, but whose westerns – including *Ride the High Country* (1962) and *The Ballad of Cable Hogue* (1970) – often feature ageing heroes and an elegiac mood.

Roy Rogers (1911–98)
Actor who, along with Gene Autry, put the singing cowboy on the western map in a string of B-movies and television programmes that co-starred his horse, Trigger.

John Wayne (1907–79)
Actor who became the western's most enduring symbol of manly bravery and traditional US values through an on- and off-screen persona combining rock-like confidence, grouchiness and old-fashioned chivalry.

Quick on the Draw

Glenn Ford, star of *The Fastest Gun Alive* (1956), was indeed credited in real life with a remarkable gun-from-holster speed of 0.4 seconds – reckoned to be the fastest of all Hollywood western stars in the 1950s.

Key films

The Iron Horse
John Ford, USA, 1924
The first clues that Ford would become the genre's major director can be found in this early tribute to the pioneer spirit.

Stagecoach
John Ford, USA, 1939
The confined space of a stagecoach shared by passengers from different social backgrounds contrasts with the iconic landscapes of Monument Valley and the drama of an Apache attack, in the film that made John Wayne a star.

My Darling Clementine
John Ford, USA, 1946
Ford downplays western myths and heroics by casting Henry Fonda as a peace-loving Wyatt Earp in the best cinematic depiction of the gunfight at the OK Corral.

Red River
Howard Hawks, USA, 1948
Hawks transfers his trademark studies of male camaraderie to a cattle drive, tapping into a darker side of John Wayne's persona as mutinous rumblings drive a wedge between his character and his adopted son (Montgomery Clift).

High Noon
Fred Zinnemann, USA, 1952
The western becomes an allegory for contemporary Communist witch hunts, as the typically taciturn Gary Cooper plays a marshal abandoned by the townsfolk and his new Quaker wife when he asks for backup in an against-the-clock showdown.

Shane
George Stevens, USA, 1953
The biggest western hit of the decade stars Alan Ladd as a gunman-drifter – the US equivalent of a knight on horseback – forced to revisit his violent past in order to protect the frontier family he has befriended.

Johnny Guitar
Nicholas Ray, USA, 1954
This bizarre, Freudian-themed western matches the intensity of its acting with the vibrancy of its colour schemes, as traditional gender roles are reversed in a showdown between casino boss Joan Crawford and lynch-mob leader Mercedes McCambridge.

The Searchers
John Ford, USA, 1956
Ford puts forward a less forgiving view of the West than ever before in the story of Ethan Edwards (John Wayne), who can find no peace in civilized society after his niece is kidnapped – and, he believes, tainted – by Native Americans.

The Magnificent Seven
John Sturges, USA, 1960
This popular western remake of Akira Kurosawa's *Seven Samurai* (1954) established a pattern for star-studded all-male ensemble films in the 1960s.

The Good, the Bad and the Ugly (Il Buono, il brutto, il cattivo)
Sergio Leone, Italy/Spain/Germany, 1966
The final part of Leone's 'Dollars' trilogy sets the scramble for a cache of gold against an epic Civil War backdrop, building to the most operatic and extended stand-off – complete with swirling cameras and Ennio Morricone score – in the genre's history.

Once Upon a Time in the West (C'era una volta il West)
Sergio Leone, Italy/USA, 1968
As harmonica-playing Charles Bronson stalks black-clad Henry Fonda like a ghostly avenger from the past, Leone paints a wider picture of the end of the Old West and the coming of a new age in the shape of the railroad and modern 'progress'.

The Wild Bunch
Sam Peckinpah, USA, 1969
The slow-motion violence of Peckinpah's bloody, destructive elegy to the passing of the Old West had a profound effect on not only the western, but all action genres.

Heaven's Gate
Michael Cimino, USA, 1980
The box-office failure of this epic tale of immigrants and powerful cattle barons ruined United Artists, and effectively killed off the Hollywood Western.

Unforgiven
Clint Eastwood, USA, 1992
Eastwood's Academy Award®-winning study of the nature of violence returned to traditional western themes, telling the story of a retired killer who picks up his gun again to avenge an abused prostitute and restore order to chaos.

Festivals

Tombstone Western Film Festival and Symposium
Held annually since 2001 in the historic mining town of Tombstone, Arizona, site of the gunfight at the OK Corral.
Website: www.tombstonewesternfilm.com

Further viewing

The Covered Wagon (1923), *The Big Trail* (1930), *Jesse James* (1939), *The Ox-Bow Incident* (1943), *She Wore a Yellow Ribbon* (1949), *Bend of the River* (1952), *Rio Bravo* (1959), *How the West Was Won* (1962), *The Man Who Shot Liberty Valance* (1962), *A Fistful of Dollars* (1964), *Django* (1966), *True Grit* (1969), *Soldier Blue* (1970), *The Shootist* (1976), *The Long Riders* (1980), *Tombstone* (1993), *Brokeback Mountain* (2005)

FILM-PRODUCING COUNTRIES

AFRICA
See also **North Africa**

History

It was not until African countries freed themselves from the shackles of colonialism in the 1960s that film-makers had a chance to counter the negative depiction of Africans as savages and slaves in European and Hollywood films. African cinema tends to deal with the simple realities of daily life, where age-old traditions rub up against modern Western influences and rural villages contrast sharply with modern cities. From the early 1960s onwards, financial support from France allowed the former French colonies (such as Senegal, Burkina Faso and Cameroon) to lead the way in feature production. By the 1980s, a second generation of film-makers was looking further back to precolonial times in order to retell African history from their own perspective and gain a deeper sense of common African heritage. In South Africa, black film-makers, denied access to the industry until the collapse of apartheid in 1990, then began to produce a handful of films with an authentic sense of street life.

The industry today

A lack of funding in some of the world's poorest countries means that African films are still more likely to be seen at festivals abroad than on home screens. On a more positive note, there are now more women entering the industry, and video technology has brought about a minor boom in low-budget 'quickies' produced for the home market in Nigeria.

Key figures

Souleymane Cissé (1940–)
Director, born in Mali, who pares down his imagery to create a beautiful, spiritual, distinctively African film-making style with the likes of *Finyé* (1982).

Med Hondo (1936–)
Director, born in Mauritania, whose politically motivated work is dedicated to breaking the 'cultural colonialism' of the white-owned cinema exhibition monopoly.

Idrissa Ouedraogo (1954–)
Director, born in Upper Volta (now Burkina Faso), who uses long shots and spare editing to convey the rhythm of village life in *Yaaba* (1989) and *Tilaï* (1990).

Darrell James Roodt (1962–)
South Africa's leading director, whose versatile career has taken in anti-apartheid themes (*A Place of Weeping*, 1986), musicals (*Sarafina!*, 1982), action thrillers (*Dangerous Ground*, 1997) and HIV drama (the Academy Award®-nominated *Yesterday*, 2004).

Ousmane Sembène (1923–)
Pioneering Senegalese director (maker of the first black African feature, 1966's *La Noire de...*) whose work challenges the legacy of colonialism and accepted notions of Africa's history.

A Varied Career

Med Hondo, one of Africa's most politically conscious film-makers, has a sideline dubbing the likes of Danny Glover and Eddie Murphy in French movies, and has also provided the voices for Rafiki in *The Lion King* (1994) and Donkey in *Shrek* (2001).

Key films

Borom Sarret
Ousmane Sembène, Senegal, 1963
Africa's first indigenous short film uses the story of a cart driver whose vehicle is seized to illustrate the difficulties that face the ordinary man when dealing with contemporary authorities.

Touki Bouki
Djibril Diop Mambety, Senegal, 1973
The social realism of the 1960s makes way for a more modern, poetic style as two lovers dream of living in Paris, but are unable to shake off the grip of Africa.

Xala
Ousmane Sembène, Senegal, 1974
A polygamist is rendered impotent on the night of his third wedding in this satirical allegory of the new bourgeoisie's inability to govern the country properly.

Yeelen
Souleymane Cissé, Mali, 1987
A shaman's son heads out on a quest for ancient knowledge. Also known as *Brightness*, this is a prime example of African cinema at its most uniquely mythical.

Mapantsula
Oliver Schmitz, South Africa, 1988
White director Schmitz and black writer-star Thomas Mogotlane capture the atmosphere of Johannesburg's streets in this story of a hustler, banned in its home country.

Tilaï
Idrissa Ouedraogo, Burkina Faso, 1990
The universal mythic power of fate clashes with African tribal law when a man is sentenced to death for beginning an incestuous relationship with his former fiancée, now his father's wife.

Keita! The Voice of the Griot
Dani Kouyaté, Burkina Faso, 1994
The subjective difference between history as taught from a Western viewpoint in schools and as told in ancient folk tales comes to the fore when a pupil skips class to listen to the words of an elderly storyteller.

Festivals

FESPACO (Pan-African Film and Television Festival of Ouagadougou)
Held biennially since 1969 in Burkina Faso. Largest competitive festival in Africa for African film-makers.

Website: www.fespaco.bf
Top prize: Étalon d'Or de Yennenga (Golden Stallion)

Academy Awards®

Best Foreign Language Film wins: *Black and White in Colour* (Ivory Coast, 1976)
Best Foreign Language Film nominations: 1 (Ivory Coast), 1 (South Africa)
Other Academy Award® wins: Charlize Theron (South Africa), Best Actress
(*Monster*, 2003)

Further viewing

Ajani-Ogun (1976), *Finyé* (1982), *The Gods Must Be Crazy* (1984), *Sarraounia* (1986),
La Vie est belle (1986), *Yaaba* (1989), *Sarafina!* (1992), *Tumult* (1996)

AUSTRALIA

History

Australia's first feature film – probably the earliest in the world – was the Tait
brothers' 1906 production of *The Story of the Kelly Gang*, the first of many screen
portraits of outlaw hero Ned Kelly. For decades, British and American companies
had a stranglehold on Australian cinemas, and it wasn't until the formation of the
Film Development Council (subsequently renamed the Australian Film Commission)
in 1970 that the situation improved for local film-makers. In the early 1980s, a group
of directors dubbed the Australian New Wave came to the fore with a rash of literary
films set in the past, but before long several of these, including Peter Weir and
Gillian Armstrong, moved to Hollywood. The same happened after another burst
of creativity in the early 1990s produced *The Piano* (1993), *Muriel's Wedding* (1994)
and *The Adventures of Priscilla, Queen of the Desert* (1994). Such is Australian
cinema's dilemma: because it shares a common language with the UK and USA, its
greatest talents are routinely snapped up by bigger industries abroad.

The industry today

By the end of the 20th century, Australian films accounted for a mere three per
cent of the home box office. However, several Hollywood blockbusters (including
Scooby-Doo (2002) and *The Matrix* and *Star Wars* sequels) have been drawn to
Australian locations by tax incentives, keeping local technicians in work.

Key figures

Gillian Armstrong (1950–   )
Leading director in the Australian New Wave who has favoured book adaptations
– *Little Women* (1994), *Charlotte Gray* (2001) – since moving to Hollywood.

Cate Blanchett (1969–   )
Actress who honed her skills with Sydney Theatre Company before impressing the
film world with her performance in the title role of *Elizabeth* (1998).

Errol Flynn (1909–59)
Actor, born in Tasmania, who made his feature film debut as Fletcher Christian in the Australian production *In the Wake of the Bounty* (1933) before proceeding to Hollywood, where he became a star in swashbucklers.

Nicole Kidman (1967–   )
Actress, born in Hawaii with dual American–Australian nationality, who brings an icy detachment to her best dramatic roles.

Baz Luhrmann (1962–   )
Flamboyant director and producer whose 'Red Curtain Trilogy' – *Strictly Ballroom* (1992), *Romeo + Juliet* (1996) and *Moulin Rouge!* (2001) – reflects a range of cultural influences including MTV, Bollywood and grand opera.

Geoffrey Rush (1951–   )
Acclaimed stage actor who shot to film stardom with his Academy Award®-winning turn in *Shine* (1996), and who now mixes blockbusters (*Pirates of the Caribbean: The Curse of the Black Pearl*, 2003) with more dramatically prestigious projects (*Quills*, 2000).

Peter Weir (1944–   )
Director whose work in Australia and Hollywood often features isolated characters at odds with their surroundings, eg schoolgirls in the outback (*Picnic at Hanging Rock*, 1975) or a cop in an Amish community (*Witness*, 1985).

Miller and Miller

Australian cinema boasts not one but two George Millers, both born in 1945. One began his career as a doctor before achieving success in the film industry as the creator of the *Mad Max* and *Babe* series. The other directed *The Man from Snowy River* (1982) and *Les Patterson Saves the World* (1987).

Key films

Jedda
Charles Chauvel, 1955
Australia's first colour film was also one of the first to centre on Aboriginal characters, telling the story of a native girl brought up by a white family who falls in love with a tribesman.

Walkabout
Nicolas Roeg, 1971
After decades of non-activity, this atmospheric story of an Aboriginal boy who helps two English children abandoned in the outback opened the world's eyes to the potential of Australian cinema.

The Adventures of Barry McKenzie
Bruce Beresford, 1972
Writer Barry Humphries's rude, crude comedy creation (played by Barry Crocker) is Australian cinema's definitive modern-day loudmouth 'ocker' stereotype.

Picnic at Hanging Rock
Peter Weir, 1975
The threatening side of Australia's wide-open landscapes is illustrated when three turn-of-the-century schoolgirls and their teacher go missing on an outing.

The Chant of Jimmie Blacksmith
Fred Schepisi, 1978
Violent period drama whose depiction of a mixed-race man caught between his Aboriginal heritage and white society, and rejected by both, alienated audiences.

Mad Max
George Miller, 1979
American-born Mel Gibson became an international star after this futuristic action movie in which a good cop avenges the murder of his family by a gang.

My Brilliant Career
Gillian Armstrong, 1979
The story of a bush farmer's daughter who chooses a career as a novelist instead of marriage was important in redefining Australia's screen image of women.

Crocodile Dundee
Peter Faiman, 1986
Australia's biggest worldwide box-office hit spawned two sequels and made a star of Paul Hogan as the no-nonsense poacher bemused by life in New York City.

The Piano
Jane Campion, 1993
This 19th-century gothic romance became Australia's most fêted film of the 1990s (despite the New Zealand setting and director) when it won the Palme d'Or at Cannes as well as Academy Awards® for Holly Hunter and Anna Paquin.

Festivals

Sydney Film Festival
Held annually since 1954 in Sydney. Major festival showing new national and international cinema across all film formats.
Website: www.sydneyfilmfestival.org
Top prize: Dendy Awards (short films), Urban Cinefile (audience awards)

National awards

Australian Film Institute: AFI Awards

Academy Awards®

Best Picture wins: 0
Best Picture nominations: *The Piano* (1993), *Babe* (1995), *Shine* (1996), *Moulin Rouge!* (2001)
Other Academy Award® wins: Geoffrey Rush, Best Actor (*Shine*, 1996), Nicole Kidman, Best Actress (*The Hours*, 2002), Cate Blanchett, Best Supporting Actress (*The Aviator*, 2004)

Further viewing

The Overlanders (1946), *The Last Wave* (1977), *Gallipoli* (1981), *The Year My Voice Broke* (1987), *The Adventures of Priscilla, Queen of the Desert* (1994), *Muriel's Wedding* (1994), *Babe* (1995), *Shine* (1996), *Lantana* (2001)

BELGIUM

History

Film production in Belgium has struggled to secure a footing, as limited audience numbers are further split by a language divide into French and Flemish. In the decades leading up to the 1960s, documentaries – particularly by Henri Storck – provided the backbone of the local industry. In 1967, international festival wins ushered in a wave of film-makers whose off-kilter style owed something to the Belgian surrealist tradition of painter René Magritte. A second wave of film-makers in the mid-1970s, including Chantal Akerman, came from a more avant-garde background.

The industry today

For a country that only produces about a dozen films each year, Belgium continues to make a good showing among the prize-winners at foreign festivals – the Dardenne brothers scooped the prestigious Palme d'Or at Cannes in 1999 and 2005.

Key figures

Chantal Akerman (1950–)
Feminist director whose minimalist style experiments with traditional film forms while also asking questions about identity and sexuality.

Jean-Pierre Dardenne (1951–) and Luc Dardenne (1954–)
Director brothers who won the Palme d'Or at the Cannes Film Festival with both *Rosetta* (1999) and *L'Enfant* (2005), using a raw, naturalistic style in which a handheld camera invades the personal space of the main characters.

André Delvaux (1926–2002)
Director who brought a dream-like surrealism to such films as *The Man Who Had His Hair Cut Short* (1966), *Rendez-vous à Bray* (1971) and *The Abyss* (1988).

Jean-Claude Van Damme (1960–)
Martial arts champion turned actor, nicknamed 'the Muscles from Brussels', who became a star in Hollywood with action flicks *Double Impact* (1991) and *Timecop* (1994).

Key films

Jeanne Dielman, 23 Quai du Commerce, 1080 Bruxelles
Chantal Akerman, 1975
One of Akerman's most determined feminist statements and narrative experiments charts two days in the life of a widow who supports herself through prostitution, reflecting the character's routine through slow minimalist touches.

Toto the Hero (Toto le héros)
Jaco Van Dormael, 1991
Rare Belgian international hit about a man who has spent his life plotting revenge for his belief that he was swapped at birth with the boy next door.

Man Bites Dog (C'est arrivé près de chez vous)
Rémy Belvaux, André Bonzel and Benoît Poelvoorde, 1992
This controversially violent pseudo-documentary about a serial killer uses black humour to make the audience feel complicit with the on-screen action.

Rosetta
Jean-Pierre Dardenne and Luc Dardenne, 1999
Palme d'Or-winning study of a white-trash teenage girl trying to hold down any available job, distinguished by long, running takes on a hand-held camera.

Festivals

Flanders International Film Festival
Held annually since 1974 in Ghent. Originally established as an alternative to the commercial Brussels Film Festival, now focusing on films not in distribution and on the use of music in films.
Website: www.filmfestival.be
Top prize: World Soundtrack Award (film music)

Academy Awards®

Best Foreign Language Film wins: 0
Best Foreign Language Film nominations: 5

Further viewing

The Man Who Had His Hair Cut Short (1965), *Le Départ* (1967), *Malpertuis* (1971), *The Sexual Life of the Belgians 1950–1978* (1995), *The Son* (2002)

CANADA

History

Traffic has always been busy across the border between Canada and America, and one wonders how strong Canadian cinema might have been had Mary Pickford, Walter Huston, James Cameron, Norman Jewison, Mike Myers, Jim Carrey, Donald Sutherland and many others remained in their homeland. Instead, from the 1940s to the 1960s, the country led the field in animation and documentaries through the support of the National Film Board of Canada. It was not until the 1970s that Canada made any impact with feature films, particularly as French-language film-makers had created what was effectively a national cinema within a larger nation. On the other hand, despite world-class work from the likes of David Cronenberg, Atom Egoyan, Patricia Rozema and Guy Maddin, the country's English-language directors cannot be said to have fashioned a cinema that is distinctively Canadian.

The industry today

Film production remains high in Canada, but consists mostly of Hollywood studios shooting films (including *Chicago* (2002), *Catch Me If You Can* (2002) and *X-Men* (2000)) in Toronto and Montreal to take advantage of tax breaks.

Key figures

Denys Arcand (1941–   )
Writer-director whose films, including Academy Award®-winner *The Barbarian Invasions* (2003), are close examinations of French-Canadian society, with polished dialogue and strong ensemble performances.

Geneviève Bujold (1942–   )
Actress equally at home working in French or English, who received an Academy Award® nomination for *Anne of a Thousand Days* (1969).

David Cronenberg (1943–   )
Director whose early fascination for 'body horror' films – *Rabid* (1976), *The Brood* (1979) – has matured into a more intellectual blend of genre and arthouse cinema.

Atom Egoyan (1960–   )
Director from an Armenian family background, whose formally-constructed films – including *The Sweet Hereafter* (1997), for which he received an Academy Award® nomination – examine alienation and isolation while keeping characters' emotions in check.

Key films

The Apprenticeship of Duddy Kravitz
Ted Kotcheff, 1974
Canadian cinema burst onto the international scene when this comic coming-of-age tale won the Golden Bear at the Berlin Film Festival.

Porky's
Bob Clark, 1981
Hugely successful college sex comedy, set in Florida in the 1950s, copied the formula set by *National Lampoon's Animal House* (1978) without adding any Canadian touches.

The Decline of the American Empire (Le Déclin de l'empire américain)
Denys Arcand, 1986
Arcand satirizes middle-class hypocrisy with this depiction of the conversations of a group of male history lecturers and their wives – characters he revisited 17 years later in the Academy Award®-winning *The Barbarian Invasions* (2003).

Crash
David Cronenberg, 1996
Cronenberg courted international controversy with this cold take on J G Ballard's novel about a group of people who find sexual gratification in car accidents.

Atanarjuat: The Fast Runner
Zacharius Kunuk, 2000
The first film in the Inukitut language is a 2,000-year-old epic about jealousy, murder

and shamanism, shot using digital Betacam in the Canadian Arctic.

Festivals

Toronto International Film Festival
Held annually since 1976 in Toronto. One of the world's top five festivals, featuring premières of major American films.
Website: www.bell.ca/filmfest
Top prize: People's Choice Award

National awards

Academy of Canadian Cinema and Television: Genies

Academy Awards®

Best Foreign Language Film wins: *The Barbarian Invasions* (2003)
Best Foreign Language Film nominations: 3
Other Academy Award® wins: Mary Pickford, Best Actress (*Coquette*, 1929), Norma Shearer, Best Actress (*The Divorcee*, 1930), Marie Dressler, Best Actress (*Min and Bill*, 1930), Best Documentary (*Churchill's Island*, 1941), James Cameron, Best Director (*Titanic*, 1997)

Further viewing

Mon Oncle Antoine (1971), *Videodrome* (1982), *I've Heard the Mermaids Singing* (1987), *Jesus of Montreal* (1989), *Léolo* (1992), *Thirty-Two Short Films About Glenn Gould* (1993), *Exotica* (1994), *Kissed* (1996), *The Barbarian Invasions* (2003)

CHINA, HONG KONG AND TAIWAN

History

It comes as no surprise to learn that China began producing martial arts films as early as 1928. Shanghai was the main production centre, and socially-aware melodramas and silent versions of Peking Operas were audience favourites. This 'golden age' of Chinese cinema came to an abrupt end when Japan bombed the city in 1937; during World War II and the civil war that followed, many of Shanghai's key players fled to Hong Kong. After the Communist victory in 1949, film-making fell under government control as a means for educating the masses. A growing cinematic sophistication was quashed in 1966, when Chairman Mao's Cultural Revolution caused a four-year halt to production, sending many directors to prison, exile or hard labour in the countryside.

As film-making ceased in mainland China, another industry was finding its feet in the then British colony of Hong Kong. Here the emphasis was on commerce, not art, and studios churned out popular comedies, swordplay epics and martial arts films, leading to a flood of kung fu films when the West caught the bug in the early 1970s. Taiwan, whose cinema had been strictly censored by the anti-communist government of Chinese Nationalist Chiang Kai-Shek, also began to make cheap martial arts movies in the 1970s. The rise of directors Hou Hsiao-Hsien and Edward Yang in the 1980s gave Taiwan an arthouse credibility on the foreign circuit. Festival acclaim also greeted the visually stunning work of the so-called Fifth Generation film-makers in China, graduates of the reopened Beijing Film Academy. Hong Kong, however, continued to impress in the popular markets, concentrating on stunt-driven comedies and stylishly choreographed gangster films.

The industry today

Although several Hong Kong stars and directors have been drawn to Hollywood, the international success of Ang Lee's *Crouching Tiger, Hidden Dragon* (2000) has rekindled interest in lavish martial arts epics, with co-production budgets now coming from both East and West. Meanwhile, China has opened its cinemas to a greater influx of Hollywood product, although it enforced a blockbuster blackout during the summers of 2004 and 2005 in order to allow local films a better run at the box office.

Key figures

Jackie Chan (1954–   )
Actor, director and producer whose underdog persona and stunt-heavy acrobatic style – seen in Hong Kong martial arts comedies and Hollywood buddy movies – owes something to silent star Buster Keaton.

Chang Cheh (1923–2002)
Director who created the male-bonding mould for Hong Kong action cinema with his martial arts films in the 1960s and 1970s, primarily for Shaw Brothers Studios.

Chow Yun-Fat (1956–   )
Leading actor of the Hong Kong 'heroic bloodshed' crime genre who is equally adept at playing tough cops (*Hard Boiled*, 1992) and noble villains (*The Killer*, 1989).

Hou Hsiao-Hsien (1947–   )
Director whose static, observational camerawork merges the political with the personal and the past with the present, building a richly textured portrait of Taiwanese society.

King Hu (1931–97)
Actor-turned-director who brought increased status to the martial arts genre in the late 1960s by marrying a literary, philosophical approach with the Peking Opera fighting style.

Chen Kaige (1952–   )
The first of the so-called 'Fifth Generation' directors to release a film (*Yellow Earth*, 1984); his work is notable for its widescreen landscapes.

Ang Lee (1954–   )
Director who made a trio of Taiwanese dramas – *Pushing Hands* (1992), *The Wedding Banquet* (1993) and *Eat Drink Man Woman* (1994) – then worked in England and Hollywood before returning east for the highly influential martial arts epic *Crouching Tiger, Hidden Dragon* (2000).

Bruce Lee (1940–73)
Actor who became an international superstar and enduring icon of kung fu cinema because of his fast fighting style, typically accompanied by a distinctive high-pitched whine.

Gong Li (1966–)
Actress who won international acclaim playing repressed but passionate women in a series of films directed by her then off-screen partner Zhang Yimou, and who later made the transition to English-language films.

Run Run Shaw (1907–)
Producer and cinema owner who, along with his older brother Run Me, established what was then the world's largest private studio in Hong Kong in 1961, the birthplace of modern martial arts cinema; he was knighted in 1977.

Wong Kar-Wai (1958–)
Hong Kong-based director who shoots his films from unfinished scripts, using post-modern editing techniques and the vivid cinematography of regular collaborator Christopher Doyle to create existential meditations on the elusive nature of love.

John Woo (1946–)
Director credited with kick-starting Hong Kong's 'heroic bloodshed' gangster genre, greatly influencing Hollywood action cinema of the 1990s and beyond with his dynamically choreographed gunfights.

Michelle Yeoh (1962–)
Malaysian-born actress who studied dance in London before her graceful stunt work in Hong Kong films brought her to international attention in the James Bond film *Tomorrow Never Dies* (1997).

Zhang Yimou (1951–)
Leading member of the Fifth Generation movement, whose early experience as a cinematographer lent a dramatic visual beauty to such films as *Raise the Red Lantern* (1991), *Hero* (2002) and *House of Flying Daggers* (2004).

All Part of the Job

Jackie Chan's commitment to doing his own stunts has come at a cost. Amongst many other injuries, he has broken his nose three times (in 1980's *The Young Master*, 1983's *Project A* and 1997's *Nice Guy*), dislocated a cheekbone (in *Police Story* 3, 1992) and fractured his skull, causing a brain haemorrhage (in *Armour of God*, 1985).

Key films

The Goddess (Shen nu)
Wu Yong-Gang, China, 1934
The social conscience of Chinese cinema in the 1930s hits home as silent movie icon Ruan Lingyu plays a single mother who resorts to prostitution to provide for her son.

The Spring River Flows East (Yi jang chun shui xiang dong liu)
Cai Chusheng and Zheng Junli, China, 1947
Two of China's top pre-communist era directors collaborated on this two-part epic, which combines melodrama and social realism in a story set against the Japanese invasion.

A Touch of Zen (Xia nü)
King Hu, Taiwan, 1969
Hu brought spectacle, grace and mysticism to the martial arts genre, also devising a bamboo-forest battle that directly influenced *Crouching Tiger, Hidden Dragon* (2000).

The Big Boss (Tang shan da xiong)
Lo Wei, Hong Kong, 1971
Also known as *Fists of Fury*, Bruce Lee's first feature on his return to Hong Kong kicked off a worldwide hysteria for kung fu films.

Yellow Earth (Huang tudi)
Chen Kaige, China, 1984
The first release from a Fifth Generation film-maker challenged Chinese film tradition with bare widescreen landscapes and an ambiguous story of a Communist soldier who falls for a village girl while collecting folk songs.

A Better Tomorrow (Yinghung boon sik)
John Woo, Hong Kong, 1986
Woo's tale of two forgers who avenge themselves on their betrayers, with its stylish depictions of gunfights, launched the 'heroic bloodshed' crime subgenre.

Red Sorghum (Hong gao liang)
Zhang Yimou, China, 1987
The international status of Fifth Generation films was secured when this period drama, starring Gong Li as a peasant woman in the years leading up to the Japanese invasion, won the Golden Bear at the Berlin Film Festival.

A City of Sadness (Beiqing chengshi)
Hou Hsiao-Hsien, Taiwan, 1989
This depiction of the 1940s Taiwan rebellion against the Nationalist authorities – and the atrocities that followed – through the eyes of four brothers, won Hou the Golden Lion at the Venice Film Festival.

Farewell My Concubine (Ba wang bie jie)
Chen Kaige, Hong Kong/China, 1993
This epic tale of two Peking Opera actors, and the prostitute who comes between them, provoked Chinese authorities with its anti-communist and gay themes.

Crouching Tiger, Hidden Dragon (Wo hu cang long)
Ang Lee, Taiwan/China/USA, 2000
A combination of spectacular action and romantic subplots made this multi-Academy Award®-winning martial arts epic popular with male and female audiences alike.

In the Mood for Love (Fa yeung nin wa)
Wong Kar-Wai, Hong Kong, 2000
With its elegiac atmosphere, rich use of colour, exotic music and stylish editing tricks, this wistful meditation on lost love played to a wide foreign audience.

Hong Kong International Film Festival
Held annually since 1977 in Hong Kong. Festival featuring cinema from across the world and a retrospective from the Hong Kong Film Archive.
Website: www.hkiff.org.hk
Top prize: Firebird Awards (for first and second-time film-makers)

Taipei Golden Horse Film Festival
Held annually since 1962 in Taipei. Began as festival to promote the domestic industry, and expanded to include international cinema in 1980 and new digital video shorts in 2000.
Website: www.goldenhorse.org.tw
Top prize: Golden Horse (Chinese-language films only)

National awards

Chinese 'Oscars' (Jin Ji Jiang): Golden Roosters

Academy Awards®

Best Foreign Language Film wins: *Crouching Tiger, Hidden Dragon* (Taiwan, 2000)
Best Foreign Language Film nominations: 2 (China), 2 (Hong Kong), 3 (Taiwan)
Other Academy Award® wins: Cong Su, Best Original Score (*The Last Emperor*, 1987), Tan Dun, Best Original Score (*Crouching Tiger, Hidden Dragon*, 2000), Peter Pau, Best Cinematography (*Crouching Tiger, Hidden Dragon*, 2000), Timmy Yip, Best Art Direction (*Crouching Tiger, Hidden Dragon*, 2000)

Further viewing

Street Angel (1937), *Crows and Sparrows* (1949), *Springtime in a Small Town* (1949), *Two Stage Sisters* (1964), *The One-Armed Swordsman* (1967), *Enter the Dragon* (1973), *Police Story* (1985), *The Killer* (1989), *A Brighter Summer Day* (1991), *Chungking Express* (1994), *Eat Drink Man Woman* (1994), *Yi Yi* (2000), *Shaolin Soccer* (2001), *Hero* (2002), *Infernal Affairs* (2002), *Kung Fu Hustle* (2004)

CUBA

History

Cuban cinema, like Cuban history, can be divided into two sections – before Castro and after Castro. The earliest images of Cuba on film were shot during the War of Independence in 1898, but a distinctively Cuban cinema was not established until the post-revolution period. Within 83 days of coming to power in 1959, the new government formed the Cuban Institute of Cinematographic Art and Industry (ICAIC), which considered cinema a vital part of rebuilding Cuban society and sent mobile cinemas into rural areas. However, the effects of the American blockade and the collapse of the USSR – Cuba's main trade partner – devastated the economy, and for many years the arts suffered from a lack of support as the government concentrated on funding health and education.

The industry today

Economically speaking, Cuba is still recovering from the hardships of the 1990s, but the success of *Strawberry and Chocolate* (1993) has opened up world markets for its cinema.

Key figures

Tomás Gutiérrez Alea (1928–96)
The first Cuban director to achieve international recognition with films such as *Death of a Bureaucrat* (1966) was once a member of a film unit attached to Castro's guerrillas.

Humberto Solás (1941–)
Director whose work often features strong women – *Lucia* (1968), *Cecilia* (1982) – in sumptuously produced, politically charged melodramas.

Juan Carlos Tabío (1943–)
Director who began making documentaries but turned to features in 1981, finding great success with screwball comedy *Plaff* (1988) and co-directing Tomás Gutiérrez Alea's final two films, *Strawberry and Chocolate* (1993) and *Guantanamera* (1995).

Key films

Lucia
Humberto Solás, 1968
The Cuban struggle for liberation is dramatized through the lives of three women (19th-century aristocrat, 1930s activist and 1960s agricultural worker) in three different genre styles (tragedy, melodrama and comedy).

Memories of Underdevelopment (Memorias del subdesarrollo)
Tomás Gutiérrez Alea, 1968
The first post-Castro film to screen in the USA mixes documentary with drama, as an alienated bourgeois intellectual dwells on the past instead of embracing the progress of the Revolution.

Strawberry and Chocolate (Fresa y chocolate)
Tomás Gutiérrez Alea and Juan Carlos Tabío, 1993
In a notable step for Cuban cinema, this Academy Award®-nominated film follows the friendship between a gay man and a politicized student.

Food on the Set

The apartment used as a location in *Strawberry and Chocolate* (1993) is now Havana's top restaurant, La Guarida, where the props and art objects used in the film are still scattered around beside the tables.

Festivals

International Festival of New Latin American Cinema
Held annually since 1979 in Havana. Showcase for feature films, videos and
unpublished scripts by Latin American and Caribbean film-makers.
Website: www.habanafilmfestival.com
Top prize: Premio Coral

Academy Awards®

Best Foreign Language Film wins: 0
Best Foreign Language Film nominations: 1

Further viewing

I Am Cuba (1964), *Death of a Bureaucrat* (1966), *Guantanamera* (1995)

CZECHOSLOVAKIA, CZECH REPUBLIC AND SLOVAKIA

History

Soon after the 1933 opening of Barrandov Studios in Prague, Czechoslovakia was
producing around 40 films a year, but the 1939 Nazi invasion brought the industry
to a sudden halt. After the Communist takeover in 1948, Czech animation – always
an area of artistic strength – began to filter political criticism into its symbolic
imagery. It wasn't until 1963 that the country became a major player in film, as
the Czech New Wave rejected the uplifting style of 'socialist realism' and seized
on something closer to the truth of everyday existence. The hopes of the Prague
Spring political movement were crushed in 1968, when Soviet tanks appeared in the
streets, and leading directors – including Miloš Forman, Ivan Passer and Ján Kádar
– left the country, while those who stayed diluted their messages. The collapse of
Communism caused a huge decline in state support, before the country's 1993 split
into the Czech Republic and Slovakia further unsettled the film industry.

The industry today

Czech cinema has rallied since the mid-1990s, with some features openly tackling
previously taboo historical subjects. Meanwhile, Prague has become a key location
for US blockbusters such as *The Bourne Identity* (2002), *xXx* (2002) and *From Hell*
(2001).

Key figures

Véra Chytilová (1929–)
Czech New Wave director with a self-consciously experimental visual style, who
was temporarily banned from working immediately after the 1968 invasion.

Miloš Forman (1932–)
Director who progressed from satirical films in the 1960s to become an important
name in Hollywood, winning Academy Awards® for *One Flew Over the Cuckoo's
Nest* (1975) and *Amadeus* (1984).

Jirí Menzel (1938–)
Director, writer and actor with a gentler comic approach than his Czech New Wave contemporaries, whose films after 1968 were more whimsical than political.

Jan Švankmajer (1934–)
Animator whose shorts and features bring human actors, puppets, clay models and natural objects to life, creating a disturbingly surreal undercurrent.

Key films

Ecstasy (Extase)
Gustav Machaty, 1933
The first major Czech film boldly explored love and sexual fulfilment from a woman's perspective, but became notorious for a nude scene featuring actress Hedwig Kiesler (soon to become Hollywood legend Hedy Lamarr).

A Shop on the High Street (Obchod na korze)
Ján Kádar and Elmar Klos, 1965
Czechoslovakia's first Academy Award®-winner examines the horror of the Holocaust through a personal moral dilemma: should easy-going Tono expose or protect a confused, deaf, old Jewish lady when the Nazis come calling?

Closely Observed Trains (Ostre sledované vlaky)
Jirí Menzel, 1966
The most charming and lightly observational of the Czech New Wave films follows the attempts of a railwayman to lose his virginity during the Nazi Occupation.

The Fireman's Ball (Hoří, má panenko)
Miloš Forman, 1967
Forman satirizes the quirks of human nature and failings of bureaucracy as a firemen's committee messes up the organization of an annual dance.

Kolya
Jan Sverák, 1996
Czech cinema re-entered the spotlight with this sentimental Academy Award®-winner about a grumpy musician who reluctantly looks after a Russian boy.

Festivals

Karlovy Vary International Film Festival
Held either annually or biennially since 1946 (not 1953 or 1955) in Karlovy Vary, Czech Republic. Once a Socialist film showcase, now the most important festival in Central and Eastern Europe.
Website: www.iffkv.cz
Top prize: Crystal Globe

National awards

Czech Film and Television Academy: Lions

Academy Awards®

Best Foreign Language Film wins: *A Shop on the High Street* (1965), *Closely Observed Trains* (1966), *Kolya* (1996)

Best Foreign Language Film nominations: 9

Other selected Academy Award® wins: Miloš Forman, Best Director (*One Flew Over the Cuckoo's Nest*, 1975), Miloš Forman, Best Director (*Amadeus*, 1984)

Further viewing

Daisies (1966), *All My Good Countrymen* (1969), *My Sweet Little Village* (1985), *The Pied Piper* (1985), *Faust* (1994), *Divided We Fall* (2000)

DENMARK

History

Along with France, Denmark dominated markets in Germany, Russia and Scandinavia during cinema's infancy. Part of the appeal of early Danish films was their racy subject matter: audiences thrilled to titles such as *The White Slave Trade's Last Sacrifice* (1910). However, the national cinema went into a quick decline after World War I, and only Carl Theodor Dreyer emerged as a director of note over the next few decades. It was not until directors Lars von Trier and Thomas Vinterberg devised the Dogme 95 Manifesto in 1995 that all eyes turned again to Danish cinema. A clever marketing exercise disguised as a break from the dominance of special-effects blockbusters, Dogme's 'vows of chastity' forbade a director's credit, external musical score, flashbacks and studio lighting. This pared-down style suited the new hand-held digital camera technology, and proved influential around the world.

The industry today

Now that the Dogme boom is officially over, established Danish directors continue to have a strong presence on the international arthouse circuit. Just as importantly, Danish audiences seem very keen to see Danish films, a situation strengthened by the government's support for exhibition and distribution as well as production.

Key figures

Bille August (1948–   )
Director whose earlier work had roots in both Denmark and Sweden, and whose English-language films are often drawn from bestselling novels – *The House of the Spirits* (1993), *Smilla's Feeling for Snow* (1997), *Les Misérables* (1998).

Henning Carlsen (1927–   )
Denmark's main director of note between Dreyer and von Trier, who began with documentaries before making his feature debut in 1962 with *Dilemma*.

Carl Theodor Dreyer (1889–1968)
Denmark's most important director, whose austere but deeply felt films use extreme close-ups to express spiritual and emotional intensity.

Asta Nielsen (1883–1972)
Denmark's most famous silent screen actress, who made her debut in future husband Urban Gad's 1910 film *The Abyss (Afgrunden)*.

Ole Olsen (1863–1943)
Cinema owner and head of the Nordisk Films Kompagni, the world's oldest surviving film company and the leader in international exports during the silent era.

Lone Scherfig (1959–)
The first female director of a Dogme film – *Italian for Beginners* (*Italiensk for begyndere*) (2000) – whose work achieves a fine balance between comedy and tragedy while showing tremendous sympathy for her characters.

Lars von Trier (1956–)
Director, screenwriter and co-founder of the Dogme 95 movement, whose technically innovative work often features unsettling subject matter.

> **"**
>
> It was all very 70s stuff ... They were so tired of it, and kept begging me to put my clothes back on, and I was like 'No – I make the rules around here'.
>
> – Lars von Trier describes stripping naked along with the cast while shooting the infamous orgy scene in *The Idiots* (1999). Quoted in a BBC article, 2000.
>
> **"**

Thomas Vinterberg (1969–)
Co-founder of the Dogme 95 movement and director of *Festen* (1998), the first film made under its 'vows of chastity'.

Key films

Day of Wrath (Vredens Dag)
Carl Theodor Dreyer, 1943
One of Dreyer's most pessimistic portraits of spiritual torment shows how accusations of witchcraft in 17th-century Denmark become an excuse for human cruelty.

The Olsen Gang (Olsen-banden)
Erik Balling, 1968
The first in a 14-film series of crime capers about a harmless gang of crooks, which has also been remade in Norwegian and Swedish versions.

Pelle the Conqueror (Pelle Erobreren)
Bille August, 1987
The most acclaimed Danish film for decades (winner of the Cannes Palme d'Or and the Best Foreign Film Academy Award[®]) dwells on the brutal misfortunes faced by a poor farm labourer and his young son in the 19th century.

Babette's Feast (Babettes Gaestebud)
Gabriel Axel, 1987
Academy Award[®]-winning story about a French servant who shows up the narrow-minded, parochial manners of her Danish employers by arranging a splendid dinner.

Festen (The Celebration)
Thomas Vinterberg, 1998
The first Dogme film uses low yellow light and intimate hand-held cameras to pull the audience into the heart of a family wrecked by pain and guilt.

Dancer in the Dark
Lars von Trier, 2000
Von Trier rewrote the rules of the musical with this film, using hand-held cameras for the story's dramatic elements and an exuberant multi-camera style for its songs; it won the Cannes Palme d'Or and a Cannes Best Actress Award for its star, Icelandic singer Björk.

Festivals

National Film Festival
Held annually since 1990 in Copenhagen. Denmark's biggest film festival, with simultaneous screenings in Copenhagen, Odense, Aalborg and Århus (and in Malmö and Lund in Sweden).
Website: www.natfilm.dk
Top Prize: Natsværmer Award (contribution to Danish cinema)

National awards

Danish Film Academy: Roberts

Academy Awards®

Best Foreign Language Film wins: *Babette's Feast* (1987), *Pelle the Conqueror* (1987)
Best Foreign Language Film nominations: 6
Other Academy Award® wins: Max Rée, Best Art Direction (*Cimarron*, 1931)

Further viewing

The Red Earth (1945), *Ordet* (1954), *Paw* (1959), *Gertrud* (1964), *Breaking the Waves* (1996), *The Idiots* (1998), *Mifune* (1999), *Open Hearts* (2002), *Dogville* (2003), *Brothers* (2004)

FINLAND

History

With a relatively small population spread out over a large area, Finland's geography has hindered the growth of its film industry. The country has, however, excelled itself with historical sagas and war films, most of which focus on the brutal 1939 conflict with the USSR. In 1969 the Finnish Film Foundation was born, allowing a freer range of subjects to emerge. Recurrent themes of isolation, poverty and alcoholism could now as easily be treated as comedy or tragedy. Comedies have fuelled Finland's recent industry, from the unrepentantly parochial humour of the long-running series beginning with Ere Kokkonen's *Uunu Turhapuro* (1973) to the deadpan cult status of the Kaurismäki brothers.

The industry today

The Finnish film industry still relies on funding from state subsidies and television to maintain an average of about ten feature films a year. A boom in children's films and documentaries has lasted since the end of the 1990s.

Key figures

Aki Kaurismäki (1957–)
Director and brother of Mika Kaurismäki, he has built up a distinctively laconic body of work identified by a deadpan sense of humour, minimalist style, sparse dialogue and tenderness for his characters.

Mika Kaurismäki (1955–)
Director and brother of Aki Kaurismäki, his style tends more towards mainstream genres, particularly road movies such as *Rosso* (1985).

Risto Orko (1899–2001)
Director of popular farces, melodramas and patriotic epics in the 1930s, who became head of film studio Suomi-Filmi in 1945.

Kati Outinen (1961–)
Actress and favoured leading lady of Aki Kaurismäki; her face conveys the downbeat, stoic misery of his stories. She won the Best Actress Award at the 2002 Cannes Film Festival for her role in his *The Man Without a Past* (2002).

Key films

The Unknown Soldier (Tuntematon sotilas)
Edvin Laire, 1955
This key Finnish war film captures the camaraderie and bitterness of the World War II campaign against the Russians, and was remade in 1985 by Rauni Mollberg.

Flame Top (Tulipää)
Pirjo Honkasalo and Pekka Lehto, 1980
Finland's most expensive film at the time of its making is a melancholy historical epic about novelist and revolutionary Maiju Lassila.

The Man Without a Past (Mies vailla menneisyyttä)
Aki Kaurismäki, 2002
Kaurismäki transcended his cult status with a Cannes Jury Prize win and Best Foreign Film Academy Award® nomination for this low-key, surreal, touching romance between an amnesiac and a Salvation Army worker.

Festivals

Tampere International Short Film Festival
Held annually since 1970 in Tampere. Oldest and largest short film festival in Northern Europe.
Website: www.tamperefilmfestival.fi
Top prize: Grand Prix

National awards

Filmiaura Awards: Jussis

Best Foreign Language Film wins: 0
Best Foreign Language Film nominations: 1

Further viewing

The Vagabond's Waltz (1941), *Leningrad Cowboys Go America* (1989), *The Winter War* (1989), *Drifting Clouds* (1996), *L.A. Without a Map* (1999)

FRANCE

History

Modern cinema as we know it was born on 28 December 1895, when the Lumière brothers presented a programme of 'moving pictures' to a paying audience in Paris. Their first films – workers leaving a factory, a gardener being squirted by a hose – were brief, one-shot affairs. Soon, however, Georges Méliès was cutting together staged scenes and experimenting with camera effects, double exposures and tracking shots. France quickly established itself as the dominant force in world cinema before World War I through a series of popular comedies starring André Deed and Max Linder. The industry responded slowly to the advent of sound, but by the late 1930s, a socially aware, fatalistic style known as 'poetic realism' had developed.

After German occupation during World War II, French cinema stuck to literary adaptations and crime stories for most of the 1950s. This was the safe 'cinéma du papa' derided by the highly influential magazine *Cahiers du Cinéma*, which argued that the director should be considered the author of a film – the 'auteur theory'. The critics writing in *Cahiers*, including François Truffaut, Jean-Luc Godard and Claude Chabrol, practised what they preached: they launched the French New Wave (Nouvelle Vague) in 1959, producing technically dynamic films that used jump-cuts and hand-held cameras to emphasize the purely cinematic quality of their work. Few cinema movements have been more influential across the world; however, by the 1970s, French cinema had again begun relying on the status quo, using bourgeois comedies and softcore pornography to fill the coffers. A new generation of directors, raised on flashy advertising and music video images, established a commercial, surface-driven style known as 'cinéma du look' in the 1980s.

The Old Jokes Are Best

The first fiction film ever made – a mere one minute long – also contained the first sight gag. In Louis Lumière's *L'Arroseur arrosé* (1895), a boy stands on a gardener's water pipe, the gardener looks at the nozzle, the boy steps off and the gardener gets drenched. The film was remade in English, and again in French, in 1897.

The industry today

At the turn of the century, France was producing more films than any other country in Europe while engaging in a fierce battle with Hollywood studios over exhibition quotas. Comedies continue to enjoy the greatest popularity at home, but middle-class mid-life dramas, period epics and the shock-art cinema of Gaspar Noé (*Irréversible*, 2002) and Catherine Breillat (*Romance*, 1999) sum up the image of French cinema abroad.

Key figures

Brigitte Bardot (1934–)
Actress who became Europe's biggest sex symbol after being cast by her then husband Roger Vadim in *And God Created Woman* (1956).

Jean-Paul Belmondo (1933–)
Actor whose boxer-style features and rugged sex appeal made him, along with Alain Delon, France's biggest male box-office draw in the 1960s.

Luc Besson (1959–)
Writer-director whose glossy, Hollywood-influenced 'cinéma du look' films – including *Nikita* (1990) and *The Fifth Element* (1997) – have been accused of post-modern emptiness, and who now serves as writer-producer on action thrillers.

Robert Bresson (1901–99)
Director with an austere, minimalist style used to express the innocence, grace, suffering and spirituality of his characters (often played by non-professional actors).

Marcel Carné (1909–96)
Director whose best films with writer Jacques Prévert – including *Le Quai des brumes* (1938) and *Le Jour se lève* (1939) – are marked by a poetic fatalism.

Catherine Deneuve (1943–)
Actress whose blonde beauty is often used to convey an icy allure, as in *Belle de jour* (1967), or impenetrable coldness, as in *Repulsion* (1965).

Gérard Depardieu (1948–)
Actor (and winemaker) who became an international arthouse icon in the 1980s and 1990s by playing heavyweight, occasionally loutish roles, and received an Academy Award® nomination for his romantic turn in *Cyrano de Bergerac* (1990).

Jean Gabin (1904–76)
Actor whose compelling physical presence, world-weary looks and restrained expression epitomized the doomed, idealistic 'everyman' heroes of the 1930s.

Abel Gance (1889–1981)
Director and writer who made a profound impact on silent films with mobile camerawork, rapid editing and spectacular staging in *La Roue* (1923) and *Napoléon* (1927), but who was reduced to remaking his classics when the sound era began.

Jean-Luc Godard (1930–)
The most technically and politically audacious of the Nouvelle Vague directors, he rewrote the rules of narrative cinema with his work from *Breathless* (1960) onwards, making the audience consciously aware of the image itself.

Auguste Lumière (1862–1954) and Louis Lumière (1864–1948)
Inventors and film pioneers who presented history's first ever moving-picture show to a paying public, using their patented camera-projector, the Cinématographe.

Jeanne Moreau (1928–)

Actress whose unconventional, sensual beauty turned her into the leading lady of the Nouvelle Vague movement, starring in *Les Amants* (1958) and *Jules et Jim* (1962).

Charles Pathé (1863–1957)

Industrialist and producer whose studio at Vincennes, opened in 1902, turned Pathé Frères into the world's biggest production company.

Jean Renoir (1894–1979)

Director (the son of painter Pierre-Auguste Renoir) whose realist films – even those made at his creative peak in the 1930s – were derided at the time, but later lauded by the Nouvelle Vague.

François Truffaut (1932–84)

Director, screenwriter and actor who worked as a critic with *Cahiers du Cinéma* in the 1950s before establishing himself at the forefront of the Nouvelle Vague.

Key films

Napoléon
Abel Gance, 1927

Taking four years to complete, France's greatest silent feature uses a mobile camera and triptych split screens to convey the vitality and spectacle of Napoleon Bonaparte's life.

Un chien andalou (An Andalusian Dog)
Luis Buñuel, 1928

Buñuel and artist Salvador Dalí collaborated on what has become the most famous art short ever made: 17 minutes of Surrealist dream imagery, from a razor pulled across an eyeball to two dead donkeys on top of pianos.

L'Atalante
Jean Vigo, 1934

A mood of poetic realism hangs over this, one of only four films made by Vigo before his early death, as three people on a barge glide through an industrialized city.

La Règle du jeu (The Rules of the Game)
Jean Renoir, 1939

At once harshly satirical and fondly sympathetic, Renoir's masterpiece depicts a country-house weekend marred by tragedy, and subverts both romance and the bedroom farce formula.

Les Enfants du paradis (Children of Paradise)
Marcel Carné, 1945

This glittering romantic epic, set in a Parisian theatre in the 1840s, is all the more remarkable for having been made beneath the noses of the occupying German Army.

La Belle et la bête (Beauty and the Beast)
Jean Cocteau, 1946
Cinema is at its most magical in this famous fairy tale, which blends fantasy with reality by using imagery specific to Cocteau's work as an artist and poet.

Monsieur Hulot's Holiday (Les vacances de Monsieur Hulot)
Jacques Tati, 1953
France's greatest director-comedian introduces his much-loved, accident-prone character, depicted here causing havoc in a seaside town in Brittany.

The 400 Blows (Les Quatre cents coups)
François Truffaut, 1959
The Nouvelle Vague movement began when Truffaut won Best Director at Cannes for this semi-autobiographical tale of a boy who runs away from an unhappy home – the first in the unique five-strong series of 'Antoine Doinel' films, all played at different ages by Jean-Pierre Léaud, up to *L'Amour en fuite* (1979).

Breathless (À bout de souffle)
Jean-Luc Godard, 1960
Godard pays homage to pulp crime movies and transforms French cinema with staccato bursts of jump-cut editing, natural lighting and on-street photography.

Betty Blue (37°2 le matin)
Jean-Jacques Beineix, 1986
Five years after Beineix established the glossy 'cinéma du look' style with *Diva* (1981), the saturated colours and luscious presence of Béatrice Dalle ensured an international cult following for this archetypal story of 'l'amour fou'.

Cyrano de Bergerac
Jean-Paul Rappeneau, 1990
French arthouse cinema of the late 20th century was never finer than in this handsomely presented classic, enhanced in English by Anthony Burgess's poetic subtitles.

Three Colours trilogy
Krzysztof Kieslowski, 1993–4
In naming his three films after the colours of the French flag and basing their stories on the ideals of the French Revolution – 'liberté, égalité, fraternité' – Polish director Kieslowski realized one of the greatest achievements of a truly European cinema.

La Haine (Hate)
Mathieu Kassovitz, 1995
Class tension and ethnic bonding in the Parisian suburbs feature in this explosively stylish black and white snapshot of modern French urban life.

Amélie (Le fabuleux destin d'Amélie Poulain)
Jean-Pierre Jeunet, 2001
A huge hit both at home and abroad, this gloriously romantic story starring the winsome Audrey Tautou confirmed Jeunet as France's most visually inventive director.

Festivals

Festival International du Film de Cannes
Held annually since 1939 in Cannes (not 1940–45, 1950 or 1968). The world's most prestigious film festival, featuring star-studded world premières, with accompanying film and home video market.
Website: www.festival-cannes.com
Top prize: Palme d'Or

Festival du Cinéma Américain
Held annually since 1975 in Deauville. Festival dedicated to US cinema, featuring tributes to Hollywood stars.
Website: www.festival-deauville.com
Top prize: Grand Jury Prize

National awards

Académie des Arts et Techniques du Cinéma: Césars

Academy Awards®

Honorary Awards for Foreign Language Film: *Monsieur Vincent* (1947), *Au-delà des grilles* (1949), *Les Jeux interdits* (1952)
Best Foreign Language Film wins: *Mon Oncle* (1958), *Black Orpheus* (1959), *Sundays and Cybèle* (1962), *Un homme et une femme* (1966), *The Discreet Charm of the Bourgeoisie* (1972), *Day for Night* (1973), *Madame Rosa* (1977), *Get Out Your Handkerchiefs* (1978)
Best Foreign Language Film nominations: 33
Other Academy Award® wins: Best Documentary Feature (*Le Monde du Silence*, 1956), Maurice Chevalier, Honorary Award, 1959, Simone Signoret, Best Actress (*Room at the Top*, 1959), Claude Lelouch, Best Original Screenplay (*Un homme et une femme*, 1966), Jean Renoir, Honorary Award, 1975, Juliette Binoche, Best Supporting Actress (*The English Patient*, 1996)

Further viewing

La Roue (1923), *The Passion of Joan of Arc* (1928), *Boudu Saved from Drowning* (1932), *La Grande illusion* (1937), *La Ronde* (1950), *Les Amants* (1958), *Last Year in Marienbad* (1961), *Jules et Jim* (1962), *Bande à part* (1964), *Belle de jour* (1967), *La Grande bouffe* (1973), *Diva* (1981), *Jean de Florette* (1986), *Beau travail* (1999)

GERMANY

History

In 1917, in order to help with the war effort, the German High Command pulled various small film companies together into one body. Named Ufa (Universum Film AG), the company became the largest film studio in Europe when denationalized after the war. This was the era of German Expressionism, an artistic style that used distorted perspectives and jagged designs to reflect troubled states of mind. As the German economy dipped in the 1920s, films began to adopt a more realistic style, focusing on crime and hardship in the cities. When the Nazi Party came to power, the industry fell under the control of Joseph Goebbels, who purged it of all Jewish talent. After its defeat in World War II, Germany was split into East and West, with the Allied Forces doing little to encourage local film production. Not until the 1960s did a new generation of film-makers give voice to the marginalized members of society. Werner Herzog, Rainer Werner Fassbinder, Wim Wenders, Alexander Kluge, Margarethe von Trotta and Volker Schlöndorff were hailed as the auteurs of New German Cinema at festivals abroad, but virtually ignored by audiences at home, who preferred smutty, cliché-ridden comedies.

An Early Attempt at Sound

Nine years before Al Jolson sang to the world in *The Jazz Singer* (1927), three Germans – Hans Vogt, Joseph Massolle and Joseph Engl – patented Tri-Ergon, a sound-on-film system that was unveiled to the public at the Alhambra Cinema in Berlin on 17 September 1922. Unfortunately, technical breakdowns at the première of the first Tri-Ergon feature, *Das Mädchen mit den Schwefelhölzern (The Little Match Girl)* (1925), made the German industry wary of adopting it and getting a head start with talkies.

The industry today

German cinema has a poor international reputation, and few of its popular commercial films screen outside its own borders. In recent years, however, directors Tom Tykwer and Oliver Hirschbiegel have found commercial success at home and abroad with, respectively, *Run Lola Run* (1998) and *Downfall* (2004).

Key figures

Marlene Dietrich (1901–92)
Actress whose bewitching aura in silents and husky voice in talkies ensured a long career that peaked in Germany with *The Blue Angel* (1930) and in Hollywood with a Best Actress Academy Award® nomination for *Morocco* (1930).

Rainer Werner Fassbinder (1946–82)
Prolific director who made over 40 films for cinema and television, treating serious social subjects in a manner close to the stylized melodrama of US director Douglas Sirk.

Werner Herzog (1942–)
Director whose documentaries and features (many of which star actor Klaus Kinski) reveal a fascination with visionaries, eccentrics and outsiders.

Emil Jannings (1884–1950)
Swiss-born actor who became silent German cinema's biggest male star with performances in *The Last Laugh* (1924) and *Tartuffe* (1926), and who also won the first ever Best Actor Academy Award® for *The Last Command* (1928).

Fritz Lang (1890–1976)
Austrian director who collaborated with his scriptwriter wife Thea von Harbou on several spectacular silent films – *Dr Mabuse the Gambler* (1922), *Die Nibelungen* (1924), *Metropolis* (1927) – before fleeing Nazi Germany for Hollywood.

Ernst Lubitsch (1892–1947)
Director who showed a distinctively light, ironic touch in both German silents and Hollywood comedies, racking up three Best Director Academy Award® nominations.

F W Murnau (1888–1931)
Director who made 17 films in Germany (including 1922's *Nosferatu*) and four in America (including his 1927 masterpiece *Sunrise*), all featuring powerful, haunting images.

G W Pabst (1885–1967)
Director whose German silent films – including *The Joyless Street* (1925) and *Pandora's Box* (1929) – use realism, rather than the dominant mode of Expressionism, to expose the hardships of city life in the years after World War I.

Wim Wenders (1945–   )
Director whose characters often undertake a physical journey in order to achieve a spiritual goal, as in *Alice in the Cities* (1974) and *Paris, Texas* (1984).

Key films

The Cabinet of Dr Caligari (Das Kabinett des Doktor Caligari)
Robert Wiene, 1920
Definitive German Expressionist film which uses twisted corridors and camera angles to convey the insanity of a fairground charlatan and his murderous somnambulist.

The Last Laugh (Der letzte Mann)
F W Murnau, 1924
Karl Freud's inventive mobile camera adds sparkle to the tragic story of an ageing hotel porter (Emil Jannings) humiliated by his employers.

Metropolis
Fritz Lang, 1927
Shot over 18 months with a budget that soared to eight million marks, this science-fiction masterpiece about love and revolution in a futuristic city boasts production designs that still influence the genre today.

The Blue Angel (Der blaue Engel)
Joseph von Sternberg, 1930
Shot simultaneously in German and English, the first of seven collaborations between director von Sternberg and Marlene Dietrich casts the actress as cabaret singer Lola Lola, a role that made her an overnight star.

People on Sunday (Menschen am Sonntag)
Robert Siodmak and Edgar G Ulmer, 1930
As well as the directors, future Hollywood players Billy Wilder, Curt Siodmak and Fred Zinnemann collaborated on this semi-dramatized portrait of a flirtatious Sunday afternoon spent in a Berlin park.

Triumph of the Will (Triumph des Willens)
Leni Riefenstahl, 1935
Propaganda meets art in this notorious but technically impeccable documentary,

which deifies the speechmaking Adolf Hitler at the Nazi Party's 1934 rally in Nuremberg.

The Murderers Are Amongst Us (Die Mörder sind unter uns)
Wolfgang Staudte, 1946
The best film made under Allied control, this East German film directly addresses the country's collective guilt amidst the rubble of a defeated city.

Fear Eats the Soul (Angst essen Seele auf)
Rainer Werner Fassbinder, 1974
Inspired by the forbidden love in Douglas Sirk's Hollywood melodrama *All That Heaven Allows* (1955), Fassbinder adds a racial divide to this story of an ageing cleaner and a Moroccan immigrant.

The Tin Drum (Die Blechtrommel)
Volker Schlöndorff, 1979
This Academy Award®-winner about a boy who refuses to grow up observes German history from a child's psychological viewpoint, placing the camera at knee-height for effect.

Das Boot
Wolfgang Petersen, 1981
Before Petersen settled in Hollywood, he enjoyed a huge box-office hit with this sympathetic and appropriately claustrophobic portrait of life on a wartime U-boat.

Fitzcarraldo
Werner Herzog, 1982
Herzog is at his most spectacular, and Klaus Kinski at his most manic, in this epic about an overreaching Irishman who decides to bring grand opera to the Amazonian jungle, even if it means dragging a steamboat over a mountain.

Downfall (Der Untergang)
Oliver Hirschbiegel, 2004
German cinema finally addresses the final days of Adolf Hitler, switching the action between the confines of his Berlin bunker and the invasion of Berlin above ground.

Festivals

Berlin International Film Festival
Held annually since 1951 in Berlin. One of the world's top five film festivals, with a large international programme.
Website: www.berlinale.de
Top prize: Golden Bear

National awards

German Film Academy: Lolas

Academy Awards®

Best Foreign Language Film wins: *The Tin Drum* (1979), *Nowhere in Africa* (2001)
Best Foreign Language Film nominations: 13
Other selected Academy Award® wins: Luise Rainer, Best Actress (*The Great Ziegfeld*, 1936), Luise Rainer, Best Actress (*The Good Earth*, 1937)

Further viewing

Nosferatu (1922), *Faust* (1926), *Die Nibelungen* (1924), *M* (1931), *Yesterday's Girl* (1966), *Jacob the Liar* (1975), *The Marriage of Maria Braun* (1978), *Wings of Desire* (1987), *Stalingrad* (1992), *Run Lola Run* (1998), *Good Bye Lenin!* (2003)

GREECE

History

For many decades, Greece's major production companies concentrated solely on musicals and comedies. It took the creation of the Thessaloniki Film Festival in 1960 to provide a platform for a new, socially aware national cinema to arise in the years that followed, although the 'Colonels' military junta, which ruled the country from 1967 until 1974, brought in strict censorship controls. Theo Angelopoulos emerged as the country's most respected director, with a trilogy of historical works – *Days of '36* (1972), *The Travelling Players* (1975) and *The Hunters* (1977) – that examined the century's key periods of turmoil. He has since continued, almost single-handedly, to fly the country's cinematic flag.

The industry today

A long fallow period in Greek cinema may soon be ending, as home-produced films such as *Safe Sex* (1999) and *A Touch of Spice* (2003) have begun to challenge the box-office grip of the Hollywood blockbusters.

Key figures

Theo Angelopoulos (1935–)
Greece's most internationally renowned director, who uses distinctively slow and measured tracking shots to take his characters on long, mythic journeys.

Michael Cacoyannis (1922–)
Greek-Cypriot director whose political films of the 1950s and popular hits (such as *Zorba the Greek*, 1964) show a fondness for working-class characters.

Costa-Gavras, Constantin (1933–)
Greek-born director who often prefers to work in French and English, tackling fiercely political subjects in the likes of *Z* (1969) and *Missing* (1982).

Melina Mercouri (1920–94)
Actress, nominated for an Academy Award® for *Never on Sunday* (1960), who left Greece during the military junta but returned in 1977 to become socialist Minister for Culture.

Vangelis (1943–)
Composer whose music for *Chariots of Fire* (1981) and *Blade Runner* (1982) gave credibility to the use of synthesizers and electronic instruments in film scores.

Key films

Never on Sunday (Pote tin Kyriaki)
Jules Dassin, 1960
This Pygmalion story of a prostitute (Melina Mercouri) who is tutored by a besotted American professor was one of Greece's biggest box-office hits.

Zorba the Greek (Alexis Zorbas)
Michael Cacoyannis, 1964
A hugely popular international hit, made as a US co-production, with Anthony Quinn in his most famous role as a larger-than-life peasant.

The Travelling Players (O thiassos)
Theo Angelopoulos, 1975
Widely regarded as the best Greek film ever made, this four-hour epic examines the turmoil of the country's civil war years through the eyes of an itinerant acting troupe.

Festivals

International Thessaloniki Film Festival
Held annually since 1960 in Thessaloniki. Long-running festival with sections for Greek and Balkan cinema.
Website: www.filmfestival.gr
Top prize: Golden Alexander

Academy Awards®

Best Foreign Language Film wins: 0
Best Foreign Language Film nominations: 4
Other Academy Award® wins: Katina Paxinou, Best Supporting Actress (*For Whom the Bell Tolls*, 1943), Manos Hadjidakis, Best Song (*Never on Sunday*, 1960), Vassilis Photopoloulos, Best Black and White Art Direction (*Zorba the Greek*, 1964)

Further viewing

Stella (1955), *Ulysses' Gaze* (1995), *Eternity and a Day* (1998)

HUNGARY

History

Silent cinema was strong in Hungary, with two figures – director Mihály Kertész and producer Sándor Laszlo Kellner – destined to go on to greater things abroad as, respectively, Michael Curtiz and Sir Alexander Korda. Under Communist rule, however, film-makers stuck closely to the socialist realism rulebook until the death of Stalin in 1953 allowed directors like Károly Makk to try out different styles. This brief relaxation of political control ended with the bloody suppression of the 1956 uprising and, throughout the 1960s and afterwards, film-makers relied on historical subjects to state their political criticisms from a safe metaphoric distance.

The industry today

Hungary has struggled to persuade its citizens to buy tickets for Hungarian films, despite the fact that several have recently won major foreign awards (*Pleasant Days* (2002), *Hukkle* (2002) and *Kontroll* (2003)).

Key figures

Michael Curtiz (1888–1962)
Director who made over 40 silent films in his native Hungary before moving to Austria and then to the USA, where he spent decades with Warner Brothers and won an Academy Award® for *Casablanca* (1942).

Miklós Jancsó (1921–   )
Director who favours historical subjects and long, complex camera movements that constantly circle and track around the actors, rarely using close-ups.

Márta Mészáros (1931–   )
One of the few women working in Hungarian cinema, her semi-autobiographical 'Diary' series of films – beginning in 1982 with *Diary for My Children* – examines the difficulties that face women living under eastern European communism.

István Szabó (1938–   )
Director who brought the energy of France's Nouvelle Vague movement to eastern European cinema during the 1960s, and used co-production money to finance large-scale, powerfully dramatic period pieces from the 1980s onwards.

Béla Tarr (1955–   )
Director whose bleak style, built through long shots lasting several minutes each, has made his films (including 1994's *Satantango*) popular with critics.

Key films

The Round-Up (Szegénylegények)
Miklós Jancsó, 1965
Jancsó's formal and dispassionate depiction of the Austrian authorities' attempts to suppress a rebellion in 1848 made coded criticisms about oppression in any form.

Mephisto
István Szabó, 1981
Hungary's sole Academy Award®-winning film, about an ambitious actor who compromises his beliefs in Nazi Germany, uses the Faust myth to reveal the seductive power of fascism.

Damnation (Kárhozat)
Béla Tarr, 1988
Black and white photography, long takes and repetitive images emphasize the despairing mood of this melancholy love story set in a grimy waterfront bar.

Festivals

Hungarian Film Week
Held annually in Pécs from 1965–82, then in Budapest since 1983. Showcase of national cinema across feature, documentary and animation formats.
Website: www.szemle.film.hu
Top prize: Best Film

Academy Awards®

Best Foreign Language Film wins: *Mephisto* (1981)
Best Foreign Language Film nominations: 8
Other Academy Award® wins: Emeric Pressburger, Best Original Story (*49th Parallel*, 1941), Paul Lukas, Best Actor (*Watch on the Rhine*, 1943), Michael Curtiz, Best Director (*Casablanca*, 1942).

Further viewing

The Red and the White (1967), *Colonel Redl* (1984), *Kontroll* (2003)

ICELAND

History

Ever since 1919, when Danish director Gunnar Sommerfeldt came to Iceland to shoot *The Story of the Borg Family* (1921), European film-makers have favoured the country's spectacular locations for their own productions. However, it was only after the establishment of the Icelandic Film Fund in 1979 that a sustainable industry managed to produce one or two home-grown films each year – a remarkable achievement, given that the country's entire population of under 300,000 is less than that of many UK cities. Icelandic films now fall roughly into three categories: ancient sagas, idiosyncratic comedies and cool, slacker-style youth movies.

The industry today

Iceland's scenery continues to entice Hollywood producers of blockbusters, including *Batman Begins* (2005) and *Die Another Day* (2002), to spend some of their location budgets here. Meanwhile, local production continues at a steady pace, with the occasional feature – such as darkly comic oddity *Nói albínói* (2003) – achieving a wider international release.

Key figures

Fridrik Thor Fridriksson (1953–   )
Iceland's most internationally renowned director whose work, including the Academy Award®-nominated *Children of Nature* (1991), makes exceptional use of natural landscapes and displays a wry sense of humour.

Björk Gudmundsdóttir (1965–   )
Singer and composer who won the Best Actress Award at the 2000 Cannes Film Festival for her role as a tragic single mother in Lars von Trier's *Dancer in the Dark* (2000).

Ágúst Gudmundsson (1947–   )
Director of sagas (*Outlaw*, 1981) and youth movies (*On Top*, 1982) whose debut *Land and Sons* (1980) put Iceland on the world film map.

Hrafn Gunnlaugsson (1948–   )
Director whose action-driven Viking sagas, including *When the Raven Flies* (1984) and *The Shadow of the Raven* (1988), paint an unheroic portrait of medieval times.

Key films

Land and Sons (Land og synir)
Ágúst Gudmundsson, 1980
This Depression-era drama about a farmer and his son not only kick-started the modern Icelandic film industry, it recouped its costs at the home box office.

Children of Nature (Börn náttúrunnar)
Fridrik Thor Fridriksson, 1991
Iceland's only Academy Award®-nominated film follows a crotchety widower who finds a new lease of life when he escapes from his old folks' home with his childhood sweetheart.

101 Reykjavik
Baltasar Kormákur, 2000
The definitive Icelandic slacker movie finds 30-year-old Hlynur digging himself into a hole when he begins an affair with his mother's lesbian-lover flamenco teacher.

Festivals

Reykjavik Short Film Festival
Held annually since 1992 in Reykjavik. International forum for fiction and documentary short films.
Website: www.icelandicfilmcentre.is
Top prize: Best Short Film

National awards

Icelandic Film and Television Academy: Eddas

Academy Awards®

Best Foreign Language Film wins: 0
Best Foreign Language Film nominations: 1

Further viewing

Cold Fever (1995), *Devil's Island* (1996), *Nói albínói* (2003)

Icelandic Investment

UK pop musician Damon Albarn (of bands Blur and Gorillaz) wrote the music for *101 Reykjavik* (2000), and is a co-owner of the Kaffibarrin bar in Iceland's capital along with the film's director, Baltasar Kormákur.

INDIA

History

Although few Indian silent features survive, history notes that reformist melodramas, lives of saints and stories from the Mahabharata and Ramayana legends were the most popular subjects. With the arrival of sound, theatrical traditions of music and dance were adapted to become distinctive elements of the national cinema. Studios were based in and around Bombay (now Mumbai), as well as in Calcutta to the east and Madras to the south, in order to cater for India's multiple languages. By the time the country had gained independence from the British Empire in 1947, the cinematic formula was set: romantic musical melodramas would feature six or seven songs, some lavish dance routines, wild switches of tone, stereotyped characters – and no kissing. While the Hindi-language films of Bombay's so-called 'Bollywood' industry were widely distributed, a more socially-dedicated art cinema, supported by public money, allowed the names of Satyajit Ray, Mrinal Sen and Shyam Benegal to represent India on screens abroad. By the 1970s, India was the most active film production centre in the world; in 1985 alone, over 900 features were made there, with major stars commanding a fervent fan base.

The industry today

Indian production has dropped dramatically in recent years, with piracy and foreign imports eroding audience figures. However, overseas box office now accounts for a major percentage of a film's receipts and Bollywood films in particular have penetrated Asian markets in the USA and the UK, although English-speaking audiences there have proved harder to win over.

Key figures

Amitabh Bachchan (1942–)
Actor whose unusually tall, dark looks made him a superstar in the 1970s, playing working-class rebels and streetwise 'men of the people'.

Raj Kapoor (1924–88)
Director and actor from the famous Kapoor family (others include his brother Shashi, son Rishi and granddaughter Kareena) whose commercially savvy films emphasize the love story angle. He occasionally casts himself as Chaplinesque tramp Raju.

Mehboob Khan (1907–64)
Leading director who created his own production company in 1942 to make social melodramas that featured big-name actors and reflected the plight of the oppressed.

Shah Rukh Khan (1965–)
Actor who has dominated the Bollywood scene from the 1990s onwards, first as morally complex anti-heroes, then as a romantic lead in films such as *Devdas* (2002).

Aishwarya Rai (1973–)
Actress and former Miss World (1994) who became Bollywood's highest-paid actress before breaking into English-language films with *Bride and Prejudice* (2004).

A Wax Doll?

In 2004, Aishwarya Rai became the first Bollywood and Indian actress to be immortalized in wax at Madame Tussauds in London. The following year, Mattel issued a limited-edition Barbie® doll based on her costumes.

Satyajit Ray (1921–92)
Director, screenwriter and composer whose potrayal of Bengali characters (particularly in the Apu trilogy) was more influenced by Italian neorealism and the work of French director Jean Renoir than by any of his Indian contemporaries.

Key films

Awara (The Tramp)
Raj Kapoor, 1951
Timelessly popular film with director Kapoor in his iconic Chaplinesque 'tramp' persona, redeeming himself in the eyes of his stern judge father after a murder.

Pather Panchali (Song of the Road)
Satyajit Ray, 1955
The first film in the Apu trilogy – followed by *Aparajito* (1956) and *Apur Sansar* (1959) – abandons the dominant Indian style in favour of Italian-influenced neorealism to capture the joy and despair of a family in a poor Bengali village.

Mother India (Bharat Mata)
Mehboob Khan, 1957
Regarded as India's answer to *Gone With The Wind*, this socially-aware melodrama casts leading actress Nargis as a physically and mentally strong woman – she tills the soil single-handedly – forced into a dramatic showdown with one of her sons.

Sholay (Embers)
Ramesh Sippy, 1975
Combines the fierce action of 1970s cinema with western-style musical spectacle and story, as Amitabh Bachchan plays a crook hired by a cop to help out a village terrorized by bandits.

Kuch Kuch Hota Hai
Karan Johar, 1998
Mega-hit example of 1990s Bollywood's desire to please a younger audience with wedding themes, additional songs and some westernized characters.

Lagaan (Once Upon a Time in India)
Ashutosh Gowariker, 2001
Major international crossover hit which sets a tale of forbidden love against a Raj backdrop, as an ethnically diverse group of Indians take on a British team at cricket.

Festivals

Mumbai International Film Festival

Held biennially since 1990 in Mumbai. Government-run festival incorporating Indian and international feature films, documentaries, shorts and retrospectives.
Website: www.filmsdivision.com
Top prize: Gold Conch

Academy Awards®

Best Foreign Language Film wins: 0
Best Foreign Language Film nominations: 3
Other Academy Award® wins: Satyajit Ray, Honorary Award, 1992

Further viewing

Devdas (1935), *The Cloud-capped Star* (1960), *Waqt* (1965), *Days and Nights in the Forest* (1970), *The Seedling* (1973), *Salaam Bombay!* (1988), *Hum* (1991), *Bandit Queen* (1994), *Dil Se* (1998), *Kabhi Khushi Kabhie Gam* (2001), *Devdas* (2002)

IRAN

History

Until the late 1960s, most Iranian films aimed for an escapist style somewhere between Hollywood and Bollywood. After the Islamic Revolution of 1979, however, foreign imports were restricted and native Iranian cinema was closely censored by the clerics. Film-makers worked around these restrictions, treating serious social subjects in an allegorical fashion, using locations rather than studio sets and hiring non-professional actors. The death of religious and political leader Ayatollah Khomeini in 1989 re-energized Iranian cinema, and by the 1990s its output was winning prizes at film festivals across the world, though it still faced bans at home.

The industry today

Iran's Islamic government has again tightened its control of the film and television industries, banning the work of leading lights such as Abbas Kiarostami and encouraging others to work abroad instead. However, foreign arthouse circuits have continued to embrace Iranian cinema's simple, unsentimental narratives, which often focus on the roles of women and children in the country's male-dominated society.

Key figures

Shohreh Aghdashloo (1952–   )

Actress in Iranian cinema of the 1970s who moved to England, then America, during the Revolution, and received an Academy Award® nomination for *House of Sand and Fog* (2003).

Abbas Kiarostami (1940–   )

Iran's most internationally acclaimed director, writer and editor, whose early philosophical films have given way to a more technically formal style with the advent of digital video.

Mohsen Makhmalbaf (1957–)
Director, producer and writer who was jailed in his teens as a radical Islamist for stabbing a policeman, and later set up a production company to teach children philosophy, cinema and aesthetics.

Samira Makhmalbaf (1980–)
Director and daughter of Mohsen Makhmalbaf, she was only 18 years old when her first feature, *The Apple*, premiered at the 1998 Cannes Film Festival.

Flashback Fever

Jafar Panahi's film *Crimson Gold* (2003) begins with a botched jewellery heist and then uses flashbacks to tell its tale. Its screenwriter Abbas Kiarostami has admitted that he was inspired by serving on the jury at the 1995 Taormina Film Festival with director Quentin Tarantino, whose film *Reservoir Dogs* (1992) featured a very similar story structure.

Key films

The House is Black (Khaneh siah ast)
Forugh Farrokhzad, 1963
Short black and white documentary about a leper colony, which influenced subsequent Iranian feature films with its simplicity and humanity.

The Cow (Gav)
Daryush Mehrjui, 1969
The first internationally acclaimed Iranian feature film tells the story of a man who becomes distraught when his cow – the only one in the village – dies.

Children of Heaven (Bacheha-Ye aseman)
Majid Majidi, 1997
This comedy about a brother and sister sharing a pair of shoes was the first Iranian film to receive an Academy Award[®] nomination for Best Foreign Language Film.

Taste of Cherry (Ta'm e guilass)
Abbas Kiarostami, 1997
Joint winner of the Cannes Film Festival Palme d'Or, Kiarostami's film about a man searching for someone to help him commit suicide questions life and Islamic law.

The Lizard (Marmoulak)
Kamal Tabrizi, 2004
Despite being withdrawn by the government for mocking religion, this satire about a thief who escapes prison dressed in clerical robes is Iran's biggest box-office success.

Festivals

Fajr International Film Festival
Held annually since 1983 in Tehran. Festival promoting Iranian cinema and showcasing other world cinema regions, with concurrent film and television markets.
Website: www.fajrfilmfest.com
Top prize: Crystal Simorgh

Academy Awards®

Best Foreign Language Film wins: 0
Best Foreign Language Film nominations: 1

Further viewing

The Runner (1984), *Where is My Friend's House?* (1987), *Close-Up* (1990), *Through the Olive Trees* (1994), *The Apple* (1998), *The Circle* (2000), *Kandahar* (2001), *Crimson Gold* (2003)

IRELAND

History

Down the years there have been far more films made by foreigners about Ireland than films made by Irishmen themselves. Indeed, footage of Dublin's O'Connell Bridge, shot by French pioneers the Lumière brothers in 1897, is thought to be the first evidence of Ireland on film. The silent era saw some attempts by actors at Dublin's famous Abbey Theatre to break into cinema. However, apart from a few dramas made by the Film Company of Ireland in the 1930s, indigenous production was almost non-existent until the 1970s. Instead, Ireland was nostalgically represented to the wider world as a green land full of comedy stereotypes, in 'foreign' films such as John Ford's *The Quiet Man* (1952). Low-budget work by directors such as Joe Comerford, Bob Quinn and Pat Murphy raised the country's profile in the 1970s and 1980s, allowing contemporary issues to be examined by native players.

The industry today

Domestic production remains a low-key affair in Ireland, and the number of foreign films shooting there has also dropped.

Key figures

Roddy Doyle (1958–)
Booker Prize-winning author and screenwriter who helped retain the feisty characters and spicy language in the film adaptations of his 'Barrytown Trilogy' of novels – *The Commitments* (1991), *The Snapper* (1993) and *The Van* (1996).

Richard Harris (1930–2002)
Actor, born in Limerick, who earned a reputation as a hellraiser for his off-screen drinking antics in the 1960s and 1970s, and who latterly reached wide audiences again with notable turns in *Gladiator* (2000) and the first two *Harry Potter* films.

Neil Jordan (1950–)
Director, screenwriter and author of three poetic novels, who dealt with IRA-related topics in *Angel* (1982), *The Crying Game* (1992) and *Michael Collins* (1996).

Peter O'Toole (1932–)
Actor with piercing blue eyes, born in Connemara but raised in the north of England, who became an international star with *Lawrence of Arabia* (1962).

Jim Sheridan (1949–   )
Director, writer and producer with a theatrical background, whose richly dramatic films – including *In the Name of the Father* (1993) and *In America* (2002) – draw the best out of his actors.

Key films

Angel
Neil Jordan, 1982
Jordan's debut brings a political edge to the thriller genre as saxophonist Stephen Rea is drawn into violence after witnessing a sectarian murder.

My Left Foot
Jim Sheridan, 1989
Irish cinema was boosted by Academy Award® wins for Brenda Fricker and Daniel Day-Lewis, stars of this biopic of disabled artist Christy Brown.

Festivals

Cork International Film Festival
Held annually since 1956 in Cork. Ireland's oldest and biggest film festival.
Website: www.corkfilmfest.org
Top prize: Best International Short Film Award

Academy Awards®

Academy Award® wins: George Bernard Shaw, Best Writing, Screenplay (*Pygmalion*, 1938), Barry Fitzgerald, Best Supporting Actor (*Going My Way*, 1944), Brenda Fricker, Best Supporting Actress (*My Left Foot*, 1989), Neil Jordan, Best Original Screenplay (*The Crying Game*, 1992), Peter O'Toole, Honorary Award, 2003

Further viewing

Pigs (1984), *December Bride* (1990), *Into the West* (1992), *I Went Down* (1997)

ISRAEL

History

In terms of politics and religion, Israel has been isolated from its Arab neighbours ever since it became an independent state in 1948. No wonder then that, in its infancy, the country's cinema reflected its people's conflicts of identity, the aftermath of the Holocaust and nationalist ideals. The Six Day War, the Yom Kippur War and the Palestinian Intifada have influenced the stories told on screen, particularly as all citizens from a certain generation onwards have had to spend time in the Israeli Army. Popular farces (known as *bourekas*) contrasted with a more serious cinema that began to emerge in the 1980s, now more openly critical of Zionism and more positive about Arab–Israeli relations.

The industry today

Audiences have not been keen to embrace local productions during recent unsettled times. However, the success of Dover Kosashvili's film *Late Marriage* (2002) has given hope to funding bodies and to a new generation of young film-makers.

Key figures

Amos Gitaï (1950–)

Director and documentarian at the forefront of Israel's new art cinema; his films tackle controversial subjects such as women in strict Hasidic society (*Kadosh*, 1999) and exiles arriving in the new state (*Kedma*, 2002).

Menahem Golan (1929–) and Yoram Globus (1941–)

Producers and cousins who made their mark with the *Lemon Popsicle* series of films, using its profits to buy up the Cannon Group and ABC cinema chain and to produce critically derided action films such as the *Death Wish* sequels.

Chaim Topol (1935–)

Actor who made the part of Tevye in *Fiddler on the Roof* (1971) his own, and who also appeared in the James Bond film *For Your Eyes Only* (1981).

Key films

Sallah (Sallah shabati)

Ephraim Kishon, 1964
Israel's first Academy Award® nomination went to this easy-going comedy about an immigrant family with a lazy but lovable patriarch, played with star-making quality by Topol.

Lemon Popsicle (Eskimo Limon)

Boaz Davidson, 1977
Modelled on the likes of *American Graffiti* (1973), this 1950s-set teen sex comedy and its many sequels did record business at domestic and international box offices.

Beyond the Walls (Me'achorei hasoragim)

Uri Barabash, 1984
A new wave of politically committed cinema began when this allegorical film about Arab and Israeli prisoners joining forces in prison won the International Critics' Prize at the Venice Film Festival.

Kippur

Amos Gitaï, 2000
Gitaï dramatizes his personal experience of being shot down in a helicopter during the 1973 Yom Kippur War, using long takes to convey the soldiers' disillusionment.

Festivals

Jerusalem Film Festival

Held annually since 1984 in Jerusalem. International feature and documentary film festival.
Website: www.jff.org.il
Top prize: Wolgin Award (Israeli cinema), In the Spirit of Freedom Award (human rights theme)

National awards

Israeli Academy of Film and Television: Ophirs

Academy Awards®

Best Foreign Language Film wins: 0
Best Foreign Language Film nominations: 6

Further viewing

The House on Chelouche Street (1973), *Cup Final* (1991), *Kadosh* (1999)

ITALY

History

During the silent era, Italian cinema had one great advantage over the rest of the world: it could use real ancient locations as settings for its costumed epics. The industry's infrastructure was strengthened under Benito Mussolini's fascist government, which in 1937 established the world-renowned Cinecittà studios, where nationalist epics and light comedies about the comfortable middle classes (known as 'white telephone' films) were produced. Immediately after World War II, the hugely influential neorealist movement rejected such escapist entertainment by drawing stories – and often actors – directly from the streets in an attempt to address the 'truth' of everyday life. During the 1950s, Italy produced an average of 140 films per year, securing an unprecedented ten per cent of the international box office thanks to the likes of Federico Fellini, Roberto Rossellini, Vittorio De Sica and Luchino Visconti. By the end of the decade, Cinecittà had become known as 'Hollywood on the Tiber', churning out sword-and-sandals adventures. The following years saw trends for 'spaghetti' westerns, political allegories that criticized the corrupt police state, 'giallo' thrillers and gory horror films. The industry underwent a general decline towards the end of the century, with a large number of Italian films – predominantly comedies – failing to make it even to Italian screens.

The industry today

Thanks to a lack of funding, the reputation of Italy's film industry is languishing both at home and abroad, despite high-profile international awards for directors Roberto Benigni and Nanni Moretti.

Key figures

Michelangelo Antonioni (1912–   )
Director who emphasizes his characters' alienation by placing them within powerful landscapes in films such as *L'Avventura* (1960), *Zabriskie Point* (1970) and *Blow-Up* (1966), for which he received a Best Director Academy Award® nomination.

Roberto Benigni (1952–   )
Comic actor and director who had a cult following, both at home and in the films of US independent director Jim Jarmusch, before unexpected Academy Award® success for his *Life Is Beautiful* (1997) raised his international profile.

Bernardo Bertolucci (1941–)
Director who became known for political films in the 1960s and 1970s before moving on to international epics in the 1980s and early 1990s.

Vittorio De Sica (1902–74)
Director and actor who established a career as a romantic lead before moving behind the camera, making his mark with neorealist classics *Shoeshine* (1946) and *Bicycle Thieves* (1948), then with glossy melodramas in the 1960s and 1970s.

Federico Fellini (1920–93)
Director who moved quickly on from neorealism to create one of world cinema's most personal and ambitious bodies of work, often casting his wife, Giulietta Masina, in central roles.

Sophia Loren (1934–)
Actress who, along with Gina Lollobrigida, became Italy's pin-up queen in the 1950s before winning credibility (and better roles) after her Academy Award® victory for *Two Women* (1960).

Marcello Mastroianni (1923–96)
Leading actor of the 1950s and 1960s who brought a suave, sophisticated presence to films including *La Dolce vita* (1960) and *Divorce Italian Style* (1961).

Ennio Morricone (1928–)
Composer whose versatile approach to a musical score can be heard in the distinctive whistle themes of spaghetti westerns and the lush orchestration of *The Mission* (1986).

Pier Paolo Pasolini (1922–75)
Director and poet whose Marxist beliefs informed films like *Accatone* (1961) and *Theorem* (1968) before he was murdered in suspicious circumstances.

Roberto Rossellini (1906–77)
Director who is most responsible for establishing neorealism in cinema through the landmark documentary style of *Rome, Open City* (1945) and *Paisa* (1946).

Vittorio Storaro (1940–)
Cinematographer with a remarkable eye for colour shading, as evidenced by his Academy Award®-winning work in *Apocalypse Now* (1979), *Reds* (1981) and *The Last Emperor* (1987).

Luchino Visconti (1906–76)
Director who worked in France with Jean Renoir before pre-empting both neorealism and film noir with *Ossessione* (1942) and moving on to grand historical themes in the 1960s.

Key films

Rome, Open City (Roma, città aperta)
Roberto Rossellini, 1945
The defining neorealist film uses real locations and spliced film stills to chronicle the last days of Nazi occupation in Rome.

Bicycle Thieves (Ladri di biciclette)
Vittorio De Sica, 1948
Moving neorealist classic about a poor man who searches Rome with his young son for the stolen bicycle on which his job depends.

La Dolce vita
Federico Fellini, 1960
The Church, and Rome's fashionably decadent social scene, are mercilessly satirized in the film that coined the word 'paparazzi' (named after a photographer character).

Divorce Italian Style (Divorzio all'italiana)
Pietro Germi, 1961
Suave black comedy that brought Bafta and Golden Globe victories (and an Academy Award® nomination) for Marcello Mastroianni as a nobleman who decides to kill his wife after falling in love with his beautiful young cousin.

A Fistful of Dollars (Per un pugno di dollar)
Sergio Leone, 1964
Leone's first spaghetti western transports Japanese samurai film *Yojimba* (1961) to America and casts imported star Clint Eastwood as the iconic 'Man with No Name', a cynical gunslinger who plays off two warring families for personal profit.

The Conformist (Il Conformista)
Bernardo Bertolucci, 1970
In this prime example of Italian political film-making, Bertolucci uses a fascist-era setting to explore the repressed thoughts and emotions of a weak-willed minion who agrees to assassinate his former teacher.

Salò (Salò, o le 120 giornate de Sodoma)
Pier Paolo Pasolini, 1975
Shocking scenes of sexual violence, drawn directly from the work of the Marquis de Sade, have ensured that Pasolini's savage attack on morally corrupt authorities remains one of the most infamous films ever made.

Cinema Paradiso (Il nuovo Cinema Paradiso)
Giuseppe Tornatore, 1988
International audiences flocked to see this nostalgic story of a projectionist and his young assistant, which fondly recreates Sicilian village life of the 1940s.

Life Is Beautiful (La Vita è bella)
Roberto Benigni, 1997
This sentimental but moving tragicomedy used the muscle of American distributor Miramax to secure Academy Awards® for Best Actor, Score and Foreign Language Film.

Festivals

Venice Film Festival (Mostra Internazionale d'Arte Cinematografia)
Held annually since 1932 (not 1933 or during World War II) in Venice. The world's oldest film festival, now second only to Cannes in industry rankings.
Website: www.labiennale.org/en/cinema/
Top prize: Golden Lion

National awards

Italian Film Academy: Davids

Academy Awards®

Honorary Awards for Foreign Language Film: *Shoeshine* (1946), *Bicycle Thieves* (1948).

Best Foreign Language Film wins: *La Strada* (1954), *Nights of Cabiria* (1957), *8½* (1963), *Yesterday, Today and Tomorrow* (1963), *Investigation of a Citizen Above Suspicion* (1970), *The Garden of the Finzi-Continis* (1970), *Amarcord* (1973), *Cinema Paradiso* (1989), *Mediterraneo* (1991), *Life Is Beautiful* (1997)

Best Foreign Language Film nominations: 26

Other Academy Award® wins: Anna Magnani, Best Actress (*The Rose Tattoo*, 1955), Sophia Loren, Best Actress (*Two Women*, 1960), Piero Gherardi, Best Costumes (*La Dolce vita*, 1960), Piero Gherardi, Best Costumes (*8½*, 1963), Danilo Donati, Best Costumes (*Fellini's Casanova*, 1976), Bernardo Bertolucci, Best Director (*The Last Emperor*, 1987)

Further viewing

Cabiria (1914), *Ossessione* (1942), *Shoeshine* (1946), *La Strada* (1954), *L'Avventura* (1960), *Accatone* (1961), *The Leopard* (1963), *8½* (1963), *The Gospel According to St Matthew* (1964), *Death in Venice* (1971), *Illustrious Corpses* (1976), *Il Postino* (1994), *The Son's Room* (2001)

JAPAN

History

As far as most of the West is concerned, Japanese cinema began when Akira Kurosawa's *Rashomon* (1950) triumphed at the Venice Film Festival. Needless to say, the country had enjoyed a rich screen tradition long before that. Japan's earliest films reflect the influence of Kabuki theatre, with stylized performances and front-on camera placements. During the silent era, highly-paid narrators known as *benshi* described the story from beside the screen, and became so popular that their influence held back the introduction of sound in Japanese cinema until well into the 1930s. This decade marked the industry's first 'golden age', when the dominant story styles were established – period epics (*jidai-geki*), swordplay adventures (*chambara*) and contemporary middle-class dramas (*shomin-geki*). Under the Allied occupation after World War II, feudal and nationalistic subjects were banned, and a wave of period feature films soon swept the world's festivals. Although some younger film-makers responded to the need for a more contemporary, youth-oriented cinema in the 1960s, the industry suffered an artistic decline and began churning out so-called 'pink' sex films. Over the next few decades, these became more openly erotic and violently extreme, forgoing art in favour of commercial success.

The industry today

Fantasy, often with a cruel edge, dominates Japanese production in animation and horror formats. The country is now one of the key markets for Hollywood blockbusters, but audiences remain loyal to home-made films.

Key figures

Kon Ichikawa (1915–   )

Director whose taste for ironic comedy and satire of post-war society darkened after his bleak anti-war drama *The Burmese Harp* (1956).

Shohei Imamura (1926–   )

Director of influential documentaries and features which often highlight the everyday lives of women, the young and the poor, and who won the Cannes Palme d'Or late in his career with *The Eel* (1997).

Takeshi Kitano (1947–   )

Actor and director, famous in his homeland as stand-up comedian and TV presenter 'Beat' Takeshi, whose work includes tough genre films (*Violent Cop*, 1989), sumptuous arthouse (*Dolls*, 2002) and samurai action (*Zatoichi*, 2003).

Akira Kurosawa (1910–98)

Director whose humanist world view filters through his samurai films and contemporary dramas of the 1940s–60s, but who went on to make period epics in the 1980s and smaller, more personal tales the following decade.

Inspired by Kurosawa

Some of Akira Kurosawa's films have famously been remade as westerns, with *Seven Samurai* (1954) becoming *The Magnificent Seven* (1960) and *Yojimbo* (1961) becoming *A Fistful of Dollars* (1964). US film-maker George Lucas has stated that Kurosawa's *Hidden Fortress* (1958) – with its story of a general, a princess and two comedy peasants travelling through enemy territory – was a major influence on Lucas's own *Star Wars* (1977).

Toshirô Mifune (1920–97)

Actor with a wide range and imposing screen presence, best known in the West for playing samurai warriors in the films of Akira Kurosawa.

Takashi Miike (1960–   )

Incredibly prolific director who often makes three or four low-budget films each year, tackling sex and violence taboos in crime, horror and sci-fi exploitation genres.

Kenji Mizoguchi (1898–1956)

Director, noted for his characteristically long takes, whose films often examine women's place in Japanese society past and present, from feudal exploitation to post-war liberation.

Nagisa Oshima (1932–   )

Leading director of the 1960s New Wave whose early, politicized films criticized Japanese society, and whose fascination with extremes of sex and violence hit a peak with *In the Realm of the Senses (Ai no corrida)* (1976).

Yasujiro Ozu (1903–63)
Director whose greatest films use static, low camera angles and a quiet, contemplative style to examine the effects of post-war changes on Japanese traditions and the family unit.

Key films

Rashomon (Rashômon)
Akira Kurosawa, 1950
The film that opened Western eyes to Japanese cinema examines the subjective nature of truth, telling the story of a rape and murder from four different perspectives.

Tokyo Story (Tokyo monogatari)
Yasujiro Ozu, 1953
This story of an elderly couple who are neglected by their busy children, but receive love and comfort from their son's widow, highlights the widening generation gap in post-war Japan.

Godzilla (Gojira)
Ishirô Hondo, 1954
The first of the long-running monster movie series, in which a dinosaur-like creature, awakened by an atom bomb, goes on the rampage and leaves cities in ruins, reflects the effects on the Japanese psyche of the Hiroshima and Nagasaki nuclear attacks.

Sansho the Bailiff (Sansho dayu)
Kenji Mizoguchi, 1954
This poetic tale of the wife and children of an 11th-century governor, who are kidnapped and separated for 20 years, examines the human response to suffering and the nature of mercy.

Seven Samurai (Shichinin no samurai)
Akira Kurosawa, 1954
Probably the most famous Japanese film, and one of the greatest action films ever – remade in western form as *The Magnificent Seven* (1960) – follows the exploits of a band of samurai hired by farmers to defend their village from bandits.

An Actor's Revenge (Yukinojo henge)
Kon Ichikawa, 1963
The influence of Kabuki theatre on Japanese cinema is still evident in this 1960s classic, in which Kazuo Hasegawa reprises the dual roles (a gangster and a stage actor) that he first played in 1935.

In the Realm of the Senses (Ai no corrida)
Nagisa Oshima, 1976
The boundary between sexual pain and pleasure is explored in a sometimes shocking film that was attacked by censors but praised by critics, who noted its gender equality.

Akira
Katsuhiro Ôtomo, 1988
This bold blend of thrilling visuals and a complicated plot, involving psychic children

and man-machines in post-Armageddon Tokyo, began a flood of *anime* (cartoon features) and *manga* (comics) to the West.

Ring (Ringu)
Hideo Nakata, 1998
Based on Koji Suzuki's novel about a videotape that kills viewers a week after they watch it, this was the highest-grossing horror film in Japanese history, its blend of ghost story and urban myth influencing the genre worldwide.

Festivals

Tokyo International Film Festival
Held annually since 1985 (biennially until 1991) in Tokyo. Asia's largest film festival, dedicated to supporting new and Asian film-makers.
Website: www.tiff-jp.net
Top prize: Governor of Tokyo Award

Academy Awards®

Honorary Awards for Foreign Language Film: *Rashomon* (1950), *Gate of Hell* (1953), *Master Swordsman* (1954)
Best Foreign Language Film wins: 0
Best Foreign Language Film nominations: 11
Other Academy Award® wins: Miyoshi Umeki, Best Supporting Actor (*Sayonara*, 1957), Ryuichi Sakamoto, Best Original Score (*The Last Emperor*, 1987), Akira Kurosawa, Honorary Award, 1990, Best Animated Feature (*Spirited Away*, 2001)

Further viewing

A Page of Madness (1926), *I Was Born, But...* (1932), *Late Spring* (1949), *Ikiru* (1952), *The Life of Oharu* (1952), *Gate of Hell* (1953), *Ugetsu monogatari* (1953), *The Burmese Harp* (1956), *Yojimbo* (1961), *Onibaba* (1964), *Ran* (1985), *Sonatine* (1993), *Audition* (1999), *Spirited Away* (2001)

MEXICO

History

Mexican cinema has always been responsive to popular demand. Early audiences flocked to see silent reels featuring actual footage of revolutionary folk hero Pancho Villa; then, in the 1940s, the industry flourished by producing melodramas starring Dolores del Rio and comedies starring the clown Cantinflas. In the decades that followed, cheap horror films and the bizarre spectacle of masked crime-fighting wrestler Santo filled the screens. Political changes in the early 1970s introduced state funding to provide a balance to the commercial mainstream, launching the careers of directors Arturo Ripstein, Jaime Humberto Hermosillo and Jorge Fons. Sex comedies and action films continued to dominate local production, but continued state support in the 1990s provided a springboard to Hollywood for the likes of Afonso Cuarón and Guillermo Del Toro – directors of, respectively, *Harry Potter and the Prisoner of Azkaban* (2004) and *Hellboy* (2004).

The industry today

After the international success of *Amores perros* (2000), Mexico proved it could make films that pleased both domestic and international markets, following up with *Y tu mamá también* (2001) and *The Crime of Father Amaro* (2002). On the arthouse circuit, the films of Carlos Reygadas – *Japón* (2002) and *Battle in Heaven* (2005) – and multi-Ariel Award winner *Duck Season* (2004) have created a buzz.

Key figures

Gael García Bernal (1978–)
Actor who was still studying in London when he was cast in *Amores perros* (2000), and who became the poster boy for the booming Latin American cinema, starring in *Y tu mamá también* (2001) and as Che Guevara in *The Motorcycle Diaries* (2004).

Emilio Fernández (1903–86)
Veteran director and actor (nicknamed 'El Indio') who aimed to create a wholly indigenous cinema, collaborating with cinematographer Gabriel Figuerora on many films including Mexico's first recognized classic, *María Candelaria* (1944).

Salma Hayek (1966–)
Actress who languished in bit-parts before Robert Rodriguez's action movie *Desperado* (1995) opened the door to Hollywood and better roles, including her Academy Award®-nominated turn as artist Frida Kahlo in *Frida* (2002), which she also produced.

Arturo Ripstein (1943–)
Director who rose to fame in the 1970s, showing a fascination for low-life characters and an understanding of the deeper social significance of popular genres.

Key films

Los Olvidados (The Young and the Damned)
Luis Buñuel, 1950
The highlight of Buñuel's stay in Mexico, and the film that brought him back to international prominence, is this juvenile delinquent film that unsentimentally refuses to blame society for its characters' repellent behaviour.

El Topo (The Mole)
Alejandro Jodorowsky, 1971
Ambiguous violent and sexual imagery made this film – part art film, part spaghetti western – an instant cult classic in the early 1970s.

Like Water for Chocolate (Como agua para chocolate)
Alfonso Arau, 1991
A distinctively Latin American flavour of magic realism permeates this popular love story about a girl who cooks for her former sweetheart, now married to her sister.

Amores perros
Alejandro González Iñárritu, 2000
Mexican cinema grabbed the world's attention once again with this fast and furious portrait of different levels of society in Mexico City, told in three linked stories.

The Netherlands

Festivals

Guadalajara International Film Festival
Held annually since 1985 in Guadalajara. Showcase for Mexican films, now also covering Ibero-American film in general.
Website: www.guadalajaracinemafest.com
Top prize: Mayahuel Awards

National awards

Academia Mexicana de Artes y Ciencias Cinematográficas: Ariels

Academy Awards®

Best Foreign Language Film wins: 0
Best Foreign Language Film nominations: 6
Other Academy Award® wins: Anthony Quinn, Best Supporting Actor (*Viva Zapata!*, 1952), Anthony Quinn, Best Supporting Actor (*Lust for Life*, 1956).

Further viewing

María Candelaria (1944), *The Exterminating Angel* (1962), *Doña Herlinda and Her Son* (1986), *Cronos* (1993), *Deep Crimson* (1996), *Y tu mamá también* (2001)

The Original Oscar

Although it's known as Oscar®, the Academy Award® statuette was actually modelled on Mexican actor and director Emilio Fernandez, who posed naked for designer Cedric Gibbons after being introduced to him by actress Dolores del Rio.

THE NETHERLANDS

History

The avant-garde shorts and documentaries of Joris Ivens first brought the Netherlands to the attention of cinema audiences in the 1920s. That documentary baton was passed on to Bert Haanstra in the 1950s, leading to what was effectively a national school of non-fiction film-making. Perhaps unsurprisingly for a country scarred by German occupation during World War II, the Netherlands' feature films have traditionally focused on themes of war and patriotism. In the 1980s, a new generation of directors attempted to reach out to a wider international market through the mainstream thriller genre. Unfortunately for the local industry, the most successful names – Rutger Hauer, Jan De Bont, Paul Verhoeven – were quickly lured to Hollywood.

The industry today

Dutch cinema lacks a strong individual identity – and a strong single figure to lead it. Co-productions with Belgium and Germany, brought about mainly because of language similarities, keep it ticking over.

Key figures

Jan De Bont (1943–)
Cinematographer who turned director with *Speed* (1994), and who favours glossy action movies in both career capacities.

Rutger Hauer (1944–)
Actor who starred in several of Paul Verhoeven's Dutch films before attracting international notice as the spiky blond-haired villain in *Blade Runner* (1982).

Paul Verhoeven (1938–)
Director whose films at home and in Hollywood – including *Turkish Delight* (1973), *RoboCop* (1987) and *Showgirls* (1995) – reflect twin obsessions with sex and violence.

Key films

Spetters
Paul Verhoeven, 1980
Verhoeven's best Dutch film mixes the thrills of an exploitative youth movie with a close study of working-class, small-town dreams.

The Assault (De Aanslag)
Fons Rademakers, 1986
The trauma of wartime occupation is expressed in this story of a man who suffers guilty flashbacks to his family's execution by the Nazis.

The Vanishing (Spoorloos)
George Sluizer, 1988
This harrowing thriller, about a man tormented by the psychopath who abducted his wife, was less successfully remade five years later in the USA by the same director.

Antonia's Line (Antonia)
Marleen Gorris, 1995
Touches of magic realism and feminism enhance this engrossing family saga, which follows five generations of women from a rural Dutch community.

Festivals

International Film Festival Rotterdam
Held annually since 1972 in Rotterdam. Major European film festival with an emphasis on arthouse cinema.
Website: www.filmfestivalrotterdam.com
Top prize: Tiger Awards

Academy Awards[®]

Best Foreign Language Film wins: *The Assault* (1986), *Antonia's Line* (1995), *Character* (1997)
Best Foreign Language Film nominations: 7
Other Academy Award[®] wins: Herman Rosse, Best Art Direction (*The King of Jazz*, 1930)

Further viewing

Soldier of Orange (1977), *The Girl with the Red Hair* (1981), *The Fourth Man* (1983), *Amsterdamned* (1988), *The Northerners* (1992), *Twin Sisters* (2002)

NEW ZEALAND

History

As part of the British Empire, and subsequently the British Commonwealth, New Zealand had no indigenous film culture to speak of until the end of the 1970s. Prior to that, a handful of independently produced features by the likes of John O'Shea and Paul Maunder were mostly ignored by local audiences, who flocked instead to imported films from the UK and USA. After the relative success of Roger Donaldson's *Sleeping Dogs* in 1977, however, a national cinema developed that reflected the country's dissatisfaction with the darker corners of its past and present. Many films emphasized the mental pressures of life on these isolated, insular, politically conservative islands, and roads and journeys frequently served as metaphors for freedom. Since the late 1980s, the Maori community has been examining its identity on screen, as seen in the internationally acclaimed *Once Were Warriors* (1993) and *Whale Rider* (2003).

The industry today

The phenomenal success of *The Lord of the Rings* (2001–3) trilogy of films has opened the door to international productions keen to use New Zealand's spectacular scenery as ready-made backdrops. Furthermore, the groundbreaking work of New Zealand-based Weta Digital on the Tolkien epics has challenged California's domination of the computer effects industry.

Key figures

Jane Campion (1954–   )
Director whose films, from *The Piano* (1993) to *In the Cut* (2003), often feature nonconformist heroines determinedly battling against hostile environments.

Russell Crowe (1964–   )
Academy Award®-winning actor who has brought a tough physicality to his roles ever since his breakthrough as a skinhead in *Romper Stomper* (1992).

Peter Jackson (1961–   )
Director, producer and writer whose early gory horror films – *Bad Taste* (1987), *Braindead* (1992) – are at the opposite end of the budget spectrum from his phenomenally successful *The Lord of the Rings* trilogy (2001–3) and *King Kong* remake (2005).

Bruno Lawrence (1941–95)
English-born actor who was regularly cast as a troubled loner in films including *Smash Palace* (1982) and *The Quiet Earth* (1985).

Key films

Sleeping Dogs
Roger Donaldson, 1977
Donaldson's vision of a totalitarian future, complete with over-zealous riot police and revolutionary guerillas, inspired a wave of modern New Zealand film-making.

Goodbye Pork Pie
Geoff Murphy, 1980
This rough and ready comedy-cum-road movie about two buddies and a stolen car was the first New Zealand film to recoup its costs at the domestic box office.

An Angel at My Table
Jane Campion, 1990
This screen version of autobiographical works by the poet Janet Frame uses an intimate, unadorned style to examine the connection between mental illness and creative genius.

Once Were Warriors
Lee Tamahori, 1993
One in three New Zealanders were thought to have seen this uncompromising portrayal of domestic violence and cultural dispossession in the Maori community.

The Lord of the Rings trilogy
Peter Jackson, 2001–3
Released in three parts (*The Fellowship of the Ring*, *The Two Towers*, *The Return of the King*) over consecutive years, this faithful adaptation of Tolkien's trilogy rejuvenated epic and fantasy cinema by pushing the boundaries of computer effects.

Festivals

Auckland International Film Festival
Held annually since July in Auckland. New Zealand's oldest, non-competitive film festival.
Website: www.enzedff.co.nz

Academy Awards®

Best Picture wins: *The Lord of the Rings: The Return of the King* (2003)
Best Picture nominations: *The Lord of the Rings: The Fellowship of the Ring* (2001), *The Lord of the Rings: The Two Towers* (2002)
Other Academy Award® wins: Jane Campion, Best Original Screenplay (*The Piano*, 1993), Russell Crowe, Best Actor (*Gladiator*, 2000), Peter Jackson, Best Director (*The Lord of the Rings: The Return of the King*, 2003).

Further viewing

Smash Palace (1982), *Utu* (1983), *Vigil* (1984), *Braindead* (1992), *Crush* (1992), *Romper Stomper* (1992), *Heavenly Creatures* (1994), *Whale Rider* (2002)

An Alien Concept

Film-maker Vincent Ward, who directed *Vigil* (1984) and *The Navigator* (1988), also worked for a while on the troubled production of *Alien³* (1992). His idea – to set the film on a man-made planet inhabited by monks and covered with wood – didn't make it to the screen, but he retains a 'story' credit on the finished film.

NORTH AFRICA

History

Although Hollywood has set numerous stories in mummies' tombs and exotic kasbahs, the only area of North Africa to have a viable film industry before World War II was Egypt. Egyptian studios, including Studio Misr – the first production facility in all of Africa, founded in Cairo in 1935 – churned out escapist musicals, comedies and melodramas for their Arab neighbours for several decades. Progress was much slower in other countries in the region, although Algeria, Tunisia and Morocco found a burst of inspiration following their independence from France. A New Arab Cinema manifesto was published at the 1972 Damascus Film Festival with the aim of creating a broad, post-colonial Arab culture through the medium of film. However, war in the Middle East stifled these ideals, with only Iran (see separate subsection) creating a sustainable industry with its own distinct style.

The industry today

The rise of Islamic fundamentalism has had a negative effect on the cinema industry in virtually every part of North Africa, forcing several key film-makers into exile and closing down local productions and cinema screens.

Key figures

Merzak Allouache (1944–)
Algerian writer-director who reached international audiences with *Bab El-Oued City* (1994) and *Salut Cousin!* (1996), and who now works in exile in France.

Youssef Chahine (1926–)
Egypt's most important director, also an actor, who followed groundbreaking melodrama *Cairo Station* (1958) with a series of films that examined Arab history and society, reaching a high point with a Cannes Palme d'Or win for *Destiny* (1997).

Salah Abu Seif (1915–96)
Prolific director, regarded as the forefather of Egyptian cinema, who brought an early touch of realism into the country's popular genres in the 1940s and 1950s.

Omar Sharif (1932–)
Egyptian actor who became a major star in his home country in the 1950s before achieving international stardom with *Lawrence of Arabia* (1962).

From Cards to Computers

Before packing his cards away in his seventies, actor Omar Sharif was a world-class tournament bridge player. As well as writing several books and newspaper columns on the subject, he has licensed his name for a computer game tie-in.

Moufida Tlatli (1947–)
Tunisian director whose directorial debut, *The Silences of the Palace* (1994), used a measured pace to capture the rhythms of Arab women's lives.

Key films

The Will (El Azima)
Kamal Selim, Egypt, 1939
One of Egyptian cinema's biggest hits presented working-class Cairo in a much more realistic light than the American and French kasbah-themed films of the day.

Cairo Station (Bab al-hadid)
Youssef Chahine, Egypt, 1958
Arab melodrama comes of age in this story of a newspaper seller infatuated with a drinks vendor, set in a bustling railway station whose richly woven minor characters form a microcosm of Egyptian society.

The Battle of Algiers
Gillo Pontecorvo, Algeria/Italy, 1965
This remarkable reconstruction of Algeria's struggle for independence does not gloss over the French Army's torture methods or the guerillas' violent revolutionary tactics.

Z
Costa-Gavras, Algeria/France, 1968
Algeria's sole Academy Award®-winner is actually a French-language political thriller about the murder of a pacifist leader in Greece.

Chronicle of the Years of Embers
Mohammed Lakhdar-Hamina, Algeria, 1975
Arab cinema appeared to be on the verge of greatness when this three-hour Algerian independence epic, which follows a peasant from his drought-stricken village into the arms of the revolution, won the Palme d'Or at Cannes.

Bab El-Oued City
Merzak Allouache, Algeria, 1994
This winner of the International Critics' Prize at Cannes attacks the rise of violent Islamic extremism through the story of a man who tears down a mosque loudspeaker positioned on the top of his apartment.

Festivals

Journées Cinématographiques de Carthage (Carthage Film Festival)
Held biennially since 1966 in Tunis. Landmark festival bringing together Arab and African cinema.
Website: www.carthage2004.org
Top prize: Tanit d'Or

Academy Awards®

Best Foreign Language Film wins: *Z* (co-production with Algeria and France, 1969).
Best Foreign Language Film nominations: 3

Further viewing

The Citadel (1988), *Halfaouine* (1990), *The Silences of the Palace* (1994), *Destiny* (1997), *West Beirut* (1998), *Fatma* (2001)

NORWAY

History

During the 1930s Norway enjoyed a golden decade of film-making, peppered with literary adaptations starring theatre actors. Despite censorship demands, the industry flourished under German occupation during World War II, although cinema 'collaborators', including director Leif Sindling, found it difficult to restart their careers in peacetime. Enjoying more generous state subsidies than its Scandinavian neighbours, Norway produced a series of worthy political features in the 1970s, but in the following decade the public increasingly began to favour action movies and comedies that stuck to a Hollywood model.

The industry today

On the back of acclaim for *Elling* (2001) and *Kitchen Stories* (2003), Norway's film industry is performing better at home as well as abroad, breaking away from mainstream genres.

Key figures

Rasmus Breistein (1890–1976)
Director credited with establishing the first truly Norwegian body of film work, including the country's first home-produced literary adaptation, *Fante-Anne* (1920).

Arne Skouen (1913– 2003)
Writer-director of 17 feature films who fled wartime occupation but returned home in 1946, turning from novels to films three years later.

Liv Ullmann (1938–   )
Actress who is best known for her collaborations with Swedish director Ingmar Bergman, whose script *Faithless* she directed in 2000.

Nine Lives (Ni liv)
Arne Skouen, 1957
Academy Award®-nominated war adventure about a wounded Norwegian commando who battles the elements and German patrols as he escapes over the border to Sweden.

Wives (Hustruer)
Anja Breien, 1975
Three 30-year-old women head out on a spree in this feminist comedy, co-written by the director and actresses, which was followed by sequels in 1985 and 1996.

Pathfinder (Veiviseren)
Nils Gaup, 1987
The first film to be made in the Sami language, this story of a young boy avenging the murder of his family by raiders brings a touch of Nordic myth to the western formula.

Insomnia
Erik Skjoldbjærg, 1997
Stellan Skarsgård plays a homicide cop with a guilty conscience in the original version of this thriller, which was later remade in Hollywood.

Norwegian International Film Festival
Held annually across Norway since 1973 and in Haugesund since 1987. International festival with New Nordic Films market.
Website: www.filmfestivalen.no
Top prize: Amanda Awards

Best Foreign Language Film wins: 0
Best Foreign Language Film nominations: 4
Other Academy Award® wins: Best Documentary Feature (*Kon-Tiki*, 1950)

Little Ida (1981), *Orion's Belt* (1985), *Kristin Lavransdattir* (1995), *Junk Mail* (1997)

POLAND

Despite producing such leading names in animation as Wladyslaw Starewicz and Walerian Borowczyk, Polish cinema did not attract the world's attention until the 1950s. For a few years after the death of Stalin in 1953, Polish film-makers turned away from Communist-sponsored socialist realism in search of more personal ways of re-examining history. Andrzej Munk and Jerzy Kawalerowicz received acclaim at home and abroad, but the key director of the period was Andrzej Wajda, whose war trilogy – *A Generation* (1955), *Kanal* (1957) and *Ashes and Diamonds* (1958)

– is a landmark of eastern European cinema. Wajda came to the fore again in the 1970s with the so-called 'Cinema of Moral Unrest', a movement that infuriated the authorities with its unflinching examinations of corruption in modern-day Poland. Indeed, until political changes in the 1990s, many of Poland's brightest talents – Roman Polanski and Jerzy Skolimowski among them – were forced to work in exile.

The industry today

The collapse of Communism means that although Polish film-makers have more artistic freedom, they also have less readily available funding to express it. The few production starts each year tend to stick to safe commercial genres.

Key figures

Zbigniew Cybulski (1927–67)
Actor, described as 'the Polish James Dean', whose aggressive yet vulnerable screen style in *Ashes and Diamonds* (1958) made him the idol of his generation.

Agnieszka Holland (1948–   )
Director, some of whose bleak political films were banned in Poland in the 1980s, causing her to move to western Europe and the USA.

Krzysztof Kieslowski (1941–96)
Director and writer whose films show a remarkable sensitivity and understanding of human nature, from his Polish films about ordinary lives under Communism to the *Three Colours* trilogy (1993–4), one of the great masterworks of European cinema.

Roman Polanski (1933–   )
Director and actor whose films, including *Rosemary's Baby* (1968) and *Chinatown* (1974), typically focus on the fears and desires of the individual. He won a Best Director Academy Award® for *The Pianist* (2002), which drew upon his own traumatic experience of wartime.

Andrzej Wajda (1926–   )
Leading director of the 'Polish school' in the 1950s and the 'Cinema of Moral Unrest' in the 1970s; his films combine politics, symbolism and a doomed romanticism.

Key films

Ashes and Diamonds (Popiół i diament)
Andrzej Wajda, 1958
The final part of Wajda's 'war trilogy' (after *A Generation* (1955) and *Kanal* (1957)) presents a complex portrait of a nation tearing itself apart, through a story of two underground fighters sent to kill a visiting communist leader.

Knife in the Water (Nóz w wodzie)
Roman Polanski, 1962
Polanski's only feature in his native tongue creates a claustrophobic, menacing mood, as a married couple and a drifter play tense mind games on a boat.

Man of Iron (Człowiek z żelaza)
Andrzej Wajda, 1981
Reflecting the political changes of its time, Wajda's follow-up to *Man of Marble* (1976) finds a hack journalist writing a smear campaign about a Solidarity activist.

A Short Film about Killing (Krótki film o zabijaniu)
Krzysztof Kieslowski, 1988
Expanded from the director's ten-part television work *Dekalog* (1988), this grim parable draws parallels between the brutal murder of a taxi driver and the state's hanging of the boy who committed the crime.

Festivals

Warsaw International Film Festival
Held annually since 1985 in Warsaw. International festival with special focus on new films and directors.
Website: www.wff.pl
Top prize: Grand Prix

National awards

Polish Film Academy: Eagle (Orly)

Academy Awards®

Best Foreign Language Film wins: 0
Best Foreign Language Film nominations: 7
Other Academy Award® wins: Janusz Kaminski, Best Cinematography (*Schindler's List*, 1993), Janusz Kaminski, Best Cinematography (*Saving Private Ryan*, 1998), Andrzej Wajda, Honorary Award, 2000, Roman Polanski, Best Director (*The Pianist*, 2002)

Further viewing

A Generation (1955), *Man on the Track* (1956), *Kanal* (1957), *Man of Marble* (1976), *The Interrogation* (1981), *The Double Life of Véronique* (1992), *Crows* (1994)

RUSSIA

History

In the years following the 1917 Russian Revolution, film became the Bolsheviks' most powerful weapon for propaganda and education. Agit-prop trains toured the country, showing newsreels and documentaries to a population that was two-thirds illiterate and therefore eager to lap up the silent images. During the 1920s, Russian film-makers were the first to embrace the unique possibilities of cinematic 'montage'. In the hands of Lev Kuleshov, Sergei Eisenstein and Vsevolod Pudovkin, editing became a means of manipulating time and space, guiding the emotions of the audience and creating symbolic meanings by placing specific images one after the other. However, towards the end of the decade and during the 1970s, 'socialist realism' with its idealized characters and earnest histories, was the only style sanctioned by the state. The few exceptions to this rule remained banned until the *glasnost* era of the 1980s. Younger film-makers then rushed to present modern life in a more sombre and realistic light, creating the dark, pessimistic and graphic genre known as *chernukha*.

The industry today

Private finance has been slow to replace state funding in Russia and the republics of the former Soviet Union, and production has been drastically reduced as a result. However, the abrasive films of Alexei Balabanov and Sergei Bodrov, and the international success of the horror film *Night Watch* (2004), offer hope for the future of the industry.

Key figures

Alexander Dovzhenko (1894–1956)
The greatest poet among the Soviet directors of the 1920s; his lyrical films – including *Arsenal* (1929) and *Earth* (1930) – reveal an obsession with death.

Sergei Eisenstein (1898–1948)
Director whose immensely influential theories on editing suited his silent political films, and who created a number of historical epics.

Elim Klimov (1933–2003)
Director of the harrowing war film *Come and See* (1985) who also arranged for the release of many previously banned films when he was Secretary of the Union of Film-makers during President Mikhail Gorbachev's *glasnost* era.

Sergei Paradjanov (1924–90)
Director, imprisoned in the 1970s, who used the folk culture, art and poetry of Georgia and Armenia to create sumptuous feasts of visual imagery in *Shadows of Our Forgotten Ancestors* (1964) and *The Colour of Pomegranates* (1968).

Vsevolod Pudovkin (1893–1953)
Director who developed a theory of unobtrusive editing in three key silent films – *Mother* (1926), *The End of St Petersburg* (1927) and *Storm over Asia* (1928).

Alexander Sokurov (1951–)
Director whose quiet, impressionistic films – including a trilogy on Hitler, Lenin and Hirohito – have a uniquely spiritual quality brought about by their distinctive 'processed' look and distorted frames.

Andrei Tarkovsky (1932–86)
Director whose seven deeply personal and spiritual feature films pose metaphysical questions about memory and the human condition.

Dziga Vertov (1896–1954)
Polish-born director who rejected fictional films in favour of newsreels and documentaries, broadening the language of early film with split screens, freeze-frames and superimposed shots.

A Working Holiday

When Soviet director and 'montage' mastermind Sergei Eisenstein visited Hollywood in 1930, he kept busy. The film-maker played tennis with Charlie Chaplin, considered pitching a screen version of James Joyce's *Ulysses* to studios, struck up a friendship with fervent anti-Communist Walt Disney and was even photographed shaking hands with capitalist icon Mickey Mouse.

Key films

Battleship Potemkin (Bronenosets Potyomkin)
Sergei Eisenstein, 1925
Widely regarded as one of the most important and influential films ever made, this story of a sailors' uprising and the subsequent slaughter of innocent citizens by tsarist soldiers uses radical editing techniques to add symbolic weight to its plot.

Mother (Mat)
Vsevolod Pudovkin, 1926
With stronger characterization than most Soviet silents, Pudovkin's masterpiece illustrates the supposed equality of women under the Bolsheviks through the story of a mother who becomes politically motivated after unwittingly betraying her son and his comrades.

Man with a Movie Camera (Chelovek s kino-apparatom)
Dziga Vertov, 1929
Vertov uses a wide array of early cinematic techniques and tricks to capture the dynamic rhythm of Moscow city life in one of the most influential documentaries in film history.

Earth (Zemlya)
Alexander Dovzhenko, 1930
Propaganda meets poetry in this story of wealthy landowners who resort to murder to stop a village collective from destroying boundary fences.

Ivan the Terrible (Ivan Grozny)
Sergei Eisenstein, 1944/1946
Eisenstein's operatic two-part account of the rise, betrayal and revenge of Ivan IV, Russia's first tsar, features spectacular set pieces and makes use of extreme close-ups.

War and Peace (Voina i mir)
Sergei Bondarchuk, 1967
The most lavish film in Soviet history transforms Tolstoy's novel into a 507-minute, 70mm spectacular, packed with balls, battles and duels (best seen in the Russian original rather than the English dubbed version).

Solaris
Andrei Tarkovsky, 1972
Touted as Russia's answer to *2001: A Space Odyssey* (1968), this enigmatic film, in which a psychiatrist on a space station sees visions of his dead wife, uses its science-fiction setting as a backdrop to a metaphysical study of guilt.

Little Vera (Malenkaya Vera)
Vasili Pichul, 1988
The first film to strip away the gloss from depictions of Russian life became a box-office sensation thanks to its strong heroine, bleak viewpoint and flashes of nudity.

Burnt by the Sun (Utomlennye solntsem)
Nikita Mikhalkov, 1994
Victims and oppressors are treated with equal sympathy in this tragic Academy Award®-winning critique of the Stalin era, when an army hero on holiday with his family is betrayed by his wife's former lover, now an officer in the secret police.

Brother (Brat)
Alexei Balabanov, 1997
The lawlessness of post-Soviet Russia is evident in this downbeat *chernukha* tale of a former soldier who becomes an amoral professional killer in St Petersburg.

Russian Ark
Alexander Sokurov, 2002
Sokurov muses on the nature of the Russian soul and his country's history by moving in a single, unedited take through the Hermitage Museum in St Petersburg, passing carefully choreographed tableaux featuring 2,000 extras.

Festivals

Moscow International Film Festival
Held irregularly since 1959 in Moscow. International festival specializing in films from Russia and the former Soviet Union.
Website: www.miff.ru
Top prize: Golden Saint George

National awards

Russian Academy of Film Arts: Golden Eagles

Academy Awards®

Best Foreign Language Film wins: *War and Peace* (1967), *Dersu Uzala* (1975), *Moscow Does Not Believe in Tears* (1979), *Burnt by the Sun* (1994)
Best Foreign Language Film nominations: 12 (Russia/USSR), 1 (Georgia)
Other Academy Award® wins: Lila Kedrova, Best Supporting Actress (*Zorba the Greek*, 1964)

Further viewing

Strike (1925), *October* (1927), *Alexander Nevsky* (1938), *The Cranes Are Flying* (1958), *Ballad of a Soldier* (1960), *Andrei Rublev* (1969), *King Lear* (1970), *Stalker* (1979), *Come and See* (1985), *Prisoner of the Mountains* (1996), *Night Watch* (2004)

SOUTH AMERICA

History

It's rare that an entire continent is united in its cinematic goals, but that was the case in South America during the late 1960s. At a time when other third world countries were fighting for their independence from colonial powers, the likes of Argentina, Brazil, Chile and Bolivia were undergoing their own political upheavals, but their film industries were rejecting the dominance of foreign films. In 1969, Argentinian film-makers Fernando Solanas and Octavio Getino published their Third Cinema manifesto, proposing an industry that was neither commercial like Hollywood nor auteur-led like Europe, but socially relevant in order to actively engage an indigenous audience. Prior to this, Latin American cinema had concentrated on musicals, newsreels, melodramas and local westerns. Influenced by Italian neorealism and its own folk myths, Brazil had produced exciting works throughout the 1960s with its Cinema Novo movement. Nelson Pereira dos Santos, Ruy Guerra and Glauber Rocha led the way, producing films that revealed the harsh poverty of rural areas and shanty towns. In the 1970s, successive right-wing and military governments cracked down on politicized film-making across Latin America, driving many talented directors into exile.

The industry today

Political liberalization and a small amount of state funding stimulated film production across South America's major countries towards the end of the 20th century. Story subjects and genre styles are now more diverse, and new films from the region are eagerly awaited on the world festival circuit.

Key figures

Hector Babenco (1946–   )
Director, born in Argentina, who captured the rough edges of Brazilian street life in *Pixote* (1981) then reached international audiences with *Kiss of the Spider Woman* (1985).

Miguel Littin (1942–   )
Chilean director whose political drive is evident in the story of a peasant-turned-criminal, *The Jackal of Nahueltoro* (1970), one of the key Third Cinema films he made before working in exile in Mexico after 1973.

Walter Salles (1956–   )
Brazilian-born director whose early documentary work laid the foundation for socially-committed features *Central Station* (1998) and *Behind the Sun* (2001).

Leopoldo Torre Nilsson (1924–78)
Leading Argentinian director of the 1950s and 1960s whose flamboyant dramas were modelled on European auteurs such as Luis Buñuel (see Spain).

Key films

Blood of the Condor (Yawar mallku)
Jorge Sanjines, Bolivia, 1969
Burning with righteous anger, Sanjines' bleak film is a portrait of the persecution
and enforced sterilization of Quechua Indians.

The Battle of Chile (La Batalla de Chile)
Patricio Guzmàn, Chile/Cuba, 1975–9
Shot in the run-up to the US-backed coup that overthrew Salvador Allende,
edited in Cuba over four years and released in three parts, this mammoth political
documentary captures history in the making.

The Official Version (La historia oficial)
Luis Puenzo, Argentina, 1986
This Academy Award®-winning story about a middle-class teacher who discovers
that the parents of the girl she adopted were 'disappeared' by Argentina's military
rulers confronted the guilt of those who feigned ignorance of their country's political
history.

Central Station (Centro do Brasil)
Walter Salles, Brazil, 1998
Salles carried the baton passed on by Cinema Novo with this internationally
successful story about the unlikely friendship between a cynical middle-aged
woman and a street urchin searching for his father.

City of God (Cidade de Deus)
Fernando Meirelles and Katia Lund, Brazil, 2002
This portrait of guns, drugs and the loss of childhood innocence in Rio's slums, or
favelas, spans three decades and is painted with a dynamic visual energy.

The Motorcyle Diaries (Diarios de motocicleta)
Walter Salles, Argentina/Chile/Peru/US/UK/Germany/France, 2004
Production companies from South America and Europe backed this adaptation of
the young Che Guevara's diaries, chronicling his consciousness-raising journey
across the borders of his home continent.

Festivals

Mar del Plata International Film Festival
Held irregularly since 1954 in Mar del Plata, Argentina. Competitive international
festival with special prizes for Latin American films.
Website: www.mardelplatafilmfest.com
Top prize: Gold Astor

Rio de Janeiro Film Festival (Festival do Rio BR)
Held annually since 1999 in Rio de Janeiro, Brazil. Largest film festival in Latin
America, with showcase for the continent's cinema.
Website: www.festivaldoriobr.com.br
Top prize: Non-competitive

Academy Awards®

Best Foreign Language Film wins: *The Official Version* (Argentina, 1985)
Best Foreign Language Film nominations: 5 (Argentina), 4 (Brazil), 1 (Uruguay, but nomination withdrawn)
Other Academy Award® wins: Jorge Drexler, Best Song (*The Motorcycle Diaries*, 2004)

Further viewing

Barren Lives (1963), *Hour of the Furnaces* (1968), *Antonio das Mortes* (1969), *Dona Flor and Her Two Husbands* (1976), *Sur* (1988), *Nine Queens* (2000)

SOUTH KOREA

History

Korea's endless political turmoil throughout the 20th century did not provide enough stability for a film industry to flourish. It is thought that no more than three feature films survive from the period between the Japanese annexation of the country in 1910 and the end of World War II. The post-war split into North Korea and South Korea, followed by the Korean War in the early 1950s, political repression under military rule in the 1970s and the Kwangju Massacre in 1980, further stifled artistic freedom. Formulaic martial arts films, war epics, melodramas and softcore pornography were South Korean cinema's staple ingredients until new laws regarding a quota system introduced in the early 1990s boosted both production and exhibition of indigenous films. A more independently minded group of film-makers began to taste commercial success at the very end of the decade by adopting the action movie model of Hong Kong cinema.

> ### *Extreme Measures*
>
> In 1978 Kim Jong-Il, film fan and son of North Korean dictator Kim Il-Sung, took a drastic approach to strengthening film production in his homeland. He arranged for the kidnap of top South Korean director Shin Sang-ok and his actress wife, forcing them to work north of the border until they managed to escape in 1986.

The industry today

Since the turn of the century, South Korea has emerged from almost nowhere to become one of the most exciting film-making nations in the world. Its arthouse dramas and stylishly violent action films are now much anticipated by audiences at festivals, in the DVD market and – crucially – in South Korea's own cinemas.

Key figures

Im Kwon-taek (1936–   )
South Korea's most internationally respected director, who made popular melodramas in the 1960s and 1970s before turning to more serious political and cultural subjects.

Kim Ki-duk (1960–   )
Director whose early fine art studies are evident in his haunting visual style, but who has earned himself a reputation as the bad boy of Korean cinema with moments of shocking violence in *The Isle* (2000), *Bad Guy* (2001) and *3-Iron* (2004).

Park Chan-wook (1963–   )
Director with remarkable visual flair and a predilection for revenge motifs, who combines dark humour, extreme violence and inventive camera set pieces in the likes of *JSA* (2000), *Sympathy for Mr Vengeance* (2002) and *Oldboy* (2003).

Key films

The Housemaid (Hanyo)
Kim Ki-young, 1960
The over-the-top melodrama of this tale of the seduction of a piano teacher by his new maid shook up the treatment of contemporary subjects in Korean cinema.

Shiri
Kang Jae-gyu, 1999
This high-octane thriller about a female assassin sent from North Korea out-grossed Hollywood's *Titanic* (1997) at the box office, and ushered in a new wave of indigenous commercial hits.

Chunhyang
Im Kwon-taek, 2000
The story of the forbidden love between a courtesan's daughter and the son of a governor became the first Korean film to screen in competition at Cannes.

Oldboy
Park Chan-wook, 2003
Winner of the Grand Jury Prize at the Cannes Film Festival, this tale of a businessman consumed by thoughts of revenge against his kidnappers has a wild visual style to match the extremes of its plot.

Festivals

Pusan International Film Festival
Held annually since 1996 in Pusan. Festival with focus on Asian cinema, also featuring Korean Panorama section.
Website: www.piff.org
Top prize: Asian Film-maker of the Year

National awards

Daejong Awards: Grand Bells

Academy Awards®

Best Foreign Language Film wins: 0
Best Foreign Language Film nominations: 0

Further viewing

Black Republic (1990), *Sopyonje* (1993), *The Day a Pig Fell into the Well* (1996), *Friend* (1999), *Chiwaseon* (2002), *Sympathy for Mr Vengeance* (2002)

SPAIN

History

Prior to World War II, Luis Buñuel was the only significant director to have come out of Spain, and most of his work was done abroad. Culturally speaking, Spain remained one of the poor cousins of European cinema for the majority of the 20th century. This was mainly because of the rigid censorship imposed by General Francisco Franco, whose right-wing Nationalist Party governed the country until his death in 1975. The likes of Juan Antonio Bardem and Luis Garcia Berlanga were lonely neorealist voices in the 1950s, and for decades films such as *Poachers* (1975) and *The Hunt* (1966) were forced to make their criticisms of the Franco regime in coded form. After the abolition of censorship in 1977 the country slowly woke up to the possibilities of a free cinema, no more so than in the flamboyant work of Pedro Almódovar.

The industry today

Younger directors such as Alejandro Amenábar and Alex de la Iglesia are happy to work within audience-friendly genres, while international stars Javier Bardem and Penélope Cruz continue to make films both at home and abroad.

Key figures

Pedro Almodóvar (1951–   )
Director whose melodramas rewrote the rules of Spanish cinematic style, subject matter and gender stereotypes, and whose later work shows increasing complexity.

Javier Bardem (1969–   )
Actor and former professional rugby player who progressed from beefy sex-symbol roles (*Jamón, jamón*, 1992) to become one of the world's leading dramatic actors in *Before Night Falls* (2000) and *The Sea Inside* (2004).

Luis Buñuel (1900–83)
Director who began his career with the Surrealists in Paris before spending long periods in Mexico and France, making satirical films that ceaselessly attacked religion and the bourgeoisie.

Penélope Cruz (1974–   )
Actress whose strong performances in European films, notably *All About My Mother* (1999) and *Don't Move* (2004), have not quite been matched by her Hollywood outings.

Déjà Vu

Alejandro Amenábar's 1997 film *Open Your Eyes* (*Abre los ojos*) was remade in Hollywood by Cameron Crowe as *Vanilla Sky* (2001). Spanish actress Penélope Cruz played the same role – the beautiful, enigmatic Sofia – in both films.

Julio Medem (1958–   )
Director from the Basque region whose elliptical films are characterized by a sense of fate as an inescapable force that binds passionate characters together.

Carlos Saura (1932–)
Director who ran into censorship problems with the films he made under the Franco regime before embarking on a series of flamenco films, beginning with *Blood Wedding* in 1981.

Key films

Viridiana
Luis Buñuel, 1961
Buñuel returned to his homeland to make this perverse satire about a novice nun exploited by the freeloading poor; immediately banned by Franco's censors, it went on to win the Palme d'Or at the Cannes Film Festival.

The Spirit of the Beehive (El Espíritu de la colmena)
Victor Erice, 1973
Childhood fantasy clashes with the deadening effect of Franco's regime in this story of a lonely little girl who imagines that Frankenstein's monster is hiding in a hut near her house.

Carmen
Carlos Saura, 1983
The middle section of Saura's flamenco trilogy – between *Blood Wedding* (1981) and *A Love Bewitched* (1986) – suggests that life imitates art for two dancers who fall in love, just like the characters they're playing.

Women on the Verge of a Nervous Breakdown (Mujeres al borde de un ataque de nervios)
Pedro Almodóvar, 1988
This perfect example of Almodóvar's early work is pop culture run riot, with neurotic characters, exaggerated emotions and absurd comedy played at a farcical pace.

All About My Mother (Todo sobre mi madre)
Pedro Almodóvar, 1999
The maturity noted in Almodóvar's *Talk to Her* (2002) and *Bad Education* (2004) first became apparent in this reworking of Hollywood classic *All About Eve* (1950).

Festivals

Donostia–San Sebastian International Film Festival
Held annually since 1953 in San Sebastian. Major European film festival featuring a focus on Latin American cinema and the 'Zabaltegi' section for new films of different formats, lengths and styles.
Website: www.sansebastianfestival.com
Top prize: Golden Shell

National awards

Academia de las Artes y las Ciencias Cinematográficas de España: Goyas

Academy Awards®

Best Foreign Language Film wins: *To Begin Again* (1982), *Belle Epoque* (1992), *All About My Mother* (1999), *The Sea Inside* (2004)
Best Foreign Language Film nominations: 19
Other Academy Award® wins: Pedro Almodóvar, Best Original Screenplay (*Talk to Her*, 2002)

Further viewing

Land Without Bread (1933), *Bienvenido Mister Marshall* (1953), *The Hunt* (1966), *Ay Carmela!* (1990), *Belle Epoque* (1992), *Jamón, jamón* (1992), *Open Your Eyes* (1997), *Talk to Her* (2002), *The Sea Inside* (2004)

SWEDEN

History

The history of Swedish cinema winds around two names – Victor Sjöström and Ingmar Bergman. Sjöström, along with Mauritz Stiller, raised the artistic threshold of silent cinema before both moved to Hollywood in the early 1920s, on the eve of a decline in Swedish cinema that lasted until World War II. Guilt over the country's wartime neutrality filtered into the films of the late 1940s and 1950s, just at the time that Ingmar Bergman was emerging as a young screenwriter. It was Bergman who, more than anyone, established the international reputation of Swedish cinema as fateful, symbolic and intellectually heavy. A new generation of film-makers, openly influenced by France's Nouvelle Vague movement, came to the fore in the 1960s through the support of the Swedish Film Institute. This was also the period when softcore sex films crept into international markets, sometimes under an 'educational' banner, giving Sweden its reputation for sexual liberty.

The industry today

Around 25 features are now made annually, with domestic films performing strongly at the box office. In Lucas Moodysson – *Together* (2000), *Lilya 4-ever* (2002) – Sweden again has a director whose every film is awaited with anticipation.

Key figures

Ingmar Bergman (1918–)
Sweden's pre-eminent director, whose very personal, symbolic, often anguished films examine major philosophical and moral questions.

Ingrid Bergman (1915–82)
Actress who found great success in Hollywood with *Casablanca* (1942) and *Notorious* (1946), but whose affair with Italian director Roberto Rossellini caused a scandal.

Greta Garbo (1905–90)
Reclusive actress whose luminous beauty shone in silent films and who proved her acting talent in talkies, with Best Actress nominations for *Anna Christie* (1930) and *Romance* (1930).

Sven Nykvist (1922–)
Cinematographer whose ability to create mood through light is at its best in collaboration with Ingmar Bergman, winning him Best Cinematography Academy Awards[®] for *Cries and Whispers* (1972) and *Fanny and Alexander* (1982).

Victor Sjöström (1879–1960)
One of the greatest directors of the silent period in Sweden and Hollywood (where he made *The Wind* with Lillian Gish in 1928), who later returned to acting in Bergman's *Wild Strawberries* (1957).

Stellan Skarsgård (1951–)
Actor who has shown himself to be equally effective in Hollywood studio films, European arthouse films and collaborations with the Danish director Lars von Trier.

Max Von Sydow (1929–)
Actor whose tall, gaunt looks have lent gravitas to characters in films as diverse as *The Seventh Seal* (1957), *The Exorcist* (1973) and *Minority Report* (2002).

Bo Widerberg (1930–97)
Writer-director whose work predominantly focuses on social and political subjects, but who is best known for the prettily photographed romantic tragedy *Elvira Madigan* (1967).

Key films

The Phantom Carriage (Körkarlen)
Victor Sjöström, 1921
With a nod to D W Griffith's classic *Intolerance* (1916), Sjöström pushed the boundaries of silent film by using flashbacks and superimposition in this tale of a drunkard looking back on his misdeeds.

The Seventh Seal (Det sjunde inseglet)
Ingmar Bergman, 1957
Bergman examines his trademark themes of loss of faith and the battle of good against evil in this story of a 12th-century Crusader who holds Death at bay by engaging him in an epic game of chess.

Persona
Ingmar Bergman, 1966
Bergman presents art cinema as psychoanalysis, letting various symbolic images spew forth as the identities of a stage actress and her nurse gradually merge.

I Am Curious – Yellow (Jag är nyfiken – en film i gult)
Vilgot Sjöman, 1967
Scenes of full-frontal nudity in this film helped break down international censorship rules, although the sex is key to understanding the film's political intent.

The Emigrants (Utvandrarna)
Jan Troell, 1971
Personal stories are treated with epic scope in this story of Swedish workers who find a new home in 19th-century America; uniquely, it was Academy Award[®]-nominated for Best Foreign Film in 1972 and Best Picture the following year.

My Life as a Dog (Mit liv som hund)
Lasse Hallström, 1985
Hallström's unsentimental depiction of a boy in 1950s Sweden coping with his mother's terminal illness led to a Best Director Academy Award® nomination.

Festivals

Göteborg Film Festival
Held annually since 1979 in Gothenburg. Scandinavia's most important film festival, including a showcase of new Nordic cinema.
Website: www.filmfestival.org
Top prize: Nordic Film Award

National awards

Swedish Film Institute: Gold Beetle (Guldbagge)

Academy Awards®

Best Foreign Language Film wins: *The Virgin Spring* (1960), *Through a Glass Darkly* (1961), *Fanny and Alexander* (1982).
Best Foreign Language Film nominations: 14
Other Academy Award® wins: Ingrid Bergman, Best Actress (*Gaslight*, 1944), Ingrid Bergman, Best Actress (*Anastasia*, 1956), Ingrid Bergman, Best Supporting Actress (*Murder on the Orient Express*, 1974)

Further viewing

Häxan (1921), *Intermezzo* (1936), *Miss Julie* (1951), *Smiles of a Summer Night* (1955), *Wild Strawberries* (1957), *Raven's End* (1963), *Elvira Madigan* (1967), *Cries and Whispers* (1972), *Fanny and Alexander* (1982), *Together* (2000)

TURKEY

History

Situated between Europe, Asia and the Middle East, Turkey has a cinematic tradition that reflects the dichotomy between the spiritual East and the materialistic West, in terms of both visual style and story content. Between 1965 and 1975, a handful of Turkish companies made popular films (known as Yeşilçam) for the local market, with almost 300 productions made in 1972 alone. These melodramas, action movies and musicals, revolving around star performers, were cheaply made and repetitive. The Turkish film industry suffered a setback during the rise of the home video market in the late 1970s, although a stream of socially conscious films, many from the pen of Yilmaz Güney, gave the nation a distinct screen identity abroad.

The industry today

A flurry of international festival awards for work by Nuri Bilge Ceylan, Zeki Demirkubuz and Fatih Akin has boosted Turkey's cinematic image in recent years. Co-productions with Italy (*Le Fate Ignoranti*, 2001) and Germany (*Lola und Bilidikid*, 1999) have opened new doors to funding.

Key figures

Zeki Demirkubuz (1964–)
Director, producer and writer at the forefront of Turkey's 21st-century art cinema renaissance, whose films – *Fate* (2001), *The Confession* (2002) – are characterized by a minimalist style and an elusive sense of happiness.

Yilmaz Güney (1937–84)
Former mainstream actor and left-wing director who achieved greater fame as screenwriter of *The Herd* (1978), *The Enemy* (1979) and *Yol* (1982), which he wrote in prison while serving an 18-year sentence for murder.

Türkan Soray (1945–)
Actress, nicknamed 'Sultan', who was at her height as *Yeşilçam*'s most famous screen diva in the late 1960s and early 1970s, usually playing a virtuous woman in love stories.

Key films

Yol (The Way)
Serif Gören, 1982
Turkey's most famous film, scripted by Yilmaz Güney and winner of the Palme d'Or at the Cannes Film Festival, tells the story of five convicts who encounter a hostile, unforgiving society while on a week's home leave.

The Turkish Bath (Hamam)
Ferzan Ozpetek, 1997
The film that opened new Turkish cinema to a wider international audience follows an Italian man to Istanbul, where he investigates a Turkish bath left to him in a will.

Uzak (Distant)
Nuri Bilge Ceylan, 2002
Double award-winner at the Cannes Film Festival (Best Actor, Grand Jury Prize) about a photographer and his unwelcome house guest, shot in a static, minimalist style.

Festivals

International Istanbul Film Festival
Held annually since 1982 in Istanbul. World cinema festival focusing on films dealing with the arts.
Website: www.iksv.org/film
Top prize: Golden Tulip

Academy Awards®

Best Foreign Language Film wins: 0
Best Foreign Language Film nominations: 0

Further viewing

The Herd (1978), *Vizontele* (2000), *Fate* (2001), *Head-On* (2004)

UNITED KINGDOM

History

In the early decades of British cinema, there was considerable overlap between stage and screen. As moving-picture reels became a music-hall attraction in the late 19th century, the theatre provided not only plays for adaptation, but also the actors to appear in them. Classically trained performers such as Ralph Richardson and John Gielgud moved on from stage productions of Shakespeare to appear in films that defined British cinema as literate and not wholly cinematic, while music-hall stars such as George Formby and Gracie Fields carried their fan bases with them to the big screen. In 1927, the Quota Act raised the number of British films that should be shown in British cinemas, leading to a flood of poor-quality product known as 'quota quickies'. American studios funded productions shot in British studios, but when they retreated during World War II, a talented group of home-grown film-makers was finally able to fill the breach.

As television ownership became the norm in the 1950s, cinema played to mainstream tastes: this was the era of Ealing comedies, routine war films and crime thrillers, the horror output of Hammer Studios and the saucy humour of the *Carry On* series. It was only when the British New Wave followed theatre's 'Angry Young Man' explosion at the end of the decade that audiences were offered films which, in terms of regional identity, class and accent, reflected their own lives. In the 1980s, the desire to compete against Hollywood saw the rise and fall of spectacular period epics, although a sideline in handsome heritage films continues to find markets at home and abroad. Romantic comedies and cockney crime flicks were a more successful formula during the 1990s.

The industry today

British films struggle to find screen space in cinemas choked with Hollywood product. Production-wise, when not making strong, low-budget, socially realistic dramas, UK film-makers still tend to be looking with an unashamedly commercial eye for the next *Four Weddings and a Funeral* (1994), *The Full Monty* (1997) or *Lock, Stock and Two Smoking Barrels* (1998).

Key figures

Sir Richard Attenborough (1923–)
Actor, director and champion of the British film industry, whose work behind the camera – such as *Gandhi* (1982) and *Chaplin* (1992) – reflects his fascination with outstandingly individual figures.

Sir Michael Caine (1933–)
Actor with a deceptively impassive screen presence and a prolific work rate that has seen him appear in turkeys (*Jaws: The Revenge*, 1987) as well as cult classics (*The Italian Job*, 1969).

Sir Sean Connery (1930–)
Actor who found fame as cinema's first James Bond, a role which has overshadowed strong performances in the likes of *The Hill* (1965) and *The Untouchables* (1987).

Peter Greenaway (1942–)
Director who uses cinema as an artist's medium, rejecting narrative in favour of visual patterns in the likes of *A Zed and Two Noughts* (1985), and whose early films used the rhythmic music of Michael Nyman to distinctive effect.

Sir Alec Guinness (1914–2000)
Actor and Ealing Studios stalwart with a chameleon-like ability to mould himself to any role, from Fagin in *Oliver Twist* (1948) to the intense colonel in *The Bridge on the River Kwai* (1957) and the noble Obi-Wan Kenobi in *Star Wars* (1977).

Sir Alfred Hitchcock (1899–1980)
Director whose taste for the macabre and ability to construct tense set pieces was evident in his early British work, notably *The Lodger* (1926) and *The Ring* (1927), two of the best UK silent films, and *Blackmail* (1929), Britain's first talkie.

Sir Anthony Hopkins (1937–)
Actor who brings a dramatic emotional intensity to every role, whether it be C S Lewis in *Shadowlands* (1993) or his Academy Award®-winning turn as Hannibal Lecter in *The Silence of the Lambs* (1991).

Sir Alexander Korda (1893–1956)
Hungarian-born producer and director who, along with his brothers – director Zoltàn and art director Vincent – raised the standards of British cinema in the 1930s with the high production values of his period dramas and heroic adventures.

Sir David Lean (1908–91)
Director and former editor who examined how class and environment controlled individual drives and desires either in muted detail (*Brief Encounter*, 1945) or on a spectacular scale (*Lawrence of Arabia*, 1962).

Mike Leigh (1943–)
Director who devises his scripts during long rehearsal periods with actors, typically creating tragicomic stories about ordinary lives in such films as *Naked* (1993).

Ken Loach (1936–)
Director who has adapted the hard-hitting style of his groundbreaking television play *Cathy Come Home* (1966) to an entire career of sociopolitical dramas about the lives of ordinary people.

Ismail Merchant (1936–2005) and James Ivory (1928–)
Indian producer and American director who, with German–Polish writer Ruth Prawer Jhabvala, examined what lies beneath the stiff upper lip of the British self-image in a series of literary adaptations.

Sir Laurence Olivier (1907–89)
Actor and director who considered the screen a secondary career to the stage until *Wuthering Heights* (1939), and will remain best known for his trio of Shakespeare adaptations – *Henry V* (1944), *Hamlet* (1948) and *Richard III* (1956).

Michael Powell (1905–90)
Director who, often with producing and writing partner Emeric Pressburger, made artistically ambitious films – including *A Matter of Life and Death* (1946) and *The Red Shoes* (1948) – which combined heightened emotion and visual excess.

Ken Russell (1927–)
Director, for decades considered the 'enfant terrible' of British cinema, who brings a flamboyant – at times vulgar – visual imagination to his work, including controversial period piece *The Devils* (1971).

Key films

The Lodger
Alfred Hitchcock, 1926
Hitchcock's third film became a huge hit due to the casting of stage star and matinee idol Ivor Novello as the prime suspect in a series of Jack the Ripper-style murders.

The Private Life of Henry VIII
Alexander Korda, 1933
British cinema's first internationally successful film helped build the Korda empire, and captured a Best Actor Academy Award® for Charles Laughton as the lusty king.

The Four Feathers
Zoltàn Korda, 1939
Belief in Britain as an imperial power lingers on in the bold heroics and stirring action of this epic about a disgraced officer regaining his dignity and honour.

In Which We Serve
Noël Coward and David Lean, 1942
The definitive British war movie aimed to raise public morale with a portrait of common loyalty across the ranks on board a destroyer.

Kind Hearts and Coronets
Robert Hamer, 1949
The best of the Ealing comedies, this tale of the illegitimate son of an aristocratic family who climbs the social ladder by killing off his relatives (eight of whom are played by Alec Guinness) uses verbal and visual wit to subvert the class system.

The Third Man
Carol Reed, 1949
Graham Greene's original screenplay, Robert Hasker's tilted cameras and Orson Welles' portrayal of shady black-marketeer Harry Lime capture the mood of bombed-out post-war Vienna.

The Curse of Frankenstein
Terence Fisher, 1957
The first of Hammer Studios' bloody, sensationalist horror cycle, followed quickly by *Dracula* (1958), made genre stars of Peter Cushing and Christopher Lee.

Saturday Night and Sunday Morning
Karel Reisz, 1960
The first of the British New Wave films to break box-office records stars Albert Finney as a Nottingham factory worker out to grab what he can from life.

FILM-PRODUCING COUNTRIES

United Kingdom

Tom Jones
Tony Richardson, 1963
Richardson's bawdy take on Henry Fielding's mammoth novel won two Academy Awards® and sparked a rush of American investment into the UK film industry.

Performance
Nicolas Roeg and Donald Cammell, 1970
British cinema outdoes European arthouse in pure modernist style, using fragmented narrative and cross-cut images to depict the merging personalities of a rock star (Mick Jagger) and petty gangster (James Fox).

A Clockwork Orange
Stanley Kubrick, 1971
As well as influencing the fashion and film industries, Kubrick's infamous depiction of teen gang violence and social conditioning allegedly inspired copycat attacks, leading to the film's withdrawal from UK circulation for almost 30 years.

Chariots of Fire
Hugh Hudson, 1981
Set to iconic music by Greek composer Vangelis, this story of two athletes competing at the 1924 Paris Olympics was the first of many British period dramas and heritage films in the 1980s.

My Beautiful Laundrette
Stephen Frears, 1985
This tale of the relationship between a National Front sympathizer and an Asian man – a critique of Thatcher's Britain – helped to establish television broadcaster Channel 4 as a major part of the UK film industry.

Four Weddings and a Funeral
Mike Newell, 1994
US backing and a script by Richard Curtis catapulted this British romantic comedy to the top of the box-office charts, establishing a formula that would later be reused in *Notting Hill* (1999) and *Bridget Jones' Diary* (2001).

Trainspotting
Danny Boyle, 1996
This adaptation of Irvine Welsh's novel about cynical young Edinburgh drug addicts married visual panache with a bestselling soundtrack album and a hip cast, providing UK cinema with its main 'Cool Britannia' contender.

Festivals

Edinburgh International Film Festival
Held annually since 1947 in Edinburgh. The world's longest continually-running film festival, with special focus on first- and second-time film-makers and new British cinema.
Website: www.edfilmfest.org.uk
Top prize: Michael Powell Award for Best New British Feature

London Film Festival
Held annually since 1957 in London. The UK's biggest film festival, from Hollywood blockbusters to experimental works.
Website: www.lff.org.uk
Top prize: Sutherland Trophy for first-time director

The Orange British Academy Film Awards: Baftas

Best Picture wins: *Hamlet* (1948), *The Bridge on the River Kwai* (1957), *Lawrence of Arabia* (1962), *Tom Jones* (1963), *Oliver!* (1968), *Chariots of Fire* (1981), *Gandhi* (1982), *The Last Emperor* (1988, China/France/UK co-production)
Best Foreign Language Film nominations: 2 (Wales)

> ### Pennan's Phone Box
> The red telephone box sitting on the quay in Bill Forsyth's comedy *Local Hero* (1983) – one of the UK's most popular destinations for cinema tourists – was actually a prop. The real phone box serving the village of Pennan in Aberdeenshire is sited closer to the harbour, in a less photogenic position.

Further viewing

Blackmail (1929), *Goodbye, Mr Chips* (1939), *The Life and Death of Colonel Blimp* (1943), *Henry V* (1944), *Brief Encounter* (1945), *Great Expectations* (1946), *Brighton Rock* (1947), *Lawrence of Arabia* (1962), *This Sporting Life* (1963), *Blow-Up* (1966), *If...* (1968), *The Italian Job* (1969), *Kes* (1969), *Get Carter* (1971), *Withnail & I* (1986), *The Crying Game* (1992), *Howards End* (1992), *Secrets & Lies* (1995)

UNITED STATES OF AMERICA

History

Although the Lumière brothers in France were first to provide moving pictures for a paying audience, the patented inventions of Thomas Alva Edison – particularly his 'Kinetoscope' – played a major role in the early days of cinema. By 1908, however, film-producing companies were looking to California for better light, cheaper land and an escape from Edison's monopoly. Soon audiences across the world were thrilling to the adventures of Douglas Fairbanks and laughing at the antics of Charlie Chaplin. Studios, often founded by European immigrants, set up exclusive contracts for their stars and technicians, working them hard and loaning them out at high fees to their rivals.

By the arrival of sound in 1927, certain studios were already becoming known for specific styles – gangster films at Warner Brothers, horror at Universal and European sophistication at Paramount. War in Europe brought an influx of fleeing talent to Hollywood, along with a darker vision that manifested itself in the 1940s as film noir. Ensuing paranoia over the Cold War and the nuclear threat fed into 1950s sciencefiction films. That same decade, the increasing presence of televisions in American homes pushed cinema screens wider and made stories bigger, resulting in a rebirth for the western, the costume epic and the musical.

Another force emerged in the 1950s: the youth market. An appetite for rock'n'roll-fuelled exploitation flicks shown at drive-in theatres confused the older generation of Hollywood film-makers, most of whom, by the end of the 1960s, had had their day. The success of counterculture films such as *Easy Rider* (1969) opened the door to a younger generation of film-makers, and by the beginning of the 1970s Hollywood rivalled Europe for adult-themed, director-led cinema. It was this group of film-school-educated 'movie brats' who created the modern blockbuster with the runaway success of *Jaws* (1975) and *Star Wars* (1977).

Marketing men and accountants gradually took over as saturation release patterns, advertising budgets and merchandising sales dwarfed artistic imagination. In the 1980s, the high-concept blockbuster took hold – 'popcorn' entertainment, with an easily understood plot and lots of glossy action. This type of big-budget 'event' movie dominates Hollywood production and summer release patterns to this day.

The industry today

Hollywood product dominates film screens across the world, thanks to a combination of big budgets, marketing savvy and cinema ownership. Such is the cost of 'event' movies, however, that the supposedly safe options of sequels and remakes tend to overshadow original ideas, although America's independent film sector remains stubbornly innovative. New advances in digital technology have revolutionized special effects, and could also lead to digital distribution as a means of eradicating film piracy.

Key figures

Marlon Brando (1924–2004)
Actor who put the method acting style on the cinema map, but who later appeared mainly in highly-paid cameos and developed a reputation for pinning his lines to nearby props.

Frank Capra (1897–1991)
Director, born in Sicily, whose films shine with idealism and celebrate the spirit of the downtrodden, decent, ordinary hero who is living out the American Dream.

Joan Crawford (1906–77)
Actress who fought her way to stardom from the bottom up, and found her niche playing similarly determined modern women such as *Mildred Pierce* (1945).

Bette Davis (1908–89)
Actress whose distinctive looks and superior acting ability made her a critics' favourite, but whose strong will brought her into conflict with Warner Brothers studios over her restrictive contract.

James Dean (1931–55)
Actor with a restless, haunted style who became an enduring icon of adolescent angst and alienation when he died in a car crash after starring in only three major films – *East of Eden* (1955), *Rebel Without a Cause* (1955) and *Giant* (1956).

Robert De Niro (1943–)
One of the foremost actors of his generation, known for his ability to immerse himself in his characters, many of whom are loners driven by intense violent urges.

Clint Eastwood (1930–)
Actor and director who made his mark in westerns and violent cop films, and who is noted for a slow-paced directorial style that gives characters room to develop.

John Ford (1894–1973)
The foremost director of westerns in the history of US cinema, whose 100-plus films occasionally betray a touch of Irish sentiment (openly so in *The Quiet Man*, 1952).

D W Griffith (1875–1948)
Director who put US silent cinema ahead of its European rivals by using such devices as close-ups, long shots and flashbacks to lend power to his films.

Howard Hawks (1896–1977)
Director with an uncanny ability to get the best from actors in films of any genre – gangster thrillers (*Scarface*, 1932), screwball comedy (*His Girl Friday*, 1940), film noir (*The Big Sleep*, 1946) and westerns (*Red River*, 1948).

Katharine Hepburn (1907–2003)
Actress whose strong, independent personality enlivened serious dramas as well as intelligent comedies, particularly with Spencer Tracy and Cary Grant as her sparring partners. She won a record four Academy Awards®.

Stanley Kubrick (1928–99)
Director, producer, writer and notorious perfectionist and recluse – latterly based in England – who brought a coldly analytical art-film style into the commercial sector with films such as *The Shining* (1980) and *2001: A Space Odyssey* (1968).

Marilyn Monroe (1926–62)
Cinema's most famous blonde actress, whose innocent expression, sweet personality, sex-symbol status and flair for light comedy made her an international icon before her early death from an overdose of barbiturates.

Martin Scorsese (1942–)
Director, famous for his New York City settings, violent gangster epics (*Goodfellas*, 1990) and period dramas (*Raging Bull*, 1980), who is also a passionate supporter of film preservation initiatives.

Steven Spielberg (1946–)
Leading director of the 'film-student generation' who reshaped Hollywood with his blockbuster hits in the 1970s before moving on to family films and epic dramas.

James Stewart (1908–97)
Actor whose early career consisted of playing charming all-American heroes brimming over with small-town values, but who developed a darker side to his post-war persona in a series of westerns and crime movies.

Orson Welles (1915–85)
Actor and director who started at the top with *Citizen Kane* (1940) but saw his studio cut *The Magnificent Ambersons* (1942); he was later forced to take cameo roles and act in commercials in order to fund his oft-delayed projects.

Billy Wilder (1906–2002)

Austrian-born director noted for his caustic wit and cynical view of his adopted homeland, whose greatest work was done in collaboration with screenwriters Charles Brackett (*Sunset Boulevard*, 1950) and I A L Diamond (*Some Like It Hot*, 1959).

Key films

The Birth of a Nation

D W Griffith, 1915

As technically innovative as it is openly racist, this Civil War epic broke box-office records and caused riots with its heroic depiction of the Ku Klux Klan.

The Jazz Singer

Alan Crosland, 1927

The talkies were born when black-faced Al Jolson mouthed not only synchronized songs, but also bursts of spoken dialogue for the first time on US screens.

Grand Hotel

Edmund Goulding, 1932

MGM utilized all of its contract resources to make Hollywood's first all-star extravaganza, casting Greta Garbo, Wallace Beery, Joan Crawford and John and Lionel Barrymore as various guests in a Berlin hotel.

King Kong

Merian C Cooper and Ernest B Schoedsack, 1933

Perhaps the greatest monster movie of all time, this uses the Beauty and the Beast myth and Willis O'Brien's groundbreaking special effects to engineer sympathy for the giant ape, taken from his home and exploited for human entertainment.

It Happened One Night

Frank Capra, 1934

The first of only three films to win all five of the top Academy Awards[®] (Best Actor, Actress, Director, Screenplay and Picture) set a high standard for all subsequent screwball comedies.

Gone with the Wind

Victor Fleming, 1939

Producer David O Selznick ensured that the entire nation was talking about his three-year search for the perfect Scarlett O'Hara, turning the resulting hype into big box-office returns for his spectacular Civil War epic.

Citizen Kane

Orson Welles, 1940

Regularly voted the 'greatest film ever made', Welles's flashback story about the rise of an enigmatic newspaper magnate is certainly a great technical achievement, making innovative use of deep focus.

Casablanca

Michael Curtiz, 1942

Part foreign adventure, part wartime morale booster, part doomed romance, this Humphrey Bogart classic has endured to become perhaps the most popular film ever.

It's a Wonderful Life
Frank Capra, 1946
Capra delivers the ultimate feelgood movie with a sentimental celebration of small-town America in this tale of a man saved from suicide by divine intervention.

All About Eve
Joseph L Mankiewicz, 1950
Hollywood scriptwriting is at its most polished in this bitchy exposé of ruthless ambition and emotional vulnerability within the acting profession.

The Wild One
Laslo Benedek, 1953
Although it was ostensibly a 'problem picture' about juvenile delinquents, young audiences seized on Marlon Brando's biker boy as an anti-hero for the times.

On the Waterfront
Elia Kazan, 1954
The new style of method acting brought Marlon Brando Academy Award® recognition for this realistically shot story of dock workers and union gangsters.

Easy Rider
Dennis Hopper, 1969
Drugs, sex, rock music and the freedom of the open road are to the fore in the film that alerted Hollywood to the box-office potential of the counterculture generation and its emerging cinema talent.

The Godfather
Francis Ford Coppola, 1972
Paramount coordinated publicity for Coppola's gangster family epic in order to strengthen a landmark same-day release in cinemas across America, giving the 'movie brat' generation of film-makers their first runaway hit.

Jaws
Steven Spielberg, 1975
This mixture of thriller and monster movie was the first ever summer blockbuster, and left a generation of moviegoers with a lasting fear of the sea and the Great White Shark.

Top Gun
Tony Scott, 1986
The epitome of 1980s high-concept Hollywood, this film cast megastar-in-the-making Tom Cruise as a cocky navy pilot, although critics argued that the glossy package owed more to the stylish use of Ray-Ban® Aviator sunglasses than to the story.

Titanic
James Cameron, 1997
The biggest-grossing film in cinema history to date mixed disaster-movie spectacle with doomed romance, and became an all-time box-office number one in almost every country on the planet.

Yugoslavia

Festivals

Seattle International Film Festival
Held annually since 1975 in Seattle. The country's biggest film festival, featuring major world premières, retrospectives and documentaries (with a special focus on music documentaries).
Website: www.seattlefilm.com
Top prizes: Golden Space Needle (audience award) and Grand Jury Prize

National awards

Academy of Motion Picture Arts and Sciences: Academy Awards®
Hollywood Foreign Press Association: Golden Globes

Further viewing

Greed (1924), *All Quiet on the Western Front* (1930), *Little Caesar* (1930), *Snow White and the Seven Dwarfs* (1937), *The Adventures of Robin Hood* (1938), *Bringing Up Baby* (1938), *Singin' in the Rain* (1952), *Ben-Hur* (1959), *The Graduate* (1967), *Bonnie and Clyde* (1967), *One Flew Over the Cuckoo's Nest* (1975), *All the President's Men* (1976), *Annie Hall* (1977), *Star Wars* (1977), *Superman* (1978), *The Deer Hunter* (1978), *Apocalypse Now* (1979), *Fight Club* (1999)

YUGOSLAVIA

History

The different languages, religions and cultures that make up the Balkan region – taking in Serbia, Bosnia, Macedonia, Croatia and other states – not only sparked some of the bloodiest disputes in 20th-century history, but also made it difficult for a single sustainable film industry to become established. Yugoslavia, created from six separate republics at the end of World War II, did make its mark, however, particularly in the fields of surreal and satirical animation. The dominance of stodgy patriotic epics in the post-war period was challenged in the 1960s by a series of radical films coming out of Zagreb Studios. By the 1970s, it was the turn of the Prague Group – film-makers, including Emir Kusturica and Goran Paskaljevic, who had studied in the Czech capital – to add their darkly comic voice to the cinema of the region. Any sense of cinematic unity disappeared in the 1990s when war broke out.

The industry today

The Balkan region is still recovering from the wars of the 1990s, but many of its best directors – Goran Paskaljevic, Srdjan Dragojevic and Danis Tanovic – have attempted to address the recent conflict from different ethnic and political perspectives.

Key figures

Emir Kusturica (1954–)
Director and sometime actor whose boisterous, chaotic, quirky style has twice won him the Palme d'Or at Cannes (*When Father Was Away on Business*, 1985, and *Underground*, 1995).

Dušan Makavejev (1932–)

Director who used a radical mix of drama and documentary footage to express themes of sexual freedom in his groundbreaking films of the 1960s and early 1970s.

Key films

W R – Mysteries of the Organism (W R – Misterije organizma)

Dušan Makavejev, 1971

The first Yugoslavian film to achieve international fame mixes documentary footage of the controversial psychologist Wilhelm Reich with old Soviet films and the explicit story of a girl trying to seduce a sexually-repressed Russian ice-skater.

Underground

Emir Kusturica, 1995

Despite being attacked as pro-Serb propaganda, Kusturica's noisy black comedy about a con man who exploits a community hiding in a cellar from the Nazis during World War II won him his second Palme d'Or.

No Man's Land

Danis Tanovic, 2001

This Academy Award®-winning black comedy about two Bosnians and a Serb trapped in a trench with an unexploded bomb satirizes the lunacy of war and the futile presence of the United Nations and western media.

Festivals

Sarajevo Film Festival

Held annually since 1995 in Sarajevo. Initiated when the city was under bombardment, and now the key film festival in the region.
Website: www.sff.ba
Top prize: Best Film

Academy Awards®

Best Foreign Language Film wins: *No Man's Land* (Bosnia, 2001)
Best Foreign Language Film nominations: 6 (Yugoslavia), 1 (Macedonia), 1 (Bosnia)

Further viewing

The Switchboard Operator (1967), *When Father Was Away on Business* (1985), *Time of the Gypsies* (1988), *Before the Rain* (1994), *Pretty Village, Pretty Flame* (1996), *Cabaret Balkan* (1998)

100 NOTABLE FILMS

AMORES PERROS (LOVE'S A BITCH)

Alejandro González Iñárritu, Mexico, 2000
Gael García Bernal, Emilio Echevarría, Goya Toledo
153 minutes; colour

The film
A car crash in Mexico City unites three stories: a novice dogfighter getting in over his head with local low-lifes, an actress awkwardly adjusting to cohabitation and a homeless street philosopher managing his menagerie of stray dogs whilst meditating on his own eventful life.

Why watch it?
Marked by a striking combination of technical precision and emotional spontaneity, this three-strand urban melodrama is in the vanguard of the current revitalization of Latin American cinema. Though the gimmick of multiple interlinked narratives threatens to grow hackneyed, González Iñárritu's debut distinguishes itself by its verve, ambition, and cross-cultural appeal.

Key quote
'When you live in a city, as I do, where violence is really in the streets and people die every day, there's nothing funny about it. We try to show that violence has a consequence – when you create violence, it turns against you.' – Alejandro González Iñárritu, quoted in *The Guardian*, 22 August 2000.

Did you know ...
Unusually, *Amores perros* has a disclaimer at its start – rather than at its end – explaining that no animals were harmed during the making of the film. Despite this the film's dogfighting scenes proved too disturbingly realistic for some detractors, including the RSPCA, who expressed disapproval of the film's depiction of 'goading or cruelty to animals'.

> ### Big Break
> In 1998, Gael García Bernal became the first Mexican to attend London's prestigious Central School of Speech and Drama. Students there are not permitted to accept professional work until their final year, but when the unknown García Bernal was offered a part in *Amores perros* during the second year of his course, he risked expulsion in order to take the job.

ANDREI RUBLEV (ANDREY RUBLYOV)

Andrei Tarkovsky, USSR, 1969
Anatoli Solonitsyn, Ivan Lapikov, Nikolai Grinko
183 minutes; b/w & colour

The film
Poetic biopic-cum-historical epic, which frames the life story of the 15th-century Russian icon painter Andrei Rublev with the turbulent events of his time. Through eight separate chapters, the film charts Rublev's efforts to sustain his faith and creativity through personal and political adversity.

Why watch it?
A key work by one of the most eloquent masters of the cinematic arts – as intellectually uncompromising as it is technically sophisticated. The sedate pacing, complex visual compositions and crisply expressive camerawork form an evocative backdrop for a painfully eloquent analysis of the position of art and religion in society.

Key quote
'We wanted the viewer to leave the film with the idea that the artist is society's conscience, as its most sensitive organ, who is most perceptive to what occurs around it. A great artist is able to make masterpieces because he is capable of seeing others clearer, and perceiving the world with joy or exaggerated pain.' – Andrei Tarkovsky, interviewed by Aleksandr Lipkov, 1 February 1967.

Did you know ...
The international acclaim that greeted *Andrei Rublev* saw Tarkovsky rated as the greatest Russian director since Sergei Eisenstein, but the Soviet authorities continued to restrict his work for political reasons. The resulting bureaucratic limitations meant that he only completed seven films in a 25-year career.

APOCALYPSE NOW

Francis Ford Coppola, USA, 1979
Martin Sheen, Marlon Brando, Robert Duvall, Laurence Fishburne
153 minutes; colour
1979 Cannes Film Festival: Palme d'Or

The film
Sprawling, luminous paean to Vietnam guilt and macho crisis, loosely based upon Joseph Conrad's 1899 novella *Heart of Darkness*. Martin Sheen stars as hardened grunt Captain Willard, who must travel into lawless jungle to assassinate Marlon Brando's deranged Green Beret, Colonel Kurtz.

Why watch it?
Posterity has rewarded those involved for the sacrifices they made during a legendarily troubled production: a heart attack for Sheen, and near-bankruptcy for Coppola. Out of chaos rose a visionary and visceral addition to the war movie canon, extraordinary on every technical and emotional level. An extended version, titled *Apocalypse Now Redux* and including two long scenes cut from the original film, was released in 2001; this is widely regarded as inferior, but of interest to fans.

Key quote
'I love the smell of napalm in the morning. It smells like victory.' – Robert Duvall as Lieutenant Colonel Bill Kilgore.

Did you know ...
Harvey Keitel was cast as Captain Willard, but replaced by Sheen two weeks into shooting. Steve McQueen and Al Pacino had also turned down the role.

L'ATALANTE

Jean Vigo, France, 1939
Dita Parlo, Michel Simon, Jean Dasté
89 minutes; b/w

The film
New love runs aground in Jean Vigo's enduringly influential masterwork, rediscovered after the director's untimely death at the age of 29. Good-time girl Juliette marries handsome sailor Jean, only to find herself ill-suited to the basic way of life on board his barge. Her desire for freedom necessitates a re-evaluation of their fledgling relationship.

Why watch it?
Vigo's only completed feature blends languid poeticism with strikingly immediate emotional drama, and remains timelessly fresh and involving. A simple morality tale – feckless urban tramp learns her lesson at sea – becomes, in Vigo's hands, a deft and sensitive study of human passions and uncertainties, aglow with unexpected wit and vivid visual detail.

Key quote
'One of the most tender and convincing love stories on film.' Marina Warner in *BFI Modern Classics: L'Atalante*, 1994.

Did you know ...
At the time of production, Vigo was languishing with the tuberculosis that would soon kill him; the film was completed and crudely recut in his absence, and met with critical indifference. Long after his death, it was fully restored according to his wishes. A screening at the 1990 Cannes Film Festival met with new-found critical appreciation.

BATTLESHIP POTEMKIN (BRONENOSETS POTYOMKIN)

Sergei Eisenstein, USSR, 1925
Aleksandr Antonov, Vladimir Barsky, Grigori Aleksandrov
75 minutes; b/w; silent

The film
The events of the failed 1905 Kronstadt revolution against the tsarist elite, revisited with a documentary aesthetic and an agit-prop agenda. A sailors' revolt on board the eponymous craft leads to rioting in the streets, and finally to a brutal massacre.

Why watch it?
Although to a modern eye it may seem to tend towards the impersonal and schematic, this precision-crafted propaganda piece displays to stunning effect Eisenstein's mastery of visual storytelling, particularly the creation of meaning

through montage. The frequency with which the film's most famous sequences are referenced elsewhere is testament to its enduring power.

Key quote
'The revolution gave me the most precious thing in life – it made an artist out of me.' – Sergei Eisenstein in *Beyond the Stars: The Memoirs of Sergei Eisenstein*, 1995.

Did you know ...
A single red flag provides the film's only splash of colour (a detail referenced by Steven Spielberg in *Schindler's List* (1993)). Eisenstein hand-tinted the flag himself, frame by frame.

BELLE DE JOUR

Luis Buñuel, France/Italy, 1967
Catherine Deneuve, Paul Sorel, Michel Piccoli
101 minutes; colour
1967 Venice Film Festival: Golden Lion

The film
Through the mysterious erotic transgressions of a beautiful Parisienne, the great Spanish surrealist Buñuel models a film as secretive, troubling and sleekly finished as its protagonist. Catherine Deneuve is Séverine: chic doctor's wife by day, debased prostitute (or lurid fantasist) by night.

Why watch it?
Whether regarded as a psychoanalytic comedy of manners, a treatise on sexual pathology, or high-class erotica, Buñuel's first colour film compels with its sheer strangeness – and pays near-obsessive tribute to the startling beauty of the young Deneuve.

Key quote
'The story is a kind of fantasy cryptogram, with countless clues – verbal puns about cats, nonsense syllables, bells, speech with motionless lips, time cues, and so on – as to when we are in a fantasy, and whose.' – Film critic Renata Adler, *The New York Times*, 11 April 1968.

Did you know ...
Early in his film-making career, Buñuel was offered a directing contract for MGM studios. However, after visiting Hollywood in 1930, he turned down the offer.

BICYCLE THIEVES (LADRI DI BICICLETTE)

Vittorio De Sica, Italy, 1948
Lamberto Maggiorani, Enzo Staiola
93 minutes; b/w

The film

Long-unemployed Antonio finally finds a job – but he requires a bicycle, and such possessions are vulnerable in a society of competing have-nots. When his is stolen, Antonio and his young son set out to track it down with increasing desperation.

Why watch it?

Distinguished by a simplicity of form that at once conveys artlessness and breathtaking skill, this has emerged as the definitive Italian neorealist text. Using non-actors, real locations and natural light, De Sica frames a piercing story of need and injustice with an invigorating portrait of a living, working Rome.

Key quote

'It is difficult – perhaps impossible – for a fully trained actor to forget his profession. It is far easier to teach it, to hand on just the little that is needed, just what will suffice for the purpose at hand.' – Vittorio De Sica, quoted in *Italian Cinema, Neorealism to the Present*, Peter Bondanella, 1990.

Did you know ...

While De Sica was preparing *Bicycle Thieves*, Hollywood producer David O Selznick showed an interest in the project – but De Sica was put off by his plan to cast Cary Grant in the lead.

THE BIG SLEEP

Howard Hawks, USA, 1946
Humphrey Bogart, Lauren Bacall, John Ridgely, Martha Vickers
114 minutes; b/w

The film

Labyrinthine but consummately stylish noir, adapted by William Faulkner from a novel by Raymond Chandler. Bogart's Philip Marlowe is enlisted by frail General Sternwood to keep an eye on his two wayward daughters; heavy-duty flirtation, blackmail and murder soon follow.

Why watch it?

Even Chandler himself reputedly lost track of who kills who, and why, in the course of this most shady and involved of narratives. But even if its triumph is one of style over substance, *The Big Sleep* remains a masterful synthesis of contrasting elements: grit and grace, sharpness and langour, Bogart and Bacall.

Key quote

'Even on the chaste screen Hawks manages to get down a good deal of the glamorous tawdriness of big-city low life, discreetly laced with hints of dope addiction, voyeurism, and fornication.' – Film critic James Agee, *Time* magazine, 1946.

Did you know ...

During shooting, Bogart was still married to his third wife, Mayo Methot. Howard Hawks tried to fix Bacall up with Clark Gable instead, but to no avail: she and Bogart were married by the time the film came out.

THE BIRTH OF A NATION

D W Griffith, USA, 1915
Lillian Gish, Henry B Walthall, Donald Crisp
190 minutes; b/w; silent

The film
Based upon Thomas J Dixon's novel and play, Griffith's controversial epic charts the effects of the American Civil War upon families, friendships and the established social order. The latter element secured the film's position as a political talking point: slavery and the Ku Klux Klan are unambiguously defended.

Why watch it?
Though its race politics are shockingly inane, and its historical perspective highly questionable – and though the resulting discomfort undoubtedly contributes to its longevity as a critical subject – *The Birth of a Nation* is a striking early example of the translation of novelistic storytelling into filmic language.

Key quote
'It is like writing history with lightning. And my only regret is that it is all so terribly true.' – US President Woodrow Wilson, after seeing *Birth of a Nation* (attributed). This quote, though no source for it is given, appears at the beginning of many prints of the film.

Did you know ...
Griffith shot *The Birth of a Nation* without a written script or even a set of notes; he claimed to have visualized the entire film in his mind.

BLADE RUNNER

Ridley Scott, USA, 1982
Harrison Ford, Sean Young, Daryl Hannah, Rutger Hauer
117 minutes; colour

The film
This adaptation of Philip K Dick's 1968 novel *Do Androids Dream of Electric Sheep?* envisages the creation of synthetic humanoid workers – 'replicants' – and the crisis that looms when they evolve beyond their masters' control.

Why watch it?
At once glitzy and darkly melancholic, Scott's dystopian sci-fi noir remains intriguing – in part because of the ambiguity attached to its central character, Deckard – and hugely influential. Its vision of a chaotic future city, in which high and low-tech lifestyles co-exist, has rarely been surpassed.

Key quote
'After I finished reading the screenplay, I got the novel out and looked through it. The two reinforce each other, so that someone who started with the novel would enjoy the movie and someone who started with the movie would enjoy the novel ... It taught me things about writing that I didn't know.' – Novelist Philip K Dick, quoted in *Rod Serling's The Twilight Zone Magazine*, June 1982.

Did you know ...
The original release imposed an explanatory voiceover and a happy ending; these were excised from Scott's director's cut, released in 1992.

BLOW-UP

Michelangelo Antonioni, UK/Italy, 1966
David Hemmings, Vanessa Redgrave, Sarah Miles, Verushka
111 minutes; colour
1967 Cannes Film Festival: Palme d'Or

The film
A shallow fashion photographer, the toast of heartlessly hip Swinging London, discovers evidence of a murder; but his fragmented investigation obscures more than it clarifies, while the world around him remains preoccupied by sensation and ephemera.

Why watch it?
A supremely elegant snail's-pace mystery that rejects conventional resolution, *Blow-Up* retains its serene confidence even as it fretfully critiques itself – pursuing the meaning of truth through a fiction, employing a surface-obsessed medium to examine a surface-obsessed society.

Key quote
'How a picture as meaningful as this one could be blackballed is hard to understand. Perhaps it is because it is too candid, too uncomfortably disturbing, about the dehumanizing potential of photography.' – Film critic Bosley Crowther, *The New York Times*, 19 December 1966.

Did you know ...
A nightclub scene features a performance by the Yardbirds, with Jeff Beck and Jimmy Page on guitar.

BLUE VELVET

David Lynch, USA, 1986
Kyle MacLachlan, Isabella Rossellini, Dennis Hopper, Laura Dern
120 minutes; colour

The film
Opening with a sequence in which maggots squirm beneath the roses in neatly-kept suburban gardens, Lynch's fourth feature charges MacLachlan's wide-eyed small-town boy with the task of freeing Rossellini's vulnerable nightclub singer from sexual slavery.

Why watch it?
The night terrors of the modern American male – violence, inadequacy, impotence, domesticity – come to life in Lynch's work, and rarely with more garish intensity than in his fourth feature. Precise in its execution, straight-faced in its hysterical excesses, it remains a seductive and unsettling vision.

Key quote
'The weirdest moments are absolutely uncalculated (which is not true of all Lynch's work) because surrealism is his natural language. *Blue Velvet* is an amazing balance of naiveté and sophistication – a boy's book mystery that is also the most genuinely erotic film since *Last Tango in Paris*.' – Film critic Charles Taylor, Salon.com, 27 June 2000.

Did you know ...
David Lynch has said that he wrote the script for *Blue Velvet* whilst listening repeatedly to Dmitri Shostakovich's Symphony No. 15 in A major.

BONNIE AND CLYDE

Arthur Penn, USA, 1967
Warren Beatty, Faye Dunaway, Gene Hackman
111 minutes; colour

The film
Showy, bloody, dazzling account of the criminal career of lovers Clyde Barrow and Bonnie Parker, the superstar bank robbers of the Depression-era South. Its juxtaposition of violence with black humour, and historical fact with dreamy fantasy, caught the jumpy mood of a generation.

Why watch it?
The success of *Bonnie and Clyde* surprised even Warner Brothers, who had envisaged it as a fly-by-night B-flick. The sensation it caused inspired a new wave of politicized rebels, earnest cinéastes and beatnik dropouts to make their move on the Hollywood mainstream.

Key quote
'They're young, they're in love, and they kill people' – Original tag line

Did you know ...
Both François Truffaut and Jean-Luc Godard were approached to direct before Penn took on the project.

BREATHLESS (À BOUT DE SOUFFLE)

Jean-Luc Godard, France, 1960
Jean-Paul Belmondo, Jean Seberg, Daniel Boulanger
87 minutes; b/w

The film
The definitive exercise in Nouvelle Vague (or French New Wave) style, Godard's debut feature is a breezy, existential anti-romance which wilfully disrupts its own narrative with jump cuts and self-aware asides. An aspiring thug with delusions of Hollywood grandeur (Belmondo) flees Paris with his girlfriend (Seberg) after committing an impetuous murder.

Why watch it?

Thrilling to watch, if lacking in human warmth, *À bout de souffle* showed that nonchalant hipster glamour and studied Brechtian detachment could occupy the same cinematic space. It has duly inspired as many fashion shoots and advertisements as learned essays.

Key quote

'At once a homage to the American gangster film, and an attack on the very ideas of Americans, gangsters and films.' – Film critic Kim Newman, *Empire* magazine, 7 July 2000.

Did you know ...

Unable to afford a proper dolly track, Godard had himself and his hand-held camera pushed in a wheelchair for moving shots.

BRIEF ENCOUNTER

David Lean, UK, 1945
Celia Johnson, Trevor Howard, Stanley Holloway
86 minutes; b/w

The film

A sober tale of near-adultery, based upon Noël Coward's play *Still Life*. Mother-of-two Laura (Johnson) is happy in her marriage, yet when dashing doctor Alec (Howard) kindly removes something from her eye, she's shocked to find herself in the grip of a most improper passion.

Why watch it?

Supposedly intended as a gentle rebuke to women with wartime lovers, Lean's earnest paean to duty over desire now tends to raise laughs – those plummy accents, that frenetic self-denial! Still, the agony of extramarital temptation has rarely been so handsomely or sympathetically evoked.

Key quote

'It's awfully easy to lie when you know that you're trusted implicitly. So very easy, and so very degrading.' – Celia Johnson as Laura.

Did you know ...

The character who loans out his flat for illicit trysts would go on to provide the premise for Billy Wilder's 1960 film *The Apartment*.

BRIGHTON ROCK

John Boulting, UK, 1947
Richard Attenborough, Hermione Baddeley, Carol Marsh
92 minutes; b/w

The film

Vicious hoodlum Pinkie Brown (Attenborough) marries a naïve waitress to prevent her from giving evidence against him in a murder case; but nosey local lush Ida (Baddeley) smells a rat, and pursues the truth herself.

Why watch it?
As tough and mournful as the source novel by Graham Greene, Boulting's seaside noir has gritty confidence and sticky post-war squalor in spades. Attenborough is unforgettable as the soulless Pinkie, but is matched by Baddeley's blowsy barfly turned amateur investigator.

Key quote
'A glittering razorblade of a movie... *Brighton Rock* feels so real you can almost smell the brine, the vinegar and the frying cod.' – Film critic Xan Brooks, *The Guardian*, 17 May 2002.

Did you know ...
Camera operator Gil Taylor would go on to work as a director of photography for Roman Polanski, Alfred Hitchcock, Stanley Kubrick and George Lucas.

Where's the Rock?
The title of *Brighton Rock* (1947) refers not to a landmark, but to the sticks of sugary 'rock' that are traditionally sold as souvenir sweets in the seaside town. As US audiences were thought unlikely to understand this reference, the film was released in America under the title *Young Scarface*.

THE CABINET OF DR CALIGARI (DAS KABINETT DES DOKTOR CALIGARI)

Robert Wiene, Germany, 1920
Lil Dagover, Friedrich Feher, Werner Krauss, Conrad Veidt
78 minutes; b/w; silent

The film
Sinister Dr Caligari displays the psychic talents of the somnambulist Cesare at travelling fairgrounds, but after Cesare accurately predicts a young man's death, the mystery of his keeper's true identity deepens.

Why watch it?
A nightmare vision wrought out of dramatic chiaroscuro, stern angles and twisted shadows, this still-startling early horror is the fullest representation of the German Expressionist aesthetic in cinema.

Key quote
'*Caligari* is one of the first films to exploit the resemblance between watching a film and dreaming' – Film critic David Thomson in *The New Biography Dictionary of Film*, 2002

Did you know ...
Anti-German feeling in the USA after World War I was so strong that the release of *The Cabinet of Dr Caligari* was greeted by angry protests.

100 NOTABLE FILMS

CASABLANCA

Michael Curtiz, USA, 1942
Humphrey Bogart, Ingrid Bergman, Paul Henreid, Claude Rains
102 minutes; b/w
1944 Academy Awards®: Best Picture, Best Director

The film
The best-loved and most frequently quoted film of Hollywood's studio era reunites pre-war lovers Rick and Ilsa in corrupt, chaotic Casablanca – a stopping-off point for European refugees en route to the USA.

Why watch it?
Neatly judged, beautifully visualized and perfectly cast, *Casablanca* may not overwhelm with its artistic ambition, but it does leave an impression of flawless balance. And though posterity chiefly celebrates the central romance, much of the magic is in the details: the vividly realized setting, the zesty supporting characters.

Key quote
'Of all the gin joints in all the towns in all the world, she walks into mine.'
– Humphrey Bogart as Rick.

Did you know ...
Bar pianist Sam, played by Dooley Wilson, was almost written as a woman; Ella Fitzgerald and Lena Horne were both considered for the role.

CHINATOWN

Roman Polanski, USA, 1974
Jack Nicholson, Faye Dunaway, John Huston
131 minutes; colour

The film
Enlisted for a bogus adultery investigation, Nicholson's volatile private eye Jake Gittes stumbles upon a colossal real-estate fraud, and is required to access a conscience he didn't know he had – though not before he gets in too deep with icy widow Dunaway, a woman with secrets of her own.

Why watch it?
Shot and styled to emulate a 1930s noir, *Chinatown* expands the grubby concerns of the obligatory cynical gumshoe to biblical proportions. Polanski, screenwriter Robert Towne and a remarkable cast conspire to create a deceptive atmosphere of arch, classy restraint before letting rip with the fire and brimstone.

Key quote
'Among the peaks of noir cinema, and probably the best movie of the 1970s.' – Film critic Anthony Quinn, *The Independent*, 2004.

Did you know ...
A sequel entitled *The Two Jakes*, also written by Towne, was directed by Nicholson in 1990. Towne also planned a third instalment called *Cloverleaf*, but this has never been filmed.

CITIZEN KANE

Orson Welles, USA, 1941
Orson Welles, Joseph Cotten, Dorothy Comingore, Agnes Moorehead
119 minutes; b/w

The film
On his deathbed, newspaper tycoon Charles Foster Kane breathes the word 'Rosebud'. Welles's wildly ambitious blend of satire, documentary-style faux-biopic, technical showcase and straight-up melodrama investigates just what he was talking about.

Why watch it?
At once flamboyant and oddly cold, *Citizen Kane* lingers in the memory more as the bravura calling card of a nascent genius than as a full-blown emotional experience in its own right. Its forceful, witty assault upon American mythology is bracing, however, and its visual flourishes still take the breath away.

Key quote
'The mechanics of movies are rarely as entertaining as they are in *Kane*, as cleverly designed to be the kind of fun that keeps one alert and conscious of the enjoyment of the artifices themselves.' – Film critic Pauline Kael in the essay 'Raising Kane', 1971.

Did you know ...
Newspaper magnate William Randolph Hearst attempted to have *Citizen Kane* suppressed, believing the central character of Kane to be an unflattering caricature of himself.

A CLOCKWORK ORANGE

Stanley Kubrick, UK, 1971
Malcolm McDowell, Patrick Magee, Michael Bates
136 minutes; colour

The film
A violent street gang, who speak in their own cultish argot, pursue a gleeful crime rampage – until their leader Alex is incarcerated and subjected to experimental treatments to rid him of his antisocial tendencies.

Why watch it?
Anthony Burgess loathed this kinetic, shocking interpretation of his 1962 novel, and bad publicity convinced Kubrick to withdraw it from circulation in the UK until after his death. Certainly its shock value remains considerable, but its stylistic bravado and emotional force are no less striking than its violent content.

Key quote
'Being the adventures of a young man whose principal interests are rape, ultra-violence and Beethoven.' – Original tag line

Did you know ...
The film's extraordinary electronic soundtrack was the work of composer Walter Carlos, who had a sex change in 1972 and re-emerged as Wendy Carlos.

CLOSE-UP (NEMA-YE NAZDIK)

Abbas Kiarostami, Iran, 1990
Hossain Sabzian, Mohsen Makhmalbaf, Abolfazl Ahankhah, Abbas Kiarostami
100 minutes; colour

The film
Kiarostami employs dramatic reconstruction to recount the tale of an impersonator, Hossain Sabzian, who passed himself off as another of Iran's most celebrated film directors, Mohsen Makhmalbaf. The real participants play themselves.

Why watch it?
Forged out of empathy, curiosity and a piercing awareness of the elusive nature of true testimony, this involving meditation on fame, status and identity offsets its own theoretical complexity with unremitting warmth towards its characters and a sympathetic fascination with their foibles and motives.

Key quote
'Film begins with DW Griffith and ends with Abbas Kiarostami.' – Film-maker Jean-Luc Godard, quoted in *The Cinema of Abbas Kiarostami*, Alberto Elena, 2005.

Did you know ...
Kiarostami has said that Hossain Sabzian is now recognized on the streets of Teheran more than he is.

DAYS OF HEAVEN

Terrence Malick, USA, 1978
Richard Gere, Brooke Adams, Sam Shepard, Linda Manz
95 minutes; colour

The film
Texas, 1916. Itinerant farm labourers Bill (Gere) and Abby (Adams) pass themselves off as brother and sister so that Abby can secure the affections of Shepard's doomed, wealthy landowner.

Why watch it?
Malick here turns a potboiler of a story into mournful, mystical folklore, while camerawork by Nestor Almendras and Haskell Wexler confers a haunted luminosity upon faces, skies and cornfields alike. The mood of the film is summed up by Linda Manz's remarkable narration: guileless, spontaneous, yet edged with dolorous poetry.

Key quote
'*Days of Heaven* is above all one of the most beautiful films ever made.' – Roger Ebert, *Chicago Sun-Times*, 7 December 1997.

Did you know ...
Days of Heaven was almost entirely filmed at the time of day known as 'magic hour' – the moments between sunset and darkness. This limited shooting to around 20 minutes a day.

DEEP THROAT

Gerard Damiano, USA, 1972
Linda Lovelace, Harry Reems
61 minutes; colour

The film
The first hardcore porn film to be successfully sold to a mainstream audience, *Deep Throat* concerns itself with a woman whose clitoris is located in her throat, and her efforts to attain sexual satisfaction.

Why watch it?
Reputedly the most profitable film of all time, *Deep Throat* recouped massively on its $25,000 production costs, although its stars paid the price in different ways. Crude and clumsy as it now appears, the sensation that it caused remains an intriguing cultural phenomenon.

Key quote
'It was the first sex film not to have the pretence of socially redeeming value. It went strictly for comedic entertainment and that's why it became the icon that it's become.' – Harry Reems, interviewed on channel4.com, 2005.

Did you know ...
Lovelace would later reinvent herself as an anti-porn activist, claiming that she was coerced into making *Deep Throat* by her violent and controlling husband Chuck Traynor.

LA DOLCE VITA

Federico Fellini, Italy/France, 1960
Marcello Mastroianni, Anita Ekberg, Anouk Aimée, Yvonne Furneaux
174 minutes; b/w
1960 Cannes Film Festival: Palme d'Or

The film
In Rome, showbiz decadence – in the startlingly pneumatic form of Anita Ekberg's visiting starlet – rubs up against religious hysteria, while a voracious paparazzi press, including rakish Marcello Mastroianni, devours it all.

Why watch it?
As intoxicating in its looseness as in its sublime imagery, *La Dolce vita* meanders like one of the tipsy socialites it portrays, shedding plotlines and characters as it goes. But if its undertone is sorrowful – a lament for disconnected lives – its atmosphere is almost jarringly vivid and celebratory.

Key quote
'A giant canvas of beauty and ugliness, seduction, melancholy, humor, imagination, and mystery.' – Film-maker Alexander Payne in his introduction to the DVD release of *La Dolce vita.*

Did you know ...
The now-familiar term 'paparazzi' is derived from the photographer character Paparazzo, played by Walter Santesso.

Behind the Glamour

Celebrity shoemaker Terry de Havilland, who watched the filming of the famous Trevi Fountain scene in *La Dolce vita*, recalled in a 2005 interview in *The Observer*, 'Anita [Ekberg] was shouting obscenities up to a friend in Swedish while she was in the fountain. She had waders on under that big dress.'

DON'T LOOK BACK

D A Pennebaker, USA, 1967
Bob Dylan, Albert Grossman, Bob Neuwirth, Joan Baez
96 minutes; b/w

The film
A jittery, bitchy travelogue in the company of a jittery, bitchy Bob Dylan, touring the UK at the height of his global fame in 1965.

Why watch it?
Pennebaker's restless hand-held camera becomes one of Dylan's entourage, absorbed into the frenzied traffic of fans, foes and other hangers-on. The result is one of cinema's most complete and unvarnished portraits of a celebrity in his pop-culture moment.

Key quote
'Keep a good head and always carry a lightbulb.' – Bob Dylan in *Don't Look Back.*

Did you know ...
After *Don't Look Back*, Pennebaker shot an 'extension' of the film, titled *Eat the Document* and directed by Dylan himself. Intended for television, it was never broadcast and has rarely been screened.

DO THE RIGHT THING

Spike Lee, USA, 1989
Danny Aiello, Rosie Perez, Spike Lee, Samuel L Jackson
120 minutes; colour

The film
Resentments simmer on a hot summer's day in Brooklyn's Bed-Stuy (Bedford-Stuyvesant) neighbourhood. Neighbour turns on neighbour as Lee's attentions flit nimbly between white cop, black street kid, Korean grocer and Italian pizza chef.

Why watch it?
Still Lee's finest film, and a key moment in the expansion of US independent cinema, this forceful, multi-layered drama represents a breathtaking synthesis of mood, message and action.

Key quote
'Established Lee as the most dedicated resistance fighter to infiltrate the Hollywood system – the filmmaker who put the fraught and disavowed issues of race and

racism at the centre of his films and refused to be ghettoized for doing so.' – Film critic Amy Taubin, *Sight and Sound* magazine, August 2002.

Did you know ...
Spike Lee's first short, *The Answer*, was a ten-minute reworking of D W Griffith's *The Birth of a Nation* (1915).

EASY RIDER

Dennis Hopper, USA, 1969
Dennis Hopper, Peter Fonda, Jack Nicholson
94 minutes; colour

The film
Two bikers ride their Harley choppers from Los Angeles to New Orleans to attend Mardi Gras, and have a variety of drug-fuelled encounters and philosophical debates along the way.

Why watch it?
By turns electrifying and stupefying, this rambling travelogue provides an intriguing record of its historical moment. Its unforeseen commercial success would help to bolster the confidence of US independent cinema and broaden the scope of the mainstream.

Key quote
'A man went looking for America and couldn't find it anywhere!' – Original tag line

Did you know ...
The marijuana was real.

8½ (OTTO E MEZZO)

Federico Fellini, Italy/France, 1963
Marcello Mastroianni, Claudia Cardinale, Anouk Aimée
138 minutes; b/w

The film
While making preparations for his new film, celebrated director Guido Anselmi is struck by paralyzing indecision. Concerns about the film soon give way to a generalized panic over his own attitudes to art, work, and, above all, women.

Why watch it?
Beautiful wife, or beautiful mistress? Big-budget studio film-making, or free artistic expression? The problems of Fellini's most explicit screen alter ego aren't exactly in the life-or-death register, but the commingling of his dreams, memories and fantasies makes for an exhilarating portrait of personal and artistic confusion.

Key quote
'I don't like the idea of "understanding" a film. I don't believe that rational understanding is an essential element in the reception of any work of art. Either a film has something to say to you or it hasn't.' – Federico Fellini quoted in *Sight and Sound* magazine, August 2004.

Did you know ...

The title refers to the number of films Fellini had made: six features, two shorts and one co-directed feature (*Luci del varietà* (1950) with Alberto Lattuada), totalling 8½.

ERASERHEAD

David Lynch, USA, 1977
Jack Nance, Charlotte Stewart, Allen Joseph, Laurel Near
89 minutes; b/w

The film

Nervy Henry Spencer ekes out a troubled existence in a squalid industrial town, plagued by noise, mess and unexplained incidents. Even his girlfriend's pregnancy provides no cause for celebration – especially when she gives birth to a deformed creature barely recognizable as human.

Why watch it?

In the manner of a dream, *Eraserhead* fashions elemental fears and quotidian worries into a warped almost-narrative that hums with subliminal significance even when we can't be sure exactly what it's saying. The sound design and special effects, achieved on a shoestring budget, are astounding in themselves.

Key quote

'Certain things are just so beautiful to me, and I don't know why. Certain things make so much sense, and it's hard to explain. I *felt Eraserhead*, I didn't think it.' – David Lynch, quoted in *Lynch on Lynch*, edited by Chris Rodley, 1993.

Did you know ...

Lynch has never revealed how the prop baby – known on set as 'Spike' – was constructed, though one theory is that it was made from an embalmed calf foetus.

E.T. THE EXTRA-TERRESTRIAL

Steven Spielberg, USA, 1982
Henry Thomas, Drew Barrymore, Dee Wallace-Stone, Peter Coyote
1983 Academy Awards®: Best Music: Original Score

The film

An alien botanist, left behind when his colleagues made a hasty exit from Earth, is befriended by a group of children who try to protect him from exposure and exploitation.

Why watch it?

A lustrous, wide-eyed suburban adventure saga that created an all-time icon in the wizened form of its title character, and taught a generation of children about the capacity of cinema to break their hearts.

Key quote

'Be good.' – E.T.

Did you know ...
For the 20th-anniversary reissue in 2002, Spielberg edited out the guns carried by the government agents in the final pursuit and removed a reference to terrorism.

THE EXORCIST

William Friedkin, USA, 1973
Linda Blair, Ellen Burstyn, Max Von Sydow, Jason Miller
122 minutes; colour

The film
The twelve-year-old daughter of a divorced actress exhibits increasingly peculiar behaviour, driving her mother to seek the services of a priest who needs a miracle to confirm his own faltering faith.

Why watch it?
Rather more tense and solemn than its schlocky reputation suggests, this most parodied, imitated and mythologized of horror films is distinguished as much by its fierce engagement with questions of faith as by its flamboyantly grotesque account of the effects of Satanic soul possession.

Key quote
'Slips from the realms of mere cinema to the arena of magical incantation.' – Mark Kermode in *BFI Modern Classics: The Exorcist*, 1997.

Did you know ...
Upon its original release, the hysterical public response to *The Exorcist* saw cinemas laying on smelling salts and ambulances for adversely affected patrons.

> *Career Change*
>
> Before adapting his own novel for the screenplay of *The Exorcist*, author William Peter Blatty was working as a very successful comedy writer. The notoriety of *The Exorcist* changed all that in an instant, and Blatty was never able to return to comedy. He later recalled, 'People would blanch when I said I wanted to. I finally got an obscure imprint to publish *Demons 5, Exorcist 0*, which was basically an Exorcist spoof, and it went absolutely nowhere' (*The Guardian*, 16 November 2000).

FAHRENHEIT 9/11

Michael Moore, USA, 2004
Michael Moore, Lila Lipscomb, George W Bush
122 minutes; colour
2004 Cannes Film Festival: Palme d'Or

The film
An irreverent primer for students of early-21st-century history that rakes over the ashes of the 11 September 2001 terrorist attacks and the Iraq war, sniffing out corruption and mendacity at the heart of the Bush administration.

Why watch it?

Though Michael Moore's aggressive, emotionally manipulative tactics bear a striking resemblance to those of the tabloid media he scorns, his particular brand of tragicomic agit-prop has made him an immeasurably influential commentator, as well as helping to shift the documentary form towards the commercial mainstream.

Key quote

'The temperature at which freedom burns.' – Original tag line

Did you know ...

Fahrenheit 9/11 was the first documentary to gross more than $100 million in the USA, and the reputed recipient of the longest standing ovation in the history of the Cannes Film Festival.

FEAR EATS THE SOUL (ANGST ESSEN SEELE AUF)

Rainer Werner Fassbinder, Germany, 1974
Brigitte Mira, El Hedi ben Salem
94 minutes; colour

The film

After impulsively straying into a late-night café, a 60-year-old woman meets and falls in love with a young Arab man, to the consternation of their friends and families. As the pressure on the couple increases, their relationship shows strain.

Why watch it?

Stylistically subdued by his flamboyant standards, Fassbinder's most widely celebrated film is based on Douglas Sirk's 1955 weepie *All That Heaven Allows*. A muted sort of melodrama, it excises sentimentality and gloss in favour of a weary, defeated tenderness, and proves all the more moving for it.

Key quote

'Think much, cry much.' – El Hedi ben Salem as Ali.

Did you know ...

By the time of his death at the age of 37, Fassbinder had made 43 feature films and written 15 plays.

THE 400 BLOWS (LES QUATRE CENTS COUPS)

François Truffaut, France, 1959
Jean-Pierre Léaud, Claire Maurier, Albert Rémy
94 minutes; b/w

The film

A 13-year-old Parisian boy, Antoine Doinel, rebels against his indifferent parents and repressive, sardonic teachers by playing truant and dabbling in petty crime.

Why watch it?

A near-documentary rawness and spontaneity infuses Truffaut's semi-autobiographical debut, from its thoroughly deglamorized view of Paris to Léaud's touchingly natural lead performance. Never forceful in its moral or emotional agenda, it approaches the mysteries of childhood with empathy, insight and immediacy.

Key quote
'Filming Antoine Doinel was a sort of complicity between François and myself... When I saw the finished film, I burst into tears, and I recognized my own story in his.' – Jean-Pierre Léaud, quoted in the *Philadelphia Citypaper*, 1999.

Did you know ...
Léaud would go on to play Antoine Doinel in four further Truffaut films.

FRANKENSTEIN

James Whale, USA, 1931
Boris Karloff, Colin Clive, Mae Clarke
71 minutes; b/w

The film
After being excluded from school for his controversial research, Dr Henry Frankenstein (Clive) succeeds in his most cherished project: to bring to life a man (Karloff) stitched together from dissected corpses. Based upon Mary Shelley's 1818 novel.

Why watch it?
This legendary early horror is now most notable not for those elements that have passed into camp cliché – the cackling mad scientist, the thunderstorm, the bolts and stitches – but for the poetic simplicity with which it conveys the monster's sad progression from childlike innocence to frustrated, destructive rage.

Key quote
'A monster science created – but could not destroy!' – Original tag line

Did you know ...
Bela Lugosi turned down the role of the monster because he didn't like the script, and recommended the little-known Karloff as his replacement. To maximize his mystique, Karloff was billed only as '?'

THE GENERAL

Clyde Bruckman and Buster Keaton, USA, 1927
Buster Keaton, Marion Mack
75 minutes; b/w; silent

The film
Railway engineer Johnnie (Keaton) is rejected for Civil War service, much to the disgust of his beloved girlfriend Annabelle (Mack). When Union spies steal his train – the eponymous General – with Annabelle on board, he has the chance to prove his heroism.

Why watch it?
One of the most enduringly witty and involving films of the silent era, this pacey action adventure displays to full advantage Keaton's remarkable gift for physical comedy, as well as the scale of his directorial ambitions.

Key quote
'Keaton is arguably the greatest film comedian the world has ever known. What is perhaps less commonly recognized is that he was also one of cinema's greatest directors.' – Film critic Geoff Andrew, *The Film Handbook*, 1989.

Did you know ...
The General includes the single most expensive shot of the entire silent era: a real train crashing through a burning bridge, filmed in one take.

THE GODFATHER TRILOGY

The Godfather
Francis Ford Coppola, USA, 1972
Marlon Brando, Al Pacino, James Caan, Robert Duvall
175 minutes; colour
1973 Academy Awards®: Best Actor (Marlon Brando), Best Picture

The Godfather Part II
Francis Ford Coppola, USA, 1974
Al Pacino, Robert De Niro, Diane Keaton, Robert Duvall
200 minutes; colour
1975 Academy Awards®: Best Picture, Best Director

The Godfather Part III
Francis Ford Coppola, USA, 1990
Al Pacino, Diane Keaton, Talia Shire, Andy Garcia
162 minutes; colour

The films
A sprawling, operatic trilogy of Mafia family life, based on Mario Puzo's 1969 novel *The Godfather*. The Corleone family battle with rival business interests, in-fighting and the law. Over time, internal power structures change, as do the values of the wider world; but the legacy of violence continues to pass from father to son.

Why watch them?
The Shakespearean dignity that Puzo and Coppola confer upon their murderous hoodlums leaves a troubling aftertaste, but the gracious sweep and throbbing emotional urgency of this modern myth can no more be denied than its extraordinary cultural impact, or the peerless acting work it displays. However, the third, later instalment conspicuously fails to match the quality of the first two films.

Key quote
'I'm going to make him an offer he can't refuse.' – Marlon Brando as Don Vito Corleone.

Did you know ...
Marlon Brando refused his Academy Award® for *The Godfather* in protest at the treatment of Native Americans by the US government and film industry.

THE GOLD RUSH

Charlie Chaplin, USA, 1925
Charlie Chaplin, Mack Swain, Tom Murray, Georgia Hale
96 minutes; b/w; silent

The film
Chaplin's winsome Little Tramp heads to the Klondike to seek his fortune as a gold prospector. Menaced by criminals, wildlife and hunger, he still finds time to fall in love with the unattainable beauty played by Hale.

Why watch it?
This was Chaplin's favourite of his own films, made at the height of his global fame. It expands the horizons of his famous protagonist beyond his poky urban milieu and into the territory of adventure saga, and features some of his most celebrated comic set pieces.

Key quote
'Chaplin at the height of his powers; in it we experience that laughter mingled with tears that is the essence of his genius.' – Maurice Bessy, *Charlie Chaplin*, 1983.

Did you know ...
The film's original leading lady, 16-year-old Lita Grey, became pregnant by Chaplin during shooting, necessitating a hurried marriage as well as a replacement actress.

GONE WITH THE WIND

Victor Fleming, USA, 1939
Vivien Leigh, Clark Gable, Leslie Howard, Olivia de Havilland
222 minutes; colour
1940 Academy Awards®: Best Picture, Best Actress: Vivien Leigh

The film
Southern belle Scarlett O'Hara scratches and bites her way through the tumult of the US Civil War, never quite shaking off her slavish love for the pallid Ashley Wilkes, nor the rumbustious sexual chemistry she shares with rakish Rhett Butler.

Why watch it?
A vivid, tumbling, alarmingly reactionary blend of war epic and domestic melodrama which offers among its many guilty pleasures one of cinema's most enduring anti-heroines, and one of its most authentically dysfunctional off-on romances.

Key quote
'I'm going to live through this and when it's all over, I'll never be hungry again. No, nor any of my folk. If I have to lie, steal, cheat or kill, as God is my witness, I'll never be hungry again!' – Vivien Leigh as Scarlett O'Hara.

Did you know ...
Black cast members were prevented from attending the film's 1939 première in Atlanta, Georgia by the state's racial segregation laws.

THE GOSPEL ACCORDING TO ST MATTHEW (IL VANGELO SECONDO MATTEO)

Pier Paolo Pasolini, Italy, 1964
Enrique Irazoqui, Margherita Caruso, Susanna Pasolini, Mario Socrate
142 minutes; b/w

The film
Pasolini's ravishing and radical telling of the Matthew Gospel approaches Christ not as an icon or sacrificial lamb, but as a passionate, mercurial young activist, stalking barren landscapes with a shifting band of followers until brought down by the oppressive forces of the status quo.

Why watch it?
Channelling both the quiet grandeur of Renaissance religious art and the raw immediacy of Italian neorealist cinema, this starkly beautiful work arguably succeeds more than any other 'Jesus film', bringing its subject and his context heart-stoppingly close.

Key quote
'I come not to bring peace, but a sword.' – Enrique Irazoqui as Jesus Christ.

Did you know ...
Irazoqui, not an actor, accepted the role in exchange for Pasolini pledging support to his student Marxist organization. He now organizes computer chess tournaments.

GREED

Erich von Stroheim, USA, 1924
Zasu Pitts, Gibson Gowland, Jean Hersholt
140 minutes; b/w; silent

The film
A young woman scoops a small fortune from a lottery, but the money brings only misery and degradation for her, her ex-lover and her husband. Based on Frank Norris's 1899 novel *McTeague: A Story of San Francisco*.

Why watch it?
A partial version of Stroheim's vision it may be (his original cut, now lost, ran to more than seven hours), but *Greed* remains an unflinching and bitterly affecting parable of moral decay, obsessively detailed in its portrayal of several deadly sins, and suffused with the infernal heat of its Death Valley setting.

Key quote
'He has one simple rule for direction. Take a close look at the world, keep on doing so, and in the end it will lay bare for you all its cruelty and its ugliness.' – Film critic André Bazin, quoted in *The Guardian*, 1999.

Did you know ...
Zasu Pitts would go on to become a noted comedienne of the 'talkies', providing the physical inspiration for the animated character of Olive Oyl in Popeye.

HIGH NOON

Fred Zinnemann, USA, 1952
Gary Cooper, Grace Kelly, Lloyd Bridges
85 minutes; b/w
1953 Academy Awards®: Best Actor: Gary Cooper, Best Original Song, Best Score

The film
About to leave town with his new bride (Kelly in her first major role), Cooper's craggy town marshal Will Kane learns that his old nemesis is being released from jail. Against the advice of the entire town, Kane opts to stay around for a showdown.

Why watch it?
Whether you regard Kane's stubborn stance as classical heroism, pointless machismo or an allegory for embattled 1950s radicalism, *High Noon*'s inexorable build-up – played in almost real time, and haunted by shots of the clock on the wall – is riveting.

Key quote
'The story of a man who was too proud to run!' – Original tag line

Did you know ...
Screenwriter Charles Foreman was blacklisted soon after filming by the House Un-American Activities Committee.

HIS GIRL FRIDAY

Howard Hawks, USA, 1940
Cary Grant, Rosalind Russell, Ralph Bellamy
92 minutes; b/w

The film
Having divorced her editor Walter Burns (Grant), and on the brink of marrying another man (Bellamy), Russell's star reporter Hildy Johnson visits her old office one last time – and promptly finds herself caught up in a new story and an old romance.

Why watch it?
Adapted from Ben Hecht and Charles MacArthur's play *The Front Page* – with a sly gender switch for the character of Hildy Johnson – this definitive screwball comedy is a giddy delight, alive with rapid-fire gags and staged and performed with impeccable confidence.

Key quote
'It takes you by the scruff of the neck in the first reel and it shakes you madly, bellowing hoarsely the while, for the remaining six or seven. Before it's over you don't know whether you have been laughing or having your ears boxed.' – Film critic Frank S Nugent, *The New York Times*, 12 January 1940.

Did you know ...

In the course of the film, a freewheeling Grant makes reference to his own real name (Archie Leach) and compares Bellamy's character to 'that film actor, Ralph Bellamy.'

IT'S A WONDERFUL LIFE

Frank Capra, USA, 1946
James Stewart, Donna Reed, Lionel Barrymore, Henry Travers
130 minutes; b/w

The film

Convinced of his own insignificance, small-town businessman George Bailey (Stewart) is on the brink of committing suicide when a guardian angel named Clarence (Travers) offers him a revelatory glimpse of the world as it would be without him.

Why watch it?

With a plot of inspired simplicity and performances that positively glow with warm-hearted enthusiasm, this Christmas perennial leaves no heartstring untugged, and displays the virtuosity of both director and star.

Key quote

'One man's life touches so many others, when he's not there it leaves an awfully big hole.' – Henry Travers as Clarence.

Did you know ...

A new type of artificial snow was developed for the film, and earned the RKO Effects Department a special award from the Academy of Motion Picture Arts and Sciences.

THE JAZZ SINGER

Alan Crosland, USA, 1927
Al Jolson, May McAvoy, Warner Oland
88 minutes; b/w

The film

The son of a Jewish cantor flees his family and their expectations to pursue his love of jazz and ragtime music, and falls in love with a fellow performer.

Why watch it?

Though primarily silent, this mild-mannered musical qualifies as the first feature-length film with audible dialogue, thanks to Jolson's impulsive on-stage ad-libs. Its massive success proved the commercial feasibility of 'talkies'.

Key quote

'Wait a minute, wait a minute, you ain't heard nothin' yet!' – Al Jolson as Jack Robin.

Did you know ...

Grossed a then considerable $3.5 million at the US box office upon its original release, and helped to establish Warner Brothers as a leading studio.

JULES ET JIM

François Truffaut, France, 1962
Jeanne Moreau, Oskar Werner, Henri Serre
105 minutes; b/w

The film
The *ménage à trois* between two young men and a capricious, free-spirited woman shifts and evolves over the early years of the 20th century. Adapted from the novel by Henri-Pierre Roché.

Why watch it?
Its narrative distorted by an unpredictably jumpy timeframe, its surface ruptured by visual gimmicks, and its story blankly expounded by a deadpan narrator, the definitive romantic tragedy of the Nouvelle Vague movement is a collage of moods and ideas, at once frolicsome and sternly intellectual.

Key quote
'Its enthusiasm for what the cinema is and can be is what makes it so special.'
– Film critic Derek Malcolm, *The Guardian*, 2000.

Did you know ...
Jeanne Moreau's mother was a dancing girl from Lancashire, who met her bartender father during a visit to Paris with the Tiller Girls variety troupe.

KING KONG

Merian C Cooper and Ernest B Schoedsack, USA, 1933
Fay Wray, Robert Armstrong, Bruce Cabot
100 minutes; b/w

The film
Searching for a new attraction to bring to life a flagging stage show, a team of explorers braves a remote tropical island and finds it populated by terrifying, oversized beasts – including the eponymous giant gorilla. They capture him and take him back to the USA, with disastrous consequences.

Why watch it?
Though its dialogue and performances are stilted (with the notable exception of Fay Wray's legendary screams), and the effects inevitably show their age, this hugely ambitious 'creature feature' was revolutionary in its use of rear projection, miniature models and stop-motion animation.

Key quote
'Possibly the most perfect blend of escapism and adventure and mystery and romance.' – Film-maker Peter Jackson, quoted in *Film Review* magazine, October 2005.

Did you know ...
Two 18-inch King Kong models were built, and had to be skinned after each day's filming to have their screws and bolts retightened.

100 *NOTABLE FILMS*

LAST TANGO IN PARIS (ULTIMO TANGO A PARIGI)

Bernardo Bertolucci, Italy/France, 1972
Marlon Brando, Maria Schneider
136 minutes; colour

The film
Slumping into depression after his wife's suicide, American expatriate Paul meets a young French woman with whom he establishes an intense rapport based on rough sex and equally wounding self-revelation.

Why watch it?
An overripe, angry paean to male mid-life angst, still fairly shocking in its depiction of sexual savagery as a last-ditch response to spiritual ennui. Brando's performance is a florid, vaguely embarrassing tour de force; the interests of Schneider's comparatively underwritten character are inevitably overshadowed.

Key quote
'The most powerfully erotic movie ever made ... Bertolucci and Brando have altered the face of an art form.' – Film critic Pauline Kael, *The New Yorker*, 1972.

Did you know ...
The infamous anal sex scene led to the film being confiscated by the Italian police. Bertolucci's civil rights were revoked for five years, and he received a four-month suspended prison sentence.

LAST YEAR IN MARIENBAD (L'ANNÉE DERNIÈRE À MARIENBAD)

Alain Resnais, France, 1961
Delphine Seyrig, Giorgio Albertazzi, Sacha Pitoeff
94 minutes; b/w
1961 Venice Film Festival: Golden Lion

The film
In a baroque spa hotel, a man – 'X' – tries to seduce or win back a woman – 'A' – with whom he may or may not have been involved on a previous holiday. In the background lurks a rival for her affections, 'M'. Adapted by Alain Robbe-Grillet from his own 1957 novella *La Jalousie*.

Why watch it?
Celebrated and reviled for its repetitiousness and its dream-like chronological imprecision, this portrait of seduction and jealousy is a glamorous conundrum that compels, befuddles, enervates and finally haunts.

Key quote
'Empty salons. Corridors. Salons. Doors. Doors. Salons. Empty chairs, deep armchairs, thick carpets. Heavy hangings. Stairs, steps. Steps, one after the other. Glass objects, objects still intact, empty glasses ...' – Giorgio Albertazzi as 'X'.

Did you know ...
The confusing matchstick game played in the film is known as Nim, and is thought to be of Chinese origin. 'X' could have beaten 'M' if he had been well versed in binary mathematics.

LAWRENCE OF ARABIA

David Lean, UK, 1962
Peter O'Toole, Alec Guinness, Anthony Quinn, Omar Sharif
216 minutes; colour
1963 Academy Awards®: Best Picture, Best Director, Best Score

The film
This sandy epic, based upon the writings of T E Lawrence, commences with his death and then explores in flashback his experiences as a British military observer in battle-torn Arabia during World War I.

Why watch it?
A visual masterpiece, albeit one framed around an enigmatic sort of hero whose military and spiritual loyalties are never wholly clear. Lean's painterly compositions are unforgettable, O'Toole's messianic flamboyance no less so.

Key quote
'If he was any prettier, they'd have had to call it Florence of Arabia.' – Playwright Noël Coward (attributed).

Did you know ...
Other credits of editor Anne V Coates, who won one of the film's seven Academy Awards®, include *The Red Shoes* (1948), *The Elephant Man* (1980), *In the Line of Fire* (1993), *Out of Sight* (1998) and *Erin Brockovich* (2000).

> ### Men Only
> Although *Lawrence of Arabia* is over three hours long, it features no women in speaking roles, and only two women appear in uncredited bit-parts.

THE LEOPARD (IL GATTOPARDO)

Luchino Visconti, Italy/France, 1963
Burt Lancaster, Claudia Cardinale, Alain Delon
183 minutes; colour
1963 Cannes Film Festival: Palme d'Or

The film
A highly decorated adaptation of Prince Giuseppe Tomasi di Lampedusa's 1958 novel about the decline of the Italian aristocracy. Lancaster plays an ageing nobleman surrendering to the new order, as symbolized by his nephew's impending marriage to nouveau-riche Angelica (Cardinale).

Why watch it?
Visconti – himself an aristocrat with Marxist sympathies – brings operatic scale and extraordinary visual splendour to this tale of displaced 'leopards', as Lancaster's Prince Salina puts it, awaiting the arrival of 'the jackals and hyenas'.

Key quote
'So incredibly moving and elegant, beautifully made and full of poetry ... it made

me realize for the first time how high a level of art cinema could achieve.' – Film-maker Sydney Pollack, quoted in *The Guardian*, 10 May 2003.

Did you know ...
Claudia Cardinale came to acting after being named 'The Most Beautiful Italian Girl in Tunis' in a 1957 beauty contest.

THE LORD OF THE RINGS TRILOGY

The Lord of the Rings: The Fellowship of the Ring
Peter Jackson, New Zealand/USA, 2001
Elijah Wood, Ian McKellen, Orlando Bloom, Christopher Lee
178 minutes; colour
2002 Academy Awards®: Best Music: Original Score

The Lord of the Rings: The Two Towers
Peter Jackson, New Zealand/USA/Germany, 2002
Elijah Wood, Ian McKellen, Viggo Mortensen, Andy Serkis
179 minutes; colour

The Lord of the Rings: The Return of the King
Peter Jackson, New Zealand/USA/Germany, 2003
Elijah Wood, Sean Astin, Orlando Bloom, Viggo Mortensen
201 minutes; colour
2004 Academy Awards®: Best Picture, Best Director, Best Music: Original Score, Best Music: Original Song

The films
In this fantasy trilogy based upon books by J R R Tolkien, hobbit Frodo Baggins (Wood) must carry the One Ring of the Dark Lord Sauron from his bucolic home in the Shire to the distant Cracks of Doom, in order to destroy it. Along the way, the irresistible and destructive power of the Ring attracts greedy interest and causes bloody conflict amid the various tribes of Middle-earth.

Why watch them?
With a background in both low-budget schlock horror (*Bad Taste*, 1987 and *Braindead*, 1992) and clever arthouse drama (*Heavenly Creatures*, 1994), Jackson brought verve and intelligence to this most ambitious and lavish of mainstream franchises. Shot back-to-back, the three instalments have a glorious stylistic unity. With imaginative casting, superb special effects, gorgeous landscape photography and nail-biting action, this is riveting stuff, even for those not customarily drawn to elfin fantasy.

Key quote
'Must have the precious. They stole it from us. Sneaky little hobbitses.' – Andy Serkis as Gollum.

Did you know ...
The New Zealand government appointed a 'Minister for Lord of the Rings' to fully exploit the economic opportunities presented by the filming of the trilogy. The estimated boost to the local economy was NZ $350,000,000.

MANHATTAN

Woody Allen, USA, 1979
Woody Allen, Diane Keaton, Mariel Hemingway, Meryl Streep
96 minutes; b/w

The film
Having lost his wife to another woman and attempted a relationship with a 17-year-old student, neurotic middle-aged writer Isaac falls for his best friend's mistress, a highly-strung intellectual.

Why watch it?
Edgy observational comedy, embattled romanticism, and New York, New York – this is Allen at his funniest and most deeply felt. If the sexual politics grate now (challenging, grown-up Keaton rejected for Hemingway's barely budding Tracy), the twitchy urban milieu is beautifully realized.

Key quote
'Chapter One: He was as tough and romantic as the city he loved. Beneath his black-rimmed glasses was the coiled sexual power of a jungle cat …' – Woody Allen as Isaac Davies.

Did you know ...
Allen initially disliked the film so much that he offered to direct another film for United Artists free of charge if they would agree to shelve it.

MAN WITH A MOVIE CAMERA (CHELOVEK S KINO-APPARATOM)

Dziga Vertov, USSR, 1929
80 minutes; b/w; silent

The film
A lone cameraman shoots, edits and screens a day in the life of the USSR in a time of dramatic change. His dynamic study takes in rich and poor, birth and death, work and leisure, urban and rural scenes.

Why watch it?
Wondrous verité observation on one level, radical exploration of the politics of entertainment and representation on another, this is a seminal work which makes astonishing use of every hip avant-garde trick far ahead of its time.

Key quote
'We must form a factory of facts… Flashes of facts! Masses of facts. Hurricanes of facts. And individual little facts. Against cinema sorcery. Against cinema mystification.' – Dziga Vertov, quoted in *Lines of Resistance: Dziga Vertov and the Twenties*, edited by Yuri Tsivian, 2004.

Did you know ...
Polish by birth, Vertov's real name was Denis Kaufman. His pseudonym means 'spinning top.'

100 NOTABLE FILMS

METROPOLIS

Fritz Lang, Germany, 1927
Brigitte Helm, Alfred Abel, Gustav Frölich
153 minutes; b/w

The film
The residents of a shimmering 21st-century city are divided into two camps: those who think above ground, and those who toil below. When a high-born 'thinker' falls in love with one of the proletariat, contact is finally made.

Why watch it?
Looking backward to German Expressionism and ahead to every glitzy dystopia in the sci-fi future, this is as influential a piece of visual design as the cinema has ever produced – even if the movement of the story is patchy and the political implications something of a puzzle.

Key quote
'There can be no understanding between the hands and the brain unless the heart acts as mediator.' – Original tag line

Did you know ...
Soundtrack maestro Giorgio Moroder released a recut and retinted version, with a new rock soundtrack, in 1984.

THE NIGHT OF THE HUNTER

Charles Laughton, USA, 1955
Robert Mitchum, Lillian Gish, Shelley Winters
93 minutes; b/w

The film
Upon emerging from prison, corrupt preacher Harry Powell seeks out and weds the widow of his dead cellmate, hoping to get his hands on a hidden fortune. However, only the dead man's children, Pearl and John, know where it is – and they prove better at keeping secrets than the bad Reverend expects.

Why watch it?
Laughton's only film as director is pure sultry, shivery Southern Gothic, centring on a thrilling performance by Mitchum and possessed of a heightened, fairytale aesthetic that does nothing to dilute its emotional intensity.

Key quote
'H-A-T-E! It was with this left hand that old brother Cain struck the blow that laid his brother low. L-O-V-E! You see these fingers, dear hearts? These fingers has veins that run straight to the soul of man.' – Robert Mitchum as Reverend Harry Powell.

Did you know ...
The film was a critical and commercial flop upon its initial release, and a depressed Laughton swore never to direct again.

NIGHT OF THE LIVING DEAD

George A Romero, USA, 1968
Duane Jones, Judith O'Dea, Karl Hardman
96 minutes; b/w

The film
A radiation leak reanimates the dead, giving them a craving for living flesh. A group of survivors take refuge in a dilapidated farmhouse, where their weakness and panic prove as dangerous as the lumbering 'undead' massing outside.

Why watch it?
This grisly progenitor of the zombie genre is low-budget legend: made for nothing by nobodies, it electrified the midnight-movie crowd as much as it inflamed respectable critics. Its unflinching refusal to allow good to triumph still chills the blood, no less than its messy flesh-eating turns the stomach.

Key quote
'During the sixties, we all thought that some kind of revolution was going to bring some sort of positive, permanent change. That's what it was about, a new society devouring the old society – in this case literally.' – George A Romero in *Filmhäftet*, issue 119, 2002.

Did you know ...
Actors who played zombies were paid $1 and a T-shirt declaring 'I Was a Zombie In *Night of the Living Dead*'.

THE PASSION OF JOAN OF ARC (LA PASSION DE JEANNE D'ARC)

Carl Theodor Dreyer, France, 1928
Maria Falconetti, Eugène Sylvain, Michel Simon, Antonin Artaud
110 minutes; b/w; silent

The film
Unconventional in virtually every regard – its oddball casting, its austere visual style, its almost exclusive use of close-ups and complete rejection of make-up – Dreyer's intimate account of the trial and martyrdom of Joan of Arc is the masterpiece of French silent cinema.

Why watch it?
This work of stark visual poetry is so intensely expressive as to render dialogue an irrelevance. Previously known only as a comic stage actress, Falconetti here conjured a performance of unvarnished frankness and staggering emotional range, widely regarded as the greatest in screen history.

Key quote
'Nothing in the world can be compared to the human face. It is a land one can never tire of exploring.' – Carl Theodor Dreyer, *Sight and Sound* magazine, 1955.

Did you know ...
The original cut of the film was believed lost for half a century, until it turned up in a Norwegian mental institution in 1981.

PATHER PANCHALI (SONG OF THE ROAD)

Satyajit Ray, India, 1955
Kanu Bannerjee, Subir Bannerjee, Karuna Bannerjee, Uma Das Gupta
115 minutes; b/w

The film
Early in the 20th century, Apu is born to a poor family in a Bengal village who struggle with dire poverty and simple personality clashes while he moves through the formative experiences of childhood. Adapted from the novel by Bibhuti Bhushan Banerjee, this is family life plainly and poignantly seen.

Why watch it?
Ray's first film, the opening of what would become known as the Apu trilogy, finds an effortless, aching beauty in the simplest daily interactions. Not that this simplicity precludes dramatic impact – with characters so subtly and powerfully rendered, emotional involvement is non-negotiable.

Key quote
'A luminous, transcendental masterpiece.' – Film critic Peter Bradshaw, *The Guardian*, 3 May 2002.

Did you know ...
Ray funded *Pather Panchali* by pawning his record collection and his wife's jewellery.

PICKPOCKET

Robert Bresson, France, 1959
Martin LaSalle, Marika Green
75 minutes; b/w

The film
A young man, Michel, is obsessively driven to commit petty crime, spurred on both by his friendship with a professional thief and his cat-and-mouse relationship with a policeman.

Why watch it?
Inspired by Dostoevsky's 1866 novel *Crime and Punishment*, this typically austere and flinty Bresson film combines a near-erotic enjoyment of Michel's graceful transgressions with a cold-eyed examination of his compromised moral character.

Key quote
'He knows what he wants but he doesn't know why. Nobody could be less dogmatic or more obstinate than he. He relies entirely on his instinct' – Actor Jean Pelegri on Bresson, quoted in *The Guardian*, 19 August 1999.

Did you know ...
Steadfastly opposed to expressive acting, Bresson referred to his performers as 'models'.

100 NOTABLE FILMS

PSYCHO

Alfred Hitchcock, USA, 1960
Anthony Perkins, Janet Leigh, Vera Miles
109 minutes; b/w

The film
Desperate to wed her lover, who is financially entrapped by alimony payments to his ex-wife, secretary Marion Crane steals $40,000 from her employer and drives into the night. But she hasn't reckoned upon the violent intervention of the motel's sinister proprietor, Norman Bates...

Why watch it?
Though its final scenes disappoint with their simplistic cod-Freudian analysis, this is Hitchcock and the horror genre at their most delightfully manipulative. Its stylistic influence is immeasurable, yet its shockingly disposable heroine, its uncomfortably sympathetic villain and its relentless dark humour keep it stunningly fresh.

Key quote
'I still don't take showers, and that's the truth.' – Janet Leigh, quoted by the Associated Press, 2001.

Did you know ...
Chocolate syrup was used to simulate blood in the iconic shower scene.

Just Another Psycho
Director Gus Van Sant's experimental 1998 remake of *Psycho* used the same score and screenplay as the original (with some slight amendments), and many scenes were reproduced exactly.

RAGING BULL

Martin Scorsese, USA, 1980
Robert De Niro, Joe Pesci, Cathy Moriarty
129 minutes; b/w
1981 Academy Awards®: Best Actor: Robert De Niro

The film
The life story of the 1949 middleweight champion Jake LaMotta (De Niro) is told here, from punch-drunk youth through burgeoning arrogance and paranoia to slobbish, defeated middle age. Pesci is his volatile brother, Moriarty his beautiful, abused wife.

Why watch it?
A brutal, beautiful meditation on men, machismo, intimacy and violence. The fights – in and out of the ring – have a visceral immediacy, thanks in no small part to Thelma Schoonmaker's brilliant editing, and the conviction of the three central performances is staggering.

Key quote

'Scorsese has never again treated the history of a form, a medium, and a culture so radically, or made so complicated a meditation on the relations among spectacle, entertainment, and art.' – Film critic Amy Taubin, *The Village Voice*, August 2000.

Did you know ...

In one of the most extreme physical transformations ever undertaken by an actor for a role, De Niro gained some 60 pounds to portray LaMotta in later life.

RAISE THE RED LANTERN (DA HONG DENG LONG GAO GAO GUA)

Zhang Yimou, China/Hong Kong/Taiwan, 1991
Gong Li, He Caifei, Ma Jingwu
125 minutes; colour

The film

In 1920s China, a young student reluctantly agrees to become the fourth wife of a wealthy older man in order to ease financial pressures on her family. Though she cares little for the attentions of her master – whom we never see – she is quickly drawn into the intrigue and paranoia that governs the lives of his other women.

Why watch it?

Intense beauty masks anger and cruelty in this vivid study of Chinese patriarchy, as admired abroad as it was decried at home. Zhang uses dazzlingly rich and vivid colours and lavish decoration to evoke a culture of elaborate ritual, repressive feudal tradition and ingrained hypocrisy.

Key quote

'A beautifully crafted and richly detailed feat of consciousness-raising and a serious drama with the verve of a good soap opera.' – Film critic Janet Maslin, *The New York Times*, 20 March 1992.

Did you know ...

Raise the Red Lantern was initially banned in China; recently, however, a ballet adapted from the film has been produced by the National Ballet of China and taken on tour around the world.

RASHOMON (RASHÔMON)

Akira Kurosawa, Japan, 1950
Toshirô Mifune, Machiko Kyô, Masayuki Mori, Takashi Shimura
88 minutes; b/w
1951 Venice Film Festival: Golden Lion

The film

In 12th-century Japan, a farmer and his wife are attacked in a forest by a notorious bandit. She is raped, he is murdered – but when the case comes to trial, the accounts of the perpetrator, the two victims (one accessed through a psychic) and a witness are all markedly different.

Why watch it?
Rashomon is undoubtedly one of the most referenced films of all time, invoked every time a film tells a story via contradictory perspectives; but Kurosawa's philosophical debate on the nature of truth and virtue is also an intensely visual and emotional experience, shot, edited and performed with thrilling grace.

Key quote
'I counsel my colleagues to resist the temptation to imitate Kurosawa blindly; it is impossible to surpass him.' – Film-maker Zhang Yimou, *TIME Asia*, 23 August 1999.

Did you know ...
Kurosawa, who trained as a painter, storyboards all of his films on full-scale canvases.

REBEL WITHOUT A CAUSE

Nicholas Ray, USA, 1951
James Dean, Natalie Wood, Sal Mineo
111 minutes; colour

The film
Misunderstood middle-class teenager Jim Stark (Dean) moves to a new town, where he falls for a similarly disaffected girl (Wood), and finds an acolyte in the no less troubled Plato (Mineo). Not everyone loves him, however – he must prove his worth to the local hoods via some very dangerous games.

Why watch it?
Lent a tragic mystique by the early deaths of all three stars, this vivid tableau of questing passions, miscommunication and violent encounters marks Dean's finest work, and showcases Ray's masterful deployment of light, space and movement in the expression of tortured relationships.

Key quote
'Teenage terror torn from today's headlines!' – Original tag line

Did you know ...
The film was released only a month after Dean's death in a road accident. Some years later, his co-stars also died in tragic circumstances – Mineo in 1976 after being stabbed by a stranger, and Wood in 1981 by drowning.

THE RED SHOES

Michael Powell and Emeric Pressburger, UK, 1948
Moira Shearer, Marius Goring, Anton Walbrook, Ludmilla Tchérina
133 minutes; colour
1949 Academy Awards®: Best Score

The film
Shearer's star ballerina Vicky Page falls for a young composer (Goring), who must then compete with her masochistic devotion to her art and her intense relationship with her authoritarian mentor (Walbrook).

Why watch it?

Powell and Pressburger, mavericks of British cinema, exuberantly bucked the trend of post-war austerity and stiff-upper-lipped restraint with this lush, lachrymose extravaganza. While it contains some of the most sumptuous imagery ever committed to film, what is most impressive is the ease with which it blends high camp and genuine emotional complexity.

Key quote

'Here ... is a visual and emotional comprehension of all the grace and rhythm and power of the ballet. Here is the color and the excitement, the strange intoxication of the dancer's life. And here is the rapture and the heartbreak which only the passionate and the devoted can know.' – Film critic Bosley Crowther, *The New York Times*, 23 October 1948.

Did you know ...

Shearer repeatedly refused the role of Vicky, because she feared for her burgeoning ballet career and didn't like the script. It took Powell a year to convince her.

LA RÈGLE DU JEU (THE RULES OF THE GAME)

Jean Renoir, France, 1939
Marcel Dalio, Nora Gregor, Paulette Dubost, Jean Renoir
110 minutes; b/w

The film

A group of aristocrats gather at a country mansion for a hunting party. Rivalries and romantic intrigues come to a head, observed with interest by the domestic staff.

Why watch it?

A sharp, layered drama of unstable attachments, shady motivations and sly social manoeuvres, from the most influential and consummately skilled director in French cinema history. It presents wise insights into hypocrisy and pretension, but evades cynicism through its lightness of touch and unshakeable empathy for its many characters.

Key quote

'A film that is ever evocative of the moral disorder and the unprogrammed ardour of men and women.' – Film critic Andrew Sarris, *The Village Voice*, 6 September 1980.

Did you know ...

Banned twice over in France – first for being 'demoralizing' at the start of the war, then again for good measure by the Nazis during the Occupation – the film was not made available again until 1956.

RESERVOIR DOGS

Quentin Tarantino, USA, 1992
Harvey Keitel, Tim Roth, Michael Madsen, Steve Buscemi
99 minutes; colour

The film
A gang of criminals comes together to plan an ambitious bank heist, but a series of misjudgements lead to dramatic dissension in the ranks, and their colour-coded pseudonyms can't protect them from the enemy within.

Why watch it?
A sensation that made an instant household name of its irrepressible tyro director, transformed the commercial possibilities of US independent film-making and spawned innumerable imitators.

Key quote
'Why do I have to be Mr Pink?' – Steve Buscemi as Mr Pink.

Did you know ...
The title – not referenced in the film – is drawn from Tarantino's days working in a video shop. Unable to pronounce the title of Louis Malle's *Au revoir les enfants* (1987), he called it 'the reservoir film'.

RUSSIAN ARK

Alexander Sokurov, Russia/Germany, 2002
Sergey Dreiden, Maria Kuznetsova, Leonid Mozgovoy
96 minutes; colour

The film
A breathtaking technical experiment: a full-length feature made in one take, without a single cut. The location is the Hermitage Museum in St Petersburg; the camera travels two kilometres in real time through its 33 rooms, where various segments of Russian history are being replayed.

Why watch it?
Radical in its technique, yet gently reactionary in its yearning for the genteel pre-revolutionary past, this dusty, scholarly, playful historical pageant is a transfixing and unexpectedly emotional experience – as well as a landmark in digital film-making.

Key quote
'I wanted to try to fit myself into the flowing of time ... to live that one and a half hours as if it were merely breathing in and out.' – Alexander Sokurov, quoted in the *International Herald Tribune*, 25 May 2002.

Did you know ...
A cast of 2,000 actors had to hit their marks on time in order for the single-take shoot to be successful.

SANS SOLEIL (SUNLESS)

Chris Marker, France, 1983
Alexandra Stewart
100 minutes; colour

100 NOTABLE FILMS

The film
Over a collage of images garnered on travels abroad (Japan dominates, but Iceland, San Francisco and Guinea-Bissau are in there too), a narrator reads out wayward, highly personal observations conveyed to her by a globetrotting friend.

Why watch it?
No dry synopsis can do justice to the myriad delights offered here by cinema's greatest living essayist. With the instinctive, flowing logic of a great conversation, *Sans soleil* slips from Vietnam to video games to Hitchcock's *Vertigo*, questioning the nature of memory, time and representation as it goes.

Key quote
'*Sans soleil* ... maps the blur between fiction and nonfiction, between an event and the memory created by the event, between a memory and its technologically mediated representation.' – Film critic Jessica Winter, *The Village Voice*, May 2003.

Did you know ...
The stubbornly enigmatic Marker reportedly chose his professional pseudonym in tribute to Magic Marker pens.

SATURDAY NIGHT AND SUNDAY MORNING

Karel Reisz, UK, 1960
Albert Finney, Shirley Anne Field, Rachel Roberts
89 minutes; b/w

The film
Nottingham factory worker Arthur Seaton is, as he puts it, 'out for a good time – all the rest is propaganda'. His pursuit of pleasure is hampered, however, by the restrictions imposed on him by work and women. Adapted by Alan Sillitoe from his own 1959 novel.

Why watch it?
One of the first popular hits of the British New Wave, this film is characteristic of the 'kitchen sink' genre in its gutsy, grubby evocation of working-class life, female frailty and masculine rage.

Key quote
'I'm a dynamite dealer waiting to blow the factory to kingdom come. Whatever you say I am, I'm not.' – Albert Finney as Arthur Seaton.

Did you know ...
Karel Reisz, who came to the UK as a wartime refugee from Czechoslovakia, began his career in film as a critic for *Sight and Sound* magazine, and was the first programmer to be appointed at London's National Film Theatre.

SCHINDLER'S LIST

Steven Spielberg, USA, 1993
Liam Neeson, Ralph Fiennes, Ben Kingsley
195 minutes; b/w & colour
1994 Academy Awards®: Best Director, Best Picture, Best Music: Original Score

The film

Polish businessman Oskar Schindler is accustomed to exploiting cheap Jewish labour in his factories. During the Holocaust, his priorities shift, and he begins to enlist workers as a covert means of saving them from the Nazi death camps. From the fact-based book *Schindler's Ark* (1982, later reissued as *Schindler's List*), by Thomas Keneally.

Why watch it?

Spielberg, Hollywood's master of heartwarming spectacle, takes on the greatest of all horrors – and still manages to conjure up a happy ending of sorts. Last-reel compromises and general discomfiting Spielberg gloss aside, this is a sincere effort to encompass the unimaginable, and to do justice to an ambiguous character.

Key quote

'I didn't want this to be an exploitation of the Holocaust. I just needed to follow Schindler's story.' – Steven Spielberg, quoted in *Inside Film* magazine, 2004.

Did you know ...

Martin Scorsese picked up the film rights to Keneally's novel from fellow film-maker Billy Wilder, who had decided to retire rather than tackle the project. Scorsese then passed the project to Spielberg in exchange for the remake rights to *Cape Fear*.

THE SEARCHERS

John Ford, USA, 1956
John Wayne, Natalie Wood, Jeffrey Hunter, Vera Miles
119 minutes; colour

The film

Ethan Edwards (Wayne) returns from the Civil War to find his family massacred and his niece taken captive by the Comanche. He resolves to find the missing girl, but in the course of a five-year quest he becomes less certain of what he should do with her when he finds her.

Why watch it?

The ultimate American hero turns darkly obsessive in Ford's endlessly ambiguous, endlessly debated western, which locates a broken man in a desolately beautiful landscape, and all his terror of loss, displacement and racial pollution in the body of a lost girl.

Key quote

'In the flawed vision of *The Searchers* we can see Ford, Wayne and the Western itself awkwardly learning that a man who hates Indians can no longer be an uncomplicated hero.' – Roger Ebert, *Chicago Sun-Times*, 25 November 2001.

Did you know ...

Ethan Edwards's repeated refrain 'That'll be the day' inspired Buddy Holly's famous lyric and song title.

SE7EN

David Fincher, USA, 1995
Morgan Freeman, Brad Pitt, Kevin Spacey, Gwyneth Paltrow
127 minutes; colour

The film
A hardened homicide cop (Freeman) and his callow new partner (Pitt) pursue a
serial killer whose victims each embody one of the seven deadly sins.

Why watch it?
With its ghastly slayings, nightmarishly squalid urban setting and apocalyptic
pessimism, this is a detective thriller that bleeds into the territory of horror.
Luridness is tempered, however, by intelligence and emotional sincerity. The film's
gloomy visual style – established from its extraordinary opening titles – has been
freely imitated.

Key quote
'We see a deadly sin on every street corner, in every home, and we tolerate it. We
tolerate it because it's common, it's trivial. We tolerate it morning, noon, and night.
Well, not any more. I'm setting the example.' – Kevin Spacey as 'John Doe'.

Did you know ...
Spacey insisted that his name be kept out of pre-publicity for the film and omitted
from the opening credits, to maximize the impact when the killer's identity is
revealed.

THE SEVENTH SEAL (DET SJUNDE INSEGLET)

Ingmar Bergman, Sweden, 1957
Max von Sydow, Gunnar Björnstrand, Bengt Ekerot
96 minutes; b/w

The film
A medieval knight returns from the Crusades to a homeland ravaged by plague.
To postpone his own end, he challenges the hooded figure of Death to a game of
chess.

Why watch it?
This weighty philosophical tract is rather oppressive in its sombreness, but
memorable in its haunting apocalyptic imagery – much of which is familiar even to
those who have never seen the film, thanks to its entry into the cinematic lexicon by
way of frequent parody.

Key quote
'An allegory with a theme that is quite simple: man, his eternal search for God, with
death as his only certainty.' – Ingmar Bergman in a programme note to *The Seventh
Seal*, 1957.

Did you know ...
The closing 'Dance of Death' was quickly improvised, with crew members and
passers-by taking part, when Bergman was struck by a dramatic evening sky.

SHADOWS

John Cassavetes, USA, 1959
Lelia Goldoni, Ben Carruthers, Hugh Hurd
81 minutes; b/w

The film
The first feature from pioneering independent director Cassavetes is a jazz-scored, free-flowing, largely improvised portrait of two black musicians and their lighter-skinned sister, pursuing love, creativity and racial identity through the beatnik underground of New York City.

Why watch it?
Unquestionably rough at the edges, but possessed of a raw elegance and a slippery, loose-limbed vibrancy, this is an exhilarating film to watch, and by no means lacking in dramatic tension despite its looseness of form.

Key quote
'Arguably the founding work of the American independent cinema.' – J Hoberman, *The Village Voice*, 18 June 2003.

Did you know ...
After a poor response to initial screenings in 1957, Cassavetes reshot much of the film. The original version was believed lost until a complete print was discovered in an attic in 2002.

SINGIN' IN THE RAIN

Stanley Donen and Gene Kelly, USA, 1952
Gene Kelly, Donald O'Connor, Debbie Reynolds, Jean Hagen
103 minutes; colour

The film
Hollywood, 1927. Silent movie star Don Lockwood (Kelly) has no trouble with the transition to sound, but his screen partner Lina Lamont (Hagen) has a voice like a cheese-grater. Enter Reynolds's fresh-faced, silken-voiced aspiring actress to dub Lina's lines and steal Don's heart.

Why watch it?
Most of the songs weren't new, the female leads were unknown, and exhaustion and sickness plagued the stars, to the extent that Kelly shot the title number with a 103° fever. Yet the outcome was a dazzling success, and remains rousing, hilarious (Hagen especially) and gorgeously choreographed.

Key quote
'*Singin' in the Rain* and childbirth were the two hardest things I ever had to do in my life.' – Debbie Reynolds, quoted in *The Saturday Evening Post*, 2003.

Did you know ...
Reynolds was herself dubbed by actress Betty Noyes for at least one song ('Would You?').

SNOW WHITE AND THE SEVEN DWARFS

USA, 1937
Voices: Adriana Caselotti, Harry Stockwell, Lucille LaVerne
83 minutes; colour

The film

Disney's first animated feature, based on the Grimms' fairy tale about a young girl who takes refuge with a group of forest-dwelling dwarf miners after escaping from her jealous stepmother, the Queen.

Why watch it?

The cultural longevity and enduring freshness of this groundbreaking, risk-taking work would astonish those industry insiders who nicknamed it 'Disney's Folly' during production. If Snow White herself is a bit of a sap, the dwarfs, the wicked Queen and those terrifying trees stand as some of cinema's most memorable creations.

Key quote

'The greatest film ever made.' – Film-maker Sergei Eisenstein (attributed).

Did you know ...

The film was given a special Academy Award®, comprising one full-sized statuette and seven miniature ones.

Rejected Dwarf Names

The original Brothers Grimm fairy tale gives no names for Snow White's dwarf companions, but in Disney's film version they are known as Bashful, Doc, Dopey, Grumpy, Happy, Sleepy and Sneezy. Other dwarf names that were reportedly considered for use in the film include Awful, Biggo-Ego, Busty, Chesty, Dirty, Hotsy, Hungry, Jumpy and Shifty.

SOME LIKE IT HOT

Billy Wilder, USA, 1959
Marilyn Monroe, Jack Lemmon, Tony Curtis, Joe E Brown
120 minutes; b/w

The film

On the run from the Mob after witnessing the St Valentine's Day massacre in 1920s Chicago, two jazz musicians drag up and join an all-girl band. Joe (Curtis) falls for Monroe's tipsy banjo player, while Jerry (Lemmon) is himself pursued by Joe E Brown's doddery tycoon.

Why watch it?

The tensions on set have been well documented – Curtis supposedly claimed that kissing Monroe was like kissing Hitler, while Wilder commented that she had 'breasts like granite and a mind like Swiss cheese'. Yet out of the maelstrom emerged a relentlessly entertaining comic treasure, beautifully judged and performed.

Key quote
'Nobody's perfect!' – Joe E Brown as Osgood Fielding III.

Did you know ...
At one stage in the troubled shoot, Monroe required 47 takes to deliver the words 'It's me, Sugar' in the correct order.

THE SOUND OF MUSIC

Robert Wise, USA, 1965
Julie Andrews, Christopher Plummer, Eleanor Parker
174 minutes; colour

The film
Having proved herself ill-suited to convent life, high-spirited Salzburg novitiate Maria is enlisted to care for the seven children of widowed Baron Von Trapp. She duly brings sunshine and music into everyone's lives; but even bright copper kettles and warm woollen mittens can't hold off the looming threat of Nazism.

Why watch it?
The final musical collaboration between Richard Rodgers and Oscar Hammerstein II was a hit on Broadway, but this film version has become a legend. Though out of critical favour due to its tooth-aching sentimentality, it has considerable visual grace (witness the famous opening sequence) and undeniably memorable musical numbers.

Key quote
'I can't seem to stop singing wherever I am. And what's worse, I can't seem to stop saying things – anything and everything I think and feel.' – Julie Andrews as Maria.

Did you know ...
Screenwriter Ernest Lehman also wrote or co-wrote the scripts for *Sweet Smell of Success* (1957), *North by Northwest* (1959) and *West Side Story* (1961).

STAR WARS TRILOGY

Star Wars
George Lucas, USA, 1977
Mark Hamill, Carrie Fisher, Harrison Ford, Peter Cushing
121 minutes; colour

The Empire Strikes Back
Irvin Kershner, USA, 1980
Mark Hamill, Carrie Fisher, Harrison Ford, Billy Dee Williams
124 minutes; colour

Return of the Jedi
Richard Marquand, USA, 1983
Mark Hamill, Carrie Fisher, Harrison Ford, Alec Guinness
134 minutes; colour

The films

A sweeping three-part account of the effort to keep control of an ancient but enlightened interplanetary civilization away from the tyrannical rule of the evil Empire, centring upon the adventures of a young Jedi Knight, Luke Skywalker.

Why watch them?

A generation of film buffs having steadfastly refused to put away childish things, this triumph of spectacle, mass marketing and modern myth-making has only gained in prominence (aided, of course, by Lucas's recent addition of three controversial new prequel episodes). Nostalgia helps to cover the cracks, but the scope is fearsomely ambitious, and the continued influence immeasurable.

Key quote

'A long time ago in a galaxy far, far away...' – Opening text scrolls

Did you know ...

In 1997, Lucas remastered and reissued the three films, with new titles corresponding to their place in the six-part series: *Episode IV: A New Hope; Episode V: The Empire Strikes Back*; and *Episode VI: Return of the Jedi*.

A STREETCAR NAMED DESIRE

Elia Kazan, USA, 1951
Vivien Leigh, Marlon Brando, Kim Hunter, Karl Malden
122 minutes; b/w
1952 Academy Awards®: Best Actress: Vivien Leigh

The film

Frail spinster Blanche Dubois turns up at the New Orleans home of her pregnant sister, seeking solace after a sex scandal and a financial crisis – only to clash violently with her brother-in-law, the brutish but passionate Stanley Kowalski. Adapted from the stage play by Tennessee Williams.

Why watch it?

A seething melodrama with performances that strain the boundaries of the characters' claustrophobic surroundings just as Brando's physique strains his iconic white T-shirt. It made him a star, showcasing a method-derived intensity that would spawn countless imitators, though it was Leigh's more mannered work that took the Academy Award®.

Key quote

'Whoever you are, I have always depended on the kindness of strangers.' – Vivien Leigh as Blanche Dubois.

Did you know ...

This was the first film to win three Academy Awards® in the acting categories – Leigh for Best Actress, Karl Malden for Best Supporting Actor and Kim Hunter for Best Supporting Actress. Only *Network* (1976) has matched this record.

From Stage to Screen

Almost all the cast of the original Broadway production of *A Streetcar Named Desire* were invited to reprise their roles in the 1951 film; the only exception was Jessica Tandy. Although Tandy's portrayal of Blanche Dubois had been highly praised by critics and audiences, even winning her a Tony award, she was replaced by the more famous Vivien Leigh in a bid to improve the film's chances at the box office.

SUNRISE: A SONG OF TWO HUMANS

F W Murnau, USA, 1927
Janet Gaynor, George O'Brien
95 minutes; b/w; silent
1929 Academy Awards®: Best Picture; Best Actress: Janet Gaynor

The film

A corrupt city girl – a prototype for countless *femmes fatales* to come – seduces a humble country farmer, and tries to persuade him to murder his virtuous wife to be with her.

Why watch it?

A quite amazing emotional odyssey – from marital boredom through sexual obsession, escape fantasies, murderous temptation, remorse and eventual redemption – related in startlingly vivid images and spare, evocative fragments of text.

Key quote

'This song of the Man and the Woman is of no place. You might hear it anywhere at any time.' – Text card from early in the film

Did you know ...

After the massive success of his German productions *The Last Laugh* (1924) and *Faust* (1926), Murnau was invited to Hollywood by William Fox and given free rein to make this, the most expensive silent film that the studio ever produced.

SUNSET BOULEVARD

Billy Wilder, USA, 1950
William Holden, Gloria Swanson, Erich von Stroheim
110 minutes; b/w
1951 Academy Awards®: Best Score

The film

A corpse is floating in a Beverly Hills swimming pool; in flashback, we learn how it got there. Luckless hack writer Joe (Holden) accepts the lavish attentions of faded screen legend Norma Desmond – but in return, Norma wants her comeback, and she's not taking no for an answer.

Why watch it?
Wilder was a master of both comedy and film noir, and elements of both genres combine to stunning effect in this black-hearted portrait of disappointment, compromise and depraved narcissism in tarnished Tinseltown. Taut, angular and fiercely absorbing, it delivers to the bitter end.

Key quote
'All right, Mr De Mille, I'm ready for my close-up...' – Gloria Swanson as Norma Desmond.

Did you know ...
Swanson's part was turned down by Mae West, Mary Pickford and Pola Negri; Holden's by Montgomery Clift and Fred MacMurray.

TAXI DRIVER

Martin Scorsese, USA, 1976
Robert De Niro, Jodie Foster, Cybill Shepherd, Harvey Keitel
113 minutes; colour
1976 Cannes Film Festival: Palme d'Or

The film
Vietnam veteran and cab driver Travis Bickle (De Niro) becomes obsessed by the sleaze and violence of nocturnal New York City. A failed romance and an encounter with Foster's hard-bitten child prostitute finally drive him to take drastic action against the depravity around him.

Why watch it?
Not so much a vigilante thriller or a social comment movie as a close-up study of one man's breakdown, the intensity and conviction of which film-makers have been striving to match ever since. De Niro combines quirky charm with blood-red menace; the supporting performances, particularly Foster's, are extraordinary.

Key quote
'Someday a real rain will come and wash all this scum off the streets.' – Robert De Niro as Travis Bickle.

Did you know ...
Screenwriter Paul Schrader wrote *Taxi Driver* in ten days, drawing on his own experiences of mental breakdown and extreme depression. He is said to have periodically stopped typing and held a gun to his own head for inspiration.

THREE COLOURS TRILOGY

Three Colours: Blue (Trois couleurs: Bleu; Trzy kolory: Niebieski)
Krzysztof Kieslowski, Poland/France/Switzerland, 1993
Juliette Binoche, Benôit Régent, Florence Pernel
100 minutes; colour
1993 Venice Film Festival: Golden Lion

Three Colours: White (Trois couleurs: Blanc; Trzy kolory: Bialy)
Krzysztof Kieslowski, Poland/France/Switzerland,1994
Julie Delpy, Zbigniew Zamachowski
91 minutes; colour

Three Colours: Red (Trois couleurs: Rouge; Trzy kolory: Czerwony)
Krzysztof Kieslowski, Poland/France/Switzerland, 1994
Irène Jacob, Jean-Louis Trintignant
99 minutes; colour

The films
This trilogy, named after the colours of the French flag, examines the ideals of the French revolution – liberty, equality, fraternity – through three intense and graceful studies of fractured lives. *Blue* sees a woman endeavour to rebuild her life after her husband and daughter are killed in an accident; *White* follows a Polish man's efforts to win back his faithless French wife; and *Red* circles the tender connection formed between an elderly loner and a troubled young model.

Why watch them?
If the awe with which Kieslowski regards his gorgeous leading ladies results in rather distant, idealized protagonists (resulting, arguably, in this trilogy seeming rather more profound to male viewers than female ones), the technical precision and elegance of this three-part arthouse fetish object cannot be disputed. For an intense character study, choose *Blue*; for astringent comedy, go for *White*; and for one of cinema's most touching platonic love affairs, stop at *Red*.

Key quote
'A monumental work of tremendous formal, moral, and dramatic sophistication.'
– Film critic Dave Kehr in *Film Comment*, 2000.

Did you know ...
When he died in 1996, Kieslowski was planning another trilogy: *Heaven*, *Purgatory* and *Hell*. The first part, *Heaven*, was directed by Tom Tykwer in 2002.

TITANIC

James Cameron, USA, 1997
Kate Winslet, Leonardo DiCaprio, Billy Zane, Gloria Stuart
194 minutes; colour
1998 Academy Awards®: Best Picture, Best Director, Best Music: Original Score, Best Music: Original Song

The film
The 1912 maritime disaster here becomes a backdrop to a fictional romance. A picture of a necklace found in the wreckage of the *Titanic* prompts its elderly owner to recall her waterlogged love affair with a social inferior on board the doomed liner.

Why watch it?
Hokum it may be, but it's impossible to deny the impact of this aggressively sentimental mega-blockbuster. Its vast expense ($200 million plus) and

corresponding profits upped the stakes for everyone; its vapid romantic theatrics may be eternally spoofed.

Key quote

'Unlike its namesake, this glossy, bombastic juggernaut will not sink. Everyone will see it ... and so they should, if only to ponder the future of mainstream cinema.' – Film critic Geoff Andrew in *Time Out*, 1997.

Did you know ...

Worldwide box-office takings for *Titanic* were staggeringly high, exceeding $1.8 billion.

TOKYO STORY (TOKYO MONOGATARI)

Yasujiro Ozu, Japan, 1953
Chishu Ryu, Cheiko Higashiyama, Setsuko Hara
136 minutes; b/w

The film

An elderly couple pay a visit to their offspring in Tokyo, only to be confronted by indifference, preoccupation and – ultimately – the aching chasm between the generations.

Why watch it?

Ozu's attention to the nuances of conversation and gesture, the niceties of emotional manipulation and the devastating legacy of regret has had immeasurable influence, and is showcased to perfection in his best-known work – no less than his rigidly controlled and sparsely beautiful visual set-ups.

Key quote

'Never before and never again since has the cinema been so close to its essence and its purpose: to present an image of man in our century, a usable, true and valid image.' – Film-maker Wim Wenders in his documentary *Tokyo-Ga* (1985).

Did you know ...

For interior shots, Ozu almost exclusively employed the same unusually low camera position. This has become known as the 'tatami shot', because it approximates the eye level of someone kneeling on a tatami mat.

TOUCH OF EVIL

Orson Welles, USA, 1958
Janet Leigh, Orson Welles, Charlton Heston
95 minutes; b/w

The film

Mexican narcotics officer Vargas (Heston), honeymooning with his young American bride (Leigh), gets caught up in a spiral of corruption when a car bomb kills a US businessman in a border town. Vargas's investigation pits him against Welles's corrupt and cynical detective.

Why watch it?
If the story – based on a novel by Whit Masterson that Welles never bothered to read – is a somewhat murky and hard-hearted affair, the style is dazzling: light and shadow in violent interplay, sinuous camerawork and an unforgiving build-up of Kafkaesque paranoia.

Key quote
'A flat-out, all-cylinders-running, eye-popping masterpiece.' – Film critic Fred Camper, *The Chicago Reader*, 1998.

Did you know ...
Janet Leigh broke her left arm just before shooting, and had to have her cast sawn off for scenes where it couldn't be concealed.

TOY STORY

John Lasseter, USA, 1995
Voices: Tom Hanks, Tim Allen, Don Rickles
81 minutes; colour

The film
The first fully computer-generated feature-length film, and the debut feature from the groundbreaking digital animation studio Pixar. When Andy gets a fancy new spaceman toy named Buzz Lightyear, Woody the cowboy is jealous. But when Buzz goes missing, all the other toys must pool their resources to save him.

Why watch it?
The replacement of traditional, painstaking flat animation by three-dimensional CGI could have proved a soul-sapping modern tragedy, were it not for the towering standards set by Pixar. The script is as dazzling as the visuals: superbly witty, sharp without cynicism and touching without sentimentality.

Key quote
'To infinity ... and beyond!' – Tim Allen as Buzz Lightyear.

Did you know ...
Pixar's six feature films to date have grossed more than $3 billion worldwide.

TRAINSPOTTING

Danny Boyle, UK, 1996
Ewan McGregor, Robert Carlyle, Ewen Bremner, Jonny Lee Miller
94 minutes; colour

The film
Episodes in the lives of a group of drug-addled Edinburgh youths, based on the 1993 novel by Irvine Welsh. Mark Renton (McGregor) attempts to kick his habit, but his ramshackle band of associates aren't much help – and when a drug deal promises to make them all rich, he's drawn back in.

Why watch it?

Though a flurry of hype turned it into a somewhat weary totem for a UK cinema revolution that didn't quite happen, *Trainspotting* is an exhilarating piece of film-making in its own right – bold in its bleakness, sharply funny, and shot and edited with dizzying imagination.

Key quote

'I chose not to choose life. I chose something else. And the reasons? There are no reasons. Who needs reasons when you've got heroin?' – Ewan McGregor as Mark Renton.

Did you know ...

Boyle plans a sequel, based on Welsh's follow-up novel *Porno*, but is waiting for his original cast to display more evidence of the ravages of time.

Dole's War on Drugs

Shortly after the release of *Trainspotting* in America, US Senator Bob Dole publicly condemned the film for what he described as its glorification of heroin use. Dole was running for President at the time, and wanted to emphasize his tough anti-drugs stance – however, this strategy backfired when he later admitted that he had not actually seen the film.

TRIUMPH OF THE WILL (TRIUMPH DES WILLENS)

Leni Riefenstahl, Germany, 1935
114 minutes; b/w

The film

Commissioned by the German Propaganda Ministry in 1934, this epic documentary covers the events of the Sixth Nuremberg Party Congress, and pays detailed tribute to both Adolf Hitler and the concept of the Aryan super-race.

Why watch it?

Groundbreaking in technical terms, grimly compelling as a propaganda piece and invaluable as a record of the collective Nazi self-image, this is a troubling but essential work, the ongoing influence of which upon cinema and advertising cannot be denied.

Key quote

'It's such an incredible burden, that to say "sorry"... it's inadequate, it expresses too little.' – Leni Riefenstahl in the documentary *Die Macht der Bilder: Leni Riefenstahl,* 1993.

Did you know ...

After the war, Riefenstahl spent four months in a French detention camp. Unable to find funding for further films, she moved into stills photography.

2001: A SPACE ODYSSEY

Stanley Kubrick, UK/USA, 1968
Keir Dullea, Gary Lockwood, William Sylvester, Douglas Rain
139 minutes; colour

The film
An epic in three ponderous parts. First, apes acquire intelligence, and through it the
awareness of their destructive capabilities. Then we join some of their descendants
on a mission to Jupiter that is disrupted by a rebellious computer. Finally, in a
mysterious, timeless realm, a man witnesses his own death and is reborn.

Why watch it?
A vast, creepy and enigmatic creation, part science-fiction thriller, part spiritual
reverie and part doom-laden meditation on mankind's inexorable progress towards
the void. Whether the ideas really mesh is a moot point in the face of such
audacious ambition and technical virtuosity.

Key quote
'If you understand *2001* completely, we failed. We wanted to raise far more
questions than we answered.' – Arthur C Clarke, co-screenwriter (attributed).

Did you know ...
The ditty performed by HAL the computer, 'A Bicycle Built for Two', really was the
first song successfully taught to a computer – an IBM 7094 in 1961.

VERTIGO

Alfred Hitchcock, USA, 1958
James Stewart, Kim Novak, Barbara Bel Geddes
128 minutes; colour

The film
Still recovering from seeing his partner perish in a fall, detective Scotty (Stewart)
takes on a private case, investigating Novak's enigmatic blonde on behalf of her
husband. Scotty promptly falls for the woman himself, and enters into a labyrinth of
obsession, illusion and betrayal.

Why watch it?
Hitchcock's most layered and disturbing study of sexual fantasy and emotional
duplicity evades his characteristic coldness via beautifully complex performances
from Stewart and Novak. It's also technically superb, with gorgeous Saul Bass
titles, Bernard Herrman's much-copied score and a remarkable, hallucinatory dream
sequence.

Key quote
'To put it plainly, the man wants to go to bed with a woman who's dead; he is
indulging in a form of necrophilia.' – Alfred Hitchcock, quoted in *Find the Director
and Other Hitchcock Games*, Thomas M Leitch, 1991.

Did you know ...
Working titles included *From Among the Dead*, *Illicit Darkening* and *Listen Darkling*.

WHISKY GALORE

Alexander Mackendrick, UK, 1949
Basil Radford, Joan Greenwood, Gordon Jackson
82 minues; b/w

The film
The inhabitants of the tiny (and fictional) Scottish island of Toddy think their ship has come in when a wrecked freighter dumps 7,000 crates of whisky on their rocky shores. But the Home Guard is determined to prevent the appropriation of the spoils.

Why watch it?
Bureaucracy versus homespun common sense, haughty English incomers versus no-nonsense Scots and a healthy glow of whimsical romance characterize this first feature by the virtually infallible Mackendrick, which remains one of the best-loved products of the legendary Ealing studios.

Key quote
'A Highland fling on a tight little island' – Original tag line

Did you know ...
The film was based on the novel by Compton MacKenzie, which was in turn inspired by the true story of the sinking of the SS *Politician* and its cargo of whisky in the Outer Hebrides in 1943.

WHITE HEAT

Raoul Walsh, USA, 1949
James Cagney, Virginia Mayo, Edmond O'Brien
114 minutes; b/w

The film
Cagney's volatile gangster kingpin Cody Jarrett escapes prison with a daring heist plan, little realizing that his closest allies are out to destroy him and his best hope of protection might just be the undercover cop who has infiltrated his gang.

Why watch it?
An extraordinary, histrionic gangster thriller, with a psychoanalytic subtext that bled into many a subsequent crime thriller (Norman Bates wasn't the first movie killer with a thing about Mom). Cagney is terrifying, while the film's climax, set in a monumental chemical plant, is simply spectacular.

Key quote
'Made it, Ma! Top of the world!' – James Cagney as Cody Jarrett.

Did you know ...
Raoul Walsh's career spanned half a century, commencing with his work as an assistant director and actor for D W Griffith.

THE WILD BUNCH

Sam Peckinpah, USA, 1969
William Holden, Ernest Borgnine, Robert Ryan, Edmond O'Brien
134 minutes; colour

The film
A group of ageing outlaws attempt a final bank job, but are forced to flee to Mexico when it goes wrong. Once there, they arrange to cover their losses by stealing a shipment of guns from a US army train for corrupt warlord General Mapeche.

Why watch it?
This punishingly violent western shows the displacement of old western values by new allegiances and new weaponry. Visually it is stunning, with remarkable editing by Peckinpah himself; morally, it's a little more confused, never quite sure whether it's celebrating the heroism of its bloodthirsty protagonists or decrying their inhumanity.

Key quote
'If they move, kill 'em.' – William Holden as Pike Bishop.

Did you know ...
An estimated 90,000 rounds of blanks were fired during the making of the film.

WINGS OF DESIRE (DER HIMMEL ÜBER BERLIN)

Wim Wenders, Germany, 1987
Bruno Ganz, Solveig Dommartin, Peter Falk, Otto Sander
127 minutes; b/w & colour

The film
Angels patrol the streets of Berlin, listening in on the troubles of humans and occasionally offering a little subliminal solace – until one of them (Ganz) falls in love with a mortal (Dommartin) and decides to give up his immortality for love.

Why watch it?
Though it contains the seeds of self-indulgent tendencies that would mar much of Wenders's subsequent work – historical portentousness, swooning romanticism, whimsy – this modern fairy tale never feels sentimental or overloaded. Gorgeous to look at, it is also funny, gently profound and deeply touching in its compassionate optimism.

Key quote
'A soaring vision that appeals to the senses and the spirit.' – Desson Howe in *The Washington Post*, 1 July 1988.

Did you know ...
Wenders cast *Columbo* star Peter Falk at the last minute, on the suggestion of assistant director Claire Denis. He had previously considered the former German Chancellor and Nobel Peace Prize winner Willy Brandt for Falk's role.

THE WIZARD OF OZ

Victor Fleming, USA, 1939
Judy Garland
101 minutes; b/w & colour
1940 Academy Awards®: Best Music: Original Score; Best Music: Original Song

The film

After quarrelling with her aunt, farm girl Dorothy wishes herself elsewhere, only for a cyclone to grant her wish by sweeping her up and away. She finds herself in the magical land of Oz, populated by Munchkins and ruled over by two witches and one all-powerful wizard.

Why watch it?

With its hectic production design, its indelible songs and the haunting oddness of some of its ideas, this most iconic of film musicals offers both straightforward pleasure and the potential for endless dubious reinterpretation. Throw in the subsequent real-life suffering of Judy Garland, and you have all the requirements for immortality.

Key quote

'Toto, I've a feeling we're not in Kansas any more!' – Judy Garland as Dorothy.

Did you know ...

Fleming was one of five directors to do stints on the film. The others were Richard Thorpe, George Cukor, King Vidor and Mervyn LeRoy.

Dorothy's Ruby Slippers

The MGM costume department made several pairs of the iconic 'ruby slippers' worn by Judy Garland in *The Wizard of Oz*. The sparkling, red-sequinned shoes have since become highly sought after by collectors, with one pair selling for $666,000 (roughly £390,000) at an auction held in 2000 by Christie's, New York.

ACADEMY AWARDS®

Awarded annually by the Academy of Motion Picture Arts and Sciences. Popularly known as Oscars®.

Year	Best Film (director)	Best Director	Best Actor	Best Actress	Best Supporting Actor	Best Supporting Actress
1927/8	Wings (William A Wellman)	Lewis Milestone Two Arabian Knights; Frank Borzage 7th Heaven	Emil Jannings The Last Command, The Way of All Flesh	Janet Gaynor 7th Heaven, Street Angel, Sunrise		
1928/9	The Broadway Melody (Harry Beaumont)	Frank Lloyd The Divine Lady	Warner Baxter In Old Arizona	Mary Pickford Coquette		
1929/30	All Quiet on the Western Front (Lewis Milestone)	Lewis Milestone All Quiet on the Western Front	George Arliss Disraeli	Norma Shearer The Divorcee		
1930/1	Cimarron (Wesley Ruggles)	Norman Taurog Skippy	Lionel Barrymore A Free Soul	Marie Dressler Min and Bill		
1931/2	Grand Hotel (Edmund Goulding)	Frank Borzage Bad Girl	Wallace Beery The Champ; Frederic March Dr Jekyll and Mr Hyde	Helen Hayes The Sin of Madame Claudet		

Year	Best Film (director)	Best Director	Best Actor	Best Actress	Best Supporting Actor	Best Supporting Actress
1932/3	*Cavalcade* (Frank Lloyd)	Frank Lloyd *Cavalcade*	Charles Laughton *The Private Life of Henry VIII*	Katharine Hepburn *Morning Glory*		
1934	*It Happened One Night* (Frank Capra)	Frank Capra *It Happened One Night*	Clark Gable *It Happened One Night*	Claudette Colbert *It Happened One Night*		
1935	*Mutiny on the Bounty* (Frank Lloyd)	John Ford *The Informer*	Victor Laglen *The Informer*	Bette Davis *Dangerous*		
1936	*The Great Ziegfeld* (Robert Z Leonard)	Frank Capra *Mr Deeds Goes to Town*	Paul Muni *The Story of Louis Pasteur*	Luise Rainer *The Great Ziegfeld*	Walter Brennan *Come and Get It*	Gale Sondergaard *Anthony Adverse*
1937	*The Life of Émile Zola* (William Dieterle)	Leo McCarey *The Awful Truth*	Spencer Tracy *Captains Courageous*	Luise Rainer *The Good Earth*	Joseph Schildkraut *The Life of Émile Zola*	Alice Brady *In Old Chicago*
1938	*You Can't Take It With You* (Frank Capra)	Frank Capra *You Can't Take It With You*	Spencer Tracy *Boys Town*	Bette Davis *Jezebel*	Walter Brennan *Kentucky*	Fay Bainter *Jezebel*
1939	*Gone with the Wind* (Victor Fleming)	Victor Fleming *Gone with the Wind*	Robert Donat *Goodbye, Mr Chips*	Vivien Leigh *Gone with the Wind*	Thomas Mitchell *Stagecoach*	Hattie McDaniel *Gone with the Wind*

Year	Best Film (director)	Best Director	Best Actor	Best Actress	Best Supporting Actor	Best Supporting Actress
1940	Rebecca (Alfred Hitchcock)	John Ford The Grapes of Wrath	James Stewart The Philadelphia Story	Ginger Rogers Kitty Foyle	Walter Brennan The Westerner	Jane Darwell The Grapes of Wrath
1941	How Green Was My Valley (John Ford)	John Ford How Green Was My Valley	Gary Cooper Sergeant York	Joan Fontaine Suspicion	Donald Crisp How Green Was My Valley	Mary Astor The Great Lie
1942	Mrs Miniver (William Wyler)	William Wyler Mrs Miniver	James Cagney Yankee Doodle Dandy	Greer Garson Mrs Miniver	Van Heflin Johnny Eager	Teresa Wright Mrs Miniver
1943	Casablanca (Michael Curtiz)	Michael Curtiz Casablanca	Paul Lukas Watch on the Rhine	Jennifer Jones The Song of Bernadette	Charles Coburn The More the Merrier	Katina Paxinou For Whom the Bell Tolls
1944	Going My Way (Leo McCarey)	Leo McCarey Going My Way	Bing Crosby Going My Way	Ingrid Bergman Gaslight	Barry Fitzgerald Going My Way	Ethel Barrymore None But the Lonely Heart
1945	The Lost Weekend (Billy Wilder)	Billy Wilder The Lost Weekend	Ray Milland The Lost Weekend	Joan Crawford Mildred Pierce	James Dunn A Tree Grows in Brooklyn	Anne Revere National Velvet
1946	The Best Years of Our Lives (William Wyler)	William Wyler The Best Years of Our Lives	Fredric March The Best Years of Our Lives	Olivia de Havilland To Each His Own	Harold Russell The Best Years of Our Lives	Anne Baxter The Razor's Edge
1947	Gentleman's Agreement (Elia Kazan)	Elia Kazan Gentleman's Agreement	Ronald Colman A Double Life	Loretta Young The Farmer's Daughter	Edmund Gwenn Miracle on 34th Street	Celeste Holm Gentleman's Agreement

Year	Best Film (director)	Best Director	Best Actor	Best Actress	Best Supporting Actor	Best Supporting Actress
1948	*Hamlet* (Laurence Olivier)	John Huston *The Treasure of the Sierra Madre*	Laurence Olivier *Hamlet*	Jane Wyman *Johnny Belinda*	Walter Huston *The Treasure of the Sierra Madre*	Claire Trevor *Key Largo*
1949	*All the King's Men* (Robert Rossen)	Joseph L Mankiewicz *A Letter to Three Wives*	Broderick Crawford *All the King's Men*	Olivia de Havilland *The Heiress*	Dean Jagger *Twelve O'Clock High*	Mercedes McCambridge *All the King's Men*
1950	*All About Eve* (Joseph L Mankiewicz)	Joseph L Mankiewicz *All About Eve*	José Ferrer *Cyrano de Bergerac*	Judy Holliday *Born Yesterday*	George Sanders *All About Eve*	Josephine Hull *Harvey*
1951	*An American in Paris* (Vicente Minnelli)	George Stevens *A Place in the Sun*	Humphrey Bogart *The African Queen*	Vivien Leigh *A Streetcar Named Desire*	Karl Malden *A Streetcar Named Desire*	Kim Hunter *A Streetcar Named Desire*
1952	*The Greatest Show on Earth* (Cecil B De Mille)	John Ford *The Quiet Man*	Gary Cooper *High Noon*	Shirley Booth *Come Back, Little Sheba*	Anthony Quinn *Viva Zapata!*	Gloria Grahame *The Bad and the Beautiful*
1953	*From Here to Eternity* (Fred Zinnemann)	Fred Zinnemann *From Here to Eternity*	William Holden *Stalag 17*	Audrey Hepburn *Roman Holiday*	Frank Sinatra *From Here to Eternity*	Donna Reed *From Here to Eternity*
1954	*On the Waterfront* (Elia Kazan)	Elia Kazan *On the Waterfront*	Marlon Brando *On the Waterfront*	Grace Kelly *The Country Girl*	Edmond O'Brien *The Barefoot Contessa*	Eva Marie Saint *On the Waterfront*
1955	*Marty* (Delbert Mann)	Delbert Mann *Marty*	Ernest Borgnine *Marty*	Anna Magnani *The Rose Tattoo*	Jack Lemmon *Mister Roberts*	Jo Van Fleet *East of Eden*

Year	Best Film (director)	Best Director	Best Actor	Best Actress	Best Supporting Actor	Best Supporting Actress
1956	*Around the World in 80 Days* (Michael Anderson)	George Stevens *Giant*	Yul Brynner *The King and I*	Ingrid Bergman *Anastasia*	Anthony Quinn *Lust for Life*	Dorothy Malone *Written on the Wind*
1957	*The Bridge on the River Kwai* (David Lean)	David Lean *The Bridge on the River Kwai*	Alec Guinness *The Bridge on the River Kwai*	Joanne Woodward *The Three Faces of Eve*	Red Buttons *Sayonara*	Miyoshi Umeki *Sayonara*
1958	*Gigi* (Vincente Minnelli)	Vincente Minnelli *Gigi*	David Niven *Separate Tables*	Susan Hayward *I Want To Live!*	Burl Ives *The Big Country*	Wendy Hiller *Separate Tables*
1959	*Ben-Hur* (William Wyler)	William Wyler *Ben-Hur*	Charlton Heston *Ben-Hur*	Simone Signoret *Room at the Top*	Hugh Griffith *Ben-Hur*	Shelley Winters *The Diary of Anne Frank*
1960	*The Apartment* (Billy Wilder)	Billy Wilder *The Apartment*	Burt Lancaster *Elmer Gantry*	Elizabeth Taylor *Butterfield 8*	Peter Ustinov *Spartacus*	Shirley Jones *Elmer Gantry*
1961	*West Side Story* (Robert Wise, Jerome Robbins)	Robert Wise, Jerome Robbins *West Side Story*	Maximilian Schell *Judgment at Nuremberg*	Sophia Loren *Two Women*	George Chakiris *West Side Story*	Rita Moreno *West Side Story*
1962	*Lawrence of Arabia* (David Lean)	David Lean *Lawrence of Arabia*	Gregory Peck *To Kill a Mockingbird*	Anne Bancroft *The Miracle Worker*	Ed Begley *Sweet Bird of Youth*	Patty Duke *The Miracle Worker*
1963	*Tom Jones* (Tony Richardson)	Tony Richardson *Tom Jones*	Sidney Poitier *Lilies of the Field*	Patricia Neal *Hud*	Melvyn Douglas *Hud*	Margaret Rutherford *The V.I.P.s*

Year	Best Film (director)	Best Director	Best Actor	Best Actress	Best Supporting Actor	Best Supporting Actress
1964	*My Fair Lady* (George Cukor)	George Cukor *My Fair Lady*	Rex Harrison *My Fair Lady*	Julie Andrews *Mary Poppins*	Peter Ustinov *Topkapi*	Lila Kedrova *Zorba the Greek*
1965	*The Sound of Music* (Robert Wise)	Robert Wise *The Sound of Music*	Lee Marvin *Cat Ballou*	Julie Christie *Darling*	Martin Balsam *A Thousand Clowns*	Shelley Winters *A Patch of Blue*
1966	*A Man for All Seasons* (Fred Zinnemann)	Fred Zinnemann *A Man for All Seasons*	Paul Scofield *A Man for All Seasons*	Elizabeth Taylor *Who's Afraid of Virginia Woolf?*	Walter Matthau *The Fortune Cookie*	Sandy Dennis *Who's Afraid of Virginia Woolf?*
1967	*In the Heat of the Night* (Norman Jewison)	Mike Nichols *The Graduate*	Rod Steiger *In the Heat of the Night*	Katharine Hepburn *Guess Who's Coming to Dinner*	George Kennedy *Cool Hand Luke*	Estelle Parsons *Bonnie and Clyde*
1968	*Oliver!* (Carol Reed)	Carol Reed *Oliver!*	Cliff Robertson *Charly*	Katharine Hepburn *The Lion in Winter*; Barbra Streisand *Funny Girl*	Jack Albertson *The Subject Was Roses*	Ruth Gordon *Rosemary's Baby*
1969	*Midnight Cowboy* (John Schlesinger)	John Schlesinger *Midnight Cowboy*	John Wayne *True Grit*	Maggie Smith *The Prime of Miss Jean Brodie*	Gig Young *They Shoot Horses, Don't They?*	Goldie Hawn *Cactus Flower*
1970	*Patton* (Franklin J Schaffner)	Franklin J Schaffner *Patton*	George C Scott *Patton*	Glenda Jackson *Women in Love*	John Mills *Ryan's Daughter*	Helen Hayes *Airport*

Year	Best Film (director)	Best Director	Best Actor	Best Actress	Best Supporting Actor	Best Supporting Actress
1971	*The French Connection* (William Friedkin)	William Friedkin *The French Connection*	Gene Hackman *The French Connection*	Jane Fonda *Klute*	Ben Johnson *The Last Picture Show*	Cloris Leachman *The Last Picture Show*
1972	*The Godfather* (Francis Ford Coppola)	Bob Fosse *Cabaret*	Marlon Brando *The Godfather*	Liza Minnelli *Cabaret*	Joel Grey *Cabaret*	Eileen Heckart *Butterflies Are Free*
1973	*The Sting* (George Roy Hill)	George Roy Hill *The Sting*	Jack Lemmon *Save the Tiger*	Glenda Jackson *A Touch of Class*	John Houseman *The Paper Chase*	Tatum O'Neal *Paper Moon*
1974	*The Godfather Part II* (Francis Ford Coppola)	Francis Ford Coppola *The Godfather Part II*	Art Carney *Harry and Tonto*	Ellen Burstyn *Alice Doesn't Live Here Anymore*	Robert De Niro *The Godfather Part II*	Ingrid Bergman *Murder on the Orient Express*
1975	*One Flew Over the Cuckoo's Nest* (Miloš Forman)	Miloš Forman *One Flew Over the Cuckoo's Nest*	Jack Nicholson *One Flew Over the Cuckoo's Nest*	Louise Fletcher *One Flew Over the Cuckoo's Nest*	George Burns *The Sunshine Boys*	Lee Grant *Shampoo*
1976	*Rocky* (John G Avildsen)	John G Avildsen *Rocky*	Peter Finch *Network*	Faye Dunaway *Network*	Jason Robards *All the President's Men*	Beatrice Straight *Network*
1977	*Annie Hall* (Woody Allen)	Woody Allen *Annie Hall*	Richard Dreyfuss *The Goodbye Girl*	Diane Keaton *Annie Hall*	Jason Robards *Julia*	Vanessa Redgrave *Julia*

Year	Best Film (director)	Best Director	Best Actor	Best Actress	Best Supporting Actor	Best Supporting Actress
1978	*The Deer Hunter* (Michael Cimino)	Michael Cimino *The Deer Hunter*	Jon Voight *Coming Home*	Jane Fonda *Coming Home*	Christopher Walken *The Deer Hunter*	Maggie Smith *California Suite*
1979	*Kramer vs Kramer* (Robert Benton)	Robert Benton *Kramer vs Kramer*	Dustin Hoffman *Kramer vs Kramer*	Sally Field *Norma Rae*	Melvyn Douglas *Being There*	Meryl Streep *Kramer vs Kramer*
1980	*Ordinary People* (Robert Redford)	Robert Redford *Ordinary People*	Robert De Niro *Raging Bull*	Sissy Spacek *Coal Miner's Daughter*	Timothy Hutton *Ordinary People*	Mary Steenburgen *Melvin and Howard*
1981	*Chariots of Fire* (Hugh Hudson)	Warren Beatty *Reds*	Henry Fonda *On Golden Pond*	Katharine Hepburn *On Golden Pond*	John Gielgud *Arthur*	Maureen Stapleton *Reds*
1982	*Gandhi* (Richard Attenborough)	Richard Attenborough *Gandhi*	Ben Kingsley *Gandhi*	Meryl Streep *Sophie's Choice*	Louis Gossett, Jr. *An Officer and a Gentleman*	Jessica Lange *Tootsie*
1983	*Terms of Endearment* (James L Brooks)	James L Brooks *Terms of Endearment*	Robert Duvall *Tender Mercies*	Shirley MacLaine *Terms of Endearment*	Jack Nicholson *Terms of Endearment*	Linda Hunt *The Year of Living Dangerously*
1984	*Amadeus* (Miloš Forman)	Miloš Forman *Amadeus*	F Murray Abraham *Amadeus*	Sally Field *Places in the Heart*	Haing S Ngor *The Killing Fields*	Peggy Ashcroft *A Passage to India*
1985	*Out of Africa* (Sydney Pollack)	Sydney Pollack *Out of Africa*	William Hurt *Kiss of the Spider Woman*	Geraldine Page *The Trip to Bountiful*	Don Ameche *Cocoon*	Anjelica Huston *Prizzi's Honor*

Year	Best Film (director)	Best Director	Best Actor	Best Actress	Best Supporting Actor	Best Supporting Actress
1986	*Platoon* (Oliver Stone)	Oliver Stone *Platoon*	Paul Newman *The Color of Money*	Marlee Matlin *Children of a Lesser God*	Michael Caine *Hannah and Her Sisters*	Dianne Wiest *Hannah and Her Sisters*
1987	*The Last Emperor* (Bernardo Bertolucci)	Bernardo Bertolucci *The Last Emperor*	Michael Douglas *Wall Street*	Cher *Moonstruck*	Sean Connery *The Untouchables*	Olympia Dukakis *Moonstruck*
1988	*Rain Man* (Barry Levinson)	Barry Levinson *Rain Man*	Dustin Hoffman *Rain Man*	Jodie Foster *The Accused*	Kevin Kline *A Fish Called Wanda*	Geena Davis *The Accidental Tourist*
1989	*Driving Miss Daisy* (Bruce Beresford)	Oliver Stone *Born on the Fourth of July*	Daniel Day-Lewis *My Left Foot*	Jessica Tandy *Driving Miss Daisy*	Denzel Washington *Glory*	Brenda Fricker *My Left Foot*
1990	*Dances With Wolves* (Kevin Costner)	Kevin Costner *Dances With Wolves*	Jeremy Irons *Reversal of Fortune*	Kathy Bates *Misery*	Joe Pesci *Goodfellas*	Whoopi Goldberg *Ghost*
1991	*The Silence of the Lambs* (Jonathan Demme)	Jonathan Demme *The Silence of the Lambs*	Anthony Hopkins *The Silence of the Lambs*	Jodie Foster *The Silence of the Lambs*	Jack Palance *City Slickers*	Mercedes Ruehl *The Fisher King*
1992	*Unforgiven* (Clint Eastwood)	Clint Eastwood *Unforgiven*	Al Pacino *Scent of a Woman*	Emma Thompson *Howards End*	Gene Hackman *Unforgiven*	Marisa Tomei *My Cousin Vinny*
1993	*Schindler's List* (Steven Spielberg)	Steven Spielberg *Schindler's List*	Tom Hanks *Philadelphia*	Holly Hunter *The Piano*	Tommy Lee Jones *The Fugitive*	Anna Paquin *The Piano*

Year	Best Film (director)	Best Director	Best Actor	Best Actress	Best Supporting Actor	Best Supporting Actress
1994	*Forrest Gump* (Robert Zemeckis)	Robert Zemeckis *Forrest Gump*	Tom Hanks *Forrest Gump*	Jessica Lange *Blue Sky*	Martin Landau *Ed Wood*	Dianne Wiest *Bullets over Broadway*
1995	*Braveheart* (Mel Gibson)	Mel Gibson *Braveheart*	Nicolas Cage *Leaving Las Vegas*	Susan Sarandon *Dead Man Walking*	Kevin Spacey *The Usual Suspects*	Mira Sorvino *Mighty Aphrodite*
1996	*The English Patient* (Anthony Minghella)	Anthony Minghella *The English Patient*	Geoffrey Rush *Shine*	Frances McDormand *Fargo*	Cuba Gooding, Jr. *Jerry Maguire*	Juliette Binoche *The English Patient*
1997	*Titanic* (James Cameron)	James Cameron *Titanic*	Jack Nicholson *As Good As It Gets*	Helen Hunt *As Good as It Gets*	Robin Williams *Good Will Hunting*	Kim Basinger *L.A. Confidential*
1998	*Shakespeare in Love* (Guy Madden)	Steven Spielberg *Saving Private Ryan*	Roberto Benigni *Life Is Beautiful*	Gwyneth Paltrow *Shakespeare in Love*	James Coburn *Affliction*	Judi Dench *Shakespeare in Love*
1999	*American Beauty* (Sam Mendes)	Sam Mendes *American Beauty*	Kevin Spacey *American Beauty*	Hilary Swank *Boys Don't Cry*	Michael Caine *The Cider House Rules*	Angelina Jolie *Girl, Interrupted*
2000	*Gladiator* (Ridley Scott)	Steven Soderbergh *Traffic*	Russell Crowe *Gladiator*	Julia Roberts *Erin Brockovich*	Benicio Del Toro *Traffic*	Marcia Gay Harden *Pollock*
2001	*A Beautiful Mind* (Ron Howard)	Ron Howard *A Beautiful Mind*	Denzel Washington *Training Day*	Halle Berry *Monster's Ball*	Jim Broadbent *Iris*	Jennifer Connelly *A Beautiful Mind*

Year	Best Film (director)	Best Director	Best Actor	Best Actress	Best Supporting Actor	Best Supporting Actress
2002	Chicago (Rob Marshall)	Roman Polanski The Pianist	Adrien Brody The Pianist	Nicole Kidman The Hours	Chris Cooper Adaptation	Catherine Zeta-Jones Chicago
2003	The Lord of the Rings: The Return of the King (Peter Jackson)	Peter Jackson The Lord of the Rings: The Return of the King	Sean Penn Mystic River	Charlize Theron Monster	Tim Robbins Mystic River	Renée Zellweger Cold Mountain
2004	Million Dollar Baby (Clint Eastwood)	Clint Eastwood Million Dollar Baby	Jamie Foxx Ray	Hilary Swank Million Dollar Baby	Morgan Freeman Million Dollar Baby	Cate Blanchett The Aviator
2005	Crash (Paul Haggis)	Ang Lee Brokeback Mountain	Philip Seymour Hoffman Capote	Reese Witherspoon Walk the Line	George Clooney Syriana	Rachel Weisz The Constant Gardener

Unavoidable Delays

The annual Academy Award® ceremonies have run like clockwork every year since 1929, with only three exceptions. In 1938, Los Angeles was struck by severe flooding that caused the ceremony to be postponed by one week. In 1968, the event was moved back by two days in order to avoid clashing with the date of Dr Martin Luther King's funeral; and in 1981 it was postponed for one day following the attempted assassination of US President Ronald Reagan.

Keeping It Brief

The shortest speech in Oscar® history was made by director Alfred Hitchcock, who upon receiving the Irving G Thalberg Memorial Award at the 1967 ceremony, simply said 'Thank you'.

BRITISH ACADEMY FILM AWARDS

The British Film Academy was founded in 1947, and in 1975 changed its name to the British Academy of Film and Television Arts (BAFTA).

Year	Best Film (director)	Best Director	Best Actor	Best Actress	Best Supporting Actor	Best Supporting Actress
1947	*The Best Years of Our Lives* (William Wyler)					
1948	*Hamlet* (Laurence Olivier)					
1949	*Bicycle Thieves* (Vittorio De Sica)					
1950	*All About Eve* (Joseph L Mankiewicz)					
1951	*La Ronde* (Max Ophuls)					
1952	*The Sound Barrier* (David Lean)		Ralph Richardson *The Sound Barrier*	Vivien Leigh *A Streetcar Named Desire*		
1953	*Forbidden Games* (René Clément)		John Gielgud *Julius Caesar*	Audrey Hepburn *Roman Holiday*		

Year	Best Film (director)	Best Director	Best Actor	Best Actress	Best Supporting Actor	Best Supporting Actress
1954	*The Wages of Fear* (Henri-Georges Clouzot)		Kenneth More *Doctor in the House*	Yvonne Mitchell *The Divided Heart*		
1955	*Richard III* (Laurence Olivier)		Laurence Olivier *Richard III*	Katie Johnson *The Ladykillers*		
1956	*Gervaise* (René Clément)		Peter Finch *A Town Like Alice*	Virginia McKenna *A Town Like Alice*		
1957	*The Bridge on the River Kwai* (David Lean)		Alec Guinness *The Bridge on the River Kwai*	Heather Sears *The Story of Esther Costello*		
1958	*Room at the Top* (Jack Clayton)		Trevor Howard *The Key*	Irene Worth *Orders to Kill*		
1959	*Ben-Hur* (William Wyler)		Peter Sellers *I'm All Right Jack*	Audrey Hepburn *The Nun's Story*		
1960	*The Apartment* (Billy Wilder)		Peter Finch *The Trials of Oscar Wilde*	Rachel Roberts *Saturday Night and Sunday Morning*		

Year	Best Film (director)	Best Director	Best Actor	Best Actress	Best Supporting Actor	Best Supporting Actress
1961	*Ballad of a Soldier* (Grigori Chukhraj); *The Hustler* (Robert Rossen)		Peter Finch *No Love for Johnnie*	Dora Bryan *A Taste of Honey*		
1962	*Lawrence of Arabia* (David Lean)		Peter O'Toole *Lawrence of Arabia*	Leslie Caron *The L-shaped Room*		
1963	*Tom Jones* (Tony Richardson)		Dirk Bogarde *The Servant*	Rachel Roberts *This Sporting Life*		
1964	*Dr Strangelove* (Stanley Kubrick)		Richard Attenborough *Séance on a Wet Afternoon; Guns at Batasi*	Audrey Hepburn *Charade*		
1965	*My Fair Lady* (George Cukor)		Dirk Bogarde *Darling*	Julie Christie *Darling*		
1966	*Who's Afraid of Virginia Woolf?* (Mike Nichols)		Richard Burton *The Spy Who Came in from the Cold*	Elizabeth Taylor *Who's Afraid of Virginia Woolf?*		
1967	*A Man for All Seasons* (Fred Zinnemann)		Paul Scofield *A Man for All Seasons*	Edith Evans *The Whisperers*		

Year	Best Film (director)	Best Director	Best Actor	Best Actress	Best Supporting Actor	Best Supporting Actress
1968	*The Graduate* (Mike Nichols)	Mike Nichols *The Graduate*	Spencer Tracy *Guess Who's Coming to Dinner?*	Katharine Hepburn *Guess Who's Coming to Dinner?; The Lion in Winter*	Ian Holm *The Bofors Gun*	Billie Whitelaw *Charlie Bubbles, Twisted Nerve*
1969	*Midnight Cowboy* (John Schlesinger)	John Schlesinger *Midnight Cowboy*	Dustin Hoffman *Midnight Cowboy; John and Mary*	Maggie Smith *The Prime of Miss Jean Brodie*	Laurence Olivier *Oh! What a Lovely War*	Celia Johnson *The Prime of Miss Jean Brodie*
1970	*Butch Cassidy and the Sundance Kid* (George Roy Hill)	George Roy Hill *Butch Cassidy and the Sundance Kid*	Robert Redford *Butch Cassidy and the Sundance Kid; Tell Them Willie Boy Is Here; Downhill Racer*	Katharine Ross *Butch Cassidy and the Sundance Kid; Tell Them Willie Boy Is Here*	Colin Welland *Kes*	Susannah York *They Shoot Horses, Don't They?*
1971	*Sunday Bloody Sunday* (John Schlesinger)	John Schlesinger *Sunday Bloody Sunday*	Peter Finch *Sunday Bloody Sunday*	Glenda Jackson *Sunday Bloody Sunday*	Edward Fox *The Go-Between*	Margaret Leighton *The Go-Between*
1972	*Cabaret* (Bob Fosse)	Bob Fosse *Cabaret*	Gene Hackman *The French Connection; The Poseidon Adventure*	Liza Minnelli *Cabaret*	Ben Johnson *The Last Picture Show*	Cloris Leachman *The Last Picture Show*

Year	Best Film (director)	Best Director	Best Actor	Best Actress	Best Supporting Actor	Best Supporting Actress
1973	Day for Night (Francois Truffaut)	Francois Truffaut Day for Night	Walter Matthau Pete 'n' Tillie; Charley Varrick	Stéphane Audran The Discreet Charm of the Bourgeoisie; Just Before Nightfall	Arthur Lowe Oh Lucky Man!	Valentina Cortese Day for Night
1974	Lacombe Lucien (Louis Malle)	Roman Polanski Chinatown	Jack Nicholson Chinatown; The Last Detail	Joanne Woodward Summer Wishes, Winter Dreams	John Gielgud Murder on the Orient Express	Ingrid Bergman Murder on the Orient Express
1975	Alice Doesn't Live Here Anymore (Martin Scorsese)	Stanley Kubrick Barry Lyndon	Al Pacino Dog Day Afternoon; The Godfather Part II	Ellen Burstyn Alice Doesn't Live Here Anymore	Fred Astaire The Towering Inferno	Diane Ladd Alice Doesn't Live Here Anymore
1976	One Flew Over the Cuckoo's Nest (Miloš Forman)	Miloš Forman One Flew Over the Cuckoo's Nest	Jack Nicholson One Flew Over the Cuckoo's Nest	Louise Fletcher One Flew Over the Cuckoo's Nest	Brad Dourif One Flew Over the Cuckoo's Nest	Jodie Foster Bugsy Malone; Taxi Driver
1977	Annie Hall (Woody Allen)	Woody Allen Annie Hall	Peter Finch Network	Diane Keaton Annie Hall	Edward Fox A Bridge Too Far	Jenny Agutter Equus
1978	Julia (Fred Zinnemann)	Alan Parker Midnight Express	Richard Dreyfuss The Goodbye Girl	Jane Fonda Julia	John Hurt Midnight Express	Geraldine Page Interiors

Year	Best Film (director)	Best Director	Best Actor	Best Actress	Best Supporting Actor	Best Supporting Actress
1979	*Manhattan* (Woody Allen)	Francis Ford Coppola *Apocalypse Now*	Jack Lemmon *The China Syndrome*	Jane Fonda *The China Syndrome*	Robert Duvall *Apocalypse Now*	Rachel Roberts *Yanks*
1980	*The Elephant Man* (Jonathan Sanger)	Akira Kurosawa *Kagemusha*	John Hurt *The Elephant Man*	Judy Davis *My Brilliant Career*	no award	no award
1981	*Chariots of Fire* (Hugh Hudson)	Louis Malle *Atlantic City*	Burt Lancaster *Atlantic City*	Meryl Streep *The French Lieutenant's Woman*	no award	no award
1982	*Gandhi* (Richard Attenborough)	Richard Attenborough *Gandhi*	Ben Kingsley *Gandhi*	Katharine Hepburn *On Golden Pond*	Jack Nicholson *Reds*	Rohini Hattangadi *Gandhi*; Maureen Stapleton *Reds*
1983	*Educating Rita* (Lewis Gilbert)	Bill Forsyth *Local Hero*	Michael Caine *Educating Rita*; Dustin Hoffman *Tootsie*	Julie Walters *Educating Rita*	Denholm Elliott *Trading Places*	Jamie Lee Curtis *Trading Places*
1984	*The Killing Fields* (Roland Joffe)	Wim Wenders *Paris, Texas*	Haing S Ngor *The Killing Fields*	Maggie Smith *A Private Function*	Denholm Elliott *A Private Function*	Liz Smith *A Private Function*
1985	*The Purple Rose of Cairo* (Woody Allen)	no award	William Hurt *Kiss of the Spider Woman*	Peggy Ashcroft *A Passage to India*	Denholm Elliott *Defence of the Realm*	Rosanna Arquette *Desperately Seeking Susan*

Year	Best Film (director)	Best Director	Best Actor	Best Actress	Best Supporting Actor	Best Supporting Actress
1986	A Room with a View (James Ivory)	Woody Allen Hannah and Her Sisters	Bob Hoskins Mona Lisa	Maggie Smith A Room with a View	Ray McAnally The Mission	Judi Dench A Room with a View
1987	Jean de Florette (Claude Berri)	Oliver Stone Platoon	Sean Connery The Name of the Rose	Anne Bancroft 84 Charing Cross Road	Daniel Auteuil Jean de Florette	Susan Wooldridge Hope and Glory
1988	The Last Emperor (Bernardo Bertolucci)	Louis Malle Au Revoir les enfants	John Cleese A Fish Called Wanda	Maggie Smith The Lonely Passion of Judith Hearne	Michael Palin A Fish Called Wanda	Olympia Dukakis Moonstruck
1989	Dead Poets Society (Peter Weir)	Kenneth Branagh Henry V	Daniel Day-Lewis My Left Foot	Pauline Collins Shirley Valentine	Ray McAnally My Left Foot	Michelle Pfeiffer Dangerous Liaisons
1990	Goodfellas (Martin Scorsese)	Martin Scorsese Goodfellas	Philippe Noiret Cinema Paradiso	Jessica Tandy Driving Miss Daisy	Salvatore Cascio Cinema Paradiso	Whoopi Goldberg Ghost
1991	The Commitments (Alan Parker)	Alan Parker The Commitments	Anthony Hopkins The Silence of the Lambs	Jodie Foster The Silence of the Lambs	Alan Rickman Robin Hood: Prince of Thieves	Kate Nelligan Frankie and Johnny
1992	Howards End (James Ivory)	Robert Altman The Player	Robert Downey Jr Chaplin	Emma Thompson Howards End	Gene Hackman Unforgiven	Miranda Richardson Damage

Year	Best Film (director)	Best Director	Best Actor	Best Actress	Best Supporting Actor	Best Supporting Actress
1993	*Schindler's List* (Steven Spielberg)	Steven Spielberg *Schindler's List*	Anthony Hopkins *The Remains of the Day*	Holly Hunter *The Piano*	Ralph Fiennes *Schindler's List*	Miriam Margolyes *The Age of Innocence*
1994	*Four Weddings and a Funeral* (Mike Newell)	Mike Newell *Four Weddings and a Funeral*	Hugh Grant *Four Weddings and a Funeral*	Susan Sarandon *The Client*	Samuel L Jackson *Pulp Fiction*	Kristin Scott-Thomas *Four Weddings and a Funeral*
1995	*Sense and Sensibility* (Ang Lee)	Michael Radford *Il Postino*	Nigel Hawthorne *The Madness of King George*	Emma Thompson *Sense and Sensibility*	Tim Roth *Rob Roy*	Kate Winslet *Sense and Sensibility*
1996	*The English Patient* (Anthony Minghella)	Joel Coen *Fargo*	Geoffrey Rush *Shine*	Brenda Blethyn *Secrets & Lies*	Paul Scofield *The Crucible*	Juliette Binoche *The English Patient*
1997	*The Full Monty* (Peter Cattaneo)	Baz Luhrmann *Romeo + Juliet*	Tom Wilkinson *The Full Monty*	Judi Dench *Mrs Brown*	Tom Wilkinson *The Full Monty*	Sigourney Weaver *The Ice Storm*
1998	*Shakespeare in Love* (John Madden)	Peter Weir *The Truman Show*	Roberto Benigni *Life Is Beautiful*	Cate Blanchett *Elizabeth*	Geoffrey Rush *Elizabeth*	Judi Dench *Shakespeare in Love*
1999	*American Beauty* (Sam Mendes)	Pedro Almodóvar *All About My Mother*	Kevin Spacey *American Beauty*	Annette Bening *American Beauty*	Jude Law *The Talented Mr Ripley*	Maggie Smith *Tea with Mussolini*

Year	Best Film (director)	Best Director	Best Actor	Best Actress	Best Supporting Actor	Best Supporting Actress
2000	*Gladiator* (Ridley Scott)	Ang Lee *Crouching Tiger, Hidden Dragon*	Jamie Bell *Billy Elliot*	Julia Roberts *Erin Brockovich*	Benicio Del Toro *Traffic*	Julie Walters *Billy Elliot*
2001	*The Lord of the Rings: The Fellowship of the Ring* (Peter Jackson)	Peter Jackson *The Lord of the Rings: The Fellowship of the Ring*	Russell Crowe *A Beautiful Mind*	Judi Dench *Iris*	Jim Broadbent *Moulin Rouge!*	Jennifer Connelly *A Beautiful Mind*
2002	*The Pianist* (Roman Polanski)	Roman Polanski *The Pianist*	Daniel Day-Lewis *Gangs of New York*	Nicole Kidman *The Hours*	Christopher Walken *Catch Me If You Can*	Catherine Zeta-Jones *Chicago*
2003	*The Lord of the Rings: The Return of the King* (Peter Jackson)	Peter Weir *Master and Commander: The Far Side of the World*	Bill Murray *Lost in Translation*	Scarlett Johansson *Lost in Translation*	Bill Nighy *Love Actually*	Renée Zellweger *Cold Mountain*
2004	*The Aviator* (Martin Scorsese)	Mike Leigh *Vera Drake*	Jamie Foxx *Ray*	Imelda Staunton *Vera Drake*	Clive Owen *Closer*	Cate Blanchett *The Aviator*
2005	*Brokeback Mountain* (Ang Lee)	Ang Lee *Brokeback Mountain*	Philip Seymour Hoffman *Capote*	Reese Witherspoon *Walk the Line*	Jake Gyllenhaal *Brokeback Mountain*	Thandie Newton *Crash*

GOLDEN RASPBERRY AWARDS

Awarded annually by the Golden Raspberry Award Foundation. Popularly known as Razzies®. Traditionally, nominations are announced one day before the Academy Award® nominations, and awards are presented one day before the Oscar® ceremony.

Year	Worst Film (director)	Worst Actor	Worst Actress
1980	*Can't Stop the Music* (Nancy Walker)	Neil Diamond *The Jazz Singer*	Brooke Shields *The Blue Lagoon*
1981	*Mommie Dearest* (Frank Perry)	Klinton Spilsbury *Legend of the Lone Ranger*	Bo Derek *Tarzan, the Ape Man*; Faye Dunaway *Mommie Dearest*
1982	*Inchon* (Terence Young)	Laurence Olivier *Inchon*	Pia Zadora *Butterfly*
1983	*The Lonely Lady* (Peter Sasdy)	Christopher Atkins *A Night in Heaven*	Pia Zadora *The Lonely Lady*
1984	*Bolero* (John Derek)	Sylvester Stallone *Rhinestone*	Bo Derek *Bolero*
1985	*Rambo: First Blood Part II* (George P Cosmatos)	Sylvester Stallone *Rambo: First Blood Part II; Rocky IV*	Linda Blair *Night Patrol; Savage Island, Savage Streets*
1986	*Howard the Duck* (Willard Huyck); *Under the Cherry Moon* (Prince)	Prince *Under the Cherry Moon*	Madonna *Shanghai Surprise*
1987	*Leonard Part 6* (Paul Weiland)	Bill Cosby *Leonard Part 6*	Madonna *Who's That Girl?*
1988	*Cocktail* (Roger Donaldson)	Sylvester Stallone *Rambo III*	Liza Minnelli *Arthur 2: On the Rocks; Rent-a-Cop*
1989	*Star Trek V: The Final Frontier* (William Shatner)	William Shatner *Star Trek V: The Final Frontier*	Heather Locklear *The Return of the Swamp Thing*
1990	*The Adventures of Ford Fairlane* (Renny Harlin); *Ghosts Can't Do It* (John Derek)	Andrew Dice Clay *The Adventures of Ford Fairlane*	Bo Derek *Ghosts Can't Do It*
1991	*Hudson Hawk* (Michael Lehmann)	Kevin Costner *Robin Hood: Prince of Thieves*	Sean Young *A Kiss Before Dying*
1992	*Shining Through* (David Seltzer)	Sylvester Stallone *Stop! Or My Mom Will Shoot*	Melanie Griffith *Shining Through*
1993	*Indecent Proposal* (Adrian Lyne)	Burt Reynolds *Cop and a Half*	Madonna *Body of Evidence*

Year	Worst Film (director)	Worst Actor	Worst Actress
1994	*Color of Night* (Richard Rush)	Kevin Costner *Wyatt Earp*	Sharon Stone *Intersection; The Specialist*
1995	*Showgirls* (Paul Verhoeven)	Pauly Shore *Jury Duty*	Elizabeth Berkley *Showgirls*
1996	*Striptease* (Andrew Bergman)	Tom Arnold *Big Bully*; *Carpool*; *The Stupids*; Pauly Shore *Bio-Dome*	Demi Moore *Striptease*
1997	*The Postman* (Kevin Costner)	Kevin Costner *The Postman*	Demi Moore *G.I. Jane*
1998	*An Alan Smithee Film: Burn Hollywood Burn* (Arthur Hiller, Alan Smithee)	Bruce Willis *Armageddon*; *Mercury Rising; The Siege*	The Spice Girls *Spice World*
1999	*Wild Wild West* (Barry Sonnenfeld)	Adam Sandler *Big Daddy*	Heather Donahue *The Blair Witch Project*
2000	*Battlefield Earth: A Saga of the Year 3000* (Roger Christian)	John Travolta *Battlefield Earth: A Saga of the Year 3000*	Madonna *The Next Best Thing*
2001	*Freddy Got Fingered* (Tom Green)	Tom Green *Freddy Got Fingered*	Mariah Carey *Glitter*
2002	*Swept Away* (Guy Ritchie)	Roberto Benigni *Pinocchio*	Madonna *Swept Away*; Britney Spears *Crossroads*
2003	*Gigli* (Martin Brest)	Ben Affleck *Gigli*	Jennifer Lopez *Gigli*
2004	*Catwoman* (Pitof)	George W Bush *Fahrenheit 9/11*	Halle Berry *Catwoman*
2005	*Dirty Love* (John Mallory Asher)	Rob Schneider *Deuce Bigalow: European Gigolo*	Jenny McCarthy *Dirty Love*

Berry's Raspberry

Although the Golden Raspberry Awards attract media coverage, it is unusual for winners to actually attend the ceremony. One of the few to have done so is Halle Berry, who accepted her 2004 Worst Actress award with good grace, explaining that her mother had taught her 'if you aren't able to be a good loser, you're not able to be a good winner.'

Continuity Chaos

Sharp-eyed movie buffs are constantly on the lookout for continuity errors, anachronisms and other mistakes in films. From camera crews reflected in plate-glass windows to Roman centurions wearing watches, some of the worst howlers have passed into film legend. These include the Von Trapp family fleeing over the mountains straight into enemy Germany at the end of *The Sound of Music* (1963), Dorothy's hair varying in length in *The Wizard of Oz* (1939) and a passenger in a lifeboat wearing a digital watch in *Titanic* (1997). Other classic gaffes include a distant aeroplane flying past in one scene in *Ben-Hur* (1959), a stormtrooper banging his head in *Star Wars* (1977) and a building marked 'Est. 1953' in World War II film *Pearl Harbor* (2001). Scenes involving food, drink and cigars or cigarettes are also a continuity nightmare for film-makers: watch the fluctuating levels of alcohol in the wine glasses in *The Godfather* (1972) and the half-eaten hamburgers in *Pulp Fiction* (1994), not to mention the lit, unlit and relit cigarettes and cigars in almost every film featuring a smoker. Fans can also spot an anachronism a mile off. One of the best-known is in *The Rocky Horror Picture Show* (1975), in which US President Richard Nixon's resignation speech can be heard on a car radio. Nixon resigned in August – but the narrator solemnly intones that the events of the film take place 'on a late November evening'.

PALME D'OR

The Cannes Film Festival began in 1946, and a Palme d'Or (Golden Palm) for best film has been awarded every year since 1955.

Year	Palme d'Or winner
1955	*Marty* (Delbert Mann)
1956	*The Silent World (Le Monde du silence)* (Jacques-Yves Cousteau)
1957	*Friendly Persuasion* (William Wyler)
1958	*The Cranes Are Flying (Letiat zhuravli)* (Mikhail Kalatozov)
1959	*Black Orpheus (Orfeu Negro)* (Marcel Camus)
1960	*La Dolce vita* (Federico Fellini)
1961	*Viridiana* (Luis Buñuel); *Une aussi longue absence* (Henri Colpi)
1962	*The Given Word (O Pagador de Promessas)* (Anselmo Duarte)
1963	*The Leopard (Il Gattopardi)* (Luchino Visconti)
1964	*The Umbrellas of Cherbourg (Les Parapluies de Cherbourg)* (Jacques Demy)
1965	*The Knack...and How to Get It* (Richard Lester)
1966	*A Man and a Woman (Un homme et une femme)* (Claude Lelouch)
1967	*Blow-Up* (Michelangelo Antonioni)
1968	*festival cancelled*
1969	*If...* (Lindsay Anderson)
1970	*M*A*S*H* (Robert Altman)
1971	*The Go-Between* (Joseph Losey)
1972	*The Mattei Affair (Il Caso Mattei)* (Francesco Rossi); *The Working Class Go to Heaven (La Classe operaia va in paradiso)* (Elio Petri)
1973	*Scarecrow* (Jerry Schatzberg); *The Hireling* (Alan Bridges)
1974	*The Conversation* (Francis Ford Coppola)

1975	*Chronicle of the Years of Embers (Ahdat sanawouach eldjamr)* (Mohammed Lakhdar Hamina)
1976	*Taxi Driver* (Martin Scorsese)
1977	*Padre padrone* (Paolo and Vittorio Taviani)
1978	*The Tree of Wooden Clogs (L'Albero degli zoccoli)* (Ermanno Olmi)
1979	*Apocalypse Now* (Francis Ford Coppola); *The Tin Drum (Die Blechtrommel)* (Volker Schlöndorff)
1980	*Kagemusha* (Akira Kurosawa); *All That Jazz* (Bob Fosse)
1981	*Man of Iron (Czlowieck z zelaza)* (Andrzej Wajda)
1982	*Missing* (Costa-Gavras); *Yol* (Yilmaz Güney)
1983	*The Ballad of Narayama (Narayama bushi ko)* (Shohei Imamura)
1984	*Paris, Texas* (Wim Wenders)
1985	*When Father Was Away on Business (Otak na sluzbenom putu)* (Emir Kusturica)
1986	*The Mission* (Roland Joffe)
1987	*Under Satan's Sun (Sous le soleil de satan)* (Maurice Pialat)
1988	*Pelle the Conqueror (Pell erobreren)* (Bille August)
1989	*sex, lies and videotape* (Steven Soderbergh)
1990	*Wild at Heart* (David Lynch)
1991	*Barton Fink* (Joel and Ethan Coen)
1992	*The Best Intentions (Den Goda vilijan)* (Bille August)
1993	*The Piano* (Jane Campion); *Farewell My Concubine* (Chen Kaige)
1994	*Pulp Fiction* (Quentin Tarantino)
1995	*Underground* (Emir Kusturica)
1996	*Secrets & Lies* (Mike Leigh)
1997	*The Eel (Unagi)* (Shohei Imamura); *A Taste of Cherry (Ta'me guilass)* (Abbas Kiarostami)
1998	*Eternity and a Day (Mia eoniotita ke mia mera)* (Theo Angelopoulos)
1999	*Rosetta* (Luc and Jean-Pierre Dardenne)
2000	*Dancer in the Dark* (Lars von Trier)
2001	*The Son's Room (La Stanza del figlio)* (Nanni Moretti)
2002	*The Pianist* (Roman Polanski)
2003	*Elephant* (Gus Van Sant)
2004	*Fahrenheit 9/11* (Michael Moore)

Better Late than Never

The first Cannes Film Festival should have taken place in 1939, but had to be cancelled when World War II broke out. In 2002, the modern Festival's organizers decided to honour some of the films that had been scheduled for screening in that first year (*The Wizard of Oz*, *Goodbye Mr Chips*, *The Four Feathers*, *La Piste du Nord*, *Union Pacific*, *Boefje* and *Lenin in October*), and a prize was belatedly awarded to *Union Pacific*.

SOME MAJOR FILM FESTIVALS

Festival	Location	Prize
Bangkok	Bangkok, Thailand	Golden Kinnaree
Berlin	Berlin, Germany	Golden Bear
Cairo	Cairo, Egypt	Golden Pyramid
Cannes	Cannes, France	Palme d'Or
Cartagena	Cartagena, Colombia	Golden India Catalina
Chicago	Chicago, Illinois, USA	Gold Hugo
Cleveland	Cleveland, Ohio, USA	Best Film
Copenhagen	Copenhagen, Denmark	Golden Swan
Edinburgh	Edinburgh, Scotland	Audience Award
Havana	Havana, Cuba	Grand Coral
Istanbul	Istanbul, Turkey	Golden Tulip
Locarno	Locarno, Switzerland	Golden Leopard
London	London, England	Sutherland Trophy
Melbourne	Melbourne, Australia	Best Film
Montreal	Montreal, Canada	Grand Prix des Amériques
Moscow	Moscow, Russia	Golden St George
Paris	Paris, France	Grand Prix
Rotterdam	Rotterdam, Netherlands	Tiger Award
San Francisco	San Francisco, California, USA	Golden Gate
San Sebastian	San Sebastian, Spain	Golden Seashell
Seattle	Seattle, Washington, USA	Golden Space Needle
Stockholm	Stockholm, Sweden	Bronze Horse
Sundance	Park City, Utah, USA	Grand Jury Prize
Tokyo	Tokyo, Japan	Grand Prix
Toronto	Toronto, Canada	People's Choice Award
Venice	Venice, Italy	Golden Lion
Vevey	Vevey, Switzerland	Golden Cane

Blink and You'll Miss It

A showcase of nine fifteen-second films, billed as 'The World's Shortest Film Festival', toured the UK in 2004. The films – winners of the Nokia Shorts competition – were screened in a booth specially designed to seat an audience of two.

FILM RECORDS

First film

Thomas Edison and William Dickson pioneered the Kinetoscope in the early 1890s, showing short films such as *The Sneeze* (1894); in 1895 Auguste and Louis Lumière patented the Cinematograph, which they demonstrated in public with such short films as *Arrival of Train at Station*.

First feature film with sound	*The Jazz Singer* (1927) featured short spoken clips and music, though other experiments with sound had been made with shorter films.
Oldest star	Jeanne Louise Calment starred in the film *Vincent and Me* (1990) at the age of 114. She lived to the age of 122.
Youngest star	Leroy Overacker appeared in the film *A Bedtime Story* (1933) at the age of six months, and received star billing.
Most leading roles in Hollywood films	John Wayne played leading roles in 142 Hollywood films, and appeared in 153. Adoor Bhasi appeared in 549 Bollywood films.
Longest continuous contract to a film studio	Lewis Stone worked as an MGM contract artist from 1924 until his death 29 years later, in 1953.
Longest career as a film director	King Vidor directed his first film (*Hurricane in Galveston*) in 1913, and his last (*The Metaphor*) 67 years later, in 1980.
Longest shot in a film	*Russian Ark* (2001) consists entirely of one long shot lasting 96 minutes.
Longest documentary film	*Grandmother Martha* (1996) runs for a total length of 24 hours 12 minutes.
Longest uninterrupted film shoot	*Eyes Wide Shut* (1999) was in production for over 15 months, including an unbroken shoot lasting 46 weeks.
Highest box office gross	*Titanic* (1997) is the most successful film of all time, and was the first to gross more than $1 billion internationally.
Largest box office loss	*Cutthroat Island* (1995) cost more than $100 million to make and distribute, but recovered only $11 million internationally.
Most Academy Awards® won by a film	Three films have won eleven Academy Awards®: *Ben-Hur* (1959), *Titanic* (1997) and *The Lord of the Rings: The Return of the King* (2003).
Most Academy Awards® for Best Actress	Katharine Hepburn won four Academy Awards® for Best Actress, in 1932, 1967, 1968 and 1981.
Most Academy Awards® for Best Actor	Seven actors have won two Academy Awards® for Best Actor: Spencer Tracy, Gary Cooper, Marlon Brando, Jack Nicholson, Fredric March, Dustin Hoffman and Tom Hanks.
Most Academy Awards® for Best Director	John Ford won four Academy Awards® for Best Director, in 1935, 1940, 1941 and 1952.
Most Academy Awards® in total	Walt Disney won 26 Academy Awards®.

Most Academy Award® nominations	Walt Disney had 64 Academy Award® nominations, while composer John Williams is the most nominated person alive today with 41.
Most unsuccessful Academy Award® nominations for a film	*The Turning Point* (1977) and *The Color Purple* (1985) were both nominated for eleven Academy Awards®, but won none.
Most unsuccessful Academy Award® nominations for an individual	Kevin O'Connell, a sound mixer, has been nominated for 17 Academy Awards® to date, but has never won.

Inspirational Incident

The idea of stars leaving their handprints and footprints in the cement outside Grauman's Chinese Theatre came about by chance. Before the theatre officially opened in 1927, actress Norma Talmadge is said to have accidentally stepped onto its wet cement, giving owner Sid Grauman the idea for a publicity stunt that still attracts tourists today.

FILM-RELATED ORGANIZATIONS

Associated Actors and Artistes of America (AAAA)	Parent organization of US actors' unions and guilds, including the SAG and SEG
L'Académie des Arts et Techniques du Cinéma	French organization; presents the Césars, France's equivalent to the Academy Awards®
Academy of Motion Picture Arts and Sciences	US organization; presents the Academy Awards®
Alliance of Motion Picture and Television Producers (AMPTP)	US labour organization
American Cinema Editors (ACE)	US honorary professional society
American Film Institute (AFI)	US organization; promotes film
American Society of Cinematographers (ASC)	US honorary professional society
American Standards Association (ASA)	US association; established technical standards known as the ASA Standards
Association Internationale du Film d'Animation (ASIFA)	International association; promotes development of animated film
Broadcasting Entertainment, Cinematograph & Theatre Union (BECTU)	UK labour organization

British Academy of Film and Television Arts (BAFTA)	UK organization; presents the BAFTA awards and promotes film
British Board of Film Classification (BBFC)	UK organization; oversees rating of films and videos
British Film Institute (BFI)	UK organization; promotes film
Centre National de la Cinématographie (CNC)	French organization; promotes film
Centro Sperimentale di Cinematografia (CSC)	Italian film research center; the oldest film school in Western Europe
Cinémathèque Française	French organization; promotes conservation and appreciation of vintage films
Directors Guild of America (DGA)	US labour organization
Federation Against Copyright Theft (FACT)	UK organization; combats film counterfeiting and piracy
Hollywood Foreign Press Association	US organization; presents the Golden Globe Awards®
International Documentary Association (IDA)	US organization; promotes documentary film
Motion Picture Association of America (MPAA)	US trade organization; oversees rating of films and videos
National Association of Theatre Owners (NATO)	US trade organization; represents film exhibitors
National Board of Review	US organization; presents the D W Griffith Awards
Screen Actors Guild (SAG)	US labour organization
Screen Extras Guild (SEG)	US labour organization
Sundance Institute	US organization; promotes independent film

Play It Again, Sam

One of the most famous lines associated with *Casablanca* (1942), 'Play it again, Sam', was never actually spoken in the film. Rick (Humphrey Bogart) declares 'Play it!' while Ilsa (Ingrid Bergman) requests 'Play it, Sam. Play "As Time Goes By"' – but neither ever utters the often-quoted version of the line.

100 AMERICAN FILMS

In 1998, the American Film Institute (AFI) polled film industry professionals to compile a list of the 100 greatest American films made during the first 100 years of American cinema (1896–1996). The list is reproduced below.

1. *Citizen Kane* (Orson Welles, 1941)
2. *Casablanca* (Michael Curtiz, 1942)
3. *The Godfather* (Francis Ford Coppola, 1972)
4. *Gone with the Wind* (Victor Fleming, 1939)
5. *Lawrence of Arabia* (David Lean, 1962)
6. *The Wizard of Oz* (Victor Fleming, 1939)
7. *The Graduate* (Mike Nichols, 1967)
8. *On the Waterfront* (Elia Kazan, 1954)
9. *Schindler's List* (Steven Spielberg, 1993)
10. *Singin' in the Rain* (Stanley Donen, Gene Kelly, 1952)
11. *It's a Wonderful Life* (Frank Capra, 1946)
12. *Sunset Boulevard* (Billy Wilder, 1950)
13. *The Bridge on the River Kwai* (David Lean, 1957)
14. *Some Like It Hot* (Billy Wilder, 1959)
15. *Star Wars* (George Lucas, 1977)
16. *All About Eve* (Joseph L Mankiewicz, 1950)
17. *The African Queen* (John Huston, 1951)
18. *Psycho* (Alfred Hitchcock, 1960)
19. *Chinatown* (Roman Polanski, 1974)
20. *One Flew Over the Cuckoo's Nest* (Miloš Forman, 1975)
21. *The Grapes of Wrath* (John Ford, 1940)
22. *2001: A Space Odyssey* (Stanley Kubrick, 1968)
23. *The Maltese Falcon* (John Huston, 1941)
24. *Raging Bull* (Martin Scorsese, 1980)
25. *E.T. the Extra-Terrestrial* (Steven Spielberg, 1982)
26. *Dr Strangelove* (Stanley Kubrick, 1964)
27. *Bonnie and Clyde* (Arthur Penn, 1967)
28. *Apocalypse Now* (Francis Ford Coppola, 1979)
29. *Mr. Smith Goes to Washington* (Frank Capra, 1939)
30. *The Treasure of the Sierra Madre* (John Huston, 1948)
31. *Annie Hall* (Woody Allen, 1977)
32. *The Godfather Part II* (Francis Ford Coppola, 1974)
33. *High Noon* (Fred Zinnemann, 1952)
34. *To Kill a Mockingbird* (Robert Mulligan, 1962)
35. *It Happened One Night* (Frank Capra, 1934)
36. *Midnight Cowboy* (John Schlesinger, 1969)
37. *The Best Years of Our Lives* (William Wyler, 1946)
38. *Double Indemnity* (Billy Wilder, 1944)
39. *Doctor Zhivago* (David Lean, 1965)
40. *North by Northwest* (Alfred Hitchcock, 1959)
41. *West Side Story* (Jerome Robbins, Robert Wise, 1961)
42. *Rear Window* (Alfred Hitchcock, 1954)
43. *King Kong* (Merian C Cooper, Ernest B Schoedsack, 1933)

44. *The Birth of a Nation* (D W Griffith, 1915)
45. *A Streetcar Named Desire* (Elia Kazan, 1951)
46. *A Clockwork Orange* (Stanley Kubrick, 1971)
47. *Taxi Driver* (Martin Scorsese, 1976)
48. *Jaws* (Steven Spielberg, 1975)
49. *Snow White and the Seven Dwarfs* (1937)
50. *Butch Cassidy and the Sundance Kid* (George Roy Hill, 1969)
51. *The Philadelphia Story* (George Cukor, 1940)
52. *From Here to Eternity* (Fred Zinnemann, 1953)
53. *Amadeus* (Miloš Forman, 1984)
54. *All Quiet on the Western Front* (Lewis Milestone, 1930)
55. *The Sound of Music* (Robert Wise, 1965)
56. *M*A*S*H* (Robert Altman, 1970)
57. *The Third Man* (Carol Reed, 1949)
58. *Fantasia* (various directors, 1940)
59. *Rebel Without a Cause* (Nicholas Ray, 1955)
60. *Raiders of the Lost Ark* (Steven Spielberg, 1981)
61. *Vertigo* (Alfred Hitchcock, 1958)
62. *Tootsie* (Sydney Pollack, 1982)
63. *Stagecoach* (John Ford, 1939)
64. *Close Encounters of the Third Kind* (Steven Spielberg, 1977)
65. *The Silence of the Lambs* (Jonathan Demme, 1991)
66. *Network* (Sidney Lumet, 1976)
67. *The Manchurian Candidate* (John Frankenheimer, 1962)
68. *An American in Paris* (Vincente Minnelli, 1951)
69. *Shane* (George Stevens, 1953)
70. *The French Connection* (William Friedkin, 1971)
71. *Forrest Gump* (Robert Zemeckis, 1994)
72. *Ben-Hur* (William Wyler, 1959)
73. *Wuthering Heights* (William Wyler, 1939)
74. *The Gold Rush* (Charles Chaplin, 1925)
75. *Dances with Wolves* (Kevin Costner, 1990)
76. *City Lights* (Charles Chaplin, 1931)
77. *American Graffiti* (George Lucas, 1973)
78. *Rocky* (John G Avildsen, 1976)
79. *The Deer Hunter* (Michael Cimino, 1978)
80. *The Wild Bunch* (Sam Peckinpah, 1969)
81. *Modern Times* (Charles Chaplin, 1936)
82. *Giant* (George Stevens, 1956)
83. *Platoon* (Oliver Stone, 1986)
84. *Fargo* (Joel Coen, 1996)
85. *Duck Soup* (Leo McCarey, 1933)
86. *Mutiny on the Bounty* (Frank Lloyd, 1935)
87. *Frankenstein* (James Whale, 1931)
88. *Easy Rider* (Dennis Hopper, 1969)
89. *Patton* (Franklin J Schaffner, 1970)
90. *The Jazz Singer* (Alan Crosland, 1927)
91. *My Fair Lady* (George Cukor, 1964)
92. *A Place in the Sun* (George Stevens, 1951)

93. *The Apartment* (Billy Wilder, 1960)
94. *Goodfellas* (Martin Scorsese, 1990)
95. *Pulp Fiction* (Quentin Tarantino, 1994)
96. *The Searchers* (John Ford, 1956)
97. *Bringing Up Baby* (Howard Hawks, 1938)
98. *Unforgiven* (Clint Eastwood, 1992)
99. *Guess Who's Coming to Dinner* (Stanley Kramer, 1967)
100. *Yankee Doodle Dandy* (Michael Curtiz, 1942)

Bathroom Breakthrough

Psycho (1960) is thought to have been the first film to show a toilet flushing on screen. Screenwriter Joseph Stefano, who felt strongly that such a shot would add to the film's realism, wrote a scene in which Janet Leigh's character flushes a crucial piece of paper away – deliberately making the flush an integral part of the plot so that it was less likely to be cut.

The Other Third Man

The title, theme music and main character of *The Third Man* (1949) were later reused for both a radio serial and a BBC television series, which ran from 1959 to 1965. In the TV version, the character of Harry Lime was transformed from the amoral charmer portrayed in the film into a businessman and art dealer who solved crimes in his spare time.

100 BRITISH FILMS

In 1999, the British Film Institute (BFI) polled film industry professionals to compile a list of the 100 favourite British films of the 20th century. The list is reproduced below.

1. *The Third Man* (Carol Reed, 1949)
2. *Brief Encounter* (David Lean, 1945)
3. *Lawrence of Arabia* (David Lean, 1962)
4. *The 39 Steps* (Alfred Hitchcock, 1935)
5. *Great Expectations* (David Lean, 1946)
6. *Kind Hearts and Coronets* (Robert Hamer, 1946)
7. *Kes* (Ken Loach, 1969)
8. *Don't Look Now* (Nicolas Roeg, 1973)
9. *The Red Shoes* (Michael Powell, Emeric Pressburger, 1948)
10. *Trainspotting* (Danny Boyle, 1996)
11. *The Bridge on the River Kwai* (David Lean, 1957)
12. *If...* (Lindsay Anderson, 1968)
13. *The Ladykillers* (Alexander Mackendrick, 1955)
14. *Saturday Night and Sunday Morning* (Karel Reisz, 1960)
15. *Brighton Rock* (John Boulting, 1947)
16. *Get Carter* (Mike Hodges, 1971)
17. *The Lavender Hill Mob* (Charles Crichton, 1951)

18. *Henry V* (Laurence Olivier, 1944)
19. *Chariots of Fire* (Hugh Hudson, 1981)
20. *A Matter of Life and Death* (Michael Powell, Emeric Pressburger, 1946)
21. *The Long Good Friday* (John Mackenzie, 1980)
22. *The Servant* (Joseph Losey, 1963)
23. *Four Weddings and a Funeral* (Mike Newell, 1994)
24. *Whisky Galore!* (Alexander Mackendrick, 1949)
25. *The Full Monty* (Peter Cattaneo, 1997)
26. *The Crying Game* (Neil Jordan, 1992)
27. *Doctor Zhivago* (David Lean, 1965) (a US production)
28. *Monty Python's Life of Brian* (Terry Jones, 1979)
29. *Withnail & I* (Bruce Robinson, 1987)
30. *Gregory's Girl* (Bill Forsyth, 1981)
31. *Zulu* (Cy Endfield, 1964)
32. *Room at the Top* (Jack Clayton, 1959)
33. *Alfie* (Lewis Gilbert, 1966)
34. *Gandhi* (Richard Attenborough, 1982)
35. *The Lady Vanishes* (Alfred Hitchcock, 1938)
36. *The Italian Job* (Peter Collinson, 1969)
37. *Local Hero* (Bill Forsyth, 1983)
38. *The Commitments* (Alan Parker, 1991)
39. *A Fish Called Wanda* (Charles Crichton, 1988)
40. *Secrets & Lies* (Mike Leigh, 1995)
41. *Dr. No* (Terence Young, 1962)
42. *The Madness of King George* (Nicholas Hytner, 1994)
43. *A Man for All Seasons* (Fred Zinnemann, 1966)
44. *Black Narcissus* (Michael Powell, Emeric Pressburger, 1947)
45. *The Life and Death of Colonel Blimp* (Michael Powell, Emeric Pressburger, 1943)
46. *Oliver Twist* (David Lean, 1948)
47. *I'm All Right Jack* (John Boulting, 1959)
48. *Performance* (Donald Cammell, Nicolas Roeg, 1970)
49. *Shakespeare in Love* (John Madden, 1998)
50. *My Beautiful Laundrette* (Stephen Frears, 1985)
51. *Tom Jones* (Tony Richardson, 1963)
52. *This Sporting Life* (Lindsay Anderson, 1963)
53. *My Left Foot* (Jim Sheridan, 1989)
54. *Brazil* (Terry Gilliam, 1985)
55. *The English Patient* (Anthony Minghella, 1996) (a US production)
56. *A Taste of Honey* (Tony Richardson, 1961)
57. *The Go-Between* (Joseph Losey, 1971)
58. *The Man in the White Suit* (Alexander Mackendrick, 1951)
59. *The Ipcress File* (Sidney J Furie, 1965)
60. *Blow-Up* (Michelangelo Antonioni, 1966)
61. *The Loneliness of the Long Distance Runner* (Tony Richardson, 1962)
62. *Sense and Sensibility* (Ang Lee, 1995)
63. *Passport to Pimlico* (Henry Cornelius, 1949)
64. *The Remains of the Day* (James Ivory, 1993)
65. *Sunday Bloody Sunday* (John Schlesinger, 1971)

66. *The Railway Children* (Lionel Jeffries, 1970)
67. *Mona Lisa* (Neil Jordan, 1986)
68. *The Dam Busters* (Michael Anderson, 1955)
69. *Hamlet* (Laurence Olivier, 1948)
70. *Goldfinger* (Guy Hamilton, 1964) (a joint UK–US production)
71. *Elizabeth* (Shekhar Kapur, 1998)
72. *Goodbye, Mr Chips* (Sam Wood, 1939)
73. *A Room with a View* (James Ivory, 1985)
74. *The Day of the Jackal* (Fred Zinnemann, 1973)
75. *The Cruel Sea* (Charles Frend, 1952)
76. *Billy Liar* (John Schlesinger, 1963)
77. *Oliver!* (Carol Reed, 1968)
78. *Peeping Tom* (Michael Powell, 1960)
79. *Far from the Madding Crowd* (John Schlesinger, 1967)
80. *The Draughtsman's Contract* (Peter Greenaway, 1982)
81. *A Clockwork Orange* (Stanley Kubrick, 1971)
82. *Distant Voices, Still Lives* (Terence Davies, 1988)
83. *Darling* (John Schlesinger, 1965)
84. *Educating Rita* (Lewis Gilbert, 1983)
85. *Brassed Off* (Mark Herman, 1996)
86. *Genevieve* (Henry Cornelius, 1953)
87. *Women in Love* (Ken Russell, 1969)
88. *A Hard Day's Night* (Richard Lester, 1964)
89. *Fires Were Started* (Humphrey Jennings, 1943)
90. *Hope and Glory* (John Boorman, 1987)
91. *My Name Is Joe* (Ken Loach, 1998)
92. *In Which We Serve* (Noel Coward, David Lean, 1942)
93. *Caravaggio* (Derek Jarman, 1986)
94. *The Belles of St. Trinian's* (Frank Launder, 1954)
95. *Life Is Sweet* (Mike Leigh, 1990)
96. *The Wicker Man* (Robin Hardy, 1973)
97. *Nil by Mouth* (Gary Oldman, 1997)
98. *Small Faces* (Gillies MacKinnon, 1995)
99. *Carry On Up the Khyber* (Gerald Thomas, 1968)
100. *The Killing Fields* (Roland Joffé, 1984)

Rosebud Rides Again

One of the most iconic film props of all time, the 'Rosebud' sled used in *Citizen Kane* (1941), is now owned by director Steven Spielberg, who reportedly paid more than $50,000 for it. Spielberg's sled is thought to be one of several balsawood copies that were constructed for the film, in which the sled is burned during the final scene.

THE *SIGHT & SOUND* TOP TEN POLL

In 1952, the magazine *Sight & Sound* (published by the British Film Institute) polled film critics around the world to compile a list of the best films of all time. The magazine has repeated the poll every ten years since then, to show which films stand the test of time in the face of shifting critical opinion. In 1992, a poll of directors was added. The results of each poll are reproduced below.

Critics' Polls

1952

1. *Bicycle Thieves* (De Sica)
2. *City Lights* (Chaplin)
2. *The Gold Rush* (Chaplin)
4. *Battleship Potemkin* (Eisenstein)
5. *Intolerance* (Griffith)
5. *Louisiana Story* (Flaherty)
7. *Greed* (von Stroheim)
7. *Le Jour se lève* (Carné)
7. *The Passion of Joan of Arc* (Dreyer)
10. *Brief Encounter* (Lean)
10. *La Règle du jeu* (Renoir)

1972

1. *Citizen Kane* (Welles)
2. *La Règle du jeu* (Renoir)
3. *Battleship Potemkin* (Eisenstein)
4. *8½* (Fellini)
5. *L'Avventura* (Antonioni)
5. *Persona* (Bergman)
7. *The Passion of Joan of Arc* (Dreyer)
8. *The General* (Keaton)
8. *The Magnificent Ambersons* (Welles)
10. *Ugetsu Monogatari* (Mizoguchi)
10. *Wild Strawberries* (Bergman)

1992

1. *Citizen Kane* (Welles)
2. *La Règle du jeu* (Renoir)
3. *Tokyo Story* (Ozu)
4. *Vertigo* (Hitchcock)
5. *The Searchers* (Ford)
6. *L'Atalante* (Vigo)
6. *The Passion of Joan of Arc* (Dreyer)
6. *Pather Panchali* (Ray)
6. *Battleship Potemkin* (Eisenstein)
10. *2001: A Space Odyssey* (Kubrick)

1962

1. *Citizen Kane* (Welles)
2. *L'Avventura* (Antonioni)
3. *La Règle du jeu* (Renoir)
4. *Greed* (von Stroheim)
4. *Ugetsu Monogatari* (Mizoguchi)
6. *Battleship Potemkin* (Eisenstein)
7. *Bicycle Thieves* (De Sica)
8. *Ivan the Terrible* (Eisenstein)
9. *La terra trema* (Visconti)
10. *L'Atalante* (Vigo)

1982

1. *Citizen Kane* (Welles)
2. *La Règle du jeu* (Renoir)
3. *Seven Samurai* (Kurosawa)
3. *Singin' in the Rain* (Kelly, Donen)
5. *8½* (Fellini)
6. *Battleship Potemkin* (Eisenstein)
7. *L'Avventura* (Antonioni)
7. *The Magnificent Ambersons* (Welles)
7. *Vertigo* (Hitchcock)
10. *The General* (Keaton)
10. *The Searchers* (Ford)

2002

1. *Citizen Kane* (Welles)
2. *Vertigo* (Hitchcock)
3. *La Règle du jeu* (Renoir)
4. *The Godfather* and *The Godfather Part II* (Coppola)
5. *Tokyo Story* (Ozu)
6. *2001: A Space Odyssey* (Kubrick)
7. *Battleship Potemkin* (Eisenstein)
7. *Sunrise* (Murnau)
9. *8½* (Fellini)
10. *Singin' in the Rain* (Kelly, Donen)

Directors' Polls

1992

1. *Citizen Kane* (Welles)
2. *8½* (Fellini)
2. *Raging Bull* (Scorsese)
4. *La strada* (Fellini)
5. *L'Atalante* (Vigo)
6. *The Godfather* (Coppola)
6. *Modern Times* (Chaplin)
6. *Vertigo* (Hitchcock)
9. *The Godfather Part II* (Coppola)
10. *The Passion of Joan of Arc* (Dreyer)
10. *Rashomon* (Kurosawa)
10. *Seven Samurai* (Kurosawa)

2002

1. *Citizen Kane* (Welles)
2. *The Godfather* and *The Godfather Part II* (Coppola)
3. *8½* (Fellini)
4. *Lawrence of Arabia* (Lean)
5. *Dr Strangelove* (Kubrick)
6. *Bicycle Thieves* (De Sica)
6. *Raging Bull* (Scorsese)
6. *Vertigo* (Hitchcock)
9. *Rashomon* (Kurosawa)
9. *La Règle du jeu* (Renoir)
9. *Seven Samurai* (Kurosawa)

Musical Chairs

The score for Alfred Hitchcock's *Vertigo* (1958) is the only one of Bernard Herrmann's film scores that the composer did not conduct himself. Herrmann, a prolific film composer and frequent Hitchcock collaborator, was prevented from conducting by a musicians' guild strike in Hollywood. Part of the score was recorded in London before the musicians there decided to join the strike too, at which point the entire unit relocated to Vienna to finish the job.

ACADEMY AWARDS® HOSTS

Since 1929, the Academy Awards® ceremony has been hosted sometimes by individual presenters and sometimes by groups of celebrities (in 1969, ten 'Friends of Oscar®', including Ingrid Bergman and Donald Duck, did the honours). Of the more than 70 people to have hosted or co-hosted the ceremony to date, only the following have done so more than twice.

Host	Ceremonies hosted	Years
Bob Hope	18	1940, 1942, 1943, 1945 (co-host), 1946 (co-host), 1953 (co-host), 1955 (co-host), 1958 (co-host), 1959 (co-host), 1960, 1961, 1962, 1965, 1966, 1967, 1968, 1975, 1978
Billy Crystal	8	1990, 1991, 1992, 1993, 1997, 1998, 2000, 2004
Johnny Carson	5	1979, 1980, 1981, 1982, 1984
Jack Lemmon	4	1958 (co-host), 1964, 1972, 1985
Whoopi Goldberg	4	1994, 1996, 1999, 2002
Conrad Nagel	3	1930 (November), 1932, 1953 (co-host)
Jerry Lewis	3	1956 (co-host), 1957 (co-host), 1959 (co-host)

David Niven	3	1958 (co-host), 1959 (co-host), 1974 (co-host)
Frank Sinatra	3	1963, 1969 (co-host), 1975 (co-host)
Walter Matthau	3	1969 (co-host), 1976 (co-host), 1983 (co-host)
Jane Fonda	3	1969 (co-host), 1977 (co-host), 1986 (co-host)

THE HOLLYWOOD TEN

When the US Government's House Un-American Activities Committee (HUAC) began its search for communist subversion in Hollywood in 1947, it set its sights not on famous stars and studio bosses, but mainly on screenwriters – one of the least glamorous professions in Hollywood. Some of the first writers to be questioned refused to answer questions about their political beliefs, and were cited for contempt of Congress and jailed for periods of up to a year. They became known as 'The Hollywood Ten'.

Alvah Bessie (1904–85)
Bessie, a volunteer with the anti-fascist Abraham Lincoln Brigade during the Spanish Civil War, wrote the story for the Errol Flynn film *Objective Burma* (1945). After the year in prison that followed his investigation by HUAC, he turned to theatre work. He also published several novels, one of which was later adapted for film as *Hard Traveling* (1985) by his son, Dan Bessie.

Herbert Biberman (1900–71)
Biberman is best remembered for a film he made while blacklisted, which was itself effectively banned for many years. *Salt of the Earth* (1954) is based on actual events, and tells the story of Hispanic mineworkers in New Mexico who struck for equal pay with their white co-workers. Many of the cast were actual participants in the events, and for this reason the film is now more often seen as innovative than, as formerly, dismissed as shallow agit-prop.

Lester Cole (1904–85)
Cole was a founder member in 1933 of the Writers Guild of America (WGA), the scriptwriters' union. He scripted numerous mainly routine films before being blacklisted, but very few thereafter, and only under pseudonyms. Ironically, one of these is his best known – the hugely successful *Born Free* (1966), based on Joy Adamson's book about raising a lion cub on a game reserve in Kenya.

Edward Dmytryk (1908–99)
Canadian-born Dmytryk had established a solid reputation with such films as *Murder, My Sweet* (1944) and *Crossfire* (1947), one of the first films to tackle the issue of anti-Semitism. After serving six months in jail and reportedly being told that he would never work in the USA again, he finally agreed to 'name names'. His subsequent film successes included *The Caine Mutiny* (1954), starring Humphrey Bogart, and *The Young Lions* (1958) with Marlon Brando. He spent much of his later life as an academic.

Ring Lardner, Jr (1915–2000)

Lardner was the son of short-story writer Ring Lardner, and his screen credits included the popular Hepburn/Tracy vehicle *Woman of the Year* (1942). After his release from jail he relocated to the UK and, in collaboration with fellow blacklistee Ian McLellan Hunter, wrote most of the first series of *The Adventures of Robin Hood* for television (neither man could be credited by name, as the series was sold to the USA). Lardner eventually returned to Hollywood work, and went on to win an Academy Award® with his script for *M*A*S*H* (1970).

John Howard Lawson (1894–1977)

Originally a successful playwright, Lawson began his Hollywood career as a dialogue writer and went on to script films including the celebrated *Algiers* (1938). **Edward Dmytryk**'s testimony implicated him as a ringleader in a supposed attempt to indoctrinate the moviegoing public with communist ideas. After prison he moved to Mexico and wrote a number of books. He adapted Alan Paton's novel *Cry the Beloved Country* for the screen (1951), but received no screen credit at the time.

Albert Maltz (1908–85)

Maltz co-wrote the crime classic *This Gun for Hire* (1942), based on a Graham Greene novel. After he was imprisoned and blacklisted, his script for *Broken Arrow* (1950) – a western groundbreaking in its portrayal of the Native American point of view – was Academy Award®-nominated, but the credit went to his friend Michael Blankfort. Maltz's later scripts include *Two Mules for Sister Sarah* (1970) and *The Beguiled* (1971).

Samuel Ornitz (1890–1957)

Originally a New York City social worker, Ornitz began writing plays and novels of Jewish immigrant life before moving to Hollywood in 1928. He was extremely politically active, and was a founder member, with **Lester Cole** and **John Howard Lawson** among others, of the Writers Guild of America (WGA). His last film credit was in 1945, and after blacklisting he returned to writing novels.

Adrian Scott (1912–73)

Scott contributed to a number of film scripts, but was most notable as producer of several of **Edward Dmytryk**'s most highly regarded films, including *Crossfire* (1947). After blacklisting, Scott made a living by writing pseudonymously for US television. A year before he died, he finally saw the television production of his play *The Great Man's Whiskers* (1972), a project he had been working on as a screenplay in the mid-1940s just as he was summoned to appear before HUAC.

Dalton Trumbo (1905–76)

One of Hollywood's most prolific and successful screenwriters, Trumbo had hits such as *Thirty Seconds over Tokyo* (1944) to his credit. After prison he moved to Mexico and continued to write, using 'fronts' (fellow writers who pretended to be the authors of a script) or pseudonyms (as 'Robert Rich', he won an Academy Award® for *The Brave One* in 1957). He finally received screen credit again for Otto Preminger's *Exodus* (1960); that same year, the producer and star of *Spartacus*, Kirk Douglas, also decided to give Trumbo screen credit, effectively ending the blacklist period. Trumbo's later successes included *Papillon* (1973).

SOME FILMS THAT HAVE BEEN BANNED OR CENSORED

The Story of the Kelly Gang (Charles Tait, 1906)
Regarded as the first feature-length film, this depiction of Australian outlaw Ned Kelly and his gang ran for over an hour. Only fragments now survive, but it was a huge success in its day. Some critics felt that it portrayed the criminal Kelly Gang as romantic figures, and it was banned in several places, including Adelaide, as a result. As with many later banned films, however, this censorship did nothing to limit its success.

Battleship Potemkin (Bronenosets Potyomkin) (Sergei Eisenstein, 1925)
Long revered as one of the most powerful films ever made, Eisenstein's depiction of a mutiny during the failed 1905 Kronstadt revolution has suffered more censorship than most. With its vivid depiction of tzarist troops descending the Odessa steps, killing civilians indiscriminately as they go, the film was for many years deemed too incendiary for public exhibition in the UK. It was refused certification in 1926, and finally granted an X rating in 1954. Today it has a PG certificate.

Extase (Gustav Machatý, 1932)
This Czech film was notorious in its day for a scene in which young actress Hedy Kiesler (later to find Hollywood fame as Hedy Lamarr) flits naked through a forest in pursuit of the runaway horse on which she thoughtlessly left her clothes before going for a swim. Lamarr later married a wealthy arms manufacturer who attempted to buy up every print in existence – an act of personal censorship in keeping with the burning of the film by US customs. Fortunately for posterity, not every copy was destroyed, and the film was recently released in the UK with a PG certificate.

La Règle du jeu (Jean Renoir, 1939)
Now commonly regarded as Renoir's finest achievement, this film was a flop on its initial release. Its depiction of the follies of all classes of French society was possibly inopportune at such a critical historical juncture, and it was branded 'demoralizing' and withdrawn from circulation by government decree when war broke out. The original negative was destroyed by Allied bombs in 1942, and the only known prints were heavily cut versions until an elaborate restoration job revealed the film in (close to) its original splendour at the 1959 Venice Film Festival.

The Wild One (László Benedek, 1953)
Marlon Brando's iconic turn as leather-clad biker Johnny Strabler (featuring the classic exchange: 'What're you rebelling against, Johnny?' 'Whaddya got?') was too much for British censors, who rejected it in 1954 and 1955. Eventually granted an X certificate (with cuts) in 1967, the now somewhat dated film is currently available as a PG-rated video.

Paths of Glory (Stanley Kubrick, 1957)
Depicting the events surrounding the trial of French troops for alleged cowardice during World War I, Kubrick's film starkly contrasts the grim conditions in the trenches with the comfortable château from which the generals direct the slaughter. The film was regarded by French authorities as a slander on the French army, and was banned there until 1975.

Setting the Scene

Though set in France, Stanley Kubrick's *Paths of Glory* (1957) was actually shot in Bavaria. A large area of pasture was rented from a local farmer and painstakingly transformed into a 'battlefield', and a special government licence had to be obtained for the huge amount of explosives used in the battle scenes.

Titicut Follies (Frederick Wiseman, 1967)
This notoriously harrowing documentary about life inside a Massachusetts institution for the criminally insane has had only limited release. Its distribution in the USA was effectively blocked by a Massachusetts Supreme Court ruling that the film invaded the privacy of prisoners and guards, a restriction which was only lifted in 1992.

Salò, or The 120 Days of Sodom (Pier Paolo Pasolini, 1975)
Pasolini's final film, completed shortly before his murder, contains some of the most extreme depictions of cruelty ever committed to celluloid. Its first UK showing, in 1977, was closed down after a few days when the cinema club (showing an uncertificated print) was raided by police. An edited version was prepared for club screenings in 1979, and was for many years the only version available in the UK, although in Sweden the film received a 15 certificate. It was finally passed, uncut, by the BBFC in 2000.

Ai no corrida (Empire of the Senses) (Nagisa Oshima, 1976)
This depiction of sexual obsession in 1930s Tokyo didn't so much push the envelope as tear it up completely, and the film was banned in numerous countries. In the UK, only cinema clubs could show it for many years, though an uncut video version was briefly made available in the early 1980s before certification became mandatory. The film was finally passed uncut by the BBFC in 1991 after one scene was reframed to comply with laws governing the portrayal of children; a shorter video version was passed in 2000.

Monty Python's Life of Brian (Terry Jones, 1979)
Despite causing much controversy in the UK with its alleged blasphemy, this satire on biblical films was passed uncut – however, several town councils took it upon themselves to ban the film anyway. Its release was delayed for a year in Norway, and in Ireland it was banned until 1987, while Italy had to wait until 1990. By the time of its rerelease in 1999 the fuss had largely died down, although the film was not shown in Jersey until as recently as 2001.

Crash (David Cronenberg, 1996)
This adaptation of a novel by J G Ballard was the subject of a heated newspaper campaign (by the *Daily Mail* and *Evening Standard*) in support of a ban. After consulting legal advisors and psychologists, the BBFC passed the film uncut (as they later did with the video version), leading to the vilification of board members as irresponsible liberals in some sections of the press. Westminster Council continued to insist on cuts, and when these were refused by distributors the film was effectively banned from London's West End cinemas. It was shown, with little fuss, almost everywhere else in the UK.

Smithee's Brilliant Career

'Alan Smithee' is a pseudonym traditionally adopted by any member of the Directors Guild of America (DGA) who wishes to disown the finished version of a particular film. The first Alan Smithee film, for which the DGA invented the name, was 1969's *Death of a Gunfighter* (actually directed by Don Siegel and Robert Totten). Other directors who have since been 'replaced' by Smithee include John Frankenheimer (on the television film *Riviera*, 1987), Dennis Hopper (on the 1990 film *Catchfire*, also known as *Backtrack*) and David Lynch (on an extended version of *Dune*, 1984). Variations on the spelling of Smithee's name are sometimes used, and he has also been known to crop up in the role of producer or writer; director Sam Raimi was credited as 'Alan Smithee, Jr' for his work on the screenplay of *The Nutt House* (1992).

SOME NOTORIOUS COMMERCIAL 'FLOPS'

Intolerance (D W Griffith, 1916)

As a follow-up to his expensive but very successful *The Birth of a Nation* (1915), Griffith planned an epic on the theme of intolerance through the ages, at least partly in response to the (entirely justified) charges of racism levelled at his earlier film. *Intolerance* came in at an estimated $380,000 (much of it Griffith's own money); the 'Fall of Babylon' scenes alone are reputed to have cost double the entire budget of *Birth of a Nation*. The film opened to admiring reviews, but its elaborate interweaving of plots set in Ancient Babylon, Palestine at the time of Christ, 16th-century France and the contemporary USA baffled many filmgoers. Audiences soon fell away, and Griffith was long burdened by the resulting debt. He would never make another film of similar scope and ambition.

Metropolis (Fritz Lang, 1927)

Fritz Lang's vision of a nightmarish, mechanized future has been hugely influential, both within cinema and beyond. It pushed contemporary special-effects technology to the limit, and in over 300 days of filming ran up an astronomical bill which almost bankrupted the Universum Film AG (Ufa) studios who backed it. Erich Pommer, the star producer at Ufa, is said to have lost his job as a result, and it was never likely that the film would make back its initial outlay. It was soon heavily cut in an attempt to improve its commercial prospects and try to recoup some of the costs, leading to a series of attempted restorations in recent decades.

The Fall of the Roman Empire (Anthony Mann, 1964)

One of the last of Hollywood's great Roman epics, this was also the most commercially disastrous – it cost $19 million, and grossed barely a quarter of that at the US box office (1963's *Cleopatra* cost more than twice as much, but had run into healthy profit by the end of the decade). The 'Roman Forum', constructed at great expense in mountains near Madrid, is believed to be the largest outdoor set ever built, and stars' salaries (Sophia Loren earned $1 million) helped to swell the budget further. After this, Roman epics were regarded as 'box-office poison' until the remarkable success of *Gladiator* (2000), which coincidentally features some of the same historical characters, such as emperor Marcus Aurelius and his deranged successor Commodus.

Heaven's Gate (Michael Cimino, 1980)

Michael Cimino's film has become a byword for directorial profligacy and a studio's suicidal passivity in the face of it. Following his success with *The Deer Hunter* (1978), Cimino was given free reign by United Artists on his next project, based on an ugly conflict between cattlemen and immigrant homesteaders in 1890s Wyoming. The budget of $2 million grew to an estimated $44 million, and stories abound of decisions to rebuild sets and ensure accuracy in tiny details at huge expense. The film opened to disastrous reviews and, despite being cut from almost four to just under two and a half hours, reclaimed less than a tenth of its budget at the US box office. United Artists was almost bankrupted by this fiasco, which paved the way for its takeover by MGM. Cimino has directed few films since, but the full-length version of *Heaven's Gate* has been reassessed, winning praise in some influential quarters.

Waterworld (Kevin Costner, 1995)

Costner's film, dubbed by some 'Mad Max on Water', is set in a post-apocalyptic world in which all land has sunk beneath the waves. Largely because of the costly demands of filming on water, its budget grew to a phenomenal $170 million, making it the most expensive Hollywood film ever made to that date. As word of its spiralling budget spread, the film was waggishly nicknamed 'Kevin's Gate'. The returns on first release were certainly ominous and disaster was widely predicted, but when video, DVD and television sales are factored in, the film has in fact more than made its money back. So far, however, the same cannot be said for Costner's other post-apocalyptic epic *The Postman* (1997), which grossed less than a quarter of its $80 million budget at the US box office.

Cutthroat Island (Renny Harlin, 1995), Town and Country (Peter Chelsom, 2001), The Adventures of Pluto Nash (Ron Underwood, 2002)

Several films compete for the title of the biggest commercial flop of recent years. *Cutthroat Island* (budget $92 million, US gross $10 million) almost put paid to the pirate-adventure genre, though this was later revived by *Pirates of the Caribbean* (2003). Despite a stellar cast led by Warren Beatty and Diane Keaton, *Town and Country* (estimated budget $90 million, world gross $10 million) was plagued by rumours of rewrites and reshoots, and languished for two years before its eventual release. A similar suspended existence was endured by Eddie Murphy's futuristic space fantasy *The Adventures of Pluto Nash*, which cost a reported $100 million but grossed only $7 million when it was finally released. While some might argue that these films have more to offer than their box-office records suggest, it is the scale of their financial losses that has earned them their place in film history.

SOME FILMS FEATURING SPECTACULAR DANCE NUMBERS

The Four Horsemen of the Apocalypse (Rex Ingram, 1921) – Valentino's tango

The iconic image of Rudolf Valentino dancing a tango comes from this film, set in Argentina and Paris around the outbreak of World War I. This is the role which brought Valentino fame after numerous bit-parts and supporting roles. His gaucho costume, complete with whip, is a historical nonsense (a pinstripe suit, slouch hat and scarf would have been more accurate) – but however unorthodox his outfit and footwork may be, his smouldering, melodramatic gaze makes this version of the dance unforgettable.

***Gold Diggers of 1935* (Busby Berkeley, 1935) – 'The Lullaby of Broadway'**
Busby Berkeley's musicals are a byword for elaborate choreography, and have
been frequently spoofed over the years; yet they still retain the power to astonish
with such numbers as 'Lullaby of Broadway', in which over 100 dancers tap and
high-kick with breathtaking precision to the Oscar®-winning song, capturing the
heady, night-into-day lifestyle of bright young things who live to party. The film has
an earlier sequence in which 50 white grand pianos cavort around the set while
being played by showgirls, so the final show-stopper had a lot to live up to; it is
generally agreed that it more than did so.

***Shall We Dance* (Mark Sandrich, 1937) – 'Let's Call the Whole Thing Off'**
The seventh in a succession of ten 'Fred and Ginger' movies produced over
a sixteen-year period, *Shall We Dance* follows the time-honoured formula of
magnificent dancing and musical numbers strung together by an implausible plot.
'Let's Call the Whole Thing Off' stands out because Fred Astaire and Ginger Rogers
perform the number on roller skates in New York's Central Park. The scene features
partnered 'skate dancing', and the metal stoppers also prove useful during a tap
dance sequence. It is said to have taken around 150 takes to film.

***Hellzapoppin'* (H C Potter, 1941) – Swing dance scene**
The most famous dance number from this farcical comedy features four couples
from the Harlem Congeroo Dancers (also known as Whitey's Lindy Hoppers)
dressed as maids, chefs and workmen. Frankie Manning's choreography mixes
lightning-speed lindy hop with breathtaking lifts and throws as well as comedy
acrobatics. Dancers from the same troupe had earlier performed in the Marx
brothers' film *A Day at the Races* (1937); this scene also features stunning dancing,
although its stereotyped portrayal of black Americans has dated badly.

***Singin' in the Rain* (Stanley Donen and Gene Kelly, 1952) – 'Make 'em Laugh'**
Although less famous than the title number performed by Gene Kelly, Donald
O'Connor's rendition of 'Make 'em Laugh' is at least as outstanding, and certainly
more exhausting. His backflips off the set walls were a trademark feat, and it
is hardly surprising that he needed several days' rest to recover after filming,
especially as he was then a heavy smoker. Film lore has it that the entire sequence
had to be reshot after the original footage was spoiled; whatever actually
happened, the stunning result remains one of the greatest pieces of clowning on
celluloid.

***The Jungle Book* (Wolfgang Reitherman, 1967) – 'I Wan'na Be Like You'**
The colourful animations and lively neo-swing music of this Walt Disney classic
have entertained generations of children. A highlight is the sight of King Louie of
the Apes (voiced by swing king Louis Prima) cavorting around the jungle while
trying to convince Mowgli to show him how to make fire as men do. Baloo the bear
joins him for some frenetic lindy hopping, disguised by the addition of coconut-
shell 'monkey lips'.

***The Cotton Club* (Francis Ford Coppola, 1984) – Gregory Hines's tap dancing**
Though not one of Coppola's best-known films, this 1920s and 30s period piece
features some dazzling song and dance routines in its depiction of the eponymous
real-life Harlem nightspot, where black musicians and dancers performed for
wealthy white audiences. In characteristic style, Coppola closes the film with a

bloodbath in which one group of hoodlums supplants another. Here, however, the killings are intercut with an astonishing tap sequence by Gregory Hines, who dances around the stage, up and down stairs at dazzling speed.

The Addams Family (Barry Sonnenfeld, 1991) – 'Mamushka'
The 'Mamushka' is a celebratory dance performed to welcome long-lost Fester Addams back into the freakish fold of the Addams family. Fester and his brother Gomez engage in a cossack-inspired frenzy of leaping, kicking and skirmishing; the dance culminates in some spectacular juggling, with Fester and Gomez passing large knives to each other and Fester finally catching them under his arms and between his teeth. Perhaps unsurprisingly, this part of the routine was carried out by stunt doubles.

SOME FILMS FEATURING A 'CAST OF THOUSANDS'

The Birth of a Nation (D W Griffith, 1915)
One of the earliest epic films, this spectacular recreation of a Civil War battle was actually accomplished with something like 500 extras – and skilful camerawork from Griffith's frequent collaborator, cinematographer G W (Billy) Bitzer.

Intolerance (D W Griffith, 1916)
Estimates of the number of extras on this film vary, but 3,000 is often quoted as the number in the 'Fall of Babylon' scenes, with their huge set framed by giant elephant statues. Griffith, who was partly funding the project, was reportedly furious when extras enthusiastically joined in with scenes they were not supposed to be paid for.

Napoléon (Abel Gance, 1927)
Abel Gance's vast film (some restored versions run to over five hours) deals with only the first stage of Napoleon Bonaparte's military career, ending as he leads his army into Italy in 1797 – a further five films were envisaged. The cast for the version that was released included 6,000 extras, armed with 4,000 rifles and 60 cannon.

Kolberg (Veit Harlan, 1945)
A pet project of Joseph Goebbels, this film depicts the legendary resistance of the people of the Baltic city of Kolberg against Napoleon's army in 1807. Few expenses were spared on its production, but Harlan's claim in his autobiography that 187,000 German troops were diverted from battlefield duties to appear as extras is undoubtedly spurious (this would have been over three times the total number involved in the actual fighting, on both sides). It is likely that the true figure was nearer 10,000 – still a bizarre use of military resources under the circumstances.

Quo Vadis? (Mervyn LeRoy, 1951)
One of the first of Hollywood's great Roman epics, Quo Vadis was based on a 19th-century Polish novel and shot at Rome's Cinecittà studios. The young Sophia Loren is said to have been among the 30,000 or so extras.

The Ten Commandments (Cecil B De Mille, 1956)
De Mille's last film as director is still one of the highest-grossing productions in Hollywood history. Some 14,000 extras and 15,000 animals were employed to recreate the trek of the Israelites out of Egyptian bondage. One of the bit-parts was

played by H B Warner, better known for his portrayal of Christ in De Mille's silent epic *King of Kings* (1927).

Spartacus (Stanley Kubrick, 1960)

This film's climactic showdown between Roman legions and an army of slaves took six weeks to film, and required over 8,000 extras. While this is certainly impressive, it would have paled in comparison to Kubrick's planned film of the life of Napoleon Bonaparte, for which he envisaged an army of 50,000 troops – almost rivalling the historical original in size.

The Longest Day (Ken Annakin, Andrew Marton, Bernhard Wicki, 1962)

Producer Darryl F Zanuck's recreation of the D-day landings was a massive undertaking, involving no fewer than three directors and a total of 23,000 British, French and US troops. The decision to shoot in 'more authentic' black and white helped to compensate for the costs of this enormous cast.

War and Peace (Voyna i mir) (Sergei Bondarchuk, 1968)

This adaptation of Leo Tolstoy's novel is over eight hours long, took seven years to shoot, and is said to be the most expensive film ever made – though, as it was a prestige project funded by the USSR, Hollywood could legitimately cry foul at the comparison. It has been claimed that as many as 120,000 extras – provided by a substantial section of the Red Army – were used in some scenes.

Waterloo (Sergei Bondarchuk, 1970)

Bondarchuk's next project was a comparatively modest affair, but as a depiction of the eponymous battle, it still required a large cast. Some 20,000 Russian soldiers were made available (at least one of these, according to eagle-eyed film buffs, can be seen sporting a wristwatch). Many of the extras, having received minimal direction, reportedly attempted to flee in an unscripted rout when charged by 'cavalry'.

Gandhi (Richard Attenborough, 1982)

It has been said that Mahatma Gandhi's funeral in 1948 was the largest gathering of people in one place for one purpose in history, making it something of a challenge to depict on film. Volunteers were dressed in white to form the massive crowd – their total number is claimed to have been as high as 400,000, certainly the largest crowd ever to appear in a feature film.

The Lord of the Rings: The Return of the King (Peter Jackson, 2003)

The final climactic battle of the Lord of the Rings trilogy featured an army of 200,000 orcs, all computer-generated, but each capable of independent movement thanks to the wonders of artificial intelligence (AI). This is almost certainly the largest army ever to appear on screen, but as computer and CGI technology advances, there is in principle no upper limit to further increases.

Clever Cameos

A tried-and-tested director's trick is to persuade a famous person – not necessarily an actor – to make a cameo appearance. A well-judged cameo gives audiences something memorable to talk about, and can even lend credibility to a film. Examples include Canadian academic and media expert Marshall McLuhan's appearance as himself (just in time to lend the hero his support in an argument about his own theories) in *Annie Hall* (1977), and Charlton Heston's brief but moving role as a 'Good Actor' in *Wayne's World 2* (1993). Perhaps the oddest cameo in cinema history, however, is Leon Trotsky's rumoured appearance as an extra in the thriller *My Official Wife* (1914); sadly, the evidence that the performer captured on film was indeed the Russian revolutionary can only be described as sketchy.

SOME MUCH-FILMED LITERARY CLASSICS

Hamlet (William Shakespeare, c.1601)
The earliest film appearance of Shakespeare's tragic student prince was in a 1907 short by cinema pioneer Georges Méliès; numerous other silent snippets were filmed in Europe during the years that followed. The Danish actress Asta Nielsen produced and starred in an extremely loose feature-length adaptation in 1921, portraying the title character as a princess forced to masquerade as a man. Laurence Olivier's more faithful 1948 version is probably still the most famous on celluloid, but it was not until Kenneth Branagh's *Hamlet* (1996) that a film adaptation of the uncut play – running to just over four hours – was produced.

Carmen (Prosper Mérimée, 1847)
Although best known as an 1875 opera by Georges Bizet (which has itself been filmed several times), *Carmen* first appeared in the form of Mérimée's novella. The enduring appeal of its story of passion, jealousy and murder is demonstrated by the sheer number of film adaptations that have been released over the years: these include numerous silent versions, by Cecil B DeMille (1915), Raoul Walsh (1915) and Ernst Lubitsch (1918) among others; looser adaptations such as Otto Preminger's *Carmen Jones* (1954) and Radley Metzger's modishly erotic *Carmen, Baby* (1967); and Vicente Aranda's comparatively 'straight' *Carmen* (2003).

Jane Eyre (Charlotte Brontë, 1847)
From 1910 onwards, several silent shorts were based on *Jane Eyre*; the first feature-length film version was by Hugo Ballin, released in 1921. R C Talwar's *Sangdil* (1952) is a loose Hindi-language adaptation of the story in which the lead characters are childhood sweethearts, separated and later reunited. An unexceptional English-language *Jane Eyre* released by Monogram Studios in 1934 was quickly forgotten, but Robert Stevenson's 1944 version, starring Orson Welles, Joan Fontaine and Agnes Moorehead, made more of an impact. The most recent big-screen adaptation, by Franco Zeffirelli, was released in 1996.

Wuthering Heights (Emily Brontë, 1847)
Emily Brontë's only novel has a universal, powerful appeal which has attracted film-makers from around the world. A feature-length silent version appeared in 1920, followed later by a Hollywood version (William Wyler, 1939) starring Laurence

Olivier, which, though it leaves out much of the original story, is widely regarded as a classic. Luis Buñuel's *Abismos de pasión* (1954) moved the action to a Mexican ranch, while Yoshishige Yoshida's *Arashi ga oka* (1988) set it in medieval Japan. Peter Kosminsky's version (1992) had the rather awkward title *Emily Brontë's Wuthering Heights* imposed upon it, in an attempt to avoid confusion with the 1939 film.

Little Women (Louisa May Alcott, 1868)

This children's classic is a natural candidate for screen adaptation, as it gives plenty of scope for a range of young female actresses to show what they can do. Stars who have been part of the March family over the years include Katharine Hepburn (in George Cukor's 1933 version); June Allyson, Janet Leigh and Elizabeth Taylor (in Mervyn LeRoy's 1949 version); and Claire Danes, Kirsten Dunst, Samantha Mathis and Winona Ryder (in Gillian Armstrong's 1994 version).

The 39 Steps (John Buchan, 1915)

Each of the three existing film versions of Buchan's fast-paced thriller (or 'shocker' as he described it) takes considerable liberties with the plot of the original book. The first and best, Alfred Hitchcock's 1935 version, introduces a beautiful blonde (Madeleine Carroll) into the mix, giving it an appealing battle-of-the-sexes quality; subsequent adaptations directed by Ralph Thomas (1959) and Don Sharp (1978) are equally free with the story but far less successful as films.

Déjà Vu

Remaking a 'classic' film is always something of a risk, as fans of the original are sure to be keeping a sharp eye out for evidence of poor directorial judgement. One possible way of winning them over is to make explicit homage to the earlier production by bringing back its star to play a small but noticeable role: hence Michael Caine's appearance in the US-set remake of *Get Carter* (2000), Richard Roundtree's role in John Singleton's *Shaft* (2000) and Kevin McCarthy's cameo in the remake of *Invasion of the Body Snatchers* (1978). A similar approach can work for big-screen adaptations of television programmes – *Starsky & Hutch* (2004), for example, concludes with an appearance by the 'real' Starsky and Hutch, complete with their trademark red and white Ford Gran Torino.

SOME ACTORS WHO HAVE PLAYED ICONIC FIGURES

For actors who have played James Bond, Sherlock Holmes and Dracula, see separate sections within the **Film genres** section.

Jesus Christ

H B Warner	*The King of Kings* (Cecil B De Mille, 1927)
Ted Neeley	*Jesus Christ Superstar* (Norman Jewison, 1973)
Kenneth Colley	*Life of Brian* (Terry Jones, 1979)
Willem Dafoe	*The Last Temptation of Christ* (Martin Scorsese, 1988)
Phil Caracas	*Jesus Christ Vampire Hunter* (Lee DeMarbre, 2001)
James Caviezel	*The Passion of the Christ* (Mel Gibson, 2004)

Satan

Peter Cook	*Bedazzled* (Stanley Donen, 1967)
Anton LaVey	*Invocation of My Demon Brother* (Kenneth Anger, 1969)
Al Pacino	*The Devil's Advocate* (Taylor Hackford, 1997)
Elizabeth Hurley	*Bedazzled* (Harold Ramis, 2000)
Harvey Keitel	*Little Nicky* (Steven Brill, 2000)
Rosalinda Celentano	*The Passion of the Christ* (Mel Gibson, 2004)

Queen Elizabeth I

Sarah Bernhardt	*Les Amours de la reine Élisabeth* (Henri Desfontaines and Louis Mercanton, 1912)
Flora Robson	*Fire Over England* (William K Howard, 1937), *The Sea Hawk* (Michael Curtiz, 1940)
Bette Davis	*The Private Lives of Elizabeth and Essex* (Michael Curtiz, 1939), *The Virgin Queen* (Henry Koster, 1955)
Quentin Crisp	*Orlando* (Sally Potter, 1992)
Cate Blanchett	*Elizabeth* (Shekhar Kapur, 1998)
Dame Judi Dench	*Shakespeare in Love* (John Madden, 1998)

Adolf Hitler

Bobby Watson	*The Devil with Hitler* (Gordon Douglas, 1942), *Hitler – Dead or Alive* (Nick Grinde, 1942), *Nazty Nuisance* (Glenn Tryon, 1943), *The Miracle of Morgan's Creek* (Preston Sturges, 1944), *The Hitler Gang* (John Farrow, 1944), *A Foreign Affair* (Billy Wilder, 1948), *The Story of Mankind* (Irwin Allen, 1957), *On the Double* (Melville Shavelson, 1961), *Four Horsemen of the Apocalypse* (Vincente Minnelli, 1962)
Alec Guinness	*Hitler: The Last Ten Days* (Ennio De Concini, 1973)
Noah Taylor	*Max* (Menno Meyjes, 2002)
Bruno Ganz	*Der Untergang (Downfall)* (Oliver Hirschbiegel, 2004)

Frankenstein's monster

Charles Ogle	*Frankenstein* (Thomas Edison, 1910)
Boris Karloff	*Frankenstein* (James Whale, 1931), *Bride of Frankenstein* (James Whale, 1935), *Son of Frankenstein* (Rowland V Lee, 1939)
Lon Chaney, Jr	*The Ghost of Frankenstein* (Erle C Kenton, 1942)
Bela Lugosi	*Frankenstein Meets the Wolf Man* (Roy William Neill, 1943)
Christopher Lee	*The Curse of Frankenstein* (Terence Fisher, 1957)
Peter Boyle	*Young Frankenstein* (Mel Brooks, 1974)
Robert De Niro	*Mary Shelley's Frankenstein* (Kenneth Branagh, 1994)

Dick und Doof

Laurel and Hardy may be famous names in the US and UK, but German audiences know them better as Dick and Doof (roughly translated as Fat and Stupid). Titles such as *Dick und Doof als Salontiroler* (better known to English speakers as *Swiss Miss*, 1938) enjoyed decades of popularity in West German cinemas, and later on television.

SOME FILM TITLES IN TRANSLATION

Original title	Foreign language title	English translation of foreign language title
Arsenic and Old Lace (Frank Capra, 1944)	*Arsénico por compasión* (Spanish)	Arsenic for pity's sake
The Blackboard Jungle (Richard Brooks, 1955)	*Die Saat der Gewalt* (German) *Semilla de maldad* (Spanish)	Seed of violence Seed of evil
Breakfast at Tiffany's (Blake Edwards, 1961)	*Diamants sur canapé* (French) *Desayuno con diamantes* (Spanish)	Diamonds on a couch Breakfast with diamonds
Bringing up Baby (Howard Hawks, 1938)	*L'Impossible monsieur bébé* (French) *La fiera de mi niña* (Spanish)	The impossible Mr Baby My girl's wild animal *or* That wild girl of mine
Butch Cassidy and the Sundance Kid (George Roy Hill, 1969)	*Dos hombres y un destino* (Spanish)	Two men and one fate
Dark Victory (Edmund Goulding, 1939)	*Victoire sur la nuit* (French) *Opfer einer großen Liebe* (German) *Amarga victoria* (Spanish)	Victory over the night Victim of a great love Bitter victory
Dial M for Murder (Alfred Hitchcock, 1954)	*Le Crime était presque parfait* (French) *Crimen perfecto* (Spanish)	The crime was almost perfect Perfect crime

Original title	Foreign language title	English translation of foreign language title
Dr Strangelove: Or, How I Learned to Stop Worrying and Love the Bomb (Stanley Kubrick, 1964)	Teléfono rojo, volamos hacia Moscú (Spanish)	Hotline, we're flying to Moscow
High Noon (Fred Zinnemann, 1952)	Le Train sifflera 3 fois (French)	The train will whistle three times
	12 Uhr mittags (German)	Twelve noon
	Solo ante el peligro (Spanish)	Alone against danger
His Girl Friday (Howard Hawks, 1940)	La Dame du vendredi (French)	The Friday woman
	Sein Mädchen für besondere Fälle (German)	His girl for special cases
	Luna Nueva (Spanish)	New moon
I Was a Male War Bride (Howard Hawks, 1949)	Allez coucher ailleurs (French)	Go and sleep somewhere else
	La novia era él (Spanish)	He was the bride
The Killing (Stanley Kubrick, 1956)	L'Ultime razzia (French)	The last raid
	Die Rechnung ging nicht auf (German)	It doesn't add up
	Atraco perfecto (Spanish)	Perfect robbery
The Lost Weekend (Billy Wilder, 1945)	Le poison (French)	Poison
	Días sin huella (Spanish)	Days without a trace
Monkey Business (Norman Z McLeod, 1931)	Monnaie de singe (French)	Funny money (literally 'monkey money')
	Pistoleros de agua dulce (Spanish)	Freshwater gunmen
Mr Smith Goes to Washington (Frank Capra, 1939)	Mr Smith au sénat (French)	Mr Smith in the Senate
	Caballero sin espada (Spanish)	Knight without a sword
Now, Voyager (Irving Rapper, 1942)	Femme cherche son destin (French)	Woman seeks her destiny
	Reise aus der Vergangenheit (German)	Voyage out of the past
	La extraña pasajera (Spanish)	The strange passenger

Original title	Foreign language title	English translation of foreign language title
Pickup on South Street (Samuel Fuller, 1953)	Le Port de la drogue (French)	Port of drugs
	Manos peligrosas (Spanish)	Dangerous hands
Scarlet Street (Fritz Lang, 1945)	Perversidad (Spanish)	Perversity
The Seven Year Itch (Billy Wilder, 1955)	Sept ans de réflexion (French)	Seven years of reflection
	La tentación vive arriba (Spanish)	Temptation lives upstairs
She Wore a Yellow Ribbon (John Ford, 1949)	La Charge héroïque (French)	The heroic charge
	La legión invencible (Spanish)	The invincible legion
Some Like It Hot (Billy Wilder, 1959)	Con faldas y a lo loco (Spanish)	In skirts and going like crazy
The Sound of Music (Robert Wise, 1965)	La Mélodie du bonheur (French)	Melody of happiness
	Meine Lieder – meine Träume (German)	My songs – my dreams
	Sonrisas y lágrimas (Spanish)	Smiles and tears
White Heat (Raoul Walsh, 1949)	L'enfer est à lui (French)	Hell is his
	Sprung in den Tod (German)	Leap into death
	Al rojo vivo (Spanish)	At boiling point

Disastrous Dubbing

English-language films of the post-World War II period often underwent substantial plot changes when German distributors, anxious to remove references to Nazis, concentration camps and anti-German feeling, adjusted their scripts for dubbing. A 1950s dubbed version of *Casablanca* (1942) presented the character of Victor Laszlo – in the original, an idealistic resistance leader – as a scientist, threatened not by the Gestapo, but by rivals in pursuit of his top-secret invention, the 'Delta Ray'. Plot stakes were similarly lowered in an early dubbing of *Notorious* (1946), which transformed Nazi spies into generic drug smugglers. Fortunately, later dubbed versions of both films were more faithful to the originals, and modern German distributors, recognizing the sophistication of today's audiences, no longer mutate films in this way.

GLOSSARY OF FILM-RELATED TERMS

See also **Film-related organizations**.

A

Abby Singer
A slang term for the penultimate shot of a day's filming. Named after veteran production manager and assistant director Abner E 'Abby' Singer, who became notorious for announcing the second-last shot of the day as the last one in order to motivate his cast and crew.

Academy leader
A type of **leader** which shows a numerical countdown to the beginning of a film.

Alan Smithee
A pseudonym traditionally used by any member of the Directors Guild of America (DGA) who is unhappy with the finished version of a particular film and does not wish to be identified in the credits as its director.

ambient light
Light that is naturally present where filming is taking place.

ambient sound
Background noise that is naturally present where filming is taking place.

anamorphic lens
A lens which gives different magnifications in horizontal and vertical directions, allowing a standard 35mm image to be expanded horizontally for **widescreen** projection.

angle shot
A shot taken with the camera tilted above or below the horizontal.

animated cartoon
A film made by photographing drawings, each showing slight changes of position, so that a series of them shown quickly together gives the effect of movement; see **CGI**.

animatic
A rough simulation of a film or sequence, produced from a **storyboard** with a **voice-over** and used to determine whether ideas work dramatically, to check timings, etc.

animator
An artist who makes drawings for **animated cartoon**s, films, etc.

anime
A style of **animated cartoon** which originated in Japan and typically features science fiction or horror stories with explicit sexual or violent content.

answer print
The first complete print of a finished film, including sound, usually shown to a **producer** for approval before a release print is made.

aperture
The opening through which light passes into a camera.

arc shot
A shot in which a camera circles around its subject.

art director	The person responsible for the design of a film's sets and sometimes its costumes and graphics; also **production designer**.
arthouse	A term for films considered to have more artistic than broadly popular appeal, including cult, experimental and foreign-language films.
articulation artist	In animation, a person who transfers an artist's designs onto computer so that they can then be animated.
aspect ratio	The ratio of the width to the height of an image on screen.
auteur	A film director who brings a recognizable personal style to his or her work, and is regarded as the 'author' of a film.
automatic dialogue replacement	The rerecording of a film's dialogue by actors in a sound studio; also **looping**.

B

baby, baby spot	A small incandescent spotlight, often used for **close-up**s.
background artist	A person who designs or creates backgrounds to be used on a film set.
backlight	Light that illuminates a subject from behind.
backlot	An outdoor area, often next to a studio, where **exterior** scenes can be shot.
back-projection	The projection of previously filmed material onto the back of a special screen, so that it appears as a background to action being filmed in front of it.
back story	The events that are supposed to have happened before the action of a film begins.
bankable	If a star or director is bankable, his or her involvement is likely to ensure that a film is profitable.
barndoors	Adjustable flaps on the front of a piece of lighting equipment, used to direct or diffuse the light.
best boy	A technician who acts as assistant to the chief electrician of a film crew.
billing	Precedence of naming in the credits of a film, eg top billing, second billing, etc.
biopic	A film telling the life story of a famous person, usually from an admiring and uncritical viewpoint.
bit-part	A small acting role in a film.

blaxploitation	The commercial exploitation of Black culture, relying on stereotypes, by US film studios in the 1970s.
blimp	A soundproof cover for a film camera that prevents the camera's noise from being picked up by sound recording equipment.
blocking (out)	The planning or rehearsal of the movements of actors in a scene; also **layout**.
bloop	A noise made by a **splice** or join in a **soundtrack** as it passes through a sound system.
blue film, blue movie	A pornographic film.
blue screen	An evenly lit blue background against which material may be filmed for later imposition onto a different background. See also **chromakeying**, **green screen**.
B-movie	A low-budget film produced to support the main feature in a cinema programme; also **supporting feature**.
body double	A person who takes the place of an actor for the filming of scenes involving only the body, especially sex scenes.
Bollywood	The commercial film industry of India (from Bombay, former name of Mumbai, and Hollywood).
bomb	A commercially unsuccessful film; compare **turkey**.
boom	A long, movable telescopic beam designed to carry a microphone, camera or light while keeping it out of shot.
boom operator	A sound technician who operates a **boom**.
brat pack	A group of young and popular film actors, especially the generation of Hollywood stars who came to prominence in the 1980s, including Robert Downey Jr, Rob Lowe and Molly Ringwald. The term is a pun on 'Rat Pack'.
breakaway furniture	Furniture (often made from balsa wood) which is designed to be smashed up in fight scenes, etc.
buddy movie	A film centred on the relationship between two friends.
buzz track	A recording of background noise on a film **soundtrack**, used to mask unnatural silence.

C

call sheet	A printed form showing all that is required for a session of filming, specifying details of **set**s, **location**s, actors and their roles.
cameo	A small film role, often played by a well-known star or a famous personality.
camera crew	The team of people involved in operating a camera, including the cameraman, **focus puller**, **grip**s, etc.

camerawork	The process or technique of filming.
can	A cylindrical container for storing film. If a film or scene is 'in the can', it has been successfully shot.
casting couch	A couch on which a **casting director** or **producer** is said to be granted sexual favours by performers in return for the promise of a role.
casting director	A person responsible for auditioning and selecting actors for the main roles in a film.
cel	A single sheet of **Celluloid®** carrying one of the drawings used to make up an animated film.
Celluloid®, celluloid	(1) Cinematographic film generally. (2) The world of film and cinema.
certificate	A classification given to a film according to the age range for which it is considered suitable.
CGI	Computer-generated imagery: a method of producing images on computer for incorporation into film, often used in **animated cartoon**s.
changeover marks	Marks made on a film to alert a projectionist that a reel is coming to an end and the next reel should be made ready.
character actor	An actor who specializes in character parts, portraying unusual or eccentric personalities.
chick flick	A slang term for a film likely to appeal mainly to women.
chromakeying	A technique which allows specific colour elements (eg **blue screen** or **green screen** backgrounds) to be removed from a picture, and different elements substituted.
Cinecittà	A studio complex in Rome, famous as the centre of the Italian film industry.
CinemaScope®	A method of film projection onto a wide screen, using film that has photographed the image at twice the normal width.
cinemathèque, cinematheque	A small, intimate cinema or a film archive.
cinematographer	The person responsible for composing the look of a film and interpreting the **director**'s wishes through such means as use of colour, light and shadow; also known as the **director of photography** or lighting cameraman.
cinematographist	A person who makes films.

cinematography	The art of making films, specifically that of using the techniques of photography to create the distinctive look of a film.
cinéma vérité	A style of film which uses natural sound and mainly hand-held cameras to give the appearance of real life. Sometimes shortened to **ciné vérité.**
cinephile	A devotee of cinema.
cineplex	A cinema with several screens, showing a range of films.
Cinerama®	A method of film projection onto a wide curved screen, giving a three-dimensional effect. Originally, three cameras (and three projectors) were used simultaneously, but the method was refined until only one of each was necessary.
ciné vérité	See **cinéma vérité**.
clapperboard	A hinged board marked with identifying details, clapped together in front of the camera before or after shooting a piece of film, to help synchronize sound and vision.
clapperboy	The person who works the **clapperboard**.
claymation	A type of **stop-motion** animation which uses clay or Plasticine® figures.
clean speech	Recorded dialogue in which no actor has made a mistake in delivery.
clip	A short segment of a film for separate showing.
close-up	A shot taken near at hand and thus detailed and large in scale, usually of a person's head and shoulders; compare **extreme close-up**, **long shot**.
coated lens	A camera lens coated with a thin film of transparent material to reduce the reflection of light from its surface.
colour consultant	A film technician who advises **cinematographer**s on film choice and processing.
colourization	A technique whereby colours are added to a film that was originally shot in black and white.
completion guarantee	An agreement, usually between a financier and a film-maker, that a film will be completed on time and within budget.
composite print	A print of a film that includes both image and sound.
continuity	The narrative structure of a film, which should flow smoothly in a logical or consistent way.
continuity man, continuity woman	A person on a film set whose job is to ensure **continuity** between different shots, especially in matters of costume, make-up, **prop**s, etc.

cookie	A perforated device that can be fitted to a light to prevent glare and cast a dappled shadow.
cowboy shot	A shot showing actors from mid-thigh upwards. Cowboy shots have been widely used in westerns, as mid-thigh is where a cowboy's gun holster hangs.
crane	A travelling platform which enables a film camera to be lifted into the air.
credits	**Titles** shown at the beginning or end of a film, listing the names and contributions of those involved in making it.
crosscutting	The cutting and fitting together of film **sequence**s so that in the finished picture the action moves from one scene to another and back again, thus increasing dramatic tension; also **intercutting**.
cut	An instantaneous switch from one **sequence** of film to another.
cutaway	A shot that shows events which are separate from but related to, or happening simultaneously with, the central events of a film.
cut-in	A shot edited into another shot.
cutting room	A place where a film is cut and edited.
cutting-room floor	The proverbial place where unwanted sequences or performances end up, rather than in the finished film.

D

dailies	See **rushes**.
day for night	The process of shooting by day scenes which are supposed to take place at night, using filters, underexposure or processing techniques to give an illusion of darkness.
deep focus	The technique of keeping in focus two or more objects or actors at different distances from the camera.
development hell	A film industry jargon term for the position of an idea or script which is constantly being discussed, rewritten, recast, etc, with no apparent prospect of ever being made.
dialogue coach	A person who teaches accents or pronunciation to an actor.
diegetic sound	Sound that is portrayed as originating from events seen on screen; compare **non-diegetic sound**.
diorama	A small-scale three-dimensional model of a **set**.

director	The person who plans and superintends the making of a film.
director of photography	See **cinematographer**.
director's cut	The version of a film preferred by its director (as opposed to one edited in line with studio requirements), often incorporating scenes omitted from the commercially released version.
dissolve	A transition effect used in film editing, in which one image **fades out** while being replaced with another; also **lap dissolve**.
distributor	A company that rents copies of films to cinemas for a fee or profit share.
Dogme 95	A movement in film-making which advocated a minimalist approach, setting strict rules including the exclusive use of hand-held camera, natural lighting and location shooting. It began in Denmark in 1995.
dolly	A trolley, truck or platform on wheels or rollers, on which a camera and its crew can be moved around while filming.
dolly grip	A person whose job is to move a **dolly**.
dolly shot	A shot taken with a **dolly**-mounted camera.
dope sheet	A list of the contents of a reel of exposed film, or of the scenes of a film that have already been shot.
double bill	A cinema programme consisting of two **feature film**s, sometimes both of equal status, sometimes comprising a main feature and a **B-movie**.
douser	A shutter for cutting off light in a cinema projector.
dub	To give a film a new **soundtrack**, eg one in a different language.
Dutch tilt	The practice of tilting the camera at an angle to the horizontal.

E

edge numbers	Numbers identifying **frame**s etc at the edge of a piece of film, used in synchronization.
editor	A person who, by careful selection and arrangement of available footage, makes up the final version of a film.
effects	Sound and lighting devices which help to suggest the place and circumstances in which the action of a film is happening.

establishing shot	A shot at the beginning of a film, showing the location or setting for subsequent action; also **master shot**.
executive producer	A producer who is in overall control of the making of a film (especially its finances), but does not take part in day-to-day filming; compare **line producer**.
exhibitor	A company that represents cinemas and rents films from a **distributor**.
exploitation film, exploitation movie	A film made quickly and cheaply to cash in on a sensational issue or social problem (eg prostitution or teenage violence), or to capitalize on the success of an existing film in the same genre. See also **blaxploitation**, **sexploitation**.
Expressionism	A movement in film-making which sought to express the inner feelings of characters through a distinctive visual style, often using distorted sets and unusual perspectives. It flourished in Germany before World War II.
exterior	A shot taken outdoors; compare **interior**.
extra	A person temporarily engaged for a minor non-speaking part in a film, eg to be one of a crowd.
extreme close-up	A shot taken nearer at hand, and showing more detail, than is usual in **close-up**.
eye light	A small light trained to create a reflective sparkle in an actor's eyes.
eyeline match	The technique of making sure that, if a character looks at something out of shot, the object looked at is placed where it logically should be when shown in another shot.

F

fade in	If an image fades in, it appears gradually.
fade out	If an image fades out, it disappears gradually.
feature, feature film	A full-length film.
featurette	A brief feature, especially a short documentary about the making of a feature film, often included on a DVD release.
fill light	A light that is less bright and softer than a **key light**; used to reduce contrast and shadows.
film à clef	A film with characters based on real people under disguised names.
film buyer	A person who buys films on behalf of an **exhibitor**.

On-Set Orders

The movie industry often portrays itself, and it is partly through films about film-making that some of the 'calls' or commands routinely used on film sets have become common knowledge. Everyone knows the meaning of 'Action!' and 'Cut!', but a few less familiar examples are listed below.

Lights	turn on lighting for the scene
Lock it down	close the set; everyone but actors must be quiet and keep out of the way
Mark it	use the clapperboard to identify a take
Print it	the take just completed is good enough to use
Roll camera	begin filming
Roll sound	begin sound recording
Second sticks	operate the clapperboard again
Speed	the camera is now running at the desired speed
That's (or **it's**) **a wrap**	filming is finished

The sequence known as 'the call', routinely used for each take, usually runs as follows: 'Roll Sound! Roll Camera! Mark it! And... Action!'

filmdom, filmland	The cinema industry.
film noir	A style of film, popular in American cinema in the 1940s and 50s, in which the darker side of human nature is presented in a bleak, often starkly urban setting.
filmography	A list of the films of a particular actor or director.
film unit	A complete team of people involved in shooting a film.
final cut	The completed version of a film, after editing.
flashback	A sequence within a film which shows events that have happened in the past, inserted as comment or explanation; compare **flash forward**.
flash forward	A sequence within a film which shows events that will happen in the future, inserted as comment or explanation; compare **flashback**.
flick	A slang word for a cinema film.
focus puller	An assistant cameraman who adjusts the focus of the camera during shooting.
foley art	The technique of adding appropriate sound effects to a film after it has been shot. Named after the pioneering sound-effects artist Jack Foley (1891–1967).
foley artist	A technician who adds sound effects to a film that has been shot.

foyer card	A still photo with credits, displayed in a cinema foyer to advertise a film; also **lobby card**.
frame	The individual unit picture in cinema film.
frame rate	The number of **frame**s of film shown per second. Most cinema films have a frame rate of 24.
Free Cinema	A movement in cinema which began in Britain in the mid-1950s, and was characterized by social realism and engagement with the lives and concerns of the working class.
freeze frame	The technique of giving an illusion of action being stopped and 'frozen', achieved by repeating a single **frame** many times.

G

gaffer	The chief electrician responsible for the lighting in a film studio.
gate	The part of a projector, printer or camera which holds the film flat behind the lens.
gel	A sheet of tinted transparent plastic used as a filter.
ghosting	The dubbing of another person's voice over an on-screen actor's, often used for singing.
giraffe	A mechanized, extendable boom microphone.
gobo	A type of device used to protect a camera lens from unwanted light, or to protect a microphone from unwanted sound.
grip	A person whose job is to move scenery, props and equipment, or a member of a camera crew who helps to move the camera.
green screen	An evenly lit green background (thought to produce better results than a **blue screen**) against which material may be filmed for later imposition on a different background. See also **chromakeying**.

H

hand-held shot	A shot filmed using a camera which is not supported or moved in any way other than by its operator.
hard light	Light from a **key light**, which typically gives deep shadow and the appearance of a single light source.

Hays Code	The Motion Picture Production Code, a first advisory (1930), then mandatory (1943) set of standards for what was permissible in US films in terms of immorality, sex, profanity or violence. Named after Will Hays (1879–1954), first president of the Motion Picture Producers and Distributors of America, the code was abandoned in 1968 in favour of a ratings system.
helm	A slang term meaning to direct a film.
high concept	A film is typically described as high concept if its main selling points are a plot that is easy to engage with and can be summed up in a few words, and a storyline in which every scene and every character contribute to driving the action forward. See also **star vehicle**.
Hollywood	Typical of or belonging to Hollywood, a suburb of Los Angeles, California and the centre of American cinema. Hollywood films are often characterized as brash and romantic, presenting the image of an affluent and often artificial society.
hot set	A film **set** on which shooting is in progress.

I

IMAX®	A system of widescreen cinema presentation in which 70mm film is projected onto a particularly large screen designed to fill the viewer's field of vision.
inbetweener	In animation, an artist who draws scenes that carry the action between one main pose and another.
indie	An independent film production company which is not tied to a major studio. Indie films often cater to non-mainstream tastes.
insert	A shot inserted within a main **sequence** with a different subject, eg to show the audience what a character is looking at.
intercutting	See **crosscutting**.
interior	A shot taken indoors; compare **exterior**.
intertitles	**Titles** shown within a film to name locations or indicate the passage of time, etc; used especially in silent films.
invisible cutting	The technique of making cuts unobtrusive to the audience, so as not to interrupt the rhythm or pace of a **sequence**.
iris shot	A shot in which the boundary of the image is a circle. Used especially in silent films, in which a scene could open with the gradual expansion of the **aperture** to

reveal the full image (known as irising in) or end with it gradually closing until nothing was visible (irising out).

iso, isolated replay A facility allowing a section of film to be isolated and the action replayed.

J

jib The boom of a **crane**.

jump-cut An abrupt change from one scene or subject to another, used to make a dramatic point.

K

key grip The chief **grip** in a film crew.

key light The brightest or most important light in a scene.

Klieg light A type of incandescent floodlighting lamp for film studio use. Named after its inventors, US lighting engineers John H Kliegl (1869–1959) and Anton T Kliegl (1872–1927).

L

lap dissolve See **dissolve**.

lavalier microphone A very small microphone that can be attached to an actor's clothing.

layout See **blocking**.

lead The main role in a film, or the person playing it.

leader A short blank strip at the beginning of a reel which allows the film to be properly fitted into a projector.

leadman The leader of a **swing gang**.

letterbox A method of formatting a film for television or video by reducing its **frame** size while maintaining its original **aspect ratio**, rather than cutting it to the proportions of a television screen.

library shot See **stock shot**.

line producer A producer in charge of the day-to-day running of a film, making sure it is on schedule and within budget.

live area The area within a camera's viewfinder that will actually be seen in the finished film, which is smaller than the full area captured by the viewfinder; compare **safe area**.

lobby card See **foyer card**.

location Any place where filming is done away from the studio.

location manager A person who makes arrangements for **location** shooting, such as obtaining permission to film.

location scout	A person whose job is to search for suitable **location**s for filming.
locked-down shot	A shot taken on a **set** that has been secured against interruption.
long shot	A shot taken at a distance from the object filmed; compare **close-up**.
looping	See **automatic dialogue replacement**.
lot	The area around a film studio used for outside filming.
louma	A portable **crane** for a lightweight camera with video replay, operated by remote control by the director.

M

MacGuffin, McGuffin	A term (coined by film-maker Alfred Hitchcock) for an element of a film's plot that is of supreme importance to the main characters, but is hardly noticed by the audience; also **weenie**.
magic hour	A brief period, around sunrise or sunset, during which natural light changes in ways that can be captured on film to dramatic effect.
major	An important film company with a large distribution network.
M and E track	A separate track on a **soundtrack**, containing only music and effects.
martini shot	The last shot of a day's filming, so-called because the next item on the agenda is traditionally a drink.
master	The original positive print of a film, from which copies are made.
master shot	See **establishing shot**.
matte	A masking device used to prevent areas of an image from being exposed while shooting, so that a different image can be superimposed in the unexposed area. See also **travelling matte**.
method acting	An approach to acting in which an actor tries to personally inhabit his or her role, rather than simply delivering a good technical performance.
mise en scène	(1) The act, result or art of setting a film scene or arranging a pictorial representation. (2) A cinematic technique which uses a relatively static camera with subjects in full shot, and very little cutting within a scene; compare **montage**.
mistake	A **take** which cannot be used because of a human or technical error.

mix	To piece together two lengths of film invisibly.
mixer	A technician whose job is to dub together different **soundtrack**s (such as for dialogue and music), creating one composite soundtrack.
montage	A cinematic technique in which a series of brief shots are shown in quick sequence with frequent **cut**s or **dissolve**s, often conveying action, plot development or the passage of time; compare **mise en scène**.
MOS	An abbreviation used in scripts to indicate a shot with no sound. It is thought to stand for 'mit out sound', a phrase supposedly used by German-accented directors in the early days of Hollywood.
motion blur	The blurring effect that results when a fast-moving object is filmed.
Moviola®	A brand of upright film-editing machine, combining image and **soundtrack** facilities.
multiplane	A technique used in animation, in which drawings on different **cel**s are photographed at varied distances from the camera to give the illusion of depth.
multiplex	A cinema with several screens showing different films.
multiscreen	Cinema projection in which the screen is divided into several **frame**s, each showing separate images.
mute print	A film print with no sound, used as part of the approval process.

N

negative	A print in which light and shade are reversed.
negative cutter	A person who works on the **negative** of a film to make it match the final version approved by the makers, thus supplying the negative from which prints are made.
neorealism	A movement which began in 1940s Italian cinema, characterized by socio-political content and the use of **mise en scène**, often using non-professional actors to achieve a starkly realistic depiction of working-class life.
New Wave	A movement in French cinema of the late 1950s and 1960s which abandoned the linear narrative and experimented with unusual framing and fluid camera movements. Also known as **Nouvelle Vague**.
non-diegetic insert	A shot or sequence cut into a main **sequence** to show an object or event that is outside the main narrative.

| non-diegetic sound | Sound that is portrayed as originating outside the main narrative of a film, such as a **voice-over** or incidental music; compare **diegetic sound**. |

Film Classification Certificates

In the UK, films are awarded ratings by the British Board of Film Classification (BBFC). Its ratings system was established in 1913 and has periodically been updated over the years. The following are the current classifications, which came into use in 2002:

UC (Universal Children)	Suitable for all, but especially suitable for young children (video only)
U (Universal)	Suitable for all
PG (Parental Guidance)	All ages admitted, but parents are advised that certain scenes may be unsuitable for small children
12A (12 Accompanied)	Suitable for those aged 12 and over, but under-12s may be admitted if they are accompanied by an adult (cinema only)
12	Suitable for those aged 12 and over (video only)
15	Suitable for those aged 15 and over
18	Suitable for those aged 18 and over
R18 (Restricted 18)	Suitable for those aged 18 and over, and only available at licensed cinemas and shops

In Ireland, the classification of films is the responsibility of the Irish Film Censor's Office (IFCO), which uses the following ratings:

G (General)	Suitable for everyone, including young children
PG	Same as UK
12A	Same as UK
15A (15 Accompanied)	Suitable for those aged 15 and over, but under-15s may be admitted if they are accompanied by an adult (cinema only)
16	Suitable for those aged 16 and over
18	Same as UK

In the USA, the classification of films is the responsibility of the Motion Picture Association of America (MPAA), which uses the following ratings:

G	General audiences – all ages admitted
PG	Parental guidance suggested. Some material may not be suitable for children
PG-13	Parents strongly cautioned. Some material may be inappropriate for children under 13
R	Restricted – under-17s may not be admitted without a parent or adult guardian
NC-17	No-one aged 17 or under admitted

FILM REFERENCE
Glossary

nose room	In a shot, the amount of space in front of an actor's head in the direction in which he or she is looking.
Nouvelle Vague	See **New Wave**.
nut	A slang term for the amount of money a film must earn in order to break even.

O

opaquer	In animation, an artist who adds colour to **cel**s.
opening weekend	The first weekend when a film can be seen by the public, often a good indication of how commercially successful it will be.
out-take	A sequence of film which is removed from the final edited version.
overcranking	The technique of speeding up the number of **frame**s shot by a camera, so that when shown at normal speed the sequence appears in slow motion; compare **undercranking**.

P

pan	To move (a camera) about (or as if pivoting about) an axis while filming, so as to follow a particular object or to produce a panoramic effect.
pic	Short for **picture**.
picture	A cinema film.
pixilation, pixillation	A technique for making figures appear to be animated artificially, eg by the use of **stop-frame camera** methods, usually to create a whimsical effect.
postproduction	The work of editing and dubbing a film that follows the shooting of it.
postsynch, postsynchronization	The process of recording and adding a **soundtrack** to a film after it has been shot.
POV	Abbreviation for point-of-view shot, a shot which appears to show what a character is looking at from his or her point of view.
preproduction	The work done on a film before it is shot.
prequel	A film produced as a follow-up to another film, showing events that happened before the original story.
prerelease	The release of a film before its official date of release, or the showing of a film so released.
preview	(1) A showing of a film before it goes on general release. (2) An advance public showing of excerpts from a

	film. (3) A short film advertising a forthcoming cinema feature; also **trailer**.
principal photography	The shooting of the most important sections of a film.
producer	Someone who exercises general control over, but does not actually make, a film.
production accountant	An accountant responsible for the finances of a film while it is being made.
production designer	See **art director**.
production number	A sequence in a musical film which involves singing and dancing by a large number of performers.
product placement	A form of advertising whereby a branded product is prominently placed within a shot in a feature film.
programmer	A fairly routine and unimaginative, usually low-budget film, often produced to form part of a **double bill** in a cinema programme.
prop, property	Any physical object needed on a film set.
property master	The person in charge of the **prop**s used in a film.

Q

quota quickie	A quickly-produced, low-budget, poor-quality film made in the UK (but usually US-financed) in the 1920s and 30s. Quota quickies were made to exploit a government measure which required UK cinemas to screen a quota of British-made films.

R

raw stock	Unused film; also **stock**.
reaction shot	A shot (often a **close-up**) showing the way in which a character responds to an event.
remake	A new version of an existing film.
reshoot	A second or subsequent attempt to film a particular scene or scenes.
residual	A payment to a performer for later use of a film in which he or she appears.
retake	A second or subsequent attempt to film a particular shot or sequence.
reverse shot	A shot taken from a position opposite to that of the preceding shot; often used in showing a conversation, alternating the point of view.

rhubarb	A word muttered repeatedly by actors to give the impression of background conversation. See also **walla**.
rigger	A person whose job is to set up lights, erect scaffolding etc on a film set.
road movie	A film with a narrative based on a journey, the latter often undertaken as an escape and having no definite destination.
rolling titles	**Titles** that scroll upwards from the bottom of the screen.
romcom, rom-com	A romantic comedy.
room tone	The ambient noise, without dialogue or action, which is present on a set or location.
rostrum	A platform used to carry a camera.
rotoscope	A device used by animators to trace **frame**s of live action for cartoons.
rough cut	A roughly edited, preliminary version of a film which allows film-makers to assess what fine-tuning is required.
running shot	A shot in which the camera moves along with the subject, either held by the operator or mounted on a vehicle or **dolly**.
running time	The duration, usually given in minutes, of a film.
rushes	Unedited prints of a film scene, or series of scenes, for immediate viewing by the film-makers; also **dailies**.

S

safe area	The part of the area captured by a camera's viewfinder that will not be seen in the film; compare **live area**.
safety film	Film with a non-flammable or slow-burning base of cellulose acetate or polyester.
scenario	A scene-by-scene outline of a film.
score	The music used in a film.
screencraft	The technique of making films.
screenplay	The written text for a film, with dialogue, stage directions and descriptions of characters and setting. See also **shooting script**.
screen test	A trial filming to determine whether an actor or actress is suitable for cinema work or for a particular role.
screenwriter	A writer of screenplays.

screwball comedy	A type of comedy popular in the 1930s, which typically features fast-moving, anarchic storylines and attractive, witty and eccentric characters.
script doctor	A writer who revises a film script in order to make it suitable for production.
script girl, script supervisor	A person (traditionally a young woman) whose job is to scan the script during filming to ensure that it is followed correctly.
second feature	A **feature film** which is shown second in a **double bill**, often but not necessarily the inferior of the two.
second unit	A camera team, usually under a second-unit director, which films location shots, action sequences and other material not requiring the director's presence.
semidocumentary	A film based on real events, but with an invented plot and dialogue.
sepmag	In sepmag recording, sound is recorded on separate magnetic tape which is then synchronized with the film as it is run.
sequence	A section of a film, roughly equivalent to a scene in a stage play.
set	(1) An area where filming takes place. (2) The scenery, furniture, etc arranged for filming.
set designer	A person who conceives and draws plans of film sets, interpreting the ideas of the **art director**.
setting	The scenery and props used for a single scene of a film.
set-up	A particular positioning of a camera in preparation for shooting a scene.
sexploitation	The commercial exploitation of sex in cinema.
shoot	The shooting of a film.
shoot-'em-up	A film featuring a large amount of gunfights and violent action.
shooting ratio	The average number of **take**s that are shot per finished scene in a film.
shooting script	A version of a script which includes instructions for the cameraman indicating the order in which scenes will be shot.
short, short subject	A film that is significantly shorter in duration than a **feature film**. Shorts were originally made to support the main feature of a programme, but are now regarded as a genre in their own right.

shot	A length of film taken by a single camera without a break.
silver screen	(1) A cinema screen. (2) The film industry.
skinflick	A film in which there is much nudity and sexual activity, especially a (cheaply made) pornographic film.
slapstick comedy	A style of comedy which relies more on knockabout physical action than on verbal wit.
slasher movie	A horror film which features graphic images of people being gorily slashed with blades.
slate	The number of a scene and take, as marked on a **clapperboard**.
sleeper	A film which becomes popular after an initial period of not being so.
sneak preview	A special private screening of a film, held before its release to the public.
snuff movie	A pornographic film which climaxes in the actual killing of an unsuspecting member of the cast.
soft focus	The deliberate slight blurring of an image, often to create a mood of romance or nostalgia, and sometimes to kindly soften the features of an ageing performer in a **close-up**.
sound effects	Sounds other than dialogue or music which are artificially produced and added to a film **soundtrack**.
sound mixer	The person who controls the tone and volume of the sound recorded for a film.
sound stage	The soundproof area of a film studio on which sets are built and actors perform.
soundtrack	(1) The magnetic tape on which sounds are recorded for a film. (2) A recording of the musical accompaniment to a film.
space opera	A slang term for a science fiction film.
spaghetti western	A film set in the American Wild West, usually made in Europe by an Italian director, and characterized by violent and melodramatic content and a baroque style.
special effects	Techniques such as **CGI**, lighting, manipulation of film, etc, which are used to create or enhance images on film.
splatter movie	A horror film which features graphic images of mutilation, amputation, etc.
splice	A place where two sections of film are joined (or spliced) together.

split screen	A technique in which different scenes are shown simultaneously on separate parts of the same screen.
squib	A small explosive device, often containing fake blood, used to simulate the strike of a bullet.
stand-in	A person who physically resembles an actor and who takes his or her place during lengthy **set-up**s.
star vehicle	A film which is conceived primarily as a way of showcasing a **bankable** star performer, attracting investment on this basis rather than because of its plot. See also **high concept**, **vehicle**.
Steadicam®	A device for steadying a hand-held camera, consisting of a shoulder and waist harness with a shock-absorbing arm to which the camera is fitted.
still	A photograph taken on a film set, or a **frame** from a film.
still man	A photographer who takes still photographs on a film set.
stock	Unused film; also **raw stock**.
stock shot, stock footage	Footage from a previously made film which is incorporated into another film; also **library shot**.
stop-frame camera	A film camera that can be adjusted to take a reduced number of **frame**s, used in creating the effect of **pixilation.**
stop-motion	In animation, a technique in which filming is repeatedly stopped to allow very slight changes of position in the subjects being filmed, creating the illusion of movement when the film is run.
storyboard	A series of rough sketches setting out the sequence of images to be used in a film.
storyline	The main plot of a film, or the line along which the plot is to develop.
straight to video	The path taken by a film that is considered to be so unlikely to make money that it is not given a cinema release.
stripe	A magnetic track for sound on a film print.
stunt double	See **stuntman**.
stuntman, stuntwoman	A person whose job is to perform dangerous and spectacular feats as a stand-in for a film actor; also **stunt double**.

subtitles	Wording superimposed onto a film image at the foot of the screen, eg a translation of foreign-language dialogue, or other descriptive text.
sun gun	A portable lamp, often attached to a camera, which is used for lighting on film sets.
Super 8®	A variety of 8mm film used in cine cameras and for home film-making.
supporting feature	See **B-movie**.
swashbuckler	A film featuring the exploits of a swaggering hero.
swing gang	A team of workers who construct and dismantle sets.
sword and sandal	A slang term used to describe epic films set in Ancient Greece or Rome.

T

take	The amount of film (eg one scene) photographed at any one time.
tear-jerker	An extravagantly sentimental film inviting pity, grief or sorrow.
technical advisor	A person with relevant practical experience or expertise who gives advice to film-makers.
Technicolor®	A process of colour photography in motion pictures in which films of the same scene, using different filters, are projected simultaneously.
third cinema	A politicized, socially-conscious movement in cinema which originated in Latin America in the 1960s, and which challenges the **Hollywood** model of film-making on ideological grounds.
threequel	A sequel to a sequel; that is, the third film in a series.
tilt	The movement of a camera up or down to produce a particular visual effect.
timecode	A sequence of number codes which are produced at set intervals by a timing system and used to synchronize sound and pictures.
time-lapse photography	A method of concisely representing long or slow processes (eg the blooming of a flower) on film by capturing a large number of images at regular intervals, then projecting the film made from these at normal speed.
titles	Text superimposed on film, often at the beginning of a film, to give the title, name the stars, etc, or at the end to list **credits**. See also **intertitles**, **rolling titles**, **subtitles**.

toon	A slang term for an animated film or cartoon.
tracking shot	A shot taken while moving a **dolly**-mounted camera in a defined path.
trailer	(1) A short film advertising a forthcoming cinema feature. (2) The blank piece of film at the end of a reel. (3) A type of mobile home in which stars are accommodated while on set.
travelling matte	A **matte** that changes shape from one **frame** to the next, eg following the silhouette of a character or object as it moves, allowing for superimposition of the resulting shot onto a different background.
treatment	A draft of a screenplay which includes camera angles, descriptions of sets and similar information.
turkey	A film that is considered a complete failure; compare **bomb**.
turnaround	The state that a film project is in if a studio decides not to go ahead with it, and its producers have to look for another studio.
two-shot	A shot in which the heads and upper bodies of two actors fill the screen.

U

| undercranking | The technique of slowing down the number of **frame**s shot by a camera, so that when shown at normal speed the sequence appears as speeded-up motion; compare **overcranking**. |

V

vehicle	A film which is conceived primarily as a way of showcasing a particular performer. See also **star vehicle**.
vérité	See **cinéma vérité**.
video nasty	A term sometimes used to describe pornographic or horror films released on video.
viewer	An apparatus used to project film for purposes of editing and cutting.
voice-over	The background voice of an unseen narrator in a film.

W

| walk-on | A brief, non-speaking role in a film. |

walla	A word muttered repeatedly by actors to give the impression of background conversation. See also **rhubarb**.
weenie	See **MacGuffin**.
weepie	See **tear-jerker**.
whip pan	A very fast panning camera movement which gives an abrupt transition between shots.
widescreen	A cinema format in which the image is projected onto a wide, curved screen, giving the viewer a greater sense of actuality in the picture.
wild sound, wild track	Sound recorded where filming is taking place, but which is not synchronized to the images, such as the sound of waves, jungle noises, etc.
wipe	A transition effect used in film editing, in which the image on the screen appears to be pushed or wiped off the screen by another.
woman's picture	A term for a genre of early- to mid-20th-century **Hollywood** films conceived to appeal mainly to women, with female protagonists and a focus on social and domestic issues.
working title	A title used to refer to a film which is still in production; not necessarily the title under which it will eventually be released.
workprint	A rough version of a film which is worked on by an **editor**.
wrangler	A person responsible for handling animals used in a film.
wrap	The completion of filming, or the end of a session of filming.
wrap party	A party which is traditionally held after a film **wrap**s.
write out	To completely remove a role or an aspect of a film's plot by rewriting.

Z

zoom lens	A lens of variable focal length, used eg for a transition from **long shot** to **close-up** without the need for camera movement.

Variety-Speak

Variety magazine is widely regarded as the 'house journal' of the US entertainment industry. Launched in 1905 to cover the New York City theatre business, it soon expanded its coverage to include the burgeoning film industry with its Los Angeles edition. From the beginning, *Variety* had its own distinctive vocabulary: partly an insiders' language designed to make its readers feel like part of an exclusive community, and partly a result of the typical journalistic preference for short words in headlines (eg *rap* instead of *censure*, or *wed* instead of *marry*). One of *Variety*'s most famous headlines was 'Sticks Nix Hick Pix' (1935) – a snappy, if rather contrived, way of saying that audiences in rural areas were not interested in films about country life. However, not all of the terminology that the magazine calls 'slanguage' is as deliberately gnomic.

Categories of 'slanguage' include nicknames for cities (**Beantown** is Boston, Massachusetts; **Beertown** is Milwaukee, Wisconsin), film genres (**horse opera** and **oater** both refer to westerns) and job titles (a songwriter is a **cleffer**, a cameraman a **lensman** and a child actor a **moppet**). Sometimes a refreshing honesty (or perhaps cynicism) is displayed, as when a publicist is dubbed a **praiser**. Money becomes **coin**, a cocktail party is a **pour**, critics are **crix**, and competition is shortened to the positively Wodehouseian **competish**.

Abbreviations are also popular, with **b.f.** and **g.f.** standing for boyfriend and girlfriend, **n.s.g.** for not so good, **the o.o.** for the once-over, and a **p.a.** for a personal appearance. Success brings its own set of terms, with **boffo, socko** and **whammo** being used to describe films that are doing excellent business, while a film said to have **legs** is expected to have a good run at the box office. The latter is an example of a *Variety* coinage which has crossed over into general slang use, as are the widely used terms **deejay**, **sex appeal** and **sitcom**, among others.

This index includes films mentioned in the Film Categories and Genres, Film-Producing Countries, 100 Notable Films and Film Reference sections.

Index of Film Titles